GENERAL MOTORS | CELEBRITY/CENTURY/CUTLASS CIERA/6000 1982-96 REPAIR MANUAL

CHILTON'S

President	Dean F. Morgantini, S.A.E.
Vice President–Finance	Barry L. Beck
Vice President–Sales	Glenn D. Potere
Executive Editor	Kevin M. G. Maher, A.S.E.
Production Manager	Ben Greisler, S.A.E.
Production Assistant	Melinda Possinger
Project Managers	George B. Heinrich III, A.S.E., S.A.E., Will Kessler, A.S.E., S.A.E., James R. Marotta, A.S.E., S.T.S., Richard Schwartz, A.S.E., Todd W. Stidham, A.S.E.
Schematics Editor	Christopher G. Ritchie
Editor	Dawn M Hoch, S.A.E.

CHILTON ™ *Automotive Books*

PUBLISHED BY **W. G. NICHOLS, INC.**

Manufactured in USA
© 1995 Chilton Book Company
1020 Andrew Drive
West Chester, PA 19380
ISBN 0-8019-9108-0
Library of Congress Catalog Card No. 94-069434
6789012345 8765432109

Contents

Contents

SAFETY NOTICE

Proper service and repair procedures are vital to the safe, reliable operation of all motor vehicles, as well as the personal safety of those performing repairs. This manual outlines procedures for servicing and repairing vehicles using safe, effective methods. The procedures contain many NOTES, CAUTIONS and WARNINGS which should be followed, along with standard procedures to eliminate the possibility of personal injury or improper service which could damage the vehicle or compromise its safety.

It is important to note that repair procedures and techniques, tools and parts for servicing motor vehicles, as well as the skill and experience of the individual performing the work vary widely. It is not possible to anticipate all of the conceivable ways or conditions under which vehicles may be serviced, or to provide cautions as to all possible hazards that may result. Standard and accepted safety precautions and equipment should be used when handling toxic or flammable fluids, and safety goggles or other protection should be used during cutting, grinding, chiseling, prying, or any other process that can cause material removal or projectiles.

Some procedures require the use of tools specially designed for a specific purpose. Before substituting another tool or procedure, you must be completely satisfied that neither your personal safety, nor the performance of the vehicle will be endangered.

Although information in this manual is based on industry sources and is complete as possible at the time of publication, the possibility exists that some car manufacturers made later changes which could not be included here. While striving for total accuracy, NP/Chilton cannot assume responsibility for any errors, changes or omissions that may occur in the compilation of this data.

PART NUMBERS

Part numbers listed in this reference are not recommendations by Chilton for any product brand name. They are references that can be used with interchange manuals and aftermarket supplier catalogs to locate each brand supplier's discrete part number.

SPECIAL TOOLS

Special tools are recommended by the vehicle manufacturer to perform their specific job. Use has been kept to a minimum, but where absolutely necessary, they are referred to in the text by the part number of the tool manufacturer. These tools can be purchased, under the appropriate part number, from your local dealer or regional distributor, or an equivalent tool can be purchased locally from a tool supplier or parts outlet. Before substituting any tool for the one recommended, read the SAFETY NOTICE at the top of this page.

ACKNOWLEDGMENTS

Portions of the materials contained herein have been reprinted with the permission of General Motors Corporation, Service Technology Group.

1

GENERAL INFORMATION AND MAINTENANCE

HOW TO USE THIS BOOK

This Chilton's Total Car Care manual is intended to help you learn more about the inner workings of your Celebrity, Century, Cutlass Ciera or 6000 while saving you money on its upkeep and operation.

The beginning of the book will likely be referred to the most, since that is where you will find information for maintenance and tune-up. The other sections deal with the more complex systems of your vehicle. Systems (from engine through brakes) are covered to the extent that the average do-it-yourselfer can attempt. This book will not explain such things as rebuilding a differential because the expertise required and the special tools necessary make this uneconomical. It will, however, give you detailed instructions to help you change your own brake pads and shoes, replace spark plugs, and perform many more jobs that can save you money and help avoid expensive problems.

A secondary purpose of this book is a reference for owners who want to understand their vehicle and/or their mechanics better.

Where to Begin

Before removing any bolts, read through the entire procedure. This will give you the overall view of what tools and supplies will be required. So read ahead and plan ahead. Each operation should be approached logically and all procedures thoroughly understood before attempting any work.

If repair of a component is not considered practical, we tell you how to remove the part and then how to install the new or rebuilt replacement. In this way, you at least save labor costs.

Avoiding Trouble

Many procedures in this book require you to "label and disconnect . . ." a group of lines, hoses or wires. Don't be think you can remember where everything goes—you won't. If you hook up vacuum or fuel lines incorrectly, the vehicle may run poorly, if at all. If you hook up electrical wiring incorrectly, you may instantly learn a very expensive lesson.

You don't need to know the proper name for each hose or line. A piece of masking tape on the hose and a piece on its fitting will allow you to assign your own label. As long as you remember your own code, the lines can be reconnected by matching your tags. Remember that tape will dissolve in gasoline or solvents; if a part is to be washed or cleaned, use another method of identification. A permanent felt-tipped marker or a metal scribe can be very handy for marking metal parts. Remove any tape or paper labels after assembly.

Maintenance or Repair?

Maintenance includes routine inspections, adjustments, and replacement of parts which show signs of normal wear. Maintenance compensates for wear or deterioration. Repair implies that something has broken or is not working. A need for a repair is often caused by lack of maintenance. for example: draining and refilling automatic transmission fluid is maintenance recommended at specific intervals. Failure to do this can shorten the life of the transmission/transaxle, requiring very expensive repairs. While no maintenance program can prevent items from eventually breaking or wearing out, a general rule is true: MAINTENANCE IS CHEAPER THAN REPAIR.

Two basic mechanic's rules should be mentioned here. First, whenever the left side of the vehicle or engine is referred to, it means the driver's side. Conversely, the right side of the vehicle means the passenger's side. Second, screws and bolts are removed by turning counterclockwise, and tightened by turning clockwise unless specifically noted.

Safety is always the most important rule. Constantly be aware of the dangers involved in working on an automobile and take the proper precautions. Please refer to the information in this section regarding SERVICING YOUR VEHICLE SAFELY and the SAFETY NOTICE on the acknowledgment page.

Avoiding the Most Common Mistakes

Pay attention to the instructions provided. There are 3 common mistakes in mechanical work:

1. Incorrect order of assembly, disassembly or adjustment. When taking something apart or putting it together, performing steps in the wrong order usually just costs you extra time; however, it CAN break something. Read the entire procedure before beginning. Perform everything in the order in which the instructions say you should, even if you can't see a reason for it. When you're taking apart something that is very intricate, you might want to draw a picture of how it looks when assembled in order to make sure you get everything back in its proper position. When making adjustments, perform them in the proper order. One adjustment possibly will affect another.

2. Overtorquing (or undertorquing). While it is more common for overtorquing to cause damage, undertorquing may allow a fastener to vibrate loose causing serious damage. Especially when dealing with aluminum parts, pay attention to torque specifications and utilize a torque wrench in assembly. If a torque figure is not available, remember that if you are using the right tool to perform the job, you will probably not have to strain yourself to get a fastener tight enough. The pitch of most threads is so slight that the tension you put on the wrench will be multiplied many times in actual force on what you are tightening.

There are many commercial products available for ensuring that fasteners won't come loose, even if they are not torqued just right (a very common brand is Loctite_). If you're worried about getting something together tight enough to hold, but loose enough to avoid mechanical damage during assembly, one of these products might offer substantial insurance. Before choosing a threadlocking compound, read the label on the package and make sure the product is compatible with the materials, fluids, etc. involved.

3. Crossthreading. This occurs when a part such as a bolt is screwed into a nut or casting at the wrong angle and forced. Crossthreading is more likely to occur if access is difficult. It helps to clean and lubricate fasteners, then to start threading the bolt, spark plug, etc. with your fingers. If you encounter resistance, unscrew the part and start over again at a different angle until it can be inserted and turned several times without much effort. Keep in mind that many parts have tapered threads, so that gentle turning will automatically bring the part you're threading to the proper angle. Don't put a wrench on the part until it's been tightened a couple of turns by hand. If you suddenly encounter resistance, and the part has not seated fully, don't force it. Pull it back out to make sure it's clean and threading properly.

Be sure to take your time and be patient, and always plan ahead. Allow yourself ample time to perform repairs and maintenance.

TOOLS AND EQUIPMENT

▶ **See Figures 1 thru 15**

Without the proper tools and equipment it is impossible to properly service your vehicle. It would be virtually impossible to catalog every tool that you would need to perform all of the operations in this book. It would be unwise for the amateur to rush out and buy an expensive set of tools on the theory that he/she may need one or more of them at some time.

The best approach is to proceed slowly, gathering a good quality set of those tools that are used most frequently. Don't be misled by the low cost of bargain tools. It is far better to spend a little more for better quality. Forged wrenches, 6 or 12-point sockets and fine tooth ratchets are by far preferable to their less expensive counterparts. As any good mechanic can tell you, there are few worse experiences than trying to work on a vehicle with bad tools. Your monetary savings will be far outweighed by frustration and mangled knuckles.

Begin accumulating those tools that are used most frequently: those associated with routine maintenance and tune-up. In addition to the normal assortment of screwdrivers and pliers, you should have the following tools:

• Wrenches/sockets and combination open end/box end wrenches in sizes ⅛–¾ in. and/or 3mm–19mm ¹³⁄₁₆ in. or ⅝ in. spark plug socket (depending on plug type).

➡ **If possible, buy various length socket drive extensions. Universal-joint and wobble extensions can be extremely useful, but be careful when using them, as they can change the amount of torque applied to the socket.**

• Jackstands for support.
• Oil filter wrench.
• Spout or funnel for pouring fluids.

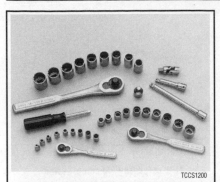

Fig. 1 All but the most basic procedures will require an assortment of ratchets and sockets

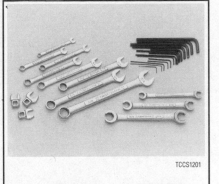

Fig. 2 In addition to ratchets, a good set of wrenches and hex keys will be necessary

Fig. 3 A hydraulic floor jack and a set of jackstands are essential for lifting and supporting the vehicle

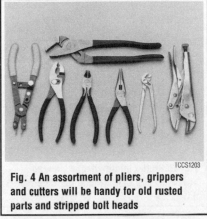

Fig. 4 An assortment of pliers, grippers and cutters will be handy for old rusted parts and stripped bolt heads

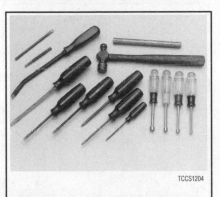

Fig. 5 Various drivers, chisels and prybars are great tools to have in your toolbox

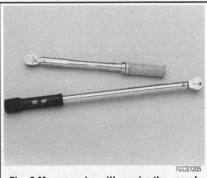

Fig. 6 Many repairs will require the use of a torque wrench to assure the components are properly fastened

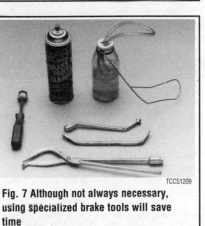

Fig. 7 Although not always necessary, using specialized brake tools will save time

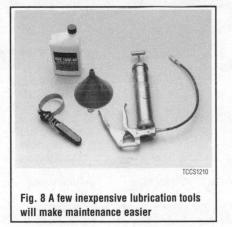

Fig. 8 A few inexpensive lubrication tools will make maintenance easier

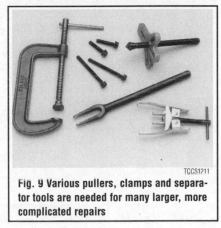

Fig. 9 Various pullers, clamps and separator tools are needed for many larger, more complicated repairs

• Grease gun for chassis lubrication (unless your vehicle is not equipped with any grease fittings)

• Hydrometer for checking the battery (unless equipped with a sealed, maintenance-free battery).

• A container for draining oil and other fluids.

• Rags for wiping up the inevitable mess.

In addition to the above items there are several others that are not absolutely necessary, but handy to have around. These include an equivalent oil absorbent gravel, like cat litter, and the usual supply of lubricants, antifreeze and fluids. This is a basic list for routine maintenance, but only your personal needs and desire can accurately determine your list of tools.

After performing a few projects on the vehicle, you'll be amazed at the other tools and non-tools on your workbench. Some useful household items are: a large turkey baster or siphon, empty coffee cans and ice trays (to store parts), a ball of twine, electrical tape for wiring, small rolls of colored tape for tagging lines or hoses, markers and pens, a note pad, golf tees (for plugging vacuum lines), metal coat hangers or a roll of mechanic's wire (to hold things out of the way), dental pick or similar long, pointed probe, a strong magnet, and a small mirror (to see into recesses and under manifolds).

A more advanced set of tools, suitable for tune-up work, can be drawn up easily. While the tools are slightly more sophisticated, they need not be outrageously expensive. There are several inexpensive tach/dwell meters on the market that are every bit as good for the average mechanic as a professional model. Just be sure that it goes to a least 1200–1500 rpm on the tach scale and that it works on 4, 6 and 8-cylinder engines. The key to these purchases is to make them with an eye towards adaptability and wide range. A basic list of tune-up tools could include:

• Tach/dwell meter.

• Spark plug wrench and gapping tool.

• Feeler gauges for valve adjustment.

• Timing light.

The choice of a timing light should be made carefully. A light which works on the DC current supplied by the vehicle's battery is the best choice; it should have a xenon tube for brightness. On any vehicle with an electronic ignition sys-

Fig. 10 A variety of tools and gauges should be used for spark plug gapping and installation

Fig. 11 Inductive type timing light

Fig. 12 A screw-in type compression gauge is recommended for compression testing

Fig. 13 A vacuum/pressure tester is necessary for many testing procedures

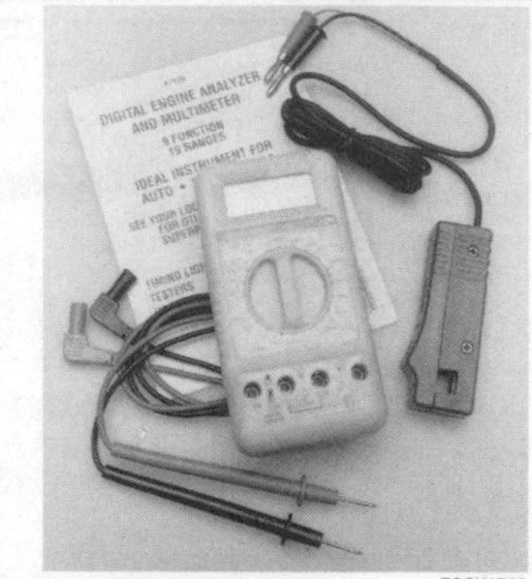

Fig. 14 Most modern automotive multimeters incorporate many helpful features

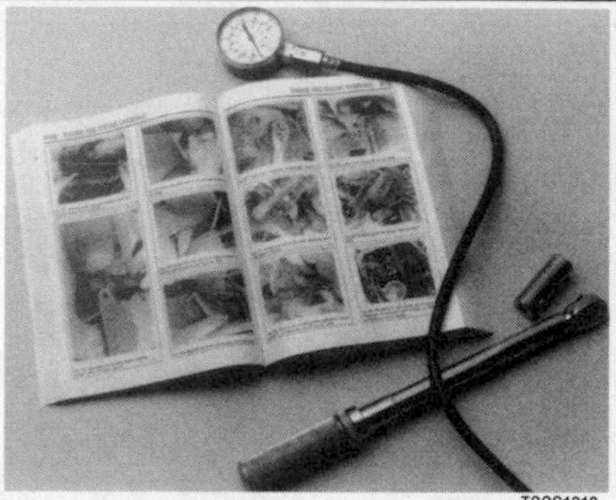

Fig. 15 Proper information is vital, so always have a Chilton Total Car Care manual handy

tem, a timing light with an inductive pickup that clamps around the No. 1 spark plug cable is preferred.

In addition to these basic tools, there are several other tools and gauges you may find useful. These include:

• Compression gauge. The screw-in type is slower to use, but eliminates the possibility of a faulty reading due to escaping pressure.

• Manifold vacuum gauge.

• 12V test light.

• A combination volt/ohmmeter

• Induction Ammeter. This is used for determining whether or not there is current in a wire. These are handy for use if a wire is broken somewhere in a wiring harness.

As a final note, you will probably find a torque wrench necessary for all but the most basic work. The beam type models are perfectly adequate, although the newer click types (breakaway) are easier to use. The click type torque wrenches tend to be more expensive. Also keep in mind that all types of torque wrenches should be periodically checked and/or recalibrated. You will have to decide for yourself which better fits your pocketbook, and purpose.

Special Tools

Normally, the use of special factory tools is avoided for repair procedures, since these are not readily available for the do-it-yourself mechanic. When it is possible to perform the job with more commonly available tools, it will be pointed out, but occasionally, a special tool was designed to perform a specific function and should be used. Before substituting another tool, you should be convinced that neither your safety nor the performance of the vehicle will be compromised.

Special tools can usually be purchased from an automotive parts store or from your dealer. In some cases special tools may be available directly from the tool manufacturer.

SERVICING YOUR VEHICLE SAFELY

♦ See Figures 16, 17 and 18

It is virtually impossible to anticipate all of the hazards involved with automotive maintenance and service, but care and common sense will prevent most accidents.

The rules of safety for mechanics range from "don't smoke around gasoline," to "use the proper tool(s) for the job." The trick to avoiding injuries is to develop safe work habits and to take every possible precaution.

Do's

• Do keep a fire extinguisher and first aid kit handy.

• Do wear safety glasses or goggles when cutting, drilling, grinding or prying, even if you have 20–20 vision. If you wear glasses for the sake of vision, wear safety goggles over your regular glasses.

• Do shield your eyes whenever you work around the battery. Batteries contain sulfuric acid. In case of contact with, flush the area with water or a mixture of water and baking soda, then seek immediate medical attention.

• Do use safety stands (jackstands) for any undervehicle service. Jacks are for raising vehicles; jackstands are for making sure the vehicle stays raised until you want it to come down.

• Do use adequate ventilation when working with any chemicals or hazardous materials. Like carbon monoxide, the asbestos dust resulting from some brake lining wear can be hazardous in sufficient quantities.

• Do disconnect the negative battery cable when working on the electrical system. The secondary ignition system contains EXTREMELY HIGH VOLTAGE. In some cases it can even exceed 50,000 volts.

• Do follow manufacturer's directions whenever working with potentially hazardous materials. Most chemicals and fluids are poisonous.

• Do properly maintain your tools. Loose hammerheads, mushroomed punches and chisels, frayed or poorly grounded electrical cords, excessively worn screwdrivers, spread wrenches (open end), cracked sockets, slipping ratchets, or faulty droplight sockets can cause accidents.

• Likewise, keep your tools clean; a greasy wrench can slip off a bolt head, ruining the bolt and often harming your knuckles in the process.

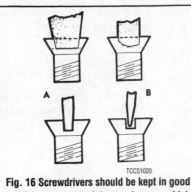

Fig. 16 Screwdrivers should be kept in good condition to prevent injury or damage which could result if the blade slips from the screw

Fig. 17 Using the correct size wrench will help prevent the possibility of rounding off a nut

Fig. 18 NEVER work under a vehicle unless it is supported using safety stands (jackstands)

• Do use the proper size and type of tool for the job at hand. Do select a wrench or socket that fits the nut or bolt. The wrench or socket should sit straight, not cocked.

• Do, when possible, pull on a wrench handle rather than push on it, and adjust your stance to prevent a fall.

• Do be sure that adjustable wrenches are tightly closed on the nut or bolt and pulled so that the force is on the side of the fixed jaw.

• Do strike squarely with a hammer; avoid glancing blows.

• Do set the parking brake and block the drive wheels if the work requires a running engine.

Don'ts

• Don't run the engine in a garage or anywhere else without proper ventilation—EVER! Carbon monoxide is poisonous; it takes a long time to leave the human body and you can build up a deadly supply of it in your system by simply breathing in a little at a time. You may not realize you are slowly poisoning yourself. Always use power vents, windows, fans and/or open the garage door.

• Don't work around moving parts while wearing loose clothing. Short sleeves are much safer than long, loose sleeves. Hard-toed shoes with neoprene soles protect your toes and give a better grip on slippery surfaces. Watches and jewelry is not safe working around a vehicle. Long hair should be tied back under a hat or cap.

• Don't use pockets for toolboxes. A fall or bump can drive a screwdriver deep into your body. Even a rag hanging from your back pocket can wrap around a spinning shaft or fan.

• Don't smoke when working around gasoline, cleaning solvent or other flammable material.

• Don't smoke when working around the battery. When the battery is being charged, it gives off explosive hydrogen gas.

• Don't use gasoline to wash your hands; there are excellent soaps available. Gasoline contains dangerous additives which can enter the body through a cut or through your pores. Gasoline also removes all the natural oils from the skin so that bone dry hands will suck up oil and grease.

• Don't service the air conditioning system unless you are equipped with the necessary tools and training. When liquid or compressed gas refrigerant is released to atmospheric pressure it will absorb heat from whatever it contacts. This will chill or freeze anything it touches.

• Don't use screwdrivers for anything other than driving screws! A screwdriver used as an prying tool can snap when you least expect it, causing injuries. At the very least, you'll ruin a good screwdriver.

• Don't use an emergency jack (that little ratchet, scissors, or pantograph jack supplied with the vehicle) for anything other than changing a flat! These jacks are only intended for emergency use out on the road; they are NOT designed as a maintenance tool. If you are serious about maintaining your vehicle yourself, invest in a hydraulic floor jack of at least a 1½ ton capacity, and at least two sturdy jackstands.

FASTENERS, MEASUREMENTS AND CONVERSIONS

Bolts, Nuts and Other Threaded Retainers

♦ See Figures 19 and 20

Although there are a great variety of fasteners found in the modern car or truck, the most commonly used retainer is the threaded fastener (nuts, bolts, screws, studs, etc.). Most threaded retainers may be reused, provided that they are not damaged in use or during the repair. Some retainers (such as stretch bolts or torque prevailing nuts) are designed to deform when tightened or in use and should not be reinstalled.

Whenever possible, we will note any special retainers which should be replaced during a procedure. But you should always inspect the condition of a retainer when it is removed and replace any that show signs of damage. Check all threads for rust or corrosion which can increase the torque necessary to achieve the desired clamp load for which that fastener was originally selected. Additionally, be sure that the driver surface of the fastener has not been compromised by rounding or other damage. In some cases a driver surface may become only partially rounded, allowing the driver to catch in only one direction. In many of these occurrences, a fastener may be installed and tightened, but the driver would not be able to grip and loosen the fastener again.

If you must replace a fastener, whether due to design or damage, you must ALWAYS be sure to use the proper replacement. In all cases, a retainer of the same design, material and strength should be used. Markings on the heads of most bolts will help determine the proper strength of the fastener. The same material, thread and pitch must be selected to assure proper installation and safe operation of the vehicle afterwards.

Thread gauges are available to help measure a bolt or stud's thread. Most automotive and hardware stores keep gauges available to help you select the proper

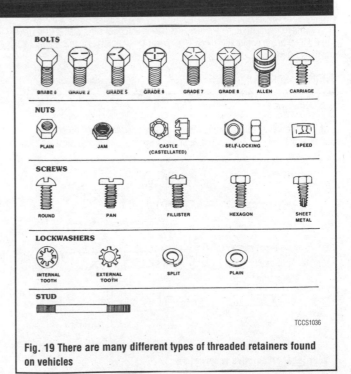

Fig. 19 There are many different types of threaded retainers found on vehicles

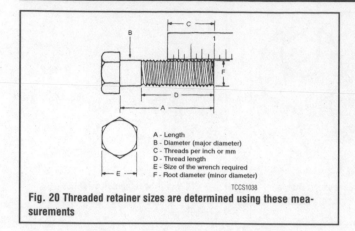

A - Length
B - Diameter (major diameter)
C - Threads per inch or mm
D - Thread length
E - Size of the wrench required
F - Root diameter (minor diameter)

TCCS1038

Fig. 20 Threaded retainer sizes are determined using these measurements

size. In a pinch, you can use another nut or bolt for a thread gauge. If the bolt you are replacing is not too badly damaged, you can select a match by finding another bolt which will thread in its place. If you find a nut which threads properly onto the damaged bolt, then use that nut to help select the replacement bolt.

✳✳ WARNING

Be aware that when you find a bolt with damaged threads, you may also find the nut or drilled hole it was threaded into has also been damaged. If this is the case, you may have to drill and tap the hole, replace the nut or otherwise repair the threads. NEVER try to force a replacement bolt to fit into the damaged threads.

Torque

Torque is defined as the measurement of resistance to turning or rotating. It tends to twist a body about an axis of rotation. A common example of this would be tightening a threaded retainer such as a nut, bolt or screw. Measuring torque is one of the most common ways to help assure that a threaded retainer has been properly fastened.

When tightening a threaded fastener, torque is applied in three distinct areas, the head, the bearing surface and the clamp load. About 50 percent of the measured torque is used in overcoming bearing friction. This is the friction between the bearing surface of the bolt head, screw head or nut face and the base material or washer (the surface on which the fastener is rotating). Approximately 40 percent of the applied torque is used in overcoming thread friction. This leaves only about 10 percent of the applied torque to develop a useful clamp load (the force which holds a joint together). This means that friction can account for as much as 90 percent of the applied torque on a fastener.

TORQUE WRENCHES

♦ See Figure 21

In most applications, a torque wrench can be used to assure proper installation of a fastener. Torque wrenches come in various designs and most automo-

tive supply stores will carry a variety to suit your needs. A torque wrench should be used any time we supply a specific torque value for a fastener. Again, the general rule of "if you are using the right tool for the job, you should not have to strain to tighten a fastener" applies here.

Beam Type

The beam type torque wrench is one of the most popular types. It consists of a pointer attached to the head that runs the length of the flexible beam (shaft) to a scale located near the handle. As the wrench is pulled, the beam bends and the pointer indicates the torque using the scale.

Click (Breakaway) Type

Another popular design of torque wrench is the click type. To use the click type wrench you pre-adjust it to a torque setting. Once the torque is reached, the wrench has a reflex signaling feature that causes a momentary breakaway of the torque wrench body, sending an impulse to the operator's hand.

Pivot Head Type

♦ See Figure 22

Some torque wrenches (usually of the click type) may be equipped with a pivot head which can allow it to be used in areas of limited access. BUT, it must be used properly. To hold a pivot head wrench, grasp the handle lightly, and as you pull on the handle, it should be floated on the pivot point. If the handle comes in contact with the yoke extension during the process of pulling, there is a very good chance the torque readings will be inaccurate because this could alter the wrench loading point. The design of the handle is usually such as to make it inconvenient to deliberately misuse the wrench.

➡ **It should be mentioned that the use of any U-joint, wobble or extension will have an effect on the torque readings, no matter what type of wrench you are using. For the most accurate readings, install the socket directly on the wrench driver. If necessary, straight extensions (which hold a socket directly under the wrench driver) will have the least effect on the torque reading. Avoid any extension that alters the length of the wrench from the handle to the head/driving point (such as a crow's foot). U-joint or wobble extensions can greatly affect the readings; avoid their use at all times.**

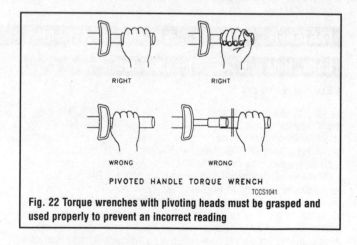

PIVOTED HANDLE TORQUE WRENCH

TCCS1041

Fig. 22 Torque wrenches with pivoting heads must be grasped and used properly to prevent an incorrect reading

Rigid Case (Direct Reading)

A rigid case or direct reading torque wrench is equipped with a dial indicator to show torque values. One advantage of these wrenches is that they can be held at any position on the wrench without affecting accuracy. These wrenches are often preferred because they tend to be compact, easy to read and have a great degree of accuracy.

TORQUE ANGLE METERS

Because the frictional characteristics of each fastener or threaded hole will vary, clamp loads which are based strictly on torque will vary as well.

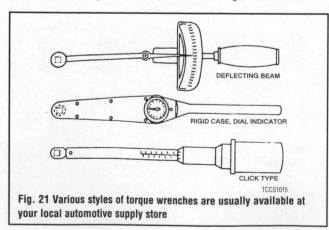

DEFLECTING BEAM

RIGID CASE, DIAL INDICATOR

CLICK TYPE

TCCS1015

Fig. 21 Various styles of torque wrenches are usually available at your local automotive supply store

In most applications, this variance is not significant enough to cause worry. But, in certain applications, a manufacturer's engineers may determine that more precise clamp loads are necessary (such is the case with many aluminum cylinder heads). In these cases, a torque angle method of installation would be specified. When installing fasteners which are torque angle tightened, a predetermined seating torque and standard torque wrench are usually used first to remove any compliance from the joint. The fastener is then tightened the specified additional portion of a turn measured in degrees. A torque angle gauge (mechanical protractor) is used for these applications.

Standard and Metric Measurements

▶ See Figure 23

Throughout this manual, specifications are given to help you determine the condition of various components on your vehicle, or to assist you in their installation. Some of the most common measurements include length (in. or cm/mm), torque (ft. lbs., inch lbs. or Nm) and pressure (psi, in. Hg, kPa or mm Hg). In most cases, we strive to provide the proper measurement as determined by the manufacturer's engineers.

Though, in some cases, that value may not be conveniently measured with what is available in your toolbox. Luckily, many of the measuring devices which are available today will have two scales so the Standard or Metric measurements may easily be taken. If any of the various measuring tools which are available to you do not contain the same scale as listed in the specifications, use the accompanying conversion factors to determine the proper value.

The conversion factor chart is used by taking the given specification and multiplying it by the necessary conversion factor. For instance, looking at the first line, if you have a measurement in inches such as "free-play should be 2 in." but your ruler reads only in millimeters, multiply 2 in. by the conversion factor of 25.4 to get the metric equivalent of 50.8mm. Likewise, if the specification was given only in a Metric measurement, for example in Newton Meters (Nm), then look at the center column first. If the measurement is 100 Nm, multiply it by the conversion factor of 0.738 to get 73.8 ft. lbs.

CONVERSION FACTORS

LENGTH–DISTANCE

Inches (in.)	x 25.4	= Millimeters (mm)	x .0394	= Inches
Feet (ft.)	x .305	= Meters (m)	x 3.281	= Feet
Miles	x 1.609	= Kilometers (km)	x .0621	= Miles

VOLUME

Cubic Inches (in3)	x 16.387	= Cubic Centimeters	x .061	= in3
IMP Pints (IMP pt.)	x .568	= Liters (L)	x 1.76	= IMP pt.
IMP Quarts (IMP qt.)	x 1.137	= Liters (L)	x .88	= IMP qt.
IMP Gallons (IMP gal.)	x 4.546	= Liters (L)	x .22	= IMP gal.
IMP Quarts (IMP qt.)	x 1.201	= US Quarts (US qt.)	x .833	= IMP qt.
IMP Gallons (IMP gal.)	x 1.201	= US Gallons (US gal.)	x .833	= IMP gal.
Fl. Ounces	x 29.573	= Milliliters	x .034	= Ounces
US Pints (US pt.)	x .473	= Liters (L)	x 2.113	= Pints
US Quarts (US qt.)	x .946	= Liters (L)	x 1.057	= Quarts
US Gallons (US gal.)	x 3.785	= Liters (L)	x .264	= Gallons

MASS–WEIGHT

Ounces (oz.)	x 28.35	= Grams (g)	x .035	= Ounces
Pounds (lb.)	x .454	= Kilograms (kg)	x 2.205	= Pounds

PRESSURE

Pounds Per Sq. In. (psi)	x 6.895	= Kilopascals (kPa)	x .145	= psi
Inches of Mercury (Hg)	x .4912	= psi	x 2.036	= Hg
Inches of Mercury (Hg)	x 3.377	= Kilopascals (kPa)	x .2961	= Hg
Inches of Water (H₂O)	x .07355	= Inches of Mercury	x 13.783	= H₂O
Inches of Water (H₂O)	x .03613	= psi	x 27.684	= H₂O
Inches of Water (H₂O)	x .248	= Kilopascals (kPa)	x 4.026	= H₂O

TORQUE

Pounds–Force Inches (in–lb)	x .113	= Newton Meters (N·m)	x 8.85	= in–lb
Pounds–Force Feet (ft–lb)	x 1.356	= Newton Meters (N·m)	x .738	= ft–lb

VELOCITY

Miles Per Hour (MPH)	x 1.609	= Kilometers Per Hour (KPH)	x .621	= MPH

POWER

Horsepower (Hp)	x .745	= Kilowatts	x 1.34	= Horsepower

FUEL CONSUMPTION*

Miles Per Gallon IMP (MPG)	x .354	= Kilometers Per Liter (Km/L)	
Kilometers Per Liter (Km/L)	x 2.352	= IMP MPG	
Miles Per Gallon US (MPG)	x .425	= Kilometers Per Liter (Km/L)	
Kilometers Per Liter (Km/L)	x 2.352	= US MPG	

*It is common to covert from miles per gallon (mpg) to liters/100 kilometers (1/100 km), where mpg (IMP) x 1/100 km = 282 and mpg (US) x 1/100 km = 235.

TEMPERATURE

Degree Fahrenheit (°F)	= (°C x 1.8) + 32
Degree Celsius (°C)	= (°F – 32) x .56

TCCS1044

Fig. 23 Standard and metric conversion factors chart

SERIAL NUMBER IDENTIFICATION

Vehicle

▶ See Figures 24, 25 and 26

The Vehicle Identification Number (VIN) is a seventeen digit alpha/numeric sequence stamped on a plate which is located at the top, left hand side of the instrument panel.

As far as the car owner is concerned, many of the digits in the VIN are of little or no value. At certain times, it may be necessary to refer to the VIN to interpret certain information, such as when ordering replacement parts or determining if your vehicle is involved in a factory service campaign (recall). In either of these instances, the following information may be helpful:
• 1ST DIGIT—Indicate the country of manufacture. A **1** designates the USA; **2** designates Canada.

• 8TH DIGIT—Indicates the type and the manufacturer of the original engine which was installed in the vehicle.
• 10TH DIGIT—Indicates the model year of the vehicle. **C** designates a 1982 model, **D** is for 1983, and so on. Certain letters such as I, O and Q are not used due to possible confusion with numbers.
• 11TH DIGIT—Indicates the specific plant at which the vehicle was assembled.
• 12TH–17TH DIGITS—This is the plant sequential number, which identifies the specific number of each vehicle within a production run. In the event of engineering change or a recall involving only a certain quantity of vehicles within a production run, the affected vehicles can be identified with this number.

The Vehicle Emission Control Information (VECI) tag is located on the front of the strut tower on most vehicles. This tag identifies the information needed to tune-up your vehicle.

86811022

Fig. 24 The VIN tag is located on the dash, behind the windshield, in the upper left hand corner

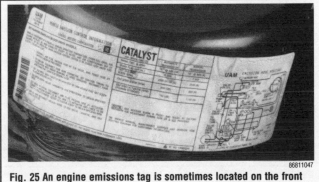

86811047

Fig. 25 An engine emissions tag is sometimes located on the front strut tower of your car

(1)(2)(3)	(4)	(5)	(6)	(7)	(8)	(9)	(10)	(11)	(12) thru (17)
DIVISION/ MAKE	CAR LINE CODE	CARLINE/ SERIES	BODY TYPE	RESTRAINT SYST.	ENGINE CODE	CHECK DIGIT	MODEL YEAR	PLANT CODE	PRODUCTION SEQUENCE NUMBER
1 G 1	G	Z	1*	1@	H	X	H	R	1 0 0 . 0 0 1

DIVISION CODE MAKE

1G1 Chevrolet Passenger
1G2 Pontiac Passenger
1G3 Oldsmobile Pass.
1G4 Buick Passenger
1G6 Cadillac Passenger
1G7 GM of Canada Pass.
1GC Chevrolet Truck
1GT GMC Truck
J8C*Chevrolet Truck
1G8 Chevrolet MPV
1G5 GMC Truck MPV
*
GM merchandised vehicle
built by Isuzu Motors.
Fujisawa Japan

CARLINE CODE

CHEVROLET

A-Celebrity
B-Impala Caprice (RWD)
F-Camaro
G-El Camino/Monte Carlo
J-Cavalier
L-
M-Sprint
R-Spectrum
S-TVX (Venture)
T-Chevette
Y-Corvette

PONTIAC

A-6000
B-Safari
F-Firebird
G-Grand Prix Brougham
H-Bonneville
J-Sunbird 2000
N-Grand Am
P-Fiero
T-T1000

OLDSMOBILE

A-Cutlass Ciera
B-Custom Cruiser (RWD)
C-98 Regency (FWD)
E-Toronado
G-Cutlass
H-Delta 88
J-Firenza
N-Calais

BUICK

A-Century
B-LeSabre Electra
  Estate Wagon (RWD)
C-Electra (FWD)
E-Riviera
G-Regal
H-LeSabre
J-Skyhawk

CAR LINE / SERIES

CHEVROLET (Code 1)

B-Chevette CS
C-Cavalier
D-Cavalier CS
E-Cavalier(Hatchback)
  (Type 10 - Convert.)
F-Spectrum - Level I
F-Cavalier Z24
G-Spectrum - Level II
K-Nova
L-Caprice
N-Caprice Classic
P-Camaro Sport Coupe
R-Sprint
S-Sprint ER
T-Corsica
U-Caprice Brougham
V-Beretta
W-Celebrity (19-27)
Y-Corvette
Z-Monte Carlo

PONTIAC (Code 2)

B-Sunbird 2000
D-Sunbird 2000 SE
E-Pontiac 6000 SE
E-Fiero Coupe
E-Grand Am
F-Fiero(SE)(37)
F-Pontiac 6000
G-Fiero GT Sport Coupe
G-Pontiac 6000 LE
H-Pontiac 6000 STE
J-Grand Prix
K-Grand Prix LE
L-T1000(08-68)
L-Safari Wagon
M-Fiero Sport Coupe
P-Grand Prix Brougham
R-Firefly
S-Firebird(87)
U-Sunbird GT
V-Grand Am LE
W-Grand AM SE
W-Firebird Trans Am
X-Bonneville
Z-Bonneville LE

OLDSMOBILE (Code 3)

C-Firenza
D-Firenza Brougham
F-Calais
J-Cutlass Ciera LS
K-Cutlass Calais
M-Cutlass Supreme
  Brougham(47-69)

OLDSMOBILE (Code 3)

M-Cutlass Ciera
  Brougham(19-27)
N-Delta 88 Royale
P-Custom Cruiser
R-Cutlass Supreme
T-Calais Supreme
W-98 Regency Brougham
  (FWD)
X-98 Regency(FWD)
Y-Delta 88 Royale
  Brougham
Z-Toronado Brougham

BUICK (Code 4)

C-Skylark
D-Skylark Limited
E-Skyhawk(T Type)
F-Electra(T Type)(FWD)
G-Century Sport(T Type)
H-Century Custom
H-LeSabre
J-Regal
J-Somerset Custom
K-Somerset(T Type)
L-Century Limited
M-Regal Limited
M-Somerset Limited
P-LeSabre Custom
R-LeSabre Limited
R-LeSabre Estate Wagon
S-Skyhawk Custom
T-Skyhawk Limited
V-Electra Estate(RWD)
W-Electra Park Ave(FWD)
X-Electra Limited(FWD)
Y-Riviera "T"
Z-Riviera Luxury

CADILLAC (Code 6)

B-Fleetwood(FWD)
D-DeVille(FWD)
G-Cimarron
H-Limousine
L-Eldorado
R-Allante
S-Seville
S-Fleetwood 60 Special
W-Fleetwood Brougham
  (RWD)

GM TRUCK & COACH
(Code 5)

W-Caballero

ENGINE CODES

CODE	LITERS		CARB	DIV USAGE
A	3.8	V6	2	1234
C	1.6	L4	2	12
D	2.3	L4	FI	3
F	5.0	V8	TPI	12
G	5.0	V8	4	12
H	5.0	V8	4	1234
K	2.0	L4	EFI	1
L	3.0	V6	MFI	234
M	2.0	L4	MFI	1
R	2.5	L4	TBI	1234
S	2.8	V6	MFI	12
U	2.5	L4	TBI	234
W	2.8	V6	MFI	12346
Y	5.0	V8	4	34
Z	4.3	V6	TBI	12 4
1	2.0	L4	EFI	1 34
2	1.0	L3	EFI	1
3	3.8	V6	MFI	34
4	1.6	L4	2	1
5	1.0	L3	2	1
6	5.7	V8	4	1
7	3.8	V6	SFI	4
7	1.5	L4	2	1
7	4.1	V8	DFI	6
8	5.7	V8	MFI	1
8	4.1	V8	DFI	6
9	2.8	V6	MFI	2
9	5.0	V8	4	3
9	3.8	V6	SFI	4

NOTE: DIVISION / MAKE
1st Position = Country
    1 = United States
    2 = Canada
    J = Japan

2nd Position = Manufacture
    G = General Motors

3rd Position = Division
    1 = Chevrolet
    2 = Pontiac
    3 = Oldsmobile
    4 = Buick
    6 = Cadillac
    7 = Canada
    Z = Isuzu (Luv)

BUICK (Cont'd)	CADILLAC
N-Somerset Regal	D-Fleetwood DeVille(RWD)
	E-Eldorado
CADILLAC	J-Cimarron
	K-Seville
C-DeVille(FWD)	V-Allante

@ RESTRAINT SYSTEM TYPE
1 MANUAL BELTS
2 MANUAL BELTS(BUILT IN SFTY)
3 MANUAL BELTS(BUILT IN SFTY-
            DRIVER ONLY)
4 AUTOMATIC BELTS

86811021

Fig. 26 General Motors vehicle identification numbering system

Body

▶ **See Figure 27**

An identification plate for body-related items is attached to the front tie bar, just behind the passenger side headlamp. Information on the body identification plate would rarely be useful to the owner. An illustration of the plate is provided.

Engine

▶ **See Figures 28 and 29**

The engine identification code will sometimes be required to order replacement engine parts. The code is stamped in different locations, depending upon the size of the engine. Refer to the accompanying illustrations to determine the code location for your engine.

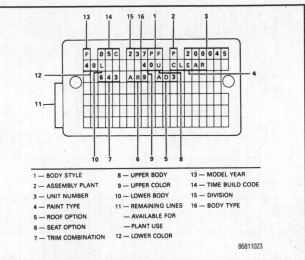

1 — BODY STYLE	8 — UPPER BODY	13 — MODEL YEAR
2 — ASSEMBLY PLANT	9 — UPPER COLOR	14 — TIME BUILD CODE
3 — UNIT NUMBER	10 — LOWER BODY	15 — DIVISION
4 — PAINT TYPE	11 — REMAINING LINES	16 — BODY TYPE
5 — ROOF OPTION	— AVAILABLE FOR	
6 — SEAT OPTION	— PLANT USE	
7 — TRIM COMBINATION	12 — LOWER COLOR	

86811023

Fig. 27 General Motors body plate identification numbering system

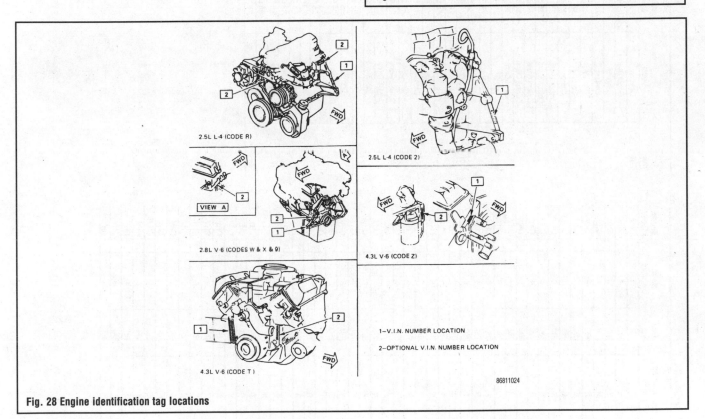

2.5L L-4 (CODE R)

2.5L L-4 (CODE 2)

VIEW A

2.8L V-6 (CODES W & X & 9)

4.3L V-6 (CODE Z)

4.3L V-6 (CODE T)

1–V.I.N. NUMBER LOCATION

2–OPTIONAL V.I.N. NUMBER LOCATION

86811024

Fig. 28 Engine identification tag locations

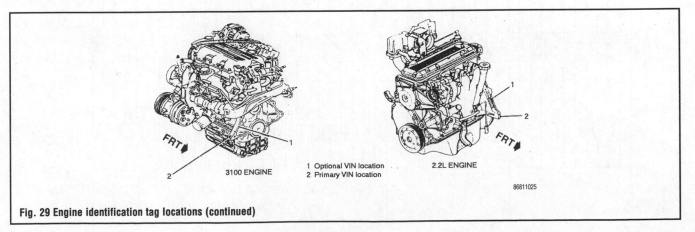

3100 ENGINE

2.2L ENGINE

1 Optional VIN location
2 Primary VIN location

86811025

Fig. 29 Engine identification tag locations (continued)

ENGINE IDENTIFICATION

Year	Model	Engine Displacement Liters (cc)	Engine Series (ID/VIN)	Fuel System	No. of Cylinders	Engine Type
1982	Celebrity	2.5 (2475)	R	TBI	4	OHV
	Celebrity	2.5 (2475)	5	2BC	4	OHV
	Celebrity	2.8 (2835)	X	2BC	6	OHV
	Century	2.5 (2475)	R	TBI	4	OHV
	Century	2.8 (2835)	X	2BC	6	OHV
	Century	3.0 (2999)	E	2BC	6	OHV
	Cutlass Ciera	2.5 (2475)	R	TBI	4	OHV
	Cutlass Ciera	2.8 (2835)	X	2BC	6	OHV
	Cutlass Ciera	3.0 (2999)	E	2BC	6	OHV
	6000	2.5 (2475)	R	TBI	4	OHV
	6000	2.8 (2835)	X	2BC	6	OHV
1983	Celebrity	2.5 (2475)	R	TBI	4	OHV
	Celebrity	2.5 (2475)	5	2BC	4	OHV
	Celebrity	2.8 (2835)	X	2BC	6	OHV
	Century	2.5 (2475)	R	TBI	4	OHV
	Century	2.8 (2835)	X	2BC	6	OHV
	Century	3.0 (2999)	E	2BC	6	OHV
	Cutlass Ciera	2.5 (2475)	R	TBI	4	OHV
	Cutlass Ciera	2.8 (2835)	X	2BC	6	OHV
	Cutlass Ciera	3.0 (2999)	E	2BC	6	OHV
	6000	2.5 (2475)	R	TBI	4	OHV
	6000	2.8 (2835)	X	2BC	6	OHV
1984	Celebrity	2.5 (2475)	R	TBI	4	OHV
	Celebrity	2.5 (2475)	5	2BC	4	OHV
	Celebrity	2.8 (2835)	X	2BC	6	OHV
	Century	2.5 (2475)	R	TBI	4	OHV
	Century	2.8 (2835)	X	2BC	6	OHV
	Century	3.0 (2999)	E	2BC	6	OHV
	Century	3.8 (3785)	3	MFI	6	OHV
	Cutlass Ciera	2.5 (2475)	R	TBI	4	OHV
	Cutlass Ciera	3.8 (3875)	3	MFI	6	OHV
	Cutlass Ciera	3.0 (2999)	E	2BC	6	OHV
	6000	2.5 (2475)	R	TBI	4	OHV
	6000	2.8 (2835)	X	2BC	6	OHV
	6000	2.8 (2835) HO	Z	2BC	6	OHV
1985	Celebrity	2.5 (2475)	R	TBI	4	OHV
	Celebrity	2.8 (2835)	X	2BC	6	OHV
	Celebrity	2.8 (2835)	W	MFI	6	OHV
	Century	2.5 (2474)	R	TBI	4	OHV
	Century	2.8 (2835)	X	2BC	6	OHV
	Century	3.0 (2999)	E	2BC	6	OHV
	Century	3.8 (3785)	3	MFI	6	OHV
	Cutlass Ciera	2.5 (2474)	R	TBI	4	OHV
	Cutlass Ciera	3.0 (2999)	E	2BC	6	OHV
	Cutlass Ciera	3.8 (3785)	3	MFI	6	OHV
	6000	2.5 (2475)	R	TBI	4	OHV
	6000	2.8 (2835)	X	2BC	6	OHV
	6000	2.8 (2835) HO	W	MFI	6	OHV

91081C01

ENGINE IDENTIFICATION

Year	Model	Engine Displacement Liters (cc)	Engine Series (ID/VIN)	Fuel System	No. of Cylinders	Engine Type
1986	Celebrity	2.5 (2475)	R	TBI	4	OHV
	Celebrity	2.8 (2835) HO	W	MFI	6	OHV
	Celebrity	2.8 (2835)	X	2BC	6	OHV
	Century	2.5 (2474)	R	TBI	4	OHV
	Century	2.8 (2835)	X	2BC	6	OHV
	Century	3.8 (3785)	3	MFI	6	OHV
	Century	3.8 (3785)	B	MFI	6	OHV
	Cutlass Ciera	2.5 (2474)	R	TBI	4	OHV
	Cutlass Ciera	2.8 (2835)	X	2BC	6	OHV
	Cutlass Ciera	2.8 (2835)	W	MFI	6	OHV
	Cutlass Ciera	3.8 (3785)	3	MFI	6	OHV
	6000	3.8 (3785)	B	MFI	6	OHV
	6000	2.5 (2475)	R	TBI	4	OHV
	6000	2.8 (2835)	X	2BC	6	OHV
	6000	2.8 (2835) HO	W	MFI	6	OHV
1987	Celebrity	2.5 (2474)	R	TBI	4	OHV
	Celebrity	2.8 (2835)	W	MFI	6	OHV
	Century	2.5 (2474)	R	TBI	4	OHV
	Century	2.8 (2835)	W	MFI	6	OHV
	Century	3.8 (3785) HO	3	MFI	6	OHV
	Cutlass Ciera	2.5 (2474)	R	TBI	4	OHV
	Cutlass Ciera	2.8 (2835)	W	MFI	6	OHV
	Cutlass Ciera	3.8 (3785)	3	MFI	6	OHV
	6000	2.5 (2475)	R	TBI	4	OHV
	6000	2.8 (2835)	W	MFI	6	OHV
1988	Celebrity	2.5 (2474)	R	TBI	4	OHV
	Celebrity	2.8 (2835)	W	MFI	6	OHV
	Century	2.5 (2474)	R	TBI	4	OHV
	Century	2.8 (2835)	W	MFI	6	OHV
	Century	3.8 (3785) HO	3	MFI	6	OHV
	Cutlass Ciera	2.5 (2474)	R	TBI	4	OHV
	Cutlass Ciera	2.8 (2835)	W	MFI	6	OHV
	Cutlass Ciera	3.8 (3785)	3	MFI	6	OHV
	6000	2.5 (2475)	R	TBI	4	OHV
	6000	2.8 (2835)	W	MFI	6	OHV

91081C02

ENGINE IDENTIFICATION

Year	Model	Engine Displacement Liters (cc)	Engine Series (ID/VIN)	Fuel System	No. of Cylinders	Engine Type
1989	Celebrity	2.5 (2474)	R	TBI	4	OHV
	Celebrity	2.8 (2835)	W	MFI	6	OHV
	Century	2.5 (2474)	R	TBI	4	OHV
	Century	2.8 (2835)	W	MFI	6	OHV
	Century	3.3 (3342)	N	MFI	6	OHV
	Cutlass Ciera	2.5 (2474)	R	TBI	4	OHV
	Cutlass Ciera	2.8 (2835)	W	MFI	6	OHV
	Cutlass Ciera	3.3 (3342)	N	MFI	6	OHV
	Cutlass Cruiser	2.5 (2474)	R	TBI	4	OHV
	Cutlass Cruiser	2.8 (2835)	W	MFI	6	OHV
	Cutlass Cruiser	3.3 (3342)	N	MFI	6	OHV
	6000	2.5 (2475)	R	TBI	4	OHV
	6000	2.8 (2835)	W	MFI	6	OHV
	6000	3.1 (3136)	T	MFI	6	OHV
1990	Celebrity	2.5 (2475)	R	TBI	4	OHV
	Celebrity	3.1 (3130)	T	MFI	6	OHV
	Century	2.5 (2474)	R	TBI	4	OHV
	Century	3.3 (3342)	N	MFI	6	OHV
	Cutlass Ciera	2.5 (2474)	R	TBI	4	OHV
	Cutlass Ciera	3.3 (3342)	N	MFI	6	OHV
	Cutlass Cruiser	2.5 (2474)	R	TBI	4	OHV
	Cutlass Cruiser	3.3 (3342)	N	MFI	6	OHV
	6000	2.5 (2475)	R	TBI	4	OHV
	6000	3.1 (3136)	T	MFI	6	OHV
1991	Century	2.5 (2474)	R	TBI	4	OHV
	Century	3.3 (3342)	N	MFI	6	OHV
	Cutlass Ciera	2.5 (2474)	R	TBI	4	OHV
	Cutlass Ciera	3.3 (3342)	N	MFI	6	OHV
	Cutlass Cruiser	2.5 (2474)	R	TBI	4	OHV
	Cutlass Cruiser	3.3 (3342)	N	MFI	6	OHV
	6000	2.5 (2475)	R	TBI	4	OHV
	6000	3.1 (3136)	T	MFI	6	OHV
1992	Century	2.2 (2195)	4	MFI	4	OHV
	Century	3.3 (3342)	N	MFI	6	OHV
	Cutlass Ciera	2.5 (2474)	R	TBI	4	OHV
	Cutlass Ciera	3.3 (3342)	N	MFI	6	OHV
	Cutlass Cruiser	2.5 (2474)	R	TBI	4	OHV
	Cutlass Cruiser	3.3 (3342)	N	MFI	6	OHV
1993	Century	3.1 (3130)	M	SFI	6	OHV
	Cutlass Ciera	2.2 (2195)	4	MFI	4	OHV
	Cutlass Ciera	3.3 (3342)	N	MFI	6	OHV
	Cutlass Cruiser	2.2 (2195)	4	MFI	4	OHV
	Cutlass Cruiser	3.3 (3342)	N	MFI	6	OHV

91081C03

ENGINE IDENTIFICATION

Year	Model	Engine Displacement Liters (cc)	Engine Series (ID/VIN)	Fuel System	No. of Cylinders	Engine Type
1994	Century	2.2 (2195)	4	MFI	4	OHV
	Century	3.1 (3130)	M	SFI	6	OHV
	Cutlass Ciera	2.2 (2195)	4	MFI	4	OHV
	Cutlass Ciera	3.1 (3130)	M	SFI	6	OHV
	Cutlass Cruiser	2.2 (2195)	4	MFI	4	OHV
	Cutlass Cruiser	3.1 (3130)	M	SFI	6	OHV
1995	Cutlass Ciera	2.2 (2195)	4	MFI	4	OHV
	Cutlass Ciera	3.1 (3130)	M	SFI	6	OHV
	Cutlass Cruiser	2.2 (2195)	4	MFI	4	OHV
	Cutlass Cruiser	3.1 (3130)	M	SFI	6	OHV
1996	Cutlass Ciera	2.2 (2195)	4	MFI	4	OHV
	Cutlass Ciera	3.1 (3130)	M	SFI	6	OHV
	Cutlass Cruiser	2.2 (2195)	4	MFI	4	OHV
	Cutlass Cruiser	3.1 (3130)	M	SFI	6	OHV

BC - Barrel carburetor
HO - High output
MFI - Multi-Port Fuel Injection
OHV - Overhead valve
SFI - Sequential Fuel Injection
TBI - Throttle Body Fuel Injection

91081C04

Transaxle

♦ **See Figures 30 and 31**

The transaxle code serves the same purpose as the engine identification code. Transaxle code locations may be determined by referring to the accompanying illustrations.

Drive Axle

The drive axle code is stamped onto the axle shaft near the CV-boot.

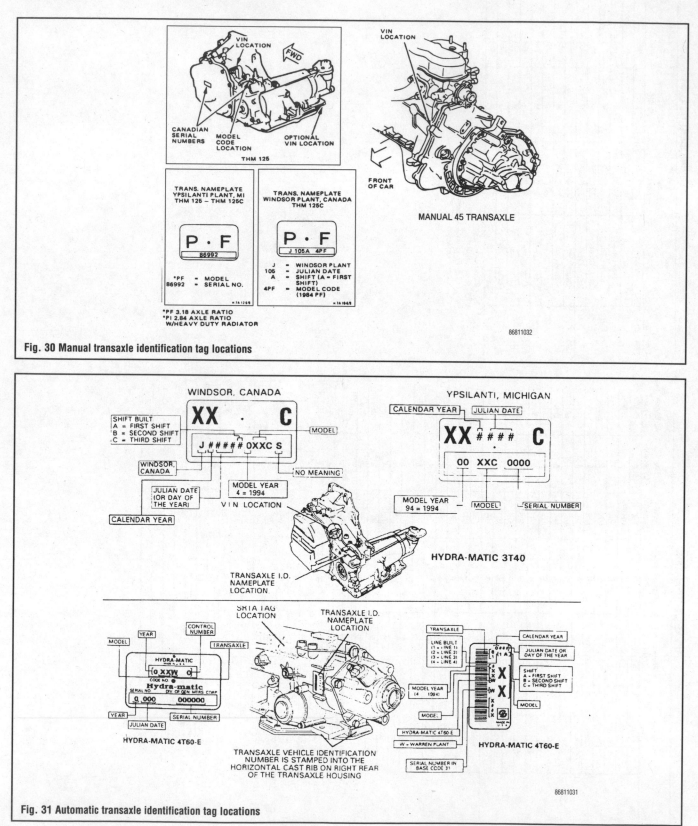

Fig. 30 Manual transaxle identification tag locations

Fig. 31 Automatic transaxle identification tag locations

ROUTINE MAINTENANCE

Proper maintenance of any vehicle is the key to long and trouble-free vehicle life. As a conscientious car owner, set aside a Saturday morning, say once a month, to check or replace items which could cause major problems later. Keep your own personal log to jot down which services you performed, how much parts cost you, the date, and the exact odometer reading at the time. Keep all receipts for such items as engine oil and filters, so that they may be referred to in case of related problems or to determine operating expenses. As a do-it-yourselfer, these receipts are the only proof you have that the required maintenance was performed. In the event of a warranty problem, these receipts will be invaluable.

The literature provided with your car when it was originally delivered includes the factory recommended maintenance schedule. If you no longer have this literature, replacement copies are usually available from the dealer.

Air Cleaner

REMOVAL & INSTALLATION

▶ **See Figures 32 and 33**

The air cleaner element should be checked periodically. Regular air cleaner element replacement is a must, since a partially clogged element will cause a performance loss, decreased fuel mileage, and engine damage (if enough dirt gets into the cylinders and contaminates the engine oil).

1. Replacement of the element is simply a matter of removing the wing nut(s) or clamps from the air cleaner lid. Some assemblies have screws to hold down the lid along with the clamps.

Fig. 32 Loosen and remove the air cleaner wing nut from the cleaner lid on a 2.8L engine

2. Once this is done lift off the lid, and remove the old filter element.
To install:
3. Wipe the inside of the housing with a damp cloth before placing the new element into the housing.
4. Place the new element in the housing.
5. Install the lid and tighten. On vehicles with wing nut(s), just snug it down with moderate finger pressure. Excessive tightening of the wing nut(s) will damage components.
6. On vehicles with screws and clamps, simply tighten the screws and hook the clamps.

➡**Never attempt to clean or soak the element in gasoline, oil, or cleaning solvent. The element is designed to be a throw-away item.**

Fuel Filter

REMOVAL & INSTALLATION

Carbureted Engines

▶ **See Figure 34**

An internal filter is located in the inlet fitting of all carburetors. The elements are spring loaded and are held against the inlet fitting gasket surface.
1. Disconnect the negative battery cable.
2. Disconnect the fuel line at the fuel inlet filter nut. Remove the inlet filter nut, the filter and the spring.
To install:
3. Install a new filter (with the check valve end facing the fuel line), the spring, the gasket and the fuel line nut.
4. Tighten the fuel filter nut to 18 ft. lbs. (24 Nm), then install the fuel line.
5. Connect the negative battery cable. Check for leaks.

Fuel Injected Engines

▶ **See Figure 35**

On throttle body vehicles, there are two kinds of in-line filters available. From 1982–85 the filter is located in the engine compartment. From 1986 the filter is located to the left of the fuel tank. On the MFI engines, the filter is located on the left side of the fuel tank also.
1. Disconnect the negative battery cable.
2. Relieve the fuel system pressure.
3. For engines other than early TBI with an engine compartment mounted filter, raise and safely support the vehicle.
4. Remove the filter bracket attaching screw(s) and filter bracket.
5. Grasp the filter and 1 fuel line fitting. Twist the quick-connect fitting ¼ turn in each direction to loosen any dirt within the fitting. Repeat for the other fuel line fitting.
6. Use compressed air, blow out dirt from the quick-connect fittings at both ends of the fuel filter.

Fig. 33 Lifting out the filter element on the 2.8L engine

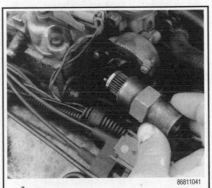

Fig. 34 Removing an internal fuel filter on a carbureted engine

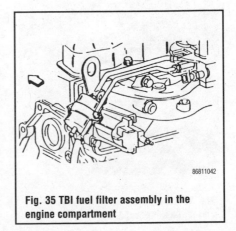

Fig. 35 TBI fuel filter assembly in the engine compartment

✻✻ CAUTION

Always wear safety goggles when using compressed air.

7. To disconnect the fuel line fittings, squeeze the plastic tabs on the male end of the connector and pull the fitting apart. Repeat for the other fitting.

8. Remove the fuel filter.

To install:

9. Remove the protective caps from the new filter.

10. Connect the filter retainers on the filter inlet and outlet pipes.

11. Install the filter and quick-connect fittings.

12. On rear mounted filters, align the filter bracket on the frame, then attach with mounting screw(s).

13. Lower the vehicle, if raised. Tighten the fuel filler cap.

14. Connect the negative battery cable.

15. Turn the ignition **ON** and inspect for leaks.

16. Reset the clock, radio and any other accessories if required.

PCV System

The Positive Crankcase Ventilation (PCV) valve regulated crankcase pressure during various engine running conditions. At high vacuum (idle speed and partial load range) it will open slightly and at low vacuum (full throttle) it will open fully. This allows vapors to be drawn from the crankcase by engine vacuum and then sucked into the combustion chamber where they are burned.

REMOVAL & INSTALLATION

PCV Valve

♦ **See Figure 36**

The PCV valve must be replaced every 30,000 miles (48,300 km). Details on the PCV system, including system tests, are given in Section 4.

The valve is located in a rubber grommet on the valve cover, connected to the air cleaner housing by a large diameter rubber hose.

1. Pull the valve (with the hose attached) from the rubber grommet in the valve cover.

2. Remove the valve from the hose.

3. Inspect the rubber grommet that houses the valve for deterioration, replace if needed.

To install:

4. Install a new valve into the hose.

5. Press the valve back into the rubber grommet in the valve cover.

PCV Filter

Some vehicles are equipped with a PCV filter which is located in the air cleaner housing and must be replaced every 50,000 miles (80,000 km).

1. Remove the air cleaner housing lid.

2. Slide back the filter retaining clip and remove the old filter.

3. Install the new filter, attach the retaining clip, then install the housing lid.

Evaporative Canister

SERVICING

♦ **See Figure 37**

The evaporator canister should be checked every 12 months or 15,000 miles (24,000 km). Check the fuel vapor lines and the vacuum hoses for proper connections and correct routing, as well as condition. Replace clogged, damaged or deteriorated parts as necessary.

For more details on the evaporative emissions system, please refer to Section 4.

Battery

PRECAUTIONS

Always use caution when working on or near the battery. Never allow a tool to bridge the gap between the negative and positive battery terminals. Also, be careful not to allow a tool to provide a ground between the positive cable/terminal and any metal component on the vehicle. Either of these conditions will cause a short circuit, leading to sparks and possible personal injury.

Do not smoke or all open flames/sparks near a battery; the gases contained in the battery are very explosive and, if ignited, could cause severe injury or death.

All batteries, regardless of type, should be carefully secured by a battery hold-down device. If not, the terminals or casing may crack from stress during vehicle operation. A battery which is not secured may allow acid to leak, making it discharge faster. The acid can also eat away at components under the hood.

Always inspect the battery case for cracks, leakage and corrosion. A white corrosive substance on the battery case or on nearby components would indicate a leaking or cracked battery. If the battery is cracked, it should be replaced immediately.

GENERAL MAINTENANCE

Always keep the battery cables and terminals free of corrosion. Check and clean these components about once a year.

Keep the top of the battery clean, as a film of dirt can help discharge a battery that is not used for long periods. A solution of baking soda and water may be used for cleaning, but be careful to flush this off with clear water. DO NOT let any of the solution into the filler holes. Baking soda neutralizes battery acid and will de-activate a battery cell.

Batteries in vehicles which are not operated on a regular basis can fall victim to parasitic loads (small current drains which are constantly drawing current from the battery). Normal parasitic loads may drain a battery on a vehicle that is in storage and not used for 6–8 weeks. Vehicles that have additional accessories such as a phone or an alarm system may discharge a battery sooner. If the vehicle is to be stored for longer periods in a secure area and the alarm system is not necessary, the negative battery cable should be disconnected to protect the battery.

86811049

Fig. 36 Remove the PCV valve, inspect and replace if needed

86811050

Fig. 37 Check the vapor lines and vacuum hoses for proper connection and correct routing, as well as condition. Replace clogged, damaged or deteriorated parts, as necessary

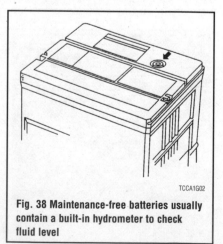

TCCA1G02

Fig. 38 Maintenance-free batteries usually contain a built-in hydrometer to check fluid level

Remember that constantly deep cycling a battery (completely discharging and recharging it) will shorten battery life.

BATTERY FLUID

♦ **See Figure 38**

Check the battery electrolyte level at least once a month, or more often in hot weather or during periods of extended vehicle operation. On non-sealed batteries, the level can be checked either through the case (if translucent) or by removing the cell caps. The electrolyte level in each cell should be kept filled to the split ring inside each cell, or the line marked on the outside of the case.

If the level is low, add only distilled water through the opening until the level is correct. Each cell must be checked and filled individually. Distilled water should be used, because the chemicals and minerals found in most drinking water are harmful to the battery and could significantly shorten its life.

If water is added in freezing weather, the vehicle should be driven several miles to allow the water to mix with the electrolyte. Otherwise, the battery could freeze.

Although some maintenance-free batteries have removable cell caps, the electrolyte condition and level on all sealed maintenance-free batteries must be checked using the built-in hydrometer "eye." The exact type of eye will vary. But, most battery manufacturers, apply a sticker to the battery itself explaining the readings.

➡ **Although the readings from built-in hydrometers will vary, a green eye usually indicates a properly charged battery with sufficient fluid level. A dark eye is normally an indicator of a battery with sufficient fluid, but which is low in charge. A light or yellow eye usually indicates that electrolyte has dropped below the necessary level. In this last case, sealed batteries with an insufficient electrolyte must usually be discarded.**

Checking the Specific Gravity

♦ **See Figures 39, 40 and 41**

A hydrometer is required to check the specific gravity on all batteries that are not maintenance-free. On batteries that are maintenance-free, the specific gravity is checked by observing the built-in hydrometer "eye" on the top of the battery case.

✳✳ CAUTION

Battery electrolyte contains sulfuric acid. If you should splash any on your skin or in your eyes, flush the affected area with plenty of clear water. If it lands in your eyes, get medical help immediately.

The fluid (sulfuric acid solution) contained in the battery cells will tell you many things about the condition of the battery. Because the cell plates must be kept submerged below the fluid level in order to operate, the fluid level is extremely important. And, because the specific gravity of the acid is an indication of electrical charge, testing the fluid can be an aid in determining if the battery must be replaced. A battery in a vehicle with a properly operating charging system should require little maintenance, but careful, periodic inspection should reveal problems before they leave you stranded.

At least once a year, check the specific gravity of the battery. It should be between 1.20 and 1.26 on the gravity scale. Most auto stores carry a variety of inexpensive battery hydrometers. These can be used on any non-sealed battery to test the specific gravity in each cell.

The battery testing hydrometer has a squeeze bulb at one end and a nozzle at the other. Battery electrolyte is sucked into the hydrometer until the float is lifted from its seat. The specific gravity is then read by noting the position of the float. If gravity is low in one or more cells, the battery should be slowly charged and checked again to see if the gravity has come up. Generally, if after charging, the specific gravity between any two cells varies more than 50 points (0.50), the battery should be replaced, as it can no longer produce sufficient voltage to guarantee proper operation.

CABLES

♦ **See Figures 42 thru 47**

Once a year (or as necessary), the battery terminals and the cable clamps should be cleaned. Loosen the clamps and remove the cables, negative cable first. On top post batteries, the use of a puller specially made for this purpose is recommended. These are inexpensive and available in most parts stores. Side terminal battery cables are secured with a small bolt.

Clean the cable clamps and the battery terminal with a wire brush, until all corrosion, grease, etc., is removed and the metal is shiny. It is especially important to clean the inside of the clamp thoroughly (an old knife is useful here), since a small deposit of oxidation there will prevent a sound connection and inhibit starting or charging. Special tools are available for cleaning these parts, one type for conventional top post batteries and another type for side terminal batteries. It is also a good idea to apply some dielectric grease to the terminal, as this will aid in the prevention of corrosion.

After the clamps and terminals are clean, reinstall the cables, negative cable last; DO NOT hammer the clamps onto battery posts. Tighten the clamps securely, but do not distort them. Give the clamps and terminals a thin external coating of grease after installation, to retard corrosion.

Check the cables at the same time that the terminals are cleaned. If the cable insulation is cracked or broken, or if the ends are frayed, the cable should be replaced with a new cable of the same length and gauge.

CHARGING

✳✳ CAUTION

The chemical reaction which takes place in all batteries generates explosive hydrogen gas. A spark can cause the battery to explode and splash acid. To avoid personal injury, be sure there is proper ventilation and take appropriate fire safety precautions when working with or near a battery.

A battery should be charged at a slow rate to keep the plates inside from getting too hot. However, if some maintenance-free batteries are allowed to discharge until they are almost "dead," they may have to be charged at a high rate to bring them back to "life." Always follow the charger manufacturer's instructions on charging the battery.

TCCA1P07

Fig. 39 On non-sealed batteries, the fluid level can be checked by removing the cell caps

TCCA1P08

Fig. 40 If the fluid level is low, add only distilled water until the level is correct

TCCA1P09

Fig. 41 Check the specific gravity of the battery's electrolyte with a hydrometer

Fig. 42 Loosen the battery cable retaining nut . . .

Fig. 43 . . . then disconnect the cable from the battery

Fig. 44 A wire brush may be used to clean any corrosion or foreign material from the cable

Fig. 45 The wire brush can also be used to remove any corrosion or dirt from the battery terminal

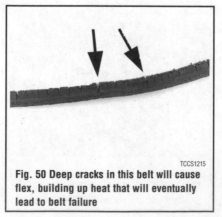

Fig. 46 The battery terminal can also be cleaned using a solution of baking soda and water

Fig. 47 Before connecting the cables, it's a good idea to coat the terminals with a small amount of dielectric grease

REPLACEMENT

When it becomes necessary to replace the battery, select one with an amperage rating equal to or greater than the battery originally installed. Deterioration and just plain aging of the battery cables, starter motor, and associated wires makes the battery's job harder in successive years. This makes it prudent to install a new battery with a greater capacity than the old.

Belts

INSPECTION

▶ **See Figures 48, 49, 50, 51 and 52**

Every 12 months or 15,000 miles (24,100 km), check the drive belts for proper tension. Also inspect the belts for signs of glazing or cracking. A glazed belt will be perfectly smooth from slippage, while a good belt will have a slight

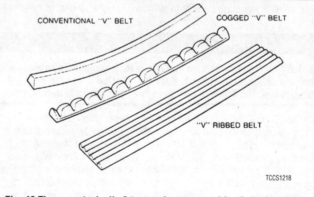

Fig. 48 There are typically 3 types of accessory drive belts found on vehicles today

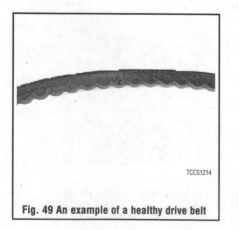

Fig. 49 An example of a healthy drive belt

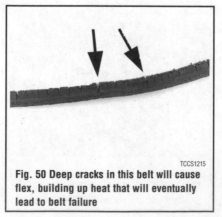

Fig. 50 Deep cracks in this belt will cause flex, building up heat that will eventually lead to belt failure

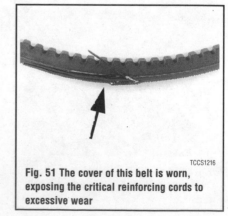

Fig. 51 The cover of this belt is worn, exposing the critical reinforcing cords to excessive wear

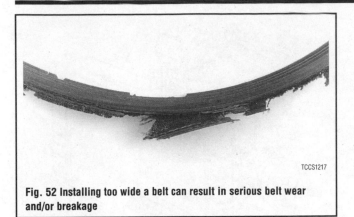

Fig. 52 Installing too wide a belt can result in serious belt wear and/or breakage

texture of fabric visible. Cracks will usually start at the inner edge of the belt and run outward. All worn or damaged drive belts should be replaced immediately. It is best to replace all drive belts at one time, as a preventive maintenance measure, during this service operation.

ADJUSTMENT

▶ **See Figure 53**

Belt tension should be checked with a gauge made for that purpose. If a gauge is not available, tension can be checked with moderate thumb pressure applied to the belt at its longest span midway between pulleys. If the belt has a free span less than 12 in. (305mm), it should deflect approximately ⅛–¼ in. (3–6mm). If the span is longer than 12 in. (305mm), deflection can range between ⅛ in. (3mm) and ⅜ in. (10mm).

➡**Models with a serpentine belt are automatically adjusted by a spring loaded belt tensioner. Adjustments are not normally required.**

1. Loosen the driven accessory's pivot and mounting bolts.
2. Move the accessory toward or away from the engine until the tension is correct. You can use a wooden hammer handle as a lever, but do not use anything metallic.
3. Tighten the bolts and recheck the tension. If new bolts have been installed, run the engine for a few minutes, then recheck and readjust, as necessary.

It is better to have belts too loose than too tight, because overtight belts will lead to bearing failure, particularly in the water pump and alternator. However, loose belts place an extremely high impact load on the driven component due to the whipping action of the belt.

REMOVAL & INSTALLATION

Except Serpentine Belt

➡**It may be necessary to loosen more than one pulley or remove another belt to access the drive belt, such as the power steering and air conditioning.**

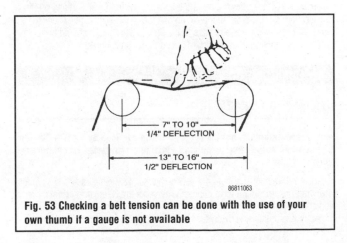

7" TO 10" 1/4" DEFLECTION

13" TO 16" 1/2" DEFLECTION

Fig. 53 Checking a belt tension can be done with the use of your own thumb if a gauge is not available

1. Loosen the driven accessory's pivot and mounting bolts.
2. Move the accessory toward or away from the engine until there is enough slack in the belt to slip it over the pulley of the driven accessory.
3. Remove the belt from the engine.
4. Install the new belt and move the accessory toward or away from the engine until the tension is correct. You can use a wooden hammer handle as a lever, but do not use anything metallic.
5. Adjust the belt tension, then tighten the bolts.

Serpentine Belt

1. Place a tool over the tensioner pulley axis bolt.
2. Rotate the tool counterclockwise to relieve belt tension.
3. Remove the drive belt.
4. Carefully release the tensioner pulley and remove the tool.
To install:
5. Route the belt over the pulleys, except tensioner.
6. Place tool over tensioner, rotate counterclockwise and install belt.
7. Remove the tool, then check alignment of tension and belt.

Hoses

The upper and lower radiator hoses, along with the heater hoses should be checked periodically for deterioration, leaks, and loose clamps. GM recommends that this be done every 12 months or 15,000 miles (24,100 km). For your own peace of mind, it may be wise to check these items at least every spring and fall, since the summer and winter months wreak the most havoc with your cooling system. Expect to replace the hoses about every 24 months or 30,000 miles (48,300 km).

REMOVAL & INSTALLATION

▶ **See Figures 54, 55, 56 and 57**

1. Drain the cooling system.

❊❊ CAUTION

When draining the coolant, keep in mind that cats and dogs are attracted by ethylene glycol antifreeze, and are quite likely to drink any that is left in an uncovered container or in puddles on the ground. This will prove fatal in sufficient quantity. Always drain the coolant into a sealable container. Coolant should be reused unless it is contaminated or several years old.

2. If so equipped, disconnect the routing bracket from the hose.
3. Loosen the hose clamps at each end of the hose to be removed. If the clamps are of the type which have a screw positioned vertically in relation to the

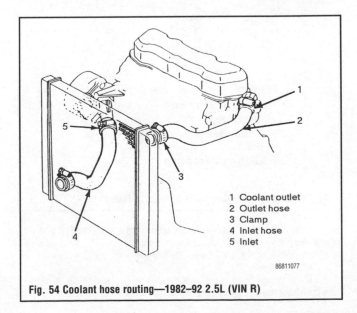

1 Coolant outlet
2 Outlet hose
3 Clamp
4 Inlet hose
5 Inlet

Fig. 54 Coolant hose routing—1982–92 2.5L (VIN R)

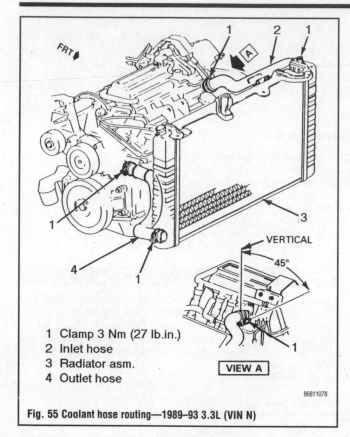

1 Clamp 3 Nm (27 lb.in.)
2 Inlet hose
3 Radiator asm.
4 Outlet hose

VIEW A

Fig. 55 Coolant hose routing—1989–93 3.3L (VIN N)

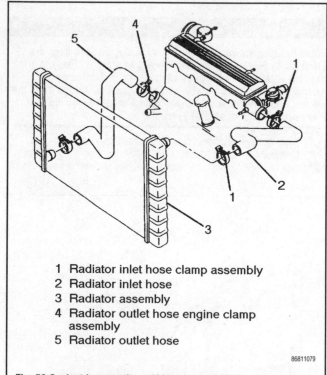

1 Radiator inlet hose clamp assembly
2 Radiator inlet hose
3 Radiator assembly
4 Radiator outlet hose engine clamp assembly
5 Radiator outlet hose

Fig. 56 Coolant hose routing—1992–96 2.2L (VIN 4)

hose, loosen the screw and gently tap the head of the screw towards the hose. Repeat this until the clamp is loose enough. If corrosion on the clamp prevents loosening in this manner, carefully cut the clamp off with cutters and replace the clamp with a new one.

4. Once the clamps are out of the way, grasp the hose and twist it off of the tube connection using only moderate force. If the hose won't break loose, DON'T

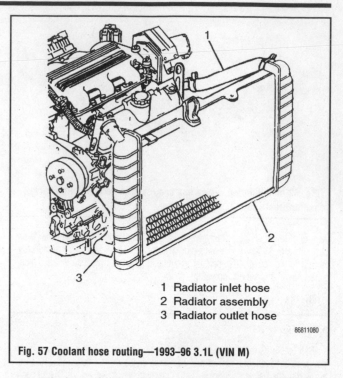

1 Radiator inlet hose
2 Radiator assembly
3 Radiator outlet hose

Fig. 57 Coolant hose routing—1993–96 3.1L (VIN M)

use excessive force—doing so can easily damage the heater core and/or radiator tubes. Using a razor blade, carefully slit the portion of the hose which covers the connection point, peel the hose off of the connection and disconnect the hose.

5. Remove the hose and clean the connection points.

To install:

6. Slip the (loosened) clamps onto the hose ends and install the new hose, being careful to position it so that there is no interference.

7. Position the clamps at the ends of the hoses, beyond the sealing bead and centered on the clamping surface. Tighten the hose clamps with a screwdriver—don't use a wrench on the screw heads to tighten them, as overtightening can damage the hose and/or connections points.

8. Refill the cooling system (detailed later) and check for leakage.

9. If so equipped, reconnect the routing bracket to the hose.

CV-Boots

INSPECTION

▶ See Figures 58 and 59

The CV (Constant Velocity) boots should be checked for damage each time the oil is changed and any other time the vehicle is raised for service. These boots keep water, grime, dirt and other damaging matter from entering the CV-joints. Any of these could cause early CV-joint failure which can be expensive to repair. Heavy grease thrown around the inside of the front wheel(s) and on the brake caliper/drum can be an indication of a torn boot. Thoroughly check the boots for missing clamps and tears. If the boot is damaged, it should be replaced immediately. Please refer to Section 7 for procedures.

Air Conditioning System

SYSTEM SERVICE & REPAIR

➡It is recommended that the A/C system be serviced by an EPA Section 609 certified automotive technician utilizing a refrigerant recovery/recycling machine.

The do-it-yourselfer should not service his/her own vehicle's A/C system for many reasons, including legal concerns, personal injury, environmental damage and cost.

According to the U.S. Clean Air Act, it is a federal crime to service or repair

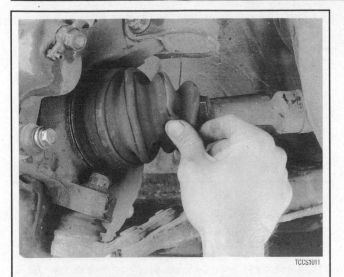

Fig. 58 CV-boots must be inspected periodically for damage

Fig. 59 A torn boot should be replaced immediately

(involving the refrigerant) a Motor Vehicle Air Conditioning (MVAC) system for money without being EPA certified. It is also illegal to vent R-12 and R-134a refrigerants into the atmosphere. State and/or local laws may be more strict than the federal regulations, so be sure to check with your state and/or local authorities for further information.

➡**Federal law dictates that a fine of up to $25,000 may be levied on people convicted of venting refrigerant into the atmosphere.**

When servicing an A/C system you run the risk of handling or coming in contact with refrigerant, which may result in skin or eye irritation or frostbite. Although low in toxicity (due to chemical stability), inhalation of concentrated refrigerant fumes is dangerous and can result in death; cases of fatal cardiac arrhythmia have been reported in people accidentally subjected to high levels of refrigerant. Some early symptoms include loss of concentration and drowsiness.

➡**Generally, the limit for exposure is lower for R-134a than it is for R-12. Exceptional care must be practiced when handling R-134a.**

Also, some refrigerants can decompose at high temperatures (near gas heaters or open flame), which may result in hydrofluoric acid, hydrochloric acid and phosgene (a fatal nerve gas).

It is usually more economically feasible to have a certified MVAC automotive technician perform A/C system service on your vehicle.

R-12 Refrigerant Conversion

If your vehicle still uses R-12 refrigerant, one way to save A/C system costs down the road is to investigate the possibility of having your system converted to R-134a. The older R-12 systems can be easily converted to R-134a refrigerant by a certified automotive technician by installing a few new components and changing the system oil.

The cost of R-12 is steadily rising and will continue to increase, because it is no longer imported or manufactured in the United States. Therefore, it is often possible to have an R-12 system converted to R-134a and recharged for less than it would cost to just charge the system with R-12.

If you are interested in having your system converted, contact local automotive service stations for more details and information.

PREVENTIVE MAINTENANCE

Although the A/C system should not be serviced by the do-it-yourselfer, preventive maintenance should be practiced to help maintain the efficiency of the vehicle's A/C system. Be sure to perform the following:
• The easiest and most important preventive maintenance for your A/C system is to be sure that it is used on a regular basis. Running the system for five minutes each month (no matter what the season) will help ensure that the seals and all internal components remain lubricated.

➡**Some vehicles automatically operate the A/C system compressor whenever the windshield defroster is activated. Therefore, the A/C system would not need to be operated each month if the defroster was used.**

• In order to prevent heater core freeze-up during A/C operation, it is necessary to maintain proper antifreeze protection. Be sure to properly maintain the engine cooling system.
• Any obstruction of or damage to the condenser configuration will restrict air flow which is essential to its efficient operation. Keep this unit clean and in proper physical shape.

➡**Bug screens which are mounted in front of the condenser (unless they are original equipment) are regarded as obstructions.**

• The condensation drain tube expels any water which accumulates on the bottom of the evaporator housing into the engine compartment. If this tube is obstructed, the air conditioning performance can be restricted and condensation buildup can spill over onto the vehicle's floor.

SYSTEM INSPECTION

Although the A/C system should not be serviced by the do-it-yourselfer, system inspections should be performed to help maintain the efficiency of the vehicle's A/C system. Be sure to perform the following:

The easiest and often most important check for the air conditioning system consists of a visual inspection of the system components. Visually inspect the system for refrigerant leaks, damaged compressor clutch, abnormal compressor drive belt tension and/or condition, plugged evaporator drain tube, blocked condenser fins, disconnected or broken wires, blown fuses, corroded connections and poor insulation.

A refrigerant leak will usually appear as an oily residue at the leakage point in the system. The oily residue soon picks up dust or dirt particles from the surrounding air and appears greasy. Through time, this will build up and appear to be a heavy dirt impregnated grease.

For a thorough visual and operational inspection, check the following:
• Check the surface of the radiator and condenser for dirt, leaves or other material which might block air flow.
• Check for kinks in hoses and lines. Check the system for leaks.
• Make sure the drive belt is properly tensioned. During operation, make sure the belt is free of noise or slippage.
• Make sure the blower motor operates at all appropriate positions, then check for distribution of the air from all outlets.

➡**Remember that in high humidity, air discharged from the vents may not feel as cold as expected, even if the system is working properly. This is because moisture in humid air retains heat more effectively than dry air, thereby making humid air more difficult to cool.**

Windshield Wipers

ELEMENT (REFILL) CARE & REPLACEMENT

♦ See Figures 60, 61 and 62

For maximum effectiveness and longest element life, the windshield and wiper blades should be kept clean. Dirt, tree sap, road tar and so on will cause streaking, smearing and blade deterioration if left on the glass. It is advisable to wash the windshield carefully with a commercial glass cleaner at least once a month. Wipe off the rubber blades with the wet rag afterwards. Do not attempt to move wipers across the windshield by hand; damage to the motor and drive mechanism will result.

To inspect and/or replace the wiper blade elements, place the wiper switch in the **LOW** speed position and the ignition switch in the **ACC** position. When the wiper blades are approximately vertical on the windshield, turn the ignition switch to **OFF**.

Examine the wiper blade elements. If they are found to be cracked, broken or torn, they should be replaced immediately. Replacement intervals will vary with usage, although ozone deterioration usually limits element life to about one year. If the wiper pattern is smeared or streaked, or if the blade chatters across the glass, the elements should be replaced. It is easiest and most sensible to replace the elements in pairs.

If your vehicle is equipped with aftermarket blades, there are several different types of refills and your vehicle might have any kind. Aftermarket blades and arms rarely use the exact same type blade or refill as the original equipment.

Regardless of the type of refill used, be sure to follow the part manufacturer's instructions closely. Make sure that all of the frame jaws are engaged as the refill is pushed into place and locked. If the metal blade holder and frame are allowed to touch the glass during wiper operation, the glass will be scratched.

Tires and Wheels

Common sense and good driving habits will afford maximum tire life. Make sure that you don't overload the vehicle or run with incorrect pressure in the tires. Either of these will increase tread wear. Fast starts, sudden stops and sharp cornering are hard on tires and will shorten their useful life span.

➡**For optimum tire life, keep the tires properly inflated, rotate them often and have the wheel alignment checked periodically.**

Inspect your tires frequently. Be especially careful to watch for bubbles in the tread or sidewall, deep cuts or underinflation. Replace any tires with bubbles in the sidewall. If cuts are so deep that they penetrate to the cords, discard the tire. Any cut in the sidewall of a radial tire renders it unsafe. Also look for uneven tread wear patterns that may indicate the front end is out of alignment or that the tires are out of balance.

TIRE ROTATION

♦ See Figure 63

Tires must be rotated periodically to equalize wear patterns that vary with a tire's position on the vehicle. Tires will also wear in an uneven way as the front steering/suspension system wears to the point where the alignment should be reset.

Rotating the tires will ensure maximum life for the tires as a set, so you will not have to discard a tire early due to wear on only part of the tread. Regular rotation is required to equalize wear.

When rotating "unidirectional tires," make sure that they always roll in the same direction. This means that a tire used on the left side of the vehicle must not be switched to the right side and vice-versa. Such tires should only be rotated front-to-rear or rear-to-front, while always remaining on the same side of the vehicle. These tires are marked on the sidewall as to the direction of rotation; observe the marks when reinstalling the tire(s).

Some styled or "mag" wheels may have different offsets front to rear. In these cases, the rear wheels must not be used up front and vice-versa. Furthermore, if these wheels are equipped with unidirectional tires, they cannot be rotated unless the tire is remounted for the proper direction of rotation.

➡**The compact or space-saver spare is strictly for emergency use. It must never be included in the tire rotation or placed on the vehicle for everyday use.**

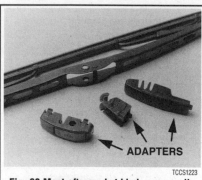

Fig. 60 Most aftermarket blades are available with multiple adapters to fit different vehicles

TCCS1223

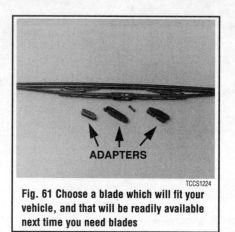

Fig. 61 Choose a blade which will fit your vehicle, and that will be readily available next time you need blades

TCCS1224

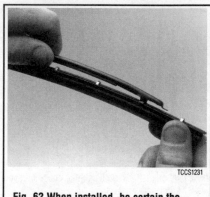

Fig. 62 When installed, be certain the blade is fully inserted into the backing

TCCS1231

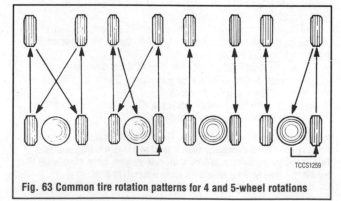

Fig. 63 Common tire rotation patterns for 4 and 5-wheel rotations

TCCS1259

TIRE DESIGN

♦ See Figure 64

For maximum satisfaction, tires should be used in sets of four. Mixing of different brands or types (radial, bias-belted, fiberglass belted) should be avoided. In most cases, the vehicle manufacturer has designated a type of tire on which the vehicle will perform best. Your first choice when replacing tires should be to use the same type of tire that the manufacturer recommends.

When radial tires are used, tire sizes and wheel diameters should be selected to maintain ground clearance and tire load capacity equivalent to the original specified tire. Radial tires should always be used in sets of four.

❋❋ CAUTION

Radial tires should never be used on only the front axle.

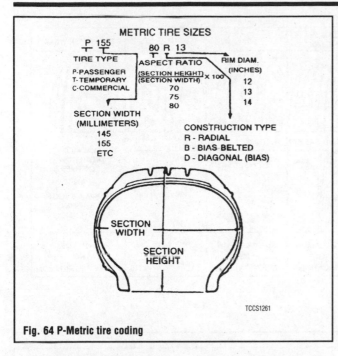

Fig. 64 P-Metric tire coding

When selecting tires, pay attention to the original size as marked on the tire. Most tires are described using an industry size code sometimes referred to as P-Metric. This allows the exact identification of the tire specifications, regardless of the manufacturer. If selecting a different tire size or brand, remember to check the installed tire for any sign of interference with the body or suspension while the vehicle is stopping, turning sharply or heavily loaded.

Snow Tires

Good radial tires can produce a big advantage in slippery weather, but in snow, a street radial tire does not have sufficient tread to provide traction and control. The small grooves of a street tire quickly pack with snow and the tire behaves like a billiard ball on a marble floor. The more open, chunky tread of a snow tire will self-clean as the tire turns, providing much better grip on snowy surfaces.

To satisfy municipalities requiring snow tires during weather emergencies, most snow tires carry either an M + S designation after the tire size stamped on the sidewall, or the designation "all-season." In general, no change in tire size is necessary when buying snow tires.

Most manufacturers strongly recommend the use of 4 snow tires on their vehicles for reasons of stability. If snow tires are fitted only to the drive wheels, the opposite end of the vehicle may become very unstable when braking or turning on slippery surfaces. This instability can lead to unpleasant endings if the driver can't counteract the slide in time.

Note that snow tires, whether 2 or 4, will affect vehicle handling in all non-snow situations. The stiffer, heavier snow tires will noticeably change the turning and braking characteristics of the vehicle. Once the snow tires are installed, you must re-learn the behavior of the vehicle and drive accordingly.

➡**Consider buying extra wheels on which to mount the snow tires. Once done, the "snow wheels" can be installed and removed as needed. This eliminates the potential damage to tires or wheels from seasonal removal and installation. Even if your vehicle has styled wheels, see if inexpensive steel wheels are available. Although the look of the vehicle will change, the expensive wheels will be protected from salt, curb hits and pothole damage.**

TIRE STORAGE

If they are mounted on wheels, store the tires at proper inflation pressure. All tires should be kept in a cool, dry place. If they are stored in the garage or basement, do not let them stand on a concrete floor; set them on strips of wood, a mat or a large stack of newspaper. Keeping them away from direct moisture is of paramount importance. Tires should not be stored upright, but in a flat position.

INFLATION & INSPECTION

▶ **See Figures 65 thru 70**

The importance of proper tire inflation cannot be overemphasized. A tire employs air as part of its structure. It is designed around the supporting strength of the air at a specified pressure. For this reason, improper inflation drastically reduces the tire's ability to perform as intended. A tire will lose some air in day-to-day use; having to add a few pounds of air periodically is not necessarily a sign of a leaking tire.

Two items should be a permanent fixture in every glove compartment: an accurate tire pressure gauge and a tread depth gauge. Check the tire pressure (including the spare) regularly with a pocket type gauge. Too often, the gauge on the end of the air hose at your corner garage is not accurate because it suffers too much abuse. Always check tire pressure when the tires are cold, as pressure increases with temperature. If you must move the vehicle to check the tire inflation, do not drive more than a mile before checking. A cold tire is generally one that has not been driven for more than three hours.

A plate or sticker is normally provided somewhere in the vehicle (door post, hood, tailgate or trunk lid) which shows the proper pressure for the tires. Never counteract excessive pressure build-up by bleeding off air pressure (letting some air out). This will cause the tire to run hotter and wear quicker.

✳✳ CAUTION

Never exceed the maximum tire pressure embossed on the tire! This is the pressure to be used when the tire is at maximum loading, but it is rarely the correct pressure for everyday driving. Con-

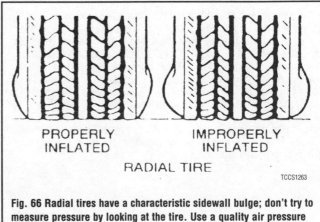

Fig. 65 Tires with deep cuts, or cuts which bulge, should be replaced immediately

PROPERLY INFLATED   IMPROPERLY INFLATED

RADIAL TIRE

Fig. 66 Radial tires have a characteristic sidewall bulge; don't try to measure pressure by looking at the tire. Use a quality air pressure gauge

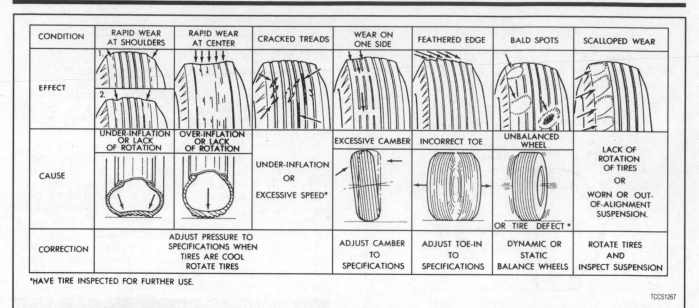

CONDITION	RAPID WEAR AT SHOULDERS	RAPID WEAR AT CENTER	CRACKED TREADS	WEAR ON ONE SIDE	FEATHERED EDGE	BALD SPOTS	SCALLOPED WEAR
EFFECT							
CAUSE	UNDER-INFLATION OR LACK OF ROTATION	OVER-INFLATION OR LACK OF ROTATION	UNDER-INFLATION OR EXCESSIVE SPEED*	EXCESSIVE CAMBER	INCORRECT TOE	UNBALANCED WHEEL OR TIRE DEFECT*	LACK OF ROTATION OF TIRES OR WORN OR OUT-OF-ALIGNMENT SUSPENSION.
CORRECTION	ADJUST PRESSURE TO SPECIFICATIONS WHEN TIRES ARE COOL ROTATE TIRES			ADJUST CAMBER TO SPECIFICATIONS	ADJUST TOE-IN TO SPECIFICATIONS	DYNAMIC OR STATIC BALANCE WHEELS	ROTATE TIRES AND INSPECT SUSPENSION

*HAVE TIRE INSPECTED FOR FURTHER USE.

TCCS1267

Fig. 67 Common tire wear patterns and causes

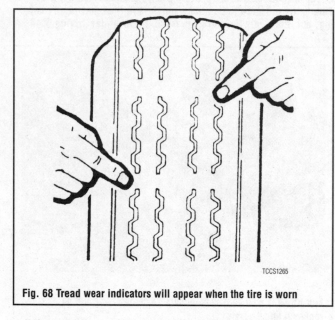

Fig. 68 Tread wear indicators will appear when the tire is worn

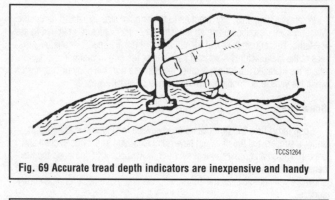

Fig. 69 Accurate tread depth indicators are inexpensive and handy

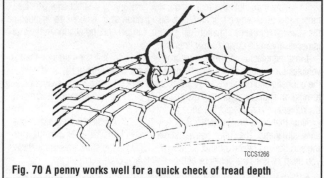

Fig. 70 A penny works well for a quick check of tread depth

sult the owner's manual or the tire pressure sticker for the correct tire pressure.

Once you've maintained the correct tire pressures for several weeks, you'll be familiar with the vehicle's braking and handling personality. Slight adjustments in tire pressures can fine-tune these characteristics, but never change the cold pressure specification by more than 2 psi. A slightly softer tire pressure will give a softer ride but also yield lower fuel mileage. A slightly harder tire will give crisper dry road handling but can cause skidding on wet surfaces. Unless you're fully attuned to the vehicle, stick to the recommended inflation pressures.

All automotive tires have built-in tread wear indicator bars that show up as ½ in. (13mm) wide smooth bands across the tire when 1⁄16 in. (1.5mm) of tread remains. The appearance of tread wear indicators means that the tires should be replaced. In fact, many states have laws prohibiting the use of tires with less than this amount of tread.

You can check your own tread depth with an inexpensive gauge or by using a Lincoln head penny. Slip the Lincoln penny (with Lincoln's head upside-down) into several tread grooves. If you can see the top of Lincoln's head in 2 adjacent grooves, the tire has less than 1⁄16 in. (1.5mm) tread left and should be replaced. You can measure snow tires in the same manner by using the "tails" side of the Lincoln penny. If you can see the top of the Lincoln memorial, it's time to replace the snow tire(s).

FLUIDS AND LUBRICANTS

Fluid Disposal

Used fluids such as engine oil, transmission fluid, antifreeze and brake fluid are hazardous wastes and must be disposed of properly. Before draining any fluids, consult with your local authorities; in many areas, waste oil, antifreeze, etc. is being accepted as a part of recycling programs. A number of service stations and auto parts stores are also accepting waste fluids for recycling.

Be sure of the recycling center's policies before draining any fluids, as many will not accept different fluids that have been mixed together.

Fuel and Engine Oil Recommendations

FUEL RECOMMENDATIONS

All cars covered by this manual must use unleaded fuel. The use of leaded fuel will plug the catalyst rendering it imperative, and will increase the exhaust back pressure to the point where engine output will be severely reduced. The minimum octane for all engines is 87 RON. All unleaded fuels sold in the U.S. and Canada are required to meet this minimum octane rating.

Use of a fuel too low in octane (a measurement of anti-knock quality) will result in spark knock. Since many factors affect operating efficiency, such as altitude, terrain, air temperature and humidity, knocking may result even though the recommended fuel is being used. If persistent knocking occurs, it may be necessary to switch to a slightly higher grade of unleaded gasoline. Continuous or heavy knocking may result in serious engine damage, for which the manufacturer is not responsible.

➡ **Your car's engine fuel requirement can change with time, due to carbon buildup, which changes the compression ratio. If your car's engine knocks, pings, or runs on, switch to a higher grade of fuel, if possible, and check the ignition timing. Sometimes changing brands of gasoline will cure the problem. If it is necessary to retard timing from specifications, don't change it more than a few degrees. Retarded timing will reduce power output and fuel mileage, and will increase engine temperature.**

OIL RECOMMENDATIONS

▶ **See Figures 71 and 72**

Under normal conditions, the engine oil and the filter should be changed at the first 7500 miles (12,000 km) or once a year whichever comes first. GM recommends that the oil filter be changed at every other oil change thereafter. For the small price of an oil filter, it's cheap insurance to replace the filter at every oil change. One of the larger filter manufacturers points out in its advertisements that not changing the filter leaves one quart of dirty oil in the engine. This claim is true and should be kept in mind when changing your oil.

	Anticipated Temperature Range	SAE Viscosity
Multi-grade	Above 32°F	10W—40
		10W—50
		20W—40
		20W—50
		10W—30
	May be used as low as −10°F	10W—30
		10W—40
	Consistently below 10°F	5W—20
		5W—30
Single-grade	Above 32°F	30
	Temperature between +32°F and −10°F	10W

Fig. 71 Oil viscosity selection chart—vehicles since 1987 are designed to use 5W-30 year-round

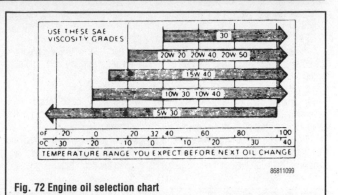

Fig. 72 Engine oil selection chart

Under severe conditions, such as:
- Driving in dusty areas
- Trailer towing
- Frequent idling or idling for extended periods
- Frequently driving short distances—4 miles (6 km) or so in freezing weather

The engine oil and filter should be changed every 3 months or 3000 miles (4800 km), whichever comes first. If dust storms are ever encountered in your area, change the oil and filter as soon as possible after the storm.

The American Petroleum Institute (API) designation (printed on the oil container) indicates the classification of engine oil for use under certain operating conditions. Oils having an API service designation of SG should be used in your car. The SG rating designates the highest quality oil meant for passenger car usage. It is okay to use an SG oil having a combination rating such as SG/CC or SG/CD. (The CC or CD indicates compatibility with diesel engines.) In addition, GM recommends the use of SG/Energy Conserving oil. Oils labeled Energy Conserving (or Saving); Fuel (Gas or Gasoline) Saving, etc. are recommended due to their superior lubricating qualities (less friction = easier and more efficient engine operation) and fuel saving characteristics. Use of engine oil additives is not recommended, because if the correct oil is purchased to begin with, the additives will be of no value.

➡ **Use of engine oils without an SG rating, or failing to change the oil and filter at the recommended intervals, will cause excessive engine wear and could affect your warranty.**

OIL LEVEL CHECK

▶ **See Figures 73, 74, 75 and 76**

The engine oil level may be checked either when the engine is cold or warm, though the latter is preferred. If you check the level while the engine is cold, DO NOT start the engine first, since the cold oil won't drain back to the engine oil pan fast enough to give an accurate reading. Even when the engine is warm, wait a couple of minutes after turning it off to let the oil drain back to the pan.

1. Raise the hood, pull the dipstick out and wipe it clean.
2. Reinsert the dipstick, being sure that you push it back in completely.
3. Pull the dipstick back out, hold it horizontally, and check the level at the end of the dipstick. Some dipsticks are marked with ADD and FULL lines, others with ADD 1 QT and OPERATING RANGE. In either case, the level must be above the ADD line. Reinsert the dipstick completely.
4. If oil must be added, it can be poured in through the rocker (valve) cover after removing the filler cap on the cover. Recheck the level a few minutes after adding oil.
5. Be sure that the dipstick and oil filler cap are installed before closing the hood.

OIL & FILTER CHANGE

Screw-on Filter

▶ **See Figures 77, 78, 79, 80 and 81**

1. Drive the car until the engine is at normal operating temperature. A run to the parts store for oil and a filter should accomplish this. If the engine is not

hot when the oil is changed, most of the acids and contaminants will remain inside the engine.

2. Raise and support the front of the vehicle safely on jackstands to access the oil filter.

3. Slide a pan of at least six quarts capacity under the oil pan.

4. Remove the drain plug from the engine oil pan, after wiping the plug area clean. The drain plug is the bolt inserted at an angle into the lowest point of the oil pan.

5. Use a rag to protect your hands from the hot plug.

6. The oil from the engine will be HOT. It will probably not be possible to hold onto the drain plug. You may have to let it fall into the pan and fish it out later. Allow all the oil to drain completely. This will take a few minutes.

7. Wipe off the drain plug, removing any traces of metal particles. Check the condition of the plastic drain plug gasket. If it is cracked or distorted in any way, replace it. Reinstall the drain plug and gasket. Tighten the drain plug snugly.

8. The oil filter for the V6 engine is right up front, just behind the radiator. The four-cylinder engine's oil filter is at the back of the engine, and is impossible to reach from above; it is almost as inaccessible from below. It may be easiest to remove the right front wheel and reach through the fender opening to get at the four-cylinder engine's oil filter. Use an oil strap wrench to loosen the oil filter; these are available at auto parts stores. It is recommended that you purchase one with as thin a strap as possible, to get into tight areas. Place the drain pan on the ground, beneath the filter. Unscrew and discard the old filter. It will be VERY HOT, so be careful.

9. If the oil filter is on so tightly that it collapses under pressure from the wrench, drive a long punch or a nail through it, across the diameter and as close to the base as possible, and use this as a lever to unscrew it. Make sure you are turning it counterclockwise.

10. Clean off the oil filter mounting surface with a rag. Apply a thin film of clean engine oil to the new filter gasket.

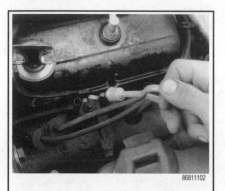

Fig. 73 Remove the oil dipstick and wipe clean

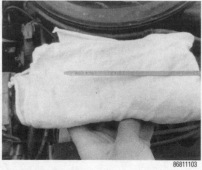

Fig. 74 When checking the oil level it should appear to be clean, not dark in color or thick. The level should be between the add and full marks

Fig. 75 Turn and remove the oil filler cap

Fig. 76 Insert a funnel into the valve cover and add the appropriate amount of engine oil needed

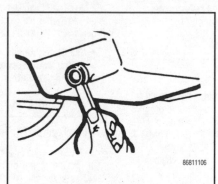

Fig. 77 Make sure you have a pan ready, loosen the drain plug with a wrench, then place the plug into the drain pan

Fig. 78 Install the plug and gasket snugly

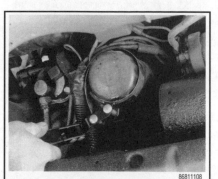

Fig. 79 Using a wrench loosen and remove the oil filter. Don't forget there is still a small amount of oil inside the filter

Fig. 80 Before installing a new oil filter, coat the rubber gasket with clean oil

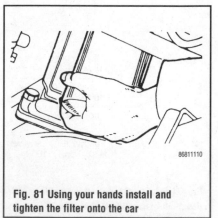

Fig. 81 Using your hands install and tighten the filter onto the car

11. Screw the filter on by hand until the gasket makes contact. Then tighten it by hand an additional ½–¾ of a turn. Do not overtighten.

12. Remove the filler cap on the rocker (valve) cover, after wiping the area clean.

13. Add the correct number of quarts of oil specified in the Capacities chart. If you don't have an oil can spout, you will need a funnel. Be certain you do not overfill the engine, which can cause serious damage. Replace the cap.

14. Check the oil level on the dipstick. It is normal for the level to be a bit above the full mark. Start the engine and allow it to idle for a few minutes.

✳✳ CAUTION

Do not run the engine above idle speed until it has built up oil pressure, indicated when the oil light goes out.

15. Shut off the engine, allow the oil to drain for a minute, and check the oil level.

16. Check around the filter and drain plug for any leaks.

Cartridge Type Filter

▶ See Figure 82

A cartridge type oil filter is found on some of the mid-model year 2.5L engines.

1. Drive the car until the engine is at normal operating temperature. A run to the parts store for oil and a filter should accomplish this. If the engine is not hot when the oil is changed, most of the acids and contaminants will remain inside the engine.

2. Raise the car and support on jackstands.

3. Remove the oil pan drain plug.

4. Drain the oil into a drain pan.

5. Slowly turn the plug to begin removal and pull downwards.

➡ Be sure to stand clear of the flowing oil from this next step.

6. With a pair of pliers, applied to the tab/boss, remove the filter.

7. Make sure the O-ring/gasket was removed with the filter; if not remove it.

To install:

8. Coat the O-ring/gasket on the end of the filter with clean engine oil.

9. Press the filter into position in the housing by hand.

10. Make sure the filter is fully seated.

11. Check the oil filter O-ring/gasket for any damage and replace it, if necessary. Lube with oil the gasket and install the drain plug.

12. Tighten the plug ¼ turn after gasket contacts, then tighten another ¼ turn.

13. Lower the car, fill engine with proper amount of oil and check for leaks.

After completing this job, you will have several quarts of oil to dispose of. The best thing to do with it is to funnel it into old plastic milk containers or bleach bottles. Then, you can locate a service station with a recycling barrel.

Manual Transaxle

FLUID RECOMMENDATIONS

Under normal conditions, the lubricant used in the manual transaxle does not require periodic changing. The fluid level in the transaxle should be checked every 12 months or 7500 miles (12,000 km), whichever comes first. The manual transaxle is designed for use with Dexron®III automatic transmission. Don't use standard manual transmission lubricant in the transaxle.

LEVEL CHECK

▶ See Figures 83 and 84

1. Park the car on a level surface. Before proceeding, the transaxle case must be cool to the touch. Due to the expansion characteristics of the Dexron®III fluid, it will be above the level of the filler plug when the transmission is hot. On your HM-282 manual 5 speeds, there is a dipstick.

2. The dipstick type can be removed in the same manner as an oil dipstick. On the drain plug type, slowly remove the filler plug from the driver's side of the transaxle (see the illustration). The lubricant level should be right at the bottom of the filler plug hole. If the fluid trickles out as the plug is removed, or if you can just touch the fluid through the filler plug hole, the level is correct.

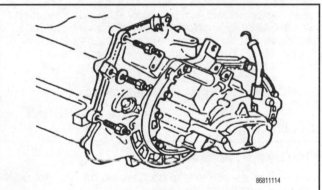

86811114

Fig. 83 Some manual transaxles have a dipstick to check the fluid level

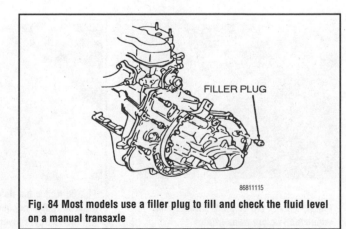

86811115

Fig. 84 Most models use a filler plug to fill and check the fluid level on a manual transaxle

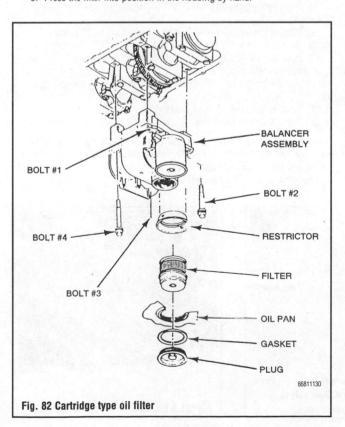

86811130

Fig. 82 Cartridge type oil filter

BALANCER ASSEMBLY

BOLT #1

BOLT #2

BOLT #4

RESTRICTOR

FILTER

BOLT #3

OIL PAN

GASKET

PLUG

3. If you cannot feel the fluid level with your finger through the filler plug hole, add Dexron®III automatic transmission through the hole until the fluid begins to trickle out of the hole.

4. When the level is correct, install the filler plug and tighten it snugly.

DRAIN & REFILL

1. Park the car on a level surface, turn **OFF** engine and apply the parking brake.

2. Place a container of adequate capacity beneath the drain plug which is located underneath the car, on the bottom of the transaxle housing.

3. Use the proper size wrench to loosen the drain plug slowly, while maintaining a slight upward pressure, to keep the oil from leaking out around the plug.

4. Allow all of the lubricant to drain from the transaxle, then clean the plug area thoroughly. Install the drain plug and gasket (if so equipped).

5. Remove the transaxle dipstick and add slowly checking the level often. Do not overfill.

6. Check the oil level as outlined above.

Automatic Transaxle

FLUID RECOMMENDATIONS

Under normal operating conditions, the automatic transmission fluid only needs to be changed every 100,000 miles (161,000 km), according to GM If one or more of the following driving conditions is encountered the fluid and filter should be changed every 15,000 miles (24,100 km):
- Driving in heavy city traffic when the outside temperature regularly reached 90°F (32°C)
- Driving regularly in hilly or mountainous areas
- Towing a trailer
- Using the vehicle as a taxi or police car, or for delivery purposes.

Remember, these are the factory recommendations, and in this case are considered to be the minimum. You must determine a change interval which fits your driving habits. If your vehicle is never subjected to these conditions, a 100,000 mile (161,000 km) change interval is adequate. If you are a normal driver, a two-year/30,000 mile (48,300 km) interval will be more than sufficient to maintain the long life for which your automatic transaxle was designed.

When replacing or adding fluid, use only fluid labeled Dexron®III or Dexron®IIE. Use of other fluids could cause erratic shifting and transmission damage.

LEVEL CHECK

▶ **See Figures 85, 86 and 87**

The fluid level may be checked with the transaxle cold, warm, or hot, as this is accounted for on the dipstick graduations.

➡**If the vehicle has just been driven in extreme conditions, allow the fluid to cool for about 30 minutes.**

1. Park the car on a level surface and set the parking brake.

2. Start the engine, apply the brake, and move the shift lever through all of the gear ranges, ending up in Park.

3. Let the engine idle for at least 5 minutes with the transaxle in Park.

4. The dipstick is located on the driver's side of the engine compartment, ahead of the engine.

5. Raise the hood, pull the dipstick out and wipe it off with a clean cloth.

6. Reinsert the dipstick, being sure that it is fully seated.

7. Again, remove the dipstick. Hold it horizontally and read the fluid level. Touch the fluid-if it feels cold or warm, the level should be between the dimples above the **FULL HOT** mark. If the fluid feels hot, the level should be in the hatched area, between the **ADD 1 PT** and **FULL HOT** marks.

8. If required, add just enough Dexron®II automatic transmission fluid to bring the level to where it should be. One pint of fluid will raise the level from **ADD** to **FULL** when the transaxle is hot. Recheck the level.

9. Reinsert the dipstick, again making sure that it is fully seated. Lower the hood.

✵ WARNING

NEVER overfill the transaxle, as fluid foaming and subsequent transaxle damage can occur!

DRAIN, FILTER SERVICE & REFILL

▶ **See Figures 88 thru 93**

➡**Some transaxle use RTV sealer in place of a gasket. Do not attempt to replace the sealer with a gasket.**

1. Jack up the front of your vehicle and support it with jackstands.

2. Remove the front and side pan bolts.

3. Loosen the rear bolts about 4 turns.

4. Carefully pry the oil pan loose, allowing the fluid to drain.

5. Remove the remaining bolts, the pan, and the gasket or RTV. Discard the gasket.

6. Clean the pan with solvent and dry thoroughly, with compressed air.

7. Remove the strainer and O-ring seal.

To install:

8. Install new strainer and new O-ring seal locating the strainer against the dipstick stop.

9. Install a new gasket or RTV. Tighten the pan bolts to: 15 ft. lbs. (20 Nm) for the 440–T4, 8 ft. lbs. (11 Nm) for the 3T40, 13 ft. lbs. (17 Nm) for the 4T60.

10. Lower the car. Add about 4 quarts of Dexron®IIE or Dexron®III transmission fluid, check your owners manual.

11. Start the engine; let it idle. Block the wheels and apply the parking brake.

12. Move the shift lever through the ranges.

13. With the lever in PARK check the fluid level. If necessary, add fluid.

➡**Always replace the filter with a new one, don't attempt to clean the old filter. The transmission fluid currently being used may appear to be darker and have a strong odor. This is normal and not a sign of required maintenance or transmission failure.**

Fig. 85 Locate the dipstick, remove and wipe clean before reinserting

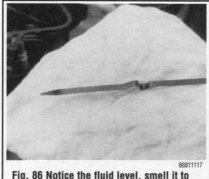

Fig. 86 Notice the fluid level, smell it to make sure it is not burnt. Add only to the full mark, NEVER overfill

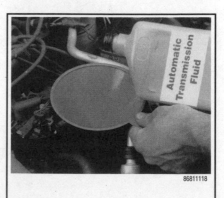

Fig. 87 A funnel is handy for adding fluid

Fig. 88 The transaxle fluid pan is usually located behind the engine oil pan (as shown here)

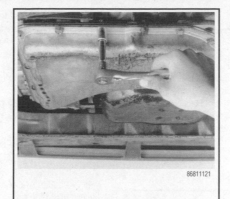

Fig. 89 Loosen and remove the pan bolts

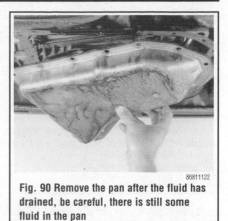

Fig. 90 Remove the pan after the fluid has drained, be careful, there is still some fluid in the pan

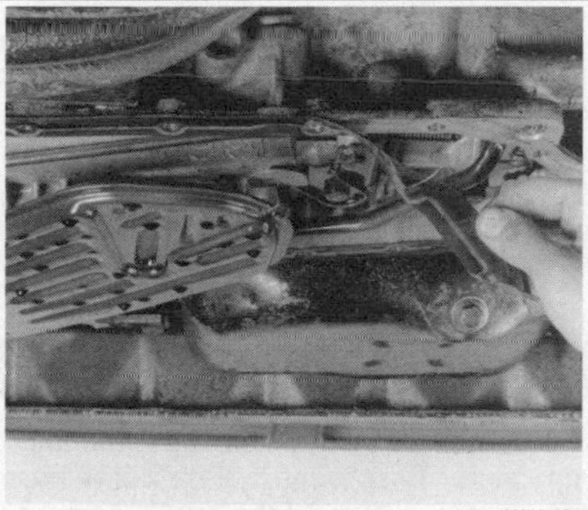

Fig. 91 Discard the gasket (if equipped)

Fig. 92 Remove the strainer

Fig. 93 Insert a new O-ring seal on the new strainer

Cooling System

General Motors recommends that you check your cooling system every 12 months or 15,000 miles (24,100 km). The following services should be performed:

1. Wash and inspect the radiator cap and the filler neck.
2. Check the coolant level and the degree of freezing protection.
3. If a pressure tester is available, pressure test the system and the radiator cap.
4. Inspect the hoses of the cooling system. Expect to replace the hoses at 24 months/30,000 miles (48,200 km).
5. Check the fins of the radiator for blockage.

FLUID RECOMMENDATIONS

▶ **See Figure 94**

The coolant used in any General Motors engine must:
- Be a high quality ethylene glycol-based solution. Do not use alcohol or methanol-based solutions at any time.
- Have built-in rust inhibitors.
- Be designed for year-round use.
- Offer complete protection for a minimum of 12 months/30,000 miles (48,300 km), without replacement, as long as the proper concentration is maintained.
- Meet GM Specification 1825-M (as specified on the container); other types of coolant could result in cooling system damage and engine damage due to overheating.
- Be mixed in the proper proportions: 50% coolant and 50% water.

✳✳ CAUTION

Adding only plain water to your cooling system can be dangerous. Plain water, or any other liquid like alcohol, can boil before the

Fig. 94 Notice the markings on your coolant reservoir

proper coolant fluid will. Your car's cooling system is designed to operate properly only with the proper coolant mixture. With plain water or the wrong mixture, your engine could get too hot but you wouldn't get the overheat warning.

The use of self-sealing coolants is not recommended. Also, the use of a coolant meeting the above requirements negates the need for supplemental additives. Use of such supplemental products is an unnecessary expense and may cause less than optimum cooling system performance.

LEVEL CHECK

♦ **See Figure 95**

Any time the hood is raised, check the level of the coolant in the see-through plastic coolant recovery tank. With the engine cold, the coolant level should be near the ADD mark on the tank. At normal engine operating temperature, the level should be at the FULL mark on the bottle. If coolant must be added to the tank, use a 50/50 mix of coolant/water to adjust the fluid level.

An inexpensive tester may be purchased to test the freezing protection of the coolant. Follow the instructions provided with the tester. The coolant should protect to -34°F (-37°C).

DRAIN & REFILL

At least every 24 months or 30,000 miles (50,000 km)-whichever comes first. The cooling system should be completely drained and refilled with the proper mixture of coolant and water. Many mechanics recommend that this be done once a year for extra protection against corrosion and subsequent overheating.

Though most coolants are labeled permanent, this only means that the coolant will retain its anti-freezing characteristics. The required rust inhibitors and other chemicals which were added to the coolant during its manufacture will become less effective over a period of time.

➡ **If you are only replacing the hoses, perform steps 1–3, and 11–16 as required.**

❋❋ CAUTION

To avoid being burned, DO NOT remove the radiator cap while the engine is at operating temperature. The cooling system will release HOT scalding fluid and steam under pressure if the cap is removed while the radiator is still hot. This could result in personal injury.

1. Park the car a level surface.
2. Remove the radiator cap. Slowly rotate the pressure cap counterclockwise to detent. Wait until the pressure (indicated by a hissing sound) is completely gone.
3. After the pressure is relieved, press down on the cap and continue to rotate counterclockwise.
4. Raise the front of the vehicle and support it safely with jackstands.
5. Place a drain pan under the car to collect the drained coolant.
6. Open the radiator fitting (located at the bottom of the radiator) by turning it counterclockwise. It may be wise to coat the fitting with penetrating lubricant before you attempt to turn it. Allow the coolant to drain from the radiator.
7. On the 3.1L engine open the air bleed vent on the throttle body return pipe (above the coolant pump). The air bleed vent should be opened two to three turns.

❋❋ CAUTION

When draining coolant, keep in mind that cats and dogs are attracted to ethylene glycol antifreeze, and are quite likely to drink any that is left in an uncovered container or in puddles on the ground. This will prove fatal in sufficient quantity. Always drain the coolant into a sealable container. Coolant should be reused unless it is contaminated or several years old.

8. Remove the drain plug(s) from the engine block (located on the engine block, above the engine oil pan) and allow the coolant to drain.
9. Close the radiator drain fitting and reinstall the engine block plugs.
10. On the 3.1L close the bleed valve on the throttle body.
11. Add clear water to the system until it is filled.
12. Start the engine and repeat steps 7–12 until the drained water is almost colorless. Turn the engine **OFF**.
13. Allow the system to drain completely and repeat step 10. Remove the cap from the coolant recovery tank, leaving the hoses connected to the cap.
14. Unbolt and remove the coolant recovery tank, drain it, and flush it with clear water. Reinstall the tank.
15. Fill the radiator to the base of the radiator filler neck with a 50/50 mixture of coolant/water.

➡ **If only the radiator was drained, use a 50/50 solution to refill it, then check the freezing protection after the level stabilizes.**

16. Fill the coolant recovery tank to the FULL mark with the 50/50 solution.
17. With the radiator cap still removed, start the engine and allow it to idle until the upper radiator hose becomes hot, indicating that the thermostat has opened.
18. With the engine still idling, fill the radiator to the base of the filler neck with the 50/50 solution.
19. Install the radiator cap, being sure to align the arrows on the cap with the overflow tube.
20. Turn the engine **OFF**, check for leakage, and double check that the radiator drain is closed and the drain plug(s) is (are) tightened.

FLUSHING AND CLEANING THE SYSTEM

Several aftermarket radiator flushing and cleaning kits can be purchased at your local auto parts store. It is recommended that the radiator be cleaned and flushed of sludge and any rust build-up once a year. Manufacturer's directions for proper use, and safety precautions, come in each kit.

RADIATOR CAP

♦ **See Figure 96**

Before removing the cap. squeeze the upper radiator hose. If it compresses easily (indicating little or no pressure in the system), the cap may be removed by turning it counterclockwise until it reaches the stop. If any hissing is noted at this point (indicating the release of pressure), wait until the hissing stops before you remove the cap. To completely remove the cap, press downward and turn it counterclockwise.

❋❋ CAUTION

To avoid being burned, DO NOT remove the radiator cap while the engine is at operating temperature. The cooling system will release HOT scalding fluid and steam under pressure if the cap is removed while the radiator is still hot. This could result in personal injury and loss of coolant.

If the upper radiator hose is hard, pressure is indicated within the system. In this case, a greater degree of caution should be used in removing the cap. Cover the radiator cap with a thick cloth, and while wearing a heavy glove, carefully turn the cap to the stop. This will allow the pressure to be relieved from the system. After the hissing stops, completely remove the cap (press and turn counterclockwise).

Check the condition of the radiator cap gasket and the seal inside of the cap. The radiator cap is designed to seal the cooling system under normal operating conditions which allows the system to build-up a certain amount of pressure (this pressure rating is stamped or printed on the cap). The pressure in the system raises the boiling point of the coolant to help prevent overheating. If the radiator cap does not seal properly, the boiling point of the coolant will be lowered and overheating will occur. If the cap must be replaced, purchase the new cap according to the pressure rating which is specified for your vehicle.

Prior to installing the cap, inspect and clean the radiator filler neck. If you are reusing the old cap, clean it thoroughly with clear water. After turning the cap, make sure that the arrows on the cap align with the overflow hose.

CLEANING RADIATOR OF DEBRIS

Periodically clean any debris—leaves, paper, insects, etc. from the radiator fins. Pick the large pieces off by hand. The smaller pieces can be washed away with water pressure from a hose.

Carefully straighten any bent radiator fins with a pair of needlenose pliers. Be careful, the fins are very soft. Don't wiggle the fins back and forth too much. Straighten them once and try not to move them again.

Master Cylinder

FLUID RECOMMENDATIONS

Only extra-heavy duty fluid meeting DOT-3 specifications must be used. Using an inferior fluid will result in component damage and reduced braking capabilities.

Fig. 95 Fill the coolant bottle using a funnel and proper a mixture of anti freeze and water

Fig. 96 Make sure you take extra care before opening a radiator. The cautions are right on the cap

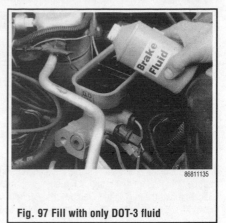

Fig. 97 Fill with only DOT-3 fluid

❊❊ CAUTION

DOT-5 silicone brake fluid can damage your car, DO NOT use it.

LEVEL CHECK

▶ **See Figure 97**

About once a month, the fluid level in the master cylinder should be checked.
1. Park the car on a level surface, turn it **OFF** and raise the hood.
2. Wipe off the master cylinder cover before you remove it, to prevent contaminating the fluid with dirt.

➥**On most models, a see-through reservoir is used, eliminating the need to remove the cover.**

3. Two types of lids are used on these master cylinders. One cover is snapped into place on the master cylinder. To remove this type, just press up on the two tabs at the side of the cover, then tilt and remove it. Be careful not to damage the rubber seal under the cover. Another type of cylinder cover has a screw on cap, simply turn the cap to remove.

❊❊ CAUTION

If you value the paint on your car, don't spill brake fluid on the finish. Brake fluid destroys paint. Should a spill accidentally occur, thoroughly flush the area with clean water.

➥**Don't leave the cover off of the master cylinder or the cap off of the brake fluid container any longer than necessary.**

4. The fluid level in each master cylinder reservoir should be ¼ in. (6mm) below the lowest edge of the filler opening. If necessary, use fresh brake fluid to adjust the level.

It is normal for the master cylinder fluid level to drop as the brake linings wear about⅛ in. (3mm) every 10,000 miles (16,100 km). If the fluid level is constantly low, the system should be checked for leaks.

5. Carefully seat the seal into the cover, then snap the cover into place on the master cylinder. Be sure that all four snaps latch completely.

Power Steering Pump

FLUID RECOMMENDATIONS

▶ **See Figure 98**

When adding power steering fluid use GM part #1050017, 1052884 or their equal. In cold climates, use GM part #12345867 and 12345866 (the system should be flushed and bled prior to using this fluid).

LEVEL CHECK

▶ **See Figures 99 and 100**

The power steering fluid level should be checked at every oil change. The power steering pump and reservoir are integrated into one unit that is bolted to the front of the engine.

To check the fluid level, run the engine until it reaches normal operating temperature, then turn the engine **OFF**. Remove the reservoir filler cap and check the oil level on the dipstick. The fluid level must be between the HOT and COLD marks on the filler cap indicator. Add power steering fluid as required then reinstall the cap.

Steering Gear

FLUID RECOMMENDATIONS AND LEVEL CHECK

All models use integral rack and pinion power steering. The power steering pump delivers hydraulic pressure through two hoses to the steering gear itself. Refer to the power steering pump fluid recommendation and level check procedures to check the steering gear fluid level.

Fig. 98 Fill the power steering pump using a funnel

Fig. 99 The power steering cap has a built-in dipstick to check the fluid level

Fig. 100 Make sure the level is in between the HOT and COLD lines on the dipstick

Chassis Greasing

FRONT SUSPENSION AND STEERING LINKAGE

These parts should be greased every 12 months or 7500 miles (12,000 km) with an EP grease meeting GM specification NLGI Grade 2, Category LB or GC-LB, or an equivalent.

If you choose to do this job yourself, you will need a hand operated grease gun, and a long flexible extension hose to reach the various grease fittings. You will also need a cartridge of the appropriate grease.

Press the fitting of the grease gun hose onto the grease fitting (zerk fitting) of the suspension or steering linkage component. Pump a few shots of grease into the fitting (zerk fitting), until the rubber boot on the joint begins to expand, indicating that the joint is full. Remove the gun from the fitting. Be careful not to overfill the joints, which will rupture the rubber boots, allowing the entry of dirt.

TRANSAXLE SHIFT LINKAGE

Lubricate the manual transaxle shift linkage contact points with the EP grease used for chassis greasing (that meets GM specification 6031M). The automatic transaxle linkage should be lubricated with clean engine oil.

Body Lubrication

Clean the latch surfaces and apply clean engine oil to the latch pilot bolts and the spring anchor. Use the engine oil to lubricate the hood, door, liftgate hinges, and rear folding seats. Use a chassis grease to lubricate all the pivot points in the latch release mechanism.

DOOR HINGES

The gas tank filler door, car door, and rear hatch or trunk lid hinges should be wiped clean and lubricated with clean engine oil. Silicone spray also works well on these parts, but must be applied more often. Use engine oil to lubricate the trunk or hatch lock mechanism and the lock bolt and striker. The door lock cylinders can be lubricated easily with a shot of silicone spray or one of the many dry penetrating lubricants commercially available.

PARKING BRAKE LINKAGE

Use chassis grease on the parking brake cable where it contacts the guides, links, levers, and pulleys. The grease should be water resistant for durability under the car.

ACCELERATOR LINKAGE

Lubricate the carburetor stud, carburetor lever, and the accelerator pedal lever at the support inside the car with clean engine oil.

Rear Wheel Bearings

The bearings used on these vehicles don't require periodic grease service. However, should a hub/bearing assembly require replacement, refer to Section 8 for details.

JUMP STARTING A DEAD BATTERY

▶ **See Figure 101**

Whenever a vehicle is jump started, precautions must be followed in order to prevent the possibility of personal injury. Remember that batteries contain a small amount of explosive hydrogen gas which is a by-product of battery charging. Sparks should always be avoided when working around batteries, especially when attaching jumper cables. To minimize the possibility of accidental sparks, follow the procedure carefully.

❋❋ CAUTION

NEVER hook the batteries up in a series circuit or the entire electrical system will go up in smoke, including the starter!

Vehicles equipped with a diesel engine may utilize two 12 volt batteries. If so, the batteries are connected in a parallel circuit (positive terminal to positive terminal, negative terminal to negative terminal). Hooking the batteries up in parallel circuit increases battery cranking power without increasing total battery voltage output. Output remains at 12 volts. On the other hand, hooking two 12 volt batteries up in a series circuit (positive terminal to negative terminal, positive terminal to negative terminal) increases total battery output to 24 volts (12 volts plus 12 volts).

Jump Starting Precautions

- Be sure that both batteries are of the same polarity (have the same terminal, in most cases NEGATIVE grounded).
- Be sure that the vehicles are not touching or a short could occur.
- On non-sealed batteries, be sure the vent cap holes are not obstructed.
- Do not smoke or allow sparks anywhere near the batteries.
- In cold weather, make sure the battery electrolyte is not frozen. This can occur more readily in a battery that has been in a state of discharge.
- Do not allow electrolyte to contact your skin or clothing.

Jump Starting Procedure

1. Make sure that the voltages of the 2 batteries are the same. Most batteries and charging systems are of the 12 volt variety.

2. Pull the jumping vehicle (with the good battery) into a position so the jumper cables can reach the dead battery and that vehicle's engine. Make sure that the vehicles do NOT touch.

3. Place the transmissions/transaxles of both vehicles in **Neutral** (MT) or **P** (AT), as applicable, then firmly set their parking brakes.

➡ **If necessary for safety reasons, the hazard lights on both vehicles may be operated throughout the entire procedure without significantly increasing the difficulty of jumping the dead battery.**

4. Turn all lights and accessories OFF on both vehicles. Make sure the ignition switches on both vehicles are turned to the **OFF** position.

5. Cover the battery cell caps with a rag, but do not cover the terminals.

6. Make sure the terminals on both batteries are clean and free of corrosion for good electrical contact.

7. Identify the positive (+) and negative (−) terminals on both batteries.

8. Connect the first jumper cable to the positive (+) terminal of the dead battery, then connect the other end of that cable to the positive (+) terminal of the booster (good) battery.

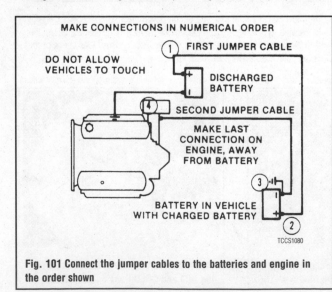

MAKE CONNECTIONS IN NUMERICAL ORDER

FIRST JUMPER CABLE

DO NOT ALLOW VEHICLES TO TOUCH

DISCHARGED BATTERY

SECOND JUMPER CABLE

MAKE LAST CONNECTION ON ENGINE, AWAY FROM BATTERY

BATTERY IN VEHICLE WITH CHARGED BATTERY

TCCS1080

Fig. 101 Connect the jumper cables to the batteries and engine in the order shown

9. Connect one end of the other jumper cable to the negative (-) terminal on the booster battery and the final cable clamp to an engine bolt head, alternator bracket or other solid, metallic point on the engine with the dead battery. Try to pick a ground on the engine that is positioned away from the battery in order to minimize the possibility of the 2 clamps touching should one loosen during the procedure. DO NOT connect this clamp to the negative (-) terminal of the bad battery.

⁕⁕ CAUTION

Be very careful to keep the jumper cables away from moving parts (cooling fan, belts, etc.) on both engines.

10. Check to make sure that the cables are routed away from any moving parts, then start the donor vehicle's engine. Run the engine at moderate speed for several minutes to allow the dead battery a chance to receive some initial charge.

11. With the donor vehicle's engine still running slightly above idle, try to start the vehicle with the dead battery. Crank the engine for no more than 10 seconds at a time and let the starter cool for at least 20 seconds between tries. If the vehicle does not start in 3 tries, it is likely that something else is also wrong or that the battery needs additional time to charge.

12. Once the vehicle is started, allow it to run at idle for a few seconds to make sure that it is operating properly.

13. Turn ON the headlights, heater blower and, if equipped, the rear defroster of both vehicles in order to reduce the severity of voltage spikes and subsequent risk of damage to the vehicles' electrical systems when the cables are disconnected. This step is especially important to any vehicle equipped with computer control modules.

14. Carefully disconnect the cables in the reverse order of connection. Start with the negative cable that is attached to the engine ground, then the negative cable on the donor battery. Disconnect the positive cable from the donor battery and finally, disconnect the positive cable from the formerly dead battery. Be careful when disconnecting the cables from the positive terminals not to allow the alligator clips to touch any metal on either vehicle or a short and sparks will occur.

JACKING

Your vehicle was supplied with a jack for emergency road repairs. This jack is fine for changing a flat tire or other short term procedures not requiring you to go beneath the vehicle. If it is used in an emergency situation, carefully follow the instructions provided either with the jack or in your owner's manual. Do not attempt to use the jack on any portions of the vehicle other than specified by the vehicle manufacturer. Always block the diagonally opposite wheel when using a jack.

A more convenient way of jacking is the use of a garage or floor jack. You may use the floor jack beneath the center of the front crossmember or rear suspension axle.

Never place the jack under the radiator, engine or transmission components. Severe and expensive damage will result when the jack is raised. Additionally, never jack under the floorpan or bodywork; the metal will deform.

Whenever you plan to work under the vehicle, you must support it on jackstands or ramps. Never use cinder blocks or stacks of wood to support the vehicle, even if you're only going to be under it for a few minutes. Never crawl under the vehicle when it is supported only by the tire-changing jack or other floor jack.

➡**Always position a block of wood or small rubber pad on top of the jack or jackstand to protect the lifting point's finish when lifting or supporting the vehicle.**

Small hydraulic, screw, or scissors jacks are satisfactory for raising the vehicle. Drive-on trestles or ramps are also a handy and safe way to both raise and support the vehicle. Be careful though, some ramps may be too steep to drive your vehicle onto without scraping the front bottom panels. Never support the vehicle on any suspension member (unless specifically instructed to do so by a repair manual) or by an underbody panel.

Jacking Precautions

The following safety points cannot be overemphasized:
- Always block the opposite wheel or wheels to keep the vehicle from rolling off the jack.
- When raising the front of the vehicle, firmly apply the parking brake.
- When the drive wheels are to remain on the ground, leave the vehicle in gear to help prevent it from rolling.
- Always use jackstands to support the vehicle when you are working underneath. Place the stands beneath the vehicle's jacking brackets. Before climbing underneath, rock the vehicle a bit to make sure it is firmly supported.

MAINTENANCE INTERVALS

Follow Schedule I if the vehicle is mainly operated under one or more of the following conditions:
  When most trips are less than 4 miles (6 kilometers)
  When most trips are less than 10 miles (16 kilometers) and outside temperatures - remain below freezing
  When most trips include extended idling and/or frequent low-speed operation as in stop-and-go traffic
  Towing a trailer**
  Operating in dusty areas

Schedule I should also be followed if the vehicle is used for delivery service, police, taxi or other commercial applications

TO BE SERVICED	WHEN TO PERFORM Miles (Kilometers) or Months whichever Occurs First	The services shown in this schedule up to 60,000 miles (100,000 km) are to be performed after 60,000 miles (100,000 km) at the same intervals																		
	MILES (000)	3	6	9	12	15	18	21	24	27	30	33	36	39	42	45	48	51	54	57	60
	KILOMETERS (000)	5	10	15	20	25	30	35	40	45	50	55	60	65	70	75	80	85	90	95	100
Engine Oil & Oil Filter Change *	Every 3,000 (5000 km) or 3 mos	•	•	•	•	•	•	•	•	•	•	•	•	•	•	•	•	•	•	•	•
Chassis Lubrication	Every other oil change		•		•		•		•		•		•		•		•		•		•
Services To Be Performed At Least Twice A Year (See Explanation)																					
Services To Be Performed At Least Once A Year (See Explanation)																					
Throttle Body Mount Bolt Torque (Some Models)*	At 6,000 mi (10,000 km) only		•																		
Tire & Wheel insp and Rotation	At 6,000 mi (10,000 km) and then every 15,000 mi (25,000 km)		•					•					•					•			
Engine Accessory Drive Belt(s) Insp *	Every 30,000 mi (50,000 km) or 24 mos										•										•
Cooling System Service*	Every 30,000 mi (50,000 km) or 24 mos										•										•
Transaxle Service	See explanation for service interval																				
Spark Plug Replacement*	LN2 every 100,000 mi (166,000 km) LB2 every 30,000 mi (50,000 km)																				•
Spark Plug Wire Insp (Some Models)*	Every 30,000 mi. (50,000 km)										•										•
EGR System Insp. *††	Every 30,000 mi (50,000 km) or 36 mos										•										•
Air Cleaner Replacement	Every 30,000 mi (50,000 km) or 36 mos										•										•
Eng. Timing Check (Some Models)*	Every 30,000 mi (50,000 km)										•										•
Fuel Tank, Cap & Lines Insp.*††	Every 30,000 mi (50,000 km)										•										•

FOOTNOTES: * An Emission Control Service
†† The U.S. Environmental Agency or the California Air Resources Board has determined that the failure to perform this maintenance item will not nullify the emission warranty or limit recall liability prior to the completion of vehicle useful life. General Motors, however, urges that all recommended maintenance services be performed at the indicated intervals and the maintenance be recorded in Section C of the owner's Maintenance Schedule.

86811154

♦ Follow Schedule II only if none of the driving conditions specified in Schedule I apply

TO BE SERVICED	WHEN TO PERFORM Miles (Kilometers) or Months whichever Occurs First	The services shown in this schedule up to 60,000 miles (100,000 km) are to be performed after 60,000 miles (100,000 km) at the same intervals							
	MILES (000)	7.5	15	22.5	30	37.5	45	52.5	60
	KILOMETERS (000)	12.54	25	37.5	50	62.5	75	87.5	100
Engine Oil Change*, Plus Other Required Services (See Explanation)	Every 7,500 mi. (12,500 km) or 12 mos.	•	•	•	•	•	•	•	•
Oil Filter Change*	At first and every other oil change or 12 mos	•		•		•		•	
Chassis Lubrication	Every 7,500 mi. (12,500 km) or 12 mos.	•	•	•	•	•	•	•	•
Services To Be Performed At Least Twice A Year (See Explanation)									
Services To Be Performed At Least Once A Year (See Explanation)									
Throttle Body Mount Bolt Torque (Some Models)*	At 7,500 mi (12,500 km) only	•							
Tire & Wheel insp. and Rotation	At 7,500 mi (12,500 km) and then every 15,000 mi. (25,000 km)	•		•		•		•	
Engine Accessory Drive Belt(s) Insp *	Every 30,000 mi. (50,000 km) or 24 mos.				•				•
Cooling System Service*	Every 30,000 mi. (50,000 km) or 24 mos.				•				•
Transaxle Service	See explanation for service interval								
Spark Plug Replacement*	LN2 every 100,000 mi (166,000 km) LB2 every 30,000 mi (50,000 km)				•				•
Spark Plug Wire Insp (Some Models)*	Every 30,000 mi. (50,000 km)				•				•
EGR System Insp. *††	Every 30,000 mi (50,000 km) or 36 mos.				•				•
Air Cleaner Replacement	Every 30,000 mi (50,000 km) or 36 mos.				•				•
Fuel Tank, Cap & Lines Insp.*††	Every 30,000 mi (50,000 km)				•				•

FOOTNOTES: * An Emission Control Service
†† The U.S. Environmental Agency or the California Air Resources Board has determined that the failure to perform this maintenance item will not nullify the emission warranty or limit recall liability prior to the completion of vehicle useful life. General Motors, however urges that all recommended maintenance services be performed at the indicated intervals and the maintenance be recorded in Section C of the owner's Maintenance Schedule.

86811155

CAPACITIES

Year	Model	Engine ID/VIN	Engine Displacement Liters (cc)	Engine Oil with Filter (qts.)	Transmission (pts.) 4-Spd	5-Spd	Auto.	Transfer Case (pts.)	Drive Axle Front (pts.)	Drive Axle Rear (pts.)	Fuel Tank (gal.)	Cooling System (qts.)
1986	Celebrity	R	2.5 (2474)	4.0 [1]	6.0	-	-	5	-	-	16.0	10.0
	Celebrity	W	2.8 (2835)	4.0 [1]	-	-	-	2	-	-	16.0	12.0
	Celebrity	X	2.8 (2835)	4.0 [1]	5.9	-	-	2	-	-	16.5	12.0
	Century	R	2.5 (2474)	4.0 [1]	-	-	8.0	2	-	-	15.5	10.0
	Century	X	2.8 (2835)	4.0 [1]	-	-	-	2	-	-	16.5	6
	Century	3	3.8 (3785)	4.0 [1]	-	-	8.0	2	-	-	15.5	6
	Century	B	3.8 (3785)	4.0 [1]	-	-	8.0	2	-	-	15.5	6
	Cutlass Ciera	R	2.5 (2474)	4.0 [1]	-	-	-	2	-	-	15.8	10.0
	Cutlass Ciera	X	2.8 (2835)	4.0 [1]	-	-	-	2	-	-	16.5	12.0
	Cutlass Ciera	W	2.8 (2835)	4.0 [1]	-	-	-	2	-	-	15.8	12.0
	Cutlass Ciera	3	3.8 (3785)	4.0 [1]	-	-	-	2	-	-	15.8	6
	Cutlass Ciera	B	3.8 (3785)	4.0 [1]	-	-	-	2	-	-	15.8	6
1987	6000	R	2.5 (2474)	4.0 [1]	-	-	8.0	2	-	-	15.8	10.0
	6000	W	2.8 (2835)	4.0 [1]	-	-	-	2	-	-	16.5	13.0
	6000	X	2.8 (2835)	4.0 [1]	-	4.5	-	2	-	-	16.5	13.0
	Celebrity	R	2.5 (2474)	3.0 [1]	-	-	8.0	2	-	-	15.8	13.0
	Celebrity	W	2.8 (2835)	4.0 [1]	-	-	13.0	2	-	-	16.0	13.0
	Century	R	2.5 (2474)	4.0 [1]	-	-	12.0	2	-	-	16.0	13.0
	Century	3	3.8 (3785)	4.0 [1]	-	-	12.0	2	-	-	16.0	13.0
	Cutlass Ciera	R	2.5 (2474)	3.0 [1]	-	-	-	2	-	-	15.8	13.0
	Cutlass Ciera	W	2.8 (2835)	4.0 [1]	-	-	-	2	-	-	16.0	13.0
	Cutlass Ciera	3	3.8 (3785)	4.0 [1]	-	-	-	2	-	-	15.8	13.0
1988	6000	R	2.5 (2474)	4.0 [1]	6.0	-	-	2	-	-	16.0	13.0
	6000	W	2.8 (2835)	4.0 [1]	6.0	-	-	2	-	-	15.8	13.0
	Celebrity	R	2.5 (2474)	3.0 [1]	4.5	-	8.0	2	-	-	16.0	13.0
	Celebrity	W	2.8 (2835)	4.0 [1]	5.3	-	10.0	2	-	-	16.0	13.0
	Century	R	2.5 (2474)	3.0 [1]	-	-	12.0	2	-	-	15.5	13.0
	Century	W	2.8 (2835)	4.0 [1]	6.0	-	-	4	-	-	15.5	13.0
	Century	3	3.8 (3785)	4.0 [1]	6.0	-	12.0	2	-	-	15.8	12.0
	Cutlass Ciera	R	2.5 (2474)	3.0 [1]	-	-	-	2	-	-	15.8	13.0
	Cutlass Ciera	W	2.8 (2835)	4.0 [1]	-	-	-	2	-	-	15.8	13.0
	Cutlass Ciera	3	3.8 (3785)	4.0 [1]	-	-	-	2	-	-	15.8	13.0
1989	5000	R	2.5 (2474)	4.0 [1]	4.5	-	12.0	5	-	-	16.0	10.0
	5000	W	2.8 (2835)	4.0 [1]	6.0	-	-	2	-	-	15.8	13.0
	Celebrity	R	2.5 (2474)	4.0 [1]	-	-	-	2	-	-	15.8	10.0
	Celebrity	W	2.8 (2835)	4.0 [1]	-	-	-	2	-	-	16.0	13.0
	Century	R	2.5 (2474)	4.0 [1]	-	-	-	5	-	-	15.8	10.0
	Century	N	3.3 (3342)	4.0 [1]	-	-	13.0	2	-	-	15.8	13.0
	Cutlass Ciera	R	2.5 (2474)	4.0 [1]	-	-	-	2	-	-	15.8	10.0
	Cutlass Ciera	W	2.8 (2835)	4.0 [1]	-	-	-	2	-	-	15.8	13.0
	Cutlass Ciera	N	3.3 (3342)	4.0 [1]	-	-	-	2	-	-	15.8	13.0
	Cutlass Cruiser	R	2.5 (2474)	4.0 [1]	-	-	-	2	-	-	15.8	13.0
	Cutlass Cruiser	W	2.8 (2835)	4.0 [1]	-	-	-	2	-	-	15.8	13.0

91081C06

CAPACITIES

Year	Model	Engine ID/VIN	Engine Displacement Liters (cc)	Engine Oil with Filter (qts.)	Transmission (pts.) 4-Spd	5-Spd	Auto.	Transfer Case (pts.)	Drive Axle Front (pts.)	Drive Axle Rear (pts.)	Fuel Tank (gal.)	Cooling System (qts.)
1982	Celebrity	R	2.5 (2474)	3.0 [1]	-	-	-	2	-	-	16.0	10.0
	Celebrity	X	2.8 (2835)	4.0	-	-	-	2	-	-	16.0	12.5
	Century	R	2.5 (2474)	3.0	6.0	-	-	2	-	-	15.7	9
	Century	X	2.8 (2835)	4.0	-	-	-	2	-	-	15.7	12.5
	Cutlass Ciera	R	2.5 (2474)	3.0	6.0	-	-	2	-	-	15.7	10.0
	Cutlass Ciera	X	2.8 (2835)	4.0	6.0	-	-	2	-	-	16.5	12.0
	6000	R	2.5 (2474)	3.0	6.0	-	-	2	-	-	15.7	10.0
	6000	X	2.8 (2835)	4.0	-	-	-	2	-	-	16.4	11.5
1983	Celebrity	R	2.5 (2474)	3.0	6.0	-	-	2	-	-	16.0	10.0
	Celebrity	5	2.5 (2474)	3.0	6.0	-	-	2	-	-	16.0	10.0
	Century	X	2.8 (2835)	4.0	6.0	-	-	2	-	-	16.0	10.0
	Century	R	2.5 (2474)	3.0	6.0	-	-	2	-	-	15.7	12.5
	Century	X	2.8 (2835)	4.0	-	-	-	2	-	-	16.0	12.5
	Cutlass Ciera	E	3.0 (2998)	4.0	6.0	-	-	2	-	-	15.7	13.0
	Cutlass Ciera	R	2.5 (2474)	3.0	6.0	-	-	2	-	-	15.7	10.0
	Cutlass Ciera	X	2.8 (2835)	4.0	6.0	-	-	2	-	-	16.5	12.0
	6000	E	3.0 (2998)	4.0	6.0	-	-	2	-	-	15.7	12.5
	6000	R	2.5 (2474)	3.0	6.0	-	-	2	-	-	15.7	13.0
	6000	X	2.8 (2835)	4.0	6.0	-	-	2	-	-	16.4	10.0
1984	Celebrity	R	2.5 (2474)	3.0	6.0	-	-	2	-	-	16.0	10.0
	Celebrity	5	2.5 (2474)	3.0	-	-	10.0	2	-	-	16.0	11.5
	Century	X	2.8 (2835)	4.0	-	-	10.0	2	-	-	16.0	10.0
	Century	R	2.5 (2474)	3.0	6.0	-	-	2	-	-	15.7	12.5
	Century	X	2.8 (2835)	4.0	-	-	10.0	2	-	-	16.5	13.0
	Cutlass Ciera	R	2.5 (2474)	3.0	6.0	-	-	2	-	-	15.7	10.0
	Cutlass Ciera	X	2.8 (2835)	4.0	6.0	-	-	2	-	-	16.0	13.0
	Cutlass Ciera	E	3.0 (2998)	4.0	6.0	-	-	2	-	-	15.7	13.0
	6000	3	3.8 (3785)	4.0	6.0	-	-	2	-	-	16.5	13.0
	6000	R	2.5 (2474)	3.0	6.0	-	-	2	-	-	15.7	10.0
1985	Celebrity	R	2.5 (2474)	3.0 [1]	6.0	6.0	-	5	-	-	16.0	13.0
	Celebrity	W	2.8 (2835)	4.0 [1]	-	-	-	5	-	-	16.0	13.0
	Century	R	2.5 (2474)	3.0 [1]	6.0	-	-	5	-	-	15.7	9.5
	Century	X	2.8 (2835)	4.0 [1]	-	-	-	5	-	-	16.4	12.0
	Century	E	3.0 (2999)	4.0 [1]	6.0	-	-	5	-	-	15.7	13.1
	Cutlass Ciera	3	3.8 (3785)	4.0 [1]	-	-	-	5	-	-	16.0	13.0
	Cutlass Ciera	R	2.5 (2474)	3.0 [1]	6.0	-	-	5	-	-	16.6	13.0
	Cutlass Ciera	E	3.0 (2999)	4.0 [1]	-	-	-	5	-	-	16.0	13.1
	6000	R	2.5 (2474)	3.0 [1]	6.0	6.0	-	5	-	-	15.7	13.0
	6000	X	2.8 (2835)	4.0 [1]	6.0	-	-	5	-	-	16.5	12.0
	6000	N	2.8 (2835)	4.0 [1]	-	-	-	5	-	-	16.5	12.0

91081C05

CAPACITIES

Year	Model	Engine ID/VIN	Engine Displacement Liters (cc)	Engine Oil with Filter (qts.)	Transmission (pts.) 4-Spd	5-Spd	Auto.	Transfer Case (pts.)	Drive Axle Front (pts.)	Rear (pts.)	Fuel Tank (gal.)	Cooling System (qts.)
1996	Century	4	2.2 (2195)	4.0 [1]	-	-	8	-	-	-	16.5	9.0
	Century	M	3.1 (3130)	4.0 [1]	-	-	8	-	-	-	16.5	12.0
	Cutlass Ciera	4	2.2 (2195)	4.0 [1]	-	-	8	-	-	-	16.5	9.0
	Cutlass Ciera	M	3.1 (3130)	4.0 [1]	-	-	8	-	-	-	16.5	12.0
	Cutlass Cruiser	4	2.2 (2195)	4.0 [1]	-	-	8	-	-	-	16.5	9.0
	Cutlass Cruiser	M	3.1 (3130)	4.0 [1]	-	-	8	-	-	-	16.5	12.0

1 Capacity is without filter replacement make sure to check fluid level to add
2 With AT 125C: 8.0
  With AT 440-T4: 13.0
3 With std. and A/C cooling: 10.0
  With heavy duty cooling (all): 12.0
4 With AT 125C: 12.0
  With AT 440-T4:13.0
5 With AT 125C: 8.0
  With AT 440-T4: 12.0
6 With std. cooling: 12.0
  With A/C: 13.0
7 With 37-40 trans: 14.0
  With 47-60 trans: 12.0
8 With 37-40 trans:8.0
  With 47-60 trans: 12.0
9 Std. cooling: 10.0
  Heavy duty cooling: 13.0
10 Sedan: 16.6 gal.
   Wagon: 15.7 gal.

91081C08

TORQUE SPECIFICATIONS

Component	US	Metric
Automatic Transaxle		
Oil pan retaining nuts:		
1982-88	15 ft. lbs.	20 Nm
1989-96	8 ft. lbs.	11 Nm
Drive Belt Tensioner Bolt:		
2.2L	37 ft. lbs.	50 Nm
2.5L	37 ft. lbs.	50 Nm
2.8L	40 ft. lbs.	54 Nm
3.1L	40 ft. lbs.	54 Nm
3.3L	33 ft. lbs.	45 Nm
Fuel Pipe Nut Fittings:		
2.5L 1990-92	22 ft. lbs.	30 Nm
3.1L 1990-91	17 ft. lbs.	23 Nm
3.1L 1993-96	13 ft. lbs.	17 Nm
3.3L 1990-93	20 ft. lbs.	27 Nm
Oil Pan Drain Plug:		
2.2L	35 ft. lbs.	45 Nm
2.5L	25 ft. lbs.	34 Nm
2.8L	18 ft. lbs.	25 Nm
3.0L	30 ft. lbs.	41 Nm
3.1L Vin-M	18 ft. lbs	25 Nm
3.3L	30 ft. lbs.	41 Nm
3.8L	30 ft. lbs.	41 Nm
Oil Filter Access Plug:		
2.5L	Hand tighten + 1/4 turn	Hand tighten + 1/4 turn
Spark Plugs:		
2.2L	11 ft. lbs.	15 Nm
2.5L to 1991	20 ft. lbs.	27 Nm
2.5L 1992 on	11 ft. lbs.	15 Nm
2.8L	15 ft. lbs.	20 Nm
3.1L Vin-M	11 ft. lbs.	15 Nm
3.1L Vin-T	18 ft. lbs.	24 Nm
3.3L to 1991	20 ft. lbs.	27 Nm
3.3L 1992 on	11 ft. lbs.	15 Nm
Wheel Lug Nuts:	100 ft. lbs.	138 Nm

86811575

CAPACITIES

Year	Model	Engine ID/VIN	Engine Displacement Liters (cc)	Engine Oil with Filter (qts.)	Transmission (pts.) 4-Spd	5-Spd	Auto.	Transfer Case (pts.)	Drive Axle Front (pts.)	Rear (pts.)	Fuel Tank (gal.)	Cooling System (qts.)
1988	Cutlass Cruiser	N	3.3 (3342)	4.0 [1]	-	-	-	-	-	-	15.8	13.0
	6000	R	2.5 (2474)	4.0 [1]	-	-	[2]	-	-	-	15.8	[3]
	6000	W	2.8 (2835)	4.0 [1]	-	-	[2]	-	-	-	15.8	13.0
	6000	T	3.1 (3136)	4.0 [1]	-	-	[2]	-	-	-	15.8	13.0
1990	Celebrity	R	2.5 (2474)	4.0 [1]	-	-	13.0	-	-	-	15.8	10.0
	Celebrity	T	3.1 (3130)	4.0 [1]	-	-	13.0	-	-	-	15.8	13.0
	Century	R	2.5 (2474)	3.0 [1]	-	-	12.0	-	-	-	15.5	10.0
	Century	N	3.3 (3342)	4.0 [1]	-	-	13.0	-	-	-	15.5	13.0
	Cutlass Ciera	R	2.5 (2474)	3.0 [1]	-	-	[2]	-	-	-	15.8	10.0
	Cutlass Ciera	N	3.3 (3342)	4.0 [1]	-	-	[2]	-	-	-	15.8	13.0
	Cutlass Cruiser	R	2.5 (2474)	3.0 [1]	-	-	[2]	-	-	-	15.8	10.0
	Cutlass Cruiser	N	3.3 (3342)	4.0 [1]	-	-	[2]	-	-	-	15.8	13.0
	6000	R	2.5 (2474)	4.0 [1]	-	-	[2]	-	-	-	15.8	10.0
	6000	T	3.1 (3136)	4.0 [1]	-	-	[2]	-	-	-	15.8	13.0
1991	Century	R	2.5 (2474)	4.0 [1]	-	-	[7]	-	-	-	15.7	10.0
	Century	N	3.3 (3342)	4.0 [1]	-	-	[7]	-	-	-	15.7	13.0
	Cutlass Ciera	R	2.5 (2474)	4.0 [1]	-	-	[7]	-	-	-	15.7	10.0
	Cutlass Ciera	N	3.3 (3342)	4.0 [1]	-	-	[7]	-	-	-	15.7	13.0
	Cutlass Cruiser	R	2.5 (2474)	4.0 [1]	-	-	[7]	-	-	-	15.7	10.0
	Cutlass Cruiser	N	3.3 (3342)	4.0 [1]	-	-	[7]	-	-	-	15.7	13.0
	6000	R	2.5 (2474)	4.0 [1]	-	-	[7]	-	-	-	15.7	10.0
	6000	T	3.1 (3136)	4.0 [1]	-	-	[7]	-	-	-	15.7	13.1
1992	Century	R	2.5 (2474)	4.0 [1]	-	-	[8]	-	-	-	15.7	10.0
	Century	N	3.3 (3342)	4.0 [1]	-	-	[8]	-	-	-	15.7	13.0
	Cutlass Ciera	R	2.5 (2474)	4.0 [1]	-	-	[8]	-	-	-	15.7	10.0
	Cutlass Ciera	N	3.3 (3342)	4.0 [1]	-	-	[8]	-	-	-	15.7	13.0
	Cutlass Cruiser	R	2.5 (2474)	4.0 [1]	-	-	[8]	-	-	-	15.7	10.0
	Cutlass Cruiser	N	3.3 (3342)	4.0 [1]	-	-	[8]	-	-	-	15.7	13.0
1993	Century	4	2.2 (2195)	4.0 [1]	-	-	[8]	-	-	-	16.5	9.0
	Century	M	3.1 (3130)	4.0 [1]	-	-	[8]	-	-	-	16.5	12.0
	Cutlass Ciera	4	2.2 (2195)	4.0 [1]	-	-	[8]	-	-	-	16.5	9.0
	Cutlass Ciera	M	3.1 (3130)	4.0 [1]	-	-	[8]	-	-	-	16.5	12.0
	Cutlass Cruiser	4	2.2 (2195)	4.0 [1]	-	-	[8]	-	-	-	16.5	9.0
	Cutlass Cruiser	M	3.1 (3130)	4.0 [1]	-	-	[8]	-	-	-	16.5	12.0
1994	Century	4	2.2 (2195)	4.0 [1]	-	-	[8]	-	-	-	16.5	9.0
	Century	M	3.1 (3130)	4.0 [1]	-	-	[8]	-	-	-	16.5	12.0
	Cutlass Ciera	4	2.2 (2195)	4.0 [1]	-	-	[8]	-	-	-	16.5	9.0
	Cutlass Ciera	M	3.1 (3130)	4.0 [1]	-	-	[8]	-	-	-	16.5	12.0
	Cutlass Cruiser	4	2.2 (2195)	4.0 [1]	-	-	[8]	-	-	-	16.5	9.0
	Cutlass Cruiser	M	3.1 (3130)	4.0 [1]	-	-	[8]	-	-	-	16.5	12.0
1995	Century	4	2.2 (2195)	4.0 [1]	-	-	[8]	-	-	-	16.5	9.0
	Century	M	3.1 (3130)	4.0 [1]	-	-	[8]	-	-	-	16.5	12.0
	Cutlass Ciera	4	2.2 (2195)	4.0 [1]	-	-	[8]	-	-	-	16.5	9.0
	Cutlass Ciera	M	3.1 (3130)	4.0 [1]	-	-	[8]	-	-	-	16.5	12.0
	Cutlass Cruiser	4	2.2 (2195)	4.0 [1]	-	-	[8]	-	-	-	16.5	9.0
	Cutlass Cruiser	M	3.1 (3130)	4.0 [1]	-	-	[8]	-	-	-	16.5	12.0

91081C07

ENGLISH TO METRIC CONVERSION: MASS (WEIGHT)

Current **mass** measurement is expressed in pounds and ounces (lbs. & ozs.). The metric unit of **mass** (or weight) is the kilogram (kg). Even although this table does not show conversion of masses (weights) larger than 15 lbs, it is easy to calculate larger units by following the data immediately below.

To convert ounces (oz.) to grams (g): multiply th number of ozs. by 28
To convert grams (g) to ounces (oz.): multiply the number of grams by .035

To convert pounds (lbs.) to kilograms (kg): multiply the number of lbs. by .45
To convert kilograms (kg) to pounds (lbs.): multiply the number of kilograms by 2.2

lbs	kg	lbs	kg	oz	kg	oz	kg
0.1	0.04	0.9	0.41	0.1	0.003	0.9	0.024
0.2	0.09	1	0.4	0.2	0.005	1	0.03
0.3	0.14	2	0.9	0.3	0.008	2	0.06
0.4	0.18	3	1.4	0.4	0.011	3	0.08
0.5	0.23	4	1.8	0.5	0.014	4	0.11
0.6	0.27	5	2.3	0.6	0.017	5	0.14
0.7	0.32	10	4.5	0.7	0.020	10	0.28
0.8	0.36	15	6.8	0.8	0.023	15	0.42

ENGLISH TO METRIC CONVERSION: TEMPERATURE

To convert Fahrenheit (°F) to Celsius (°C): take number of °F and subtract 32; multiply result by 5; divide result by 9

To convert Celsius (°C) to Fahrenheit (°F): take number of °C and multiply by 9; divide result by 5; add 32 to total

Fahrenheit (F)		Celsius (C)		Fahrenheit (F)		Celsius (C)		Fahrenheit (F)		Celsius (C)	
°F	°C	°C	°F	°F	°C	°C	°F	°F	°C	°C	°F
−40	−40	−38	−36.4	80	26.7	18	64.4	215	101.7	80	176
−35	−37.2	−36	−32.8	85	29.4	20	68	220	104.4	85	185
−30	−34.4	−34	−29.2	90	32.2	22	71.6	225	107.2	90	194
−25	−31.7	−32	−25.6	95	35.0	24	75.2	230	110.0	95	202
−20	−28.9	−30	−22	100	37.8	26	78.8	235	112.8	100	212
−15	−26.1	−28	−18.4	105	40.6	28	82.4	240	115.6	105	221
−10	−23.3	−26	−14.8	110	43.3	30	86	245	118.3	110	230
−5	−20.6	−24	−11.2	115	46.1	32	89.6	250	121.1	115	239
0	−17.8	−22	−7.6	120	48.9	34	93.2	255	123.9	120	248
1	−17.2	−20	−4	125	51.7	36	96.8	260	126.6	125	257
2	−16.7	−18	−0.4	130	54.4	38	100.4	265	129.4	130	266
3	−16.1	−16	3.2	135	57.2	40	104	270	132.2	135	275
4	−15.6	−14	6.8	140	60.0	42	107.6	275	135.0	140	284
5	−15.0	−12	10.4	145	62.8	44	112.2	280	137.8	145	293
10	−12.2	−10	14	150	65.6	46	114.8	285	140.6	150	302
15	−9.4	−8	17.6	155	68.3	48	118.4	290	143.3	155	311
20	−6.7	−6	21.2	160	71.1	50	122	295	146.1	160	320
25	−3.9	−4	24.8	165	73.9	52	125.6	300	148.9	165	329
30	−1.1	−2	28.4	170	76.7	54	129.2	305	151.7	170	338
35	1.7	0	32	175	79.4	56	132.8	310	154.4	175	347
40	4.4	2	35.6	180	82.2	58	136.4	315	157.2	180	356
45	7.2	4	39.2	185	85.0	60	140	320	160.0	185	365
50	10.0	6	42.8	190	87.8	62	143.6	325	162.8	190	374
55	12.8	8	46.4	195	90.6	64	147.2	330	165.6	195	383
60	15.6	10	50	200	93.3	66	150.8	335	168.3	200	392
65	18.3	12	53.6	205	96.1	68	154.4	340	171.1	205	401
70	21.1	14	57.2	210	98.9	70	158	345	173.9	210	410
75	23.9	16	60.8	212	100.0	75	167	350	176.7	215	414

TCCS1C01

ENGLISH TO METRIC CONVERSION: LENGTH

To convert inches (ins.) to millimeters (mm): multiply number of inches by 25.4

To convert millimeters (mm) to inches (ins.): multiply number of millimeters by .04

Inches		Decimals	Milli-meters	Inches to millimeters inches	mm	Inches		Decimals	Milli-meters	Inches to millimeters inches	mm
	1/64	0.051625	0.3969	0.0001	0.00254		33/64	0.515625	13.0969	0.6	15.24
	1/32	0.03125	0.7937	0.0002	0.00508	17/32		0.53125	13.4937	0.7	17.78
	3/64	0.046875	1.1906	0.0003	0.00762		35/64	0.546875	13.8906	0.8	20.32
1/16		0.0625	1.5875	0.0004	0.01016	9/16		0.5625	14.2875	0.9	22.86
	5/64	0.078125	1.9844	0.0005	0.01270		37/64	0.578125	14.6844	1	25.4
	3/32	0.09375	2.3812	0.0006	0.01524	19/32		0.59375	15.0812	2	50.8
	7/64	0.109375	2.7781	0.0007	0.01778		39/64	0.609375	15.4781	3	76.2
1/8		0.125	3.1750	0.0008	0.02032	5/8		0.625	15.8750	4	101.6
	9/64	0.140625	3.5719	0.0009	0.02286		41/64	0.640625	16.2719	5	127.0
	5/32	0.15625	3.9687	0.001	0.0254	21/32		0.65625	16.6687	6	152.4
	11/64	0.171875	4.3656	0.002	0.0508		43/64	0.671875	17.0656	7	177.8
3/16		0.1875	4.7625	0.003	0.0762	11/16		0.6875	17.4625	8	203.2
	13/64	0.203125	5.1594	0.004	0.1016		45/64	0.703125	17.8594	9	228.6
	7/32	0.21875	5.5562	0.005	0.1270	23/32		0.71875	18.2562	10	254.0
	15/64	0.234375	5.9531	0.006	0.1524		47/64	0.734375	18.6531	11	279.4
1/4		0.25	6.3500	0.007	0.1778	3/4		0.75	19.0500	12	304.8
	17/64	0.265625	6.7469	0.008	0.2032		49/64	0.765625	19.4469	13	330.2
	9/32	0.28125	7.1437	0.009	0.2286	25/32		0.78125	19.8437	14	355.6
	19/64	0.296875	7.5406	0.01	0.254		51/64	0.796875	20.2406	15	381.0
5/16		0.3125	7.9375	0.02	0.508	13/16		0.8125	20.6375	16	406.4
	21/64	0.328125	8.3344	0.03	0.762		53/64	0.828125	21.0344	17	431.8
	11/32	0.34375	8.7312	0.04	1.016	27/32		0.84375	21.4312	18	457.2
	23/64	0.359375	9.1281	0.05	1.270		55/64	0.859375	21.8281	19	482.6
3/8		0.375	9.5250	0.06	1.524	7/8		0.875	22.2250	20	508.0
	25/64	0.390625	9.9219	0.07	1.778		57/64	0.890625	22.6219	21	533.4
	13/32	0.40625	10.3187	0.08	2.032	29/32		0.90625	23.0187	22	558.8
	27/64	0.421875	10.7156	0.09	2.286		59/64	0.921875	23.4156	23	584.2
7/16		0.4375	11.1125	0.1	2.54	15/16		0.9375	23.8125	24	609.6
	29/64	0.453125	11.5094	0.2	5.08		61/64	0.953125	24.2094	25	635.0
	15/32	0.46875	11.9062	0.3	7.62	31/32		0.96875	24.6062	26	660.4
	31/64	0.484375	12.3031	0.4	10.16		63/64	0.984375	25.0031	27	690.6
1/2		0.5	12.7000	0.5	12.70						

ENGLISH TO METRIC CONVERSION: TORQUE

To convert foot-pounds (ft. lbs.) to Newton-meters: multiply the number of ft. lbs. by 1.3

To convert inch-pounds (in. lbs.) to Newton-meters: multiply the number of in. lbs. by .11

in lbs	N·m	in lbs	N·m	in lbs	N·m	in lbs	N·m	in lbs	N·m
0.1	0.01	1	0.11	10	1.13	19	2.15	28	3.16
0.2	0.02	2	0.23	11	1.24	20	2.26	29	3.28
0.3	0.03	3	0.34	12	1.36	21	2.37	30	3.39
0.4	0.04	4	0.45	13	1.47	22	2.49	31	3.50
0.5	0.06	5	0.56	14	1.58	23	2.60	32	3.62
0.6	0.07	6	0.68	15	1.70	24	2.71	33	3.73
0.7	0.08	7	0.78	16	1.81	25	2.82	34	3.84
0.8	0.09	8	0.90	17	1.92	26	2.94	35	3.95
0.9	0.10	9	1.02	18	2.03	27	3.05	36	4.0

2

ENGINE PERFORMANCE AND TUNE-UP

TUNE-UP PROCEDURES

In order to extract the full measure of performance and economy from your car's engine it is essential that it be properly tuned at regular intervals. Although the tune-up intervals for these cars have been stretched to limits which would have been thought impossible a few years ago, periodic maintenance is still required. A regularly scheduled tune-up will keep your car's engine running smoothly and will prevent the annoying minor breakdowns and poor performance associated with an untuned engine.

A complete tune-up should be performed at the interval specified in the Maintenance Intervals chart in Section 1. This interval should be halved if the car is operated under severe conditions, such as trailer towing, prolonged idling, continual stop-and-start driving, or if starting and running problems are noticed. It is assumed that the routine maintenance described in the first section has been kept up, as this will have a decided effect on the results of a tune-up. All of the applicable steps should be followed in order, as the result is a cumulative one.

If the specifications on the tune-up label in the engine compartment of your vehicle disagree with the Tune-Up Specifications chart in this section, the figures on the sticker must be used. The label often reflects changes made during the production run.

Spark Plugs

♦ **See Figures 1 and 2**

A typical spark plug consists of a metal shell surrounding a ceramic insulator. A metal electrode extends downward through the center of the insulator and protrudes a small distance. Located at the end of the plug and attached to the side of the outer metal shell is the side electrode. The side electrode bends in at a 90⁻ angle so that its tip is just past and parallel to the tip of the center electrode. The distance between these two electrodes (measured in thousandths of an inch or hundredths of a millimeter) is called the spark plug gap.

The spark plug does not produce a spark, but instead provides a gap across which the current can arc. The coil produces anywhere from 20,000 to 50,000 volts (depending on the type and application) which travels through the wires to the spark plugs. The current passes along the center electrode and jumps the gap to the side electrode, and in doing so, ignites the air/fuel mixture in the combustion chamber.

SPARK PLUG HEAT RANGE

♦ **See Figure 3**

Spark plug heat range is the ability of the plug to dissipate heat. The longer the insulator (or the farther it extends into the engine), the hotter the plug will operate; the shorter the insulator (the closer the electrode is to the block's cooling passages) the cooler it will operate. A plug that absorbs little heat and remains too cool will quickly accumulate deposits of oil and carbon since it is not hot enough to burn them off. This leads to plug fouling and consequently to misfiring. A plug that absorbs too much heat will have no deposits but, due to the excessive heat, the electrodes will burn away quickly and might possibly lead to preignition or other ignition problems. Preignition takes place when plug

tips get so hot that they glow sufficiently to ignite the air/fuel mixture before the actual spark occurs. This early ignition will usually cause a pinging during low speeds and heavy loads.

The general rule of thumb for choosing the correct heat range when picking a spark plug is: if most of your driving is long distance, high speed travel, use a colder plug; if most of your driving is stop and go, use a hotter plug. Original equipment plugs are generally a good compromise between the 2 styles and most people never have the need to change their plugs from the factory-recommended heat range.

REMOVAL & INSTALLATION

♦ **See Figures 4 and 5**

A set of spark plugs usually requires replacement after about 20,000–30,000 miles (32,000–48,000 km), depending on your style of driving. In normal operation plug gap increases about 0.001 in. (0.025mm) for every 2500 miles (4000 km). As the gap increases, the plug's voltage requirement also increases. It requires a greater voltage to jump the wider gap and about two to three times as much voltage to fire the plug at high speeds than at idle. The improved air/fuel ratio control of modern fuel injection combined with the higher voltage output of modern ignition systems will often allow an engine to run significantly longer on a set of standard spark plugs, but keep in mind that efficiency will drop as the gap widens (along with fuel economy and power).

When you're removing spark plugs, work on one at a time. Don't start by removing the plug wires all at once, because, unless you number them, they may become mixed up. Take a minute before you begin and number the wires with tape.

Before you replace your spark plugs make sure your engine is cool. If you do attempt to remove the plugs on a hot engine, several things could occur. The spark plugs could seize, causing damage to the cylinder head threads which can be expensive. You can also burn yourself severely. Also, make sure you clean the recess area thoroughly **before** removing the plugs. Any dirt entering the plug area will prevent the plug not to seat properly.

1. Number the wires with pieces of adhesive tape so that you won't cross them when you replace them.

2. The spark plug boots have large grips to aid in removal. Grasp the wire by the rubber boot and twist the boot ½ turn in either direction to break the tight seal between the boot and the plug. Then twist and pull on the boot to remove the wire from the spark plug. Do not pull on the wire itself or you will damage the carbon cord conductor.

3. Some of the engines may have one or more plugs which are difficult to access. The use of special tools can aid in the removal and installation. There are two tools made for these kinds of problems: J-38491, to prevent damage to the wire by breaking the plug/boot bond, and J-39294, to remove the plug wire from the rear bank of the engine.

4. If compressed air is available, apply it to the area around the spark plug holes. Otherwise, use a rag or a brush to clean the area. Doing this now will help from dirt entering into the plug chamber after removal.

5. Use a correct size spark plug socket to loosen all of the plugs about two turns. A universal joint installed at the socket end of the extension will ease the

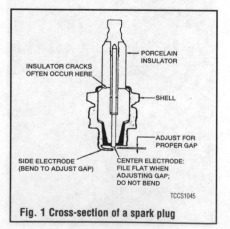

Fig. 1 Cross-section of a spark plug

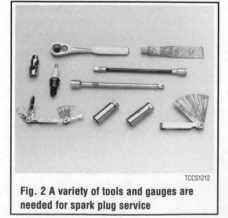

Fig. 2 A variety of tools and gauges are needed for spark plug service

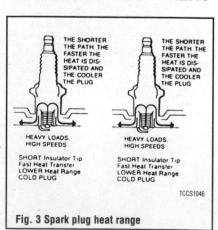

Fig. 3 Spark plug heat range

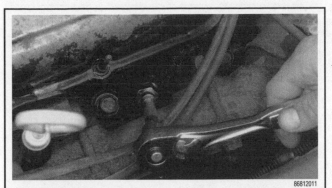

Fig. 4 Using the correct size socket is VERY important to prevent stripping the wrenching surface of the plug

Fig. 5 Spark plugs can be removed with your hand after they are loosened

process. If removal of the plugs is difficult, apply a few drops of penetrating oil or silicone spray to the area around the base of the plug, and allow it a few minutes to work.

6. Remove the plugs by unscrewing them the rest of the way.

To install:

7. Check and adjust the gap. This includes old and new plugs. Never rely on "pre-gapped" plugs. Also, use a wire gauge as opposed to a flat feeler gauge.

8. Lubricate the threads of the spark plugs with a drop of oil or a shot of silicone spray. Install the plugs and tighten them hand-tight. Take care not to cross-thread them.

9. Tighten the spark plugs with the socket. Do not apply the same amount of force you would use for a bolt; just snug them in. These spark plugs do not use gaskets, and over-tightening will make future removal difficult. If a torque wrench is available, tighten to 10–20 ft. lbs. (13–27 Nm).

➡While over-tightening the spark plug is to be avoided, under-tightening is just as bad. If combustion gases leak past the threads, the spark plug will overheat and rapid electrode wear will result.

10. Install the wires on their respective plugs. Make sure the wires are firmly connected. You will be able to feel them click into place. Spark plug wiring diagrams are in this section if you get into trouble.

INSPECTION & GAPPING

▶ **See Figures 6, 7, 8 and 9**

Check the plugs for deposits and wear. If they are not going to be replaced, clean the plugs thoroughly. Remember that any kind of deposit will decrease the efficiency of the plug. Plugs can be cleaned on a spark plug cleaning machine, which can sometimes be found in service stations, or you can do an acceptable job of cleaning with a stiff brush. If the plugs are cleaned, the electrodes must be filed flat. Use an ignition points file, not an emery board or the like, which will leave deposits. The electrodes must be filed perfectly flat with sharp edges; rounded edges reduce the spark plug voltage by as much as 50%.

Check spark plug gap before installation. The ground electrode (the L-shaped one connected to the body of the plug) must be parallel to the center electrode and the specified size wire gauge (please refer to the Tune-Up Specifications chart for details) must pass between the electrodes with a slight drag.

➡**NEVER adjust the gap on a used platinum type spark plug.**

Always check the gap on new plugs as they are not always set correctly at the factory. Do not use a flat feeler gauge when measuring the gap on a used plug, because the reading may be inaccurate. A round-wire type gapping tool is the best way to check the gap. The correct gauge should pass through the electrode gap with a slight drag. If you're in doubt, try one size smaller and one larger. The smaller gauge should go through easily, while the larger one shouldn't go through at all. Wire gapping tools usually have a bending tool attached. Use that to adjust the side electrode until the proper distance is obtained. Absolutely never attempt to bend the center electrode. Also, be careful not to bend the side electrode too far or too often as it may weaken and break off within the engine, requiring removal of the cylinder head to retrieve it.

Spark Plug Wires

INSPECTION & TESTING

▶ **See Figure 10**

Every 15,000 miles (24,000 km), inspect the spark plug wires for burns, cuts, or breaks in the insulation. Check the boots and the nipples on the distributor cap. Replace any damaged wiring. General Motors requests that you replace your spark plug wires every 30,000 miles (50,000 km).

The resistance of the wires should be checked with an ohmmeter. Wires with excessive resistance will cause misfiring, and may make the engine difficult to start in damp weather.

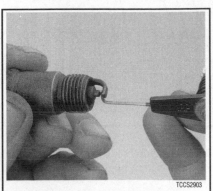

Fig. 6 Checking the spark plug gap with a feeler gauge

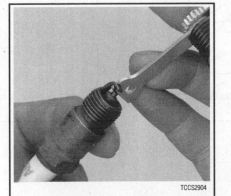

Fig. 7 Adjusting the spark plug gap

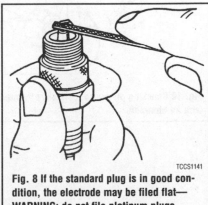

Fig. 8 If the standard plug is in good condition, the electrode may be filed flat— WARNING: do not file platinum plugs

A normally worn spark plug should have light tan or gray deposits on the firing tip.

A physically damaged spark plug may be evidence of severe detonation in that cylinder. Watch that cylinder carefully between services, as a continued detonation will not only damage the plug, but could also damage the engine.

An oil fouled spark plug indicates an engine with worn poston rings and/or bad valve seals allowing excessive oil to enter the chamber.

This spark plug has been **left in the engine too long,** as evidenced by the extreme gap- Plugs with such an extreme gap can cause misfiring and stumbling accompanied by a noticeable lack of power.

A carbon fouled plug, identified by soft, sooty, black deposits, may indicate an improperly tuned vehicle. Check the air cleaner, ignition components and engine control system.

A bridged or almost bridged spark plug, identified by a build-up between the electrodes caused by excessive carbon or oil build-up on the plug.

TCCA1P40

Fig. 9 Inspect the spark plug to determine engine running conditions

To check resistance, remove the distributor cap, leaving the wires in place. Connect one lead of an ohmmeter to an electrode within the cap; connect the other lead to the corresponding spark plug terminal (remove it from the spark plug for this test). The following chart gives resistance values as a function of length. Replace any wire which shows a resistance over 30,000 ohms.

- 0–15 in. (0–38cm): 3,000–10,000 ohms
- 15–25 in. (38–64cm): 4,000–15,000 ohms
- 25–35 in. (64–89cm): 6,000–20,000 ohms
- Over 35 in. (89cm): 25,000 ohms

It should be remembered that resistance is a function of length; the longer the wire, the greater the resistance. Thus, if the wires on your car are longer than the factory originals, resistance will be higher, quite possibly outside these limits.

REMOVAL & INSTALLATION

◆ **See Figures 11, 12 and 13**

When installing new wires, replace them one at a time to avoid mix-ups. Start by replacing the longest one first. Install the boot firmly over the spark plug. Route the wire over the same path as the original. Insert the nipple firmly onto the tower on the distributor cap or coil, then install the cap cover and latches to secure the wires, if applicable.

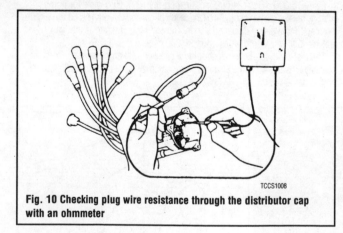
TCCS1008

Fig. 10 Checking plug wire resistance through the distributor cap with an ohmmeter

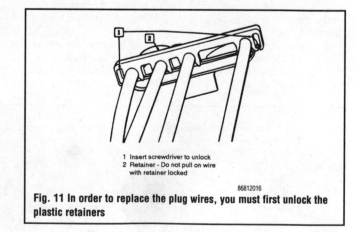
1 Insert screwdriver to unlock
2 Retainer - Do not pull on wire with retainer locked

86812016

Fig. 11 In order to replace the plug wires, you must first unlock the plastic retainers

Fig. 12 Grasp only the boot when removing the wires, never tug on the wire itself!

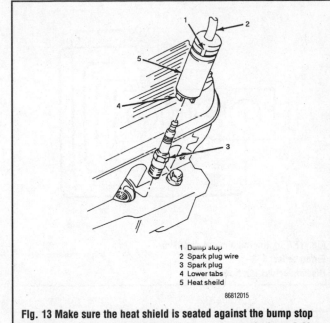

1 Bump stop
2 Spark plug wire
3 Spark plug
4 Lower tabs
5 Heat shield

Fig. 13 Make sure the heat shield is seated against the bump stop and lower the tabs extended over the hex on the spark plug—3.3L engine

FIRING ORDERS

⬥ See Figures 14 thru 22

➡To avoid confusion, remove and tag the spark plug wires one at a time, for replacement.

If a distributor is not keyed for installation with only one orientation, it could have been removed previously and rewired. The resultant wiring would hold the correct firing order, but could change the relative placement of the plug towers in relation to the engine. For this reason, it is imperative that you label all wires before disconnecting any of them. Also, before removal, compare the current wiring with the accompanying illustrations. If the current wiring does not match, make notes in your book to reflect how your engine is wired.

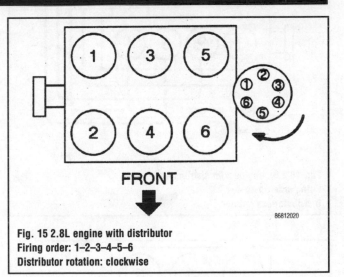

Fig. 15 2.8L engine with distributor
Firing order: 1–2–3–4–5–6
Distributor rotation: clockwise

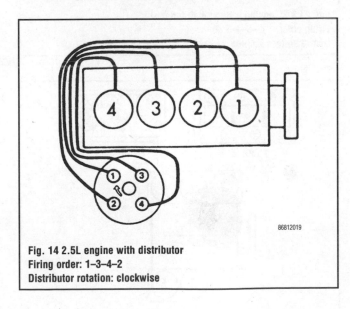

Fig. 14 2.5L engine with distributor
Firing order: 1–3–4–2
Distributor rotation: clockwise

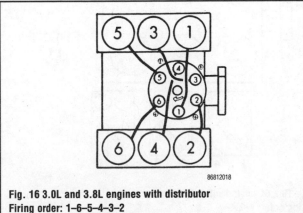

Fig. 16 3.0L and 3.8L engines with distributor
Firing order: 1–6–5–4–3–2
Distributor rotation: clockwise

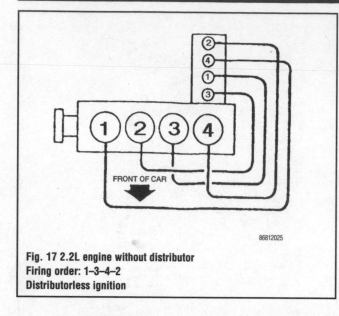

Fig. 17 2.2L engine without distributor
Firing order: 1–3–4–2
Distributorless ignition

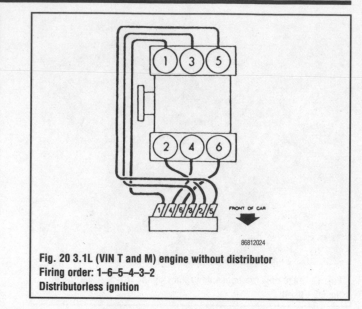

Fig. 20 3.1L (VIN T and M) engine without distributor
Firing order: 1–6–5–4–3–2
Distributorless ignition

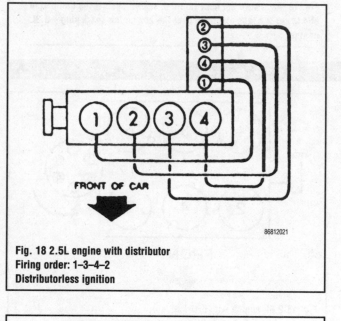

Fig. 18 2.5L engine with distributor
Firing order: 1–3–4–2
Distributorless ignition

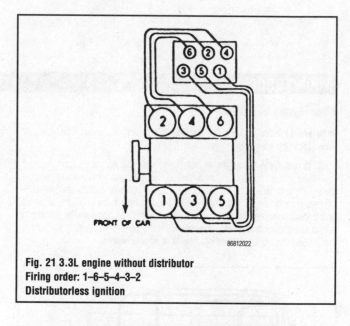

Fig. 21 3.3L engine without distributor
Firing order: 1–6–5–4–3–2
Distributorless ignition

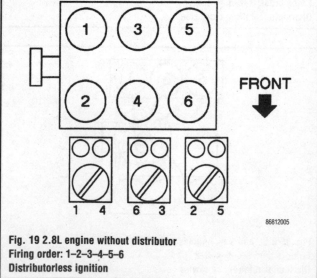

Fig. 19 2.8L engine without distributor
Firing order: 1–2–3–4–5–6
Distributorless ignition

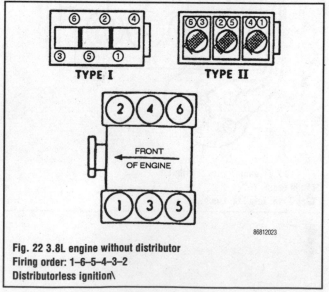

Fig. 22 3.8L engine without distributor
Firing order: 1–6–5–4–3–2
Distributorless ignition\

ELECTRONIC IGNITION SYSTEMS

General Information

General Motors uses two basic ignition systems on these vehicles: a high energy distributor type system or a high energy distributorless type system. The High Energy Ignition (HEI) distributor type system is virtually maintenance-free, since it is electronic and, therefore, uses no breaker points. The only required service for the HEI distributor is to check the distributor cap and rotor for cracks, carbon tracking, and corrosion every 30,000 miles (48,300 km).

On distributorless systems, even less maintenance is required. Since there is no distributor, there is no cap or rotor to wear out. The only normal maintenance required on these systems will be the spark plug and wires. Diagnosis of no start conditions may require testing the ignition module or coil assemblies. These items are not much different than the ignition module or coil used on HEI systems.

The distributorless ignition systems used by General Motors go by two names, either DIS or C³I. DIS simply stands for Distributorless Ignition System, while C³I stands for Computer Controlled Coil Ignition. Both of these systems function the same way; by connecting a coil pack to a pair of spark plugs and firing the proper coil each time the a specific plug should spark, instead of using a distributor cap and rotor.

The distributorless ignition system is far better than previous system. It allows for more accurate spark control and a higher spark output. This is important at the high rpm's generated by newer engines.

HIGH ENERGY IGNITION (HEI) SYSTEM

The General Motors HEI system is a pulse-triggered, transistor-controlled, inductive discharge ignition system. The entire HEI system is contained within the distributor cap.

The distributor contains the ignition coil and electronic control module; the magnetic pick-up assembly contains a permanent magnet, pole piece with internal teeth, and pick-up coil (not to be confused with the ignition coil).

For 1982 and later models, an HEI distributor with Electronic Spark Timing (EST) is used. (For more information on EST, refer to Section 4).

All spark timing changes in the 1982 and later distributors are done electronically by the Ignition Control Module (ICM) which monitors information from various engine sensors, computes the desired spark timing and then signals the distributor to change the timing accordingly. No vacuum or mechanical advance systems are used whatsoever.

In the HEI system, as in other electronic ignition systems, the breaker points have been replaced with an electronic switch, (a transistor), which is located within the control module. This switching transistor performs the same function the points did in a conventional ignition system; it simply turns coil primary current on and off at the correct time. Essentially then, electronic and conventional ignition systems operate on the same principle.

The module which houses the switching transistor is controlled (turned on and off) by a magnetically generated impulse induced in the pick-up coil. When the teeth of the rotating timer align with the teeth of the pole piece, the induced voltage in the pick-up coil signals the electronic module to open the coil primary circuit. The primary current then decreases, and a high voltage is induced in the ignition coil secondary windings which is then directed through the rotor and spark plug wires to fire the spark plugs.

In essence then, the pick-up coil module system simply replaces the conventional breaker points and condenser. The condenser found within the distributor is for radio suppression purposes only and has nothing to do with the ignition process. The module automatically controls the dwell period, increasing it with increasing engine speed. Since dwell is automatically controlled, it cannot be adjusted. The module itself is non-adjustable and non-repairable, and must be replaced if found defective.

DISTRIBUTORLESS IGNITION SYSTEMS

Starting in 1987, some models came with engines equipped with a Computer Controlled Coil Ignition (C³I) or Distributorless Ignition System (DIS).

Both DIS and C³I system consists of the coil pack, ignition module, crankshaft sensor, interrupter rings and ignition control module (ICM). All components are serviced as complete assemblies, although individual coils are available for Type 2 coil packs. Since the ICM controls the ignition timing, no timing adjustments are necessary or possible.

Diagnosis and Testing

▶ See Figure 23

The ignition, fuel, electrical and emission systems are all interrelated on vehicles that have computer control engines. Testing these systems has become very involved because of this. When using this manual, it's important to realize that these systems overlap. Some testing or component replacement that may affect the ignition system may be found in Section 4.

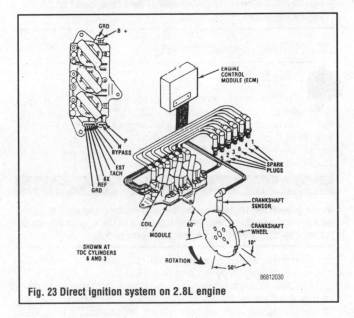

Fig. 23 Direct ignition system on 2.8L engine

HEI SYSTEM PRECAUTIONS

This is an extremely high voltage system and contact with the spark plug wires with the ignition switch **ON** can give a very dangerous shock. Never service the or test the spark plug wires, distributor cap or coil with the key **ON** or engine running unless instructed to perform a specific test. Before going on to troubleshooting, it might be a good idea to take note of the following precautions:

➡**To avoid damage to the ICM or other ignition system components, do not use electrical test equipment such as battery or AC powered voltmeter, ohmmeter, etc. or any type of tester other than specified.**

• When performing electrical tests on the system, use a high impedance multimeter, digital voltmeter (DVM) J-34029-A or equivalent.

• To prevent electrostatic discharge damage, when working with the Computer Control Module (ECM/PCM), do not touch the connector pins or soldered components on the circuit board.

• When handling a PROM, CAL-PAK or MEM-CAL, do not touch the component leads. Also, do not remove the integrated circuit from the carrier.

• Never pierce a high tension lead or boot for any testing purpose; otherwise, future problems are guaranteed.

• Leave new components and modules in the shipping package until ready to install them.

• Never disconnect any electrical connection with the ignition switch **ON** unless instructed to do so in a test.

Timing Light Use

▶ See Figure 24

Inductive pick-up timing lights are the best kind of use with HEI. Timing light which connect between the spark plug and the spark plug wire occasionally (not always) give false readings.

Fig. 24 Aim the inductive timing light at the timing marks on the engine and pulley

DISTRIBUTOR COMPONENT TESTING

▶ **See Figure 25**

Not all tachometers will operate or indicate correctly when used on a HEI system. While some tachometers may give a reading, this does not necessarily mean the reading is correct. In addition, some tachometers hook up differently from others. If you can't figure out whether or not your tachometer will work on your car, check with the tachometer manufacturer. The following procedure is for internal coils; see the illustrations for external coils.

✳✳ WARNING

Never ground the TACH terminal; serious module and ignition coil damage will result. If there is any doubt as to the correct tachometer hookup, check with the tachometer manufacturer.

1. Connect an ohmmeter between the TACH and BAT terminals in the distributor cap. The primary coil resistance should be less than 1 ohm.
2. To check the coil secondary resistance, connect an ohmmeter between the rotor button and BAT terminal. Note the reading. Connect the ohmmeter between the rotor button and the TACH terminal. Note the reading. The resistance in both cases should be 6000–30,000 ohms. Be sure to test between the rotor button and both the BAT and TACH terminals.
3. Replace the coil only if the readings in Step 1 and 2 are infinite.

➡**These resistance checks will not disclose shorted coil windings. This condition can only be detected with scope analysis or a suitably designed coil tester. If these instruments are unavailable, replace the coil with a known good coil as a final test.**

4. To test the pick-up coil, first disconnect the white and green module leads. Set the ohmmeter on the high scale and connect it between a ground and either the white or green lead. Any resistance measurement less than infinity requires replacement of the pick-up coil.

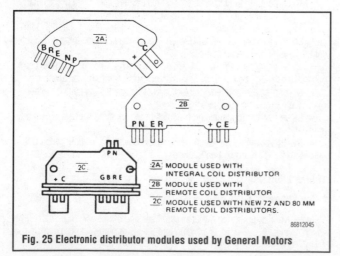

Fig. 25 Electronic distributor modules used by General Motors

5. Pick-up coil continuity is tested by connecting the ohmmeter (on low range) between the white and green leads. Normal resistance is between 800–1500 ohms. Move the vacuum advance arm while performing this test, if equipped. This will detect any break in coil continuity. Such a condition can cause intermittent misfiring. Replace the pick-up if the reading is outside the specified limits.

6. If no defects have been found at this time, and you still have a problem, then the module will have to be checked. If you do not have access to a module tester, the only possible alternative is a substitution test or have the module tested by a professional.

HEI System Testers

Instruments designed specifically for testing HEI systems are available from several tool manufacturers. Some of these will even test the module itself. For specific details, refer to the instruments' instructions.

HEI System Parts Replacement

REMOVAL & INSTALLATION

Integral Coil

▶ **See Figures 26, 27 and 28**

1. Disconnect the negative battery cable.
2. Disconnect the feed and module wire terminal connectors from the distributor cap.
3. Remove the ignition set retainer.
4. Remove the 4 coil cover-to-distributor cap screws.
5. Using a blunt drift, press the coil wire spade terminals out of the distributor cap.
6. Lift the coil out of the distributor cap.
7. Remove and clean the coil spring, rubber seal washer and coil cavity of the distributor cap.
To install:
8. Coat the rubber seal with a dielectric lubricant furnished. This is usually in the replacement ignition coil package.
9. Install the coil spring, rubber seal washer and coil cavity into the distributor cap.
10. Place the coil into the cap, connect the spade terminals.
11. Install the 4 cover-to distributor cap screws, install the ignition set retainer.
12. Connect the feed and module wire terminal connectors to the distributor cap.
13. Connect the negative battery cable.
14. Reset the clock, radio and any other accessories if required.

External Coil

▶ **See Figures 29, 30, 31, 32 and 33**

1. Disconnect the negative battery cable.
2. Loosen the bolts securing the coil assembly.
3. Remove the wires attached to the mounting screw.
4. Disconnect the wire harnesses connected to the coil assembly.
5. Disconnect the coil wire from the coil, then remove the coil.
To install:
6. Place the new coil in position, attach the wires to the mounting bolts and tighten.
7. Attach the wiring harnesses to the coil, and connect the coil wire.
8. Connect the negative battery cable.
9. Reset the clock, radio and any other accessories if required.

Distributor Cap

INTEGRAL COIL

1. Disconnect the negative battery cable.
2. Remember to number the cap and wires before removal.
3. Remove the feed and module wire terminal connectors from the distributor cap.
4. Remove the retainer and spark plug wires from the cap.

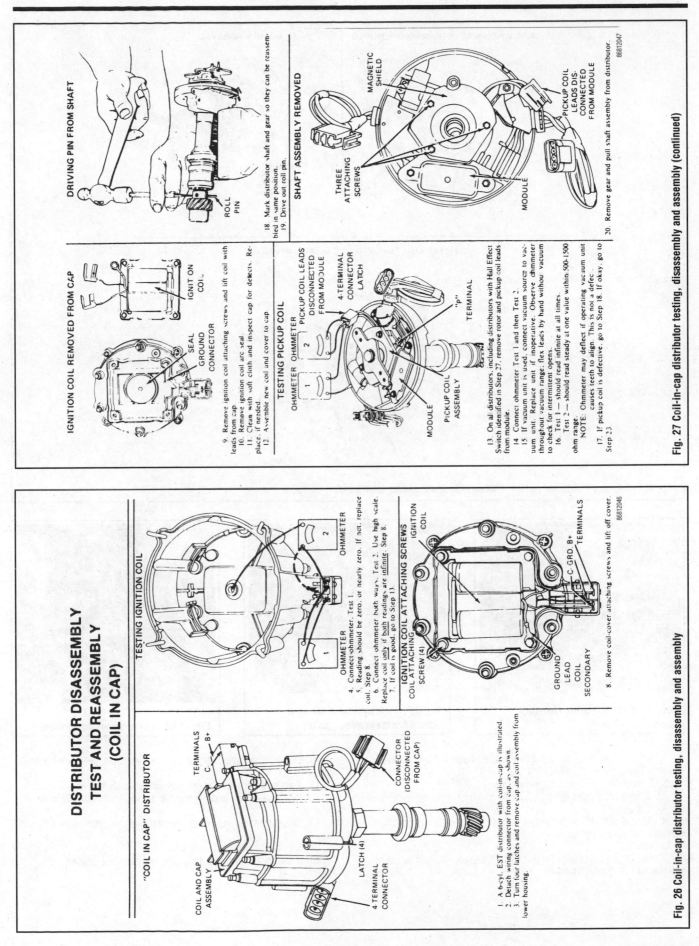

DRIVING PIN FROM SHAFT

ROLL PIN

18. Mark distributor shaft and gear so they can be reassembled in same position.
19. Drive out roll pin.

SHAFT ASSEMBLY REMOVED

MAGNETIC SHIELD

PICKUP COIL LEADS DISCONNECTED FROM MODULE

THREE ATTACHING SCREWS

MODULE

20. Remove gear and pull shaft assembly from distributor.

IGNITION COIL REMOVED FROM CAP

IGNIT ON COIL

SEAL GROUND CONNECTOR

9. Remove ignition coil attaching screws and lift coil with leads from cap.
10. Remove ignition coil arc seal.
11. Clean with soft cloth and inspect cap for defects. Replace, if needed.
12. Assemble new coil and cover to cap.

TESTING PICKUP COIL

OHMMETER OHMMETER

PICKUP COIL LEADS DISCONNECTED FROM MODULE

4-TERMINAL CONNECTOR LATCH

"P" TERMINAL

MODULE

PICKUP COIL ASSEMBLY

13. On all distributors, including distributors with Hall Effect Switch identified in Step 27, remove rotor and pickup coil leads from module.
14. Connect ohmmeter Test 1 and then Test 2.
15. If vacuum unit is used, connect vacuum source to vacuum unit. Replace unit if inoperative. Observe ohmmeter throughout vacuum range; flex leads by hand withour vacuum to check for intermittent opens.
16. Test 1 — should read infinite at all times.
    Test 2 — should read steady at one value within 500-1500 ohm range.
    NOTE: Ohmmeter may deflect if operating vacuum unit causes teeth to align. This is not a defect.
17. If pickup coil is defective, go to Step 18. If okay, go to Step 23.

Fig. 27 Coil-in-cap distributor testing, disassembly and assembly (continued)

DISTRIBUTOR DISASSEMBLY TEST AND REASSEMBLY (COIL IN CAP)

"COIL IN CAP" DISTRIBUTOR

COIL AND CAP ASSEMBLY

TERMINALS C. B+

LATCH (4)

4-TERMINAL CONNECTOR

CONNECTOR (DISCONNECTED FROM CAP)

1. A 6-cyl. EST distributor with coil-in-cap is illustrated.
2. Detach wiring connector from cap, as shown.
3. Turn four latches and remove cap and coil assembly from lower housing.

TESTING IGNITION COIL

OHMMETER 2

OHMMETER 1

4. Connect ohmmeter, Test 1.
5. Reading should be zero, or nearly zero. If not, replace coil. Step 8.
6. Connect ohmmeter both ways. Test 2. Use high scale. Replace coil only if both readings are infinite. Step 8.
7. If coil is good, go to Step 13.

IGNITION COIL ATTACHING SCREWS

IGNITION COIL

C- GRD. B+

TERMINALS

IGNITION COIL ATTACHING SCREW (4)

GROUND LEAD COIL SECONDARY

8. Remove coil-cover attaching screws and lift off cover.

Fig. 26 Coil-in-cap distributor testing, disassembly and assembly

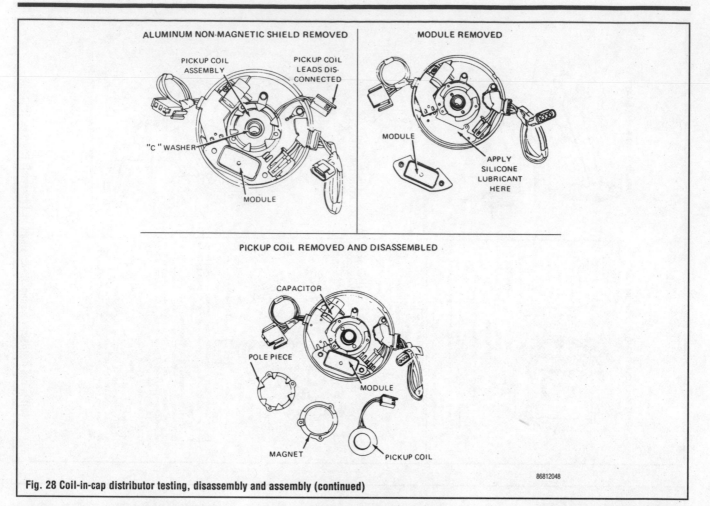

ALUMINUM NON-MAGNETIC SHIELD REMOVED

MODULE REMOVED

PICKUP COIL ASSEMBLY

PICKUP COIL LEADS DISCONNECTED

"C" WASHER

MODULE

MODULE

APPLY SILICONE LUBRICANT HERE

PICKUP COIL REMOVED AND DISASSEMBLED

CAPACITOR

POLE PIECE

MODULE

MAGNET

PICKUP COIL

Fig. 28 Coil-in-cap distributor testing, disassembly and assembly (continued)

86812048

Fig. 29 Loosen the coil's mounting bolts . . .

86812051

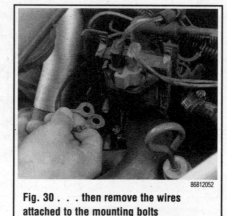

Fig. 30 . . . then remove the wires attached to the mounting bolts

86812052

86812053

Fig. 31 Disengage the wiring harnesses

5. Depress and release the 4 distributor cap-to-housing retainers and lift off the cap assembly.

6. Remove the 4 coil cover screws and cover.

7. Using a finger or a blunt drift, push the spade terminals out of the distributor cap.

8. Remove all 4 coil screws and lift the coil, coil spring and rubber seal washer out of the cap coil cavity.

To install:

9. Position the new cap on the distributor. Clean and lubricate the rubber seal washer with dielectric lubricant.

10. Install the coil spring, rubber seal washer and coil cavity into the distributor cap.

11. Position the coil into the cap, connect the spade terminals.

12. Install the 4 cover-to distributor cap screws, install the ignition set retainer.

13. Connect the feed and module wire terminal connectors to the distributor cap.

14. Connect the negative battery cable.

15. Reset the clock, radio and any other accessories if required.

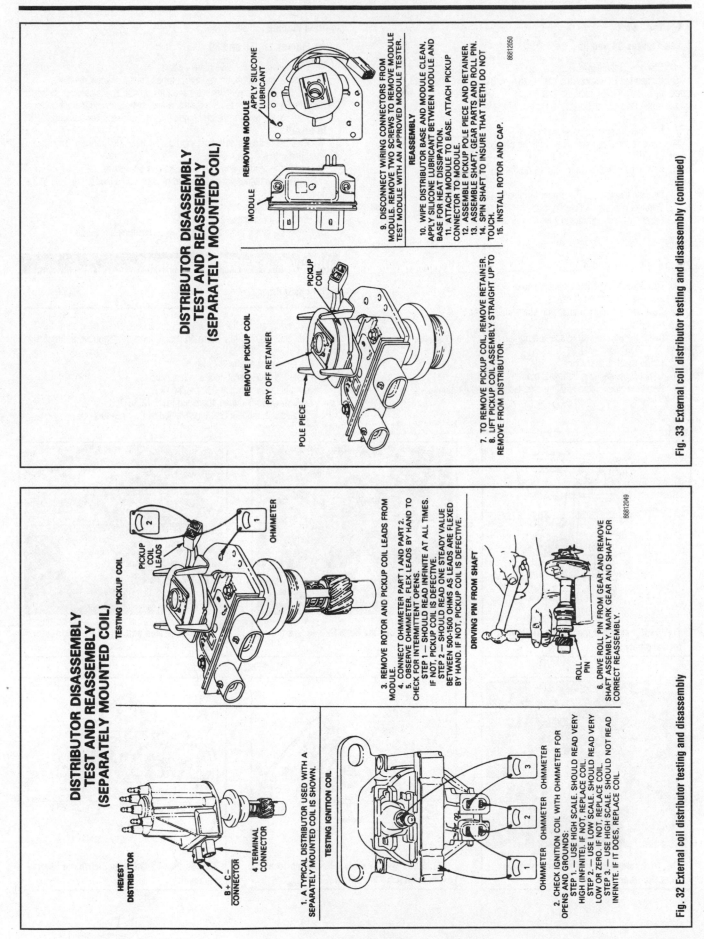

DISTRIBUTOR DISASSEMBLY TEST AND REASSEMBLY (SEPARATELY MOUNTED COIL)

REMOVING MODULE

APPLY SILICONE LUBRICANT

MODULE

REMOVE PICKUP COIL

PRY OFF RETAINER

PICKUP COIL

POLE PIECE

9. DISCONNECT WIRING CONNECTORS FROM MODULE. REMOVE TWO SCREWS TO REMOVE MODULE TEST MODULE WITH AN APPROVED MODULE TESTER.

REASSEMBLY

10. WIPE DISTRIBUTOR BASE AND MODULE CLEAN. APPLY SILICONE LUBRICANT BETWEEN MODULE AND BASE FOR HEAT DISSIPATION.
11. ATTACH MODULE TO BASE. ATTACH PICKUP CONNECTOR TO MODULE.
12. ASSEMBLE PICKUP POLE PIECE AND RETAINER.
13. ASSEMBLE SHAFT, GEAR PARTS AND ROLL PIN.
14. SPIN SHAFT TO INSURE THAT TEETH DO NOT TOUCH.
15. INSTALL ROTOR AND CAP.

7. TO REMOVE PICKUP COIL, REMOVE RETAINER.
8. LIFT PICKUP COIL ASSEMBLY STRAIGHT UP TO REMOVE FROM DISTRIBUTOR.

Fig. 33 External coil distributor testing and disassembly (continued)

DISTRIBUTOR DISASSEMBLY TEST AND REASSEMBLY (SEPARATELY MOUNTED COIL)

TESTING PICKUP COIL

OHMMETER 2

OHMMETER 1

PICKUP COIL LEADS

3. REMOVE ROTOR AND PICKUP COIL LEADS FROM MODULE.
4. CONNECT OHMMETER PART 1 AND PART 2.
5. OBSERVE OHMMETER. FLEX LEADS BY HAND TO CHECK FOR INTERMITTENT OPENS.
   STEP 1 — SHOULD READ INFINITE AT ALL TIMES. IF NOT, PICKUP COIL IS DEFECTIVE.
   STEP 2 — SHOULD READ ONE STEADY VALUE BETWEEN 500-1500 OHMS AS LEADS ARE FLEXED BY HAND. IF NOT, PICKUP COIL IS DEFECTIVE.

DRIVING PIN FROM SHAFT

ROLL PIN

6. DRIVE ROLL PIN FROM GEAR AND REMOVE SHAFT ASSEMBLY. MARK GEAR AND SHAFT FOR CORRECT REASSEMBLY.

HEI/EST DISTRIBUTOR

B+ C– CONNECTOR

4 TERMINAL CONNECTOR

TESTING IGNITION COIL

OHMMETER   OHMMETER   OHMMETER

1. A TYPICAL DISTRIBUTOR USED WITH A SEPARATELY MOUNTED COIL IS SHOWN.

2. CHECK IGNITION COIL WITH OHMMETER FOR OPENS AND GROUNDS:
   STEP 1.— USE HIGH SCALE. SHOULD READ VERY HIGH (INFINITE). IF NOT, REPLACE COIL.
   STEP 2.— USE LOW SCALE. SHOULD READ VERY LOW OR ZERO. IF NOT, REPLACE COIL.
   STEP 3.— USE HIGH SCALE. SHOULD NOT READ INFINITE. IF IT DOES, REPLACE COIL.

Fig. 32 External coil distributor testing and disassembly

EXTERNAL COIL

▶ **See Figures 34 and 35**

1. Disconnect the negative battery cable.
2. Remember to number the cap and wires before removal. It might be a good idea to match the caps up and insert the wires into the new cap prior to installation. This could aid you in replacing the wires on the correct terminals.
3. Remove the spark plug wires from the cap.
4. Remove the 2 cap screws and lift the cap off.

To install:

5. Install the new distributor cap using the cap screws and tighten until snug.
6. Replace the wires to the proper terminals.
7. Connect the negative battery cable.
8. Reset the clock, radio and any other accessories if required.

Rotor

▶ **See Figures 36 and 37**

1. Disconnect the negative battery cable.
2. Remove the distributor cap.
3. Remove the two rotor attaching screws and rotor.

To install:

4. Insert the new rotor in place and tighten the mounting screws until snug.
5. Install the distributor cap.
6. Connect the negative battery cable.
7. Reset the clock, radio and any other accessories if required.

Ignition Module

▶ **See Figures 25, 38 and 39**

1. Disconnect the negative battery cable.
2. Remove the distributor cap and rotor as previously described.
3. Unplug the harness connector and pick-up coil spade connectors from the module. Be careful not to damage the wires when removing the connector.
4. Remove the two screws and module from the distributor housing.

To install:

5. Coat the bottom of the new module with dielectric lubricant. This is usually supplied with the new module.
6. Install the module and tighten the screws until snug.
7. Engage the harness connector and pick-up coil spade connectors to the module.
8. Install the cap and rotor.
9. Connect the negative battery cable.
10. Reset the clock, radio and any other accessories if required.

DIS System Parts Replacement

IDLE LEARN PROCEDURE

This procedure allows the ICM memory to be updated with the correct IAC valve pintle position. The Idle Learn procedure must be performed on the 3.1L engine as follows:

1. Place the transaxle in **P** or **N**.
2. Install the Tech 1 scan tool or equivalent.
3. Turn the ignition switch **ON**, engine OFF.
4. Select IAC system, then Idle Learn in the MISC Test mode.
5. Proceed with the Idle Learn as directed by the scan tool.

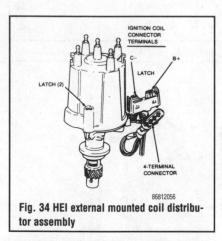

Fig. 34 HEI external mounted coil distributor assembly

Fig. 35 Remove the bolts that secure the cap for removal

Fig. 36 Unfasten and lift off the distributor cap

Fig. 37 Remove the two mounting screws from the rotor

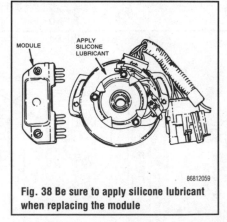

Fig. 38 Be sure to apply silicone lubricant when replacing the module

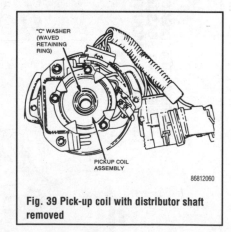

Fig. 39 Pick-up coil with distributor shaft removed

REMOVAL & INSTALLATION

DIS Assembly

2.2L, 2.5L, 2.8L, 3.1L AND 3.8L ENGINES

♦ See Figures 40 and 41

1. Disconnect the negative battery cable.
2. Unplug the DIS electrical connectors.
3. Tag and disconnect the spark plug wires.
4. Remove the DIS assembly attaching bolts.
5. Remove the DIS assembly from the engine.

To install:

6. Install the DIS assembly and attaching bolts.
7. Connect the spark plug wires.
8. Engage the DIS electrical connectors.
9. Connect the negative battery cable.
10. On 3.1L (VIN T) engine, perform the idle learn procedure.
11. Reset the clock, radio and any other accessories if required.

Ignition Coils

2.2L ENGINE

1. Disconnect the negative battery cable.
2. Raise the car and support with jackstands.
3. Disconnect the ICM electrical connectors.
4. Mark and disconnect the spark plug wires.
5. Remove the 3 coil assembly-to-block bolts.
6. Remove the coil assembly from the engine.

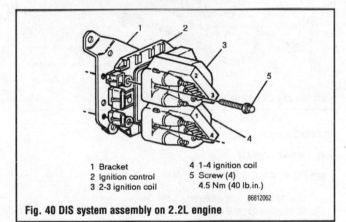

1 Bracket
2 Ignition control
3 2-3 ignition coil
4 1-4 ignition coil
5 Screw (4)
4.5 Nm (40 lb.in.)

86812062

Fig. 40 DIS system assembly on 2.2L engine

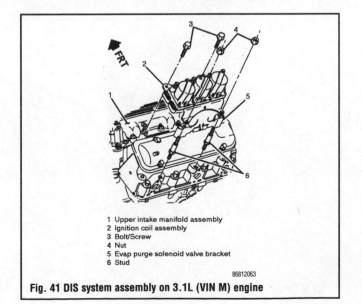

1 Upper intake manifold assembly
2 Ignition coil assembly
3 Bolt/Screw
4 Nut
5 Evap purge solenoid valve bracket
6 Stud

86812063

Fig. 41 DIS system assembly on 3.1L (VIN M) engine

To install:

7. Install the coil assembly to the engine with the mounting bolts.
8. Connect the 3 ignition coil assembly-to-the block bolts.
9. Tighten the coil assembly mounting bolts to 15–22 ft. lbs. (20–30 Nm).
10. Install the plug wires to the proper coils.
11. Install the ICM connectors.
12. Lower the car, connect the negative battery cable.
13. Reset the clock, radio and any other accessories if required.

2.5L, 2.8L, 3.1L AND 3.8L ENGINES

1. Disconnect the negative battery cable.
2. Disconnect and tag spark plug wires.
3. Remove ignition coil attaching bolts, then the ignition coil from the module.

To install:

4. Install the coil(s) and attaching bolts, tighten to 40 inch lbs. (4–5 Nm).
5. Connect the spark plug wires.
6. Connect the negative battery cable.
7. On 3.1L engine perform the idle learn procedure.
8. Reset the clock, radio and any other accessories if required.

3.3L ENGINE

1. Disconnect the negative battery cable.
2. Tag and disconnect spark plug wires.
3. Remove ignition coil(s) attaching bolts, then the ignition coil from the module.

To install:

4. Install the coil(s) and attaching bolts, torque to 27 inch lbs. (3 Nm).
5. Connect the spark plug wires.
6. Connect the negative battery cable.
7. Reset the clock, radio and any other accessories if required.

Ignition Module

2.2L ENGINE

1. Disconnect the negative battery cable.
2. Raise and support the car.
3. Remove the ignition coil assembly from the engine. Disconnect the coils from the assembly.
4. Remove the module from the assembly plate.

To install:

5. Install the new module to the plate.
6. Install the coils to the assembly, and install the coil assembly on the engine.
7. Lower the car. Connect the negative battery cable, then reset the clock, radio and any other accessories.

2.5L, 2.8L, 3.1L (VIN T) AND 3.8L ENGINES

1. Disconnect the negative battery cable.
2. Remove the DIS assembly from the engine.
3. Remove the coils from the assembly.
4. Remove the DIS module from the assembly plate.

To install:

5. Install the DIS module to the assembly plate.
6. Install the coils to the assembly.
7. Install the DIS assembly to the engine.
8. Connect the negative battery cable, then reset the clock, radio and any other accessories.
9. On 3.1L engine perform the idle learn procedure.

3.1L (VIN M) ENGINE

1. Disconnect the negative battery cable.
2. Remove the 6-way, 3-way and 2-way connectors at the ignition control module.
3. Remove the plug wires from the coil assembly.
4. Disconnect the 6 screws that secure the coil assemblies to the ICM.
5. Remove the nuts and washers securing the ICM assembly to the bracket and remove the ICM.

To install:

6. Install the coils to the ICM installing the 6 screws.
7. Tighten the screws to 40 inch lbs. (4–5 Nm).

8. Install the nuts and washers securing the assembly to the bracket and torque them to 70 inch lbs. (8 Nm).

9. Engage the 2, 3, and 6 way connectors to the ICM.

10. Connect the negative battery cable, then reset the clock, radio and any other accessories.

Crankshaft Position Sensor (CKP)

2.2L ENGINE

1. Disconnect the negative battery cable.
2. Raise the car and support.
3. Disconnect the harness at the sensor.
4. Remove the bolt to the sensor.
5. Remove the sensor from the engine.

To install:

6. Inspect the O-ring and replace if needed. Lubricate the O-ring with engine oil.
7. Install the sensor to the block.
8. Insert the bolt and tighten to 71 inch lbs. (8 Nm).
9. Engage the harness on the sensor.
10. Lower the car, Connect the negative battery cable, then reset the clock, radio and any other accessories.

2.5L, 2.8L, 3.1L (VIN T) AND 3.8L ENGINES

1. Disconnect the negative battery cable.
2. Disconnect crankshaft sensor electrical connector.
3. Remove the crankshaft sensor attaching bolt, then remove the crankshaft sensor from the vehicle.

To install:

4. Inspect the sensor O-ring for wear, cracks or leakage. Replace as necessary. Lubricate the new O-ring with engine oil prior to installation.
5. Install the sensor into the hole in the engine block and install retaining bolt.
6. Engage the electrical connector.
7. Connect the negative battery cable, then reset the clock, radio and any other accessories.
8. On 3.1L engine perform the idle learn procedure.

3.1L (VIN M) ENGINE WITH 3X CKP

▶ See Figure 42

➡ On cars equipped with manual transaxles, the CKP is easily accessed from beneath the engine. For automatic transaxles, the rack and pinion heat shield and the converter intermediate exhaust assembly must be removed.

1. Disconnect the negative battery cable.
2. Unplug the sensor connector.
3. Remove the sensor bolts and the sensor from the engine.
4. Inspect the O-ring and replace if needed. This is always advisable anyway.

To install:

5. Install the sensor to the engine, tighten the mounting bolt to 88 inch lbs. (10 Nm).

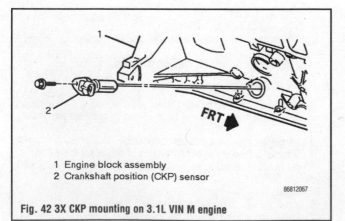

1 Engine block assembly
2 Crankshaft position (CKP) sensor

86812067

Fig. 42 3X CKP mounting on 3.1L VIN M engine

6. Insert the connector to the sensor, then connect the negative battery cable.
7. Reset the clock, radio and any other accessories.

3.1L (VIN M) ENGINE WITH 24X CKP

▶ See Figure 43

1. Disconnect the negative battery cable.
2. Remove the serpentine belt from the crankshaft pulley.
3. Raise the car on a hoist.
4. Remove the crankshaft harmonic balancer retaining bolt. Use tool J-38197 or equivalent.
5. Unplug the crankshaft sensor connector.
6. Remove the 2 sensor mounting bolts, then remove the sensor.

To install:

7. Connect the sensor with the 2 mounting bolts. Tighten the bolts to 8 ft. lbs. (10 Nm).
8. Reattach the sensor connector.
9. Install the balancer on the crankshaft.
10. Apply thread sealer GM# 1052080 or equivalent to the threads of the balancer bolt. Tighten the bolt to 110 ft. lbs. (150 Nm).
11. Lower the car.
12. Install the serpentine belt.
13. Connect the negative battery cable, then reset the clock, radio and any other accessories.

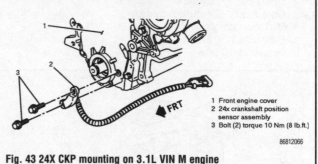

1 Front engine cover
2 24x crankshaft position sensor assembly
3 Bolt (2) torque 10 Nm (8 lb.ft.)

86812066

Fig. 43 24X CKP mounting on 3.1L VIN M engine

Camshaft Position Sensor

3.1L ENGINE (VIN M)

▶ See Figure 44

1. Disconnect the negative battery cable.
2. Remove the serpentine belt.
3. Remove the power steering pump.

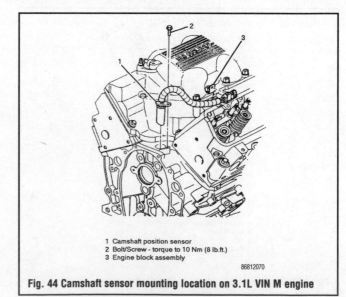

1 Camshaft position sensor
2 Bolt/Screw - torque to 10 Nm (8 lb.ft.)
3 Engine block assembly

86812070

Fig. 44 Camshaft sensor mounting location on 3.1L VIN M engine

4. Unplug the connector to the sensor.

5. Remove the mounting bolt for the sensor, and remove the sensor.

To install:

6. Install the camshaft sensor.

7. Insert the bolt, tighten down to 8 ft. lbs. (10 Nm).

8. Insert the electrical connector to the sensor.

9. Install the power steering pump, and the serpentine belt.

10. Connect the negative battery cable, then reset the clock, radio and any other accessories.

C³I System Parts Replacement

The 3.3L engine is the only one with the C³I system.

REMOVAL & INSTALLATION

C³I Module

▶ **See Figure 45**

1. Disconnect the negative battery cable.

2. Unplug the 14-way connector at the ignition module.

3. Tag and disconnect the spark plug wires at the coil assembly.

4. Remove the nuts and washers securing the C³I module assembly to the bracket.

5. Remove the 6 bolts attaching the coil assemblies to the ignition module.

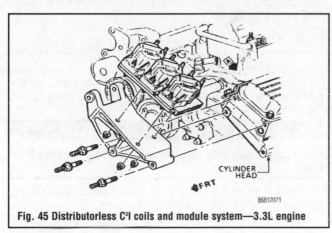

Fig. 45 Distributorless C³I coils and module system—3.3L engine

To install:

6. Install the coil assemblies to the ignition module and install the 6 attaching bolts.

7. Install the nuts and washers attaching the assembly to the bracket.

8. Connect the spark plug wires.

9. Engage the 14-way connector to the module.

10. Connect the negative battery cable, then reset the clock, radio and any other accessories.

Ignition Coil(s)

1. Disconnect the negative battery cable.

2. Tag and disconnect the spark plug wires.

3. Remove ignition coil attaching bolts, then the ignition coil from the module.

To install:

4. Install the coil(s) and attaching bolts.

5. Connect the spark plug wires.

6. Connect the negative battery cable, then reset the clock, radio and any other accessories.

Dual Crankshaft Sensor

▶ **See Figure 46**

1. Disconnect battery negative cable.

2. Remove serpentine belt from crankshaft pulley.

3. Raise and safely support the vehicle.

4. Remove right front tire and wheel assembly, then the inner access cover.

5. Remove crankshaft harmonic balancer retaining bolt and crankshaft harmonic balancer.

6. Unplug the electrical connector from the sensor and remove the crankshaft sensor from the vehicle.

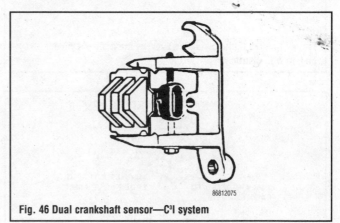

Fig. 46 Dual crankshaft sensor—C³I system

To install:

7. Loosely install the crankshaft sensor on the pedestal.

8. Position the sensor with the pedestal attached on special tool J-37089.

9. Position the tool on the crankshaft.

10. Install the bolts to hold the pedestal to the block face. Tighten to 14–28 ft. lbs. (20–40 Nm).

11. Tighten the pedestal pinch bolt to 30–35 inch lbs. (3–4 Nm).

12. Remove special tool J-37089.

13. Place special tool J-37089 on the harmonic balancer and turn. If any vane of the harmonic balancer touches the tool, replace the balancer assembly.

➡**A clearance of 0.025 inch is required on either side of the interrupter ring. Be certain to obtain the correct clearance. Failure to do so will damage the sensor. A misadjusted sensor of bent interrupter ring could cause rubbing of the sensor, resulting in potential driveability problems, such as rough idle, poor performance, or a no start condition.**

14. Install the balancer on the crankshaft and install the crankshaft balancer bolt. Tighten to 200–239 ft. lbs. (270–325 Nm).

15. Install the inner fender shield.

16. Install the tire and wheel assembly. Tighten to 100 ft. lbs. (140 Nm).

17. Lower the vehicle.

18. Install the serpentine belt.

19. Connect the negative battery cable, then reset the clock, radio and any other accessories.

IGNITION TIMING

General Information

▶ **See Figures 47, 48 and 49**

Ignition timing is the point at which each spark plug fires in relation to its respective piston, during the compression stroke of the engine.

As far as ignition timing is concerned, the position of the piston can be related (in degrees) to the following reference terms: Top Dead Center (TDC), After Top Dead Center (ATDC), and Before Top Dead Center (BTDC). The movement of the piston is expressed in degrees due to the rotation of the crankshaft. Even though the crankshaft turns 720° to complete one entire 4-stroke cycle, all we're concerned about here is the compression stroke, since this is when the ignition of the air/fuel mixture takes place (or more accurately, should take place).

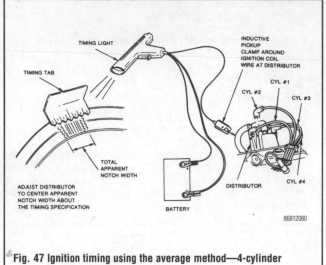

Fig. 47 Ignition timing using the average method—4-cylinder engine with distributor

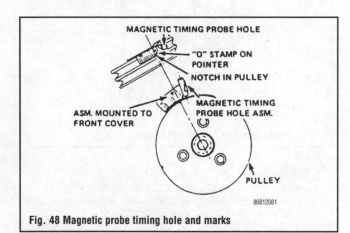

Fig. 48 Magnetic probe timing hole and marks

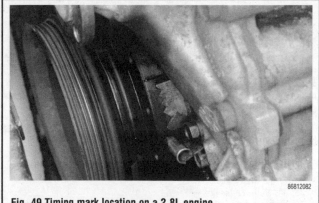

Fig. 49 Timing mark location on a 2.8L engine

Because it takes a fraction of a second for the spark (at the spark plug) to ignite the air/fuel mixture and for the mixture to burn completely, the spark should ideally occur just before the piston reaches TDC. If the spark didn't occur until exactly TDC or ATDC, the piston would already be on its way down before the mixture explosion and would not exert as much downward force on the piston as it would if the ignition timing was properly set. The result of this would be reduced power and fuel economy.

Should ignition of the air/fuel mixture occur too far BTDC (advanced), the mixture explosion will try to force the piston downward before it can mechanically do so. This contest between the explosion forcing the piston downward

and the crankshaft forcing the piston upward will result in a pinging sound if you're lucky; severe engine damage if you're not so lucky. If you experience pinging, check with a reputable
mechanic to determine if the pinging is mild or severe. Only a trained car mechanic can safely determine this.

➡**Pinging can also be caused by inferior gasoline, since lower octane gas burns at a faster, more uncontrolled rate than a higher octane fuel.**

In order to compensate for low quality gas, the ignition timing may be retarded a couple of degrees, though this is not recommended since performance and fuel economy will suffer.

On federal emissions engines, after the initial (base) timing is set, the computer and related components electronically determine and adjust the degree of spark advance under all conditions. On Canadian models, total ignition timing advance is determined by three things: initial timing setting, distributor vacuum control and distributor mechanical control.

Inspection and Adjustment

DIS AND C³I SYSTEMS

On vehicles equipped with either the Direct or Distributorless Ignition System (DIS) or the Computer Controlled Coil Ignition (C³I) system, timing advance and retard are accomplished through the ICM with the Electronic Spark Timing (EST) and Electronic Spark Control (ESC) circuitry. No ignition timing adjustment is required or possible.

HEI SYSTEM

Because your car has electronic ignition, you should use a timing light which has an inductive pick-up. This type of pick-up merely clamps around the No. 1 spark plug wire, eliminating any kind of adapter. Other types of timing lights may cause false timing readings when used with ignition systems.

✳✳ CAUTION

NEVER use a timing light which requires piercing of the spark plug wire.

1. Refer to the instructions listed on the emission control label inside the engine compartment. Follow all instructions on the label.
2. Locate the timing marks on the front of the engine and on the crankshaft balances.
3. Clean off the marks so that they are readable. Chalk or white paint on the balancer mark (line) and at the correct point on the timing scale will make the marks much easier to accurately align.
4. If specified on the emissions label, attach a tachometer to the engine according to the tachometer manufacturer's instructions.

➡**On 4-cylinder engines, the TACH terminal is at the brown wire connection at the ignition coil; on V6's, it is next to the BAT connector on the distributor cap.**

5. Attach a timing light according to the timing light manufacturer's instructions. Remember that the inductive pick-up is clamped around the No. 1 spark plug wire.
6. Check that all wiring is clear of the fan, then start the engine. Allow the engine to reach normal operating temperature.
7. Aim the timing light at the timing marks. The line on the crankshaft balancer should align the correct timing mark. If the line is within 1° of where it should be, no adjustment is necessary.
8. If adjustment is necessary, loosen the distributor hold-down bolt slightly. Slowly rotate the distributor until the proper setting is attained.
9. Tighten the hold-down bolt, recheck the timing and readjust if required.
10. Turn the engine off and disconnect the timing light (and tachometer, if in use).

➡**Disregard the short tube which may be integral with the timing scale on some engines. This tube is used to connect magnetic timing equipment which is marketed to professional shops.**

VALVE LASH

Adjustment

All models utilize an hydraulic valve lifter system to obtain zero lash. No adjustment is necessary. An initial adjustment is required anytime that the lifters are removed or the valve train is disturbed, this procedure is covered in Section 3.

IDLE SPEED AND MIXTURE

Adjustments

IDLE SPEED

Carbureted Models

On non-A/C models not equipped with Idle Speed Control (ISC), the idle speed is adjusted at the idle speed screw on the carburetor. Before adjusting, check the underhood sticker for any preparations required. On A/C equipped models which do not have an ISC motor, an idle speed solenoid is used. This solenoid is adjusted at the solenoid screw. Consult the underhood specifications sticker for special instructions. If the sticker is missing, consult your dealer for specifications.

1. All idle settings are made with the engine operating in the closed loop. The air cleaner must be removed, along with the A/C and cooling fan **OFF**.
2. Apply the parking brake and block the drive wheels.
3. Disconnect and plug the vacuum hoses at the EGR valve and purge hose at the canister.
4. For the fast idle speed adjustment:
   a. With the automatic in PARK, manual in NEUTRAL, place the adjusting screw on the highest step of the fast idle cam.
   b. Adjust if needed, to recommended rpm in PARK or NEUTRAL.
5. For the curb idle speed adjustment:
   a. Adjust the curb idle speed screw to recommended rpm in DRIVE (AT) or NEUTRAL (MT).
6. For the idle speed actuator plunger adjustment:
   a. Disconnect and plug the vacuum hose at the actuator.
   b. Connect a vacuum source (a hand vacuum pump) and apply, 6 in. Hg. vacuum minimum to the actuator. The actuator plunger must be fully extended.
   c. Adjust if needed, recommended rpm in DRIVE (AT) or NEUTRAL (MT).
7. Unplug and reconnect the all the vacuum hoses: EGR valve, canister purge, and the idle speed actuator.

Fuel Injected Models

THROTTLE BODY

No idle speed or mixture adjustments are possible on fuel injected engines unless the following:

This procedure should be performed only when the throttle body parts have been replaced. Newer models may not provide for this adjustment as the computer is responsible for idle control.

➡**The following procedure requires the use of a special tool.**

1. Remove the air cleaner and gasket.
2. Plug the vacuum port on the TBI marked THERMAC.
3. If the car is equipped with a tamper resistant plug cover the throttle stop screw, the TBI unit must be removed as instructed above, to remove the plug.
4. Remove the throttle valve cable from the throttle control bracket to allow access to the throttle stop screw.
5. Connect a tachometer to the engine.
6. Start the engine and run it to normal operating temperature.
7. Install tool J-33047 into the idle air passage of the throttle body. Be sure that the tool is fully seated and that no air leaks exist.
8. Using a #20 Torx bit (0.16 in.–4mm), turn the minimum air screw until the engine speed is 675–725 rpm for automatic transaxle models in PARK, or 725–825 rpm for manual transaxle models in NEUTRAL.
9. Stop the engine and remove the special tool.
10. Install the cable on the throttle body.
11. Use RTV sealant to cover the throttle stop screw.

MULTI-PORT/SEQUENTIAL INJECTION

The engine should be at normal operating temperature before making this adjustment. Newer engines do not provide for this adjustment as the idle is completely computer controlled. If the computer cannot control the idle, the most likely cause a defective idle air control valve. Test the IAC valve, check the engine for mechanical problems (for basic tune-up, vacuum leaks, proper compression) and check the rest of the fuel control system. The least likely cause is the computer itself, unless someone has recently worked on the computer or the electrical system. For models that are adjustable following the following procedures:

1. Using an awl, pierce the idle stop screw plug (located on the side of the throttle body) and remove it by prying it from the housing.
2. Using a jumper wire, ground the diagnostic lead of the IAC motor.
3. Turn on the ignition, DO NOT start the engine and wait for 30 seconds, then disconnect the IAC electrical connector. Remove the diagnostic lead ground lead and start the engine. Allow the system to go to closed loop.
4. Adjust the idle set screw to 550 rpm for the automatic transaxle in Drive, and 650 rpm for the manual transaxle in Neutral.
5. Turn the ignition **OFF** and reconnect the IAC motor lead.
6. Using a voltmeter, adjust the TPS to 0.45–0.65 volt and secure the TPS.
7. Recheck the setting, then start the engine and check for proper idle operation.
8. Seal the idle stop screw with silicone sealer.

IDLE MIXTURE

Carbureted Models

Mixture adjustments are a function of the Computer Command Control (CCC) system. The idle speed on models equipped with an Idle Speed Control (ISC) motor is also automatically adjusted by the Computer Command Control System, making manual adjustment unnecessary. The underhood specifications sticker will indicate ISC motor use. We strongly recommend that mixture adjustments be referred to a qualified, professional technician.

The idle mixture screws are concealed under hardened plugs and mixture adjustments are not normally required. Since carburetor removal is necessary in order to gain access to the screws, the plug removal and adjustment procedures are covered in Section 5.

1. Perform the carburetor pre-set procedure. See Section 5.
2. Run the engine on high step of the fast idle cam. until the engine cooling fan starts to cycle.
3. Run the engine at 3000 rpm and adjust the lean mixture screw slowly in small increments allowing time for dwell to stabilize after turning the screw to obtain an average dwell of 35°. If the dwell is too low, back the screw out, if too high, turn it in. If you are unable to adjust it to specifications, inspect the main metering circuit for leaks or restrictions.
4. Return to idle.
5. Adjust the mixture screw to obtain the average dwell of 25° with the cooling fan in the off cycle. If the reading is too low, back the screw out. If the reading is too high, turn it in. Allow time for reading to stabilize after each adjustment. Adjustment is very sensitive. Make a final check with the adjusting tool removed.
6. If you are unable to adjust to specifications, inspect the idle system for leaks, or restrictions.
7. Disconnect the mixture control solenoid when the cooling fan is in the off cycle, then check for an rpm change of at least 50 rpm. If the rpm does not change enough, inspect the idle air bleed circuit for restrictions or leaks.
8. Run the engine at 3000 rpm for a few moments, then note the dwell reading. Dwell should be varying with the average reading of 35°.
9. If the 35° is not the average dwell, reset the lean mixture screw pre step 3. Then reset the idle mixture screw to obtain a 25° dwell per steps 5 and 6.

10. If you have an average dwell, reconnect the systems disconnected (purge and vent hoses, EGR valve etc.), then reinstall the vent screen and set the idle speed.

Fuel Injected Models

No mixture adjustments are possible on fuel injected engines.

GASOLINE ENGINE TUNE-UP SPECIFICATIONS

Year	Engine ID/VIN	Engine Displacement Liters (cc)	Spark Plugs Gap (in.)	Ignition Timing (deg.) MT	AT	Fuel Pump (psi)	Idle Speed (rpm) MT	AT	Valve Clearance In.	Ex.
1982	R	2.5 (2474)	0.060	8B	8B	6-8	950	750	HYD	HYD
	X	2.8 (2835)	0.045	10B	10B	6-7.5	800	600	HYD	HYD
	Z [7]	2.8 (2835)	0.045	6B	10B	6-7.5	850 [7]	750	HYD	HYD
	E	3.0 (2999)	0.080	-	15B	6-8	-	-	HYD	HYD
1983	R	2.5 (2474)	0.060	8B	8B	6-8	950	750	HYD	HYD
	X	2.8 (2835)	0.045	10B	10B	6-7.5	800	600	HYD	HYD
	Z [7]	2.8 (2835)	0.045	6B	10B	6-7.5	850 [7]	750	HYD	HYD
	E	3.0 (2999)	0.080	-	15B	6-8	-	-	HYD	HYD
1984	R	2.5 (2474)	0.060	8B	8B	6-8	950	750	HYD	HYD
	X	2.8 (2835)	0.045	10B	10B	6-7.5	800	600	HYD	HYD
	Z [7]	2.8 (2835)	0.045	6B	10B	6-7.5	850 [7]	750	HYD	HYD
	E	3.0 (2999)	0.080	-	15B	6-8	-	-	HYD	HYD
1985	R	2.5 (2474)	0.060	8B	8B	9-13	900-1000	675-775	HYD	HYD
	X	2.8 (2835)	0.045	10B	10B	6-7	800	600D	HYD	HYD
	W	2.8 (2835)	0.045	10B	10B	30-37	600-700	500-600D	HYD	HYD
	E	3.0 (2999)	0.060	15B	15B	4-6.5	-	- [2]	HYD	HYD
	3	3.8 (3785)	0.080	-	15B	34-40	-	- [2]	HYD	HYD
1986	R	2.5 (2474)	0.060	8B	8B	9-13	850-950	750-850D	HYD	HYD
	X	2.8 (2835)	0.045	10B	10B	5.5-6.5	775	600D	HYD	HYD
	W	2.8 (2835)	0.045	10B	10B	30-37	600-700	500-600D	HYD	HYD
	B	3.8 (3735)	0.045	-	[1]	34-40	-	- [2]	HYD	HYD
	3	3.8 (3735)	0.080	-	[1]	34-40	-	- [2]	HYD	HYD
1987	R	2.5 (2474)	0.060	[1]	[1]	9-13	600 [3]	600 [3]	HYD	HYD
	W	2.8 (2835)	0.045	[1]	[1]	40-46	-	550D [3]	HYD	HYD
	3	3.8 (3785)	0.045	[1]	[1]	34-44	-	500D [3]	HYD	HYD
1988	R	2.5 (2474)	0.060	[1]	[1]	9-13	550-650 [3]	550-650 [3]	HYD	HYD
	W	2.8 (2835)	0.045	[1]	[1]	40-46	550-650 [3]	500-600D [3]	HYD	HYD
	3	3.8 (3785)	0.045	[1]	[1]	34-40	-	500D [3]	HYD	HYD
1989	R	2.5 (2474)	0.060	[1]	[1]	9-13	550-650 [3]	550-650 [3]	HYD	HYD
	W	2.8 (2835)	0.045	[1]	[1]	41-47	600-700 [3]	500-600D [3]	HYD	HYD
	T	3.1 (3146)	0.045	[1]	[1]	41-47	[4]	[4]	HYD	HYD
	N	3.3 (3342)	0.045	[1]	[1]	41-47	[4]	[4]	HYD	HYD
1990	R	2.5 (2474)	0.060	[1]	[1]	9-13	550-650 [3]	550-650 [3]	HYD	HYD
	T	3.1 (3146)	0.045	[1]	[1]	41-47	[4]	[4]	HYD	HYD
	N	3.3 (3342)	0.060	[1]	[1]	41-47	[4]	[4]	HYD	HYD
1991	R	2.5 (2474)	0.060	[1]	[1]	9-13	550-650 [6]	550-650 [6]	HYD	HYD
1991	T	3.1 (3146)	0.045	[1]	[1]	41-47	[9]	[9]	HYD	HYD
	N	3.3 (3342)	0.060	[1]	[1]	41-47	[5]	[5]	HYD	HYD
1992	4	2.2 (2195)	0.045	[1]	[1]	41-47	[5]	[5]	HYD	HYD
	R	2.5 (2474)	0.060	[1]	[1]	9-13	550-650 [4]	550-650 [4]	HYD	HYD
	N	3.3 (3342)	0.060	[1]	[1]	41-47	[5]	[5]	HYD	HYD
1993	4	2.2 (2195)	0.045	[1]	[1]	41-47	[5]	[5]	HYD	HYD
	N	3.3 (3342)	0.060	[1]	[1]	41-47	[4]	[4]	HYD	HYD
	M	3.1 (3130)	0.060	[1]	[1]	41-47	[4]	[4]	HYD	HYD
1994	4	2.2 (2195)	0.060	[1]	[1]	41-47	[5]	[5]	HYD	HYD
	M	3.1 (3130)	0.060	[1]	[1]	41-47	[5]	[5]	HYD	HYD
1995	4	2.2 (2195)	0.060	[1]	[1]	41-47	[5]	[5]	HYD	HYD
	M	3.1 (3130)	0.060	[1]	[1]	41-47	[5]	[5]	HYD	HYD
1996	4	2.2 (2195)	0.060	[1]	[1]	41-47	[5]	[5]	HYD	HYD
	M	3.1 (3130)	0.060	[1]	[1]	41-47	[5]	[5]	HYD	HYD

NOTE: The Vehicle Emission Control Information label often reflects specification changes made during production. The label figures must be used if they differ from those in this chart.

B - Before top dead center
D - Drive
HYD - Hydraulic

[1] Direct ignition system timing is not adjustable
[2] Minimum idle speed: 450-550 in drive; Refer to manual for adjustment procedure
[3] Minimum idle speed setting; Refer to manual for procedure
[4] Idle speed is controlled by ECM; Minimum air rate is adjusted by IAC centering; Refer to manual for procedure
[5] Idle speed is maintained by the ECM. There is no recommended adjustment procedure
[6] Idle specification is minimum air rate; Refer to manual for procedure
[7] High output
[8] California: 750
[9] Refer to emmisions label

91082C00

3

ENGINE AND ENGINE OVERHAUL

ENGINE ELECTRICAL

Distributor

REMOVAL

4-Cylinder Engines

♦ **See Figure 1**

1. Disconnect the negative battery cable.
2. Raise the front of the vehicle and support is safely with jackstands. DO NOT place the jackstands under the engine cradle.
3. Remove the two rear engine cradle attaching bolts and lower the cradle just enough to gain access to the distributor.
4. Remove the five screws which attach the brake line support to the floorpan.
5. Remove the coil wire from the distributor.
6. Remove the distributor cap.
7. Mark the position of the rotor firing tip on the distributor body, then mark the relationship between the distributor body and the engine.
8. Loosen the distributor hold-down clamp bolt and slide the hold-down clamp aside to clear the distributor body.
9. Lift the distributor out of the engine and mark the point at which the rotor stops turning while you're pulling upward. The rotor will have to be positioned at this same spot in order to install the distributor correctly.

V6 Engines

♦ **See Figure 2**

1. Disconnect the negative battery cable at the battery.
2. Release the distributor and ignition coil electrical connections at the distributor cap.
3. Remove the distributor clamp screw and hold-down clamp. Note position of the rotor. Pull distributor up until the rotor just stops turning clockwise. Note the position of rotor again.

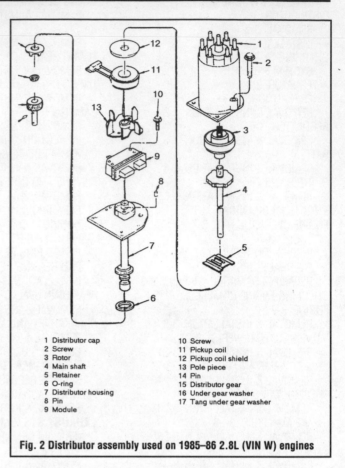

1 Distributor cap	10 Screw
2 Screw	11 Pickup coil
3 Rotor	12 Pickup coil shield
4 Main shaft	13 Pole piece
5 Retainer	14 Pin
6 O-ring	15 Distributor gear
7 Distributor housing	16 Under gear washer
8 Pin	17 Tang under gear washer
9 Module	

Fig. 2 Distributor assembly used on 1985–86 2.8L (VIN W) engines

➠ **The rotor will have to be positioned at this same spot in order to install the distributor correctly.**

INSTALLATION

Engine Disturbed

1. Remove the spark plug from the No. 1 cylinder.
2. Place your thumb over the spark plug hole and turn the crankshaft by hand with a wrench until pressure is felt at the plug hole.
3. Look at the timing marks on the front of the engine and check to see if the balancer slash is aligned with the **0** on the timing scale. If necessary, turn the crankshaft until it does align.
4. Position the firing tip of the rotor between the No.1 and 6 towers of the cap on 6-cylinder engines or the No. 1 tower, on 4-cylinder engine.
5. Install the distributor into the engine.
6. Reposition the hold-down clamp on the distributor body and tighten the bolt until the distributor is snug, but can be moved with a little effort.
7. On 4-cylinder models, jack the engine cradle back into place. Install the engine cradle bolts and the brake line support bolts.
8. Connect all wiring to the distributor.
9. Connect the battery cable, tighten the cable bolt to 11 ft. lbs. (15 Nm).
10. Adjust the ignition timing.

Engine Not Disturbed

1. Align the ignition rotor with the mark made during the removal procedure.
2. Install the distributor into the engine, noting that the marks made previously must align. If they don't line up the first time, remove the distributor and try again.
3. Reposition the hold-down clamp on the distributor body and tighten the bolt until the distributor is snug, but can be moved with a little effort.

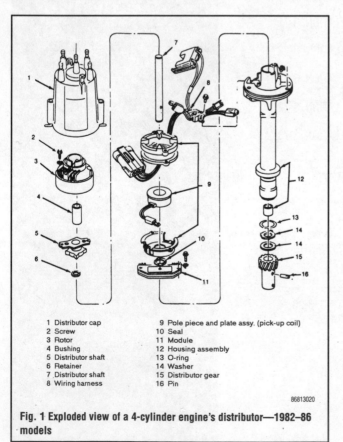

1 Distributor cap	9 Pole piece and plate assy. (pick-up coil)
2 Screw	10 Seal
3 Rotor	11 Module
4 Bushing	12 Housing assembly
5 Distributor shaft	13 O-ring
6 Retainer	14 Washer
7 Distributor shaft	15 Distributor gear
8 Wiring harness	16 Pin

86813020

Fig. 1 Exploded view of a 4-cylinder engine's distributor—1982–86 models

4. On 4-cylinder models, jack the engine cradle back into place. Install the engine cradle bolts and the brake line support bolts.
5. Connect all wiring to the distributor.
6. Connect the battery cable, tighten the cable bolt to 11 ft. lbs. (15 Nm).
7. Adjust the ignition timing.

Charging System

The automobile charging system provides electrical power for operation of the vehicle's ignition and starting systems and all the electrical accessories. The battery serves as an electrical surge or storage tank, storing (in chemical form) the energy originally produced by the engine-driven A.C. generator (alternator). The system also provides a means of regulating alternator output to protect the battery from being overcharged and to avoid excessive voltage to the accessories.

The storage battery is a chemical device incorporating parallel lead plates in a tank containing a sulfuric acid/water solution. Adjacent plates are slightly dissimilar, and the chemical reaction of the two dissimilar plates produces electrical energy when the battery is connected to a load such as the starter motor. The chemical reaction is reversible, so that when the alternator is producing a voltage (electrical pressure) greater than that produced by the battery, electricity is forced into the battery, and the battery is returned to its fully charged state.

The vehicle's alternator is driven mechanically, through belts, by the engine crankshaft. It consists of two coils of fine wire, stationary (the stator), and one movable (the rotor). The rotor may also be known as the armature, and consists of fine wire wrapped around an iron core which is mounted on a shaft. In an alternator, the field rotates while all the current produced passes only through the stator windings. The brushes bear against continuous slip rings. This causes the current produced to periodically reverse the direction of its flow. Diodes (electrical one-way switches) block the flow of current from traveling in the wrong direction. A series of diodes is wired together to permit the alternating flow of the stator to be converted to a pulsating, but unidirectional flow at the alternator output. The alternator's field is wired in series with the voltage regulator. Alternators are self-limiting as far as maximum current is concerned.

SYSTEM PRECAUTIONS

Observing these precautions will ensure safe handling of the electrical system components, and will avoid damage to the vehicle's electrical system:
1. Be absolutely sure of the polarity of a battery before making connections. Connect the cables positive to positive, and negative to negative. Connect positive cables first and disconnect negative cables first.
2. Disconnect both vehicle battery cables before attempting to charge a battery.
3. Never ground the alternator output or battery terminal. Be cautious when using metal tools around a battery to avoid creating a short circuit between the terminals.
4. Never run an alternator without load unless the field circuit is disconnected.
5. Never attempt to polarize an alternator.

Alternator

PRECAUTIONS

1. When installing a battery, make sure that the positive and negative cables are not reversed.
2. When jump-starting the car, be sure that like terminals are connected. This also applies to using a battery charger. Reverse polarity will burn out the alternator and regulator in a matter of seconds.
3. Never operate the alternator with the battery disconnected or on an otherwise uncontrolled open circuit.
4. Do not short across or ground any alternator or regulator terminals.
5. Do not try to polarize the alternator.
6. Do not apply full battery voltage to the field (brown) connector.
7. Always disconnect the battery ground cable before disconnecting the alternator lead.
8. Always disconnect the battery (negative cable first) when charging it.
9. Never subject the alternator to excessive heat or dampness. If you are steam cleaning the engine, cover the alternator.
10. Never use arc-welding equipment on the car with the alternator connected.

REMOVAL & INSTALLATION

▶ See Figures 3, 4, 5 and 6

SI Series

4-CYLINDER ENGINES

1. Disconnect the negative battery cable.
2. Remove the two-terminal plug and the battery leads from the rear of the alternator.
3. Remove the adjusting bolt from the alternator.
4. Remove the drive belt.
5. Remove the upper alternator bracket.
6. Loosen and remove the alternator pivot bolt, remove the alternator.
To install:
7. Position the alternator and install the pivot bolt.
8. Install upper mounting bracket, insert the adjusting bolt.
9. Place belt into position.
10. Be sure to adjust the tension of the drive belt properly, then tighten the adjusting bolt(s).
11. Install alternator terminal plug and battery leads to the alternator.
12. Connect the negative battery cable, tighten the cable bolt to 11 ft. lbs. (15 Nm).

6-CYLINDER ENGINES

1. Disconnect the negative battery cable.
2. Remove the two-terminal plug and the battery leads from the rear of the alternator.
3. Remove the adjusting bolt from the alternator.

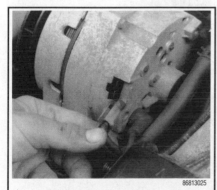

Fig. 3 Unplug the field terminal connector from the alternator

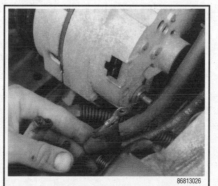

Fig. 4 Loosen the nut to disconnect the "BAT" lead

Fig. 5 Remove the adjusting bolt to release the belt

Fig. 6 After disconnecting all terminals and removing the mounting bolts, pull the alternator from its bracket

4. Move the alternator to loosen the drive belt, then remove the belt.
5. On some models you may need to remove the upper alternator bracket.
6. Remove the alternator pivot bolt and remove the alternator.

To install:

7. Position the alternator and install the pivot bolt.
8. Insert upper mounting bracket with the adjusting bolt.
9. Place the belt into position.
10. Be sure to adjust the tension of the drive belt properly, then tighten the adjusting bolt.
11. Install the terminal plug and battery leads to the alternator.
12. Connect the negative battery cable, tighten the cable bolt to 11 ft. lbs. (15 Nm).

CS Series

※※ CAUTION

Failure to disconnect the negative battery cable when working on the CS alternator can result in personal injury. If a tool is shorted at the alternator output or battery terminal, the tool will heat up enough to cause skin damage.

2.2L ENGINE

♦ See Figure 7

1. Disconnect the negative battery cable.
2. Disconnect the electrical connector at the alternator.
3. Lift or rotate the tensioner using a 15mm socket to remove the belt.
4. Loosen and remove all the bolts to alternator.
5. Remove bolts from brace(s) to alternator.
6. Remove the nut from alternator battery terminal BAT.
7. Remove the alternator.

To install:

8. Install the alternator with mounting bolts. Tighten the front bolts to, 37 ft. lbs. (50 Nm) and rear bolts 18 ft. lbs. (25 Nm).
9. Connect battery positive lead and nut to alternator output BAT terminal. Tighten nut 71 inch lbs. (8 Nm).
10. Insert electrical connector to alternator.
11. Install drive belt by lifting or rotating tensioner using a 15mm socket.
12. Connect the negative battery cable, tighten the cable bolt to 11 ft. lbs. (15 Nm).

2.5L ENGINE

♦ See Figure 8

1. Disconnect the negative battery cable.
2. Remove the belt by lifting or rotating the tensioner using a 15mm socket.

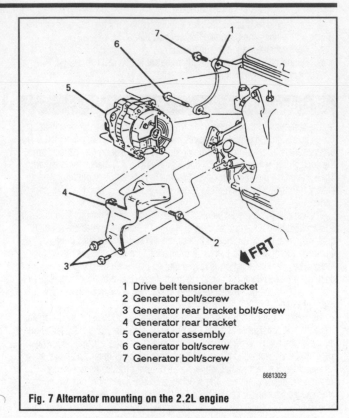

1 Drive belt tensioner bracket
2 Generator bolt/screw
3 Generator rear bracket bolt/screw
4 Generator rear bracket
5 Generator assembly
6 Generator bolt/screw
7 Generator bolt/screw

Fig. 7 Alternator mounting on the 2.2L engine

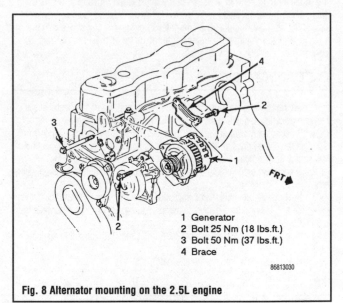

1 Generator
2 Bolt 25 Nm (18 lbs.ft.)
3 Bolt 50 Nm (37 lbs.ft.)
4 Brace

Fig. 8 Alternator mounting on the 2.5L engine

3. Disconnect the electrical connector at the alternator.
4. Remove the nut from alternator battery terminal BAT.
5. Remove the rear attaching bolt, front attaching bolt and rear brace.
6. Remove the alternator.

To install:

7. Install the alternator with mounting bolts but do not tighten.
8. Install the rear brace and attaching bolt.
9. Tighten the long bolts 37 ft. lbs. (50 Nm), short bolts 18 ft. lbs. (25 Nm), rear bolts 18 ft. lbs. (25 Nm).
10. Connect battery positive lead and nut to alternator output BAT terminal. Tighten nut 71 inch lbs. (8 Nm).
11. Insert electrical connector to alternator.
12. Install drive belt by lifting or rotating tensioner using a 15mm socket.
13. Connect the negative battery cable, tighten the cable bolt to 11 ft. lbs. (15 Nm).

3.1L ENGINE

♦ See Figure 9

1. Disconnect the negative battery cable.
2. Detach the electrical connector at the alternator.
3. Disconnect the belt shield bolt, remove shield (if equipped).
4. Lift or rotate tensioner using a breaker bar.
5. Untighten and remove the nuts, bolt along with the stud for alternator braces.
6. The alternator bolts may be removed now.
7. Remove the nut from alternator battery terminal BAT.
8. Remove the alternator, bracket bolts and the bracket.

To install:

9. Install bracket to alternator, tighten to 37 ft. lbs. (50 Nm).
10. Position the alternator. Install the BAT lead and nut on alternator. Tighten to 71 inch lbs. (8 Nm).
11. Install the alternator bolt, do not tighten.
12. Install the brace stud, nuts and bolts to alternator.

➡ **Make sure when tightening the brace stud, it does not bind the alternator.**

13. Tighten the alternator pivot to 37 ft. lbs. (50 Nm), the other bolts to 18 ft. lbs. (25 Nm), Install brace nuts and studs to 18 ft. lbs. (25 Nm).
14. Lift or rotate tensioner with breaker bar and install the belt. Install the bolt shield, tighten to 89 inch lbs. (10 Nm).
15. Connect the electrical connector at alternator.
16. Connect the negative battery cable, tighten the cable bolt to 11 ft. lbs. (15 Nm).

3.3L ENGINE

1. Disconnect the negative battery cable.
2. Disconnect the electrical connector at the alternator.
3. Lift or rotate the tensioner to remove the belt.
4. Loosen and remove all the bolts to alternator.
5. Next remove bolts from brace(s) to alternator.
6. Remove the nut from alternator battery terminal BAT, remove alternator.

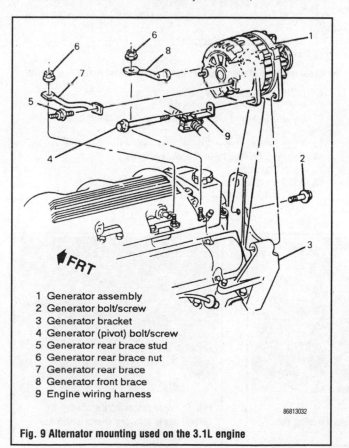

1 Generator assembly
2 Generator bolt/screw
3 Generator bracket
4 Generator (pivot) bolt/screw
5 Generator rear brace stud
6 Generator rear brace nut
7 Generator rear brace
8 Generator front brace
9 Engine wiring harness

86813032

Fig. 9 Alternator mounting used on the 3.1L engine

To install:

7. Connect battery positive lead and nut to alternator output BAT terminal. Tighten nut to 71 inch lbs. (8 Nm).
8. Install the alternator with mounting bolts but do not tighten.
9. After inserting all bolts, tighten the long bolts to 37 ft. lbs. (50 Nm), short bolts to 18 ft. lbs. (25 Nm), and the brace bolt to 37 ft. lbs. (50 Nm). Make sure when tightening brace bolt, it does not bind the alternator.
10. Install drive belt by lifting or rotating tensioner using a 15mm socket.
11. Insert electrical connector to alternator.
12. Connect the negative battery cable, tighten the cable bolt to 11 ft. lbs. (15 Nm).

Regulator

A solid-state regulator is mounted within the alternator. It is non-adjustable.

REMOVAL & INSTALLATION

1982–87 SI Series

1. Remove the alternator from the vehicle. Position the assembly in a suitable holding fixture.
2. Make scribe marks on the case end frames to aid in reassembly.
3. Remove the through bolts. Separate the drive end frame assembly from the rectifier end frame assembly.
4. Remove the rectifier attaching nuts and the regulator attaching screws from the end frame assembly. Note the position of the screws with the insulated washers for reassembly.
5. Remove the voltage regulator from the end frame assembly.

To install:

6. Position the brushes in the brush holder and retain them in place using a brush retainer wire or equivalent.
7. Assemble the brush holder, regulator, resistor, diode trio and rectifier bridge to the end frame. Be sure to assemble the screws with the insulated washers in the correct locations.
8. Assemble the end frames together with the through bolts. Remove the brush retainer wire.

1988–96 CS Series

TYPE 130

1. Remove the alternator from the vehicle. Scribe marks on the end frames to facilitate assembly. Remove the through bolts and separate the end frames.
2. Remove the cover rivets or pins and remove the cover.
3. Unsolder the stator leads at the three terminals on the rectifier bridge. Avoid excessive heat, as damage to the assembly will occur. Remove the stator.
4. Remove the brush holder screw. Disconnect the terminal and remove the brush holder assembly.
5. Unsolder and pry open the terminal between the regulator and the rectifier bridge. Remove the terminal and the retaining screws. Remove the regulator and the rectifier bridge from the end frame.

To install:

6. Position the brushes in the brush holder and retain them in place using a brush retainer wire or equivalent.
7. Assembly is the reverse of disassembly. Be sure to remove the brush retainer wire when the alternator has been reassembled.

TYPE 144

1. Remove the alternator from the vehicle. Scribe marks on the end frames to facilitate assembly. Remove the through bolts and separate the end frames.
2. Remove the stator attaching nuts and the stator from the end frame.
3. Unsolder the connections, remove the retaining screws and connector from the end frame. Separate the regulator and brush holder from the end frame.

To install:

4. Position the brushes in the brush holder and retain them in place using a brush retainer wire or equivalent.
5. Assembly is the reverse of disassembly. Be sure to remove the brush retainer wire when the alternator has been reassembled.

Battery

REMOVAL & INSTALLATION

1. Raise the hood and remove the front end diagonal brace(s) from above the battery(ies).
2. On some vehicles, it will be necessary to remove the air cleaner and duct assembly.
3. Disconnect the battery cables from the battery(ies). Use a small box end wrench or a ¼ in. (6mm) drive ratchet. Avoid using an open-end wrench for the cable bolts.
4. Loosen and remove the battery hold-down bolt and block. The use of a long extension which places the ratchet above the battery makes it easier to reach to the hold-down bolt.
5. Carefully lift the battery from the engine compartment.

To install:

6. Install the new battery in the vehicle. Attach the retainer and hold-down bolt. Tighten to 13 ft. lbs. (17 Nm).
7. Connect the positive battery cable, tighten to 11 ft. lbs. (15 Nm).
8. Connect the negative battery cable, tighten to 11 ft. lbs. (15 Nm).
9. Attach the air cleaner and duct assembly if removed.
10. Install the cross brace and bolts, then tighten to 52 ft. lbs. (70 Nm).
11. Reset the radio, clock and any other components in need.

Starter

REMOVAL & INSTALLATION

1982–85 Models

1. Disconnect the negative battery cable.
2. Raise the front of the vehicle and support it safely with jackstands.
3. From underneath the vehicle, remove the two starter motor-to-engine bolts and carefully lower the starter. Note the location of shims (if so equipped). On the four cylinder engine, remove the nut that holds the starter bracket to the rear of the starter.
4. Mark and disconnect all wiring at the starter.

To install:

5. Position and install then new starter assembly into the vehicle.
6. Insert the starter bolts, tighten to specification.
7. Attach the starter wires in the proper locations.
8. Lower the vehicle, connect the negative battery cable, then reset the radio and clock.

1986–96 Models

2.2L ENGINE

1. Disconnect the negative battery cable.
2. Remove the engine torque strut brace.
3. Raise and support the vehicle.

4. Loosen and remove the bolts for the inspection cover, then the cover itself.
5. Remove the bolt from the bracket, then the bolts from the starter motor.
6. If used remove the shims from the starter as you lower the starter from the vehicle, then disconnect the starter wiring.
7. Remove the starter bracket.

To install:

➥Before you install the starter to the vehicle, be sure the solenoid battery terminal is secure. Tighten the nut next to the cap on the solenoid battery terminal. If it is not tight in the solenoid cap, the cap may be damaged during installation of the electrical connection and cause the starter to fail later.

8. Connect the wiring and nuts to the solenoid battery terminal and the solenoid S terminal. Tighten the nuts on the solenoid battery terminal to 84 inch lbs. (10 Nm). Then tighten the nut on the S terminal to 22 inch lbs. (3 Nm).
9. Attach the bracket to the starter, tighten the nuts to 76 inch lbs. (9 Nm).
10. Install the shims (if used).
11. Position the starter on the engine, then tighten the two starter mounting bolts to 32 ft. lbs. (43 Nm).
12. Install the starter bracket to engine bolt, tighten to 26 ft. lbs. (32 Nm).
13. Install the flywheel cover and tighten the bolts to 89 inch lbs. (10 Nm).
14. Lower the vehicle, then install the engine torque strut brace.
15. Connect the negative battery cable, tighten the cable bolt to 11 ft. lbs. (15 Nm).

2.5L AND 2.8L ENGINES

▶ See Figures 10, 11 and 12

1. Disconnect the negative battery cable.
2. Raise and safely support the vehicle.
3. Disconnect the solenoid wires and battery cable from the starter.
4. Remove the bolt from the engine cross brace.
5. Place a prybar tool between the upper engine mount and engine to pry rearward. Support the engine.
6. Remove the 4 bolts holding the dust covers. Remove the dust covers.
7. Remove the 2 bolts attaching the starter.
8. On the 2.5L engine, remove the bolt attaching the starter bracket to the engine.
9. Remove the starter and any shims.

To install:

➥If replacing the starter, transfer the starter bracket to the new starter.

10. Install the starter and any applicable shims.
11. Install the 2 starter attaching bolts.
12. On the 2.5L engine, install the bolt attaching the starter bracket to the engine.
13. Install the dust cover and 4 attaching bolts.
14. Connect the battery cable and solenoid wires.
15. Lower the vehicle.
16. Roll the engine forward and install the engine brace bolts.
17. Connect the negative battery cable.

Fig. 10 Disconnect the wires from the solenoid. Limited access can make this difficult

Fig. 11 Remove the bolts securing the starter to the engine

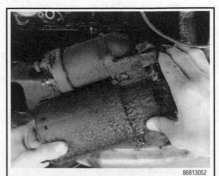

Fig. 12 When removing the starter, be careful not to lose any shims which may be used

3.1L ENGINE (VIN T)

1. Disconnect the negative battery cable.
2. Raise and safely support the vehicle.
3. If equipped, remove the nut from the brace at the air conditioning compressor.
4. If equipped, remove the nuts from the starter-to-engine brace.
5. Remove the drain pan under the engine oil pan.
6. Disconnect the oil pressure sending unit electrical connector. Remove the oil pressure sending unit.
7. Remove the oil filter.
8. Remove the bolts from the flywheel inspection cover. Remove the inspection cover.
9. Remove the bolts from the starter motor.
10. Remove the starter motor and any shims.
11. Disconnect the starter motor electrical connectors.

To install:

12. Connect the starter motor electrical connectors.
13. Install the starter motor and any shims.
14. Install the starter motor attaching bolts. Tighten to 32 ft. lbs. (43 Nm).
15. Install the flywheel inspection cover and attaching bolts.
16. Install the oil filter.
17. Attach the oil pressure sending unit. Connect the electrical wire.
18. Bolt on the drain pan.
19. Install the nuts to the starter-to-engine brace.
20. Install the nut to brace at the air conditioner compressor.
21. Lower the vehicle.
22. Connect the negative battery cable.
23. Check the engine oil level, add as required.

3.1L ENGINE (VIN M)

1. Disconnect the negative battery cable.
2. Raise and safely support the vehicle.
3. Remove the starter mounting bolts and lower the starter until the solenoid wiring is accessible.

4. Disconnect the electrical leads.
5. Remove the starter.

To install:

6. Install the starter.
7. Connect the electrical leads to the starter.
8. Install the starter mounting bolts and tighten to 32 ft. lbs. (43 Nm).
9. Lower the vehicle.
10. Connect the negative battery cable.

3.3L ENGINE

1. Disconnect the negative battery cable.
2. Properly discharge the air conditioning system into a recycling recovery machine. Refer to Section 1.
3. Remove the cooling fan assembly.
4. Remove the front exhaust manifold.
5. Raise and support the vehicle safely.
6. Remove the bolts from the flywheel inspection cover and remove the cover.
7. Disconnect the air conditioner condenser hose from the compressor and position aside. Cap the opening.
8. Disconnect the starter motor electrical wiring.
9. Remove the 2 bolts attaching the starter.
10. Remove the starter and any shims.

To install:

11. Install the starter motor and any shims.
12. Install the 2 bolts attaching the starter. Tighten to 30 ft. lbs. (40 Nm).
13. Connect the starter motor electrical wiring.
14. Replace the condenser O-ring. Lubricate with refrigerant oil. Connect the air conditioner condenser hose to the compressor.
15. Install the flywheel inspection cover and attaching bolts.
16. Lower the vehicle.
17. Install the front exhaust manifold.
18. Install the cooling fan assembly.
19. Evacuate, recharge and leak test the air conditioning system.
20. Connect the negative battery cable.

ENGINE MECHANICAL

Engine Overhaul Tips

Most engine overhaul procedures are fairly standard. In addition to specific parts replacement procedures and specifications for your individual engine, this section also is a guide to acceptable rebuilding procedures. Examples of standard rebuilding practice are shown and should be used along with specific details concerning your particular engine.

Competent and accurate machine shop services will ensure maximum performance, reliability and engine life. In most instances it is more profitable for the do-it-yourself mechanic to remove, clean and inspect the component, buy the necessary parts and deliver these to a shop for actual machine work.

On the other hand, much of the rebuilding work (crankshaft, block, bearings, piston rods, and other components) is well within the scope of the do-it-yourself mechanic's tools and abilities. You will have to decide for yourself the depth of involvement you desire in an engine repair or rebuild.

TOOLS

The tools required for an engine overhaul or parts replacement will depend on the depth of your involvement. With a few exceptions, they will be the tools found in a mechanic's tool kit (see Section 1 of this manual). More in-depth work will require some or all of the following:

- a dial indicator (reading in thousandths) mounted on a universal base
- micrometers and telescope gauges
- jaw and screw-type pullers
- scraper
- valve spring compressor
- ring groove cleaner
- piston ring expander and compressor
- ridge reamer
- cylinder hone or glaze breaker

- Plastigage®
- engine stand

The use of most of these tools is illustrated in this chapter. Many can be rented for a one-time use from a local parts jobber or tool supply house specializing in automotive work.

Occasionally, the use of special tools is called for. See the information on Special Tools and the Safety Notice in the front of this book before substituting another tool.

INSPECTION TECHNIQUES

Procedures and specifications are given in this chapter for inspecting, cleaning and assessing the wear limits of most major components. Other procedures such as Magnaflux® and Zyglo® can be used to locate material flaws and stress cracks. Magnaflux® is a magnetic process applicable only to ferrous materials. The Zyglo® process coats the material with a fluorescent dye penetrant and can be used on any material. Checking for suspected surface cracks can be more readily made using spot check dye. The dye is sprayed onto the suspected area, wiped off and the area sprayed with a developer. Cracks will show up brightly.

OVERHAUL TIPS

Aluminum has become extremely popular for use in engines, due to its low weight. Observe the following precautions when handling aluminum parts:
- Never hot tank aluminum parts (the caustic hot tank solution will eat the aluminum.
- Remove all aluminum parts (identification tag, etc.) from engine parts prior to the tanking.
- Always coat threads lightly with engine oil or anti-seize compounds before installation, to prevent seizure.
- Never overtighten bolts or spark plugs especially in aluminum threads.

Stripped threads in any component can be repaired using any of several commercial repair kits (Heli-Coil®, Microdot®, Keenserts®, etc.).

When assembling the engine, any parts that will be exposed to frictional contact, the parts must be prelubed to provide lubrication at initial start-up. Any product specifically formulated for this purpose can be used, but engine oil is not recommended as a prelube in most cases.

When semi-permanent (locked, but removable) installation of bolts or nuts is desired, threads should be cleaned and coated with Loctite® or other similar, commercial non-hardening sealant.

REPAIRING DAMAGED THREADS

♦ See Figures 13, 14, 15, 16 and 17

Several methods of repairing damaged threads are available. Heli-Coil® (shown here), Keenserts® and Microdot® are among the most widely used. All involve basically the same principle—drilling out stripped threads, tapping the hole and installing a prewound insert—making welding, plugging and oversize fasteners unnecessary.

Two types of thread repair inserts are usually supplied: a standard type for most inch coarse, inch fine, metric course and metric fine thread sizes and a spark lug type to fit most spark plug port sizes. Consult the individual manufacturer's catalog to determine exact applications. Typical thread repair kits will contain a selection of prewound threaded inserts, a tap (corresponding to the outside diameter threads of the insert) and an installation tool. Spark plug inserts usually differ because they require a tap equipped with pilot threads and a combined reamer/tap section. Most manufacturers also supply blister-packed thread repair inserts separately in addition to a master kit containing a variety of taps and inserts plus installation tools.

Before attempting to repair a threaded hole, remove any snapped, broken or damaged bolts or studs. Penetrating oil can be used to free frozen threads. The offending item can be removed with locking pliers or using a screw/stud extractor. After the hole is clear, the thread can be repaired, as shown in the series of accompanying illustrations and in the kit manufacturer's instructions.

Checking Engine Compression

♦ See Figure 18

A noticeable lack of engine power, excessive oil consumption and/or poor fuel mileage measured over an extended period are all indicators of internal engine war. Worn piston rings, scored or worn cylinder bores, blown head gaskets, sticking or burnt valves and worn valve seats are all possible culprits here. A check of each cylinder's compression will help you locate the problems.

As mentioned in the Tools and Equipment portion of Section 1, a screw-in type compression gauge is more accurate than the type you simply hold against the spark plug hole, although it takes slightly longer to use. The extra time is worth it, however, to obtain a more accurate reading.

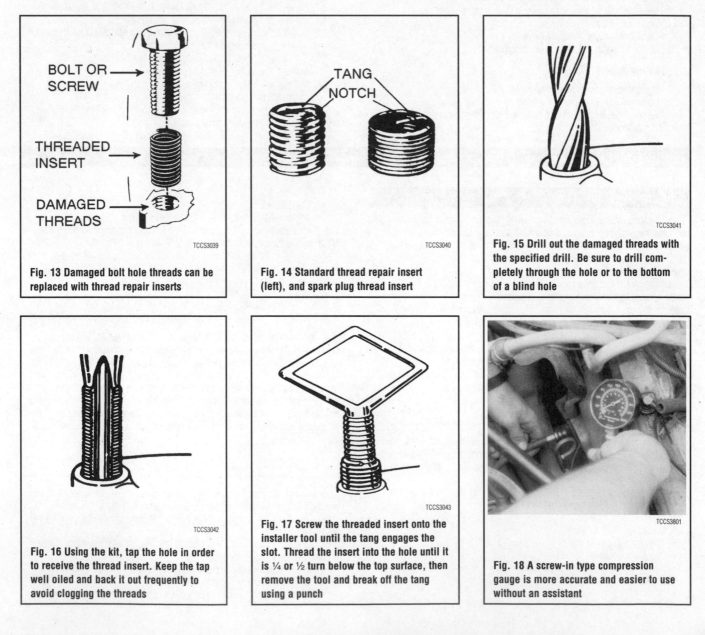

TCCS3039

Fig. 13 Damaged bolt hole threads can be replaced with thread repair inserts

TCCS3040

Fig. 14 Standard thread repair insert (left), and spark plug thread insert

TCCS3041

Fig. 15 Drill out the damaged threads with the specified drill. Be sure to drill completely through the hole or to the bottom of a blind hole

TCCS3042

Fig. 16 Using the kit, tap the hole in order to receive the thread insert. Keep the tap well oiled and back it out frequently to avoid clogging the threads

TCCS3043

Fig. 17 Screw the threaded insert onto the installer tool until the tang engages the slot. Thread the insert into the hole until it is ¼ or ½ turn below the top surface, then remove the tool and break off the tang using a punch

TCCS3801

Fig. 18 A screw-in type compression gauge is more accurate and easier to use without an assistant

1. Warm up the engine to normal operating temperature.
2. Remove all spark plugs.
3. Disconnect the high tension lead from the ignition coil.
4. Fully open the throttle either by operating the carburetor throttle linkage by hand or by having an assistant floor the accelerator pedal.
5. Screw the compression gauge into the No.1 spark plug hole until the fitting is snug.

➡ **Be careful not to crossthread the plug hole. On aluminum cylinder heads use extra care, as the threads in these heads are easily ruined.**

6. While you read the compression gauge, ask the assistant to crank the engine two or three times in short bursts using the ignition switch.
7. Read the compression gauge at the end of each series of cranks, and record the highest of these readings. Repeat this procedure for each of the engine's cylinders. Compare the highest reading of each cylinder to the compression pressure specification in the Tune-Up Specifications chart in Section 2. The specs in this chart are maximum values. A cylinder's compression pressure is usually acceptable if it is not less than 80% of maximum. The difference between each cylinder should be no more than 12–14 psi (83–97 kPa).
8. If a cylinder is unusually low, pour a tablespoon of clean engine oil into the cylinder through the spark plug hole and repeat the compression test. If the compression comes up after adding the oil, it appears that the cylinder's piston rings or bore are damaged or worn. If the pressure remains low, the valves may not be seating properly (a valve job is needed), or the head gasket may be blown near that cylinder. If compression in any two adjacent cylinders is low, and if the addition of oil doesn't help the compression, there is leakage past the head gasket. Oil and coolant water in the combustion chamber can result from this problem. There may be evidence of water droplets on the engine dipstick when a head gasket has blown.

Engine

REMOVAL & INSTALLATION

❄ CAUTION

When draining the coolant, keep in mind that cats and dogs are attracted by ethylene glycol antifreeze, and are quite likely to drink any that is left in an uncovered container or in puddles on the ground. This will prove fatal in sufficient quantity. Always drain the coolant into a sealable container. Coolant should be reused unless it is contaminated or several years old.

2.2L Engine

❄ CAUTION

The fuel system is under pressure and must have the pressure relieved prior to disconnecting the fuel lines. Failure to properly bleed the system can lead to personal injury.

1. Relieve the fuel pressure.
2. Disconnect the negative battery cable.
3. Drain the cooling system into a suitable container.
4. While supporting the hood, disconnect the hydraulic shock from the cowl pan and secure the hood in a fully open position.
5. Remove the air cleaner and air duct assembly.
6. Disconnect the control cables from the throttle body and remove the control cable bracket from the intake manifold and rocker arm cover. Set the assembly out of the way.
7. Disconnect and cap the fuel lines from the throttle body and manifold mounting bracket.
8. Tag and disconnect any vacuum hoses that will interfere with the engine removal.
9. Remove the upper and lower radiator hoses.
10. Disconnect the heater hoses from the intake manifold and the water pump, then secure them out of the way.
11. Remove the torque strut.
12. Disconnect the engine harness wiring, then rotate the engine forwards.

13. Remove the power steering pump from the engine an support it out of the way with the power steering lines attached.
14. Disconnect the electrical wiring from the rear of the engine.
15. Remove the transaxle oil fill tube.
16. Remove the transaxle-to-engine bolts leaving in only the two upper bolts.
17. Rotate the engine to it's normal position.
18. Loosen the right front wheel lug nuts, then raise and support the vehicle.
19. Remove the right front tire and wheel assembly.
20. Remove the right inner fender well splash shield.
21. Disconnect the exhaust pipe from the exhaust manifold.
22. Remove the flywheel cover.
23. Disconnect and remove the starter.
24. Remove the engine mount-to-frame nuts.
25. Remove the torque converter-to-flywheel bolts.
26. Remove the A/C compressor from the mounting bracket and secure out of the way to the side without disconnecting the refrigerant lines.
27. Remove the front pipe support bracket from the transaxle.
28. Remove the transaxle support bracket from the transaxle and frame.
29. Lower the vehicle.
30. Remove the two remaining engine-to-transaxle mounting bolts.
31. Attach a suitable lifting device and slowly remove the engine. While lifting out the engine, make sure that no hoses or electrical connectors are still attached.

To install:
32. Lower the engine into the vehicle and connect the engine to the transaxle.
33. Install the two upper engine-to-transaxle bolts. Tighten the bolts only until snug.
34. Raise and safely support the vehicle.
35. Install the transaxle support bracket and tighten the mounting bolts to 38 ft. lbs. (52 Nm).
36. Install the front exhaust pipe-to-transaxle mounting bolt.
37. Install the A/C compressor in the mounting bracket.
38. Secure the torque converter-to-flywheel bolts, then tighten to 46 ft. lbs. (62 Nm).
39. Secure the engine mount-to-frame nuts, then tighten them to 33 ft. lbs. (45 Nm).
40. Connect and install the starter, then tighten the mounting bolts to 33 ft. lbs. (45 Nm).
41. Connect the exhaust pipe to the exhaust manifold, then tighten the mounting bolts to 22 ft. lbs. (30 Nm).
42. Attach the right inner fender well splash shield.
43. Install the tire and wheel assembly, then lower the vehicle.
44. Tighten the lug nuts to 100 ft. lbs. (136 Nm).
45. Install the remainder of the engine-to-transaxle bolts, then tighten all the bolts to 37 ft. lbs. (50 Nm).
46. Insert the transaxle fill tube.
47. Connect the electrical harness to the rear of the engine.
48. Install the power steering pump onto it's mounting bracket.
49. Connect the engine harness.
50. Attach the power steering pump onto the bracket.
51. Install the torque strut, then tighten the mounting bolts to 41 ft. lbs. (51 Nm).
52. Attach the heater hoses to the intake manifold and the water pump.
53. Attach the upper and lower radiator hoses.
54. Connect any vacuum hoses disconnected at removal.
55. Connect the fuel lines to the throttle body and the fuel line brackets.
56. Install the throttle cable bracket on the intake manifold and rocker arm cover, then connect the control cables to the throttle body.
57. Install the air cleaner and air inlet duct work.
58. Connect the hood hydraulic shock to the cowl panel.
59. Refill the cooling system and engine oil if needed.
60. Connect the negative battery cable.
61. Start the vehicle, top the cooling system as it warms up.
62. Check for leaks.

2.5L Engine With Manual Transaxle

❄ CAUTION

The fuel system is under pressure and must have the pressure relieved prior to disconnecting the fuel lines. Failure to properly bleed the system can lead to personal injury.

1. Relieve the fuel pressure.
2. Disconnect the battery cables at the battery.
3. Raise and support the vehicle.
4. Remove the front mount-to-cradle nuts.
5. Remove the forward exhaust pipe.
6. Remove the starter assembly, make sure the wires are attached, then swing to the side.
7. Remove the flywheel inspection cover.
8. Lower the car.
9. Remove the air cleaner assembly.
10. Remove all the bell housing bolts.
11. Remove the forward torque rod from the engine and the core support.
12. If equipped with air conditioning, remove the air conditioning belt and compressor, then put to the side.
13. Unfasten the emission hoses at the canister.
14. Remove the power steering hoses (if so equipped).
15. Detach the vacuum hoses and the electrical harness at solenoid.
16. Remove the heater blower motor.
17. Disconnect the throttle cable.
18. Drain the heater hose.
19. Disconnect the heater hose.
20. Disconnect the radiator hoses.
21. Disconnect engine harness at the bulkhead.
22. With an engine lifting tool, hoist the engine (remove heater hose at intake manifold, then disconnect the fuel line).

To install:

23. Lower the engine into the engine compartment.
24. Connect engine the harness at the bulkhead.
25. Install the radiator hoses.
26. Connect the heater hoses.
27. Attach the throttle cable.
28. Install the heater blower motor.
29. Install the vacuum hoses and electrical connectors at the solenoid.
30. Connect the power steering hose.
31. Install the emission hoses at the canister.
32. Install the air conditioning compressor and belt.
33. Install the forward torque reaction rod to the engine and core support.
34. Secure all of the bell housing bolts.
35. Install the air cleaner.
36. Raise and support the vehicle.
37. Install the flywheel inspection cover.
38. Install the starter assembly.
39. Connect the forward exhaust pipe.
40. Install the front mount-to-cradle nuts.
41. Lower the vehicle and install the battery.
42. Fill the engine oil and cooling system, start the engine, then top off the fluids.

2.5L Engine With Automatic Transaxle

❊❊ CAUTION

The fuel system is under pressure and must have the pressure relieved prior to disconnecting the fuel lines. Failure to properly bleed the system can lead to personal injury.

1. Relieve the fuel pressure.
2. Disconnect the battery cables at battery.
3. Drain the cooling system.
4. Remove the air cleaner and pre-heat tube.
5. Disconnect the engine harness.
6. Disconnect and tag all of the external vacuum hoses.
7. Remove the throttle and transaxle linkage at E.F.I. assembly and the intake manifold.
8. Remove the upper radiator hose.
9. If equipped with air conditioning, remove the air conditioning compressor from it's mounting brackets, then set aside. Do not disconnect the hoses.
10. Unsecure and remove the front engine strut assembly.
11. Disconnect the heater hose at intake manifold.
12. Remove the transaxle-to-engine bolts, make sure to leave the upper two bolts in place.

13. Remove the front mount-to-cradle nuts.
14. Disconnect and drop the forward exhaust pipe.
15. Remove the flywheel inspection cover, then remove the starter motor.
16. Remove the torque converter-to-flywheel bolts.
17. Remove the power steering pump and bracket, then move aside.
18. Detach the heater hose and lower radiator hose.
19. Remove the two rear transaxle support bracket bolts.
20. Remove the fuel supply line at the fuel filter.
21. Using a floor jack, and a block of wood placed under the transaxle, raise engine and transaxle until the engine front mount studs clear the cradle.
22. Connect the engine lift equipment and put tension on engine.
23. Remove the two remaining transaxle bolts.
24. Slide the engine forwards and lift it from the vehicle.

To install:

25. Lower the engine into the vehicle. Do not completely lower the engine while the jack is supporting the transaxle.
26. Install the two transaxle bolts.
27. Remove the floor jack and lower the engine completely into the vehicle.
28. Connect the fuel supply line and install the filter.
29. Install the two transaxle rear support bracket bolts.
30. Install the heater and lower radiator hoses.
31. Connect the power steering bracket and pump.
32. Install the torque converter-to-flywheel bolts.
33. Install the starter motor and the flywheel inspection cover.
34. Connect the forward exhaust pipe.
35. Install the front mount-to-cradle nuts.
36. Install the transaxle to engine bolts.
37. Connect the heater hose at intake manifold.
38. Install the front engine strut assembly.
39. Install the air conditioning compressor mounting brackets and the compressor.
40. Install the upper radiator hose.
41. Connect the throttle and transaxle linkage at the E.F.I. assembly and intake manifold.
42. Connect all the external vacuum hose connections.
43. Connect the engine harness.
44. Install the air cleaner and pre-heat tube.
45. Fill the cooling system.
46. Connect battery cables at battery.
47. Start the engine, top the cooling system, check for leaks.

2.8L Engine With Manual Transaxle

❊❊ CAUTION

The fuel system is under pressure and must have the pressure relieved prior to disconnecting the fuel lines. Failure to properly bleed the system can lead to personal injury.

1. Relieve the fuel pressure.
2. Disconnect the cables from the battery.
3. Remove the air cleaner assembly.
4. Drain the cooling system.
5. Disconnect and tag the vacuum hoses to all of the non-engine mounted components.
6. Disconnect the accelerator linkage from the carburetor.
7. Disconnect the engine harness from the ECM/PCM, then pull the connector through the front of the dash.
8. Disconnect the radiator hoses from radiator.
9. Disconnect the heater hoses from the engine.
10. If equipped, remove the power steering pump and bracket assembly from the engine.
11. Disconnect the clutch cable from the transaxle.
12. Disconnect the shift linkage from the transaxle shift levers. Remove the cables from the transaxle bosses.
13. Disconnect the speedometer cable from the transaxle.
14. Raise and support the vehicle on jackstands.
15. Remove the exhaust crossover pipe.
16. Remove all but one of the transaxle-to-engine retaining bolts.
17. Remove the side and crossmember assembly.
18. Disconnect the exhaust pipe.

19. Remove all the powertrain mount-to-cradle attachments.
20. Disconnect the engine harness from the junction block at the left side of the dash.
21. Lower the vehicle. If equipped with MFI, disconnect the throttle, T.V. and cruise control cables at the throttle body.
22. Install the engine support fixture. Raise the engine until the weight is relieved from the mount assembled.
23. Lower the left side of the engine/transaxle assembly.
24. Place a jack under the transaxle.
25. Remove the final transaxle-to-engine attaching bolt, then separate the transaxle from the engine and lower.
26. Lower the vehicle.
27. Install the engine lifting device.
28. If equipped with air conditioning, remove the compressor from the mounting bracket and swing aside.
29. Disconnect the forward strut bracket from the radiator support. Swing aside.
30. Lift the engine out of the vehicle.

To install:
31. Lower the engine into the vehicle.
32. Connect the forward strut bracket to radiator support.
33. Install the air conditioning compressor and mounting bracket.
34. Raise the vehicle and place the transaxle jack under the transaxle.
35. Raise the transaxle flush with the engine, then install the engine-to-transaxle attaching bolts.
36. Remove the transaxle jack and lower the vehicle just enough to install the engine support fixture.
37. Raise the engine until the weight is relieved from the mount assemblies.
38. Connect all of the powertrain mount-to-cradle attachments.
39. Connect the exhaust pipe.
40. Install the side and crossmember assembly. Connect the engine harness to the junction block at the left side of the dash.
41. Install all remaining transaxle-to-engine retaining bolts.
42. Install the exhaust crossover.
43. Remove the engine support fixture.
44. Lower the vehicle.
45. Connect the speedometer cable to the transaxle.
46. Install the cables to the transaxle bosses.
47. Connect the transaxle shift linkage.
48. Connect the clutch cable.
49. Install the power steering bracket and pump assembly.
50. Connect the heater hoses to the engine.
51. Install the radiator hoses to the radiator.
52. Feed the engine harness through the front of the dash, then attach it to the ECM/PCM.
53. Connect the throttle, T.V. and the cruise control cables at the throttle body.
54. Connect the accelerator linkage to the carburetor.
55. Connect vacuum hosing to all non-engine mounted components.
56. Fill the cooling system.
57. Install the air cleaner.
58. Connect the battery cables.
59. Start the engine, top off the cooling system, check for leaks.

2.8L Engine With Automatic Transaxle

❋❋❋ CAUTION

The fuel system is under pressure and must have the pressure relieved prior to disconnecting the fuel lines. Failure to properly bleed the system can lead to personal injury.

1. Relieve the fuel pressure.
2. Disconnect the battery cables from the battery.
3. Remove the air cleaner.
4. Drain the cooling system.
5. Disconnect and tag the vacuum hoses to all non-engine mounted components.
6. Disconnect the detent cable from the carburetor lever.
7. Disconnect the accelerator linkage. If equipped with MFI, disconnect the throttle at the T.V. and the cruise control cables at the throttle body.

8. Disconnect the engine harness from the ECM/PCM, then pull the connector through the front of the dash, then disconnect it from the junction block at the left side of the dash.
9. Disconnect the ground strap from the engine at the engine forward strut.
10. Remove the radiator hoses from radiator.
11. Disconnect the heater hoses from engine.
12. Remove the power steering pump and bracket assembly from the engine, if equipped.
13. Raise and support the vehicle.
14. Disconnect the exhaust pipe.
15. Disconnect the fuel lines at their rubber hose connections at the right side of the engine.
16. Remove the engine front mount-to-cradle retaining nuts (right side of vehicle).
17. Disconnect the battery cables from the engine (starter and transaxle housing bolt).
18. Remove the flex plate cover, then disconnect the torque converter from the flex plate.
19. Remove the transaxle case-to-cylinder case support bracket bolts.
20. Lower the vehicle. Place a support under the transaxle rear extension.
21. Remove the engine strut bracket from the radiator support and swing rearward.
22. Remove the exhaust crossover pipe.
23. Remove the transaxle-to-cylinder case retaining bolts. Make note of ground stud location.
24. If air conditioning equipped, remove the compressor from the mounting bracket and lay aside.
25. Install a lift fixture to the engine, then remove engine from the vehicle.

To install:
26. Lower the engine into the vehicle.
27. Install the compressor mounting bracket and the compressor.
28. Install the transaxle to cylinder case retaining bolts and the ground stud.
29. Install the exhaust crossover pipe.
30. Install the engine stud bracket to the radiator support.
31. Raise the vehicle and remove the support from the transaxle rear extension.
32. Install the transaxle case to cylinder case support bracket bolts.
33. Connect the torque converter to the flex plate and install the flex plate cover.
34. Connect the battery cables to the engine (starter and transaxle housing bolt).
35. Install the engine front mount to cradle retaining nuts (right side of vehicle).
36. Connect the fuel lines at the rubber hose connections at the right side of the engine.
37. Connect the exhaust pipe.
38. Lower the vehicle.
39. Install the power steering pump and bracket assembly to the engine.
40. Connect the heater hoses to the engine.
41. Connect the radiator hoses to the radiator.
42. Attach the ground strap to the engine at the engine forward strut.
43. Connect the engine harness connector to the junction block at the left side of the dash then push the connector through the front of the dash and connect it to the ECM/PCM.
44. Attach the accelerator linkage. If equipped with MFI, connect the throttle at the T.V. and the cruise control cables at the throttle body.
45. Connect the detent cable from the carburetor lever.
46. Connect the vacuum hosing to all non-engine mounted components.
47. Fill the cooling system.
48. Install the air cleaner.
49. Connect battery cables.
50. Start the engine, top off the cooling system, then check for leaks.

3.0L Engine

❋❋❋ CAUTION

The fuel system is under pressure and must have the pressure relieved prior to disconnecting the fuel lines. Failure to properly bleed the system can lead to personal injury.

1. Relieve the fuel pressure.
2. Disconnect the battery cables from the battery.
3. Remove the air cleaner.
4. Drain the cooling system.
5. Disconnect and tag the vacuum hoses to all non-engine mounted components.
6. Remove the detent cable from the carburetor lever.
7. Unsecure the accelerator linkage.
8. Disconnect the engine harness.
9. Loosen and remove the ground strap from the engine at the engine forward strut.
10. Disconnect the radiator hoses from radiator.
11. Disconnect all heater hoses from engine.
12. Remove the power steering pump and bracket assembly from the engine.
13. Raise and support the vehicle.
14. Disassemble the exhaust pipe at the manifold.
15. Disconnect all fuel lines at the rubber hose connections.
16. Remove the engine front mount-to-cradle retaining nuts (right side of vehicle).
17. Disconnect the battery cables from engine (starter and transaxle housing bolt).
18. Remove the flex plate cover, then disconnect the torque converter from the flex plate.
19. Remove the transaxle case-to-cylinder case support bracket bolts.
20. Lower the vehicle. Place a support under the transaxle rear extension.
21. Remove the engine strut bracket from the radiator support and swing rearwards.
22. Remove transaxle to cylinder case retaining bolts. Make note of ground stud location.
23. If air conditioning equipped, remove the compressor from the mounting bracket and lay aside.
24. Install a lift fixture to the engine.
25. Remove the engine from the vehicle.

To install:

26. Lower the engine into the vehicle.
27. Attach the compressor mounting bracket and the compressor to the vehicle.
28. Install the transaxle-to-cylinder case retaining bolts and the ground stud.
29. Install the exhaust crossover pipe.
30. Install the engine stud bracket to the radiator support.
31. Raise the vehicle and remove the support from the transaxle rear extension.
32. Install the transaxle case to cylinder case support bracket bolts.
33. Connect the torque converter to the flex plate and install the flex plate cover.
34. Connect the battery cables to the engine (starter and transaxle housing bolt).
35. Install the engine front mount to cradle retaining nuts (right side of vehicle).
36. Connect fuel lines at rubber hose connections at right side of engine.
37. Connect exhaust pipe.
38. Lower the vehicle.
39. Install the power steering pump and bracket assembly to the engine.
40. Connect the heater hoses to the engine.
41. Connect the radiator hoses to the radiator.
42. Assemble the ground strap to the engine at the engine forward strut.
43. Connect the engine harness connector to the junction block at the left side of the dash then push the connector through the front of the dash and connect it to the ECM/PCM.
44. Connect the accelerator linkage.
45. Connect detent cable from carburetor lever.
46. Connect vacuum hosing to all non-engine mounted components.
47. Fill the cooling system.
48. Install the air cleaner.
49. Connect battery cables.

3.1L Engine (VIN T)

⁕⁕⁕ CAUTION

The fuel system is under pressure and must have the pressure relieved prior to disconnecting the fuel lines. Failure to properly bleed the system can lead to personal injury.

1. Relieve the fuel system pressure.
2. Disconnect the negative battery cable. Scribe reference marks at the hood supports and remove the hood. Install covers on both fenders.
3. Remove the airflow tube at the air cleaner and throttle valve.
4. Drain the cooling system.
5. Disconnect and tag all vacuum hoses from all non-engine mounted components.
6. Disassemble the accelerator linkage and TV cable, then disconnect the cruise control cable, if equipped.
7. Disconnect the engine harness connector from the ECM/PCM and pull the connector through the front of dash. Disconnect the engine harness from the junction block at the dash panel.
8. Remove the engine strut bracket from the radiator support and position aside, as required.
9. Disconnect the radiator hoses from radiator and heater hoses from engine. Disconnect and plug the transaxle cooler lines.
10. Remove the serpentine belt cover and belt.
11. On vehicles with the air conditioning compressor mounted on the upper portion of the engine, remove the AIR pump and bracket. Then, remove the air conditioning compressor from the mounting bracket and position aside.
12. If equipped, remove power steering pump from engine and set it aside. Disconnect and cap any power steering lines.
13. Disconnect and plug the fuel lines.
14. Disconnect the EGR at the exhaust, as required.
15. Raise and safely support the vehicle.
16. On vehicles with the air conditioning compressor mounted on the lower portion of the engine, remove the air conditioning compressor from the engine. Do not discharge the air conditioning system.
17. Remove the engine front mount-to-cradle and mount-to-engine bracket retaining nuts, as required.
18. Disconnect and tag all electrical wiring at the starter. Remove the starter retaining bolts and remove the starter.
19. If equipped with automatic transaxle, remove the transaxle inspection cover and disconnect the torque converter from the flexplate.
20. Disconnect the exhaust pipe.
21. Remove the 1 transaxle-to-engine bolt from the back side of the engine.
22. Disconnect the power steering cut-off switch, if equipped.
23. Lower the vehicle.
24. Remove the exhaust crossover pipe.
25. Remove the remaining transaxle-to-engine bolts.
26. Support the transaxle by positioning a floor jack and a block of wood under the transaxle. Install an engine lift tool and remove the engine from the vehicle.

To install:

27. Position the engine in the vehicle while aligning the transaxle. Install the transaxle-to-engine bolts.
28. Position the front engine mount studs in the cradle and engine bracket.
29. Remove the engine lift tool. Raise and support the vehicle safely.
30. Install the engine mount retaining nuts.
31. If equipped, connect the power steering cut-off switch.
32. Install the 1 transaxle-to-engine bolt from the back side of the engine.
33. Connect the exhaust pipe.
34. If equipped with automatic transaxle, connect the torque converter to the flexplate and install the transaxle inspection cover.
35. Install the starter and retaining bolts. Connect the starter electrical connectors.
36. Install the engine front mount-to-cradle and mount-to-engine bracket retaining nuts.
37. On vehicles with the air conditioning compressor mounted on the lower portion of the engine, install the air conditioning compressor.
38. Lower the vehicle.
39. Connect the EGR at the exhaust, if removed.
40. Connect the fuel lines.
41. If equipped, install power steering pump.
42. On vehicles with the air conditioning compressor mounted on the upper portion of the engine, install the air conditioner compressor. Install the AIR pump and bracket.
43. Install the serpentine belt cover and belt.
44. Connect the radiator and heater hoses. Connect the transaxle cooler lines.
45. Install the engine strut bracket to the radiator support.

46. Connect the engine harness connector to the ECM/PCM.
47. Connect the accelerator linkage and TV cable. Connect the cruise control cable, if equipped.
48. Connect vacuum hoses to all non-engine mounted components.
49. Install the airflow tube at the air cleaner and throttle valve.
50. Install the hood using the reference marks made upon removal.
51. Connect the negative battery cable.
52. Fill cooling system and check for leaks. Start the engine and allow to come to normal operating temperature. Check for leaks and refill the cooling system.

3.1L Engine (VIN M)

✳✳ CAUTION

Fuel injection systems remain under pressure, even after the engine has been turned OFF. The fuel system pressure must be relieved before disconnecting any fuel lines. Failure to do so may result in fire and/or personal injury.

1. Relieve the fuel system pressure.
2. Disconnect the negative battery cable.
3. Remove the top half of the air cleaner assembly and the throttle body inlet duct.
4. Drain the cooling system.
5. Remove the upper and lower radiator hoses.
6. Disconnect the coolant inlet line from the coolant surge tank.
7. Disconnect and tag the vacuum hoses from the EVAP canister purge valve, vacuum modulator and power brake booster
8. Disconnect the heater outlet hose from the water pump.
9. Remove the serpentine drive belt.
10. Disconnect the control cables from the throttle body lever and intake manifold bracket and position the cables out of the way.
11. Disconnect the following electrical connectors from their related components:
   - Ignition assembly
   - Oxygen sensor
   - Fuel injectors
   - Idle Air Control (IAC) valve
   - Throttle Position Sensor (TPS)
   - Coolant sensor
   - Park neutral switch
   - TCC solenoid
   - Shift solenoid
   - EGR valve
   - Transaxle ground
12. Remove the alternator.
13. Disconnect and cap the power steering lines from the power steering pump.
14. Disconnect and cap the fuel lines from the fuel rail.
15. Remove the cooling fan assembly.
16. Disconnect the shift control cable from the transaxle shift lever and cable bracket.
17. Detach the transaxle vent tube from the transaxle.
18. Disconnect the vacuum hose from the vacuum reservoir.
19. Install an engine support fixture, J-28467-A, or the equivalent.
20. Loosen, but do not remove the top 2 A/C compressor mounting bolts.
21. Raise and safely support the vehicle.
22. Remove the front tire and wheel assemblies.
23. Remove the right and left inner fender splash shields.
24. Remove the engine mount strut.
25. Disconnect the ABS sensor wires from the wheel sensors and suspension member supports, if equipped.
26. Remove the cotter pins and castle nuts from the lower ball joints. Using a suitable tool, separate the lower ball joints from the steering knuckles.
27. Remove the lower suspension support assemblies with the lower control arms attached.
28. Disconnect the halfshafts from the transaxle and support out of the way.
29. Remove the oil filter and oil filter adapter.
30. Remove the flywheel cover.

31. Remove the starter.
32. Disconnect the following electrical connectors from their related components:
   - Knock sensor
   - Front crankshaft position sensor
   - Side crankshaft position sensor
   - Oil level sensor
   - Vehicle speed sensor
   - Transaxle ground
33. Disconnect the heater hoses from the heater core.
34. Remove the A/C compressor lower mounting bolts and remove the compressor from the mounting bracket and position aside. DO NOT disconnect the refrigerant lines from the compressor or allow the lines top support the weight of the compressor.
35. Remove the vacuum reservoir tank.
36. Disconnect the exhaust pipe from the exhaust manifold and position the pipe aside.
37. Remove the engine mount strut bracket from the engine.
38. Disconnect the transaxle cooler lines from the radiator.
39. Remove the transaxle oil fill tube.
40. Lower the vehicle until the powertrain assembly is resting on a suitable engine table.
41. Unbolt the transaxle mount-to-body bolts.
42. Remove the intermediate bracket from the right engine mount.
43. Remove the engine support fixture.
44. Raise the vehicle leaving the powertrain assembly on the engine table.
45. Separate the engine and transaxle assemblies.
To install:
46. Connect the transaxle to the engine and tighten the mounting bolts to 55 ft. lbs. (75 Nm).
47. Position the powertrain assembly under the vehicle and lower the vehicle into position.
48. Loosely install the serpentine belt.
49. Install the intermediate bracket to the right side engine mount.
50. Install the transaxle-to-body bolts.
51. Raise and safely support the vehicle.
52. Install the transaxle fill tube.
53. Connect the transaxle cooler lines to the radiator.
54. Install the engine strut bracket to the engine and tighten the mounting bolts to 44 ft. lbs. (60 Nm).
55. Connect the exhaust pipe to the exhaust manifold and tighten the mounting bolts to 18 ft. lbs. (25 Nm).
56. Install the vacuum reserve tank.
57. Install the A/C compressor in the mounting bracket. Install the upper bolts loosely and tighten the lower bolts.
58. Connect the heater hoses to the heater core.
59. Connect the following electrical connectors to their related components:
   - Knock sensor
   - Front crankshaft position sensor
   - Side crankshaft position sensor
   - Oil level sensor
   - Vehicle speed sensor
   - Transaxle ground
60. Attach the starter to the engine.
61. Install the flywheel cover.
62. Install the oil filter adapter and after coating the oil filter seal with clean engine oil, install the oil filter.
63. Connect the drive axles to the transaxle.
64. Install the suspension support assemblies and lower control arms.
65. Connect the lower ball joints to the steering knuckles and tighten the castle nuts to 41 ft. lbs. (55 Nm).
66. Connect the ABS sensor wires to the wheel sensors and suspension support wire clips.
67. Install the engine mount strut.
68. Reinstall the left and right inner fender splash shields.
69. Install the right front tire and wheel assemblies.
70. Lower the vehicle.
71. Tighten the upper A/C compressor mounting bolts.
72. Remove the engine support fixture.
73. Connect the vacuum hose to the reservoir.
74. Connect the transaxle vent hose to the transaxle.

75. Connect the shift cable linkage to the cable bracket and shift lever on the transaxle.
76. Install the cooling fan assembly.
77. Connect the fuel lines to the fuel rail.
78. Connect the power steering lines to the power steering pump.
79. Install the alternator.
80. Connect the following electrical connectors to their related components:
- Ignition assembly
- Oxygen sensor
- Fuel injectors
- Idle Air Control (IAC) valve
- Throttle Position Sensor (TPS)
- Coolant sensor
- Park neutral switch
- TCC solenoid
- Shift solenoid
- EGR valve
- Transaxle ground

81. Connect the control cables to the throttle body lever and cable bracket.
82. Install the serpentine belt.
83. Connect the heater outlet hose to the water pump.
84. Connect the vacuum hoses to the power brake booster, vacuum modulator and EVAP purge solenoid.
85. Connect the coolant inlet line to the surge tank.
86. Install the upper and lower radiator hoses.
87. Install the top half of the air cleaner assembly and the throttle body air inlet duct.
88. Connect the negative battery cable.
89. Check and fill all the engine fluids as necessary.
90. Start the vehicle and bleed the power steering system.

3.3L Engine

✳✳ CAUTION

The fuel system is under pressure and must have the pressure relieved prior to disconnecting the fuel lines. Failure to properly bleed the system can lead to personal injury.

1. Disconnect the negative battery cable. Scribe reference marks at the hood supports and remove the hood. Install covers on both fenders.
2. Relieve the fuel system pressure.
3. Disconnect the negative battery cable.
4. Drain the cooling system. Disconnect the radiator and heater hoses. Disconnect and plug the transaxle cooler lines.
5. Remove the upper engine strut and engine cooling fan.
6. Remove the intake duct from the throttle body. Disconnect and tag the vacuum hoses from all non-engine mounted components. Disconnect all electrical connections.
7. Remove the cable bracket and cables from the throttle body.
8. Remove the serpentine belt. If equipped, remove the power steering pump and locate to the side.
9. Unfasten the upper transaxle-to-engine retaining bolts.
10. Raise and support the vehicle safely.
11. Remove the air conditioning compressor and locate to the side.
12. Remove the engine mount-to-frame nuts, flywheel dust cover and flywheel-to-converter bolts.
13. Remove the lower engine-to-transaxle bolts; 1 bolt is located behind the transaxle case and engine block.
14. Lower the vehicle. Install an engine lift tool and remove the engine from the vehicle.

To install:
15. Install the engine in the engine compartment. Install the upper engine-to-transaxle bolts. Remove the engine lift tool.
16. Raise and safely support the vehicle.
17. Install the lower engine-to-transaxle bolts; 1 bolt is located behind the transaxle case and engine block.
18. Install the flywheel-to-converter bolts, flywheel dust cover and engine mount-to-frame nuts.
19. Install the air conditioning compressor.
20. Lower the vehicle.

21. If equipped, install the power steering pump. Install the serpentine belt.
22. Install the cable bracket and cables to the throttle body.
23. Install the intake duct to the throttle body. Connect vacuum hoses to all non-engine mounted components. Connect all electrical connections.
24. Install the upper engine strut and engine cooling fan.
25. Connect the radiator and heater hoses. Connect the transaxle cooler lines.
26. Install the hood.
27. Connect the negative battery cable.
28. Fill cooling system and check for leaks. Start the engine and allow to come to normal operating temperature. Recheck for leaks and fill the cooling system.

3.8L Engine

✳✳ CAUTION

The fuel system is under pressure and must have the pressure relieved prior to disconnecting the fuel lines. Failure to properly bleed the system can lead to personal injury.

1. Relieve the fuel pressure.
2. Disconnect the negative battery cable. Scribe reference marks at the hood supports and remove the hood. Install covers on both fenders.
3. Remove the air cleaner assembly and drain the cooling system.
4. Disconnect and tag the vacuum hoses to all non-engine mounted components.
5. Disconnect the detent cable and accelerator linkage.
6. Disconnect the engine electrical harness and ground strap.
7. Disconnect the heater hoses from the engine and radiator hoses from the radiator. Disconnect the transaxle cooler lines, if equipped.
8. If equipped, remove the power steering pump and bracket assembly.
9. Raise and safely support the vehicle.
10. Disconnect the exhaust pipe from the manifold.
11. Disconnect the fuel lines.
12. Remove the engine front mount-to-cradle retaining nuts.
13. Disconnect and tag all electrical wiring at the starter. Remove the starter retaining bolts and remove the starter.
14. Remove the flexplate cover and disconnect the flexplate from the torque converter.
15. Remove the retaining bolts from the transaxle rear support bracket.
16. Lower the vehicle and place a support under the transaxle rear extension.
17. Remove the engine strut bracket from the radiator support and position aside.
18. Remove the transaxle-to-engine retaining bolts.
19. If equipped with air conditioning, remove the air conditioning compressor from the mounting bracket and lay aside.
20. Install an engine lift tool and remove the engine from the vehicle.

To install:
21. Position the engine in the vehicle and align the engine front mount studs. Align the transaxle and install the transaxle-to-engine retaining bolts.
22. Remove the engine lift tool.
23. If equipped, install the air conditioning compressor to the mounting bracket.
24. Raise and safely support the vehicle. Install the retaining bolts to the transaxle rear support bracket.
25. Connect the flexplate to the torque converter and install the flexplate cover.
26. Install the starter and retaining bolts. Connect the starter electrical connectors.
27. Install the engine front mount-to-cradle retaining nuts.
28. Connect the fuel lines.
29. Connect the exhaust pipe to the manifold.
30. Lower the vehicle.
31. If equipped, install the power steering bracket assembly and pump.
32. Connect the heater and radiator hoses. Connect the transaxle cooler lines, if equipped.
33. Connect the engine electrical harness and ground strap.
34. Connect the detent cable and accelerator linkage.
35. Connect vacuum hoses to all non-engine mounted components.

36. Install the air cleaner assembly.
37. Install the hood.
38. Connect the negative battery cable.

39. Fill cooling system and check for leaks. Start the engine and allow to come to normal operating temperature. Check for leaks and refill the cooling system.

GENERAL ENGINE SPECIFICATIONS

Year	Engine ID/VIN	Engine Displacement Liters (cc)	Fuel System Type	Net Horsepower @ rpm	Net Torque @ rpm (ft. lbs.)	Bore x Stroke (in.)	Compression Ratio	Oil Pressure @ rpm
1982	R	2.5 (2474)	TBI	92@4000	134@2800	4.00x3.00	8.2:1	38.5@2000
	X	2.8 (2835)	2BC	112@4800	145@2100	3.50x3.00	8.5:1	50-65@1200
	Z	2.8 (2835) HO	2BC	135@5400	145@2400	3.50x3.00	8.9:1	50-65@1200
	E	3.0 (2999)	2BC	110@4800	145@2600	3.80x2.66	8.45:1	35-42@2000
1983	R	2.5 (2474)	TBI	92@4000	134@2800	4.00x3.00	8.2:1	37.5@2000
	X	2.8 (2835)	2BC	112@4800	145@2100	3.50x3.00	8.5:1	50-65@1200
	Z	2.8 (2835) HO	2BC	135@5400	145@2400	3.50x3.00	8.9:1	50-65@1200
	E	3.0 (2999)	2BC	110@4800	145@2600	3.80x2.66	8.45:1	35-42@2000
1984	R	2.5 (2835)	TBI	92@4000	164@2800	4.00x3.00	9.0:1	38.5@2000
	X	2.8 (2835)	2BC	112@4800	145@2100	3.50x3.00	8.5:1	50-65@1200
	Z	2.8 (2835) HO	2BC	135@5400	145@2400	3.50x3.00	8.9:1	50-65@2000
	E	3.0 (2999)	2BC	110@4800	145@2600	3.80x2.66	8.45:1	35-42@2000
1985	R	2.5 (2835)	TBI	92@4000	134@2800	4.00x3.00	9.0:1	38.5@2000
	X	2.8 (2835)	2BC	112@4800	145@2100	3.50x3.00	8.5:1	50-65@1200
	E	3.0 (2999)	2BC	110@4800	145@2600	3.80x2.66	8.45:1	35-42@2000
	3	3.8 (3785)	MFI	150@4400	200@2000	3.80x3.40	8.5:1	37@2400
1986	R	2.5 (2474)	TBI	92@4000	134@2800	4.00x3.00	9.0:1	38.5@2000
	X	2.8 (2835)	2BC	112@4800	144.5@2100	3.50x3.00	8.5:1	50-65@1200
	3	3.8 (3785)	MFI	150@4400	200@2000	3.80x3.40	8.5:1	37@2400
	B	3.8 (3785)	MFI	150@4400	200@2000	3.80x3.40	8.5:1	37@2400
1987	R	2.5 (2474)	TBI	98@4800	135@3200	4.00x3.00	8.3:1	38.5@2000
	W	2.8 (2835)	MFI	125@4800	160@3600	3.50x2.99	8.9:1	50-65@2400
	3	3.8 (3785)	MFI	150@4400	200@2000	3.80x3.40	8.5:1	37@2400
1988	R	2.5 (2474)	TBI	92@4000	134@2800	4.00x3.00	8.3:1	50.@2000
	W	2.8 (2835)	MFI	130@4800	155@3600	3.50x2.99	8.9:1	50-65@2400
	3	3.8 (3785)	MFI	150@4400	200@2000	3.80x3.40	8.5:1	37@2400
1989	R	2.5 (2474)	TBI	98@4500	134@2800	4.00x3.00	8.3:1	50@2000
	W	2.8 (2835)	MFI	125@4500	160@3600	3.50x2.99	8.9:1	15@1100
	N	3.3 (3342)	MFI	160@5200	185@3200	3.70x3.16	9.0:1	45@2000
	T	3.1 (3130)	MFI	120@4200	175@2200	3.50x3.31	8.8:1	15@1100
1990	R	2.5 (2474)	MFI	110@5200	135@3200	4.00x3.00	8.3:1	26@800
	T	3.1 (3130)	MFI	120@4200	175@2200	3.50x3.31	8.8:1	15@1100
	N	3.3 (3342)	MFI	160@5200	185@2200	3.70x3.16	9.0:1	40@1850
1991	R	2.5 (2474)	TBI	110@5200	135@3200	4.00x3.00	8.3:1	26@800
	N	3.3 (3342)	MFI	160@5200	185@2000	3.70x3.16	9.0:1	60@1850
	T	3.1 (3130)	MFI	120@4200	175@2200	3.50x3.31	8.8:1	15@1100
1992	4	2.2 (2195)	MFI	110@5200	130@3200	3.50x3.346	9.0:1	56@3000
	R	2.5 (2474)	TBI	110@5200	135@3200	4.00x3.00	8.3:1	26@800
	N	3.3 (3342)	MFI	160@5200	185@2000	3.70x3.16	9.0:1	60@1850
1993	4	2.2 (2195)	MFI	110@5200	130@3200	3.50x3.346	9.0:1	56@3000
	M	3.1 (3130)	MFI	160@5200	185@4000	3.50x3.31	9.5:1	15@1100
	N	3.3 (3342)	MFI	160@5200	185@4000	3.50x3.31	9.5:1	15@1100
1994	4	2.2 (2195)	MFI	120@5200	130@4000	3.50x3.46	9.0:1	56@3000
	M	3.1 (3130)	MFI	160@5200	185@4000	3.50x3.31	9.5:1	15@1100
1995	4	2.2 (2195)	MFI	120@5200	130@4000	3.50x3.46	9.0:1	56@3000
	M	3.1 (3130)	MFI	160@5200	185@4000	3.50x3.31	9.5:1	15@1100
1996	4	2.2 (2195)	MFI	120@5200	130@4000	3.50x3.46	9.0:1	56@3000
	M	3.1 (3130)	MFI	160@5200	185@4000	3.50x3.31	9.5:1	15@1100

TBI - Throttle body fuel injection

MFI - Multiport fuel injection

BC - barrel carburetor

91083C01

VALVE SPECIFICATIONS

Year	Engine ID/VIN	Engine Displacement Liters (cc)	Seat Angle (deg.)	Face Angle (deg.)	Spring Test Pressure (lbs. @ in.)	Spring Installed Height (in.)	Stem-to-Guide Clearance (in.) Intake	Stem-to-Guide Clearance (in.) Exhaust	Stem Diameter (in.) Intake	Stem Diameter (in.) Exhaust
1982	R	2.5 (2474)	46	45	176@1.254	1.660	0.0010-0.0027	0.0010-0.0027	0.3418-0.3425	0.3418-0.3425
	X, Z	2.8 (2835)	46	45	155@1.160	1.610	0.0010-0.0027	0.0010-0.0027	0.3410-0.3416	0.3410-0.3416
	E	3.0 (2999)	45	45	220@1.340	1.727	0.0015-0.0035	0.0015-0.0032	0.3412-0.3401	0.3412-0.3405
1983	R	2.5 (2474)	46	45	176@1.254	1.660	0.0010-0.0027	0.0010-0.0027	0.3418-0.3425	0.3418-0.3425
	X, Z	2.8 (2835)	46	45	195@1.181	1.575	0.0010-0.0027	0.0010-0.0027	0.3410-0.3416	0.3410-0.3416
	E	3.0 (2999)	45	45	220@1.340	1.727	0.0015-0.0035	0.0015-0.0032	0.3412-0.3401	0.3412-0.3405
1984	R	2.5 (2474)	46	45	176@1.254	1.660	0.0010-0.0027	0.0010-0.0027	0.3418-0.3425	0.3418-0.3425
	X, Z	2.8 (2835)	46	45	195@1.181	1.575	0.0010-0.0027	0.0010-0.0027	0.3410-0.3416	0.3410-0.3416
	E	3.0 (2999)	45	45	220@1.340	1.727	0.0015-0.0035	0.0015-0.0032	0.3410-0.3401	0.3412-0.3405
1985	R	2.5 (2474)	46	45	176-180@1.260	1.69	0.0010-0.0027	0.0010-0.0027	0.3420-0.3430	0.3420-0.3430
	X	2.8 (2835)	46	45	195@1.181	1.575	0.0010-0.0027	0.0010-0.0027	0.3410-0.3416	0.3410-0.3416
	W	2.8 (2835)	46	45	195@1.181	1.575	0.0010-0.0027	0.0010-0.0027	0.3410-0.3416	0.3410-0.3416
	E	3.0 (2999)	45	45	220@1.340	1.727	0.0015-0.0035	0.0015-0.0027	0.3412-0.3401	0.3412-0.3405
1986	R	2.5 (2474)	46	45	176-180@1.260	1.690	0.0010-0.0027	0.0010-0.0027	0.3420-0.3430	0.3420-0.3430
	X	2.8 (2835)	46	45	195@1.181	1.575	0.0010-0.0027	0.0010-0.0027	0.3410-0.3416	0.3410-0.3416
	B	3.8 (3785)	45	45	185@1.340	1.727	0.0015-0.0035	0.0015-0.0032	0.3412-0.3401	0.3412-0.3405
	3	3.8 (3785)	45	45	185@1.340	1.727	0.0010-0.0027	0.0010-0.0027	0.3412-0.3401	0.3412-0.3405
1987	R	2.5 (2474)	46	45	158-170@1.040	1.440	0.0010-0.0027	0.0010-0.0027	0.3130-0.3140	0.3120-0.3130
	W	2.8 (2835)	46	45	215@1.291	1.575	0.0010-0.0027	0.0010-0.0027	0.3412-0.3401	0.3412-0.3416
	3	3.8 (3785)	46	45	175-195@1.340	1.697-1.757	0.0015-0.0035	0.0015-0.0032	0.3412-0.3401	0.3412-0.3405
1988	R	2.5 (2474)	46	45	158-170@1.040	1.440	0.0010-0.0027	0.0010-0.0027	0.3130-0.3140	0.3120-0.3130
	W	2.8 (2835)	46	45	215@1.291	1.575	0.0010-0.0027	0.0010-0.0027	NA	NA
	3	3.8 (3785)	46	45	185@1.340	1.720	0.0015-0.0035	0.0015-0.0032	0.3412-0.3401	0.3412-0.3405

NA - Not Available

91083C02

VALVE SPECIFICATIONS

Year	Engine ID/VIN	Engine Displacement Liters (cc)	Seat Angle (deg.)	Face Angle (deg.)	Spring Test Pressure (lbs. @ in.)	Spring Installed Height (in.)	Stem-to-Guide Clearance (in.) Intake	Stem-to-Guide Clearance (in.) Exhaust	Stem Diameter (in.) Intake	Stem Diameter (in.) Exhaust
1989	R	2.5 (2474)	46	45	173@1.240	1.680	0.0010-0.0026	0.0013-0.0041	NA	NA
	W	2.8 (2835)	46	45	215@1.291	1.575	0.0010-0.0027	0.0010-0.0027	NA	NA
	T	3.1 (3146)	46	45	215@1.291	1.701	0.0010-0.0027	0.0010-0.0027	NA	NA
	N	3.3 (3342)	45	45	200-220@1.315	1.690-1.750	0.0015-0.0035	0.0015-0.0032	NA	NA
1990	R	2.5 (2474)	46	45	173@1.240	1.680	0.0010-0.0026	0.0013-0.0041	NA	NA
	T	3.1 (3146)	46	45	215@1.291	1.575	0.0010-0.0027	0.0010-0.0027	NA	NA
	N	3.3 (3342)	45	45	200-220@1.315	1.690-1.750	0.0015-0.0032	0.0015-0.0032	NA	NA
1991	R	2.5 (2474)	46	45	173@1.240	1.680	0.0010-0.0026	0.0013-0.0041	NA	NA
	T	3.1 (3146)	46	45	215@1.291	1.575	0.0010-0.0027	0.0010-0.0027	NA	NA
	N	3.3 (3342)	45	45	210@1.315	1.690-1.720	0.0010-0.0027	0.0010-0.0027	NA	NA
1992	4	2.2 (2195)	46	45	215-233@1.247	1.637	0.0011-0.0026	0.0014-0.0031	NA	NA
	R	2.5 (2474)	46	45	173@1.240	1.680	0.0010-0.0028	0.0013-0.0041	NA	NA
	T	3.1 (3146)	46	45	215@1.291	1.575	0.0010-0.0027	0.0010-0.0027	NA	NA
	N	3.3 (3342)	45	45	210@1.315	1.690-1.720	0.0015-0.0035	0.0015-0.0032	NA	NA
1993	4	2.2 (2195)	46	45	215-233@1.247	1.637	0.0011-0.0026	0.0011-0.0031	NA	NA
	M	3.1 (3130)	45	45	250@1.239	1.71C	0.0001-0.0027	0.0010-0.0027	NA	NA
1994	N	3.3 (3342)	46	45	210@1.315	1.690-1.720	0.0015-0.0035	0.0015-0.0035	NA	NA
	4	2.2 (2195)	46	45	220-236@1.278	1.710	0.0001-0.0027	0.0014-0.0031	NA	NA
1995	M	3.1 (3130)	45	45	250@1.239	1.710	0.0001-0.0027	0.0010-0.0027	NA	NA
	4	2.2 (2195)	46	45	220-236@1.278	1.710	0.0001-0.0027	0.0014-0.0031	NA	NA
	M	3.1 (3130)	45	45	250@1.315	1.710	0.0001-0.0027	0.0010-0.0027	NA	NA
1996	4	2.2 (2195)	46	45	220-236@1.278	1.710	0.0001-0.0027	0.0014-0.0031	NA	NA
	M	3.1 (3130)	45	45	250@1.239	1.710	0.0001-0.0027	0.0010-0.0027	NA	NA

NA - Not Available

91083C03

CAMSHAFT SPECIFICATIONS
All measurements given in inches.

Year	Engine ID/VIN	Engine Displacement Liters (cc)	Journal Diameter 1	2	3	4	5	Elevation In.	Ex.	Bearing Clearance	Camshaft End Play
1989	R	2.5 (2474)	1.8690	1.8690	1.8690	1.8690	1.8690	0.248	0.248	0.0007-0.0027	0.0015-0.0050
	W	2.8 (2835)	1.8678-1.8815	1.8678-1.8815	1.8678-1.8815	1.8678-1.8815	1.8678-1.8815	0.263	0.273	0.0010-0.0040	NA
	T	3.1 (3146)	1.8678-1.8815	1.8678-1.8815	1.8678-1.8815	1.8678-1.8815	1.8678-1.8815	0.263	0.273	0.0010-0.0040	NA
	N	3.3 (3342)	1.7850-1.7860	1.7850-1.7860	1.7850-1.7860	1.7850-1.7860	1.7850-1.7860	0.250	0.255	0.0005-0.0035	NA
1990	R	2.5 (2474)	1.8690	1.8690	1.8690	1.8690	1.8690	0.248	0.248	0.0007-0.0027	0.0020-0.0090
	T	3.1 (3146)	1.8678-1.8815	1.8678-1.8815	1.8678-1.8815	1.8678-1.8815	1.8678-1.8815	0.2626	0.2732	0.0010-0.0040	NA
	N	3.3 (3342)	1.7850-1.7860	1.7850-1.7860	1.7850-1.7860	1.7850-1.7860	1.7850-1.7860	0.250	0.255	0.0005-0.0035	NA
1991	R	2.5 (2474)	1.8690	1.8690	1.8690	1.8690	1.8690	0.248	0.248	0.0007-0.0027	0.0015-0.0050
	T	3.1 (3146)	1.8678-1.8815	1.8678-1.8815	1.8678-1.8815	1.8678-1.8815	1.8678-1.8815	0.2626	0.2732	0.0010-0.0040	NA
	N	3.3 (3342)	1.7850-1.7860	1.7850-1.7860	1.7850-1.7860	1.7850-1.7860	1.7850-1.7860	0.250	0.255	0.0005-0.0035	NA
1992	R	2.5 (2474)	1.8690	1.8690	1.8690	1.8690	1.8690	0.248	0.248	0.0007-0.0027	0.0015-0.0050
	T	3.1 (3146)	1.8678-1.8815	1.8678-1.8815	1.8678-1.8815	1.8678-1.8815	1.8678-1.8815	0.262	0.273	0.0010-0.0040	NA
	N	3.3 (3342)	1.7850-1.7860	1.7850-1.7860	1.7850-1.7860	1.7850-1.7860	1.7850-1.7860	0.250	0.255	0.0005-0.0035	NA
1993	4	2.2 (2195)	1.8670-1.8690	1.8660-1.8690	1.8660-1.8690	1.8660-1.8690	1.8660-1.8690	0.259	0.250	0.0010-0.0039	NA
	M	3.1 (3130)	1.8660-1.8690	1.8660-1.8690	1.8660-1.8690	1.8660-1.8690	1.8660-1.8690	0.273	0.273	0.0010-0.0040	NA
1994	4	2.2 (2195)	1.8680-1.8690	1.8680-1.8690	1.8680-1.8690	1.8680-1.8690	1.8680-1.8690	0.288	0.288	0.0005-0.0035	NA
	M	3.1 (3130)	1.8680-1.8690	1.8680-1.8690	1.8680-1.8690	1.8680-1.8690	1.8680-1.8690	0.273	0.273	0.0010-0.0039	NA
1995	4	2.2 (2195)	1.8680-1.8690	1.8680-1.8690	1.8680-1.8690	1.8680-1.8690	1.8680-1.8690	0.288	0.288	0.0010-0.0040	NA
	M	3.1 (3130)	1.8680-1.8690	1.8680-1.8690	1.8680-1.8690	1.8680-1.8690	1.8680-1.8690	0.273	0.273	0.0010-0.0039	NA
1996	4	2.2 (2195)	1.8680-1.8690	1.8680-1.8690	1.8680-1.8690	1.8680-1.8690	1.8680-1.8690	0.288	0.288	0.0010-0.0040	NA
	M	3.1 (3130)	1.8680-1.8690	1.8680-1.8690	1.8680-1.8690	1.8680-1.8690	1.8680-1.8690	0.273	0.273	0.0010-0.0039	NA

NA - Not Available
1 No. 1 bearing: 0.0005-0.0025; Bearing Nos. 2-5: 0.0005-0.0035

91083C05

CAMSHAFT SPECIFICATIONS
All measurements given in inches.

Year	Engine ID/VIN	Engine Displacement Liters (cc)	Journal Diameter 1	2	3	4	5	Elevation In.	Ex.	Bearing Clearance	Camshaft End Play
1982	R	2.5 (2474)	1.8690	1.8690	1.8690	1.8690	1.8690	0.398	0.398	0.0001-0.0027	0.0015-0.0050
	X	2.8 (2835)	1.8678-1.8815	1.8678-1.8815	1.8678-1.8815	1.8678-1.8815	1.8678-1.8815	0.231	0.263	0.0010-0.0040	NA
	Z	2.8 (2835)	1.8690	1.8690	1.8660	1.8690	NA	0.231	0.263	0.0010-0.0040	NA
	E	3.0 (2999)	1.7860	1.7860	1.7860	1.7860	1.7860	0.406	0.406	0.0010-0.0040	NA
1983	R	2.5 (2474)	1.8690	1.8690	1.8690	1.8690	1.8690	0.398	0.398	0.0001-0.0027	0.0015-0.0050
	X	2.8 (2835)	1.8678-1.8815	1.8678-1.8815	1.8678-1.8815	1.8678-1.8815	1.8678-1.8815	0.231	0.263	0.0010-0.0040	NA
	Z	2.8 (2835)	1.8690	1.8690	1.8690	1.8690	NA	0.231	0.263	0.0010-0.0040	NA
	E	3.0 (2999)	1.7860	1.7860	1.7860	1.7860	1.7860	0.406	0.405	0.0010-0.0040	NA
1984	R	2.5 (2474)	1.8690	1.8690	1.8690	1.8690	1.8690	0.398	0.398	0.0001-0.0027	0.0015-0.0050
	X	2.8 (2835)	1.8678-1.8815	1.8678-1.8815	1.8678-1.8815	1.8678-1.8815	1.8678-1.8815	0.231	0.263	0.0010-0.0040	NA
	Z	2.8 (2835)	1.8690	1.8690	1.8690	1.8690	NA	0.231	0.263	0.0010-0.0040	NA
	E	3.0 (2999)	1.7860	1.7860	1.7860	1.7860	1.7860	0.406	0.406	0.0010-0.0040	NA
1985	R	2.5 (2474)	1.8690	1.8690	1.8690	1.8690	1.8690	0.398	0.398	0.0001-0.0027	0.0015-0.0050
	X	2.8 (2835)	1.8678-1.8815	1.8678-1.8815	1.8678-1.8815	1.8678-1.8815	1.8678-1.8815	0.231	0.263	0.0010-0.0040	NA
	Z	2.8 (2835)	1.8690	1.8690	1.8690	1.8690	NA	0.231	0.263	0.0010-0.0040	NA
	E	3.0 (2999)	1.7860	1.7860	1.7860	1.7860	1.7860	0.406	0.406	0.0010-0.0040	NA
1986	R	2.5 (2474)	1.8690	1.8690	1.8690	1.8690	1.8690	0.398	0.398	0.0001-0.0027	0.0015-0.0050
	X	2.8 (2835)	1.8678-1.8815	1.8678-1.8815	1.8678-1.8815	1.8678-1.8815	1.8678-1.8815	0.231	0.263	0.0010-0.0040	NA
	B	3.8 (3785)	1.7850-1.7860	1.7850-1.7860	1.7850-1.7860	1.7850-1.7860	1.7850-1.7860	0.392	0.392	[1]	NA
	3	3.8 (3785)	1.7850-1.7860	1.7850-1.7860	1.7850-1.7860	1.7850-1.7860	1.7850-1.7860	0.368	0.384	[1]	NA
1987	R	2.5 (2474)	1.8690	1.8690	1.8690	1.8690	1.8690	0.398	0.398	0.0001-0.0027	0.0015-0.0050
	W	2.8 (2835)	1.8678-1.8815	1.8678-1.8815	1.8678-1.8815	1.8678-1.8815	1.8678-1.8815	0.263	0.273	0.0010-0.0040	NA
	3	3.8 (3785)	1.7850-1.7860	1.7850-1.7860	1.7850-1.7860	1.7850-1.7860	1.7850-1.7860	0.397	0.397	[1]	NA
1988	R	2.5 (2474)	1.8690	1.8690	1.8690	1.8690	1.8690	0.232	0.232	0.0007-0.0027	0.0015-0.0050
	W	2.8 (2835)	1.8670-1.8690	1.8670-1.8690	1.8670-1.8690	1.8670-1.8690	1.8670-1.8690	0.263	0.273	0.0010-0.0030	NA
	3	3.8 (3785)	1.7850-1.7860	1.7850-1.7860	1.7850-1.7860	1.7850-1.7860	1.7850-1.7860	0.210	0.240	0.0005-0.0035	NA

91083C04

CRANKSHAFT AND CONNECTING ROD SPECIFICATIONS

All measurements are given in inches.

Year	Engine ID/VIN	Engine Displacement Liters (cc)	Main Brg. Journal Dia.	Crankshaft Main Brg. Oil Clearance	Shaft End-play	Thrust on No.	Journal Diameter	Connecting Rod Oil Clearance	Side Clearance
1989	R	2.5 (2474)	2.3000	0.0005-0.0022	0.0006-0.0110	5	2.0000	0.0005-0.0030	0.0060-0.0220
	W	2.8 (2835)	2.6473-2.6483	0.0012-0.0027	0.0024-0.0083	3	1.9994-1.9983	0.0014-0.0036	0.0140-0.0270
	T	3.1 (3146)	2.6473-2.6483	0.0012-0.0027	0.0024-0.0083	3	1.9994-1.9983	0.0014-0.0036	0.0140-0.0270
	N	3.3 (3342)	2.4988-2.4998	0.0003-0.0018	0.0030-0.0110	2	2.2487-2.2495	0.0005-0.0026	0.0030-0.0150
1990	R	2.5 (2474)	2.3000	0.0005-0.0022	0.0006-0.0110	5	2.0000	0.0005-0.0030	0.0060-0.0240
	T	3.1 (3146)	2.6473-2.6483	0.0012-0.0030	0.0024-0.0083	3	1.9983-1.9994	0.0110-0.0340	0.0140-0.0270
	N	3.3 (3342)	2.4988-2.4998	0.0003-0.0018	0.0030-0.0110	2	2.2487-2.2499	0.0003-0.0026	0.0030-0.0150
1991	R	2.5 (2474)	2.3000	0.0005-0.0022	0.0006-0.0110	5	2.0000	0.0005-0.0030	0.0060-0.0240
	T	3.1 (3146)	2.6473-2.6483	0.0012-0.0030	0.0024-0.0083	3	1.9983-1.9994	0.0011-0.0034	0.0140-0.0270
	N	3.3 (3342)	2.4988-2.4998	0.0003-0.0018	0.0030-0.0110	2	2.2487-2.2499	0.0003-0.0026	0.0030-0.0150
1992	4	2.2 (2195)	2.4945-2.4954	0.0006-0.0019	0.0020-0.0070	4	1.9983-1.9994	0.0010-0.0031	0.0039-0.0149
	R	2.5 (2474)	2.3000	0.0005-0.0022	0.0005-0.0100	5	2.0000	0.0005-0.0030	0.0060-0.0240
	N	3.3 (3342)	2.4988-2.4998	0.0008-0.0022	0.0030-0.0110	2	2.2487-2.2499	0.0008-0.0022	0.0030-0.0150
1993	4	2.2 (2195)	2.4945-2.4954	0.0006-0.0019	0.0020-0.0070	4	1.9983-1.9994	0.0010-0.0031	0.0039-0.0149
	M	3.1 (3130)	2.6473-2.6483	0.0012-0.0030	0.0024-0.0083	3	1.9982-1.9994	0.0011-0.0037	0.0071-0.0173
	N	3.3 (3342)	2.4988-2.4998	0.0008-0.0022	0.0030-0.0110	2	2.2487-2.2499	0.0008-0.0022	0.0030-0.0150
1994	4	2.2 (2195)	2.4945-2.4954	0.0006-0.0019	0.0020-0.0070	4	1.9983-1.9994	0.00098-0.0031	0.0039-0.0149
	3	2.3 (2261)	2.0470-2.0480	0.0005-0.0023	0.0034-0.0095	3	1.8887-1.8897	0.0005-0.0020	0.0059-0.0177
	M	3.1 (3130)	2.6473-2.6483	0.0012-0.0030	0.0024-0.0083	3	1.9982-1.9994	0.0011-0.0037	0.0071-0.0173
1995	4	2.2 (2195)	2.4945-2.4954	0.0006-0.0019	0.0020-0.0070	4	1.9983-1.9994	0.00098-0.0031	0.0039-0.0149
	M	3.1 (3130)	2.6473-2.6483	0.0012-0.0030	0.0024-0.0083	3	1.9982-1.9994	0.0011-0.0037	0.0071-0.0173
1996	4	2.2 (2195)	2.4945-2.4954	0.0006-0.0019	0.0020-0.0070	4	1.9983-1.9994	0.00098-0.0031	0.0039-0.0149
	M	3.1 (3130)	2.6473-2.6483	0.0012-0.0030	0.0024-0.0083	3	1.9982-1.9994	0.0011-0.0037	0.0071-0.0173

1 Engine ID code on front of block
Codes A, T: 2.6473-2.6483
Code K: 2.4937-2.4947
2 Measured at thrust bearing
No. 1: 2.6473-2.6483
3 No. 1: 2.4698-2.4698

91083C07

CRANKSHAFT AND CONNECTING ROD SPECIFICATIONS

All measurements are given in inches.

Year	Engine ID/VIN	Engine Displacement Liters (cc)	Main Brg. Journal Dia.	Crankshaft Main Brg. Oil Clearance	Shaft End-play	Thrust on No.	Journal Diameter	Connecting Rod Oil Clearance	Side Clearance
1982	R	2.5 (2474)	2.2995-2.3005	0.0005-0.0022	0.0035-0.0085	5	1.9995-2.0005	0.0005-0.0026	0.0060-0.0220
	X, Z	2.8 (2835)	2.4937-2.4946	0.0017-0.0030	0.0020-0.0067	3	1.9984-1.9994	0.0014-0.0036	0.0060-0.0170
	E	3.0 (2999)	2.4990-2.5000	0.0003-0.0018	0.0030-0.0090	2	2.2487-2.2495	0.0005-0.0026	0.0023-0.0220
1983	R	2.5 (2474)	2.2995-2.3005	0.0005-0.0022	0.0035-0.0085	5	1.9995-2.0005	0.0005-0.0026	0.0060-0.0220
	X, Z	2.8 (2835)	2.4397-2.4946	0.0017-0.0030	0.0020-0.0067	3	1.9984-1.9994	0.0014-0.0036	0.0060-0.0170
	E	3.0 (2999)	2.4990-2.5000	0.0003-0.0018	0.0030-0.0090	2	2.2487-2.2495	0.0005-0.0026	0.0060-0.0170
1984	R	2.5 (2474)	2.2995-2.3005	0.0005-0.0022	0.0035-0.0085	5	1.9995-2.0005	0.0005-0.0026	0.0060-0.0220
	X, Z	2.8 (2835)	2.4397-2.4946	0.0017-0.0030	0.0020-0.0067	3	1.9984-1.9994	0.0014-0.0036	0.0060-0.0170
	E	3.0 (2999)	2.4990-2.5000	0.0003-0.0018	0.0030-0.0090	2	2.2487-2.2495	0.0005-0.0026	0.0023-0.0220
1985	R	2.5 (2474)	2.2995-2.3005	0.0005-0.0022	0.0035-0.0085	5	1.9995-2.0005	0.0005-0.0026	0.0060-0.0220
	X	2.8 (2835)	[1]	0.0016-0.0033	0.0020-0.0085	3	1.9993-1.9983	0.0014-0.0037	0.0060-0.0170
	E	3.0 (2999)	2.4990-2.5000	0.0003-0.0018	0.0030-0.0090	2	2.2487-2.2495	0.0005-0.0026	0.0023-0.0170
	3	3.8 (3785)	2.4990-2.4995	0.0003-0.0018	0.0030-0.0090 [2]	2	2.2487-2.2495	0.0005-0.0026	0.0060-0.0230
1986	R	2.5 (2474)	2.2995-2.3005	0.0005-0.0022	0.0035-0.0085	5	1.9995-2.0005	0.0005-0.0026	0.0060-0.0220
	X	2.8 (2835)	[1]	0.0016-0.0033	0.0020-0.0033	3	1.9993-1.9983	0.0014-0.0037	0.0060-0.0170
	B	3.8 (3785)	2.4995	0.0003-0.0018	0.0030-0.0110	2	2.2487-2.2495	0.0005-0.0026	0.0060-0.0230
	3	3.8 (3785)	2.4995	0.0003-0.0032	0.0024-0.0083	3	1.9994-1.9983	0.0013-0.0026	0.0060-0.0170
1987	R	2.5 (2474)	2.2995-2.3005	0.0005-0.0022	0.0035-0.0085	5	1.9995-2.0005	0.0005-0.0026	0.0060-0.0220
	W	2.8 (2835)	2.6473-2.6483	0.0016-0.0032	0.0024-0.0083	3	1.9994-1.9983	0.0013-0.0026	0.0060-0.0170
	3	3.8 (3785)	2.4995	0.0003-0.0018	0.0030-0.0090	2	2.2487-2.2495	0.0005-0.0026	0.0040-0.0150
1988	R	2.5 (2474)	2.2995-2.3005	0.0005-0.0022	0.0035-0.0085	5	1.9995-2.0005	0.0005-0.0026	0.0060-0.0220
	W	2.8 (2835)	2.6473-2.6438	0.0016-0.0033	0.0020-0.0080	3	1.9983-1.9993	0.0013-0.0026	0.0066-0.0170
	3	3.8 (3785)	2.4988-2.4998	0.0003-0.0018	0.0030-0.0110 [3]	2	2.2487-2.2499	0.0003-0.0028	0.0030-0.0150

91083C06

PISTON AND RING SPECIFICATIONS
All measurements are given in inches.

Year	Engine ID/VIN	Engine Displacement Liters (cc)	Piston Clearance	Ring Gap Top Compression	Ring Gap Bottom Compression	Ring Gap Oil Control	Ring Side Clearance Top Compression	Ring Side Clearance Bottom Compression	Ring Side Clearance Oil Control
1989	R	2.5 (2474)	0.0014-0.0022 [1]	0.010-0.020	0.010-0.020	0.020-0.060	0.0020-0.0030	0.0010-0.0030	0.0150-0.0550
	W	2.8 (2835)	0.0009-0.0022	0.010-0.020	0.010-0.020	0.001-0.020	0.0020-0.0030	0.0020-0.0035	0.0008-0.0035
	T	3.1 (3146)	0.0009-0.0022	0.010-0.020	0.010-0.020	0.001-0.020	0.0020-0.0030	0.0020-0.0035	0.0008-0.0035
	N	3.3 (3342)	0.0004-0.0022	0.0-0.0	0.010-0.025	0.010-0.040	0.0013-0.0031	0.0013-0.031	0.0011-0.0081
1990	R	2.5 (2474)	0.0028-0.0048	0.0-0.0	0.010-0.020	0.020-0.060	0.0020-0.0030	0.0010-0.0030	0.0150-0.0550
	T	3.1 (3146)	0.0009-0.0022	0.0-0.020	0.010-0.020	0.010-0.060	0.0020-0.0030	0.0020-0.0030	0.0080 MAX
	N	3.3 (3342)	0.0004-0.0220	0.0-0.025	0.010-0.025	0.010-0.040	0.0013-0.031	0.0013-0.0031	0.0011-0.0081
1991	R	2.5 (2474)	0.0014-0.0022	0.010-0.020	0.010-0.020	0.010-0.060	0.0020-0.0030	0.0010-0.0030	0.0150-0.0550
	T	3.1 (3146)	0.0009-0.0022	0.010-0.020	0.010-0.020	0.010-0.030	0.0020-0.0035	0.0020-0.0035	0.0080 MAX
1992	N	3.3 (3342)	0.0004-0.0022	0.010-0.025	0.010-0.025	0.010-0.040	0.0013-0.031	0.0013-0.031	0.0011-0.0081
	4	2.2 (2195)	0.0007-0.0017	0.010-0.025	0.010-0.020	0.010-0.050	0.0019-0.0027	0.0019-0.0027	0.0019-0.0082
	R	2.5 (2474)	0.0014-0.0022 [1]	0.010-0.020	0.010-0.020	0.020-0.060	0.0020-0.0030	0.0010-0.0030	0.0150-0.0550
1993	N	3.3 (3342)	0.0004-0.0022 [1]	0.010-0.025	0.010-0.025	0.015-0.055	0.0013-0.0031	0.0013-0.031	0.0011-0.0081
	4	2.2 (2195)	0.0007-0.0017	0.010-0.020	0.010-0.020	0.010-0.050	0.0019-0.0027	0.0019-0.0027	0.0019-0.0082
	M	3.1 (3130)	0.0013-0.0027	0.007-0.016	0.020-0.028	0.010-0.030	0.0020-0.0035	0.0020-0.0035	0.0080 MAX
1994	N	3.3 (3342)	0.0004-0.0022 [1]	0.010-0.025	0.010-0.025	0.015-0.055	0.0013-0.0031	0.0013-0.031	0.0011-0.0081
	4	2.2 (2195)	0.0007-0.0017	0.010-0.025	0.010-0.020	0.010-0.050	0.0019-0.0027	0.0019-0.0027	0.0019-0.0082
1995	M	3.1 (3130)	0.0013-0.0027	0.007-0.216	0.020-0.028	0.010-0.030	0.0020-0.0035	0.0020-0.0035	0.0080 MAX
	4	2.2 (2195)	0.0007-0.0017	0.010-0.020	0.010-0.020	0.010-0.050	0.0019-0.0027	0.0019-0.0027	0.0019-0.0082
1996	4	2.2 (2195)	0.0007-0.0017	0.010-0.020	0.010-0.020	0.010-0.050	0.0019-0.0027	0.0019-0.0027	0.0019-0.0082
	M	3.1 (3130)	0.0013-0.0027	0.007-0.216	0.020-0.028	0.010-0.030	0.0020-0.0035	0.0020-0.0035	0.0080 MAX

NA - Not Available
1 Measured 1/8 down from top of piston
2 Measured at top of piston skirt

PISTON AND RING SPECIFICATIONS
All measurements are given in inches.

Year	Engine ID/VIN	Engine Displacement Liters (cc)	Piston Clearance	Ring Gap Top Compression	Ring Gap Bottom Compression	Ring Gap Oil Control	Ring Side Clearance Top Compression	Ring Side Clearance Bottom Compression	Ring Side Clearance Oil Control
1982	R	2.5 (2474)	0.0025-0.0033	0.010-0.022	0.010-0.020	0.015-0.055	0.0015-0.0030	0.0015-0.0030	SNUG
	X, Z	2.8 (2835)	0.0017-0.0027	0.010-0.020	0.010-0.020	0.020-0.055	0.0012-0.0028	0.0016-0.0037	0.008
	E	3.0 (2999)	0.0008-0.0020	0.013-0.023	0.013-0.023	0.015-0.035	0.0030-0.0050	0.0030-0.0050	0.0035
1983	R	2.5 (2474)	0.0025-0.0033	0.010-0.022	0.010-0.027	0.015-0.055	0.0015-0.0030	0.0015-0.0030	SNUG
	X, Z	2.8 (2835)	0.0017-0.0027	0.010-0.020	0.010-0.020	0.020-0.055	0.0012-0.0028	0.0016-0.0037	0.008
	E	3.0 (2999)	0.0008-0.0020	0.013-0.023	0.013-0.023	0.015-0.035	0.0030-0.0050	0.0030-0.0050	0.0035
1984	R	2.5 (2474)	0.0025-0.0033	0.010-0.022	0.010-0.020	0.015-0.055	0.0015-0.0030	0.0015-0.0030	SNUG
	X, Z	2.8 (2835)	0.0017-0.0027	0.010-0.020	0.010-0.020	0.020-0.055	0.0012-0.0028	0.0016-0.0037	0.008
	E	3.0 (2999)	0.0008-0.0020	0.013-0.023	0.013-0.023	0.015-0.035	0.0030-0.0050	0.0030-0.0050	0.0035
1985	R	2.5 (2474)	0.0014-0.0022 [1]	0.010-0.020	0.010-0.020	0.020-0.060	0.0020-0.0030	0.0010-0.0030	0.0150-0.0550
	X	2.8 (2835)	0.0007-0.0017	0.010-0.020	0.010-0.020	0.020-0.055	0.0012-0.0027	0.0016-0.0037	0.0078
	E	3.0 (2999)	[2]	0.010-0.020	0.010-0.020	0.015-0.055	0.0030-0.0050	0.0030-0.0050	0.0035
	3	3.8 (3785)	[2]	0.010-0.020	0.010-0.020	0.015-0.055	0.0030-0.0050	0.0030-0.0050	0.0035
1986	R	2.5 (2474)	0.0014-0.0022 [1]	0.010-0.020	0.010-0.020	0.020-0.060	0.0020-0.0030	0.0010-0.0030	0.0150-0.0550
	X	2.8 (2835)	0.0007-0.0017	0.010-0.020	0.010-0.020	0.020-0.055	0.0012-0.0027	0.0016-0.0037	0.0076 MAX
	3	3.8 (3785)	[2]	0.010-0.020	0.010-0.020	0.015-0.055	0.0030-0.0050	0.0030-0.0050	0.0035
1987	R	2.5 (2474)	0.0014-0.0022 [1]	0.010-0.020	0.010-0.020	0.020-0.060	0.0020-0.0030	0.0010-0.0030	0.0150-0.0550
	W	2.8 (2835)	0.0012-0.0022	0.010-0.020	0.010-0.020	0.020-0.060	0.0010-0.0030	0.0010-0.0030	0.0080
	3	3.8 (3785)	[2]	0.010-0.020	0.010-0.020	0.015-0.055	0.0030-0.0050	0.0030-0.0050	0.0035
1988	R	2.5 (2474)	0.0014-0.0022 [1]	0.010-0.020	0.010-0.020	0.020-0.060	0.0020-0.0030	0.0010-0.0030	0.0150-0.0550
	W	2.8 (2835)	0.0012-0.0028	0.010-0.020	0.010-0.020	0.020-0.060	0.0010-0.0030	0.0010-0.0030	0.0080 MAX
	3	3.8 (3785)	0.0004-0.0022 [2]	0.010-0.020	0.010-0.022	0.015-0.055	0.0010-0.0030	0.0010-0.0030	0.0005-0.0065

TORQUE SPECIFICATIONS
All readings in ft. lbs.

9103C11

Year	Engine ID/VIN	Engine Displacement Liters (cc)	Cylinder Head Bolts	Main Bearing Bolts	Rod Bearing Bolts	Crankshaft Damper Bolts	Flywheel Bolts	Manifold Intake	Manifold Exhaust	Spark Plugs	Lug Nut
1991	R	2.5 (2474)	[7]	65	29	162 [1]	22	25	[8]	15	100
	T	3.1 (3146)	[5]	73	39	76	52	11	18	20	100
	N	3.3 (3342)	[10]	[12]	[9]	[13]	[21]	7	41 [3]	20	100
1992	R	2.5 (2474)	[7]	65	29	162 [1]	55	25	[3]	12	100
	N	3.3 (3342)	[10]	[12]	[9]	[14]	[15]	7	38	11	100
1993	4	2.2 (2195)	[17]	66	38	77	54	24	10	20	100
	N	3.3 (3342)	[10]	[12]	[9]	[16]	[15]	7	38	20	100
1994	4	2.2 (2195)	[17]	70	38	77	55	24	10	18	100
	M	3.1 (3130)	[5]	[19]	[20]	76	61	11	10	18	100
1995	4	2.2 (2195)	[17]	70	38	77	55	24	10	18	100
	M	3.1 (3130)	[5]	[19]	[20]	76	61	11	10	18	100
1996	4	2.2 (2195)	[17]	70	38	77	55	24	10	18	100
	M	3.1 (3130)	[5]	[19]	[20]	76	61	11	10	18	100

1 Sprocket retaining bolt
2 Step 1: Tighten all head bolts to 18 ft. lbs.
   Step 2: Tighten all bolts to 22 ft. lbs. except No. 9
   Tighten No. 9 to 29 ft. lbs.
   Step 3: Tighten all 120 degrees (two flats) except No. 9
   Tighten No. 9 1/4 turn (90 degrees)
3 Inner bolts: 37 ft. lbs.
   Outer bolts: 28 ft. lbs.
4 Refer to text
5 Coat threads with sealer. Torque to 33 ft. lbs. then turn 90 degrees
6 Torque all bolts to 25 ft. lbs.
   Tighten 180 degrees in two steps, not exceeding a total of 60 ft. lbs.
7 Step 1: 18 ft. lbs.
   Step 2: 26 ft. lbs. except I bolt. Retorque I bolt to 18 ft. lbs.
   Step 3: Plus 90 degrees
8 Inner bolts: 37 ft. lbs
   Outer bolts: 28 ft. lbs.
9 20 ft. lbs. plus 50 degrees
10 Step 1: 35 ft. lbs.
   Step 2: Plus 130 degrees
   Step 3: Rotate four center bolts an additional 30 degrees
11 Step 1: 15 ft. lbs.
   Step 2: 24 ft. lbs.
12 26 ft. lbs. plus 50 degrees
13 105 ft. lbs. plus 76 degrees
14 100 ft. lbs. plus 76 degrees
15 11 ft. lbs. plus 50 degrees
16 111 ft. lbs. plus 76 degrees
17 Short bolts: 43 ft. lbs. plus 90 degrees
   Long bolts: 46 ft. lbs. plus 90 degrees
18 New cylinder head:
   1st-time installation: 20 ft. lbs.
   All other installations: 11 ft. lbs.
19 37 ft. lbs. plus 77 degrees
20 15 ft. lbs. plus 75 degrees
21 7 ft. lbs. plus 90 degrees
22 Automatic transaxle: 55 ft. lbs.
   Manual transaxle: 69 ft. lbs.

TORQUE SPECIFICATIONS
All readings in ft. lbs.

9103C10

Year	Engine ID/VIN	Engine Displacement Liters (cc)	Cylinder Head Bolts	Main Bearing Bolts	Rod Bearing Bolts	Crankshaft Damper Bolts	Flywheel Bolts	Manifold Intake	Manifold Exhaust	Spark Plugs	Lug Nut
1982	R	2.5 (2474)	92	70	32	200	44	29	44	NA	100
	X	2.8 (2835)	70	68	37	75	50	23	25	7-15	100
	Z	2.8 (2835)	70	68	37	75	50	23	25	7-15	100
	E	3.0 (2999)	80	100	40-45	225	60	32	25-37	13	100
1983	R	2.5 (2474)	92	70	32	200	44	29	44	NA	100
	X	2.8 (2835)	70	68	37	75	50	23	25	7-15	100
	Z	2.8 (2835)	70	68	37	75	50	23	25	7-15	100
	E	3.0 (2999)	80	100	40-45	225	60	32	25-37	13	100
1984	R	2.5 (2474)	92	70	32	200	44	29	44	NA	100
	X	2.8 (2835)	70	68	37	75	50	23	25	7-15	100
	Z	2.8 (2835)	70	68	37	75	50	23	25	7-15	100
	E	3.0 (2999)	80	100	40-45	225	60	32	25-37	13	100
1985	R	2.5 (2474)	[1]	70	32	200 [2]	22	[4]	[4]	15	100
	W	2.8 (2835)	65-90	63-74	34-40	67-85	45	23	22-28	11	100
	X	2.8 (2835)	65-90	63-74	34-40	67-85	[6]	23	22-28	11	100
	E	3.0 (2999)	72	97	40	200	60	35	37	20	100
	3	3.8 (3785)	[6]	100	45	200	60	32	37	20	100
1986	R	2.5 (2474)	[2]	70	32	200 [1]	22	[4]	[4]	15	100
	X	2.8 (2835)	65-90	63-74	34-40	67-85	22	23	22-28	11	100
	B	3.8 (3785)	[6]	100	45	200	60	32	37	20	100
	3	3.8 (3785)	[6]	100	45	200	60	32	37	20	100
1987	R	2.5 (2474)	[2]	70	32	200 [1]	22	[4]	[4]	15	100
	W	2.8 (2835)	[5]	63-83	34-40	67-85	25	15-23	15-23	10-25	100
	3	3.8 (3785)	[6]	100	45	219	32	37	37	20	100
1988	R	2.5 (2474)	[7]	70	32	162 [1]	45	18	19	15	100
	W	2.8 (2835)	[5]	70	37	77	60	32	37	10-25	100
	3	3.8 (3785)	[6]	100	45	219	45	18	[8]	20	100
1989	R	2.5 (2474)	[5]	65	29	162 [1]	45	25	[8]	15	100
	W	2.8 (2835)	[5]	70	37	77	45	18	[8]	10-25	100
	T	3.1 (3146)	[5]	70	37	77	45	18	[8]	20	100
	N	3.3 (3342)	[8]	90	[9]	219	61	7	30	20	100
1990	R	2.5 (2474)	[7]	70	32	162 [1]	45	25	18	15	100
	T	3.1 (3146)	[5]	73	39	76	45	25 [11]	30	20	100
	N	3.3 (3342)	[10]	90	[9]	219	61	7	30	20	100

Valve/Rocker Cover(s)

REMOVAL & INSTALLATION

♦ See Figure 19

✳✳ CAUTION

When draining the coolant, keep in mind that cats and dogs are attracted by ethylene glycol antifreeze, and are quite likely to drink any that is left in an uncovered container or in puddles on the ground. This will prove fatal in sufficient quantity. Always drain the coolant into a sealable container. Coolant should be reused unless it is contaminated or several years old.

2.2L Engine

1. Clean all the dirt from around the mating area of the valve cover.
2. Disconnect the PCV valve from the valve cover.
3. Remove the valve cover bolts.
4. Remove the valve cover by tapping it with a rubber mallet. This must be done to break the seal. DON'T attempt to pry the cover off, as it is easily damaged.
5. Clean the sealing surface on the head and the valve cover with a degreaser.

To install:

6. Attach a new gasket in the mating area of the head.
7. Install the valve cover to the head, tighten the cover bolts to 89 inch lbs. (10 Nm).
8. Install the PCV valve.
9. Add engine oil if needed. Start the engine and check for leaks.

Fig. 19 Always make sure you completely remove all traces of gasket and sealant before installing a valve cover

2.5L Engine

♦ See Figure 20

1. Clean all the dirt from around the mating area of the valve cover.
2. Remove the air cleaner assembly, being sure to tag all disconnected hoses for reassembly purposes.
3. Remove the PCV valve and hose from the valve cover grommet.
4. Remove the spark plug wires from the spark plugs and the locating clips. Be sure to tag the wires so that they may be attached properly.
5. Remove the crankcase vent tube from the cover.
6. Remove the EGR valve.
7. Remove the cover retaining bolts, then the valve cover by tapping it with a rubber mallet. This must be done to break the seal. DON'T attempt to pry the cover off, as it is easily damaged.

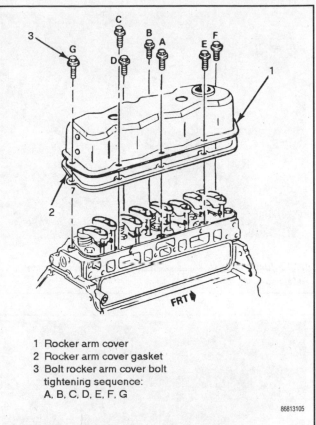

1. Rocker arm cover
2. Rocker arm cover gasket
3. Bolt rocker arm cover bolt
   tightening sequence:
   A, B, C, D, E, F, G

Fig. 20 Valve cover assembly used on 2.5L engines

8. Clean the mating surface on the head and valve cover assembly.

To install:

9. Install a new valve cover gasket on the cylinder head mating surface, then the cover.
10. Install the valve cover bolts, tighten to 80 inch lbs. (9 Nm).
11. Install the EGR valve with a new gasket.
12. Install the crankcase vent tube to the valve cover.
13. Attach the spark plug wires to the spark plugs, then attach the clip on the cover.
14. Install the air cleaner assembly.
15. Start the engine, check for leaks.

2.8L Engine

♦ See Figures 21 and 22

1. Disconnect the negative battery cable at the battery.
2. Clean all the dirt from around the mating area of the valve cover.
3. Remove the air cleaner assembly, being sure to tag all disconnected hoses for reassembly purposes.

➡ If equipped with an MFI system, remove any component which will interfere with the valve cover removal.

4. Remove the spark plug wires from the spark plugs and the locating clips. Be sure to tag the wires so that they may be attached properly.
5. Disconnect the accelerator linkage and springs from the carburetor.
6. If your vehicle has an automatic transaxle, disconnect the T.V. (throttle valve) linkage at the carburetor.
7. If your vehicle has cruise control, remove the diaphragm actuator mounting bracket.
8. Remove the air management valve and the necessary hoses (see Section 4).
9. Remove the valve cover retaining bolts, then remove the valve cover. If the cover sticks, tap it loose with a rubber mallet. DON'T attempt to pry it off of the head, as the cover may be easily damaged.

To install:

10. Clean the mating surfaces of the cylinder head and intake manifold with degreaser.

Fig. 21 Use a deep socket or extension to remove the valve cover retaining bolts

Fig. 22 Lift the valve cover off the head. If necessary, use a rubber mallet to loosen it

11. Place RTV sealer all around the valve cover sealing surface. When going around the holes always follow the inboard side of the holes.

12. Install the cover and tighten the bolts to 8 ft. lbs. (10 Nm).

13. Install the front engine strut bracket-to-cylinder head. Tighten the bolts to 35 ft., lbs. (48 Nm).

14. Connect all the vacuum hoses and the spark plug wires.

15. Install the front engine strut at the radiator support and engine bracket.

16. Install the air cleaner.

17. Connect the negative battery cable, start the engine, check for leaks.

3.0L and 3.8L Engines

FRONT COVER

1. Disconnect the negative battery cable.
2. Clean all the dirt from around the mating area of the valve cover.
3. Remove the crankcase breather tube.
4. Remove the spark plug wire harness cover and disconnect the spark plug wires at the spark plugs.
5. Remove the valve cover nuts, washers, seals and valve cover.
6. Using a putty knife, clean the gasket mounting surfaces.

To install:

7. Install a new gasket to the clean mating area of the cylinder head, then put the valve cover on.

8. Install the valve cover seals, washers and nuts. Tighten the nuts to 7 ft. lbs. (10 Nm).

9. Install the spark plug wire harness on the valve cover, then insert the wires in there proper places. Connect the plug wires to the spark plugs.

10. Connect the crankcase breather tube.

11. Fill the engine oil to the proper fill mark, connect the negative battery cable.

12. Start the engine, check for leaks.

REAR COVER

1. Disconnect the negative battery cable.
2. Clean all the dirt from around the mating area of the valve cover.
3. Remove the C_3I ignition coil module, the spark plug cables, the wiring connectors, the EGR solenoid wiring and vacuum hoses.

➡ If equipped with an MFI system, remove any component which will interfere with the valve cover removal.

4. Remove the serpentine drive belt.
5. Remove the alternator's wiring connectors, then the mounting bolt and swing the alternator toward the front of the vehicle.
6. Remove the power steering pump from the belt tensioner (move it aside) and the belt tensioner assembly.
7. Remove the engine lift bracket and the rear alternator brace.
8. Drain the cooling system below the level of the heater hose, then disconnect the throttle body heater hoses.
9. Remove the valve cover nuts, the washers, the seals, the valve cover and the gasket.
10. Using a putty knife, clean the gasket mounting surfaces.
11. To install, use a new gasket and reverse the removal procedures. Tighten the valve cover nuts to 7 ft. lbs. (10 Nm.).

3.1L Engine (VIN T)

FRONT COVER

1. Release fuel system pressure and disconnect the negative battery cable.
2. Clean all the dirt from around the mating area of the valve cover.
3. Remove the air cleaner assembly.
4. Drain the cooling system.
5. Disconnect the ignition wire clamps from the coolant tube.
6. Remove the coolant tube mount at head and coolant tube from each end.
7. Remove the coolant tube at the coolant pump and remove the tube.
8. Remove the ignition wire guide.
9. Remove the spark plug wire harness cover and disconnect the spark plug wires at the spark plugs, as needed.
10. Remove the valve cover nuts, washers, seals and valve cover.
11. Using a putty knife, clean the gasket mounting surfaces.

To install:

12. Install a new gasket to the clean mating area of the cylinder head, then put the valve cover on.

13. Install the valve cover seals, washers and nuts. Tighten the nuts to 7 ft. lbs. (10 Nm).

14. Install the spark plug wire harness on the valve cover, then insert the wire in there proper places. Attach the spark plug wires to the plugs if removed.

15. Install the ignition wires and guides.

16. Attach the air cleaner assembly on the engine.

17. Fill the coolant system.

18. Fill the engine oil to the proper fill mark, connect the negative battery cable.

19. Start the engine, top off the cooling system, then check for leaks.

REAR COVER

1. Release fuel system pressure and disconnect the negative battery cable.
2. Drain the cooling system below the level of the heater hose.
3. Clean all the dirt from around the mating area of the valve cover.
4. Remove the hoses at the intake plenum.
5. Remove the airflow tube.
6. Remove the EGR valve crossover pipe.
7. Remove the ignition wire guide.
8. Tag and remove the ignition wires.
9. Disconnect the coolant hoses at the throttle body.

10. Tag and disconnect all electrical connectors to throttle body and that will ease the operation by moving aside.

11. Disconnect the throttle body cables.

12. Remove the bracket at the right side of the intake plenum.

13. Disconnect the power brake booster supply hose.

14. Remove the serpentine belt.

15. Remove the coolant recovery bottle.

16. Remove the exhaust crossover pipe.

17. Remove the alternator and support it out of the way.

18. Remove the PCV valve from the valve cover.

19. Remove the valve cover nuts, the washers, the seals, the valve cover and the gasket.

20. Using a putty knife, clean the gasket mounting surfaces.

To install:

21. Use a new gasket and reverse the removal procedures. Tighten the valve cover nuts to 7 ft. lbs. (10 Nm.).

22. Insert the PCV valve.

23. Install the alternator, exhaust crossover and coolant recovery tank.

24. Install the serpentine drive belt.

25. Attach the brake booster hose.

26. Install the bracket to the right side of the intake plenum.

27. Connect the throttle body cables, electrical connectors and hoses.

28. Install the ignition wires and guides.

29. Install the EGR valve crossover pipe and the airflow tube.

30. Install the vacuum hoses.

31. Fill the radiator and check for leaks.

32. Connect the negative battery cable, install air cleaner. Tighten the air cleaner bolt to 11 ft. lbs. (15 Nm).

3.1L Engine (VIN M)

FRONT COVER

♦ **See Figure 23**

1. Disconnect the negative battery cable.

2. Drain the cooling system to a level below the coolant pipe on the front of the engine.

3. Remove the coolant bypass hose clamp at the coolant tube.

4. Remove the two bolts and nut securing the coolant tube to the cylinder head and position the tube out of the way.

5. Clean all the dirt from around the mating area of the valve cover.

6. Disconnect the PCV valve from the valve cover.

7. Remove the four valve cover bolts and remove the valve cover.

8. Remove the rocker arm nuts, balls, rocker arms and pushrods.

To install:

9. Clean all the gasket surfaces completely.

10. Coat all the valve train components with engine oil prior to installation.

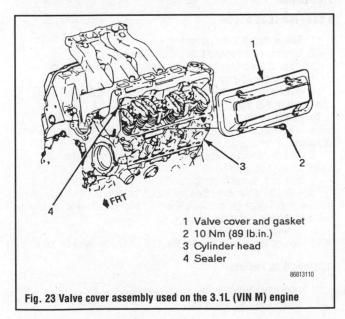

1 Valve cover and gasket
2 10 Nm (89 lb.in.)
3 Cylinder head
4 Sealer

86813110

Fig. 23 Valve cover assembly used on the 3.1L (VIN M) engine

11. Install the pushrods and install the rocker arms on the studs. Install the rocker arm balls and mounting nuts. Make sure the pushrods are properly seated in the lifter and rocker arm. Tighten the mounting nuts to 18 ft. lbs. (24 Nm).

12. Install the valve cover using a new gasket and tighten the rocker cover bolts to 89 inch lbs. (10 Nm).

13. Connect the PCV valve to the valve cover.

14. Position the coolant tube and connect the thermostat bypass hose.

15. Install the coolant tube mounting nut and bolts. Tighten the screw at the water pump to 106 inch lbs. (12 Nm), the bolt at the corner of the cylinder head to 18 ft. lbs. (25 Nm) and the nut to 18 ft. lbs. (25 Nm).

16. Refill the cooling system.

17. Connect the negative battery cable.

18. Start the vehicle and verify no leaks.

REAR COVER

1. Disconnect the negative battery cable.

2. Disconnect the spark plug wires from the spark plugs and upper intake plenum wire retainer and position out of the way.

3. Disconnect the power brake booster vacuum pipe from the intake plenum.

4. Remove the serpentine belt.

5. Remove the alternator.

6. Disconnect and remove the ignition assembly and EVAP canister purge solenoid as an assembly.

7. Clean all the dirt from around the mating area of the valve cover.

8. Remove the four valve cover bolts and remove the valve cover.

9. Remove the rocker arm nuts, balls, rocker arms and pushrods.

To install:

10. Clean all the gasket surfaces completely.

11. Coat all the valve train components with engine oil prior to installation.

12. Install the pushrods and install the rocker arms on the studs. Install the rocker arm balls and mounting nuts. Make sure the pushrods are properly seated in the lifter and rocker arm. Tighten the mounting nuts to 18 ft. lbs. (25 Nm).

13. Install the valve cover using a new gasket and tighten the rocker cover bolts to 90 inch lbs. (10 Nm).

14. Install the alternator.

15. Install the serpentine belt.

16. Connect the power brake booster vacuum pipe to the plenum.

17. Install the EVAP solenoid and ignition assembly.

18. Connect the spark plug wires to the wire retainers on the plenum and the spark plugs.

19. Refill the cooling system.

20. Connect the negative battery cable.

21. Start the vehicle, top off the cooling system, then verify there are no leaks.

3.3L Engine

FRONT COVER

1. Disconnect the negative battery cable.

2. Remove the serpentine drive belt.

3. Remove the alternator brace bolt and brace.

4. Remove the engine torque strut at the radiator support, then the strut bracket bolts and nuts from the intake and exhaust manifolds.

5. Remove the engine lift bracket, then loosen the engine lift bracket brace bolt.

6. Remove the spark plug wire harness cover and disconnect the spark plug wires at the spark plugs.

7. Clean all the dirt from around the mating area of the valve cover.

8. Remove the valve cover nuts, washers, seals and valve cover.

9. Using a putty knife, clean the gasket mounting surfaces.

To install:

10. Install a new gasket to the cylinder head mating surface, then install the valve cover.

11. Apply thread locking compound to the bolt threads.

12. Insert the valve cover retainer bolts. Tighten the bolts to 89 inch lbs. (10 Nm).

13. Connect the spark plug wires to the plugs and cover.

14. Install the engine lift bracket brace bolt, then the bracket.

15. Secure the engine strut mount bracket bolts and nuts to the intake and exhaust manifolds.

16. Attach the engine torque strut at the radiator support, tighten the bolt to 18 ft. lbs. (24 Nm).

17. Position the alternator, then install the mounting bolts and support brace.

18. Install the serpentine drive belt.

19. Install the negative battery cable, start engine and check for leaks.

REAR COVER

1. Disconnect the negative battery cable.

2. Remove the serpentine drive belt.

3. Loosen the power steering pump bolts and slide the pump forward. Remove the pump braces.

4. Remove the power steering pump from the belt tensioner (move it aside) and the belt tensioner assembly.

5. Clean all the dirt from around the mating area of the valve cover.

6. Remove the valve cover nuts, the washers, the seals, the valve cover and the gasket.

7. Using a putty knife, clean the gasket mounting surfaces.

To install:

8. To install, use a new gasket and reverse the removal procedures. Tighten the valve cover nuts to 7 ft. lbs. (10 Nm.).

9. Reinstall the power steering pump and install the serpentine drive belt.

10. Install the negative battery cable, start engine and check for leaks.

Rocker Arms and Pushrods

REMOVAL & INSTALLATION

➡When removing the valve train components, they should be kept in the order they were removed.

2.2L Engine

1. Disconnect the negative battery cable.

2. Remove the air cleaner and air duct assembly.

3. Tag and disconnect the spark plug wires from the spark plugs, then disconnect the plug wire clips from the valve cover and position aside.

4. Disconnect the throttle cables from the throttle body, then remove the cable bracket from the intake plenum and move aside.

5. Remove the valve cover bolts, then remove the cover.

6. Remove the rocker arm nuts, balls and rocker arms.

To install:

7. Clean the gasket surfaces thoroughly.

8. Coat the bearing surfaces of the rocker arms and the arm balls with Molykote® or it's equivalent.

9. Seat the pushrods in the lifters.

10. Install the rocker arms, balls and nuts in the same positions they were removed from. Tighten the nuts to 22 ft. lbs. (30 Nm).

11. Install a new gasket in the valve cover.

12. Install the valve cover on the cylinder head, then tighten the cover bolts to 89 inch lbs. (10 Nm).

13. Install the throttle cable bracket on the intake plenum, then connect the throttle control cables to the throttle body.

14. Attach the spark plug wire clips to the valve cover, then connect the plug wires to the spark plugs.

15. Install the air cleaner an air duct assembly.

16. Connect the negative battery cable.

17. Install fresh oil to the fill line on the dipstick, then start the engine to verify no leaks.

2.5L Engine

◗ **See Figure 24**

1. Remove the air cleaner assembly.

2. Tag and remove the spark plug wires from the plugs and the cover clips.

3. Disconnect and remove the EGR valve.

4. Remove the valve cover.

5. On fuel injected engines relieve pressure in the fuel system before disconnecting any fuel lines.

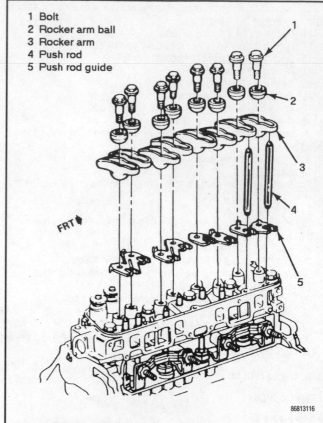

1 Bolt
2 Rocker arm ball
3 Rocker arm
4 Push rod
5 Push rod guide

FRT

86813116

Fig. 24 Rocker arm assembly on 2.5L engines

6. Loosen and remove the rocker arm bolt and balls.

7. Lift the rocker arm off the stud, keeping rocker arms in order for installation.

To install:

8. Position the rocker arms on the studs, then install the arm balls and bolts. Tighten the bolts to 20 ft. lbs. (27 Nm).

9. Attach the valve cover.

10. Install the EGR valve.

11. Attach the plug wire clip to the cover, then attach all the plug wires in there proper locations.

12. Install the air cleaner assembly.

2.8L Engine

◗ **See Figures 25 and 26**

1. Relieve the fuel system pressure.

2. Disconnect the negative battery cable at the battery.

3. Clean all the dirt from around the mating area of the valve cover.

4. Remove the valve cover.

5. Remove the rocker arm nuts, balls and rocker arms, then pull the pushrods from their seats.

To install:

6. Clean the mating surfaces of the cylinder head and intake manifold with degreaser.

7. Coat the bearing surfaces of the rocker arms and the arm balls with Molykote® or it's equivalent.

8. Seat the pushrods in the lifters.

9. Install the rocker arms, balls and nuts in the same positions they were removed from. Tighten the nuts to 22 ft. lbs. (30 Nm). Be sure to adjust valve lash after replacing rocker arms.

10. Install the valve covers.

11. Connect the negative battery cable, start the engine, check for leaks.

3.0L and 3.8L Engines

1. Remove the valve cover(s).

2. Remove the rocker arm shaft(s).

Fig. 25 After the nut and ball is removed, lift the rocker arm off the stud

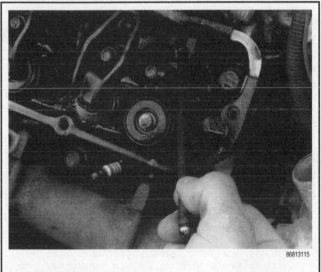

Fig. 26 If necessary, the pushrod can now be removed as well

3. Place the shaft on a clean surface.
4. Remove the nylon rocker arm retainers.
5. Slide the rocker arms off the shaft and inspect them for wear or damage. Keep them in order!

To install:

6. To install, reverse the removal steps. If new rocker arms are being installed, note that they are stamped R (right) or L (left), meaning that they be used on the right or left of each cylinder, NOT right and left cylinder banks. Each rocker arm must be centered over its oil hole. New nylon retainers must be used.

3.1L Engine (VIN T)

1. Release fuel pressure and disconnect the negative battery cable.
2. Remove the valve covers.
3. Remove the rocker arm nuts.
4. Remove rocker are pivot ball and arms. Keep the parts in order.
5. Remove the pushrods.

➡ **Keep all components separated. The pushrods are not the same length. Intake pushrods are 6 in. (152mm) long and marked orange, while the exhaust pushrods are 6 ⅜ in. (162mm) long and marked blue.**

To install:

6. Install the pushrods taking care they are in the proper locations.

7. Make sure the pushrods are seated in the lifters.
8. Install the rocker arms, pivots and nuts. They should be coated with pre-lube (GM 1052365 or equivalent).
9. Tighten the rocker arm nuts to 18 ft. lbs. (25 Nm).
10. Install the valve covers. Install the battery cable.

3.1L Engine (VIN M)

▶ **See Figure 27**

LEFT SIDE ROCKER ARMS (FRONT)

1. Disconnect the negative battery cable.
2. Remove the valve cover.
3. Remove the rocker arm nuts, balls, rocker arms and pushrods. Keep them in order.

To install:

4. Clean all the gasket surfaces completely.
5. Coat all the valve train components with engine oil prior to installation.
6. Install the pushrods and install the rocker arms on the studs. Install the rocker arm balls and mounting nuts. Make sure the pushrods are properly seated in the lifter and rocker arm. Tighten the mounting nuts to 18 ft. lbs. (24 Nm).
7. Install the valve cover.
8. Connect the negative battery cable.
9. Start the vehicle and verify no leaks.

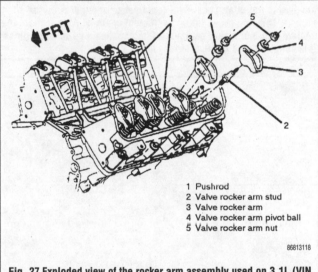

1 Pushrod
2 Valve rocker arm stud
3 Valve rocker arm
4 Valve rocker arm pivot ball
5 Valve rocker arm nut

Fig. 27 Exploded view of the rocker arm assembly used on 3.1L (VIN M) engines

RIGHT SIDE ROCKER ARMS (REAR)

1. Disconnect the negative battery cable.
2. Remove the valve cover.
3. Remove the rocker arm nuts, balls, rocker arms and pushrods.

To install:

4. Clean all the gasket surfaces completely.
5. Coat all the valve train components with engine oil prior to installation.
6. Install the pushrods and install the rocker arms on the studs. Install the rocker arm balls and mounting nuts. Make sure the pushrods are properly seated in the lifter and rocker arm. Tighten the mounting nuts to 18 ft. lbs. (25 Nm).
7. Install the rocker arm cover using a new gasket and tighten the rocker cover bolts to 90 inch lbs. (10 Nm).
8. Connect the negative battery cable.
9. Start the vehicle and verify no leaks.

3.3L Engine

1. Release fuel pressure and disconnect the negative battery cable.
2. Remove the valve covers.
3. Remove the rocker arm pedestal bolts.
4. Remove rocker arm and pedestal assembly.

➡Keep all components in order, if old parts are to be reinstalled they must be installed in the same locations.

5. Remove the pushrods.

To install:

6. Install the pushrods taking care they are in the proper locations.
7. Make sure the pushrods are seated in the lifters.
8. Install the rocker arm assembly. Coat threads with lock compound (GM 12345493 or equivalent).
9. Tighten the rocker arm bolts to 28 ft. lbs. (38 Nm).
10. Install the valve covers. Install the battery cable.

Thermostat

REMOVAL & INSTALLATION

♦ **See Figures 28, 29, 30 and 31**

1. Disconnect the negative battery cable.
2. Drain the cooling system.

✳✳ CAUTION

When draining the coolant, keep in mind that cats and dogs are attracted by ethylene glycol antifreeze, and are quite likely to drink any that is left in an uncovered container or in puddles on the ground. This will prove fatal in sufficient quantity. Always drain the coolant into a sealable container. Coolant should be reused unless it is contaminated or several years old.

Fig. 28 Loosen the clamp securing the hose to the thermostat housing

3. Some models require you to remove the air cleaner assembly from the throttle body.
4. Some models with cruise control have a vacuum modulator attached to the thermostat housing with a bracket. It your vehicle is equipped as such, remove the bracket from the housing.
5. On the 4-cylinder engines, unbolt the water outlet from the thermostat housing, remove the outlet from the housing and lift the thermostat out of the housing. On all other models, unbolt the water outlet from the intake manifold, remove the outlet and lift the thermostat out of the manifold.

To install:

6. Clean both of the mating surfaces and run a ⅛ in. (3mm) bead of R.T.V. (Room Temperature Vulcanizing) sealer in the groove of the water outlet.
7. Install the thermostat (spring towards engine) and bolt the water outlet into place while the R.T.V. sealer is still wet. Tighten the bolts 17–21 ft. lbs. (23–28 Nm) on all but the 2.2L engine. Other engines tighten to 89 inch lbs. (10 Nm).
8. The remainder of the installation is the reverse of removal. Fill the cooling system, start the engine and top off. Check for leaks after the car is started and correct as required.

Intake Manifold

REMOVAL & INSTALLATION

✳✳ CAUTION

When draining the coolant, keep in mind that cats and dogs are attracted by ethylene glycol antifreeze, and are quite likely to drink any that is left in an uncovered container or in puddles on the ground. This will prove fatal in sufficient quantity. Always drain the coolant into a sealable container. Coolant should be reused unless it is contaminated or several years old.

2.2L Engine

♦ **See Figure 32**

UPPER INTAKE

1. Disconnect the throttle body from the air cleaner air inlet duct.
2. Remove the accelerator control cable bracket at the manifold and valve cover.
3. Remove the brake vacuum booster hose from the manifold.
4. Disconnect the MAP sensor connection and, then remove the sensor.
5. Disconnect the vacuum harness at the throttle body.
6. Remove the electrical connections at the throttle body and intake manifold.
7. Remove the intake manifold bolts and studs.
8. Remove the manifold and gasket.

To install:

9. Install the manifold and gasket.
10. Install the bolts and studs, tighten to 22 ft. lbs. (30 Nm).

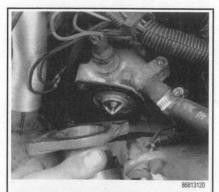

Fig. 29 Remove the bolts securing the housing, then pull it away

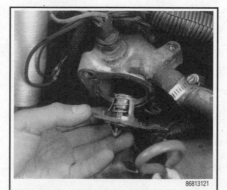

Fig. 30 Make a note as to which end of the thermostat fits in the housing

Fig. 31 Make sure both of the mating surfaces are free of any old gasket material

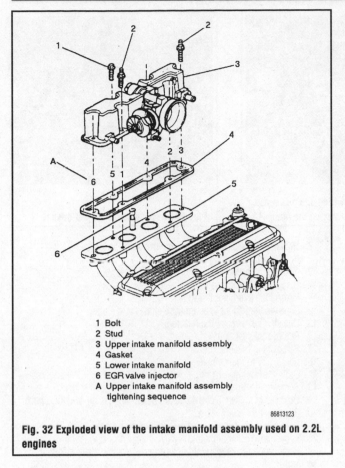

1 Bolt
2 Stud
3 Upper intake manifold assembly
4 Gasket
5 Lower intake manifold
6 EGR valve injector
A Upper intake manifold assembly
   tightening sequence

86813123

Fig. 32 Exploded view of the intake manifold assembly used on 2.2L engines

11. Attach the electrical connections to the throttle body and intake manifold.
12. Reinstall the vacuum harness to the throttle body.
13. Install the MAP sensor and connection.
14. Install the brake booster hose to the manifold.
15. Attach the accelerator cable bracket to the manifold and valve cover. Tighten the bolts to 18 ft. lbs. (25 Nm).
16. Install the throttle body to the air cleaner.

LOWER INTAKE

1. Disconnect the negative battery cable.
2. Drain the cooling system.
3. Remove the air cleaner and duct assembly.
4. Rotate the engine forwards.
5. Disconnect the throttle control cable bracket.
6. Remove the electrical connections from the:
- Throttle body
- Fuel injector
- Wiring harness clip from under the manifold
7. Remove the vacuum hoses from:
- Intake manifold
- Plenum
- EGR valve
8. Remove the power steering pump bracket from the intake manifold brace.
9. Tag and remove the spark plug wires.
10. Relieve the fuel system pressure. This is extremely important.
11. Disconnect the fuel lines, set aside.
12. Remove the transaxle fluid level indicator tube retaining nut, position aside.
13. Remove the nuts and manifold with the plenum attached, then clean all the gasket surfaces on the cylinder head and intake manifold.
To install:
14. Install a new gasket and intake manifold with the plenum attached, then install and tighten the retaining nuts to 24 ft. lbs. (33 Nm).
15. Install the transaxle fluid level indicator tube retaining nut.

16. Attach the fuel lines.
17. Connect the spark plug wires in their proper locations.
18. Attach the power steering pump bracket to the intake manifold brace.
19. Install the vacuum hoses from:
- Intake manifold
- Plenum
- EGR valve
20. Attach the electrical connections to the:
- Throttle body
- Fuel injector
- Wiring harness clip from under the manifold
21. Attach the throttle body cable bracket, then connect the cables to the throttle body.
22. Rotate the engine to it's proper position.
23. Assemble the air cleaner and air duct to the engine.
24. Refill the engine coolant.
25. Connect the negative battery cable, then start the engine, top off the coolant.

2.5L Engine

▶ See Figure 33

1. Relieve the fuel system pressure.
2. Remove the air cleaner and the PCV valve.
3. Drain the cooling system into a clean container.
4. Disconnect the fuel and vacuum lines and the electrical connections at the carburetor/throttle body and manifold.
5. Disconnect the throttle linkage at the EFI unit and disconnect the transaxle downshift linkage and cruise control linkage.
6. Remove the carburetor and the spacer.
7. Remove the bell crank and the throttle linkage. Position to the side for clearance.
8. Remove the heater hose at the intake manifold.
9. Remove the pulse air check valve bracket from the manifold.
10. Remove the manifold attaching bolt and remove the manifold.
11. To install, reverse the removal procedure.

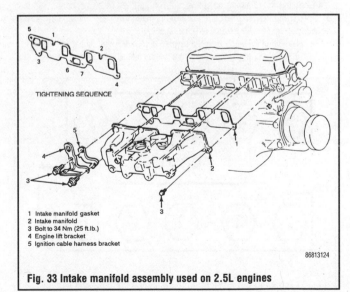

1 Intake manifold gasket
2 Intake manifold
3 Bolt to 34 Nm (25 ft.lb.)
4 Engine lift bracket
5 Ignition cable harness bracket

TIGHTENING SEQUENCE

86813124

Fig. 33 Intake manifold assembly used on 2.5L engines

2.8L Engine

CARBURETED ENGINE

▶ See Figures 34, 35, 36 and 37

1. Remove the rocker covers.
2. Drain the cooling system.
3. If equipped, remove the AIR pump and bracket.
4. Remove the distributor cap. Mark the position of the ignition rotor in relation to the distributor body, and remove the distributor. Do not crank the engine with the distributor removed.

Fig. 34 Use a deep socket to loosen the manifold retainers

Fig. 35 Make sure all wiring and hoses are disconnected before removing the manifold

Fig. 36 Always discard the old gasket

5. Remove the heater and radiator hoses from the intake manifold.
6. Remove the power brake vacuum hose.
7. Disconnect and label the vacuum hoses. Remove the EFE pipe from the rear of the manifold.
8. Remove the carburetor linkage. Disconnect and plug the fuel line.
9. Remove the manifold retaining bolts/nuts.
10. Remove the intake manifold. Remove and discard the gaskets, and scrape off the old silicone seal from the front and rear ridges.

To install:

11. The gaskets are marked for right and left side installation; do not interchange them. Clean the sealing surface of the engine block, and apply a 3/16 in. (5mm) bead of silicone sealer to each ridge.
12. Install the new gaskets onto the heads. The gaskets will have to be cut slightly to fit past the center pushrods. Do not cut any more material than necessary. Hold the gaskets in place by extending the ridge bead of sealer 1/4 in. (6mm) onto the gasket ends.
13. Install the intake manifold. The area between the ridges and the manifold should be completely sealed.
14. Install the retaining bolts and nuts, and tighten in sequence to 23 ft. lbs. (31 Nm). Do not overtighten; the manifold is made from aluminum, and can be warped or cracked with excessive force.
15. The rest of installation is the reverse of removal. Adjust the ignition timing after installation, and check the coolant level after the engine has warmed up.

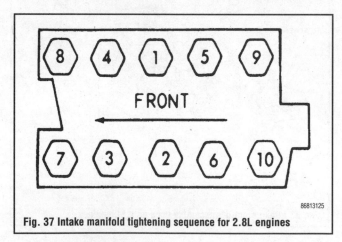

Fig. 37 Intake manifold tightening sequence for 2.8L engines

FUEL INJECTED ENGINE

▶ See Figure 37

1. Relieve the pressure in the fuel system before disconnecting any fuel line connections.
2. Disconnect the negative battery cable.
3. Remove the accelerator and TV cable bracket at the intake plenum.
4. Unsecure the throttle body at the intake plenum.
5. Disconnect the EGR valve at the intake plenum.
6. Remove the intake plenum.

7. Unfasten the fuel inlet and return pipes at the fuel rail.
8. Remove the serpentine belt.
9. Remove the power steering pump and lay it aside.
10. Disconnect the alternator and lay it aside.
11. Loosen the alternator bracket.
12. Separate the idle air vacuum hose at the throttle body.
13. Unfasten the wires at the injectors.
14. Remove the fuel rail.
15. Remove the breather tube.
16. Remove both rocker covers.
17. Drain the cooling system.
18. Separate the radiator hose at the thermostat housing.
19. Disconnect the wires at the coolant sensor and the oil sending switch.
20. Remove the coolant sensor.
21. Disconnect the bypass hose at the fill neck and head.
22. Loosen the rocker arms and remove the pushrods.
23. Remove the intake manifold bolts and remove the intake manifold.

To install:

24. Place a 3/16 in. (5mm) diameter bead of GM sealer 1052917 or equivalent, on each ridge.
25. Position a new intake manifold gasket.
26. Install the pushrods and tighten the rocker arm nuts to 14–20 ft. lbs. (19–27 Nm).
27. Install the intake manifold and tighten the bolts in sequence.
28. Connect the bypass hose to the filler neck and head.
29. Install the coolant sensor.
30. Attach the wires to the coolant sensor and the oil sending switch.
31. Connect the radiator hose to the thermostat housing.
32. Install both rocker covers.
33. Install the breather tube.
34. Connect the fuel rail.
35. Connect the wires to the injectors.
36. Connect the idle air vacuum hose to the throttle body.
37. Tighten the alternator bracket.
38. Attach the alternator electrical connectors.
39. Install the power steering pump.
40. Install the serpentine belt.
41. Connect the fuel inlet and return pipes to the fuel rail.
42. Install the intake plenum.
43. Attach the EGR valve to the intake plenum.
44. Connect the throttle body to the intake plenum.
45. Connect the accelerator and TV cable bracket to the intake plenum.
46. Connect the negative battery cable.
47. Fill cooling system and check for leaks. Start the engine and allow to come to normal operating temperature. Check for leaks and top off the coolant.
48. Adjust the valves, as required.

3.0L Engine

▶ See Figure 38

1. Relieve the fuel system pressure.
2. Disconnect the battery ground.
3. Drain the cooling system.

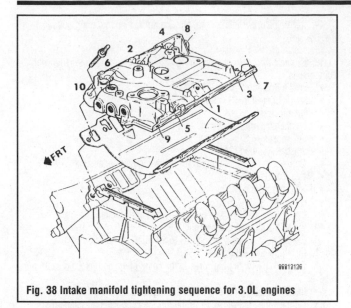

Fig. 38 Intake manifold tightening sequence for 3.0L engines

4. Remove the air cleaner.
5. Disconnect all hoses and wiring from the manifold.
6. Disconnect the accelerator linkage and cruise control chain.

➡**If equipped with an MFI system, remove any component which will interfere with the intake manifold removal.**

7. Disconnect the fuel line.
8. Remove the distributor cap and rotor to remove the Torx® head bolt from the left side of the manifold.
9. Unbolt and remove the manifold.

To install:

10. Place a new intake manifold gasket and rubber manifold seals in position at the front and rear rails of the cylinder block. Make sure the pointed end of the seal fits snugly against the block and head.
11. Before installing the intake seals, apply silicone sealer to each ends of the seals.
12. Install the one piece manifold gasket, then carefully set the intake on the engine block.
13. Insert the head to manifold bolts. A new gasket and seals must be used when a manifold is removed.
14. When installing the manifold, start with number 1 and 2 bolts, then gradually tighten both bolts until snug. Continue with the rest of the bolts in sequence, tighten to 41 ft. lbs. (55 Nm).
15. Reverse the removal for installation.
16. Connect the negative battery cable.
17. Close the drain plug and fill the radiator. Start the engine, top off the coolant.

3.1L Engine (VIN T)

▶ **See Figure 39**

1. Relieve the pressure in the fuel system before disconnecting any fuel line connections.
2. Disconnect the negative battery cable.
3. Separate the accelerator and TV cable bracket at the intake plenum.
4. Disconnect the throttle body at the intake plenum.
5. Remove the EGR valve at the intake plenum.
6. Remove the intake plenum.
7. Detach the fuel inlet and return pipes at the fuel rail.
8. Remove the serpentine belt.
9. Remove the power steering pump and lay it aside.
10. Disconnect the alternator and lay it aside.
11. Loosen the alternator bracket.
12. Unsecure the idle air vacuum hose at the throttle body.
13. Disconnect the wires at the injectors.
14. Separate the fuel rail from the vehicle.
15. Remove the breather tube.

16. Remove both rocker covers.
17. Drain the cooling system.
18. Separate the radiator hose from the thermostat housing.
19. Disconnect the wires at the coolant sensor and the oil sending switch.
20. Remove the coolant sensor.
21. Disconnect the bypass hose at the fill neck and head.
22. Loosen the rocker arms and remove the pushrods.
23. Remove the intake manifold bolts and remove the intake manifold.

To install:

24. Place a ³⁄₁₆ in. (5mm) diameter bead of GM sealer 1052917 or equivalent, on each ridge.
25. Position a new intake manifold gasket.
26. Install the pushrods and tighten the rocker arm nuts to 14–20 ft. lbs. (19–27 Nm).
27. Install the intake manifold and tighten the bolts to specifications.
28. Attach the bypass hose to the filler neck and head.
29. Install the coolant sensor.
30. Connect the wires to the coolant sensor and the oil sending switch.
31. Secure the radiator hose to the thermostat housing.
32. Install both rocker covers.
33. Install the breather tube.
34. Connect the fuel rail.
35. Connect the wires to the injectors.
36. Connect the idle air vacuum hose to the throttle body.
37. Tighten the alternator bracket.
38. Connect the alternator electrical connectors.
39. Install the power steering pump.
40. Install the serpentine belt.
41. Connect the fuel inlet and return pipes to the fuel rail.
42. Install the intake plenum.
43. Connect the EGR valve to the intake plenum.
44. Connect the throttle body to the intake plenum.
45. Connect the accelerator and TV cable bracket to the intake plenum.
46. Connect the negative battery cable.
47. Fill cooling system and check for leaks. Start the engine and allow to come to normal operating temperature. Recheck for leaks, then top-up the coolant.
48. Adjust the valves, as required.

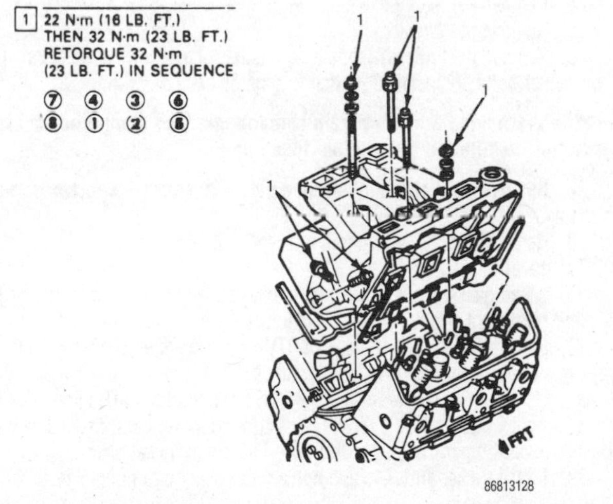

Fig. 39 Tightening sequence for 3.1L engines

3.1L Engine (VIN M)

▶ **See Figure 39**

⁂ **CAUTION**

The fuel system is under pressure and must be properly relieved before disconnecting the fuel lines. Failure to properly relieve the fuel system pressure can lead to personal injury and component damage.

1. Relieve the fuel system pressure.
2. Disconnect the negative battery cable.
3. Remove top half of the air cleaner assembly and throttle body duct.
4. Drain the cooling system.
5. Remove the EGR pipe from exhaust manifold.
6. Remove the serpentine belt.
7. Remove the brake vacuum pipe at the intake plenum.
8. Disconnect the control cables from the throttle body and intake plenum mounting bracket.
9. Remove the power steering lines at the alternator bracket.
10. Remove the alternator.
11. Disconnect the spark plug wires from the spark plugs and wire retainers on the intake plenum.
12. Remove the ignition assembly and the EVAP canister purge solenoid together.
13. Disconnect the upper engine wiring harness connectors at the following components:
   - Throttle Position Sensor (TPS)
   - Idle Air Control (IAC) valve
   - Fuel Injectors
   - Coolant temperature sensor
   - MAP sensor
   - Camshaft Position (CMP) sensor
14. Disconnect the vacuum lines from the following components:
   - Vacuum modulator
   - Fuel pressure regulator
   - PCV valve
15. Remove the MAP sensor from upper intake manifold.
16. Remove the upper intake plenum mounting bolts and remove the plenum.
17. Disconnect the fuel lines from the fuel rail and fuel line bracket.
18. Install engine support fixture special tool J 28467-A or an equivalent.
19. Remove the right side engine mount.
20. Remove the power steering mounting bolts and support the pump out of the way without disconnecting the power steering lines.
21. Disconnect the coolant inlet pipe from coolant outlet housing.
22. Remove the coolant bypass hose from the water pump and the cylinder head.
23. Disconnect the upper radiator hose at thermostat housing.
24. Remove the thermostat housing.
25. Remove both rocker arm covers.
26. Remove the lower intake manifold bolts. Make sure the washers on the four center bolts are installed in their original locations.

➡ **When removing the valve train components they should be kept in order for installation the original locations.**

27. Remove the rocker arm retaining nuts and remove the rocker arms and pushrods.
28. Remove the intake manifold from the engine.
To install:
29. Clean gasket material from all mating surfaces. Remove all excess RTV sealant from front and rear ridges of cylinder block.
30. Place a 0.1 in. (3mm) bead of RTV, on each ridge, where the front and rear of the intake manifold contact the block.
31. Using a new gasket, install the intake manifold to the engine.
32. Install the pushrods, rocker arms and mounting nuts. Make sure the pushrods are properly seated in the valve lifters and rocker arms.
33. Install rocker arm nuts and tighten the rocker arm nuts to 18 ft. lbs. (24 Nm).
34. Install lower the intake manifold attaching bolts. Apply sealant GM part no. 12345739 or equivalent to the threads of bolts, and tighten bolts to 115 inch lbs. (13 Nm).
35. Install the front rocker arm cover.
36. Install the thermostat housing.
37. Connect the upper radiator hose to the thermostat housing.
38. Install the coolant inlet pipe to thermostat housing.
39. Install coolant bypass pipe at the water pump and cylinder head.
40. Install the power steering pump in the mounting bracket.
41. Connect the right side engine mount.
42. Remove the special engine support tool.
43. Connect the fuel lines to fuel rail and bracket.

44. Install the upper intake manifold and tighten the mounting bolts to 18 ft. lbs. (25 Nm).
45. Install the MAP sensor.
46. Connect the upper engine wiring harness connectors to the following components:
   - Throttle Position Sensor (TPS)
   - Idle Air Control (IAC) valve
   - Fuel Injectors
   - Coolant temperature sensor
   - MAP sensor
   - Camshaft Position (CMP) sensor
47. Connect the vacuum lines to the following components:
   - Vacuum modulator
   - Fuel pressure regulator
   - PCV valve
48. Install the EVAP canister purge solenoid and ignition assembly.
49. Install the alternator assembly.
50. Connect the power steering line to the alternator bracket.
51. Install the serpentine belt.
52. Connect the spark plug wires to the spark plugs and intake plenum wire retainer.
53. Install the EGR pipe to the exhaust manifold.
54. Connect the control cables to the throttle body lever and upper intake plenum mounting bracket.
55. Install air intake assembly and top half of the air cleaner assembly.
56. Install the brake vacuum pipe.
57. Fill the cooling system.
58. Connect the negative battery cable.
59. Start the vehicle and verify no leaks exist.

3.3L Engine

▶ **See Figure 40**

1. Relieve the pressure in the fuel system before disconnecting any fuel line connections.
2. Disconnect the negative battery cable.
3. Drain the cooling system.
4. Remove the serpentine belt, alternator and braces and power steering pump braces.
5. Remove the coolant bypass hose, heater pipe and upper radiator hose.
6. Remove the air inlet duct, throttle cable bracket and cables.
7. Disconnect and tag all vacuum hoses and electrical connectors, as necessary.
8. Remove the fuel rail, vapor canister purge line and heater hose from the throttle body.
9. Remove the intake manifold retaining bolts and intake manifold.

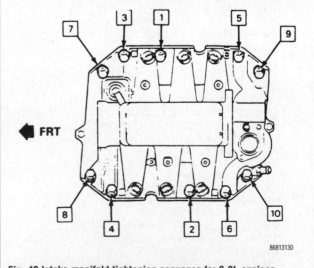

Fig. 40 Intake manifold tightening sequence for 3.3L engines

To install:

10. Clean the cylinder head and intake manifold surfaces from any foreign matter, nicks or heavy scratches.

11. Apply sealer GM part no. 12345336 or equivalent, to the ends of the manifold seals. Clean the intake manifold bolts and bolt holes. Apply thread lock compound GM part no. 1052624 or equivalent, to the intake manifold bolt threads before assembly.

12. Install the new gasket and intake manifold. Tighten the intake manifold bolts twice to 88 inch lbs. (10 Nm) in the proper sequence.

13. Install the fuel rail, vapor canister purge line and heater hose from the throttle body.

14. Connect all vacuum hoses and electrical connectors.

15. Install the air inlet duct, throttle cable bracket and cables.

16. Install the coolant bypass hose, heater pipe and upper radiator hose.

17. Install the serpentine belt, alternator and braces and power steering pump braces.

18. Connect the negative battery cable.

19. Fill cooling system and check for leaks. Start the engine and allow to come to normal operating temperature. Recheck for leaks.

3.8L Engine

♦ See Figure 41

1. Relieve the pressure in the fuel system before disconnecting any fuel line connections.

2. Disconnect the negative battery cable.

3. Remove the mass air flow sensor and air intake duct.

4. Remove the serpentine accessory drive belt, alternator and bracket.

5. Remove the ignition coil module, TV cable, throttle cable and cruise control cable.

6. Disconnect and tag all vacuum hoses and electrical wiring, as necessary.

7. Drain the cooling system. Remove the heater hoses from the throttle body and upper radiator hose.

8. Disconnect the fuel lines from the fuel rail and injectors.

9. Remove the intake manifold retaining bolts and remove the intake manifold and gasket.

To install:

10. Clean the cylinder head and intake manifold surfaces from any foreign matter, nicks or heavy scratches.

11. Install the intake manifold gasket and rubber seals. Apply sealer GM part no. 1050026 or equivalent, on the gasket. Apply sealer/lubricant GM part no. 1052080 or equivalent, to all pipe thread fitting.

12. Carefully install the intake manifold to cylinder block. Install the intake manifold bolts and tighten in sequence to the specified value.

13. Connect the fuel lines to the fuel rail and injectors.

14. Install the heater hoses to the throttle body and upper radiator hose.

15. Connect all vacuum hoses and electrical wiring.

16. Install the ignition coil module, TV cable, throttle cable and cruise control cable.

17. Install the bracket, alternator and serpentine belt.

18. Install the mass air flow sensor and air intake duct.

19. Connect the negative battery cable.

20. Fill cooling system and check for leaks. Start the engine and allow to come to normal operating temperature. Recheck for leaks.

Exhaust Manifold

REMOVAL & INSTALLATION

2.2L Engine

♦ See Figure 42

1. Disconnect the negative battery cable.

2. Remove the air cleaner and air inlet duct.

3. Remove the lower air inlet duct.

4. Remove the engine drive belt, then remove the alternator.

5. Unsecure the engine torque strut bracket from the cylinder head.

6. Loosen and remove the alternator bracket.

7. Raise and support the vehicle safely.

8. Remove the two bolts securing the exhaust pipe to the exhaust manifold.

9. Lower the vehicle.

10. Remove the dipstick tube mounting bolt, then the dipstick tube and stick.

11. Disconnect the electrical harness to the Oxygen sensor (O_2) sensor.

12. Unsecure the manifold mounting bolts/nuts, then remove the manifold.

To install:

13. Clean all the gasket surfaces completely.

14. Install the exhaust manifold, then tighten the mounting bolts to 116 inch lbs. (13 Nm).

15. Connect the O_2 sensor harness to the sensor.

16. Attach the dipstick tube with it's mounting bolt.

17. Raise and support the vehicle.

18. Connect the front exhaust pipe to the exhaust manifold, then tighten the mounting bolts to 18 ft. lbs. (25 Nm).

19. Lower the vehicle.

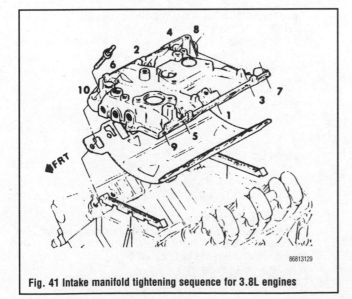

86813129

Fig. 41 Intake manifold tightening sequence for 3.8L engines

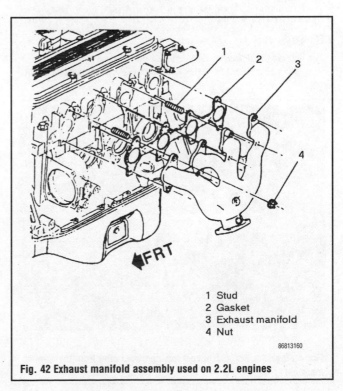

1 Stud
2 Gasket
3 Exhaust manifold
4 Nut

86813160

Fig. 42 Exhaust manifold assembly used on 2.2L engines

20. Install the alternator rear support bracket, then tighten the three mounting bolts to 74 ft. lbs. (100 Nm).

21. Install the engine torque strut bracket to the engine, then tighten the nuts to 41 ft. lbs. (56 Nm) and the bolt to 40 ft. lbs. (55 Nm).

22. Attach the torque strut, then tighten the bolts to 40 ft. lbs. (55 Nm).

23. Attach the alternator to the engine.

24. Install the drive belt.

25. Attach the lower air intake duct, then the air intake resonator to the upper tie bar.

26. Install the air cleaner and duct work.

27. Connect the negative battery cable.

28. Start the vehicle, then check for leaks.

2.5L Engine

1. Disconnect the negative battery cable. Remove the air cleaner and the preheat tube.

2. Remove the manifold strut bolts from the radiator support panel and the cylinder head.

3. Remove the air conditioning compressor bracket to one side. Do not disconnect any of the refrigerant lines.

4. If necessary, remove the dipstick tube attaching bolt and the engine mount bracket from the cylinder head.

5. Raise the vehicle and support safely. Disconnect the exhaust pipe from the manifold.

6. Remove the manifold attaching bolts, then remove the manifold and gasket.

To install:

7. Clean all the gasket surfaces completely.

8. Install the exhaust manifold and gasket to the cylinder head. Tighten all bolts in sequence to the specified value. The outside bolts to 28 ft. lbs. (38 Nm), and the inside bolts to 37 ft. lbs. (50 Nm).

9. Connect the exhaust pipe to the manifold. Lower the vehicle.

10. Install the dipstick tube attaching bolt and the engine mount bracket to the cylinder head.

11. Install the air conditioning compressor bracket.

12. Install the manifold strut bolts to the radiator support panel and the cylinder head.

13. Install the air cleaner and the preheat tube.

14. Connect the negative battery cable.

2.8L Engine

▶ See Figures 43 and 44

LEFT SIDE

1. Remove the air cleaner. Remove the exhaust crossover pipe.

2. Remove the air supply plumbing from the exhaust manifold, if equipped.

Fig. 43 If necessary, disconnect the crossover pipe from the exhaust manifold

Fig. 44 Once the retaining bolts are removed, the exhaust manifold can be removed from the engine

3. Raise and support the car. Unbolt and remove the exhaust pipe at the manifold.

4. Unbolt and remove the manifold and gasket.

To install:

5. Clean the mating surfaces of the cylinder head and manifold. Install the manifold and gasket to the head, then install the retaining bolts finger-tight.

6. Tighten the manifold bolts in a circular pattern, working from the center to the ends, to 25 ft. lbs. (34 Nm) in two stages.

7. Connect the exhaust pipe to the manifold.

8. The remainder of installation is the reverse of removal.

RIGHT SIDE

1. Disconnect the negative battery cable.

2. Raise and safely support the vehicle.

3. Disconnect the exhaust pipe and lower the vehicle.

4. Remove the air cleaner assembly, breather, mass air flow sensor and heat shield.

5. Remove the crossover at the manifold.

6. Remove the accelerator and TV cables and brackets, as required.

7. Remove the exhaust manifold retaining bolts, then remove the manifold and gasket.

To install:

8. Clean all the gasket surfaces completely.

9. Install the exhaust manifold and gasket with the retaining bolts. Tighten to 15–22 ft. lbs. (20–30 Nm).

10. If removed, install the accelerator, TV cables and brackets.

11. Install the crossover at the manifold.

12. Install the air cleaner assembly, breather, mass air flow sensor and heat shield.

13. Raise and safely support the vehicle.

14. Connect the exhaust pipe and lower the vehicle.

15. Connect the negative battery cable.

3.0L Engine

LEFT SIDE

1. Disconnect the battery ground.

2. Unbolt and remove the crossover pipe.

3. Remove the upper engine support strut.

4. Unbolt and remove the manifold and gasket.

To install:

5. Clean all the gasket surfaces completely.

6. Install the exhaust manifold, making sure the new gasket is in place.

7. Tighten the mounting bolts for the manifold to 25 ft. lbs. (34 Nm).

8. Attach the upper engine support to the vehicle.

9. Install the engine crossover pipe.

10. Connect the negative battery cable.

RIGHT SIDE

1. Disconnect the negative battery cable.
2. Remove the intermediate shaft pinch bolt and separate the intermediate shaft from the stub shaft.

> ✳✳ **CAUTION**
>
> **Failure to disconnect the intermediate shaft from the rack and pinion stub shaft can result in damage to the steering gear and/or the intermediate shaft. This damage can cause loss of steering control.**

3. Raise the support the vehicle on jackstands.
4. Remove the exhaust pipe-to-manifold bolts, then lower the vehicle.
5. Place a jack under the front crossmember of the cradle, then raise the jack until it starts to raise the vehicle and remove the two front body mount bolts.
6. With the cushions removed, thread the body mount bolts and retainers at least three turns into the cage nuts, then slowly release the jack.
7. Remove the power steering pump and bracket, then move it aside.
8. Disconnect the oxygen sensor connector.
9. Remove the crossover pipe-to-manifold nuts and the exhaust manifold bolts.
10. Remove the manifold and gasket.
11. To install, reverse the removal procedures.
12. Clean all the gasket surfaces completely.

3.1L Engine (VIN T)

LEFT SIDE

1. Disconnect the negative battery cable.
2. Loosen and remove the air supply plumbing from the exhaust manifold, as required.
3. Remove the coolant recovery bottle, if necessary.
4. Remove the serpentine belt cover and belt, as required.
5. Remove the air conditioning compressor and lay aside, if necessary.
6. Remove the right side torque strut, air conditioning and torque strut mounting bracket, as required.
7. Disconnect the heat shield, if equipped.
8. Separate the exhaust crossover pipe at the manifold.
9. Remove the exhaust manifold retaining bolts, then the manifold and gasket.

To install:

10. Clean all the gasket surfaces completely.
11. Attach the exhaust manifold and gasket to the vehicle with the retaining bolts. Tighten to 15–20 ft. lbs. (20–30 Nm).
12. Attach the exhaust crossover pipe at the manifold, then tighten the mounting nuts to 18 ft. lbs. (25 Nm).
13. Install the heat shield, if equipped.
14. If removed, install the right side torque strut, air conditioning and torque strut mounting bracket.
15. If removed, install the air conditioning compressor.
16. If removed, install the serpentine belt and cover.
17. If removed, attach the coolant recovery bottle.
18. Install the air supply plumbing to the exhaust manifold.
19. Connect the negative battery cable.

RIGHT SIDE

1. Disconnect the negative battery cable.
2. Raise and safely support the vehicle.
3. Disconnect the exhaust pipe and lower the vehicle.
4. Remove the air cleaner assembly, breather, mass air flow sensor and heat shield.
5. Remove the crossover at the manifold.
6. Remove the accelerator and TV cables and brackets, as required.
7. Remove the exhaust manifold retaining bolts, then remove the manifold and gasket.

To install:

8. Clean all the gasket surfaces completely.
9. Install the exhaust manifold, gasket and retaining bolts. Tighten to 15–20 ft. lbs. (20–30 Nm).

10. If removed, install the accelerator, TV cables and brackets.
11. Install the crossover at the manifold.
12. Install the air cleaner assembly, breather, mass air flow sensor and heat shield.
13. Raise and safely support the vehicle.
14. Connect the exhaust pipe and lower the vehicle.
15. Connect the negative battery cable.

3.1L Engine (VIN M)

FRONT

1. Disconnect the negative battery cable.
2. Remove the top half of the air cleaner assembly and throttle cable duct.
3. Partially drain the cooling system.
4. Separate the radiator hose from the thermostat housing.
5. Remove the coolant bypass hose at the coolant pump and from the exhaust manifold.
6. Loosen and remove the exhaust crossover heat shield.
7. Remove the exhaust crossover pipe from the manifold.
8. Tag and disconnect the secondary ignition wires from the spark plugs.
9. Remove the exhaust manifold heat shield.
10. Unsecure the exhaust manifold retaining nuts.
11. Remove the exhaust manifold and gasket.

To install:

12. Clean mating surfaces at the cylinder head and manifold.
13. Install the exhaust manifold gasket and the exhaust manifold. Tighten the manifold mounting nuts to 12 ft. lbs. (16 Nm).
14. Attach the exhaust manifold heat shield.
15. Install the exhaust crossover pipe to the manifold.
16. Attach the exhaust crossover pipe heat shield.
17. Connect the secondary ignition wires to the appropriate spark plug.
18. Connect the coolant bypass pipe to the coolant pump and exhaust manifold.
19. Secure the radiator hose to the coolant outlet housing.
20. Install the top half of the air cleaner and the throttle body duct.
21. Connect the negative battery cable.

REAR

1. Disconnect the negative battery cable.
2. Remove the top half of the air cleaner assembly and throttle cable duct.
3. Remove the exhaust crossover heat shield.
4. Separate the exhaust crossover pipe from the manifold.
5. Remove the oxygen sensor.
6. Separate the EGR pipe from the exhaust manifold.
7. Raise and safely support the vehicle.
8. Remove the transaxle oil fill tube and lever indicator assembly.
9. Disassemble the front exhaust pipe from the exhaust manifold.
10. Disconnect the exhaust pipe from the converter flange and support the converter.
11. Remove the converter heat shield from the body.
12. Loosen and remove the exhaust manifold heat shield.
13. Unsecure the exhaust manifold nuts.
14. Remove the exhaust manifold from the bottom of vehicle and the gasket.

To install:

15. Clean mating surfaces at the cylinder head and manifold.
16. Install the exhaust manifold gasket.
17. Install the exhaust manifold loosely and install heat shield at this time.
18. Install the manifold nuts, then tighten to 12 ft. lbs. (16 Nm).
19. Install the exhaust manifold heat shield nuts.
20. Install the converter heat shield to the body.
21. Connect the exhaust pipe to the converter flange.
22. Connect the exhaust pipe to the exhaust manifold.
23. Install the transaxle oil level indicator and fill tube assembly.
24. Safely lower the vehicle.
25. Connect the oxygen sensor.
26. Connect the EGR pipe to exhaust manifold.
27. Install top half of the air cleaner assembly and throttle body duct.
28. Connect the negative battery cable.

3.3L Engine

LEFT SIDE

1. Disconnect the negative battery cable.
2. Remove the air cleaner inlet ducting. Install the spark plug wires.
3. Loosen and remove the 2 bolts attaching the exhaust crossover pipe to the manifold.
4. Remove the engine lift hook, manifold heat shield and oil level indicator.
5. Remove the exhaust manifold retaining bolts and remove the manifold.

To install:

6. Clean all the gasket surfaces completely.
7. Install the exhaust manifold and retaining bolts, then tighten to 30 ft. lbs. (41 Nm).
8. Install the engine lift hook, manifold heat shield and oil level indicator.
9. Secure the 2 bolts attaching the exhaust crossover pipe to the manifold.
10. Install the air cleaner inlet ducting. Install the spark plug wires.
11. Connect the negative battery cable.

RIGHT SIDE

1. Disconnect the negative battery cable.
2. Remove the spark plug wires, oxygen sensor connector, throttle cable bracket and cables.
3. Remove the brake booster hose from the manifold.
4. Unsecure the 2 bolts attaching the exhaust crossover pipe to the manifold.
5. Remove the exhaust pipe-to-manifold bolts, engine lift hook and transaxle oil level indicator tube.
6. Remove the manifold heat shield. Remove the exhaust manifold retaining bolts and remove the manifold.

To install:

7. Clean all the gasket surfaces completely.
8. Install the exhaust manifold and retaining bolts, then tighten to 30 ft. lbs. (41 Nm). Install the manifold heat shield.
9. Install the exhaust pipe-to-manifold bolts, engine lift hook and transaxle oil level indicator tube.
10. Secure the 2 bolts attaching the exhaust crossover pipe to the manifold.
11. Attach the brake booster hose to the manifold.
12. Install the spark plug wires, oxygen sensor connector, throttle cable bracket and cables.
13. Connect the negative battery cable.

3.8L Engine

1. Disconnect the negative battery cable.

✳✳ WARNING

Failure to disconnect the intermediate shaft from the rack and pinion stub shaft may result in damage to the steering gear and/or intermediate shaft.

2. Remove the pinch bolt from the intermediate shaft and separate the intermediate shaft from the stub shaft.
3. Raise and safely support the vehicle.
4. Remove the 2 bolts attaching the exhaust pipe to the manifold.
5. Lower the vehicle.
6. Remove the upper engine support strut.
7. Place a jack under the front crossmember of the cradle and raise the jack until it starts to raise the vehicle.
8. Remove the 2 front body mount bolts.
9. With the cushions removed, thread the body mount bolts and retainers a minimum of 3 turns into the cage nuts.
10. Release the jack slowly.

➡**To avoid damage, do not lower the cradle without it being restrained.**

11. Remove the power steering pump and bracket from the cylinder head and exhaust manifold.
12. Disconnect the oxygen sensor.
13. If removing the left side exhaust manifold, remove the upper engine support strut.
14. Remove the 2 nuts retaining the crossover pipe to the exhaust manifold.

15. Remove the 6 bolts attaching the manifold to the cylinder head.
16. Remove the exhaust manifold.

To install:

17. Carefully, clean the gasket sealing surfaces of old gasket material.
18. Install the exhaust manifold and the manifold-to-cylinder head bolts, then tighten to 37 ft. lbs. (50 Nm).
19. If the left side exhaust manifold was removed, install the crossover pipe to the manifold.
20. If the right side exhaust manifold was removed, install the upper engine support strut.
21. Connect the oxygen sensor wire.
22. Install the power steering pump and bracket.
23. Support the cradle with the jack. Remove the 2 body mount bolts and install the cushions.
24. Raise the cradle into position and install the 2 body mount bolts.
25. Remove the jack.
26. Connect the intermediate shaft to the stub shaft and install the pinch bolt.
27. Raise and safely support the vehicle.
28. Install the exhaust pipe-to-manifold bolts.
29. Lower the vehicle.
30. Connect the negative battery cable.

Radiator

REMOVAL & INSTALLATION

▶ **See Figures 45, 46, 47, 48 and 49**

1. Disconnect the negative battery cable. On some vehicles you will need to remove the air cleaner assembly.
2. Drain the cooling system.

✳✳ CAUTION

When draining the coolant, keep in mind that cats and dogs are attracted by ethylene glycol antifreeze, and are quite likely to drink any that is left in an uncovered container or in puddles on the ground. This will prove fatal in sufficient quantity. Always drain the coolant into a sealable container. Coolant should be reused unless it is contaminated or several years old.

3. Unplug the fan electrical connector.
4. Remove the attaching bolts for the fan, then remove the fan assembly.
5. Remove the forward strut brace for the engine at the radiator. Loosen the bolt to prevent shearing the rubber bushing, then swing the strut rearward.
6. On 2.5L engine, remove the resonator mounting and resonator. Disconnect the headlamp wiring harness from the fan frame.
7. Some vehicles will require you to scribe the hood latch location on the radiator support, then remove the latch.
8. Disconnect the coolant hoses from the radiator. Keep rags handy for this step. Remove the coolant recovery tank hose from the radiator neck. Disconnect and plug the automatic transmission fluid cooler lines from the radiator, if so equipped.
9. Remove the upper mounting panel mounting bolts and the panel.
10. Remove the radiator attaching bolts and remove the radiator. If the car has air conditioning, if first may be necessary to raise the left side of the radiator so that the radiator neck will clear the compressor.

To install:

➡**If a new radiator is going to be installed, check that all the fittings and brackets from the old radiator are removed, you'll need them on the new one.**

11. Install the radiator in the car, tightening the mounting bolts to 7 inch lbs. (0.8 Nm). Connect the transmission cooler lines and hoses. Install the coolant recovery hose.
12. Secure the upper and lower radiator hoses.
13. Install the hood latch. Tighten to 6 ft. lbs. (8 Nm).
14. Install the fan, making sure the bottom leg of the frame fits into the rubber grommet at the lower support. Tighten the fan bolts to 80 inch lbs. (10 Nm).

Fig. 45 Remove the bolts securing the engine strut . . .

Fig. 46 . . . then lift and position it aside

Fig. 47 On automatic transaxles, disconnect the cooler lines from the radiator

Fig. 48 Remove the bolts securing the upper mounting panel

Fig. 49 After the attaching bolts are removed, the radiator can be pulled from the engine compartment

Fig. 50 Remove the attaching bolts for the fan . . .

15. Install the fan wires and the headlamp wiring harness. Swing the strut and brace forward, tightening the bolt to 11–18 ft. lbs. (15–24 Nm) and the nut to 39 ft. lbs. (53 Nm).
16. Connect the negative battery cable.
17. Fill the cooling system with clean coolant.
18. Start the vehicle, top off the coolant.
19. Pressure test the system to verify no leaks.

Electric Cooling Fan

REMOVAL & INSTALLATION

▶ **See Figures 50 and 51**

1. Disconnect the negative battery cable.
2. Drain the cooling system.
3. Remove the cooling fan mounting bolt.
4. Disconnect the electrical connector from the fan.
5. Remove the radiator inlet hose from the radiator.
6. Remove the radiator mounting bolt.
7. On some models you may need to pull the windshield washer fluid bottle fill tube from the bottle.
8. Remove the vacuum tank, then the bracket if needed.
9. Remove the cooling fan by sliding fan leg into area left from the vacuum tank.
   To install:
10. Install the cooling fan assembly.
11. Install the vacuum tank bracket.
12. Secure the vacuum tank.
13. Attach the windshield washer fluid bottle fill tube, if removed.
14. Install the radiator mounting bolt.
15. Connect the radiator inlet hose to the radiator.
16. Connect the electrical connector to cooling fan.
17. Install the cooling fan mounting bolt.

Fig. 51 . . . then remove the fan assembly

18. Install the air intake duct assembly.
19. Connect the negative battery cable.

Auxiliary Engine Cooling Fan

REMOVAL & INSTALLATION

➡ **Only the 3.1L (VIN M) engine uses the auxiliary fan.**

1. Remove the grille assembly from the vehicle.
2. Disconnect the electrical harness from the cooling fan.

3. Unbolt the front end upper support.
4. Remove the bolts from the top of the fan.
5. Raise and support the vehicle safely.
6. Unbolt the front end lower bolts.
7. Remove the bolts from the bottom of the fan.
8. Remove the fan.
To install:
9. Attach the fan to the vehicle, then tighten the bolt at the bottom of the fan to 80 inch lbs.
10. Attach the front end lower support bolts, then lower the vehicle.
11. Attach the remaining bolts to the fan, tighten them to 80 inch lbs. (9 Nm).
12. Attach the bolts for the front end upper support.
13. Install the electrical harness for the fan.
14. Install the grille to the front of the vehicle.

Water Pump

REMOVAL & INSTALLATION

✳ CAUTION

When draining the coolant, keep in mind that cats and dogs are attracted by ethylene glycol antifreeze, and are quite likely to drink any that is left in an uncovered container or in puddles on the ground. This will prove fatal in sufficient quantity. Always drain the coolant into a sealable container. Coolant should be reused unless it is contaminated or several years old.

2.2L Engine

▶ See Figure 52

1. Partially drain the engine coolant from the vehicle.
2. Remove the serpentine drive belt from the vehicle.
3. Loosen and position the alternator to one side.
4. Unbolt the water pump pulley, then remove the pulley.
5. Unbolt the water pump, then remove the pump and gasket.
6. Clean the gasket areas thoroughly.
To install:
7. Install a new gasket to the water pump mating surface.
8. Attach the water pump to the engine with the retaining bolts, tighten them to 18 ft. lbs. (25 Nm).
9. Attach the water pump pulley, then tighten the bolts to 22 ft. lbs. (30 Nm).
10. Properly position the alternator.

11. Install the serpentine drive belt.
12. Fill the coolant system, start the engine, then top off the fluid.

2.5L Engine

1. Disconnect the negative battery cable.
2. Drain the cooling system.
3. Remove the serpentine belt. Removal of the alternator and/or bracket may help give more room for easier access.
4. Remove water pump attaching bolts and nut, then remove pump.
To install:
5. Clean the sealing surfaces, then place a ³⁄₃₂ in. (2mm) bead of RTV sealant or equivalent on the water pump sealing surface.
6. Coat the bolt threads with a pipe sealant GM part no. 1052080 or equivalent.
7. Install the water pump, then tighten the bolts to 10–24 ft. lbs. (14–33 Nm).
8. Connect the negative battery cable.
9. Fill the cooling system, then check for leaks. Start the engine and allow to come to normal operating temperature. Recheck for leaks, then top off the coolant.

2.8L Engine

▶ See Figure 53

1. Disconnect battery negative cable.
2. Drain cooling system and remove heater hose.
3. Remove the pump pulley.
4. When replacing the water pump, the timing cover must be clamped to the cylinder block prior to removing the water pump bolts. Use special tool J29176 or its equivalent.
5. Remove water pump attaching bolts and nut and remove pump.
To install:
6. With the sealant surfaces cleaned, place a ³⁄₃₂ in. (2mm) bead of sealant GM part no. 1052357 or equivalent on the water pump sealing surface.
7. Coat bolt threads with pipe sealant GM part no. 1052080 or equivalent.
8. Install the new water pump, then tighten the bolts to 10–18 ft. lbs. (14–24 Nm).
9. Attach the pulley to the water pump, tighten the bolts to 15 ft. lbs. (21 Nm).
10. Connect the negative battery cable.

3.0L Engine

1. Disconnect the negative battery cable, then drain the coolant.
2. Remove accessory drive belts. Remove the radiator and heater hoses from the water pump.
3. Remove the water pump attaching bolts.

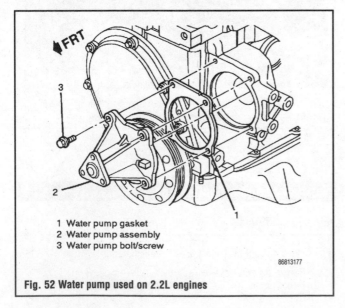

1 Water pump gasket
2 Water pump assembly
3 Water pump bolt/screw

86813177

Fig. 52 Water pump used on 2.2L engines

86813175

Fig. 53 After the water pump attaching bolts are removed, the pump can be pulled from its housing

4. Remove the engine support strut.

5. Place a floor jack under the front crossmember of the cradle and raise the jack until the jack just starts to raise the car.

6. Disconnect the front two body mount bolts with the lower cushions and retainers.

7. Remove the cushions from the bolts.

8. Thread the body mount bolts with retainers a minimum of three (3) turns into the cage nuts so that the bolts restrain cradle movement.

9. Release the floor jack slowly until the crossmember contacts the body mount bolts retainers. As the jack is being lowered watch and correct any interference with hoses, lines, pipes and cables.

➡**Do not lower the cradle without its being restrained as possible damage can occur to the body and underhood items.**

10. Remove water pump from engine.

To install:

11. To install, reverse the removal procedure. Tighten the water pump bolts to 25 ft. lbs. (34 Nm).

12. Connect negative battery cable.

13. Fill with coolant, start the engine. Top off the coolant system and check for leaks.

3.1L Engine (VIN T)

1. Disconnect the negative battery cable.
2. Drain cooling system in to a drain pan.
3. Remove the serpentine belt.
4. Remove the heater hose and radiator hose.
5. Remove the water pump cover attaching bolts and remove the cover.
6. Remove the water pump attaching bolts and remove the water pump.

To install:

7. Position the water pump on the engine and install the attaching bolts. Tighten bolts to 89 inch lbs. (10 Nm).

8. Install the water pump cover and attaching bolts.
9. Install the heater hose and radiator hose.
10. Install the serpentine belt.
11. Connect the negative battery cable.
12. Fill cooling system and check for leaks. Start the engine and allow to come to normal operating temperature. Recheck for leaks.

3.1L Engine (VIN M)

1. Partially drain the coolant from the vehicle.
2. Remove the serpentine drive belt from the vehicle.
3. Unbolt the pulley from the pump.
4. Remove the water pump mounting bolts.
5. Remove the pump from the engine, then clean the gasket area.

To install:

6. Attach the water pump with gasket to the engine with the mounting bolts.

7. Tighten the mounting bolts to 89 inch lbs. (10 Nm).

8. Attach the pulley with it's mounting bolts. Tighten them to 18 ft. lbs. (25 Nm).

9. Install the serpentine drive belt.
10. Fill the coolant system, start the engine and top off the fluid. Check for leaks.

3.3L Engine

1. Disconnect the negative battery cable.
2. Drain the cooling system.
3. Remove the serpentine drive belt.
4. Disconnect the coolant hose at the water pump.
5. Unsecure the water pump pulley bolts. The long bolt should be removed through the access hole provided in the body side rail. Remove the pulley.
6. Remove the water pump attaching bolts, then remove the water pump.

To install:

7. Install the water pump with the attaching bolts. Tighten the bolts to 22 ft. lbs. (30 Nm).

8. Install the pulley. Install the water pump pulley bolts. The long bolt should be installed through the access hole provided in the body side rail.

9. Install the coolant hose at the water pump.

10. Install the serpentine drive belt.
11. Connect the negative battery cable.
12. Fill cooling system and check for leaks. Start the engine and allow to come to normal operating temperature. Recheck for leaks.

3.8L Engine

1. Disconnect the negative battery cable.
2. Drain the cooling system.
3. Remove the serpentine drive belt.
4. Disconnect the radiator and heater hoses at the water pump.
5. Remove the water pump pulley bolts, the long bolt is removed through the access hole provided in the body side rail. Remove the pulley.
6. Remove the water pump attaching bolts, then remove the water pump.

To install:

7. Clean all gasket mating surfaces.
8. Using a new gasket, install the water pump to the engine.
9. Install the water pump pulley.
10. Connect the radiator and heater hoses to the water pump.
11. Install the serpentine drive belt.
12. Connect the negative battery cable.
13. Fill cooling system and check for leaks. Start the engine and allow to come to normal operating temperature. Check for leaks and top-off the coolant.

Cylinder Head

REMOVAL & INSTALLATION

❄ CAUTION

When draining the coolant, keep in mind that cats and dogs are attracted by ethylene glycol antifreeze, and are quite likely to drink any that is left in an uncovered container or in puddles on the ground. This will prove fatal in sufficient quantity. Always drain the coolant into a sealable container. Coolant should be reused unless it is contaminated or several years old.

2.2L Engine

▶ **See Figure 54**

1. Relieve the fuel system pressure.
2. Disconnect the negative battery cable.
3. Drain the cooling system into a suitable container.
4. Separate the air cleaner and air duct assembly from the vehicle.
5. Remove the lower air inlet.
6. Remove the serpentine drive belt.
7. Unsecure the alternator, and remove from the vehicle.
8. Remove the power steering pump, then position it aside without disconnecting the power steering lines.
9. Disconnect the spark plug wires, lay them aside.
10. Detach the control cables from the throttle body, then remove the cable bracket at the throttle body and valve cover.

➡**When removing the valve train components, they must be kept in order for installation, in the same locations as they were removed from.**

11. Remove the valve cover, rocker arm nuts, rocker arms and pushrods.
12. Disconnect the electrical harness from the intake manifold, throttle body and cylinder head.
13. Remove the O_2 sensor connection.
14. Unsecure the power steering pump bracket from the intake brace, located under the manifold.
15. Remove the torque strut and the engine side torque strut mounting bracket.
16. Unfasten the alternator rear bracket.
17. Tag and disconnect the vacuum lines at the intake manifold and cylinder head.
18. Disconnect the upper radiator hose from the engine.
19. Raise and safely support the vehicle.

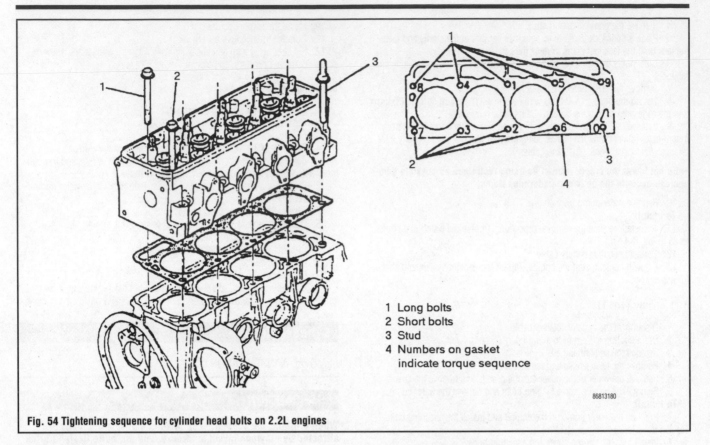

1 Long bolts
2 Short bolts
3 Stud
4 Numbers on gasket
  indicate torque sequence

86813180

Fig. 54 Tightening sequence for cylinder head bolts on 2.2L engines

20. Disconnect the exhaust pipe from the exhaust manifold.
21. Lower the vehicle.
22. Disconnect and cap the fuel lines at the quick disconnects.
23. Remove the transaxle fill tube.
24. Remove the cylinder head bolts.
25. Remove the cylinder head with both manifolds, then remove the intake and exhaust manifolds from the cylinder head.

To install:

26. Clean all the gasket surfaces completely. Clean the threads on the cylinder head bolts and the block threads.
27. Install the intake and exhaust manifolds on the cylinder head.
28. Place a new cylinder head gasket in position over the dowel pins on the block. Carefully guide the cylinder head into position.
29. Install the head bolts finger-tight. The long bolts go in bolts positions 1, 4, 5, 8, and 9. The short bolts are in the positions 2, 3, 6 and 7. The stud is in position 10.
30. Tighten the bolts in sequence. The long bolts to 23 ft. lbs. (32 Nm) and the short bolts and stud to 22 ft. lbs. (29 Nm). Make a second pass tightening the long bolts to 46 ft. lbs. (58 Nm). Maker a final pass over all the bolts tightening each an additional 100°.
31. Install the transaxle fill tube.
32. Connect the fuel lines to the throttle body.
33. Raise and support the vehicle.
34. Connect the exhaust pipe to the exhaust manifold. Tighten the mounting bolts to 22 ft. lbs. (30 Nm).
35. Lower the vehicle.
36. Attach the upper radiator hose.
37. Install the vacuum lines to the intake manifold.
38. Attach the engine side torque strut bracket and torque strut to the engine.
39. Install the alternator rear bracket.
40. Install the power steering pump bracket to the intake manifold brace, located under the intake manifold.
41. Connect the electrical harness at the intake manifold, throttle body and cylinder head.
42. Attach the O$_2$sensor wiring harness.
43. Install the pushrods, rocker arms and rocker arm nuts, then tighten to 22 ft. lbs. (30 Nm).

44. Install the valve cover.
45. Connect the control cables to the throttle body, then install the cables brackets at the throttle body and valve cover.
46. Attach the spark plug wires to there proper locations.
47. Install the power steering pump in the mounting bracket.
48. Attach the alternator to the engine.
49. Install the serpentine drive belt.
50. Connect the lower air inlet duct.
51. Attach the air inlet resonator tie bar.
52. Install the air cleaner and duct assembly.
53. Refill the cooling system.
54. Connect the negative battery cable.
55. Start the vehicle, top off the coolant. Verify there are no leaks.

2.5L Engine

▶ See Figure 55

❈❈ CAUTION

On fuel injected engines, relieve the pressure in the fuel system before disconnecting any fuel line connections.

➡The engine should be not be warm, it is best to leave engine sit overnight to cool before removing the cylinder head.

1. Drain the cooling system into a clean container.
2. Remove the air cleaner, the negative battery cable, the oil dipstick tube, the ignition coil, the engine-to-upper strut rod bolt and the power steering pump bracket.
3. Remove the intake and exhaust manifolds as previously outlined.
4. Remove the alternator bracket bolts.
5. Remove the air conditioning compressor bracket bolts and position the compressor to one side. Do not disconnect any of the refrigerant lines.
6. Disconnect and tag all vacuum and electrical connections from the cylinder head.
7. Disconnect the upper radiator hose.
8. Disconnect the spark plug wires and remove the plugs.

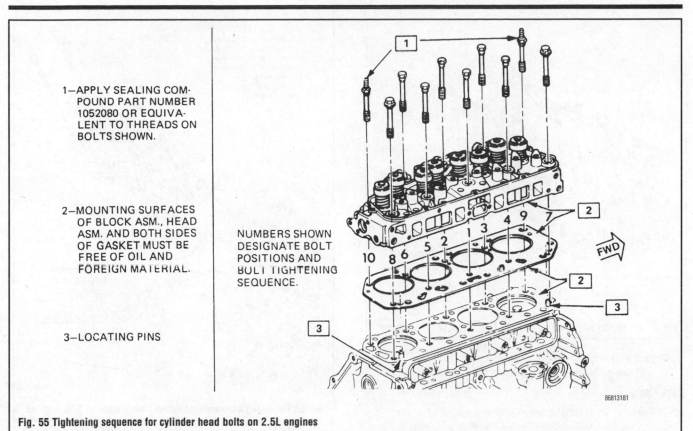

1—APPLY SEALING COMPOUND PART NUMBER 1052080 OR EQUIVALENT TO THREADS ON BOLTS SHOWN.

2—MOUNTING SURFACES OF BLOCK ASM., HEAD ASM. AND BOTH SIDES OF GASKET MUST BE FREE OF OIL AND FOREIGN MATERIAL.

NUMBERS SHOWN DESIGNATE BOLT POSITIONS AND BOLT TIGHTENING SEQUENCE.

3—LOCATING PINS

Fig. 55 Tightening sequence for cylinder head bolts on 2.5L engines

9. Remove the valve cover, rocker arms, and pushrods.
10. Unbolt and remove the cylinder head.
11. Clean the gasket surfaces thoroughly.
12. Install a new gasket over the dowels with the right side facing up.
13. Coat the head bolt threads with sealer and install finger-tight.
14. Tighten the bolts in sequence, in equal steps to the specified torque.
15. On vehicles from:
    a. 1982–84 final torque is 85 ft. lbs. (115 Nm).
    b. 1985–86 final torque is 92 ft. lbs. (125 Nm).
    c. 1987–92 first torque to 18 ft. lbs. (25 Nm), then repeat 26 ft. lbs. (35 Nm) excluding No. 9, which is 18 ft. lbs. (25 Nm).
16. Reverse the removal procedure to install.

2.8L Engine

▶ See Figures 56 and 57

LEFT SIDE

1. Disconnect the negative battery cable.
2. Raise and support the car.
3. Drain the coolant and lower the car.
4. Remove the valve covers.
5. Remove the intake manifold and plenum.
6. Remove the crossover pipe.
7. Remove the left exhaust manifold.
8. Remove the oil dipstick.
9. Remove the alternator and AIR pump brackets.
10. Remove the dipstick tube.
11. Loosen the rocker arm bolts and remove the pushrods. Keep the pushrods in the same order as removed.
12. Remove the cylinder head bolts in stages using the reverse order of the tightening sequence.
13. Remove the cylinder head. Do not pry on the head to loosen it.

To install:

14. Clean all mating surfaces on the cylinder head block and intake manifold.
15. Place the gasket into position over the dowel pins, with the correct side facing up, if marked.

16. Install the cylinder head.
17. Coat the head bolt threads with GM part no. 1052080 sealer or an equivalent.
18. Tighten the head bolts in proper sequence to 70 ft. lbs. (90 Nm) on 1982–86 models and 1987–89 models to 33 ft. lbs. (45 Nm).
19. Attach the intake manifold gasket.
20. Install the pushrods loosely retained with the rocker arms. Make sure the pushrods seat in the lifter.
21. Install the rocker arm nuts.
22. Attach the intake manifold and plenum.
23. Install the valve covers, then connect the oil level indicator tube bracket.
24. Install the crossover pipe and the left exhaust manifold.
25. Connect the engine strut bracket top the engine.
26. Fill the cooling system, connect the negative battery cable.

Fig. 56 Remove the cylinder head. Do not pry on the head to loosen it

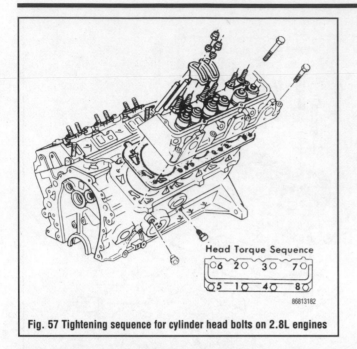

Fig. 57 Tightening sequence for cylinder head bolts on 2.8L engines

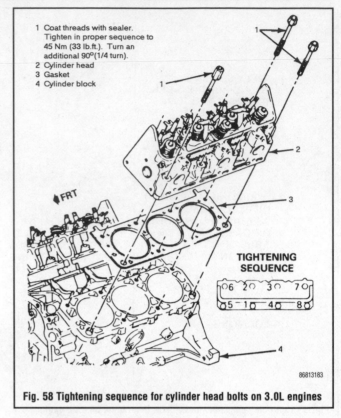

1 Coat threads with sealer.
  Tighten in proper sequence to
  45 Nm (33 lb.ft.). Turn an
  additional 90°(1/4 turn).
2 Cylinder head
3 Gasket
4 Cylinder block

Fig. 58 Tightening sequence for cylinder head bolts on 3.0L engines

27. Double check no connections have been missed.
28. Start the vehicle, top off the coolant, then check for leaks.

RIGHT SIDE

1. Raise the car and drain the coolant from the block.
2. Disconnect the exhaust pipe and lower the car.
3. If equipped, remove the cruise control servo bracket.
4. Remove the air management valve and hose.
5. Remove the intake manifold.
6. Remove the exhaust crossover.
7. Loosen the rocker arm nuts and remove the pushrods. Keep the pushrods in the order in which they were removed.
8. Remove the cylinder head bolts in stages using the reverse order of the tightening sequence.
9. Remove the cylinder head. Do not pry on the cylinder head to loosen it.

To install:

10. Clean all mating surfaces on the cylinder head block and intake manifold.
11. Place the gasket into position over the dowel pins, with the correct side facing up, if marked.
12. Install the cylinder head.
13. Coat the head bolt threads with GM part no. 1052080 sealer or an equivalent.
14. Tighten the head bolts in proper sequence to 70 ft. lbs. (90 Nm) on 1982–86 models and 1987–89 models to 33 ft. lbs. (45 Nm).
15. Attach the intake manifold gasket.
16. Install the pushrods loosely retained with the rocker arms. Make sure the pushrods seat in the lifter.
17. Install the rocker arm nuts.
18. Attach the intake manifold and plenum.
19. Install the valve covers, then connect the spark plug wires.
20. Install the crossover pipe and the right exhaust manifold. The crossover heat shield needs to be installed.
21. Raise and support the vehicle.
22. Install the exhaust at the crossover. Lower the vehicle.
23. Attach the cruise control servo bracket, if removed.
24. Fill the cooling system, connect the negative battery cable.
25. Double check no connections have not been missed.
26. Start the vehicle, top off the coolant, then check for leaks.

3.0L Engine

♦ See Figure 58

1. Disconnect negative battery cable.
2. Remove intake manifold.

3. Loosen and remove the belt(s).
4. When removing LEFT cylinder head;
   a. Remove oil dipstick.
   b. Remove air and vacuum pumps with mounting bracket if present, and move out of the way with hoses attached.
5. When removing RIGHT cylinder head:
   a. Remove alternator.
   b. Disconnect power steering gear pump and brackets attached to cylinder head.
6. Disconnect wires from spark plugs, and remove the spark plug wire clips from the valve cover studs.
7. Remove exhaust manifold bolts from head being removed.
8. Clean dirt off cylinder head and adjacent area to avoid getting dirt into engine. It is extremely important to avoid getting dirt into the hydraulic valve lifters.
9. Remove valve cover and rocker arm and shaft assembly from cylinder head. Lift out pushrods.
10. Loosen all cylinder head bolts, then remove bolts and lift off the cylinder head.
11. With cylinder head on bench, remove all spark plugs for cleaning and to avoid damaging them during work on the head.
12. Installation is the reverse of removal. Clean all gasket surfaces thoroughly. Always use a new head gasket. The head gasket is installed with the bead downward. Coat the head bolt threads with heavy-bodied thread sealer. Tighten the head bolts in equal stages. Recheck head bolt torque after the engine has been warmed to operating temperature.

3.1L Engine (VIN T)

♦ See Figure 59

LEFT SIDE

※※ CAUTION

Care should be taken when working around the fuel system. DO NOT smoke or expose the fuel system to any flames or sparks. The fuel system is under pressure and must be relieved prior to performing any service work on the system components. Failure to properly bleed the system can lead to personal injury or component damage.

Always keep a suitable fire extinguisher handy when servicing the fuel system.

1. Relieve the pressure in the fuel system before disconnecting any fuel line connections. Disconnect the fuel lines.
2. Disconnect the negative battery cable.
3. Remove the air cleaner assembly. Raise and safely support the vehicle.
4. Drain the cylinder block and lower the vehicle.
5. Remove the oil level indicator tube, valve cover, intake manifold and plenum, as required.
6. Remove the exhaust crossover, alternator bracket, AIR pump and brackets.
7. Disconnect and tag all electrical wiring and vacuum hoses that may interfere with the removal of the left cylinder head.
8. Loosen the rocker arm until the pushrods can be removed. Remove the pushrods. Keep the pushrods in the same order as removed.
9. Remove the cylinder head bolts. Remove the cylinder head. Do not pry on the head to loosen it.

To install:

10. Clean the cylinder head and block from any foreign matter, nicks or heavy scratches. Clean the cylinder head bolt threads and threads in the cylinder block.
11. Place the gasket into position over the dowel pins, with the correct side facing up, if marked.
12. Install the cylinder head bolts and tighten in sequence to 33 ft. lbs. (45 Nm). Turn an additional 90° in sequence.
13. Install the pushrods. Make sure the lower ends of the pushrods are in the lifter seats. Install the rocker arm nuts and tighten the nuts to 14–20 ft. lbs. (20–27 Nm).
14. Install the intake manifold.
15. Connect all electrical wiring and vacuum hoses.
16. Install the exhaust crossover, alternator and AIR pump brackets, alternator and AIR pump.
17. If removed, install the oil level indicator tube, valve cover, intake manifold and plenum.
18. Connect the fuel lines.
19. Connect the negative battery cable.
20. Adjust the valve lash, as required.
21. Install the air cleaner assembly.

RIGHT SIDE

1. Relieve the pressure in the fuel system before disconnecting any fuel line connections.
2. Disconnect the negative battery cable. Remove the air cleaner assembly. Raise the vehicle and support it safely.
3. Drain the cylinder block and lower the vehicle.
4. If equipped, remove the cruise control servo bracket, the air management valve and hose and the intake manifold.
5. Remove the exhaust pipe at crossover, crossover and heat shield, as required.
6. Disconnect and tag all electrical wiring and vacuum hoses that may interfere with the removal of the right cylinder head.
7. Remove the rocker cover. Loosen the rocker arm nuts and remove the pushrods. Keep the pushrods in the order in which they were removed.
8. Remove the cylinder head bolts. Remove the cylinder head. Do not pry on the head to loosen it.

To install:

9. Clean the cylinder head and block from any foreign matter, nicks or heavy scratches. Clean the cylinder head bolt threads and threads in the cylinder block.
10. Place the gasket into position over the dowel pins, with the correct side facing up, if marked.
11. Install the cylinder head bolts and tighten in sequence to 33 ft. lbs. (45 Nm). Turn an additional 90° in sequence.
12. Install the pushrods. Make sure the lower ends of the pushrods are in the lifter seats. Install the rocker arm nuts and tighten the nuts to 14–20 ft. lbs. (20–27 Nm).
13. Install the intake manifold.
14. Install the rocker cover.
15. Connect all electrical wiring and vacuum hoses.
16. If removed, install the crossover exhaust pipe and heat shield.
17. If equipped, install the cruise control servo bracket, the air management valve and hose.
18. Connect the negative battery cable.

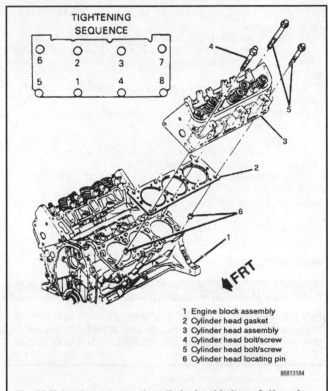

1 Engine block assembly
2 Cylinder head gasket
3 Cylinder head assembly
4 Cylinder head bolt/screw
5 Cylinder head bolt/screw
6 Cylinder head locating pin

86813184

Fig. 59 Tightening sequence for cylinder head bolts on 3.1L engines

19. Fill cooling system and check for leaks. Start the engine and allow to come to normal operating temperature. Recheck for leaks.
20. Adjust the valve lash, as required.
21. Install the air cleaner assembly.

3.1L Engine (VIN M)

LEFT SIDE (FRONT)

◗ **See Figure 59**

◗ See Figure 59

> **❖ CAUTION**

Fuel Injection systems remain under pressure, even after the engine has been turned OFF. The fuel system pressure must be relieved before disconnecting any fuel lines. Failure to do so may result in fire and/or personal injury.

1. Relieve the fuel system pressure.
2. Disconnect the negative battery cable.
3. Drain the cooling system.
4. Remove the top half of the air cleaner assembly and remove the throttle body air inlet duct.
5. Remove the exhaust crossover pipe heat shield and crossover pipe.
6. Disconnect the spark plug wires from spark plugs and wire looms and route the wires out of the way.
7. Remove the rocker arm covers.
8. Remove upper intake plenum and lower intake manifold.
9. Remove the left side exhaust manifold.
10. Remove oil level indicator tube.

➡ **When removing the valve train components they must be kept in order for installation in the same locations they were removed from.**

11. Remove rocker arms nut, rocker arms, balls and pushrods.
12. Remove the cylinder head bolts evenly.
13. Remove the cylinder head.

To install:

14. Clean all the gasket surfaces completely. Clean the threads on the cylinder head bolts and block threads.

15. Place the gasket into position over the dowel pins, with the correct side facing up, if marked.

16. Coat the bolt threads with sealer and install finger-tight.

17. Tighten the cylinder head bolts in sequence to 33 ft. lbs. (45 Nm). With all the bolts tightened make a second pass tightening all the bolts an additional 90°.

18. Install the pushrods, rocker arms, balls and rocker arm nuts. Tighten the rocker arm nuts to 18 ft. lbs. (25 Nm).

19. Install the lower intake manifold and upper intake plenum.

20. Install the rocker arm covers.

21. Install the oil level indicator tube.

22. Connect the spark plug wires to spark plugs and wire looms.

23. Install the left side exhaust manifold.

24. Install the exhaust crossover pipe and crossover pipe heat shield.

25. Refill the cooling system.

26. Install the top half of the air cleaner assembly and the throttle body air inlet duct.

27. Connect negative battery cable.

28. Start vehicle and verify no leaks.

RIGHT SIDE (REAR)

> ⁕⁕ **CAUTION**
>
> **Fuel Injection systems remain under pressure, even after the engine has been turned OFF. The fuel system pressure must be relieved before disconnecting any fuel lines. Failure to do so may result in fire and/or personal injury.**

1. Relieve the fuel system pressure.

2. Disconnect the negative battery cable.

3. Drain the cooling system.

4. Remove the top half of the air cleaner assembly and remove the throttle body air inlet duct.

5. Remove the exhaust crossover pipe heat shield and crossover pipe.

6. Raise and safely support the vehicle.

7. Disconnect the oxygen (O_2) sensor connector.

8. Disconnect the exhaust pipe from the exhaust manifold.

9. Remove the right side exhaust manifold.

10. Lower the vehicle.

11. Disconnect the spark plug wires from spark plugs and wire looms and route the wires out of the way.

12. Remove the rocker arm covers.

13. Remove upper intake plenum and lower intake manifold.

➡ When removing the valve train components they must be kept in order for installation in the same locations they were removed from.

14. Remove rocker arms nut, rocker arms, balls and pushrods.

15. Remove the cylinder head bolts evenly.

16. Remove the cylinder head.

To install:

17. Clean all the gasket surfaces completely. Clean the threads on the cylinder head bolts and block threads.

18. Place the gasket into position over the dowel pins, with the correct side facing up, if marked.

19. Coat the bolt threads with sealer and install finger-tight.

20. Tighten the cylinder head bolts in sequence to 33 ft. lbs. (45 Nm). With all the bolts tightened make a second pass tightening all the bolts an additional 90°.

21. Install the pushrods, rocker arms, balls and rocker arm nuts. Tighten the rocker arm nuts to 18 ft. lbs. (25 Nm).

22. Install the lower intake manifold and upper intake plenum.

23. Install the rocker arm covers.

24. Connect the spark plug wires to spark plugs and wire looms.

25. Raise vehicle and safely support.

26. Install the exhaust manifold.

27. Connect the exhaust pipe to the exhaust manifold.

28. Lower the vehicle.

29. Connect the oxygen (O_2) sensor connector.

30. Install the exhaust crossover pipe and heat shield.

31. Refill the cooling system.

32. Install the top half of the air cleaner assembly and the throttle body air inlet duct.

33. Connect negative battery cable.

34. Start vehicle and verify no leaks.

3.3L Engine

◆ See Figure 60

RIGHT SIDE

1. Relieve the pressure in the fuel system before disconnecting any fuel line connections.

2. Disconnect the negative battery cable. Raise the vehicle and support it safely.

3. Drain the cylinder block and lower the vehicle.

4. Remove the intake manifold.

5. Remove the exhaust crossover pipe.

6. Disconnect the heater pipe retaining nut, then slide the pipe from the front of the cover housing.

7. Unsecure the power steering pump bolts at the mounting bracket, then remove the ground wires.

8. Unsecure the engine lift bracket and coolant pipe.

9. Remove the exhaust manifold heat shield.

10. Unbolt the transaxle fill tube.

11. Remove the spark plug loom, wires and spark plugs.

12. Raise and support the vehicle.

13. Disconnect the exhaust pipe to the manifold.

14. Lower the vehicle.

15. Unbolt the exhaust manifold and the heat shield, then remove.

16. Remove the valve cover, then remove the rocker arm assemblies.

17. Disconnect and tag all electrical wiring and vacuum hoses, as necessary.

18. If equipped with air conditioning, remove the air conditioning compressor and position to the side.

19. Remove the cylinder head bolts, then remove the cylinder head.

To install:

20. Clean the cylinder head and block of any foreign matter, nicks or heavy scratches. Clean the cylinder head bolt threads and threads in the cylinder block.

21. Position the new cylinder head gasket on the block. Apply sealant GM part no. 1052080, to the under side of the bolt heads, and thread locker GM part no. 12345382, to the bolt threads.

22. Carefully guide the cylinder head into place.

23. Coat the cylinder head bolts with sealing compound and install into the head. Tighten the cylinder head bolts according to the following procedure:

  a. Tighten in sequence to 35 ft. lbs. (47 Nm).

  b. Using an appropriate torque angle gauge, rotate each bolt in sequence an additional 130°.

  c. Rotate the center 4 bolts an additional 30° in sequence.

24. Install the pushrods, guide plate and rocker arm assembly. Tighten the rocker arm pivot bolts to 28 ft. lbs. (38 Nm).

25. Install the exhaust manifold and heat shield, tighten the mounting bolts to 38 ft. lbs. (52 Nm).

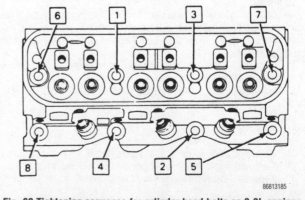

Fig. 60 Tightening sequence for cylinder head bolts on 3.3L engines

86813185

26. Raise and support the vehicle.
27. Attach the exhaust pipe to the manifold.
28. Lower the vehicle.
29. Install the spark plug, wires and looms to the engine.
30. Bolt the transaxle fill tube to the engine.
31. Attach the exhaust manifold heat shield.
32. Install the coolant pipe and the engine lift bracket.
33. Connect the ground wires, then install the power steering pump bolts to the mounting bracket.
34. Slide the heater pipe to the front of the cover housing, then install the pipe retaining nut.
35. Attach the exhaust crossover pipe.
36. Install the intake manifold.
37. Connect all electrical wiring and vacuum hoses.
38. If equipped with air conditioning, install the air conditioning compressor.
39. Connect the negative battery cable.
40. Fill cooling system and check for leaks. Start the engine and allow to come to normal operating temperature. Recheck for leaks.

LEFT SIDE

1. Relieve the pressure in the fuel system before disconnecting any fuel lines.
2. Disconnect the negative battery cable. Raise the vehicle and support it safely.
3. Drain the cylinder block and lower the vehicle.
4. Unbolt the intake manifold.
5. Remove the spark plug loom and wires.
6. Unsecure the engine lift bracket and coolant pipe.
7. Unbolt the valve cover.
8. Remove the spark plugs.
9. Unfasten the exhaust crossover pipe.
10. Remove the oil level indicator.
11. Remove the cooling fan assembly.
12. Disconnect the exhaust manifold heat shield.
13. Remove the exhaust manifold support bracket.
14. Unbolt the exhaust manifold.
15. Remove the rocker arm assemblies.
16. Disconnect the A/C bracket bolt from the cylinder head.
17. Disconnect the bolts holding the alternator and ignition coil mounting bracket, push aside.
18. Remove the vacuum line bolt at the cylinder head (rear).
19. Remove the cylinder head bolts, then remove the cylinder head.
To install:
20. Clean the cylinder head and block of any foreign matter, nicks or heavy scratches. Clean the cylinder head bolt threads and threads in the cylinder block.
21. Position the new cylinder head gasket on the block. Apply sealant GM part no. 1052080, to the under side of the bolt heads, and thread locker GM part no. 12345382, to the bolt threads.
22. Carefully guide the cylinder head into place.
23. Coat the cylinder head bolts with sealing compound and install into the head. Tighten the cylinder head bolts according to the following procedure:
  a. Tighten in sequence to 35 ft. lbs. (47 Nm).
  b. Using an appropriate torque angle gauge, rotate each bolt in sequence an additional 130°.
  c. Rotate the center 4 bolts an additional 30° in sequence.
24. Attach the vacuum line bolt at the cylinder head.
25. Connect the A/C bracket bolt from the head.
26. Install the pushrods, guide plate and rocker arm assembly. Tighten the rocker arm pivot bolts to 28 ft. lbs. (38 Nm).
27. Install the exhaust manifold, gasket and heat shield, tighten the mounting bolts to 38 ft. lbs. (52 Nm).
28. Attach the manifold support bracket and the heat shield, tighten the nuts fro the heat shield to 20 ft. lbs. (27 Nm).
29. Install the cooling fan assembly.
30. Attach the oil level indicator, tighten to 20 ft. lbs. (27 Nm).
31. Install the exhaust crossover.
32. Install the spark plugs.
33. Attach the intake manifold and gasket.

3.8L Engine

▶ **See Figure 61**

1. Relieve the pressure in the fuel system before disconnecting any fuel lines.
2. Disconnect the negative battery cable. Raise the vehicle and support it safely.
3. Drain the cylinder block and lower the vehicle.
4. Remove the serpentine belt.
5. Remove the alternator, AIR pump, oil indicator and power steering pump, as required. Position to the side.
6. Remove the throttle cable. Remove the cruise control cable, if equipped.
7. Disconnect the fuel lines and fuel rail, as required.
8. Loosen and remove the heater hoses and radiator hoses.
9. Disconnect and tag all vacuum and electrical wiring.
10. Remove the radiator and cooling fan, if necessary.
11. Remove the intake manifold and valve cover.
12. Disconnect the exhaust manifold(s).
13. Remove the rocker arm assembly and pushrods.
14. Unbolt the cylinder head, then remove the cylinder head and gasket.
To install:
15. Clean the cylinder head and block from any foreign matter, nicks or heavy scratches. Clean the cylinder head bolt threads and threads in the cylinder block.
16. Position the new cylinder head gasket on the block.
17. Carefully guide the cylinder head into place. Coat the cylinder head bolts with sealing compound and install.
18. Tighten the cylinder head bolts according to the following procedure:
  a. Tighten the cylinder head bolts in sequence to 25 ft. lbs. (34 Nm).
  b. Do not exceed 60 ft. lbs. (81 Nm) at any point during the next 2 steps.
  c. Using a torque angle gauge, tighten each bolt an additional 90° in sequence.
19. Install the exhaust manifold.
20. Install the intake manifold, pushrods and rocker arm assembly.
21. Install the valve cover.
22. Install the radiator and cooling fan, as required.
23. Connect all vacuum and electrical wiring.
24. Install the heater hoses and radiator hoses.

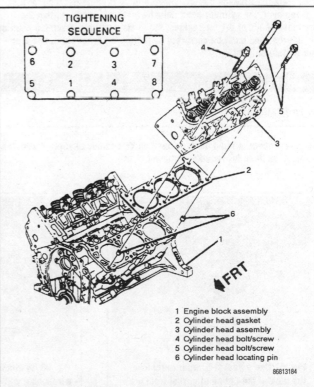

TIGHTENING SEQUENCE

1 Engine block assembly
2 Cylinder head gasket
3 Cylinder head assembly
4 Cylinder head bolt/screw
5 Cylinder head bolt/screw
6 Cylinder head locating pin

86813184

Fig. 61 Tightening sequence for cylinder head bolts on 3.8L engines

25. Connect the fuel lines and fuel rail.
26. Attach the throttle cable. Install the cruise control cable, if equipped.
27. Install the alternator, AIR pump, oil indicator and power steering pump.
28. Install the serpentine belt.
29. Connect the negative battery cable.
30. Fill cooling system and check for leaks. Start the engine and allow to come to normal operating temperature. Check for leaks and top off the coolant.

CLEANING & INSPECTION

▶ **See Figures 62 and 63**

Chip carbon away from the valve heads, combustion chambers, and ports, using a chisel made of hardwood. Remove the remaining deposits with a stiff wire brush.

> ※ **WARNING**
>
> **DO NOT use a steel wire brush to clean an aluminum cylinder head. Special brushes are sold just for use on aluminum. Always wear eye protection when grinding chipping or wire brushing.**

Be sure that the deposits are actually removed, rather than burnished. Have the cylinder head cleaned to remove grease, corrosion, and scale from the water passages. Clean the remaining cylinder head parts in an engine cleaning solvent. Do not remove the protective coating from the springs.

RESURFACING

▶ **See Figures 64 and 65**

➥**All machine work should be performed by a competent, professional machine shop.**

Place a straightedge across the gasket surface of the cylinder head. Using feeler gauges, determine the clearance at the center of the straightedge. If warpage is between 0.002 in. (0.05mm) to 0.010 in. (0.25mm) in a 6 in. (152mm) span, or 0.004 in. (0.1mm) to 0.010 in. (0.25mm) over all, resurface the cylinder head. If warpage exceeds 0.010 in. (0.25mm) in a 6 in. (152mm) span, the cylinder head must be replaced.

➥**If warpage exceeds the manufacturer's maximum tolerance for material removal, the cylinder head must be replaced. When milling the cylinder heads of V-type engines, the intake manifold mounting position is altered, and must be corrected by milling the manifold flange a proportionate amount.**

Valves and Springs

ADJUSTMENT

➥**This procedure must be performed on V6 engines anytime the rocker arms have been loosened or removed.**

1. Remove the valve cover and the No. 1 spark plug.
2. Rotate the engine until the **0** mark on the crankshaft pulley aligns with the timing tab and the No. 1 cylinder is on the TDC of the compression stroke.
3. With the engine in this position, adjust the exhaust valves of No. 1, 2 and 3 and the intake valves of No. 1, 5 and 6. Back out the adjusting nut until lash is felt at the pushrod, then turn the nut to remove the lash. With the lash removed, turn the nut an additional 1½ turns.
4. Rotate the engine 1 complete revolution until the **0** mark on the crankshaft pulley aligns with the timing tab and the No. 4 piston is on the TDC of the compression stroke.
5. With the engine in this position, adjust the exhaust valves of No. 2, 3 and 4; adjust the valves the same way as in Step No. 3.
6. Install the valve covers and the spark plugs.

REMOVAL & INSTALLATION

▶ **See Figures 66 and 67**

1. Remove the cylinder head(s) from the vehicle as previously outlined.
2. Using a suitable valve spring compressor, compress the valve spring and remove the valve keys using a magnetic retrieval tool.
3. Slowly release the compressor and remove the valve spring caps (or rotators) and the valve springs.
4. Fabricate a valve arrangement board to use when you remove the valves, which will indicate the port in which each valve was originally installed (and which cylinder head on V6 models). Also note that the valve keys, rotators, caps, etc. should be arranged in a manner which will allow you to reinstall them on the valve on which they were originally used.
5. Remove and discard the valve seals. On models using the umbrella type seals, note the location of the large and small seals for assembly purposes.
6. Thoroughly clean the valves on the wire wheel of a bench grinder, then clean the cylinder head mating surface. Avoid using a metallic scraper, since this can cause damage to the cylinder head mating surface, especially on models with aluminum heads.
7. Using a valve guide cleaner chucked into a drill, clean all of the valve guides.

To install:

8. Lubricate all of the valve stems with a light coating of engine oil, then install the valves into the proper ports/guides.
9. Install the valve seals. Be sure to use a seal protector to prevent damage to the seals as they are pushed over the valve keeper grooves. Install O-ring seals in the second groove closest to the head.
10. Install the valve springs and the spring retainers (or rotators), and using the valve compressing tool, compress the springs.
11. After all of the valves are installed and retained, tap each valve spring retainer with a rubber mallet to seat the keepers in the retainer.

INSPECTION

▶ **See Figures 68, 69 and 70**

1. Reinstall each valve into its respective port (guide) of the cylinder head.

TCCS3132

Fig. 62 Use a gasket scraper to remove the bulk of the old head gasket from the mating surface

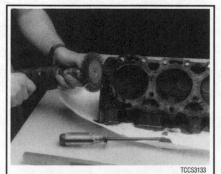

TCCS3133

Fig. 63 An electric drill equipped with a wire wheel will expedite complete gasket removal

TCCS3134

Fig. 64 Check the cylinder head for warpage along the center using a straight-edge and a feeler gauge

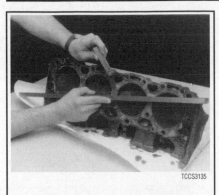

Fig. 65 Be sure to check for warpage across the cylinder head at both diagonals

Fig. 66 A small magnet will help in removal of the valve keys

Fig. 67 Once the spring has been removed, the O-ring may be removed from the valve stem

Fig. 68 A dial gauge may be used to check valve stem-to-guide clearance

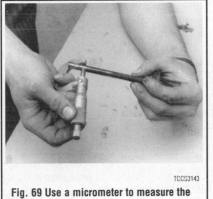

Fig. 69 Use a micrometer to measure the valve stem diameter

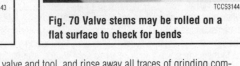

Fig. 70 Valve stems may be rolled on a flat surface to check for bends

2. Mount a dial indicator so that the stem is at 90° to the valve stem, as close to the valve guide as possible.

3. Move the valve off its seat, and measure the valve guide-to-stem clearance by rocking the stem back and forth to actuate the dial indicator.

4. Measure the valve stems using a micrometer, and compare to specifications, to determine whether stem or guide wear is responsible for excessive clearance.

REFACING

Using a valve grinder, resurface the valves according to specifications in this section. All machine work should be performed by a competent, professional machine shop.

➡**Valve face angle is not always identical to valve seat angle.**

A minimum margin of ³⁄₃₂ in. (0.8mm) should remain after grinding the valve. The valve stem top should also be squared and resurfaced, by placing the stem in the V-block of the grinder, and turning it while pressing lightly against the grinding wheel. Be sure to chamfer the edge of the tip so that the squared edges don't dig into the rocker arm.

LAPPING

This procedure should be performed after the valves and seats have been machined, to insure that each valve mates to each seat precisely.

1. Invert the cylinder head, lightly lubricate the valve stems, and install the valves in the head as numbered.

2. Coat valve seats with fine grinding compound, and attach the lapping tool suction cup to a valve head.

➡**Moisten the suction cup.**

3. Rotate the tool between the palms, changing position and lifting the tool often to prevent grooving.

4. Lap the valve until a smooth, polished seat is evident.

5. Remove the valve and tool, and rinse away all traces of grinding compound.

Valve Seals

REPLACEMENT

➡ **See Figure 71**

The valve seals can be replaced with the cylinder head on or off the engine. But great care and skill must be used to perform this procedure with the cylin-

Fig. 71 An umbrella type seal is used on some engines

der head on the engine. With the cylinder head off the engine, compress the valve spring using tool J26513 or equivalent. Remove the keeper, spring and seal. All parts must be return to their original locations.

If the cylinder head is on the vehicle, 60 psi or more of compressed air must be used. The procedure will require bringing the piston of the cylinder to be serviced up to top dead center on compression stoke. Then apply compressed air through the spark plug hole using a compressor gauge fitting. The valve spring and seal can now be removed.

➡If the air pressure is too low or drops during this procedure the valve will fall into the engine, requiring complete removal of the cylinder head. Also if the valve is pressed downward at all, pressure will be lost and the valve will fall in.

Valve Lifters

REMOVAL & INSTALLATION

2.2L Engine

1. Disconnect the negative battery cable.
2. Drain the engine coolant in a suitable container.
3. Remove the valve cover and gasket.
4. Loosen and remove the rocker arm nuts. Remove the rocker arms and balls.
5. Remove the pushrods.
6. Remove the engine lift bracket from the rear of the engine.
7. Disconnect the spark plug wires, route them under the intake manifold.
8. Remove the cylinder head with the intake and exhaust manifolds attached.
9. Unbolt the anti-rotation brackets then remove them.
10. Remove the lifters. Keep all components separated so they may be reinstalled in the same location.

To install:

When ever new valve lifters are being installed, coat the foot of the valve lifters with camshaft assembly lube GM part no. 1052365 or equivalent.

The lifter foot is slightly convex. This can be detected by holding a straight edge to the surface while looking into a light source. If the lifter foot is worn flat or grooved, it must be replaced.

11. Lubricate the bearing surfaces with GM part no. 1052365 or equivalent.
12. Install the lifters in the same bores they were taken from.
13. Install the anti-rotation brackets, tighten the mounting bolts to 97 inch lbs. (11 Nm).
14. Install the spark plug wires to the correct plugs.
15. Install the pushrods making sure they seat in the lifters correctly.
16. Install the rocker arms, balls and mounting nuts, tighten the nuts to 22 ft. lbs. (30 Nm).
17. Secure the valve cover and gasket, tighten the bolts to 89 inch lbs. (10 Nm).
18. Connect the negative battery cable.

2.5L Engine

1. Disconnect the negative battery cable.
2. Remove the intake manifold, valve and side covers.
3. Loosen the rocker arms and rotate to clear the pushrods.
4. Remove the pushrods, retainer and guide.
5. Remove the lifters. Keep all components separated so they may be reinstalled in the same location.

To install:

6. Lubricate the lifters with engine oil and install the lifters in their bore.
7. Install the guides, retainers and pushrods.
8. With the lifter on the base circle of the camshaft, tighten the rocker arm bolts to 24 ft. lbs. (32 Nm).
9. Install the intake manifold, valve and side covers.
10. Connect battery negative cable.

3.1L Engine (VIN M)

1. Disconnect the negative battery cable.
2. Drain the cooling system.
3. Remove the rocker arm covers and the intake manifold.

➡Be sure to keep all valve train parts in order so they may be reinstalled in their original locations and with the same mating surfaces as when removed.

4. Remove the rocker arm retaining nuts, rocker arm balls, rocker arms and pushrods.
5. Remove the 2 bolts from the right or left side lifter guide and remove the guide.
6. Remove the valve lifter(s) from the lifter bores.

To install:

7. Lubricate the bearing surfaces with Molykote® or equivalent.
8. Install the lifters in their original locations.
9. Install the lifter guide and lifter guide bolts and tighten the guide bolts to 89 inch lbs. (10 Nm).
10. Install the pushrods, rocker arms, rocker balls and rocker arm nuts. Tighten the rocker arm nuts to 18 ft. lbs. (25 Nm).
11. Install the intake manifold and rocker arm covers.
12. Refill the cooling system.
13. Connect the negative battery cable.
14. Start the vehicle and verify no leaks.

Except 2.2L, 2.5L and 3.1L (VIN M) Engines

1. Disconnect the negative battery cable.
2. Drain the cooling system.
3. Remove the valve cover and the intake manifold.
4. If the engine is equipped with individual rocker arms, loosen the rocker arm adjusting nut and rotate the arm so as to clear the pushrod.
5. If the engine is equipped with a rocker shaft assembly, remove the rocker shaft retaining bolts/nuts and remove the shaft assembly.

➡Be sure to keep all valve train parts in order so they may be reinstalled in their original locations and with the same mating surfaces as when removed.

6. Remove the pushrods and valve lifters using tool J-3049 or equivalent.

To install:

7. Lubricate the bearing surfaces with Molykote® or equivalent.
8. Install the lifters in their original locations.
9. With the lifter on the base circle of the camshaft, tighten the rocker arm bolts to 14–20 ft. lbs. (20–27 Nm).
10. Connect the negative battery cable.
11. Adjust the valves, as required.

Oil Pan

REMOVAL & INSTALLATION

✳✳ CAUTION

The EPA warns that prolonged contact with used engine oil may cause a number of skin disorders, including cancer! You should make every effort to minimize your exposure to used engine oil. Protective gloves should be worn when changing the oil. Wash your hands and any other exposed skin areas as soon as possible after exposure to used engine oil. Soap and water, or waterless hand cleaner should be used.

2.2L Engine

▶ See Figure 72

1. Disconnect the negative battery cable.
2. Remove the air cleaner and air duct form the vehicle.
3. Remove the serpentine belt.
4. Detach the engine torque strut.
5. Install the engine support fixture J-28467-A.
6. Loosen the right front lug nuts.
7. Raise and support the vehicle safely.
8. Remove the right front tire.
9. Detach the right front inner fender well splash shield.

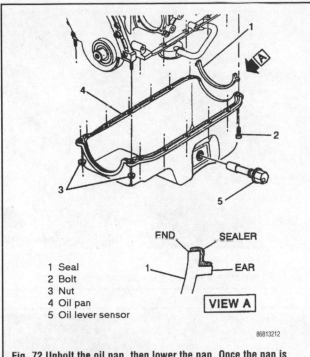

1 Seal
2 Bolt
3 Nut
4 Oil pan
5 Oil lever sensor

FND   SEALER

1 ━━ EAR

VIEW A

86813212

Fig. 72 Unbolt the oil pan, then lower the pan. Once the pan is removed, don't forget to discard the gasket

10. Remove the flywheel cover bolts.
11. Disconnect and remove the starter and starter bracket.
12. Unbolt the A/C compressor mounting bolts, then set the compressor aside without detaching the lines.
13. Remove the front engine mount nuts from the frame.
14. Remove the front engine mount bolts from the engine.
15. Lower the vehicle.
16. Raise the engine about three inches using the support fixture.
17. Raise and safety support the vehicle.
18. Drain the engine oil.
19. Remove the front engine mount bracket.
20. Unbolt the oil pan, then lower the pan.
To install:
21. Clean all the gasket surfaces completely.
22. Apply a thin bead of sealer around the outside edge of the oil pan and install the oil pan gasket onto the sealer.
23. Install the oil pan onto the engine and loosely install all the fasteners.
24. Tighten the nuts and bolts to 89 inch lbs. (10 Nm).
25. Install the front engine mount bracket and loosely install the mount-to-engine bolts.
26. Lower the vehicle.
27. Lower the engine into place.
28. Raise and safely support the vehicle.
29. Tighten the front engine mount bolts.
30. Install and tighten the engine mount nuts to 33 ft. lbs. (45 Nm).
31. Install the A/C compressor in the mounting bracket and tighten to 37 ft. lbs. (50 Nm).
32. Install the exhaust pipe and converter.
33. Connect the starter and install the starter and support bracket.
34. Install the flywheel cover and cover mounting bolts.
35. Install the right fender well splash shield.
36. Install the right front tire and wheel assembly and tighten to specification.
37. Lower the vehicle.
38. Remove the engine support fixture.
39. Install the engine torque strut.
40. Refill the crankcase with oil.
41. Install the serpentine belt.
42. Install the air cleaner and air duct assembly.
43. Connect the negative battery cable.
44. Start the vehicle and verify no leaks.

2.5L Engine

1982–85 MODELS

▶ See Figure 73

1. Raise and support the car. Drain the oil.
2. Remove the engine cradle-to-front engine mounts.
3. Disconnect the exhaust pipe at both the exhaust manifold and at the front of the converter.
4. Disconnect and remove the starter. Remove the flywheel housing or torque converter cover.
5. Remove the alternator upper bracket. Remove the splash shield.
6. Install an engine lifting chain and raise the engine. If equipped, remove the power steering pump and bracket and move it aside.
7. Remove the lower alternator bracket. Remove the engine support bracket.
8. Remove the oil pan retaining bolts and remove the pan.
To install:
9. Clean all gasket surfaces thoroughly.
10. Install the rear oil pan gasket into the rear main bearing cap, then apply a thin bead of silicone sealer to the pan gasket depressions.
11. Install the front pan gasket into the timing cover.
12. Install the side gaskets onto the pan, not the block. They can be retained in place with grease. Apply a thin bead of silicone seal to the mating joints of the gaskets.
13. Install the oil pan, then attach the timing gear bolts last, after the other bolts have been snugged down.
14. Attach the alternator bracket and the engine support bracket.
15. Reverse to install the remaining components.

1986–92 MODELS

▶ See Figure 73

1. Disconnect the negative battery cables.
2. Remove the coolant recovery reservoir.
3. Unbolt and remove the engine torque strut.
4. If needed detach the air cleaner and air inlet assemblies.
5. Remove the serpentine drive belt.
6. If equipped, remove the air conditioning compressor from it's brackets and set aside.

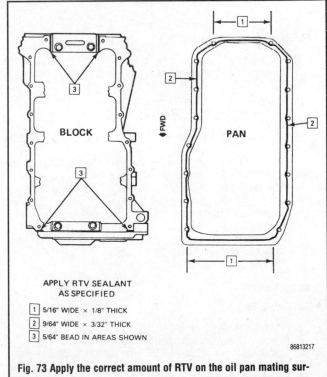

BLOCK

←FWD

PAN

APPLY RTV SEALANT AS SPECIFIED

1 5/16" WIDE × 1/8" THICK
2 9/64" WIDE × 3/32" THICK
3 5/64" BEAD IN AREAS SHOWN

86813217

Fig. 73 Apply the correct amount of RTV on the oil pan mating surfaces as shown

7. Remove the oil level indicator.
8. Raise and support the vehicle.
9. Drain the engine oil from the vehicle.
10. On some models you may need to remove the nuts from the engine mount-to-cradle.
11. Detach the exhaust pipe at the manifold and front of the converter.
12. Detach the starter and flywheel cover, then set aside.
13. Turn the front wheels to the extreme right, then disconnect the engine wiring harness screws under the oil pan right and left sides.
14. Detach the right side engine splash shield.
15. On some models you will need to remove the power steering pump and bracket.
16. Lower the vehicle, then support the engine and raise approximately 2 inches.
17. Disconnect the engine front mount and bracket.
18. Unbolt the oil pan, then lower the pan from the vehicle.
19. Clean the oil pan mounting area and oil pan of any old gasket material (RTV).
20. Reverse to install. Using RTV, apply as shown in the illustration to the oil pan. Tighten the mounting bolts on the oil pan to 89 inch lbs. (10 Nm).
21. Fill the crank case with fresh engine oil.
22. Connect the negative battery cable, then start the engine and check for leaks.

2.8L Engine

▶ See Figures 74 and 75

1. Disconnect the battery ground.
2. Raise and support the car on jackstands.
3. Drain the oil.
4. Remove the bell housing cover.
5. Remove the starter.
6. Support the engine.
7. Unbolt the engine from its mounts.
8. Remove the oil pan bolts.
9. Raise the engine with a jack, just enough to remove the oil pan.
10. Installation is the reverse of removal. The pan is installed using RTV gasket material in place of a gasket. Make sure that the sealing surfaces are free of old RTV material. Use a ⅛ in. (3mm) bead of RTV material on the pan sealing flange. Tighten the pan bolts to 6mm bolts to 6–9 ft. lbs. (8–12 Nm) and 8mm bolts to 14–22 ft. lbs. (19–30 Nm).
11. Fill the crank case with fresh engine oil.
12. Connect the negative battery cable, then start the engine and check for leaks.

3.0L Engine

1. Disconnect the battery ground cable.
2. Raise and support the car on jackstands.
3. Drain the oil.
4. Remove the bell housing cover.
5. Unbolt and remove the oil pan.

To install:
6. Clean the mating area well, then install RTV gasket material in place of a gasket.
7. Make sure that the sealing surfaces are free of all old RTV material. Use a ⅛ in. (3mm) bead of RTV material on the oil pan sealing flange.
8. Install the oil pan to the block, then tighten the pan bolts to 10 ft. lbs. (14 Nm).
9. Attach the bell housing cover.
10. Lower the vehicle.
11. Add engine oil to the engine.
12. Connect the negative battery cable.
13. Start the engine, check for leaks.

3.1L Engine (VIN T)

▶ See Figure 76

1. Disconnect the battery ground.
2. Remove the serpentine belt cover, belt and tensioner.
3. Support the engine with tool J-28467-A or equivalent, using an extra support leg.
4. Raise and safely support the vehicle.

Fig. 74 An extension is necessary to reach many of the bolts

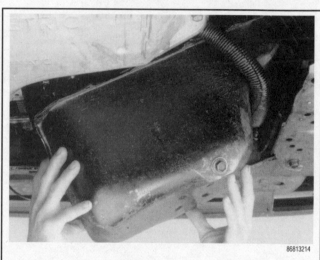

Fig. 75 The oil pan will require some maneuvering before it will come off

5. Drain the oil.
6. Remove the right tire and wheel assembly. Remove the splash shield.
7. Remove the steering gear pinch bolt, as required.

❊❊ CAUTION

Failure to disconnect the intermediate shaft from the rack and pinion stub shaft can result in damage to the steering gear and/or the intermediate shaft. This damage can result in loss of steering control, this could cause personal injury.

8. Remove the transaxle mount retaining nuts and engine-to-frame mount retaining nuts, as required.
9. Remove the front engine horse collar bracket from the block, as required.
10. Remove the bell housing cover and remove the starter.
11. Position a jackstand under the frame front center crossmember.
12. Loosen but do not remove the rear frame bolts.
13. Remove the front frame bolts and lower the front frame.
14. Remove the DIS sensor wire.
15. Remove the oil pan retaining bolts and nuts, then remove the oil pan.

To install:
16. Clean and inspect the oil pan flanges, oil pan rail, front cover, rear main bearing cap and the threaded holes.

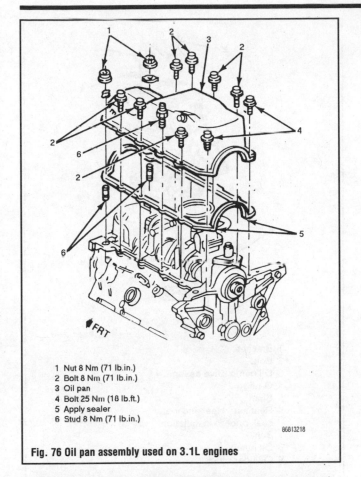

1 Nut 8 Nm (71 lb.in.)
2 Bolt 8 Nm (71 lb.in.)
3 Oil pan
4 Bolt 25 Nm (18 lb.ft.)
5 Apply sealer
6 Stud 8 Nm (71 lb.in.)

86813218

Fig. 76 Oil pan assembly used on 3.1L engines

➡The oil pan on some vehicles may not require a gasket. If a gasket is not required, the oil pan is installed using RTV gasket material. Make sure the sealing surfaces are free of old RTV material. Use a ⅛ inch (3mm) bead of RTV material on the pan sealing flange.

17. Install the oil pan using a new gasket or RTV gasket material. Tighten the pan nuts to 89 inch lbs. (10 Nm), rear bolts; 18 ft. lbs. (25 Nm) and remaining bolts to 89 inch lbs. (10 Nm).
18. Attach the DIS sensor wire.
19. Raise the front frame and install the front frame bolts.
20. Tighten the rear frame bolts.
21. Remove the jackstand from the front center crossmember.
22. Install the starter and bell housing cover.
23. If removed, install the front engine horse collar bracket from the block.
24. Install the transaxle mount retaining nuts and engine to frame mount retaining nuts.
25. If removed, install the steering gear pinch bolt.
26. Install the splash shield. Install the right tire and wheel assembly.
27. Lower the vehicle.
28. Install the tensioner, serpentine belt and cover.
29. Fill the crankcase with oil.
30. Connect the negative battery cable.
31. Start the vehicle and check for leaks.

3.1L Engine (VIN M)

▸ See Figure 76

1. Disconnect the negative battery cable.
2. Remove the serpentine belt.
3. Unbolt the upper A/C compressor bolts, if equipped.
4. Raise and safely support the vehicle.
5. Drain the engine oil.
6. Remove the right front tire and wheel assembly.
7. Detach the right inner fender splash shield.

8. Remove the engine mount strut from the suspension support.
9. Remove the cotter pin and castle nut from the lower ball joint and separate the joint from the steering knuckle.
10. Unbolt and remove the right side sway bar link.
11. Disconnect the ABS sensor from the right subframe.
12. Remove the right side subframe mounting bolts and remove the right side subframe and control arm as an assembly.
13. Remove the lower A/C compressor mounting bolts and position the compressor aside. DO NOT disconnect the refrigerant lines or allow the compressor to hang unsupported.
14. Remove the engine mount strut bracket from the engine.
15. Remove the engine to transaxle brace.
16. Remove the oil filter.
17. Remove the starter.
18. Remove the flywheel cover.
19. Remove the oil pan flange retaining bolts and the oil pan side retaining bolts. Remove the oil pan.

To install:
20. Clean the gasket mating surfaces.
21. Install a new gasket on the oil pan. Apply silicon sealer to the portion of the pan that contacts the rear of the block.
22. Install the oil pan and install the mounting bolts finger-tight.
23. With all the bolts in place, tighten the oil pan flange bolts to 18 ft. lbs. (25 Nm) and the oil pan side bolts to 37 ft. lbs. (50 Nm).
24. Install the flywheel cover.
25. Install the starter.
26. Coat the seal on the oil filter with clean engine oil and install the filter on the engine.
27. Install the engine-to-transaxle brace and tighten the mounting bolts to 68 ft. lbs. (93 Nm).
28. Install the engine mount strut bracket. Tighten the mounting bolt at the engine bracket to 85 ft. lbs. (115 Nm).
29. Install the A/C compressor in the mounting bracket and tighten the lower mounting bolts.
30. Attach the right side subframe and control arm assembly. Tighten the subframe mounting bolts to 89 ft. lbs. (120 Nm).
31. Install the right side sway bar link and tighten to 22 ft. lbs. (30 Nm).
32. Connect the ball joint to the steering knuckle and tighten the castle nut to 48 ft. lbs. (60 Nm). Install a new cotter pin.
33. Connect the ABS sensor from the right subframe assembly.
34. Connect the engine mount strut bracket and tighten the mounting bolt at the frame to 89 ft. lbs. (120 Nm).
35. Install the right inner fender well splash shield.
36. Install the right front tire and wheel assembly and tighten to specification.
37. Lower the vehicle.
38. Install the serpentine belt.
39. Fill the crankcase to the correct level.
40. Connect the negative battery cable.
41. Start the vehicle and verify no leaks.

3.3L Engine

1. Disconnect the negative battery cable.
2. Raise and support the vehicle safely.
3. Drain the engine oil.
4. Remove the transaxle converter cover and starter motor.
5. Remove the oil filter, oil pan retaining bolts and oil pan assembly.

To install:
6. Clean the oil pan and cylinder block mating surfaces.
7. Install a new oil pan gasket to the oil pan flange.
8. Install the oil pan and tighten the retaining bolts 8–10 ft. lbs. (11–14 Nm).
9. Lower the vehicle.
10. Fill the crankcase with oil.
11. Connect the negative battery cable.

3.8L Engine

1. Disconnect the battery ground cable.
2. Raise and safely support the vehicle.

3. Drain the oil.
4. Remove the bell housing cover.
5. Unbolt and remove the oil pan.

To install:

6. RTV gasket material is used in place of a gasket. Make sure the sealing surfaces are free of all old RTV material. Use a ⅛ inch (3mm) bead of RTV material on the oil pan sealing flange. Tighten the pan bolts to 10–14 ft. lbs. (14–19 Nm).
7. Install the bell housing cover.
8. Lower the vehicle.
9. Fill the crankcase with oil.
10. Connect the negative battery cable.

Oil Pump

REMOVAL & INSTALLATION

> **CAUTION**
>
> The EPA warns that prolonged contact with used engine oil may cause a number of skin disorders, including cancer! You should make every effort to minimize your exposure to used engine oil. Protective gloves should be worn when changing the oil. Wash your hands and any other exposed skin areas as soon as possible after exposure to used engine oil. Soap and water, or waterless hand cleaner should be used.

2.2L Engine

▶ See Figure 77

1. Disconnect the negative battery cable.
2. Raise and support the vehicle safely.
3. Drain the engine oil into a suitable container.
4. Remove the oil pan.
5. Remove the oil pump-to-main bearing cap bolt, then the oil pump and extension shaft.

To install:

> **WARNING**
>
> Heat the extension shaft retainer in hot water prior to assembly. Be sure the retainer does not crack upon installation. Wear heavy gloves when handling the hot retainer.

> **WARNING**
>
> To avoid engine damage, all oil pump cavities must be filled with petroleum jelly before installing the gears into the pump body. Also use only original equipment gaskets. Gasket thickness is critical to proper oil pump operation.

6. Install the extension shaft, oil pump and pump-to-rear main cap bolt. Tighten the oil pump-to-bearing cap bolt to 25–38 ft. lbs. (34–54 Nm) and the upper oil pump drive bolt to 14–22 ft. lbs. (19–30 Nm).
7. Install the oil pan and attaching bolts.
8. Lower the vehicle.
9. Fill the crankcase with clean engine oil.
10. Connect the negative battery cable.
11. Start the engine, check the oil pressure, then check for leaks.
12. Check the oil level, add as needed.

2.5L Engine

1. Disconnect the negative battery cable.
2. Raise and support the vehicle safely.
3. Drain the engine oil and remove the oil pan.
4. Remove the 2 flange mounting bolts and nut from the main bearing cap bolt.
5. Remove the pump and screen as an assembly.

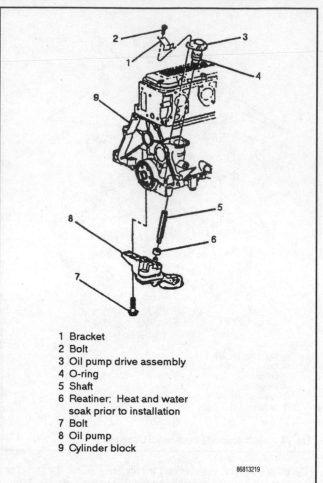

1 Bracket
2 Bolt
3 Oil pump drive assembly
4 O-ring
5 Shaft
6 Reatiner: Heat and water soak prior to installation
7 Bolt
8 Oil pump
9 Cylinder block

86813219

Fig. 77 Oil pump assembly used on 2.2L engines

To install:

6. Remove the 4 cover attaching screws and cover from the oil pump assembly.
7. Pack the space around the oil pump gears completely full of petroleum jelly. There must be no air space left inside the pump. If the pump is not packed, it may not begin to pump oil as soon as the engine is started and engine damage may result.

> **WARNING**
>
> To avoid engine damage, all oil pump cavities must be filled with petroleum jelly before installing the gears into the pump body. Also use only original equipment gaskets. Gasket thickness is critical to proper oil pump operation.

8. Align the oil pump shaft to match with the oil pump drive shaft tang, then install the oil pump to the block positioning the flange over the oil pump driveshaft lower bushing. Do not use any gasket. Tighten the bolts to 20 ft. lbs. (30 Nm).
9. Install the oil pan using a new gasket and seals.
10. Install the 2 flange mounting bolts and nut to the main bearing cap bolt.
11. Lower the vehicle.
12. Fill the crankcase with oil.
13. Connect the negative battery cable.

2.8L Engine

▶ See Figures 78, 79 and 80

1. Disconnect the negative battery cable.
2. Raise and support the vehicle safely.
3. Drain the engine oil and remove the oil pan.

Fig. 78 Once the oil pan is removed, you have access to the oil pump

Fig. 79 Remove the bolts securing the oil pump

Fig. 80 The pump assembly may now be pulled out

4. Remove the pump-to-rear main bearing cap bolt and remove the pump and extension shaft.

To install:

5. Remove the 4 cover attaching screws and cover from the oil pump assembly.

6. Pack the space around the oil pump gears completely full of petroleum jelly. There must be no air space left inside the pump. If the pump is not packed, it may not begin to pump oil as soon as the engine is started and engine damage may result.

> ✳✳ **WARNING**
>
> To avoid engine damage, all oil pump cavities must be filled with petroleum jelly before installing the gears into the pump body. Also use only original equipment gaskets. Gasket thickness is critical to proper oil pump operation.

7. Assemble the pump and extension shaft with retainer to rear main bearing cap, aligning the top end of the extension shaft with the lower end of the drive gear.

8. Install the pump-to-the rear bearing cap bolt. Tighten to 30 ft. lbs. (40 Nm).

9. Install the oil pan.

10. Lower the vehicle.

11. Fill the crankcase with oil.

12. Connect the negative battery cable.

3.0L Engines

1. Remove the oil filter.

2. Unbolt the oil pump cover from the timing chain cover.

3. Slide out the oil pump gears. Clean all parts thoroughly in solvent and check for wear. Remove the oil pressure relief valve cap, spring and valve.

4. Installation is the reverse of removal. Tighten the pressure relief valve cap to 35 ft. lbs. (47 Nm). Place a straightedge across the face of the pump cover and check that it is flat to within 0.001 in. (0.025mm). Pack the oil pump cavity with petroleum jelly so that there is no air space. Install the cover and tighten the bolts to 10 ft. lbs. (14 Nm).

> ✳✳ **WARNING**
>
> To avoid engine damage, all oil pump cavities must be filled with petroleum jelly before installing the gears into the pump body. Also use only original equipment gaskets. Gasket thickness is critical to proper oil pump operation.

3.1 Engine (VIN T)

1. Disconnect the negative battery cable.

2. Raise and support the vehicle safely.

3. Drain the engine oil and remove the oil pan.

4. Remove the pump-to-rear main bearing cap bolt and remove the pump and extension shaft.

To install:

5. Remove the 4 cover attaching screws and cover from the oil pump assembly.

6. Pack the space around the oil pump gears completely full of petroleum jelly. There must be no air space left inside the pump. If the pump is not packed, it may not begin to pump oil as soon as the engine is started and engine damage may result.

> ✳✳ **WARNING**
>
> To avoid engine damage, all oil pump cavities must be filled with petroleum jelly before installing the gears into the pump body. Also use only original equipment gaskets. Gasket thickness is critical to proper oil pump operation.

7. Assemble the pump and extension shaft with retainer to rear main bearing cap, aligning the top end of the extension shaft with the lower end of the drive gear.

8. Install the pump-to-the rear bearing cap bolt. Tighten to 30 ft. lbs. (41 Nm).

9. Install the oil pan.

10. Lower the vehicle.

11. Fill the crankcase with oil.

12. Connect the negative battery cable.

3.1 Engine (VIN M)

1. Disconnect the negative battery cable.

2. Raise and safely support the vehicle.

3. Drain the engine oil into a suitable container.

4. Unbolt the oil pan, then remove it from the vehicle.

5. Remove the crankshaft oil deflector bolts.

6. Remove the crankshaft oil deflector.

7. Remove the oil pump retaining bolts and remove the oil pump and pump driveshaft.

To install:

8. Install the oil pump and pump driveshaft. Tighten the oil pump mounting bolts to 30 ft. lbs. (41 Nm).

9. Install the crankshaft oil deflector and mounting nuts. Tighten the mounting nuts to 18 ft. lbs. (25 Nm).

10. Attach the oil pan.

11. Lower the vehicle.

12. Fill the crankcase to the correct level with oil.

13. Start the engine, check the oil pressure and check for leaks.

3.3L and 3.8L Engines

1. Disconnect the negative battery cable.

2. Drain the engine oil.

3. Remove the oil filter adapter, pressure regulator valve and spring.

4. Remove the oil pump cover attaching screws and cover.

5. Remove the gears.

To install:

6. Lubricate the gears with petroleum jelly.

7. Assemble the gears in the housing.
8. Pack the gear cavity with petroleum jelly.
9. Install the oil pump cover and screws. Tighten to 97 inch lbs. (11 Nm).
10. Install the pressure regulator and spring valve.
11. Install the oil filter adapter with a new gasket. Tighten the oil filter adapter bolts to 24 ft. lbs. (33 Nm).
12. Install the front cover on the engine.
13. Fill the crankcase with oil.
14. Connect the negative battery cable.

Crankshaft Damper

REMOVAL & INSTALLATION

2.2L Engine

1. Remove the drive belt from the vehicle.
2. Loosen the lug nuts on the right front tire.
3. Raise and support the vehicle safely.
4. Remove the right front tire and wheel from the vehicle.
5. Detach the right engine splash shield.
6. Loosen and remove the crankshaft bolt.
7. Pull the crankshaft balancer hub and balancer off the vehicle. Make sure to use a suitable tool to hold the flywheel from rotating.
8. Remove the balancer using a suitable puller.

To install:

9. Install the balancer hub and balancer, tighten the hub bolts to 37 ft. lbs. (40 Nm).
10. Install the balancer bolt, tighten to 77 ft. lbs. (105 Nm).
11. Attach the right engine splash shield.
12. Install the right front tire and wheel assembly, lower the vehicle, then tighten the lug nuts to 100 ft. lbs. (136 Nm).
13. Install the drive belt.

2.5L, 3.3L and 3.8L Engines

▶ See Figure 81

1. Disconnect the negative battery cable, and remove the serpentine belt.
2. Raise and safely support the vehicle.
3. Remove the flywheel or torque converter cover.
4. Remove the right front tire and wheel assembly.
5. Detach the right front engine splash shield.
6. Use a suitable tool on the flywheel to keep engine from rotating and remove the bolt and washer from the damper.
7. Remove the balancer and the key using a suitable puller.

To install:

8. Install the key and balancer.
9. Install the bolt and washer, tighten the bolt to 162 ft. lbs. (220 Nm).

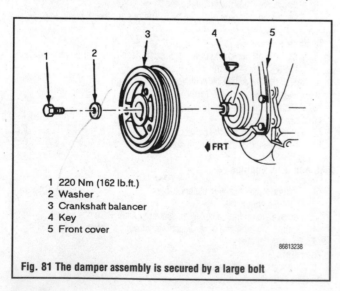

1 220 Nm (162 lb.ft.)
2 Washer
3 Crankshaft balancer
4 Key
5 Front cover

86813238

Fig. 81 The damper assembly is secured by a large bolt

10. Attach the engine splash shield.
11. Install the tire and wheel assembly.
12. Install the flywheel or torque converter cover.
13. Lower the vehicle.
14. Install the serpentine belt.
15. Connect the negative battery cable.

2.8L Engine

1. Disconnect the negative battery cable, and remove the serpentine belt.
2. Raise and safely support the vehicle.
3. Remove the flywheel or torque converter cover.
4. Right front tire and wheel assembly.
5. Remove the right front engine splash shield.
6. Remove the AIR pump, if equipped.
7. Use a suitable tool on the flywheel to keep engine from rotating and remove the bolt and washer from the damper.
8. With tool J-29113, or equivalent, installed on the damper, turn the puller screw.

➡ **The inertia weight section of the damper is assembled to the hub with a rubber sleeve. A proper puller must be used to avoid damaging the damper assembly.**

9. Remove the damper.

To install:

10. Coat the cover seal with clean engine oil before installing the damper using tool J-29113 or equivalent.
11. Apply sealant to the key and keyway.
12. Place the damper into position and pull into place with tool.
13. Install the retaining bolt and tighten to 110 ft. lbs. (149 Nm).
14. Install the right front tire and wheel.
15. Install the AIR pump, inner splash shield and lower the vehicle.
16. Tighten the lug nuts on the right front to 100 ft. lbs. (136 Nm).
17. Install the serpentine drive belt.
18. Install the negative battery cable.

3.1L Engine (VIN T)

1. Disconnect the negative battery cable, and remove the serpentine belt.
2. Raise and safely support the vehicle.
3. Remove the flywheel or torque converter cover.
4. Right front tire and wheel assembly.
5. Remove the right front engine splash shield.
6. Use a suitable tool on the flywheel to keep engine from rotating and remove the bolt and washer from the damper.
7. Remove the balancer and the key. With tool J-24420-B or equivalent, turn the puller screw to remove the balancer.

To install:

8. Install the key and balancer.
9. Install the bolt and washer, tighten the bolt to 76 ft. lbs. (103 Nm).
10. Attach the engine splash shield.
11. Install the tire and wheel assembly.
12. Install the flywheel or torque converter cover.
13. Lower the vehicle.
14. Tighten the right wheel lug nuts to 100 ft. lbs. (136 Nm).
15. Install the serpentine belt.
16. Connect the negative battery cable.

Timing Gear/Chain Cover

REMOVAL & INSTALLATION

2.2L Engine

1. Disconnect the negative battery cable.
2. Remove the serpentine drive belt.
3. Remove the drive belt tensioner as follows:
   a. Remove the coolant reservoir.
   b. Unbolt the front alternator mounting bolts.
   c. Remove the three power steering pump mounting bolts. These bolts

can be accessed by working through the holes in the drive pulley on the pump. Lay the pump aside, without disconnecting the power steering lines.

   d. Unsecure the four tensioner mounting bolts, then remove the tensioner.

4. Raise and safely support the vehicle.

5. Remove the oil pan.

6. Remove the crankshaft pulley and hub as follows:

   a. Remove the right front tire and wheel assembly.

   b. Detach the right inner fender well splash shield.

   c. Remove the bolts from the crankshaft pulley and hub, then remove the pulley from the pulley hub.

   d. Install tool J-24420-B, or an equivalent puller and remove the hub from the crankshaft.

7. Unbolt the front cover.

8. Lift the front cover off. If it is difficult to remove, use a soft faced mallet to lightly strike the cover loose.

9. After removing the timing cover, pry oil seal from front of cover. Lubricate the seal lip and install new lip seal with lip, open side of seal, facing toward the cylinder block. Carefully drive or press seal into place

To install:

10. Clean all gasket surfaces completely.

11. Apply a thin bead of sealer around the gasket area of the front cover, then install a new front cover gasket on the cover.

12. Attach the front cover making sure the dowel pins line up with the holes in the cover. Tighten the mounting bolts to 97 inch lbs. (11 Nm).

13. Attach the crankshaft pulley and hub as follows;

   a. Coat the seal contact area of the hub with clean engine oil.

   b. Line up the notch in the hub with the crankshaft key, then slide the hub on until the key is in the notch.

   c. Using a suitable puller, J-29113 or an equivalent, seat the hub on the crankshaft.

   d. Install the pulley on the hub. Tighten the three pulley mounting bolts to 37 ft. lbs. (50 Nm) and the center hub bolt to 77 ft. lbs. (105 Nm).

   e. Install the right fender splash shield.

   f. Install the right tire and wheel assembly.

14. Attach the oil pan, then lower the vehicle.

15. Tighten the lug nuts to 100 ft. lbs. (136 Nm).

16. Install the serpentine drive belt tensioner as follows:

   a. Attach the tensioner on the front of the engine, then tighten the mounting bolts to 37 ft. lbs. (50 Nm).

   b. Position the power steering pump against the tension so the bolt hoes are lined up. Mount the three bolts tightening them to 25 ft. lbs. (34 Nm).

   c. Install the two alternator bolts removed. Tighten the upper bolt to 22 ft. lbs. (30 Nm) and the lower bolt to 37 ft. lbs. (50 Nm).

   d. Install the coolant reservoir.

17. Install the serpentine drive belt.

18. Connect the negative battery cable.

19. Top off the coolant reservoir as needed.

20. Start the vehicle and verify there are no oil or coolant leaks.

2.5L Engine

♦ **See Figures 82 and 83**

1. Relieve the pressure in the fuel system before disconnecting any fuel line connections.

2. Disconnect the negative battery cable.

3. On some models you will need to remove the drive belt tensioner.

4. Raise and support the vehicle.

5. Remove the right tire assembly.

6. Remove the inner fender splash shield. Remove the crankshaft balancer.

7. On some models you will need to:

   a. Remove the alternator lower bracket and the front engine mounts.

   b. Using a floor jack, raise the engine.

   c. Remove the engine mount mounting bracket-to-cylinder block bolts. Remove the bracket and mount as an assembly.

8. Remove the oil pan-to-front cover screws and front cover-to-block screws.

9. Pull the cover slightly forward, just enough to allow cutting of the oil pan front seal flush with the block on both sides.

10. Remove the front cover and attached portion of the pan seal.

11. Clean all of the gasket surfaces thoroughly.

To install:

12. Pry oil seal from front of cover, then lubricate the seal lip. Install the new lip seal facing toward the cylinder block. Carefully drive or press seal into place with tool J-34995 or equivalent will help.

13. Coat the new gasket with sealer and position it on the front cover.

14. Apply a ⅛ in. (3mm) bead of silicone sealer to the joint formed at the oil pan and stock.

15. Attach the front cover, partially tighten the two opposing cover screws. Install the remaining block to cover screws, then tighten those screws in proper sequence. See the Illustration.

16. Remove the tool J-34995.

17. If removed:

   a. Install the alternator lower bracket and the front engine mounts.

   b. Using a floor jack, raise the engine.

   c. Attach the bracket and mount as an assembly, by installing the engine mount mounting bracket-to-cylinder block bolts.

18. Install the harmonic balancer.

19. Attach the right splash shield.

20. Install the right tire assembly.

21. Lower the vehicle, then tighten the lug nuts.

22. Install the drive belt tensioner.

23. Connect the negative battery cable.

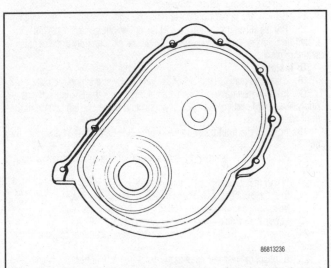

86813236

Fig. 82 Coat the new gasket with sealer and position it on the front cover

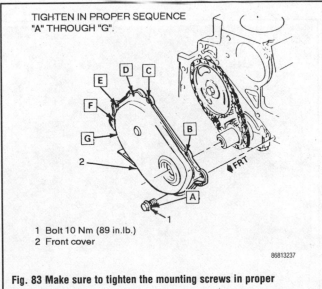

TIGHTEN IN PROPER SEQUENCE "A" THROUGH "G".

1 Bolt 10 Nm (89 in.lb.)
2 Front cover

86813237

Fig. 83 Make sure to tighten the mounting screws in proper sequence

2.8L Engine

◆ **See Figure 84**

1. Relieve the pressure in the fuel system before disconnecting any fuel line connections. Disconnect the negative battery cable.
2. Drain the cooling system.
3. Remove the serpentine belt and tensioner.
4. Remove the alternator and power steering pump. Locate and support these accessories to the side, remove the AIR pump and hoses, as needed.
5. Remove the A/C compressor without disconnecting any air conditioning lines and lay it aside. If equipped, remove the A.I.R. pump. Raise and support the vehicle safely.
6. Remove the inner splash shield. Remove the torsion damper using tool J-24420-B or equivalent.
7. Remove the flywheel cover at the transaxle and starter.
8. Remove the serpentine belt idler pulley.
9. Drain the engine oil. Remove the oil pan and lower front cover bolts.
10. Lower the vehicle.
11. Remove the radiator hose at the water pump. Remove the heater hose at fill pipe.
12. Remove the bypass hose and overflow hoses. Remove the canister purge hose.
13. Remove the crankshaft damper.
14. Remove the upper front cover retaining bolts and remove the front cover.
15. Pry the oil seal from the front of the cover. Lubricate the seal lip and install new lip seal facing toward the cylinder block. Carefully drive or press seal into place.

To install:

16. Clean the mating surfaces of the front cover and cylinder block.
17. Install a new gasket. Make sure not to damage the sealing surfaces. Apply sealer GM part no. 1052080 or equivalent, to the sealing surface of the front cover.
18. Position the front cover on the engine block and install the upper cover bolt.
19. Raise and safely support the vehicle. Install the oil pan and lower cover bolts.
20. Install the serpentine belt idler pulley.
21. Bolt the flywheel cover to the transaxle. Install the starter.
22. Install the torsion damper. Install the inner splash shield.
23. Lower the vehicle.
24. Attach the bypass hose and overflow hoses. Install the canister purge hose.
25. Connect the radiator hose to the water pump. Connect the heater hose to fill pipe.
26. Mount the alternator and power steering pump.
27. Install the tensioner serpentine belt.
28. Connect the negative battery cable.

Fig. 84 Remove the upper front cover retaining bolts and remove the front cover

3.0L Engine

◆ **See Figure 85**

1. Drain the cooling system.
2. Disconnect the radiator hoses and the heater hose at the water pump.
3. Remove the water pump pulley and all drive belts. Remove the front engine mount-to-cradle bolts and raise the engine.
4. Unbolt the alternator and brackets.
5. Remove the distributor.
6. Remove the balancer bolt and washer, and using a puller, remove the balancer.
7. Unsecure the cover-to-block bolts. Remove the two oil pan-to-cover bolts.
8. Remove the cover and gasket.
9. Installation is the reverse of removal. Always use a new gasket coated with sealer. Tighten the timing cover bolts to 30 ft. lbs. (41 Nm).

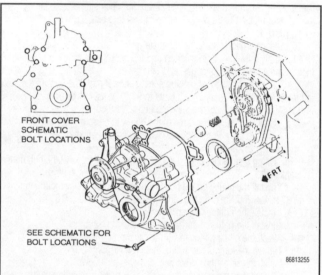

FRONT COVER SCHEMATIC BOLT LOCATIONS

FRT

SEE SCHEMATIC FOR BOLT LOCATIONS →

Fig. 85 Bolt locations for the 3.0L engine on the timing cover

3.1L Engine (VIN M)

◆ **See Figure 86**

1. Disconnect the negative battery cable.
2. Drain the cooling system into a suitable container.
3. Remove the right engine mount bracket.
4. Remove the serpentine belt.
5. Remove the crankshaft balancer.
6. Remove the serpentine belt tensioner mounting bolt and tensioner.
7. Remove the oil pan.
8. Remove coolant bypass pipe from the water pump and the intake manifold.
9. Disconnect the lower radiator hose to from the front cover outlet.
10. Remove the front cover mounting bolts and remove the front cover.

To install:

11. Clean all gasket surfaces completely.
12. Apply a thin bead of sealer around the gasket sealing area of the front cover. Install a new front cover seal on the front cover.
13. Install the front cover on the engine and tighten the mounting bolts to 15 ft. lbs. (21 Nm).
14. Connect the radiator hose to the coolant outlet.
15. Install coolant bypass pipe to the water pump and the intake manifold.
16. Install the oil pan following the recommended procedure.
17. Install crankshaft balancer.
18. Install the serpentine belt tensioner and tighten the mounting bolt to 40 ft. lbs. (54 Nm).
19. Install the serpentine belt.
20. Install the right engine mount bracket and tighten the bracket-to-mount bolts to 96 ft. lbs. (130 Nm).
21. Refill the cooling system.

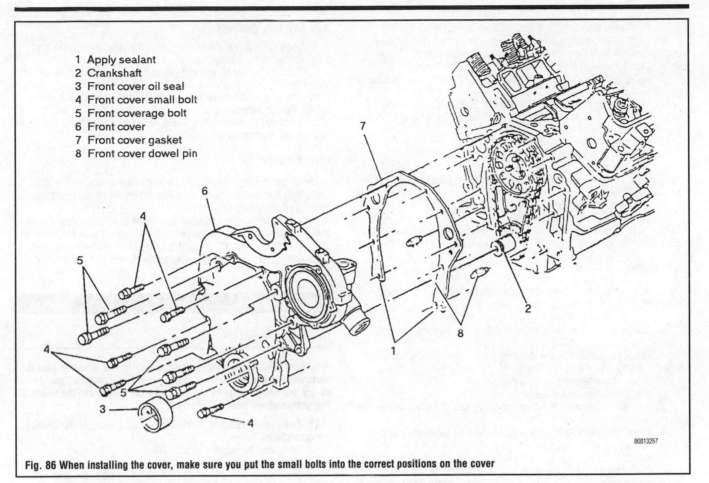

1 Apply sealant
2 Crankshaft
3 Front cover oil seal
4 Front cover small bolt
5 Front coverage bolt
6 Front cover
7 Front cover gasket
8 Front cover dowel pin

Fig. 86 When installing the cover, make sure you put the small bolts into the correct positions on the cover

22. Check the engine oil level and top off as necessary.
23. Connect the negative battery cable.
24. Start the vehicle and verify no oil leaks.

3.1L Engine (VIN T)

1. Relieve the pressure in the fuel system before disconnecting any fuel line connections. Disconnect the negative battery cable.
2. Drain the cooling system.
3. Remove the serpentine belt and tensioner.
4. Remove the alternator and power steering pump. Locate and support these accessories to the side, remove the AIR pump and hoses, as needed.
5. Remove the A/C compressor without disconnecting any air conditioning lines and lay it aside. If equipped, remove the A.I.R. pump. Raise and support the vehicle safely.
6. Remove the inner splash shield. Remove the torsion damper using tool J-24420-B or equivalent.
7. Remove the flywheel cover at the transaxle and starter.
8. Remove the serpentine belt idler pulley.
9. Remove the crankshaft damper.
10. Drain the engine oil. Remove the oil pan and lower front cover bolts.
11. Lower the vehicle.
12. Remove the radiator hose at the water pump. Remove the heater hose at fill pipe.
13. Remove the bypass hose and overflow hoses. Remove the canister purge hose.
14. Remove the upper front cover retaining bolts and remove the front cover.
To install:
15. Pry the oil seal from the front of the cover. Lubricate the seal lip and install new lip seal with lip, open side of seal, facing toward the cylinder block. Carefully drive or press seal into place.
16. Clean the mating surfaces of the front cover and cylinder block.
17. Install a new gasket. Make sure not to damage the sealing surfaces. Apply sealer GM part no. 1052080 or equivalent, to the sealing surface of the front cover.

18. Position the front cover on the engine block and install the upper cover bolt.
19. Raise and safely support the vehicle. Install the oil pan and lower cover bolts.
20. Install the crankshaft damper.
21. Install the serpentine belt idler pulley.
22. Bolt the flywheel cover to the transaxle. Install the starter.
23. Install the torsion damper. Install the inner splash shield.
24. Lower the vehicle.
25. Attach the bypass hose and overflow hoses. Install the canister purge hose.
26. Connect the radiator hose to the water pump. Connect the heater hose to fill pipe.
27. Mount the alternator and power steering pump.
28. Install the tensioner serpentine belt.
29. Connect the negative battery cable.

3.3L Engine

1. Relieve the pressure in the fuel system before disconnecting any fuel line connections. Disconnect the negative battery cable.
2. Drain the cooling system.
3. Remove the serpentine belt.
4. Remove the heater pipes. Remove the coolant bypass hose and lower radiator hose from cover.
5. Raise and support the vehicle safely.
6. Remove the inner splash shield.
7. Remove the crankshaft balancer.
8. Disconnect all electrical connectors at the camshaft sensor, crankshaft sensor and oil pressure sender.
9. Remove the oil pan-to-front cover retaining bolts, front cover retaining bolts and remove the front cover.
To install:
10. Pry the oil seal from the front of the cover. Lubricate the seal lip and install new lip seal with lip, open side of seal, facing toward the cylinder block. Carefully drive or press seal into place.

11. Clean the mating surfaces of the front cover and cylinder block.

12. Install a new gasket on the cylinder block. Install the front cover. Apply sealer to the threads of the cover retaining bolts and secure the cover. Tighten the bolts to 22 ft. lbs. (30 Nm).

13. Install the oil pan-to-front cover bolts. Tighten the bolts to 88 inch lbs. (10 Nm).

14. Reconnect the camshaft sensor, crankshaft sensor and oil pressure sender electrical connectors. Adjust the crankshaft sensor using tool J-37087 or equivalent.

15. Install the crankshaft balancer.

16. Install the inner splash shield.

17. Lower the vehicle.

18. Install the heater pipes. Install the coolant bypass hose and lower radiator hose from cover.

19. Install the serpentine belt.

20. Connect the negative battery cable.

21. Fill cooling system and check for leaks. Start the engine and allow to come to normal operating temperature. Recheck for leaks.

3.8L Engine

1. Relieve the pressure in the fuel system before disconnecting any fuel line connections. Disconnect the negative battery cable.

2. Drain the cooling system.

3. Disconnect the lower radiator hose and the heater hose from the water pump.

4. Remove the 2 nuts from the front engine mount from the cradle and raise the engine using a suitable lifting device.

5. Remove the water pump pulley and the serpentine belt.

6. Unbolt the alternator and brackets.

7. Remove the balancer bolt and washer. Using a puller, remove the balancer.

8. Unbolt the cover-to-block bolts. Remove the 2 oil pan-to-cover bolts.

9. Remove the cover and gasket.

To install:

10. Pry the oil seal from the front of the cover. Lubricate the seal lip and install new lip seal with lip, open side of seal, facing toward the cylinder block. Carefully drive or press seal into place.

11. Clean the mating surfaces of the front cover and cylinder block.

➡Remove the oil pump cover and pack the space around the oil pump gears completely with petroleum jelly. There must be no air space left inside the pump. If the pump is not packed, it may not begin to pump oil as soon as the engine is started and engine damage may result.

12. Install a new gasket to the oil pan and cylinder block. Install the front cover. Apply sealer to the threads of the cover retaining bolts and secure the cover.

13. Install the cover-to-block bolts, then the 2 oil pan-to-cover bolts.

14. Install the balancer, washer and balancer bolt.

15. Attach the alternator brackets and the alternator.

16. Install the water pump pulley and the serpentine belt.

17. Lower the engine into position and install the 2 nuts to the front engine mount at the cradle.

18. Connect the lower radiator hose and the heater hose to the water pump.

19. Connect the negative battery cable.

20. Fill cooling system and check for leaks. Start the engine and allow to come to normal operating temperature. Check for leaks.

Oil Seal

REMOVAL & INSTALLATION

Cover Removed

EXCEPT 3.0L AND 3.8L ENGINES

1. After removing the timing cover, pry oil seal out of front of cover.

2. Install new lip seal with lip (open side of seal) inside and drive or press seal carefully into place. The use of tools J-34995, J-35468 or an equivalent can be helpful.

3.0L AND 3.8L ENGINES

1. Using a drift punch, drive the oil seal and the shedder from the front toward the rear of the timing cover.

2. To install the new oil seal, coil it around the opening with the ends toward the top. Using a punch, drive in the oil seal and stake it at three places. Rotate a hammer handle inside the seal until the crankshaft balancer can be inserted through the opening.

3. To complete the installation, reverse the removal procedures. Tighten the balancer bolt to proper torque.

Cover Installed

The oil seal may be removed from the timing cover without removing the cover. To do this, remove the damper pulley and pry the oil seal from the timing cover, using a small pry bar.

Place a seal installation tool J-34995, J-35468 or equivalent on the crankshaft (to prevent damaging the seal) when installing the new oil seal or the front cover. To install the new oil seal, place the seal's open end toward the inside of the cover and drive it into the cover. Tighten the damper pulley bolt to proper torque.

Timing Gear

REMOVAL & INSTALLATION

➡On early 2.5L engines without a timing chain, the camshaft gear is press fitted on the camshaft. If replacement of the camshaft gear is necessary, the engine must be removed from the vehicle and the camshaft and gear removed from the engine.

1. Relieve the pressure in the fuel system before disconnecting any fuel line connections.

2. Disconnect the negative battery cable.

3. Remove the engine from the vehicle.

4. Remove the camshaft and gear assembly from the engine block.

5. Using an arbor press and adapter, remove the gear from the camshaft. Position the thrust plate to avoid damage by interference with the Woodruff® key as the gear is removed.

To install:

6. Support the camshaft at the back of the front journal in the arbor press using press plate adapters.

7. Position the spacer ring thrust plate over the end of the shaft and key.

8. Press the gear on the shaft with the bottom against the spacer ring. Measure the end clearance at the thrust plate. Clearance should be within 0.0015–0.0050 in. (0.0381–1.270mm).

   a. If the clearance is less than 0.0015 in. (0.0381mm), replace the spacer ring.

   b. If more than 0.0050 in. (1.270mm), make certain the gear is seated properly against the spacer. If the clearance is still excessive, replace the thrust plate.

9. Lubricate the camshaft journals with a high quality engine oil supplement. Install the camshaft and gear into the engine block.

10. Rotate the camshaft and crankshaft so the timing marks on the gear teeth align. The engine is now in No. 4-cylinder firing position.

11. Install the camshaft thrust plate-to-block screws and tighten to 90 inch lbs. (10 Nm).

12. Install the engine in the vehicle.

13. Connect the negative battery cable.

Timing Chain and Sprockets

REMOVAL & INSTALLATION

2.2L Engine

♦ **See Figure 87**

1. Disconnect the negative battery cable.

2. Remove the timing chain front cover.

3. Rotate the crankshaft until the piston in No. 1 cylinder is at TDC on the compression stroke. The marks on the camshaft and crankshaft sprockets should be in alignment.

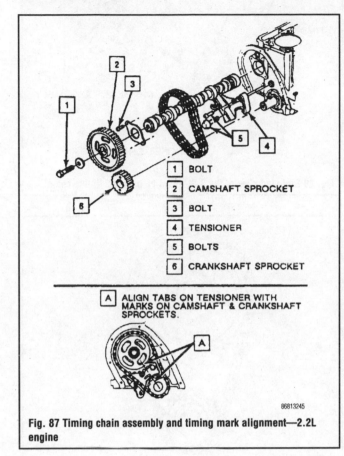

Fig. 87 Timing chain assembly and timing mark alignment—2.2L engine

4. Loosen but do not remove, the timing chain tensioner nut.

5. Unbolt the camshaft sprocket bolt, then remove the sprocket and chain together. If the sprocket does not slide from the camshaft easily, a light blow with a soft mallet at the lower edge of the sprocket will dislodge it.

6. Use a puller such as J-22888 or equivalent and remove the crankshaft sprocket.

To install:

7. Install the crankshaft sprocket, using the installation tool J-5590 or equivalent.

8. Install the timing chain over the camshaft sprocket and then around the crankshaft sprocket. Make sure the marks on the two sprockets are in alignment.

9. Lubricate the thrust surface with Molykote® or it's equivalent.

10. Align the dowel in the camshaft with the dowel hole in the sprocket and then install the sprocket onto the camshaft. Use the mounting bolt to draw the sprocket onto the camshaft and then tighten to 77 ft. lbs. (105 Nm).

11. Lubricate the timing chain with clean engine oil. Tighten the bolts on the chain tensioner to 18 ft. lbs. (24 Nm).

12. Install the timing chain front cover.

13. Connect the negative battery cable.

2.5L Engine

♦ **See Figure 88**

1. Disconnect the negative battery cable.
2. Remove the crankcase front cover.
3. Loosen the camshaft bolt.
4. Place the No. 1 piston at TDC with the marks on the camshaft and crankshaft sprockets aligned.
5. Remove the camshaft sprocket and chain.

➡ **If the sprocket does not come off easily, a light blow with a plastic mallet on the lower edge of the sprocket should dislodge the sprocket.**

To install:

6. Aligning the timing marks with the engine at TDC, install the timing chain and sprocket.
7. Insert and tighten the camshaft bolt to 43 ft. lbs. (58 Nm).
8. Lubricate the timing chain with engine oil. Install the crankcase front cover. Connect battery negative cable.

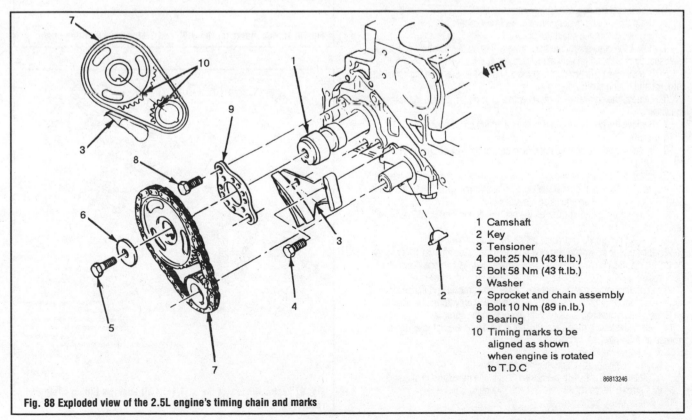

1 Camshaft
2 Key
3 Tensioner
4 Bolt 25 Nm (43 ft.lb.)
5 Bolt 58 Nm (43 ft.lb.)
6 Washer
7 Sprocket and chain assembly
8 Bolt 10 Nm (89 in.lb.)
9 Bearing
10 Timing marks to be aligned as shown when engine is rotated to T.D.C

Fig. 88 Exploded view of the 2.5L engine's timing chain and marks

2.8L Engine

1. Relieve the pressure in the fuel system before disconnecting any fuel line connections. Disconnect the negative battery cable.
2. Remove the crankcase front cover.
3. Place the No. 1 piston at TDC with the marks on the camshaft and crankshaft sprockets aligned.
4. Remove the camshaft sprocket and chain.

➡**If the sprocket does not come off easily, a light blow with a plastic mallet on the lower edge of the sprocket should dislodge the sprocket.**

5. Remove the crankshaft sprocket.
To install:
6. Install the crankshaft sprocket. Apply Molykote® or equivalent, to the sprocket thrust surface.
7. Hold the sprocket with the chain hanging down and align the marks on the camshaft and crankshaft sprockets.
8. Align the dowel in the camshaft with the dowel hole in the camshaft sprocket.
9. Draw the camshaft sprocket onto the camshaft using the mounting bolts. Tighten the camshaft sprocket mounting bolts to 18 ft. lbs. (25 Nm).
10. Lubricate the timing chain with engine oil. Install the crankcase front cover. Connect battery negative cable.

3.0L Engine

▶ See Figures 89 and 90

1. Remove the timing chain cover.
2. Turn the crankshaft so that the timing marks are aligned.
3. Remove the crankshaft oil slinger.
4. Remove the camshaft sprocket bolts.
5. Use two prybars to alternately pry the camshaft and crankshaft sprocket free along with the chain.
6. Installation is the reverse of removal. If the engine was turned, make sure that the No. 1 cylinder is at TDC.

3.1L Engine (VIN M)

▶ See Figure 91

1. Disconnect the negative battery cable.
2. Drain the cooling system into a suitable container.
3. Remove the timing chain front cover.
4. Rotate the crankshaft until the timing marks on the camshaft and crankshaft sprockets are in alignment at their closest approach.
5. Remove the camshaft sprocket mounting bolt and remove the camshaft sprocket and timing chain.
6. Remove the crankshaft sprocket with a gear puller, J-5825-A, or the equivalent.
7. Remove the two bolts and remove the timing chain damper.
To install:
8. Install the timing chain damper and tighten the mounting bolts to 15 ft. lbs. (21 Nm).
9. Install the crankshaft sprocket onto the crankshaft making sure the notch in the sprocket fits over the crankshaft key. Fully seat the sprocket on the crankshaft using J-38612, or an equivalent gear installer.
10. Make sure the timing mark on the crankshaft sprocket is still pointing straight up.
11. Install the camshaft sprocket inside the timing chain.
12. Pick up the chain and sprocket and hold the sprocket in such a way that the timing mark is pointing down and the timing chain is hanging down off of the sprocket.
13. Loop the timing chain under the crankshaft sprocket and install the camshaft sprocket on the camshaft. The sprocket will only fit on the camshaft if the dowel on the camshaft lines up with the hole in the sprocket.
14. Verify the timing marks are aligned. If the marks are not in alignment proceed as follows:
   a. Remove the chain and sprocket.
   b. Install the sprocket and mounting bolt loosely.
   c. Rotate the crankshaft and camshaft until the marks are in alignment.
   d. Remove the camshaft sprocket and mounting bolt.
15. Repeat steps 13 and 14.

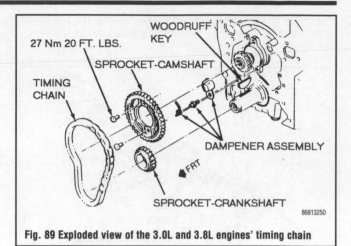

Fig. 89 Exploded view of the 3.0L and 3.8L engines' timing chain

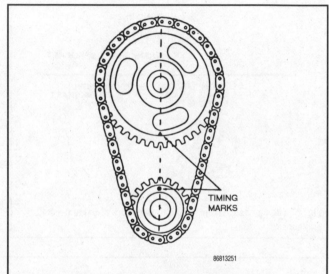

Fig. 90 Timing marks for the 3.0L and 3.8L engines' timing chain

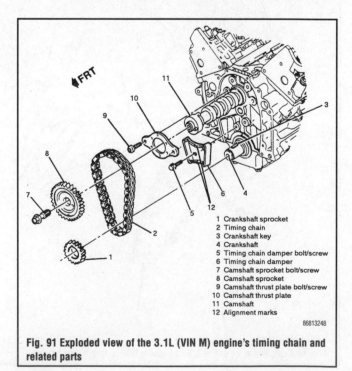

1 Crankshaft sprocket
2 Timing chain
3 Crankshaft key
4 Crankshaft
5 Timing chain damper bolt/screw
6 Timing chain damper
7 Camshaft sprocket bolt/screw
8 Camshaft sprocket
9 Camshaft thrust plate bolt/screw
10 Camshaft thrust plate
11 Camshaft
12 Alignment marks

Fig. 91 Exploded view of the 3.1L (VIN M) engine's timing chain and related parts

16. Tighten the camshaft sprocket mounting bolt to 74 ft. lbs. (100 Nm).
17. Lubricate the timing chain components with engine oil.
18. Install the timing chain front cover.
19. Refill the cooling system.
20. Connect the negative battery cable.
21. Start the vehicle and verify no leaks.

3.1L Engine (VIN T)

♦ See Figure 92

1. Disconnect the negative battery cable.
2. Remove the crankcase front cover.
3. Place the No. 1 piston at TDC with the marks on the camshaft and crankshaft sprockets aligned.
4. Remove the camshaft sprocket and chain.

➡**If the sprocket does not come off easily, a light blow with a plastic mallet on the lower edge of the sprocket should dislodge the sprocket.**

5. Remove the crankshaft sprocket.

To install:

6. Install the crankshaft sprocket. Apply Molykote® or equivalent, to the sprocket thrust surface.
7. Hold the sprocket with the chain hanging down and align the marks on the camshaft and crankshaft sprockets.
8. Align the dowel in the camshaft with the dowel hole in the camshaft sprocket.
9. Draw the camshaft sprocket onto the camshaft using the mounting bolts. Tighten the camshaft sprocket mounting bolts to 18 ft. lbs. (25 Nm).
10. Lubricate the timing chain with engine oil. Install the crankcase front cover. Connect battery negative cable.

3.3L Engine

♦ See Figure 93

1. Relieve the pressure in the fuel system before disconnecting any fuel line connections.
2. Disconnect the negative battery cable.
3. Remove the crankcase front cover and camshaft thrust bearing.
4. Turn the crankshaft so the timing marks are aligned.
5. Remove the timing chain damper and camshaft sprocket bolts.
6. Remove the camshaft sprocket and chain. Remove the crankshaft sprocket.

To install:

7. Make sure the crankshaft is positioned so No. 1 piston is at TDC on compression stroke.
8. Rotate the camshaft with the sprocket temporarily installed, so the timing mark is straight down.

9. Assembly the timing chain on the sprockets with the timing marks aligned. Install the timing chain and sprocket.
10. Install the camshaft sprocket bolts. Tighten the bolts to 27 ft. lbs. (37 Nm).
11. Install the timing chain damper and engine front cover. Connect battery negative cable.

3.8L Engine

♦ See Figures 89 and 90

1. Relieve the pressure in the fuel system before disconnecting any fuel line connections.
2. Disconnect the negative battery cable.
3. Remove the crankcase front cover.
4. Turn the crankshaft so the timing marks are aligned.
5. Remove the crankshaft oil slinger, as required.
6. Remove the camshaft sprocket bolts.
7. Remove the cam sensor magnet assembly.
8. Use 2 prybars to alternately pry the camshaft and crankshaft sprocket free along with the chain.

To install:

9. Make sure the crankshaft is positioned so No. 1 piston is at TDC.
10. Rotate the camshaft with the sprocket temporarily installed, so the timing mark is straight down.
11. Assemble the timing chain on the sprockets with the timing marks aligned. Install the timing chain and sprocket.
12. Install the cam sensor magnet assembly.
13. Install the oil slinger with the large part of the cone toward the front of the engine, as required.
14. Secure the camshaft sprocket bolt, thrust button and spring.
15. Attach the timing chain damper and engine front cover.

Camshaft

REMOVAL & INSTALLATION

2.2L Engine

♦ See Figure 94

The engine must be removed from the vehicle for this procedure.
1. Disconnect the negative battery cable.
2. Remove the engine assembly from the vehicle. Mount the engine on a suitable engine stand.
3. Remove the serpentine drive belt.
4. Remove the serpentine drive belt tensioner assembly with the alternator attached.

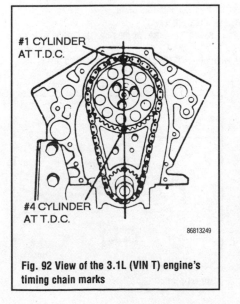

Fig. 92 View of the 3.1L (VIN T) engine's timing chain marks

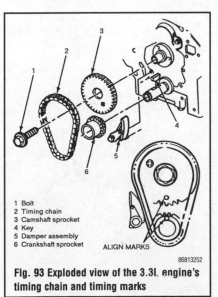

1 Bolt
2 Timing chain
3 Camshaft sprocket
4 Key
5 Damper assembly
6 Crankshaft sprocket

Fig. 93 Exploded view of the 3.3L engine's timing chain and timing marks

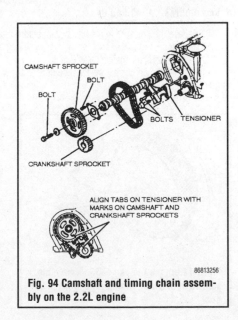

Fig. 94 Camshaft and timing chain assembly on the 2.2L engine

5. Detach the strut bracket and the rear alternator bracket.
6. Unbolt the front engine mount bracket.
7. Remove the oil level indicator tube.
8. Unbolt and remove the oil pan.
9. Remove the crankshaft balancer and front cover.
10. Remove the timing chain and camshaft sprocket.
11. Disconnect the spark plug wires.
12. Remove the rocker arm cover.

➡**When removing the valve train components they must be kept in order for installation in the same locations from which they were removed.**

13. Remove the rocker arm nuts, rocker arms, balls and pushrods.
14. Remove the power steering pump brace.
15. Disconnect the cylinder head with the intake and exhaust manifolds attached.
16. Remove the valve lifters.
17. Remove the camshaft thrust plate mounting bolts and the thrust plate.
18. Remove the oil pump assembly.
19. Remove the camshaft carefully from the engine.

To install:
20. Coat the camshaft lobes and bearings with GM Engine Oil Supplement (E.O.S.) 1051396 or equivalent, then insert the camshaft carefully into the engine.
21. Install the oil pump drive assembly.
22. Install the thrust plate, then tighten the mounting bolts to 106 inch lbs. (12 Nm).
23. Install the valve lifters.
24. Attach the cylinder head and manifold assemblies to the engine.
25. Connect the power steering pump brace.
26. Install the pushrods, rocker arms, balls and rocker arms nuts. Tighten the nuts to 22 ft. lbs. (30 Nm).
27. Install the valve cover.
28. Connect the spark plug wires.
29. Install the timing chain and camshaft sprocket. Verify that the camshaft and crankshaft sprocket timing marks are correctly aligned.
30. Install the timing chain front cover and crankshaft balancer.
31. Install the oil pan.
32. Bolt down the oil level indicator.
33. Attach the front engine bracket, rear alternator bracket and strut bracket.
34. Install the drive belt tensioner and alternator assembly, then install the serpentine drive belt.
35. Install the engine assembly into the vehicle.
36. Attach a new oil filter on the engine, then fill the engine crankcase with clean oil.
37. Connect the negative battery cable.
38. Fill the cooling system with new coolant.
39. Start the vehicle, top off the coolant, check for leaks.

2.5L Engine

◆ **See Figures 95, 96 and 97**

1. Relieve the pressure in the fuel system before disconnecting any fuel line connections.
2. Disconnect the negative battery cable.
3. Remove the engine as previously outlined, and support it on a suitable engine stand.

4. Unbolt the rocker cover, rocker arms and pushrods.
5. Remove the spark plugs and fuel pump on carbureted models.
6. Unsecure the pushrod cover and gasket. Remove the lifters.
7. Remove the alternator, the alternator lower bracket and the front engine mount bracket assembly.
8. Remove the oil pump driveshaft and gear assembly.
9. Remove the crankshaft hub and timing gear cover.
10. Unfasten and remove the 2 camshaft thrust plate screws by working through the holes in the gear.
11. Remove the camshaft and gear assembly by pulling it through the front of the block. Take care not to damage the bearings.
12. If replacement of the camshaft gear is necessary, use the following procedure:
  a. Remove the camshaft gear using an arbor press and adapter.
  b. Position the thrust plate to avoid damage by interference with the key as the gear is removed.
  c. When assembling the gear onto the camshaft, support the camshaft at the back of the front journal in the arbor press using press plate adapters.
  d. Press the gear on the shaft until it bottoms against the spacer ring.
  e. Measure the end clearance of the thrust plate. End clearance should be 0.0015–0.0050 in. (0.0381–0.1270mm).
  f. If clearance is less than 0.0015 in. (0.0381mm), replace the spacer ring.
  g. If clearance is more than 0.0050 in. (0.127mm), replace the thrust plate.

To install:
13. Lubricate the camshaft journals with a high quality engine oil supplement and carefully install the camshaft and gear into the cylinder block.
14. Rotate the camshaft and crankshaft so the timing marks on the gear teeth align. The engine is now in No. 4-cylinder firing position.
15. Install the camshaft thrust plate-to-block screw. Tighten the screw to 90 inch lbs. (10 Nm).
16. Attach the crankshaft hub and timing gear cover.
17. Install the oil pump driveshaft and gear assembly.
18. Attach the lower alternator bracket, alternator and the front engine mount bracket assembly.
19. Install the spark plugs and fuel pump.
20. Install the lifters. Install the pushrod cover and gasket.
21. Install the pushrods, rocker arms and rocker cover.
22. Place and attach the engine in the vehicle.
23. Connect the negative battery cable.

2.8L Engine

1. Relieve the pressure in the fuel system before disconnecting any fuel line connections.
2. Disconnect the negative battery cable.
3. Remove the engine as previously outlined, and support it on a suitable engine stand.
4. Remove the intake manifold, valve cover, rocker arms, pushrods and valve lifters.
5. Remove the crankshaft balancer and front cover.
6. Remove the timing chain and sprockets.
7. Carefully remove the camshaft. Avoid marring the camshaft bearing surfaces.

To install:
8. Coat the camshaft with lubricant 1052365 or equivalent, and install the camshaft.

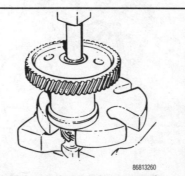

Fig. 95 Remove the camshaft thrust plate screws by working through the holes in the gear

86813259

Fig. 96 A press is needed to remove the camshaft timing gear

86813260

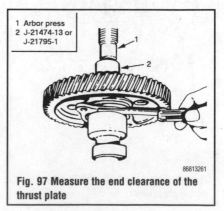

1 Arbor press
2 J-21474-13 or
  J-21795-1

Fig. 97 Measure the end clearance of the thrust plate

86813261

9. Install the timing chain and sprocket.
10. Install the camshaft thrust button and front cover.
11. Install the crankshaft balancer.
12. Install the intake manifold, valve cover, rocker arms, pushrods and valve lifters.
13. Install the engine in the vehicle.
14. Connect the negative battery cable.
15. Adjust the valves, as required.

3.0L Engine

1. Disconnect the battery cables.
2. Remove the engine as described earlier.
3. Remove the intake manifold.
4. Remove the valve covers.
5. Remove the rocker arm assemblies, pushrods and lifters.
6. Remove the timing cover, chain and camshaft sprocket. This will avoid burring of the camshaft journals by the crankshaft during removal. Slide the camshaft forward out of the bearing bores carefully to avoid marring the bearing surfaces.

To install:

7. When replacing the camshaft, take extra care to avoid marring the bearing surfaces.
8. Install the valve mechanism.
9. Attach the intake manifold to the engine.
10. Install the engine.
11. Connect the battery cables, start the engine, and check for leaks.

3.1L Engine (VIN T)

1. Remove the engine as previously outlined earlier in this section.
2. Remove the valve lifters, then remove the front cover.
3. Remove the timing chain and sprocket.
4. Slide the camshaft from the engine, take care not to damage the camshaft bearings. The journals are the same diameter.

To install:

5. Coat the camshaft lobes and bearings with GM Engine Oil Supplement (E.O.S.) 1051396 or equivalent, then insert the camshaft carefully into the engine.
6. Lubricate the camshaft journals with engine oil.
7. Install the camshaft.
8. Attach the timing chain and sprocket.
9. Install the crankcase front cover.
10. Install the lifters.
11. Install the engine.
12. Fill the engine crankcase with clean engine oil. Fill the cooling system.
13. Double check everything has been connected, start the engine, top off the cooling system, then check for leaks.

3.1L Engine (VIN M)

✳✳ CAUTION

Fuel Injection systems remain under pressure, even after the engine has been turned OFF. The fuel system pressure must be relieved before disconnecting any fuel lines. Failure to do so may result in fire and/or personal injury.

1. Relieve the fuel system pressure.
2. Disconnect the negative battery cable.
3. Remove the engine assembly.

➡**When removing valve train components they must be marked for installation in the same location they are removed from. When the camshaft is being replaced the valve lifters should also be replaced.**

4. Remove the intake manifold, valve cover, rocker arms, pushrods and valve lifters.
5. Remove the crankshaft balancer and front cover.
6. Remove the timing chain and sprockets.
7. Remove the oil pump driven gear mounting bolt and remove the oil pump driven gear.
8. Remove the two bolts and remove the camshaft thrust plate.
9. Carefully remove the camshaft. Avoid marring the camshaft bearing surfaces.

To install:

10. Coat the camshaft with lubricant 1052365 or equivalent, and install the camshaft.
11. Attach the camshaft thrust plate and tighten the mounting bolts to 89 inch lbs. (10 Nm).
12. Install the oil pump driven gear and tighten the mounting bolt to 27 ft. lbs. (36 Nm).
13. Install the timing chain and sprocket.
14. Attach the camshaft thrust button and front cover.
15. Install the crankshaft balancer.
16. Install the intake manifold, valve cover, rocker arms, pushrods and valve lifters.
17. Install the engine assembly.
18. Connect the negative battery cable.
19. Adjust the valves, as required.
20. Add engine and coolant as required.
21. Start the engine and verify no oil leaks.

3.8L Engine

1. Relieve the pressure in the fuel system before disconnecting any fuel line connections.
2. Disconnect the negative battery cable.
3. Remove the engine as previously outlined, and support it on a suitable engine stand.
4. Remove the intake manifold.
5. Unbolt and remove the valve covers.
6. Remove the rocker arm assemblies, pushrods and lifters.
7. Unbolt and remove the timing chain cover.

➡**Align the timing marks of the camshaft and crankshaft sprockets to avoid burring the camshaft journals by the crankshaft.**

8. Remove the timing chain, camshaft sensor magnet assembly and sprockets.

To install:

9. Coat the camshaft with lubricant 1052365 or equivalent, and install the camshaft.
10. Install the timing chain, camshaft sensor magnet assembly and sprockets.
11. Install the camshaft thrust button and front cover.
12. Complete installation by reversing the removal procedure.
13. Add engine oil and coolant as required.
14. Connect battery negative cable.

INSPECTION

Degrease the camshaft, using solvent, and clean out all oil holes. Visually inspect cam lobes and bearing journals for excessive wear. If a lobe is questionable, check all lobes as indicated below. If a journal or lobe is worn, the camshaft must be reground or replaced.

Inspect the sprocket, key way and threads, bearing surfaces and lobes for: wear, galling, gouges, and overheating.

Do not attempt to repair a camshaft, replace it if damaged. If a new camshaft is installed, all the valve lifters must be replaced.

Measure the bearing journals, with a micrometer, measure the diameter and run-out. If out of specification, replace the camshaft. Measure the camshaft lift, lubricate the journal bearings with GM 1052365 or equivalent. Carefully set the camshaft on "V" blocks or between the camshaft centers. With dial indicators, measure the cam lift. If out of specification, replace the cam.

Camshaft Bearings

REMOVAL & INSTALLATION

2.2L Engine

▶ **See Figure 98**

1. Remove the engine from the vehicle.
2. Remove the camshaft from the engine as previously outlined.
3. Assemble the camshaft remover and installer tool, J-33049 or an equivalent.

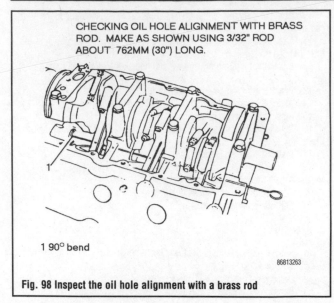

CHECKING OIL HOLE ALIGNMENT WITH BRASS ROD. MAKE AS SHOWN USING 3/32" ROD ABOUT 762MM (30") LONG.

1 90° bend

86813263

Fig. 98 Inspect the oil hole alignment with a brass rod

4. Select the proper pilot, nut and thrust washer.
5. Make sure the puller nut engages a sufficient number of threads.
6. Pull out the bearings.

➡**It is very important that you do not use the old camshaft bearings once they are removed from the engine.**

To install:
7. Separate the front, rear and intermediate camshaft bearings.
8. Assemble the camshaft remover and installer tool, J-33049 or an equivalent.
9. Place the bearing onto the J-33049 and index the oil hole(s) of the bearing with the oil passage(s) in the cylinder block. Pull the bearing into place.
10. Select the proper pilot, nut and thrust washer.

➡**Proper alignment of the oil holes is critical. Restriction of the oil flow will cause severe engine damage.**

11. Install the camshaft plug, then apply GM sealer 1052914 or equivalent to the plug before installing.
12. Inspect with a piece of ³⁄₃₂ inch brass rod with a 90° bend at the end. Probe the bearing oil holes and verify that they are properly aligned.

2.5L Engine

1982–90 MODELS

1. Remove the engine from the vehicle as previously outlined.
2. Remove the camshaft from the engine as previously outlined.
3. Unbolt and remove the engine flywheel.
4. Drive the rear camshaft expansion plug out of the engine block from the inside.
5. Using a camshaft bearing service tool, J-21473-1 (1982–84) or J-33049 (1985–90), drive the front camshaft bearing towards the rear and the rear bearing towards the front.
6. Install the appropriate extension tool J-21054-1 on the service tool and drive the center bearing out towards the rear.
To install:
7. Drive all of the new bearings into place in the opposite direction of which they were removed, making sure to align the oil holes of each bearing with each of the feed holes in the engine block bores.

➡**The front camshaft bearing must be driven approximately ⅛ in. (3mm) behind the front of the cylinder block to uncover the oil hole to the timing gear oiling nozzle.**

8. Install the camshaft into the engine then reinstall the engine as previously outlined.

1991–93 MODELS

1. Remove the engine from the vehicle.
2. Remove the camshaft from the engine as previously outlined.

3. Assemble the camshaft remover and installer tool, J-33049 or an equivalent.
4. Select the proper pilot, nut and thrust washer.
5. Make sure the puller nut engages a sufficient number of threads.
6. Pull out the bearings.

➡**It is very important that you do not use the old camshaft bearings once they are removed from the engine.**

To install:
7. Separate the front, rear and intermediate camshaft bearings.
8. Assemble the camshaft remover and installer tool, J-33049 or an equivalent.
9. Place the bearing onto the J-33049 and index the oil hole(s) of the bearing with the oil passage(s) in the cylinder block. Pull the bearing into place.
10. Select the proper pilot, nut and thrust washer.

➡**Proper alignment of the oil holes is critical. Restriction of the oil flow will cause sever engine damage.**

11. Install the camshaft plug, then apply GM sealer 1052914 or equivalent to the plug before installing.
12. Inspect with a piece of ³⁄₃₂ inch brass rod with a 90° bend at the end, probe the bearing oil holes and verify that they are properly aligned.

2.8L Engine

1. Remove the camshaft rear cover.
2. Using Tool J-6098 (1982–84) or J-33049 (1985 and later) or its equivalent, index the pilot in the camshaft front bearing, then install the puller screw through the pilot.
3. Install the remover and installer tool with the shoulder towards the bearing, make sure a sufficient amount of threads are engaged.
4. Using two wrenches, hold puller the screw while turning the nut. When the bearing has been pulled from the bore, remove the remover and installer tool, then the bearing from the puller screws.
5. Remove the remaining bearings (except front and rear) in the same manner. It will be necessary to index the pilot in the camshaft rear bearing to remove the rear intermediate bearing.
6. Assemble the remover and installer tool on the driver handle and remove the camshaft front and rear bearings by driving towards the center of the cylinder block.
The camshaft front and rear bearings should be installed first. These bearings will act as guides for the pilot and center the remaining bearings being pulled into place.
To install:
7. Assemble the remover and installer tool on the driver handle, then install the camshaft front and rear bearings by driving towards center of the cylinder block.
8. Use tool set J-6098 (1982–84 models) or J-33049 (1985 and later), or its equivalent, index the pilot in the camshaft front bearing, then install the puller screw through the pilot.
9. Index the camshaft bearing in the bore (with oil hole aligned as outlined below), then install the remover and installer tool on the puller screw with the shoulder towards the bearing.
• The rear and intermediate bearing oil holes must be aligned at the 2:30 o'clock position.
• The front bearing oil holes must be aligned at the 1:00 and 2:30 o'clock (two holes) positions.
10. Using two wrenches, hold the puller screw while turning the nut. After the bearing has been pulled into the bore, remove the remover and installer tool from the puller screw, then check alignment of the oil hole in the camshaft bearing.
11. Install the remaining bearings in the same manner. It will be necessary to index pilot in the camshaft rear bearing to install the rear intermediate bearing. Clean the rear cover mating surfaces and bolt holes then apply a ⅛ in. (3mm) bead of R.T.V. to the cover. Install the cover.

3.0L Engine

1. Remove the camshaft as previously outlined.
2. Assemble the puller screw to the required length.
3. Select the proper size expanding collet and back-up nut.

4. Install the expanding collet on the expanding mandrel. Install the back-up nut.

5. Insert this assembly into the camshaft bearing to be removed. Tighten the back-up nut to expand the collet to fit the I.D. of the bearing.

6. Thread the end of the puller screw assembly into the end of the expanding mandrel and collet assembly.

7. Install the pulling plate, thrust bearing, and pulling nut on the threaded end of the puller screw.

8. The bearing can then be removed by turning the pulling nut.

➡**Make certain to grip the ⅝ in. hex end of the puller screw with a wrench to keep it from rotating when the pulling nut is turned. Failure to do this will result in the locking up of all threads in the pulling assembly and possible over expansion of the collet.**

9. Repeat the above procedure to remove any other bearings, except the front bearing, which may be pulled from the rear of the engine.

➡**When removing rear cam bearing, it is necessary to remove the welch plug at the back of the cam bore. However, if only the front bearing is being replaced, it is not necessary to remove the engine or welch plug. The front bearing can be removed by using a spacer between the pulling plate and the cylinder block.**

To install:

10. Assemble the puller screw to the required length.

11. Select the proper size expanding collet and back-up nut.

12. Install the expanding collet on the expanding mandrel.

13. Install the back-up nut.

14. Place the new camshaft bearing on the collet and GENTLY hand-tighten the back-up nut to expand the collet to fit the bearing. Do not over-tighten the back-up nut. A loose sliding fit between the collet and the bearing surface is adequate. This will provide just enough clearance to allow for the collapse which will occur when the new bearing is pulled into the engine block.

15. Slide the mandrel assembly and bearing into the bearing bore as far as it will go without force.

16. Thread the end of puller screw onto the end of the mandrel. Make certain to align the oil holes in bearing and block properly. One of the collet separation lines may be used as a reference point.

17. Install the pulling plate, thrust bearing and pulling nut on threaded end of puller screw.

18. Install the bearing in the same manner as described in the previous under bearing removal.

➡**When installing rear cam bearing, install new welch plug at back of cam bore. Coat outside diameter of plug with non-hardening sealer before installation.**

3 1L Engine (VIN T)

1. Remove the engine from the vehicle as previously outlined.

2. Remove the camshaft from the engine as previously outlined.

3. Remove the camshaft rear plug.

4. Assemble the removal tool. Using care and follow proper tool instructions remove camshaft bearings.

5. Select the proper pilot, nut and thrust washer.

6. Assemble to J-33049. Make certain the puller engages a sufficient number of threads and pull the bearing.

7. Install the appropriate extension tool J-21054-1 on the service tool and drive the center bearing out towards the rear.

3.1L Engine (VIN M)

1. Remove the engine from the vehicle.

2. Remove the camshaft from the engine as previously outlined.

3. Assemble the camshaft remover and installer tool, J-33049 or an equivalent.

4. Select the proper pilot, nut and thrust washer.

5. Make sure the puller nut engages a sufficient number of threads.

6. Pull out the bearings.

➡**It is very important that you do not use the old camshaft bearings once they are removed from the engine.**

To install:

7. Separate the front, rear and intermediate camshaft bearings.

8. Assemble the camshaft remover and installer tool, J-33049 or an equivalent.

9. Place the bearing onto the J-33049 and index the oil hole(s) of the bearing with the oil passage(s) in the cylinder block. Pull the bearing into place.

10. Select the proper pilot, nut and thrust washer.

➡**Proper alignment of the oil holes is critical. Restriction of the oil flow will cause sever engine damage.**

11. Install the camshaft plug, then apply GM sealer 1052914 or equivalent to the plug before installing.

12. Inspect with a piece of ³⁄₃₂ inch brass rod with a 90° bend at the end, probe the bearing oil holes and verify that they are properly aligned.

3.3L Engine

1. Remove the engine from the vehicle as previously outlined.

2. Remove the camshaft from the engine as previously outlined.

3. Remove the camshaft rear plug.

4. Assembly the removal tool. Using care and follow proper tool instructions remove camshaft bearings.

5. Select the proper pilot, nut and thrust washer.

6. Assemble to J-33049. Make certain the puller engages a sufficient number of threads and pull the bearing.

7. Install the appropriate extension tool J-21054-1 on the service tool and drive the center bearing out towards the rear.

3.8L Engine

1. Remove the camshaft as previously outlined.

2. Assemble the puller screw to the required length.

3. Select the proper size expanding collet and back-up nut.

4. Install the expanding collet on the expanding mandrel. Install the back-up nut.

5. Insert this assembly into the camshaft bearing to be removed. Tighten the back-up nut to expand the collet to fit the I.D. of the bearing.

6. Thread the end of the puller screw assembly into the end of the expanding mandrel and collet assembly.

7. Install the pulling plate, thrust bearing, and pulling nut on the threaded end of the puller screw.

8. The bearing can then be removed by turning the pulling nut.

➡**Make certain to grip the ⅝ in. hex end of the puller screw with a wrench to keep it from rotating when the pulling nut is turned. Failure to do this will result in the locking up of all threads in the pulling assembly and possible over expansion of the collet.**

9. Repeat the above procedure to remove any other bearings, except the front bearing, which may be pulled from the rear of the engine.

➡**When removing rear cam bearing, it is necessary to remove welch plug at the back of cam bore. However, if only the front bearing is being replaced, it is not necessary to remove the engine or welch plug. The front bearing can be removed by using a spacer between the pulling plate and the cylinder block.**

To install:

10. Assemble the puller screw to the required length.

11. Select the proper size expanding collet and back-up nut.

12. Install the expanding collet on the expanding mandrel.

13. Install the back-up nut.

14. Place the new camshaft bearing on the collet and GENTLY hand-tighten the back-up nut to expand the collet to fit the bearing. Do not overtighten the back-up nut. A loose sliding fit between the collet and the bearing surface is adequate. This will provide just enough clearance to allow for the collapse which will occur when the new bearing is pulled into the engine block.

15. Slide the mandrel assembly and bearing into the bearing bore as far as it will go without force.

16. Thread the end of puller screw onto the end of the mandrel. Make certain to align the oil holes in bearing and block properly. One of the collet separation lines may be used as a reference point.

17. Install the pulling plate, thrust bearing and pulling nut on threaded end of puller screw.

18. Install the bearing in the same manner as described in under bearing removal.

➡**When installing rear cam bearing, install new welch plug at back of cam bore. Coat outside diameter of plug with non-hardening sealer before installation.**

Pistons and Connecting Rods

✳✳ CAUTION

The EPA warns that prolonged contact with used engine oil may cause a number of skin disorders, including cancer! You should make every effort to minimize your exposure to used engine oil. Protective gloves should be worn when changing the oil. Wash your hands and any other exposed skin areas as soon as possible after exposure to used engine oil. Soap and water, or waterless hand cleaner should be used.

REMOVAL

◆ **See Figures 99, 100, 101 and 102**

1. Disconnect the negative battery cable.
2. Remove the engine assembly from the vehicle and secure on a suitable workstand.
3. Remove the intake manifold and cylinder heads.
4. Remove the oil pan and oil pump.
5. The position of each piston, connecting rod and connecting rod cap should be noted before any are removed, so they can be reinstalled in the same location.
6. Check the tops of the pistons and the sides of the connecting rods for identifying marks. In some engines, the top of the piston will be numbered to correspond with the cylinder number. The connecting rod and connecting rod cap should have numbers stamped on the machined surfaces next to the rod bolts that correspond with their cylinder number.
7. If no numbers are visible, use a number punch set and stamp the cylinder number on the connecting rod and connecting rod cap. The 2.2L and 2.5L engines are numbered 1–4 front to rear. On the 3.0L, 3.3L and 3.8L V6s, the right (rear) bank is numbered 2, 4, 6, and the left (front) bank 1, 3, 5. The 2.8L and 3.1L engines are numbered 1, 3, 5 on the right bank, and 2, 4, 6 on the left bank.
8. Rotate the crankshaft until the piston to be removed is at the bottom of the cylinder. Examine the cylinder bore above the ring travel. If the bore is worn so that a shoulder or ridge exists at the top of the cylinder, remove the ridge with a ridge reamer to avoid damaging the rings or cracking the ring lands in the piston during removal. Before operating the ridge reamer, place a shop towel on top of the piston to catch the metal shavings.

✳✳ WARNING

Be very careful when using a ridge reamer. Only remove the cylinder bore material that is necessary to remove the ridge. If too much

cylinder bore material is removed, cylinder overboring and piston replacement may be necessary.

9. Loosen the connecting rod bolt nuts until the nuts are flush with the ends of the bolts. Using a hammer and a brass drift or piece of wood, lightly tap on the nuts/bolts until the connecting rod cap is loosened from the connecting rod. Remove the nuts, rod cap and lower bearing shell.

➡**All caps and rods are matched pairs and must be assembled together. They must also return to their original locations. Match mark all caps to rods, for both location and direction. Installing the caps on the wrong rod or facing the wrong way will cause permanent engine damage.**

10. Slip a piece of snug fitting rubber hose over each rod bolt, to prevent the bolt threads from damaging the crankshaft during removal. Using a hammer handle or piece of wood or plastic, push the rod and piston upward in the bore until the connecting rod is clear of the crankshaft journal.
11. Inspect the rod bearings for scoring, chipping or other wear.
12. Inspect the crankshaft rod bearing journal for wear. Measure the journal diameter in several locations around the journal and compare to specification. If the crankshaft journal is scored or has deep ridges, or its diameter is below specification, the crankshaft must be removed from the engine and reground.
13. If the crankshaft journal appears usable, clean it and the rod bearing shells until they are completely free of oil. Blow any oil from the oil hole in the crankshaft.

➡**The journal surfaces and bearing shells must be completely free of oil to get an accurate reading with Plastigage®.**

14. Pull the connecting rod back onto the crankshaft rod journal and remove the rubber hoses.
15. Place a strip of Plastigage® lengthwise along the bottom center of the lower bearing shell, then install the cap with the shell and torque the connecting rod nuts to specification. Do not turn the crankshaft with the Plastigage® installed in the bearing.
16. Remove the bearing cap with the shell. The flattened Plastigage® will either be sticking to the bearing shell or the crankshaft journal.
17. Using the printed scale on the Plastigage® package, measure the flattened Plastigage® at its widest point. The number on the scale that most closely corresponds to the width of the Plastigage® indicates the bearing clearance in thousandths of an inch or hundredths of a millimeter.
18. Compare the actual bearing clearance with the bearing clearance specification. If the bearing clearance is excessive, the bearing must be replaced or the crankshaft must be ground and the bearing replaced.

➡**If the crankshaft is still at standard size (has not been ground undersize), bearing shell sets of 0.001, (0.0254mm) 0.002 (0.050mm) and 0.003 in. (0.0762mm) over standard size may be available to correct excessive bearing clearance.**

19. After clearance measuring is completed, be sure to remove the Plastigage® from the crankshaft and/or bearing shell.
20. Again remove the connecting rod cap and install the rubber hose on the rod bolts. Push the rod and piston upward in the bore until the piston rings clear the cylinder block. Remove the piston and connecting rod assembly from the top of the cylinder bore.

86813304

Fig. 99 Use a brass drift and hammer to loosen the cap

86813305

Fig. 100 Remove the nuts, rod cap and lower bearing shell

TCCS3803

Fig. 101 Place lengths of rubber hose over the connecting rod studs in order to protect the crankshaft and cylinders from damage

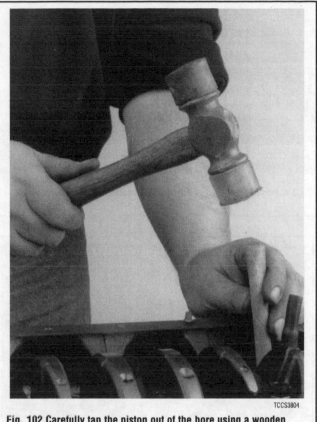

Fig. 102 Carefully tap the piston out of the bore using a wooden dowel

CLEANING & INSPECTION

▶ See Figures 103, 104, 105, 106 and 107

1. Remove the piston rings from the piston. The compression rings must be removed using a piston ring expander, to prevent breakage.

2. Clean the ring grooves with a ring groove cleaner, being careful not to cut into the piston metal. Heavy carbon deposits can be cleaned from the top of the piston with a scraper or wire brush, however, do not use a wire wheel on the ring grooves or lands. Clean the oil drain holes in the ring grooves. Clean all remaining dirt, carbon and varnish from the piston with a suitable solvent and a brush; do not use a caustic solution.

3. After cleaning, inspect the piston for scuffing, scoring, cracks, pitting or excessive ring groove wear. Replace any piston that is obviously worn.

4. If the piston appears okay, measure the piston diameter using a micrometer. Measure the piston diameter in the thrust direction, 90° to the piston pin axis, 3/4 in. below the center line of the piston pin bore.

5. Measure the cylinder bore diameter using a bore gauge, or with a telescope gauge and micrometer. The measurement should be made in the piston thrust direction at the top, middle and bottom of the bore.

➡ Piston diameter and cylinder bore measurements should be made with the parts at room temperature, 70°F (21°C).

6. Subtract the piston diameter measurement made in Step 4 from the cylinder bore measurement made in Step 5. This is the piston-to-bore clearance. If the clearance is within specification, light finish honing is all that is necessary. If the clearance is excessive, the cylinder must be bored and the piston replaced. If the pistons are replaced, the piston rings must also be replaced.

7. If the piston-to-bore clearance is okay, check the ring groove clearance. Roll the piston ring around the ring groove in which it is to be installed and check the clearance with a feeler gauge. Compare the measurement with specification. High points in the ring groove that may cause the ring to bind may be cleaned up carefully with a points file. Replace the piston if the ring groove clearance is not within specification.

8. Check the connecting rod for damage or obvious wear. Check for signs of fractures and check the bearing bore for out-of-round and taper.

9. A shiny surface on the pin boss side of the piston usually indicates that the connecting rod is bent or the wrist pin hole is not in proper relation to the piston skirt and ring grooves.

10. Abnormal connecting rod bearing wear can be caused by either a bent connecting rod, an improperly machined journal, or a tapered connecting rod bore.

11. Twisted connecting rods will not create an easily identifiable wear pattern, but badly twisted rods will disturb the action of the entire piston, rings, and connecting rod assembly and may be the cause of excessive oil consumption.

12. If the piston must be removed from the connecting rod, mark the side of the connecting rod that corresponds with the side of the piston that faces the front of the engine, so the new piston will be installed facing the same direction. Most pistons have an arrow or notch on the top of the piston, indicating that this side should face the front of the engine. If the original piston is to be reinstalled, use paint or a marker to indicate the cylinder number on the piston, so it can be reinstalled on the same connecting rod.

13. The piston pin is a press fit in the connecting rod. If the piston and/or connecting rod must be replaced, the pin must be pressed into the connecting rod using a fixture that will not damage or distort the piston and/or connecting rod. The piston must move freely on the pin after installation.

HONING

▶ See Figures 108 and 109

1. After the piston and connecting rod assembly have been removed, check the clearances as explained in the cleaning and inspection procedure, to determine whether boring and honing or just light honing are required.

2. Honing is best done with the crankshaft removed. This prevents damage to the crankshaft and makes post-honing cleaning easier, as the honing process will scatter metal particles. However, if the crankshaft is in the cylinder block, position the connecting rod journal for the cylinder being honed as far away from the bottom of the cylinder bore as possible, and wrap a shop cloth around the journal.

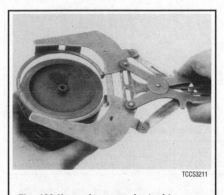

Fig. 103 Use a ring expander tool to remove the piston rings

Fig. 104 Clean the piston grooves using a ring groove cleaner

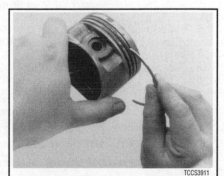

Fig. 105 You can use a piece of an old ring to clean the ring grooves, BUT be careful the ring is sharp

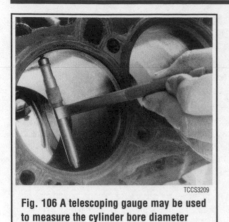

Fig. 106 A telescoping gauge may be used to measure the cylinder bore diameter

TCCS3209

Fig. 107 Measure the piston's outer diameter using a micrometer

TCCS3210

Fig. 108 Removing cylinder glazing using a flexible hone

TCCS3213

3. Honing can be done either with a flexible glaze breaker type hone or with a rigid hone that has honing stones and guide shoes. The flexible hone removes the least amount of metal, and is especially recommended if the piston-to-cylinder bore clearance is on the loose side. The flexible hone is useful to provide a finish on which the new piston rings will seat. A rigid hone will remove more material than the flexible hone and requires more operator skill.

4. Regardless of the type of hone used, carefully follow the manufacturers instructions for operation.

5. The hone should be moved up and down the bore at sufficient speed to obtain a uniform finish. A rigid hone will provide a more definite cross-hatch finish; operate the rigid hone at a speed to obtain a 45° included angle in the cross-hatch. The finish marks should be clean but not sharp, free from embedded particles and torn or folded metal.

6. Periodically during the honing procedure, thoroughly clean the cylinder bore and check the piston-to-bore clearance with the piston for that cylinder.

7. After honing is completed, thoroughly wash the cylinder bores and the rest of the engine with hot water and detergent. Scrub the bores well with a stiff bristle brush and rinse thoroughly with hot water. Thorough cleaning is essential, for if any abrasive material is left in the cylinder bore, it will rapidly wear the new rings and the cylinder bore. If any abrasive material is left in the rest of the engine, it will be picked up by the oil and carried throughout the engine, damaging bearings and other parts.

8. After the bores are cleaned, wipe them down with a clean cloth coated with light engine oil, to keep them from rusting.

PISTON PIN REPLACEMENT

◗ See Figure 110

Use care at all times when handling and servicing connecting rods and pistons To prevent possible damage to these units, do not clamp rod or piston is vise since they may become distorted. Do not allow pistons to strike against one another, against hard objects or bench surfaces, since distortion of piston contour or nicks in the soft aluminum material may result.

1. Remove the piston rings using a suitable piston ring remover.
2. Install the guide bushing of the piston pin removing and installing tool.
3. Install the piston and connecting rod assembly on the support, then place the assembly in an arbor press. Press the pin out of the connecting rod, using tool J-24086-B or equivalent.
4. Clean all disassembled parts completely.
5. Use a micrometer to measure the diameter of the piston pin. Use an inside micrometer to measure to piston pin bore.

➥If the piston pin-to-piston clearance is in excess of 0.001 in. (0.0254mm), the piston and pin assembly must be replaced.

6. Lubricate the piston and pin assembly and press fit together.

➥Never exceed 5000 lbs. of pressure when press fitting piston and pins.

7. After installing the piston pins, check that the piston has freedom of motion.

Fig. 109 A properly cross-hatched cylinder bore

TCCS3216

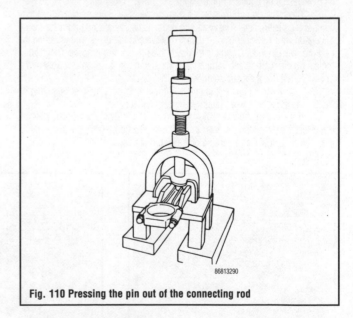

86813290

Fig. 110 Pressing the pin out of the connecting rod

PISTON RING REPLACEMENT

1. After the cylinder bores have been finish honed and cleaned, check the piston ring end-gap. Compress the piston rings to be used in the cylinder, one

at a time, into that cylinder. Using an inverted piston, push the ring down into the cylinder bore area where normal ring wear is not encountered.

2. Measure the ring end-gap with a feeler gauge and compare to specification. A gap that is too tight is more harmful than one that is too loose (If ring end-gap is excessively loose, the cylinder bore is probably worn beyond specification).

3. If the ring end-gap is too tight, carefully remove the ring and file the ends squarely with a fine file to obtain the proper clearance.

4. Install the rings on the piston, lowest ring first. The lowest (oil) ring is installed by hand; the top 2 (compression) rings must be installed using a piston ring expander tool. There is a high risk of breaking or distorting the compression rings if they are installed by hand.

5. Install the oil ring expander in the bottom ring groove. Make sure the ends butt together and do not overlap. The expander end-gap should be parallel to the piston pin, facing the right cylinder bank.

6. Start the end of an oil ring rail ring into the oil ring groove above the expander. The rail end-gap should be positioned 135° from the expander end-gap. Finish installing the rail ring by spiraling it the remainder of the way on. Repeat the rail installation with the other rail ring. Its gap position must be 135° from the other side of the expander end-gap, 90° from the other rail ring end-gap.

➡**If the instructions on the ring packaging differ from this information regarding ring gap positioning, follow the ring manufacturers instructions.**

7. Install the lower compression ring in the piston ring expander tool with the proper side up (usually the manufacturer's mark faces UP). The piston ring packaging should contain instructions as to the directions the ring sides should face. Spread the ring with the expander tool and install it on the piston. Position the end-gap 180° from the oil ring expander end-gap.

8. Repeat Step 7 to install the top compression ring. Position the end-gap in line with the oil ring expander end-gap. The compression ring end-gaps must not be aligned.

ROD BEARING REPLACEMENT

If you have already removed the connecting rod and piston assemblies from the engine, follow only Steps 3–7 of the following procedure.

The connecting rod bearings are designed to have a slight projection above the rod and cap faces to insure a positive contact. The bearings can be replaced without removing the rod and piston assembly from the engine.

1. Remove the oil pan. It may be necessary to remove the oil pump to provide access to rear connecting rod bearings.

2. With the connecting rod journal at the bottom, stamp the cylinder number on the machined surfaces of connecting rod and cap for identification when reinstalling, then remove caps.

3. Inspect journals for roughness and wear. Slight roughness may be removed with a fine grit polishing cloth saturated with engine oil. Burrs may be removed with a fine oil stone by moving the stone on the journal circumference. Do not move the stone back and forth across the journal. If the journals are scored or ridged, the crankshaft must be replaced.

4. The connecting rod journals should be checked for out-of-round and correct size with a micrometer.

➡**Crankshaft rod journals will normally be standard size. If any under-sized crankshafts are used, all will be 0.254mm undersize and 0.254mm will be stamped the number 4 counterweight.**

If a plastic gauging material (Plastigage® or equivalent) is to be used:

5. Clean oil from the journal bearing cap, connecting rod and outer and inner surface of the bearing inserts. Position insert so that tang is properly aligned with notch in rod and cap.

6. Place a piece of plastic gauging material in the center of lower bearing shell.

7. Remove bearing cap and determine bearing clearances by comparing the width of the flattened plastic gauging material at its widest point with the graduation on the container. The number within the graduation on the envelopes indicates the clearance in thousandths of an inch or millimeters. If this clearance is excessive, replace the bearing and recheck clearance with plastic gauging material. Lubricate bearing with engine oil before installation. Repeat Steps 2 through 7 on remaining connecting rod bearings. All rods must be connected to their journals when rotating the crankshaft to prevent engine damage.

INSTALLATION

1. Make sure the connecting rod and rod cap bearing saddles are clean and free of nicks or burrs. Install the bearing shells in the connecting rod, making sure the bearing shell tangs are seated in the notches.

➡**Be careful when handling any bearings. Hands and working area should be clean. Dirt is easily embedded in the bearing surface and the bearings are easily scratched or damaged.**

2. Make sure the cylinder bore and crankshaft journal are clean.

3. Position the crankshaft journal at its furthest position away from the bottom of the cylinder bore.

4. Coat the cylinder bore with light engine oil.

5. Install the rubber hoses over the connecting rod bolts to protect the crankshaft during installation.

6. Make sure the piston rings are properly installed and the ring end-gaps are correctly positioned. Install a piston ring compressor over the piston and rings and compress the piston rings into their grooves. Follow the ring compressor manufacturers instructions.

7. Place the piston and connecting rod assembly into the cylinder bore. Make sure the assembly is the correct one for that bore and that the piston and connecting rod are facing in the proper direction. Most pistons have an arrow or notch on the top of the piston, indicating that this side should face the front of the engine.

8. Make sure the ring compressor is seated squarely on the block deck surface. If the compressor is not seated squarely, a ring could pop out from beneath the compressor and hang up on the deck surface. As the piston is tapped into the bore, possibly breaking the ring.

9. Make sure that the connecting rod is not hung up on the crankshaft counterweights and is in position to come straight on to the crankshaft.

10. Tap the piston slowly into the bore, making sure the compressor remains squarely against the block deck. When the piston is completely in the bore, remove the ring compressor.

➡**If the connecting rod bearings were replaced, recheck the bearing clearance as described during the removal procedure, before proceeding further.**

11. Coat the crankshaft journal and the bearing shells with engine assembly lube or clean engine oil. Pull the connecting rod onto the crankshaft journal. After the rod is seated, remove the rubber hoses.

12. Install the rod bearing cap, making sure it is the correct one for the connecting rod. Lightly oil the connecting rod bolt threads and install the rod nuts, then tighten the nuts.

13. After each piston and connecting rod assembly is installed, turn the crankshaft over several times and check for binding. If there is a problem and the crankshaft will not turn, or turns with great difficulty, it will be easier to find the problem (rod cap on backwards, broken ring, etc.) than if all the assemblies are installed.

14. Check the clearance between the sides of the connecting rods and the crankshaft using a feeler gauge. Spread the rods slightly with a screwdriver to insert the gauge. If the clearance is below the minimum specification, the connecting rod will have to be removed and machined to provide adequate clearance. If the clearance is excessive, substitute an unworn rod and recheck. If the clearance is still excessive, the crankshaft must be welded and reground, or replaced.

15. Install the oil pump and oil pan.

16. Install the cylinder heads and intake manifold.

17. Install the engine in the vehicle.

18. Run the engine and check for leaks and proper engine operation.

Rear Main Seal

REMOVAL & INSTALLATION

2.2L and 2.5L Engines

◆ **See Figures 111 and 112**

The rear main bearing seal is a one piece seal and can be removed without removal of the oil pan or the crankshaft.

1. Disconnect the negative battery cable.
2. Drain the engine oil from the vehicle.
3. Support the engine and remove the transaxle and flywheel.
4. Loosen the seal by inserting a flat bladed tool into the dust lip. Pry the seal out by moving the tool around the seal as required until the seal is removed.

➡**Care must be taken not to damage the crankshaft seal surface with the prytool.**

5. Clean all of the block and crankshaft-to-seal mating areas.
6. Inspect the inside diameter bore for nicks or burrs.
7. Inspect the crankshaft for nicks or burrs on the seal contact surface. Repair or replace the crankshaft as needed.

To install:

8. Lubricate the seal bore to the seal surface with engine oil.
9. Install the new seal using tool J-34686 or equivalent.
10. Slide the new seal over the mandrel until the dust lip bottoms squarely against the tool collar.
11. Next align the dowel pin of the tool with the dowel pin hole in the crankshaft, then attach the tool to the crankshaft. Tighten the screws to 45 inch lbs. (5 Nm).
12. Tighten the T-handle of the tool. Push the seal into the bore. Continue until the collar is flush against the cylinder block.

13. Loosen the T-handle completely, then remove the attaching screws and the tool.
14. Check to be sure the seal is seated properly into the bore.
15. Install the flywheel, then reverse to install the remaining components.
16. Add engine oil to the crankcase, as necessary.
17. Connect the negative battery cable.
18. Start the engine and check for leaks.

2.8L Engine

2-PIECE SEAL

▶ **See Figures 113 and 114**

1. Drain the engine oil.
2. Remove the oil pan and pump.
3. Remove the rear main bearing cap.
4. Gently pack the upper seal into the groove approximately ¼–¾ in. (6–19mm) on each side.
5. Measure the amount the seal was driven in on one side, then add ¹⁄₁₆ in. (1.6mm). Cut this length from the old lower cap seal. Be sure to get a clean cut. Repeat for the other side.
6. Place the piece of cut seal into the groove and pack the seal into the block. Do this for each side.

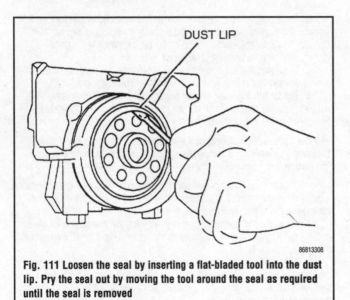

Fig. 111 Loosen the seal by inserting a flat-bladed tool into the dust lip. Pry the seal out by moving the tool around the seal as required until the seal is removed

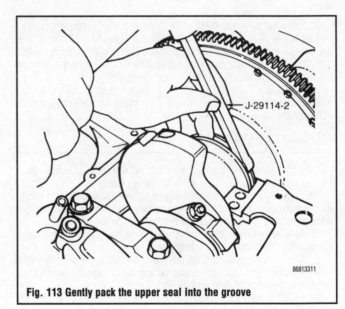

Fig. 113 Gently pack the upper seal into the groove

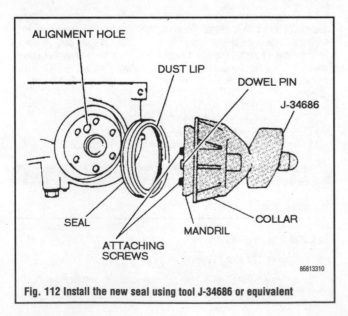

Fig. 112 Install the new seal using tool J-34686 or equivalent

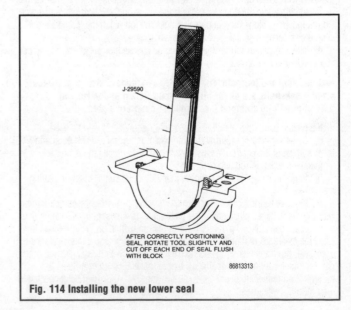

Fig. 114 Installing the new lower seal

➡GM makes a guide tool (J-29114-1) which bolts to the block via an oil pan bolt hole, and a packing tool (J-29114-2) which is machined to provide a built-in stop for the installation of the short cut pieces. Using the packing tool, work the short pieces of seal onto the guide tool, then pack them into the block with the packing tool.

7. Install a new lower seal in the rear main cap.

8. Install a piece of Plastigage® or the equivalent on the bearing journal. Install the rear cap and tighten to 70 ft. lbs. (95 Nm). Remove the cap and check the gauge for bearing clearance. If out of specification, the ends of the seal may be frayed or not flush, preventing the cap from proper sealing. Correct as required.

9. Clean the journal, and apply a thin film of sealer to the mating surfaces of the cap and block. Do not allow any sealer to get onto the journal or bearing. Install the bearing cap and tighten to 70 ft. lbs. (95 Nm), Install the pan and pump.

10. Add engine oil to the crankcase.

11. Start the engine and check for leaks.

1-PIECE SEAL

1. Drain the engine oil.
2. Remove the transaxle and the flexplate.
3. Using a small pry bar, pry the seal from the block.

❊❊ CAUTION

Be careful not to damage the crankshaft surface when removing the oil seal.

4. Clean and inspect the seal mounting surface for nicks and burrs.
5. Coat the new seal with engine oil. Using tool J-34686, press the seal into the block, until it seats.
6. To complete the installation, reverse the removal procedures.
7. Add engine oil to the crankcase.
8. Start the engine and check for leaks.

3.0L Engine

LOWER OIL SEAL

1. Remove the crankshaft.
2. Remove the old seal and place a new seal in the groove with both ends projecting the surface of the cap.
3. Force the seal into the groove rubbing down with a hammer handle or smooth stick until the seal projects above the groove not more than $\frac{1}{16}$ in. (1.6mm). Cut ends off flush with surface of cap, using sharp knife or razor blade.
4. The engine must be operated at slow speed when first started after a new braided seal is installed. Neoprene composition seals are placed in grooves in the sides of bearing cap to seal against leakage in the joints between cap and crankcase. The neoprene composition swells in the presence of oil and heat. The seals are undersize when newly installed and may even leak for a short time until the seals have had time to swell and seal the opening.
5. The neoprene seals are slightly longer than the grooves in the bearing cap. The seals must not be cut to length. Before installation of seals, soak for 1 to 2 minutes in light oil or kerosene. After installation of bearing cap in crankcase, install seal in bearing cap.
6. To help eliminate oil leakage at the joint where the cap meets the crankcase, apply sealer, to the rear main bearing cap split line. When applying sealer, use only a thin coat as an over abundance will not allow the cap to seat properly.

UPPER OIL SEAL

1. Drain the engine oil.
2. Remove oil pan.
3. Insert packing tool (J-21526-2 or equivalent) against one end of the seal in the cylinder block. Drive the old seal gently into the groove until it is packed tight. This varies from ¼ in. (6mm) to ¾ in. (19mm) depending on the amount of pack required.
4. Repeat on the other end of the seal in the cylinder block.
5. Measure the amount the seal was driven up on one side and add $\frac{1}{16}$ in. (1.6mm). Using a single edge razor blade, cut that length from the old seal removed from the rear main bearing cap. Repeat the procedure for the other

side. Use the rear main bearing cap as a holding fixture when cutting the seal.
6. Install guide tool (J-21526-1 or equivalent) onto cylinder block.
7. Using packing tool, work the short pieces cut previously into the guide tool and then pack into cylinder block. The guide tool and packing tool have been machined to provide a built-in stop. Use this procedure for both sides. It may help to use oil on the short pieces of the rope seal when packing into the cylinder block.
8. Remove the guide tool.
9. Install a new fabric seal in the rear main bearing cap. Install cap and tighten to specifications.
10. Install oil pan.
11. Add engine oil to the crankcase, as necessary.
12. Start the engine and check for leaks.

3.1L and 3.3L Engines

1. Disconnect the negative battery cable.
2. Drain the engine oil.
3. Remove the transaxle.
4. Remove the flywheel mounting bolts and remove the flywheel and spacer.
5. Using a small pry bar, pry the seal from the block.

❊❊ CAUTION

Be careful not to damage the crankshaft surface when removing the oil seal.

6. Clean the seal mounting surface.
To install:
7. Coat the inside and outside of the new rear main oil seal with engine oil.
8. Install the new seal on tool J-34686 (or equivalent) until the seal bottom is squarely against the collar of the tool.
9. Align the dowel pin of the tool with the dowel pin hole in the crankshaft. Tighten the attaching screws to 45 inch lbs. (5 Nm).
10. Turn the handle of the tool until the collar is tight against the case. This will ensure the seal is fully seated.
11. Back the tool off and remove the attaching screws.
12. Install the flywheel and spacer and tighten the flywheel mounting bolts.
13. Install the transaxle assembly.
14. Connect the negative battery cable.
15. Add engine oil to the crankcase.
16. Start the engine and check for leaks.

3.8L Engine

1. Disconnect the negative battery cable.
2. Raise and support the vehicle safely.
3. Drain the engine oil and remove the oil pan.
4. Remove the rear main bearing cap. Remove the oil seal from the bearing cap.
To install:
5. Insert a packing tool (J-21526-2 or equivalent) against one end of the seal in the cylinder block. Pack the old seal in until it is tight. Pack the other end of seal in the same manner.
6. Measure the amount the seal was driven up into the block on one side and add approximately $\frac{3}{32}$ in. (2mm). With a single edge razor blade, cut this amount off of the old lower seal. The bearing cap can be used as a holding fixture.
7. Install the packing guide tool J-21526-1 or equivalent, onto the cylinder block.
8. Using the packing tool, work the short pieces of the seal into the guide tool and pack into the cylinder block until the tool hits the built in stop. Repeat this step on the other side. A small amount of oil on the pieces of seal may be helpful when packing into the cylinder block.
9. Remove the guide tool.
10. Install a new rope seal in the bearing cap and install the cap. Tighten the retaining bolts to specification.
11. Install the oil pan.
12. Fill the crankcase with oil.
13. Connect the negative battery cable.
14. Start the vehicle and check for leaks.

Crankshaft and Main Bearings

REMOVAL & INSTALLATION

▶ **See Figure 115**

1. Remove the engine assembly as previously outlined.
2. Remove the engine front cover.
3. Remove the timing chain and sprockets or gears.
4. Remove the oil pan.
5. Remove the oil pump.
6. Stamp the cylinder number on the machined surfaces of the bolt bosses of the connecting rods and caps for identification when reinstalling. If the pistons are to be removed from the connecting rod, mark cylinder number on piston with a silver pencil or quick drying paint for proper cylinder identification and cap to rod location.
7. Remove the connecting rod caps and install thread protectors.
8. Mark the main bearing caps so that they can be reinstalled in their original positions.
9. Remove all the main bearing caps. They all must go back to their original locations and they must all face the same direction. Any cap install incorrectly will cause engine damage when reassembled.
10. Note position of keyway in crankshaft so it can be installed in the same position.
11. Lift crankshaft out of block. Rods will pivot to the center of the engine when the crankshaft is removed.
12. Remove both halves of the rear main oil seal if two piece design. If a one piece design, remove the seal.

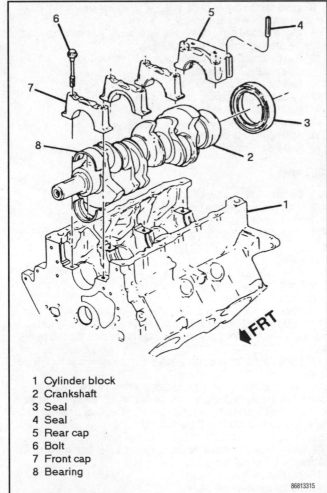

1 Cylinder block
2 Crankshaft
3 Seal
4 Seal
5 Rear cap
6 Bolt
7 Front cap
8 Bearing

86813315

Fig. 115 The crankshaft is secured in the block by the main bearing caps

To install:

13. Clean all of the oil sludge and carbon deposits. Probe the oil passages for any obstructions.
14. Inspect the bearing journals for; cracks, chips, gouges, roughness, grooves, and overheating (discoloration).
15. Inspect the corresponding bearing inserts for any imbedded foreign materials, then determine it's source.
16. If cracks, burned spots or gouges are found, you must replace the crankshaft.
17. Measure the crankshaft journals with a micrometer to determine the correct size rod and main bearings to be used. Whenever a new or reconditioned crankshaft is installed, new connect rod bearings and main bearings should be installed.
18. Clean all oil passages in the block (and crankshaft if it is being reused).

➡**A new rear main seal should be installed anytime the crankshaft is removed or replaced. If any engine repair is made, any related seals or gaskets should be replaced. It's not worth the time lost to repeat a repair job due to an old seal or gasket leaking.**

19. Install sufficient oil pan bolts in the block to align with the connecting rod bolts. Use rubber bands between the bolts to position the connecting rods as required. Connecting rod position can be adjusted by increasing the tension on the rubber bands with additional turns around the pan bolts or thread protectors.
20. Position the upper half of main bearings in the block and lubricate with engine oil.
21. Position crankshaft keyway in the same position as removed and lower into block. The connecting rods will follow the crank pins into the correct position as the crankshaft is lowered.
22. Lubricate the thrust flanges with GM part no. 1050169 lubricant or equivalent. Install caps with lower half of bearings lubricated with engine oil. Lubricate cap bolts with engine oil and install, but do not tighten.
23. With a block of wood, bump the shaft in each direction to align thrust flanges of main bearing. After bumping shaft in each direction, wedge the shaft to the front and hold it while tightening the thrust bearing cap bolts.

➡**In order to prevent the possibility of cylinder block and/or main bearing cap damage, the main bearing caps are to be tapped into their cylinder block cavity using a brass or leather mallet before attaching bolts are installed. Do not use attaching bolts to pull main bearing caps into their seat.**

24. Tighten all main bearing caps to specification.
25. Remove the connecting rod bolt thread protectors and lubricate the connecting rod bearings with engine oil.
26. Install the connecting rod bearing caps in their original position. Tighten the nuts to specification.
27. Complete the installation by reversing the removal steps.

CHECKING BEARING CLEARANCE

1. Remove bearing cap and wipe oil from crankshaft journal and outer and inner surfaces of bearing shell.
2. Place a piece of plastic gauging material (Plastigage® or equivalent) in the center of bearing. Position the crankshaft in the saddles.
3. Reinstall bearing cap and bearing. Place engine oil on cap bolts and install. Tighten bolts to specification.
4. Remove bearing cap and determine bearing clearance by comparing the width of the flattened plastic gauging material at its widest point with graduations on the gauging material container. The number within the graduation on the envelope indicates the clearance in millimeters or thousandths of an inch. If the clearance is greater than allowed, REPLACE BOTH BEARING SHELLS AS A SET. Recheck clearance after replacing shells.

BEARING REPLACEMENT

Engine Installed

Main bearing clearances must be corrected by the use of selective upper and lower shells. To install main bearing shells, proceed as follows:

1. Remove the oil pan. On some models, the oil pump may also have to be removed.

2. Loosen all main bearing caps.

3. Remove bearing cap and remove lower shell.

4. Insert a flattened cotter pin or roll out pin in the oil passage hole in the crankshaft in the direction opposite to cranking rotation. The pin will contact the upper shell and roll it out.

5. The main bearing journals should be checked for roughness and wear. Slight roughness may be removed with a fine grit polishing cloth saturated with engine oil. Burrs may be removed with a fine oil stone. If the journals are scored or ridged, the crankshaft must be replaced.

6. Clean crankshaft journals and bearing caps thoroughly before installing new main bearings.

7. Apply lubricant GM part no.1050169 or equivalent to the thrust flanges of bearing shells.

8. Place new upper shell on crankshaft journal with locating tang correctly positioned and rotate shaft to turn it into place. Use the cotter pin or roll out pin as during removal.

9. Place new bearing shell in bearing cap.

10. Install a new oil seal in the rear main bearing cap and block.

11. Lubricate the removed or replaced main bearings with engine oil. Lubricate the thrust surface with lubricant GM part no. 1050109 or equivalent.

12. Lubricate the main bearing cap bolts with engine oil.

➡In order to prevent the possibility of cylinder block and/or main bearing cap damage, the main bearing caps are to be tapped into their cylinder block cavity using a brass or leather mallet before attaching bolts are installed. Do not use attaching bolts to pull main bearing caps into their seats.

13. Tighten the main bearing cap bolts.

EXHAUST SYSTEM

General Information

➡Safety glasses should be worn at all times when working on or near the exhaust system. Older exhaust systems will almost always be covered with loose rust particles which will shower you when disturbed. These particles are more than a nuisance and could injure your eye.

Whenever working on the exhaust system always keep the following in mind:

1. Check the complete exhaust system for open seams, holes loose connections, or other deterioration which could permit exhaust fumes to seep into the passenger compartment.

2. The exhaust system is usually supported by free-hanging rubber mountings which permit some movement of the exhaust system, but does not permit transfer of noise and vibration into the passenger compartment. Do not replace the rubber mounts with solid ones.

3. Before removing any component of the exhaust system, ALWAYS squirt a liquid rust dissolving agent onto the fasteners for ease of removal. A lot of knuckle skin will be saved by following this rule. It may even be wise to spray the fasteners and allow them to sit overnight.

4. Annoying rattles and noise vibrations in the exhaust system are usually caused by misalignment of the parts. When aligning the system, leave all bolts and nuts loose until all parts are properly aligned, then tighten, working from front to rear.

5. When installing exhaust system parts, make sure there is enough clearance between the hot exhaust parts and pipes and hoses that would be adversely affected by excessive heat. Also make sure there is adequate clearance from the floor pan to avoid possible overheating of the floor.

Front Pipe

REMOVAL & INSTALLATION

Pipe Without Catalytic Converter

◆ See Figure 116

1. Before removing any component of the exhaust system, always squirt a liquid rust dissolving agent onto the fasteners for ease of removal..

2. Raise and support the front of the vehicle on jackstands.

Engine Removed

The bearings can easily be replaced after the crankshaft is removed. Simply remove the bearing inserts from the saddles and main bearing caps, and install the new ones. Be sure to check for proper bearing clearances.

Flywheel and Ring Gear

REMOVAL & INSTALLATION

The ring gear is an integral part of the flywheel and is not replaceable.

1. Remove the transaxle.

2. Remove the bolts attaching the flywheel to the crankshaft flange. Remove the flywheel.

3. Inspect the flywheel for cracks, and inspect the ring gear for burrs or worn teeth. Replace the flywheel if any damage is apparent. Remove burrs with a mill file.

4. Clean the flywheel bolt threads and bolt holes.

To install:

5. Apply thread locker GM part no.12345382 or an equivalent to all of the flywheel bolts.

6. Attach the flywheel and start bolts. The flywheel will only attach to the crankshaft in one position, as the bolt holes are unevenly spaced. Use a suitable tool to prevent the rotation of the crankshaft.

7. Tighten the bolts to specifications.

8. Install the transaxle.

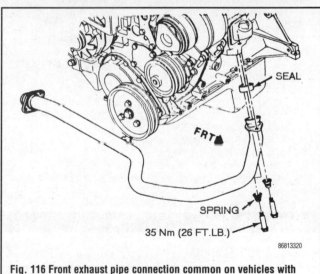

Fig. 116 Front exhaust pipe connection common on vehicles with the catalytic converter not included

3. Remove the exhaust pipe-to-manifold nuts.

4. Support the catalytic converter, then disconnect the pipe from the converter. Remove the pipe.

5. Remove the exhaust gaskets.

To install:

6. Be sure to use all new gaskets when required. Assemble the system, check the clearance and tighten the bolts to about 15–30 ft. lbs. (20–41 Nm).

7. All clamps should be tightened to about 18–25 ft. lbs. (24–34 Nm). Do overtighten the clamps. If pipes become dented they can leak.

Pipe With Catalytic Converter

1. Before removing any component of the exhaust system, always squirt a liquid rust dissolving agent onto the fasteners for ease of removal.

2. Raise and support the vehicle.

3. On some vehicles you will need to remove the brace from the transaxle.

4. Remove the exhaust pipe nuts from the manifold.
5. Support the catalytic converter pipe bolts from the rear of the converter.
6. Lower the catalytic converter/front pipe assembly from the vehicle.

To install:

7. Be sure to use all new gaskets when required.
8. Attach the new catalytic converter/front pipe assembly to the vehicle. Tighten the pipe to manifold nuts to 20–40 ft. lbs. (27–55 Nm).
9. Attach the bolts at the rear of the catalytic converter/front pipe. Tighten them to 30–35 ft. lbs. (41–47 Nm).
10. Connect the brace at the transaxle if removed.
11. Lower the vehicle.

Crossover Pipe

REMOVAL & INSTALLATION

V6 Engines

> ✳✳ **CAUTION**
>
> **Fuel Injection systems remain under pressure, even after the engine has been turned OFF. The fuel system pressure must be relieved before disconnecting any fuel lines. Failure to do so may result in fire and/or personal injury.**

1. Drain the cooling system.
2. Remove the air cleaner assembly. Relieve the fuel system pressure.
3. Disconnect the fuel lines.
4. Remove the upper radiator hose.
5. Disconnect the shift control cables, then remove the bracket.
6. Detach the electrical connectors.
7. Unfasten the heat shield.
8. Remove the crossover pipe nuts, then remove the crossover pipe.

To install:

9. Attach the new crossover pipe to the vehicle, then tighten the mounting nuts to 18 ft. lbs. (25 Nm).
10. Attach the heat shield.
11. Connect the electrical harness to the vehicle.
12. Install the shift control cables and bracket in their proper locations.
13. Attach the upper radiator hose.
14. Connect the fuel lines that were detached.
15. Install the air cleaner assembly.
16. Refill the cooling system.
17. Start the engine. Fill the cooling system, then check for exhaust and cooling leaks.

Intermediate Pipe

REMOVAL & INSTALLATION

▶ **See Figure 117**

1. Before removing any component of the exhaust system, always squirt a liquid rust dissolving agent onto the fasteners for ease of removal.
2. Raise and support the front of the vehicle.
3. Support the exhaust system.
4. Disconnect the intermediate pipe from the catalytic converter. If the pipe is original you may have to cut the pipe from the catalytic converter.
5. At the muffler, remove the clamp and the intermediate pipe.

To install:

6. Use a new clamp, nuts and bolts, then assemble the system. Be sure to use all new gaskets when required. Check the clearances, then tighten the connectors.
7. All clamps should be tightened to about 18–25 ft. lbs. (24–34 Nm). Do overtighten the clamps. If pipes become dented they can leak.

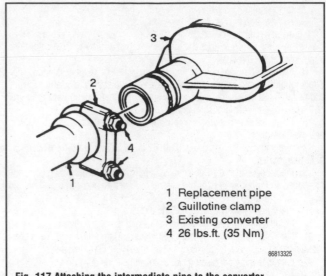

1 Replacement pipe
2 Guillotine clamp
3 Existing converter
4 26 lbs.ft. (35 Nm)

86813325

Fig. 117 Attaching the intermediate pipe to the converter

Catalytic Converter

REMOVAL & INSTALLATION

▶ **See Figure 118**

For vehicles with the catalytic converter included with the front pipe, see front pipe removal and installation.

1. Before removing any component of the exhaust system, always squirt a liquid rust dissolving agent onto the fasteners for ease of removal.
2. Raise and support the front of the vehicle on jackstands and place a support under the catalytic converter.
3. Remove the clamp at the front of the converter. then cut the pipe at the front of the converter.

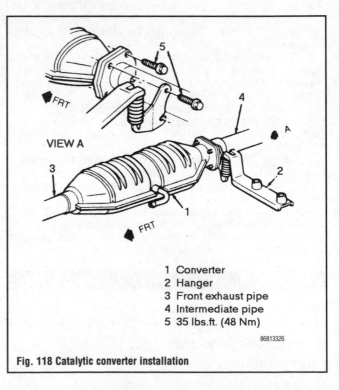

1 Converter
2 Hanger
3 Front exhaust pipe
4 Intermediate pipe
5 35 lbs.ft. (48 Nm)

86813326

Fig. 118 Catalytic converter installation

4. Remove the converter-to-intermediate pipe nuts/bolts.

5. Disconnect the converter-to-crossover pipe or front pipe.

To install:

6. Reverse to install.

7. Use new clamps and nuts/bolts. Make sure to use all new gaskets if required. Assemble the system, then check the clearances and tighten all of the attachments.

8. All clamps should be tightened to about 18–25 ft. lbs. (24–34 Nm). Do overtighten the clamps. If pipes become dented they can leak.

Muffler

REMOVAL & INSTALLATION

1. Before removing any component of the exhaust system, always squirt a liquid rust dissolving agent onto the fasteners for ease of removal.

2. Raise and support the vehicle on jackstands.

3. On the single pipe system, cut the exhaust pipe near the front of the muffler. On the dual pipe system, remove the U-bolt clamp at the front of the muffler and disengage the muffler from the exhaust pipe.

➡**Before cutting the exhaust pipe, measure the service muffler exhaust pipe extension and make certain to allow 1½ in. (38mm) for the exhaust pipe-to-muffler extension engagement.**

4. At the rear of the muffler, remove the U-bolt clamp and disengage the muffler from the tailpipe.

5. Remove the tailpipe clamps and the tailpipe.

6. Inspect the muffler and the tailpipe hangers, replace if necessary.

To install:

7. Always use all new gaskets if required when installing an exhaust system.

8. Assemble the system. Check the clearances, then tighten all of the attachments.

9. All clamps should be tightened to about 18–25 ft. lbs. (24–34 Nm). Do overtighten the clamps. If pipes become dented they can leak.

Tailpipe

REMOVAL & INSTALLATION

▶ **See Figure 119**

1. Before removing any component of the exhaust system, always squirt a liquid rust dissolving agent onto the fasteners for ease of removal.

2. Raise and support the vehicle on jackstands.

3. Remove the hanger clamps from the tail pipe.

4. Remove the tailpipe-to-muffler clamp.

5. Disengage the tailpipe from the muffler and remove the tailpipe.

6. Inspect the tailpipe hangers and replace, if necessary.

To install:

7. Assemble the system. Check the clearances, then tighten all of the attachments.

8. All clamps should be tightened to about 18–25 ft. lbs. (24–34 Nm). Do overtighten the clamps. If pipes become dented they can leak.

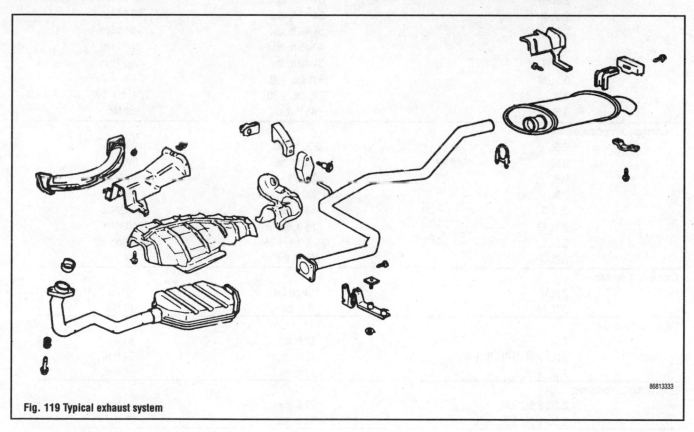

Fig. 119 Typical exhaust system

86813333

TORQUE SPECIFICATIONS

Component		US	Metric
Alternator bolts:			
	Front:	37 ft. lbs.	50 Nm
	Rear:	18 ft. lbs.	25 Nm
Battery cable:		11 ft. lbs.	15 Nm
Camshaft sprocket:			
	2.2L	77 ft. lbs.	105 Nm
	2.8L	15-20 ft. lbs.	20-27 Nm
	3.1L- T	15-20 ft. lbs.	20-27 Nm
	3.1L- M	74 ft. lbs.	100 ft. lbs.
	3.3L, 3.8L	52 ft. lbs. + 110°	70 Nm + 110°
Camshaft thrust bolt:			
	2.2L	106 inch lbs.	12 Nm
	2.5L, 2.8L, 3.0L, 3.1L	89 inch lbs.	10 Nm
	3.3L, 3.8L	110 inch lbs.	15 Nm
Camshaft sensor:		8 ft. lbs.	10 Nm
Camshaft rear cover:		6-9 ft. lbs.	8-12 Nm
Connecting rod cap nuts:			
	2.2L	38 ft. lbs.	52 Nm
	2.5L	29 ft. lbs.	40 Nm
	2.8L-W	34-40 ft. lbs.	46-54 Nm
	2.8L-X	34-40 ft. lbs.	46-54 Nm
	2.8L-Z	34-40 ft. lbs.	46-54 Nm
	3.0L	40-45 ft. lbs.	54-61 Nm
	3.1L-T	34-40 ft. lbs.	46-54 Nm
	3.1L-M	15 ft. lbs. + 75°	20 Nm + 75°
	3.3L	20 ft. lbs. + 50°	27 Nm + 50°
	3.8L	45 ft. lbs.	61 Nm
Crankshaft dampner/balancer:			
	2.5L 1982-87	200 ft. lbs.	260 Nm
	2.5L 1988-93	162 ft. lbs.	220 Nm
	2.8L	75 ft. lbs.	102 Nm
	3.0L	200 ft. lbs.	260 Nm
	3.1L-T	75 ft. lbs.	102 Nm
	3.1L-M	76 ft. lbs.	103 Nm
	3.3L	105 ft. lbs. + 56°	140 Nm + 56°
	3.8L	220 ft. lbs.	290 Nm
Crankshaft sensor:			
	2.2L	71 inch lbs.	8 Nm
	3.1L-M	8 ft. lbs.	10 Nm
Engine mount-to-engine:			
	2.2L	39 ft. lbs.	53 Nm
	2.5L, 2.8L, 3.0L, 3.1L	40 ft. lbs.	54 Nm
	3.3L, 3.8L	70 ft. lbs.	95 Nm
Engine mount-to-frame:			
	2.2L, 3.3L, 3.8L	32 ft. lbs.	43 Nm
	2.5L, 2.8L, 3.0L, 3.1L	35 ft. lbs.	47 Nm

91083C12

TORQUE SPECIFICATIONS

Component			US	Metric
Exhaust manifold:				
	2.2L		39 ft. lbs.	53 Nm
	2.5L	Inner:	37 ft. lbs.	50 Nm
		Outer:	28 ft. lbs.	38 Nm
	2.8L-W		15-23 ft. lbs.	20-30 Nm
	2.8L-X		25 ft. lbs.	34 Nm
	2.8L-Z		25 ft. lbs.	34 Nm
	3.0L		25-37 ft. lbs.	34-50 Nm
	3.1L-N		15-23 ft. lbs.	20-30 Nm
	3.1L-T		35 ft. lbs.	47 Nm
	3.3L		39 ft. lbs.	55 Nm
	3.8L		37 ft. lbs.	50 Nm
Exhaust clamps:			20-25 ft. lbs.	27-34 Nm
Flywheel bolts:				
	2.2L		55 ft. lbs.	75 Nm
	2.5L	1982-86	47 ft. lbs.	61 Nm
		1987-93	55 ft. lbs.	75 Nm
	2.8L		52 ft. lbs.	70 Nm
	3.0L		60 ft. lbs.	80 Nm
	3.1L-T		76 ft. lbs.	108 Nm
	3.1L-M		61 ft. lbs.	83 Nm
	3.3L		89 inch lbs + 90 °	10 Nm + 90°
	3.8L		60 ft. lbs.	80 Nm
Front cover:				
	2.2L		97 inch lbs.	11 Nm
	2.5L, 2.8L, 3.0L,3.1L-T		89 inch lbs.	10 Nm
	3.1L-M	Large	35 ft. lbs.	47 Nm
		Small	15 ft. lbs.	21 Nm
Ignition coil:				
	2.2L		15-22 ft. lbs.	20-30 Nm
	2.5L, 2.8L, 3.1L-T		40 inch lbs.	4-5 Nm
	3.1L-M		40 inch lbs.	4-5 Nm
	3.3L		27 inch lbs.	3 Nm
Intake manifold:				
	2.2L	Lower	24 ft. lbs.	33 Nm
		Upper	22 ft. lbs.	30 Nm
	2.5L, 2.8-W, 3.1-T		25 ft. lbs.	32 Nm
	3.0L, 3.8L		47 ft. lbs.	65 Nm
	3.1L-M		115 inch lbs.	13 Nm
	3.3L		89 inch lbs.	10 Nm
Lifter guide retaining stud:			89 inch lbs.	10 Nm
Main bearing caps:				
	2.2L		70 ft. lbs.	95 Nm
	2.5L	1982-89	70 ft. lbs.	95 Nm
		1990-93	65 ft. lbs.	88 Nm
	2.8L-W		63-83 Nm	85-112 Nm
	2.8L-X		68 ft. lbs.	90 Nm
	2.8L-Z		68 ft .lbs.	90 Nm
	3.0L		100 ft. lbs.	85-112 Nm
	3.1L-T		63-83 ft. lbs.	85-112 Nm
	3.1L-M		37 ft. lbs + 77°	50 Nm + 77°
	3.3L		26 ft. lbs.+ 45°	35 Nm +45°
	3.8L		100 ft. lbs.	135 Nm

91083C13

TORQUE SPECIFICATIONS

Component	US	Metric
Oil pan:		
2.2L	89 inch lbs.	10 Nm
3.1L-M	18 ft. lbs.	25 Nm
3.3L	124 inch lbs.	14 Nm
All others		
M6	6-9 ft. lbs.	8-12 Nm
M8	15-23 ft. lbs.	20-30 Nm
Oil pump hold down:	67-85 ft. lbs.	27-41 Nm
Oil cover-to-timing cover:	89 inch lbs.	11 Nm
Oxygen sensor:	30 ft. lbs.	41 Nm
Spark plugs:		
2.2L		
new	20 ft. lbs.	27 Nm
used	11 ft. lbs.	15 Nm
2.5L	10-25 ft. lbs.	
2.8L-W	10-25 ft. lbs.	
2.8L-X, Z	7-15 ft. lbs.	
3.0L	7-15 ft. lbs.	
3.1L-T	10-25 ft. lbs.	
3.1L-M		
new	20 ft. lbs.	27 Nm
used	11 ft. lbs.	15 Nm
3.3L, 3.8L	20 ft. lbs.	27 Nm
Starter mounting bolts:	32 ft. lbs.	43 Nm
Thermostat housing:	8-23 ft. lbs.	10-30 Nm
Timing chain dampner:	14-19 ft. lbs.	18-24 Nm
Water pump:		
2.2L	18 ft. lbs.	25 Nm
2.5L		
1982-86	25 ft. lbs.	30 Nm
1987-93	10 ft. lbs.	11 Nm
3.0L	8 ft. lbs.	10 Nm
M6 bolts	6-9 ft. lbs.	8-12 Nm
M8 bolts	25 ft. lbs.	34 Nm
Valve cover:		
2.2L	89 inch lbs.	10 Nm
2.5L	80 inch lbs.	9 Nm
2.8L-W	6-9 ft. lbs.	8-12 Nm
2.8L-X	10 ft. lbs.	11 Nm
2.8L-Z	10 ft. lbs.	11 Nm
3.0L	14 ft. lbs.	19 Nm
3.1L-T	6-9 ft. lbs.	8-12 Nm
3.1L-M	18 ft. lbs.	24 Nm
3.3L	14 ft. lbs.	19 Nm
3.8L	14-20 ft. lbs.	19-27 Nm

91083C14

ENGINE REBUILDING SPECIFICATIONS CHART

Component	US	Metric
CAMSHAFT		
2.2L (VIN 4)		
End play:	NA	
Bearing diameter:	1.868-1.869 in.	47.45-47.48 mm
Bearing clearance:	0.001-0.0039 in.	0.026-0.101 mm
Lobe lift		
Intake:	0.288 in.	7.309 mm
Exhaust:	0.288 in.	7.307 mm
2.5L (VIN R)		
End play:	0.0015-0.005 in.	NA
Bearing diameter:	1.869 in.	47.45-47.48 mm
Bearing clearance:	0.0007-0.0027 in.	0.026-0.101 mm
Lobe lift (1982-88)		
Intake:	0.398 in.	7.309 mm
Exhaust:	0.398 in.	7.307 mm
Lobe lift (1989)		
Intake:	0.232 in.	5.8882 mm
Exhaust:	0.232 in.	5.8882 mm
Lobe lift (1990-93)		
Intake:	0.248 in.	6.302 mm
Exhaust:	0.248 in.	6.302 mm
2.8L (VIN W)		
End play:	NA	NA
Bearing diameter:	1.8678-1.8815 in.	47.44-47.79 mm
Bearing clearance:	0.001-0.004 in.	0.026-0.101 mm
Lobe lift		
Intake:	0.2626 in.	6.67 mm
Exhaust:	0.2732 in.	6.94 mm
2.8L (VIN X)		
End play:	NA	NA
Bearing diameter:	1.8876-1.8996 in.	47.44-47.49 mm
Bearing clearance:	0.001-0.004 in.	0.026-0.101 mm
Lobe lift		
Intake:	0.2348 in.	5.87 mm
Exhaust:	0.2668 in.	6.67 mm
2.8L (VIN Z)		
End play:	NA	NA
Bearing diameter:	1.8876-1.8996 in.	47.44-47.49 mm
Bearing clearance:	0.001-0.004 in.	0.026-0.101 mm
Lobe lift		
Intake:	0.2348 in.	5.87 mm
Exhaust:	0.2668 in.	6.67 mm
3.0L (VIN E)		
End play:	NA	NA
Bearing diameter:	1.785-1.786 in.	45.339-45.364 mm
Bearing clearance		
Number 1:	0.0005-0.0025 in.	0.0127-0.0635 mm
Numbers 2, 3, 4:	0.0005-00035 in.	0.0127-0.0889 mm
3.1L (VIN T)		
End play:	NA	NA
Bearing diameter:	1.8678-1.8815 in.	47.44-47.79 mm

ENGINE REBUILDING SPECIFICATIONS CHART

Component	US	Metric
3.1L (VIN T) Bearing clearance:	0.001-0.004 in.	0.026-0.101 mm
Lobe lift		
Intake:	0.2626 in.	6.67 mm
Exhaust:	0.2732 in.	6.94 mm
3.1L (VIN M)		
End play:	NA	NA
Bearing diameter:	1.871-1.872 in.	47.523-47.549 mm
Bearing clearance:	0.001-0.004 in.	0.026-0.101 mm
Lobe lift		
Intake:	0.2727 in.	6.9263 mm
Exhaust:	0.2727 in.	6.9256 mm
3.3L (VIN N)		
End play:	NA	NA
Bearing diameter:	1.785-1.786 in.	45.339-45.364 mm
Bearing clearance:	0.0005-0.0035 in.	0.013-0.089 mm
Lobe lift		
Intake:	0.250 in.	6.43 mm
Exhaust:	0.255 in.	6.48 mm
3.8L (VIN 3)		
End play:	NA	NA
Bearing diameter:	1.785-1.786 in.	45.339-45.364 mm
Bearing clearance		
Number 1:	0.0005-0.0025 in.	0.0127-0.0635 mm
Numbers 2, 3, 4:	0.0005-0.0035 in.	0.0127-0.0889 mm
VALVES		
2.2L (VIN 4)		
Face angle:	45°	
Face runout:	0.0012 in.	0.03 mm
Seat angle:	46°	
Seat runout:	0.002 in.	0.05 mm
Seat width		
Intake:	0.049-0.059 in.	1.25-1.50 mm
Exhaust:	0.063-0.075 in.	1.60-1.90 mm
Stem clearance		
Intake:	0.0010-0.0027 in.	0.025-0.069 mm
Exhaust:	0.0014-0.0031 in.	0.035-0.081 mm
2.5L (VIN R)		
Face angle:	45°	
Seat angle:	46°	
Seat runout:	0.002 in.	0.05 mm
Seat width		
Intake:	0.035-0.075 in.	0.889-1.905 mm
Exhaust: (1982-89)	0.058-0.097 in.	1.473-2.642 mm
Exhaust: (1990-93)	0.058-0.105 in.	1.473-2.667 mm
Stem clearance		
Intake:	0.001-0.0028 in.	0.028-0.071 mm
Exhaust: (1982-89)	0.0013-0.0041 in.	0.033-0.104 mm
Exhaust: (1990-93)	0.0013-0.0041 in.	0.033-0.104 mm

91083C15

ENGINE REBUILDING SPECIFICATIONS CHART

Component		US	Metric
2.8L (VIN W)			
Face angle:		45°	45°
Seat angle:		46°	46°
Seat runout:		0.001 in.	0.25 mm
Seat width			
	Intake:	0.061-0.073 in.	1.550-1.850 mm
	Exhaust:	0.067-0.079 in.	1.70-2.0 mm
Stem clearance			
	Intake:	0.001-0.0027 in.	0.026-0.068 mm
	Exhaust:	0.001-0.0027 in.	0.026-0.068 mm
2.8L (VIN X)			
Face angle:		45°	45°
Seat angle:		46°	46°
Seat runout:		0.002 in.	0.05 mm
Seat width			
	Intake:	0.049-0.059 in.	1.250-1.50 mm
	Exhaust:	0.049-0.059 in.	1.250-1.50 mm
Stem clearance			
	Intake:	0.001-0.0027 in.	0.026-0.068 mm
	Exhaust:	0.001-0.0027 in.	0.026-0.068 mm
2.8L (VIN Z)			
Face angle:		45°	45°
Seat angle:		46°	46°
Seat runout:		0.002 in.	0.05 mm
Seat width			
	Intake:	0.049-0.059 in.	1.250-1.50 mm
	Exhaust:	0.049-0.059 in.	1.250-1.50 mm
Stem clearance			
	Intake:	0.001-0.0027 in.	0.026-0.068 mm
	Exhaust:	0.001-0.0027 in.	0.026-0.068 mm
3.0 (VIN E)			
Face angle:		45°	45°
Seat angle:		46°	46°
Seat runout:		0.002 in.	0.05 mm
Seat width			
	Intake:	0.3412-0.3401 in.	8.666-8.638 mm
	Exhaust:	0.3412-0.3405 in.	8.666-8.649 mm
Stem clearance			
	Intake:	0.0015-0.0035 in.	0.038-0.089 mm
	Exhaust:	0.0015-0.0032 in.	0.038-0.081 mm
3.0L (VIN E) **3.1L (VIN T)**			
Face angle:		45°	45°
Seat angle:		46°	46°
Seat runout:		0.001 in.	0.25 mm
Seat width			
	Intake:	0.061-0.073 in.	1.150-1.850 mm
	Exhaust:	0.067-0.079 in.	1.70-2.0 mm

91083C17

ENGINE REBUILDING SPECIFICATIONS CHART

Component		US	Metric
3.1L (VIN T) Stem clearance			
	Intake:	0.001-0.0027 in.	0.026-0.068 mm
	Exhaust:	0.001-0.0027 in.	0.026-0.068 mm
3.1L (VIN M)			
Face angle:		45°	45°
Seat angle:		45°	45°
Seat runout:		0.001 in.	0.025 mm
Seat width			
	Intake:	0.061-0.071 in.	1.55-1.80 mm
	Exhaust:	0.067-0.079 in.	1.70-2.0 mm
Stem clearance			
	Intake:	0.001-0.0027 in.	0.026-0.068 mm
	Exhaust:	0.001-0.0027 in.	0.026-0.068 mm
3.3L (VIN N)			
Face angle:		45°	45°
Seat angle:		45°	45°
Seat runout:		0.002 in.	0.05 mm
Seat width			
	Intake:	0.060-0.080 in.	1.53-2.030 mm
	Exhaust:	0.090-0.110 in.	2.29-2.79 mm
Stem clearance			
	Intake:	0.0015-0.0035 in.	0.038-0.089 mm
	Exhaust:	0.0015-0.0032 in.	0.038-0.081 mm
3.8L (VIN 3)			
Face angle:		45°	45°
Seat angle:		46°	46°
Seat runout:		0.002 in.	0.05 mm
Seat width			
	Intake:	0.3412-0.3401 in.	8.666-8.638 mm
	Exhaust:	0.3412-0.3405 in.	8.666-8.649 mm
Stem clearance			
	Intake:	0.0015-0.0035 in.	0.038-0.089 mm
	Exhaust:	0.0015-0.0035 in.	0.038-0.081 mm
VALVE SPRING			
2.2L (VIN 4)			
Free length		1.95 in.	49.5 mm
2.5L (VIN R)			
Free length:		2.01 in.	51 mm
Installed height:		1.68 in.	42.64 mm
2.8L (VIN W)			
Free length:		1.191 in.	48.5 mm
Installed height:		1.5748 in.	40.0 mm

91083C18

ENGINE REBUILDING SPECIFICATIONS CHART

Component	US	Metric
2.8L (VIN X)		
Free length:	1.191 in.	48.5 mm
2.8L (VIN Z)		
Free length:	1.191 in.	48.5 mm
3.1L (VIN T)		
Free length:	1.191 in.	48.5 mm
Installed height:	1.5748 in.	40.0 mm
3.1L (VIN M)		
Free length:	1.89 in.	48.5 mm
Installed height:	1.710 in.	43 mm
3.3L (VIN N)		
Free length:	1.93 in.	50.32 mm
Installed height:	1.69-1.72 in.	42.93-44.45 mm
SPRING LOAD		
2.2L (VIN 4)		
Closed	78-81 lbs @ 1.710 in.	332-362 N @ 43.43 mm
Open	220-236 lbs. @ 1.278 in.	979-1049 N @ 32.47 mm
2.5L (VIN R)		
Closed	75 lbs. @ 1.68 in.	532 N @ 42.64 mm
Open	173 lbs. @ 1.24 in.	770 N @ 31.46 mm
2.8L (VIN W)		
Closed	90 lbs. @ 1.70 in.	400 N @ 43.0 mm
Open	215 lbs. @ 1.29 in.	956 N @ 33.0 mm
2.8L (VIN X)		
Closed	88 lbs. @ 1.70 in.	40 Kg @ 40.0 mm
Open	195 lbs. @ 1.57 in.	88 Kg @ 30.0 mm
2.8L (VIN Z)		
Closed	88 lbs. @ 1.70 in.	40 Kg @ 40.0 mm
Open	195 lbs. @ 1.57 in.	88 Kg @ 30.0 mm
3.0L (VIN E)		
Closed	93 lbs. @ 1.727 in.	413 N @ 43.9 mm
Open	220 lbs. @ 1.340 in.	978 N @ 34.0 mm
3.1L (VIN T)		
Closed	90 lbs. @ 1.701 in.	400 N @ 43.0 mm
Open	215 lbs. @ 1.291 in.	956 N @ 33.0 mm
3.1L (VIN M)		
Closed	80 lbs @ 1.710 in.	356 N @ 43 mm
Open	250 lbs. @ 1.239 in.	1111 N @ 31.5 mm
3.3L (VIN N)		
Closed	80 lbs @ 1.750 in.	356 N @ 43.7 mm
Open	210 lbs. @ 1.315 in.	935 N @ 33.4 mm
3.8L (VIN 3)		
Closed	64 lbs @ 1.727 in.	285 N @ 43.9 mm
Open	182 lbs. @ 1.340 in.	810 N @ 34 mm

91083C19

ENGINE REBUILDING SPECIFICATIONS CHART

Component	US	Metric
LIFTER		
2.2L (VIN 4)	NA	NA
2.5L (VIN R)		
Body diameter:	0.841-0.843 in.	211.3668-21.4046 mm
Bore diameter:	0.844-0.845 n.	21.425-21.450 mm
Bore clearance:	0.002-0.0006 in.	0.06-0.016 mm
2.8L (VIN W)	NA	NA
2.8L (VIN X)	NA	NA
2.8L (VIN Z)	NA	NA
3.0L (VIN E)	NA	NA
3.1L (VIN T)		
Body diameter:	0.820-0.8427 in.	21.3668-21.4046 mm
Bore clearance:	0.008-0.0025 in.	0.0203-0.0635 mm
3.1L (VIN M)	NA	NA
3.3 (VIN N)	NA	NA
OIL PUMP		
2.2L (VIN 4)		
Gear pocket depth:	1.195-1.198 in.	30.36-30.44 mm
Gear pocket diameter:	1.503-1.506 in.	38.18-38.25 mm
Gear lash:	0.004-0.008 in.	0.094-0.195 mm
Gear length:	1.199-1.20 in.	30.45-30.48 mm
Gear diameter:	1.498-1.5 in.	38.05-38.10 mm
Side clearance:	0.0015-0.004 in.	0.038-0.102 mm
End clearance:	0.002-0.007 in.	0.05-0.18 mm
Valve to bore:	0.0015-0.0035 in.	0.038-0.089 mm
2.5L (VIN R)		
Gear pocket depth:	0.512-0.516 in.	13.05-13.10 mm
Gear pocket diameter:	0.511-0.512 in.	12.973-12.998 mm
2.8L (VIN W)	NA	NA
2.8L (VIN X)		
Gear pocket depth:	1.195-1.198 in.	30.36-30.44 mm
Gear pocket diameter:	1.503-1.506 in.	38.18-38.25 mm
Gear length:	1.200-1.199 in.	30.48-30.45 mm
Gear diameter:	1.498-1.500 in.	38.05-38.10 mm
Side clearance:	0.003-0.004 in.	0.08-0.10 mm
End clearance:	0.002-0.005 in.	0.05-0.13 mm
Valve to bore:	0.0015-0.0035 in.	0.089-0.038 mm
2.8L (VIN Z)		
Gear pocket depth:	1.195-1.198 in.	30.36-30.44 mm
Gear pocket diameter:	1.503-1.506 in.	38.18-38.25 mm
Gear length:	1.200-1.199 in.	30.48-30.45 mm

91083C20

ENGINE REBUILDING SPECIFICATIONS CHART

Component		US	Metric
2.8L (VIN Z)	Gear diameter:	1.498-1.500 in.	38.05-38.10 mm
	Side clearance:	0.003-0.004 in.	0.08-0.10 mm
	End clearance:	0.002-0.005 in.	0.05-0.13 mm
	Valve to bore:	0.0015-0.0035 in.	0.089-0.038 mm
3.0L (VIN E)		NA	NA
3.1L (VIN T)		NA	NA
3.1L (VIN M)			
	Gear pocket depth:	1.202-1.204 in.	30.52-30.58 mm
	Gear pocket diameter:	1.503-1.505 in.	38.176-38.226 mm
	Gear length:	1.199-1.200 in.	30.45-30.48 mm
	Gear diameter:	1.498-1.500 in.	38.05-38.10 mm
	Side clearance:	0.001-0.003 in.	0.038-0.088 mm
	End clearance:	0.002-0.005 in.	0.040-0.125 mm
	Valve to bore:	0.0015-0.0035 in.	0.038-0.089 mm
3.3L (VIN N)			
	Gear pocket depth:	0.461-0.4625 in.	11.71-11.75 mm
	Gear pocket diameter:	3.508-3.512 in.	89.10-89.20 mm
	Inner gear clearance:	0.006 in.	0.152 mm
	Outer gear end clearance:	0.001-0.0035 in.	0.025-0.089 mm
	Diameter clearance:	0.08-0.015 in.	0.203-0.381 mm
	Valve to bore:	0.0015-0.0035 in.	0.089-0.038 mm
3.8L (VIN 3)		NA	NA
CYLINDER BORE			
2.2L (VIN 4)			
	Diameter:	3.5036-3.5043 in.	88.991-89.009 mm
	Out of round:	0.0005 in.	0.013 mm
	Taper:	0.0005 in.	0.013 mm
2.5 L (VIN R)			
	Diameter:	4.0 in.	101.6 mm
	Out of round:	0.001 in	0.02 mm
	Taper:	0.005 in.	0.13 mm
2.8L (VIN W)			
	Diameter:	3.504-3.5033 in.	89.016-89.034 mm
	Out of round:	0.0005 in.	0.13 mm
	Taper:	0.0005 in.	0.13 mm
2.8L (VIN X)			
	Diameter:	3.504-3.5033 in.	88.90-89.07 mm
	Out of round:	0.001 in.	0.02 mm
	Taper:	0.001 in.	0.02 mm
2.8L (VIN Z)			
	Diameter:	3.504-3.5033 in.	88.90-89.07 mm
	Out of round:	0.001 in.	0.02 mm
	Taper:	0.001 in.	0.02 mm

9108C21

ENGINE REBUILDING SPECIFICATIONS CHART

Component		US	Metric
3.0L (VIN E)	Diameter:	3.8 in.	96.52 mm
	Out of round:	0.001 in.	0.02 mm
	Taper:	0.001 in.	0.02 mm
3.1L (VIN T)			
	Diameter:	3.504-3.5033 in.	88.90-89.07 mm
	Out of round:	0.0005 in.	0.13 mm
	Taper:	0.0005 in.	0.13 mm
3.1L (VIN M)			
	Diameter:	3.504-3.5033 in.	89.016-89.034 mm
	Out of round:	0.0005 in.	0.014 mm
	Taper:	0.0008 in.	0.020 mm
3.3L (VIN N)			
	Diameter:	3.7 in.	93.9 mm
	Out of round:	0.0004 in.	0.10 mm
	Taper:	0.0005 in.	0.13 mm
3.8L (VIN 3)			
	Diameter:	3.8 in.	96.52 mm
	Out of round:	0.001 in.	0.02 mm
	Taper:	0.001 in.	0.02 mm
PISTON			
2.2L (VIN 4)	Clearance to bore:	0.0007-0.0017 in.	0.015-0.045 mm
2.5 L (VIN R)	Clearance to bore:	0.0014-0.0022 in.	0.036-0.056 mm
2.8L (VIN W)	Clearance to bore:	0.00093-0.00222 in.	0.0235-0.0565 mm
2.8L (VIN X)	Clearance to bore:	0.0017-0.003 in.	0.043-0.069 mm
2.8L (VIN Z)	Clearance to bore:	0.0017-0.003 in.	0.043-0.069 mm
3.0L (VIN E)	Clearance to bore:	0.0008-0.0020 in.	0.020-0.051 mm
3.1L (VIN T)	Clearance to bore:	0.0022-0.0028 in.	0.057-0.072 mm
3.1L (VIN M)	Clearance to bore:	0.0013-0.0027 in.	0.032-0.068 mm
3.3L (VIN N)	Clearance to bore:	0.0004-0.0022 in.	0.010-0.056 mm
3.8L (VIN 3)	Clearance to bore:	0.0008-0.0020 in.	0.020-0.051 mm
PISTON RINGS			
2.2L (VIN 4)	End gap		
	Compression:	0.010-0.020 in.	0.25-0.50 mm
	Oil:	0.010-0.050 in.	0.25-1.27 mm
	Groove Clearance		
	Compression:	0.0019-0.0027 in.	0.05-0.07 mm
	Oil:	0.0019-0.0082 in.	0.05-0.21 mm

9108C22

ENGINE REBUILDING SPECIFICATIONS CHART

Component		US	Metric
2.5L (VIN R)			
Gap	Top:	0.01-0.02 in.	0.30-0.50 mm
	Second:	0.01-0.02 in.	0.030-0.050 mm
	Oil:	0.02-0.06 in.	0.50-1.50 mm
Side clearance	Top:	0.002-0.003 in.	0.05-0.08 mm
	Second:	0.001-0.003 in.	0.03-0.08 mm
	Oil:	0.015-0.055 in.	0.38-1.40 mm
2.8L (VIN W)			
Gap	Top:	0.01-0.02 in.	0.30-0.50 mm
	Second:	0.01-0.02 in.	0.30-0.50 mm
	Oil:	0.02-0.55 in.	0.50-1.40 mm
Side clearance	Top:	0.001-0.003 in.	0.03-0.08 mm
	Second:	0.001-0.003 in.	0.03-0.08 mm
	Oil:	0.008 in.	0.20 mm
2.8L (VIN X)			
Gap	Top:	0.01-0.02 in.	0.30-0.50 mm
	Second:	0.02-0.55 in.	0.50-1.40 mm
	Oil:	NA	NA
Side clearance	Top:	0.001-0.003 in.	0.03-0.08 mm
	Second:	0.001-0.003 in.	0.03-0.08 mm
	Oil:	0.008 in.	0.20 mm
2.8L (VIN Z)			
Gap	Top:	0.01-0.02 in.	0.30-0.50 mm
	Second:	0.02-0.55 in.	0.50-1.40 mm
	Oil:	NA	NA
Side clearance	Top:	0.001-0.003 in.	0.03-0.08 mm
	Second:	0.001-0.003 in.	0.03-0.08 mm
	Oil:	0.008 in.	0.20 mm
3.0L (VIN E)			
Gap	Top:	0.01-0.20 in.	0.254-0.508 mm
	Second:	0.10-0.020 in.	0.254-0.508 mm
	Oil:	0.015-0.55 in.	0.381-0.397 mm
Grove width	Top:	0.0770-0.0780 in.	1.955-1.987 mm
	Second:	0.0770-0.0780 in.	1.955-1.981 mm
	Oil:	0.183-0.189 in.	4.684-4.80 mm
Ring depth	Top:	0.184-0.194 in.	4.674-4.928 mm
	Second:	0.186-0.194 in.	4.724-4.928 mm
	Oil:	0.188-0.196 in.	4.7752-4.987 mm

91083C23

ENGINE REBUILDING SPECIFICATIONS CHART

Component		US	Metric
3.1L (VIN T)			
Gap	Top:	0.01-0.02 in.	0.30-0.50 mm
	Second:	0.01-0.02 in.	0.30-0.50 mm
	Oil:	0.01-0.50 in.	0.25-1.27 mm
Side clearance	Top:	0.002-0.0035 in.	0.05-0.09 mm
	Second:	0.002-0.0035 in.	0.05-0.09 mm
	Oil:	0.008 in.	0.20 mm
3.1L (VIN M)			
Groove clearance	1 st.	0.002-0.0035 in.	0.05-0.08 mm
	2nd.	0.002-0.0035 in.	0.05-0.09 mm
Gap	1 st.	0.007-0.016 in.	0.18-0.41 mm
	2nd.	0.0197-0.0280 in.	0.50-0.71 mm
Oil groove clearance:		0.008 in.	0.20 mm
Gap:		0.0098-0.0295 in.	0.25-0.75 mm
3.3L (VIN N)			
Gap	Top:	0.01-0.25 in.	0.30-0.63 mm
	Second:	0.01-0.25 in.	0.30-0.63 mm
	Oil:	0.01-0.40 in.	0.25-0.40 mm
Side clearance	Top:	0.00163-0.0031 in.	0.033-0.079 mm
	Second:	0.0013-0.0031 in.	0.033-0.079 mm
	Oil:	0.0011-0.0081 in.	0.28-0.206 mm
Ring width	Top:	0.0581-0.0589 in.	1.476-1.497 mm
	Second:	0.0581-0.0589 in.	1.476-1.497 mm
	Oil:	0.1122-0.01182 in.	2.850-3.002 mm
3.8L (VIN 3)			
Gap	Top:	0.01-0.20 in.	0.254-0.508 mm
	Second:	0.10-0.020 in.	0.254-0.508 mm
	Oil:	0.015-0.55 in.	0.381-0.397 mm
Grove width	Top:	0.0770-0.0780 in.	1.955-1.987 mm
	Second:	0.0770-0.0780 in.	1.955-1.981 mm
	Oil:	0.183-0.189 in.	4.684-4.80 mm
Ring depth	Top:	0.184-0.194 in.	4.674-4.928 mm
	Second:	0.186-0.194 in.	4.724-4.928 mm
	Oil:	0.188-0.196 in.	4.7752-4.987 mm
PISTON PINS			
2.2L (VIN 4)			
	Diameter:	0.8000-0.8002 in.	20.320-20.325 mm
	Fit in piston:	0.0004-0.0009 in.	0.010-0.022 mm
	Press fit in roc:	0.00098-0.0017 in.	0.025-0.045 mm
2.5 L (VIN R)			
	Diameter:	0.927-0.928 in.	23-546-213.561 mm

91083C24

ENGINE REBUILDING SPECIFICATIONS CHART

Component	US	Metric
2.5 L (VIN R) Fit in piston:	0.0003-0.0005 in.	0.008-0.013 mm
Press fit in rod:	press fit	press fit
2.8L (VIN W)		
Diameter:	0.9052-0.9056 in.	22.937-23.001 mm
Fit in piston:	0.00025-0.0037 in.	0.0065-0.091 mm
Press fit in rod:	0.00078-0.0021 in.	0.020-0.0515 mm
2.8L (VIN X)		
Diameter:	0.9052-0.9056 in.	22.937-23.001 mm
Fit in piston:	0.00026-0.00037 in.	0.0065-0.091 mm
Press fit in rod:	0.00078-0.0021 in.	0.20-0.515 mm
2.8L (VIN Z)		
Diameter:	0.9052-0.9056 in.	22.937-23.001 mm
Fit in piston:	0.0002-0.0037 in.	0.0065-0.0091 mm
Press fit in rod:	0.00078-0.0021 in.	0.020-0.0515 mm
3.0L (VIN E)		
Diameter:	0.931-0.9394 in.	23.853-23.860 mm
Fit in piston:	0.0004-0.0007 in.	0.0100-0.0177 mm
Press fit in rod:	0.00078-0.0017 in.	0.017-0.0432 mm
Pin off-set:	0.040 in. thrust side	1.016 mm thrust side
3.1L (VIN T)		
Diameter:	0.9052-0.9054 in.	22.937-22.964 mm
Fit in piston:	0.0004-0.0008 in.	0.0096-0.0215 mm
Press fit in rod:	0.00078-0.0021 in.	0.020-0.0515 mm
3.1L (VIN M)		
Diameter:	0.9052-0.9054 in.	22.9915-22.9964 mm
Fit in piston:	0.0005-0.0010 in.	0.0126-0.0245 mm
Press fit in rod:	0.0006-0.0018 in.	0.0165-0.0464 mm
3.3L (VIN N)		
Diameter:	0.9053-0.9055 in.	22.995-23.000 mm
Fit in piston:	0.0004-0.0008 in.	0.0096-0.0215 mm
Press fit in rod:	0.0007-0.0017 in.	0.018-0.043 mm
3.8L (VIN 3)		
Diameter:	0.9391-0.9394 in.	23.853-23.860 mm
Fit in piston:	0.0004-0.0007 in.	0.0100-0.0177 mm
Press fit in rod:	0.00078-0.0017 in.	0.017-0.0432 mm
Pin off-set:	0.040 in. thrust side	1.016 mm thrust side
CRANKSHAFT		
2.2L (VIN 4)		
Main journal		
Diameter:	2.4945-2.4954 in.	63.360-63.384 mm
Taper:	0.00019 in.	0.005 mm
Out of round:	0.00019 in.	0.005 mm
Main bearing		
Clearance:	0.0006-0.0019 in.	0.015-0.047 mm
End play:	0.002-0.007 in.	0.0511-0.1780 mm
Connecting rod		
Journal diameter:	1.9983-1.9994 in.	50.758-50.784 mm
Taper:	0.00019 in.	0.005 mm
Out of round:	0.00019 in.	0.0005 mm
Clearance:	0.00098-0.0031 in.	0.025-0.079 mm
Side clearance:	0.0039-0.0149 in.	0.10-0.38 mm

91083C25

ENGINE REBUILDING SPECIFICATIONS CHART

Component	US	Metric
2.5L (VIN R)		
Main journal		
Diameter:	2.3 in.	58.399-58.400 mm
Taper:	0.0005 in.	0.013 mm
Out of round:	0.0005 in.	0.013 mm
Clearance:	0.0005-0.0022 in.	0.013-0.056 mm
End-play:	0.0051-0.010 in.	0.13-0.26 mm
Crankpin		
Diameter:	2.0 in.	50.708-50.805 mm
Taper:	0.0005 in.	0.013 mm
Out of round:	0.0005 in.	0.013 mm
Clearance		
Bearing:	0.0005-0.003 in.	0.013-0.07 mm
Side:	0.006-0.024 in.	0.015-0.06 mm
2.8L (VIN W)		
Main journal		
Diameter:	2.6473-2.4683 in.	67.241-67.265 mm
Taper:	0.0002 in.	0.005 mm
Out of round:	0.0002 in.	0.005 mm
Clearance:	0.0012-0.0027 in.	0.032-0.069 mm
Thrust:	0.0016-0.0031 in.	0.042-0.079 mm
End-play:	0.0024-0.0083 in.	0.06-0.21 mm
Crankpin		
Diameter:	1.9994-1.9983 in.	50-784-50.758 mm
Taper:	0.00002 in.	0.005 mm
Out of round:	0.0002 in.	0.005 mm
Clearance		
Bearing:	0.0015-0.0036 in.	0.038-0.083 mm
Side:	0.014-0.027 in.	0.360-0.680 mm
2.8L (VIN X)		
Main journal		
Diameter:	2.5850-2.5860 in.	63.340-63.364 mm
Taper:	0.0002 in.	0.005 mm
Out of round:	0.00002 in.	0.005 mm
Clearance:	0.002-0.003 in.	0.05-0.08 mm
End-play:	0.002-0.007 in.	0.05-0.18 mm
Crankpin		
Diameter:	2.0713-2.0715 in.	50.784-50.758 mm
Taper:	0.0002 in.	0.005 mm
Out of round:	0.0002 in.	0.005 mm
Clearance		
Bearing:	0.0014-0.0037 in.	0.040-0.083 mm
Side:	0.0065-0.018 in.	0.160-0.440 mm
2.8L (VIN Z)		
Main journal		
Diameter:	2.5850-2.5860 in.	63.340-63.364 mm
Taper:	0.0002 in.	0.005 mm
Out of round:	0.00002 in.	0.005 mm
Clearance:	0.002-0.003 in.	0.05-0.08 mm
End-play:	0.002-0.007 in.	0.05-0.18 mm

91083C26

ENGINE REBUILDING SPECIFICATIONS CHART

Component	US	Metric
2.8L (VIN Z) Crankpin		
Diameter:	2.0713-2.0715 in.	50.784-50.758 mm
Taper:	0.0002 in.	0.005 mm
Out of round:	0.0002 in.	0.005 mm
Clearance		
Bearing:	0.0014-0.0037 in.	0.040-0.083 mm
Side:	0.0065-0.018 in.	0.160-0.440 mm
3.0L (VIN E)		
Main journal		
Diameter:	2.4995 in.	63.4873 mm
Taper:	0.0002 in.	0.005 mm
Out of round:	0.0002 in.	0.005 mm
Clearance:	0.003-0.0018 in.	0.08-0.0457 mm
End-play:	0.003-0.0011 in.	0.08-0.2794 mm
Length		
Numbers 1, 3, 4:	0.864 in.	21.9456 mm
Number 2:	1.057 in.	28.8478 mm
Crankpin		
Diameter:	2.2487-2.2495 in.	57.1169-57.1373 mm
Taper:	0.0002 in.	0.005 mm
Out of round:	0.0002 in.	0.005 mm
Clearance:	0.0005-0.0026 in.	0.0127-0.066 mm
Bearing:	0.003-0.015 in.	0.0762-0.381 mm
Side:	0.654 in.	16.611 mm
3.1L (VIN T)		
Main journal		
Diameter:	2.6473-2.6483 in.	67.241-67.265 mm
Taper:	0.0003 in.	0.008 mm
Out of round:	0.0002 in.	0.005 mm
Clearance:	0.0012-0.0027 in.	0.032-0.069 mm
Thrust:	0.0012-0.0027 in.	0.032-0.069 mm
End-play:	0.0024-0.0083 in.	0.06-0.21 mm
Crankpin		
Diameter:	1.9994-1.9983 in.	50.784-50.758 mm
Taper:	0.0003 in.	0.008 mm
Out of round:	0.0002 in.	0.005 mm
Clearance		
Bearing:	0.0013-0.0031 in.	0.032-0.079 mm
Side:	0.014-0.027 in.	0.360-0.680 mm
3.1L (VIN M)		
Main journal		
Diameter:	2.6473-2.6483 in.	67.239-67.257 mm
Taper:	0.0002 in.	0.005 mm
Out of round:	0.0002 in.	0.005 mm
Flange runout:	0.0016 in.	0.04 mm
Main bearing		
Bore diameter:	2.8407-2.8412 in.	72.155-72.168 mm
Inside diameter:	2.6492-2.6502 in.	67.289-67.316 mm
Bearing clearance:	0.0012-0.0030 in.	0.032-0.077 mm
Thrust bearing		
Clearance:	0.0012-0.0030 in.	0.032-0.077 mm
Crankshaft End-play:	0.0024-0.0083 in.	0.060-0.210 mm

91083C27

ENGINE REBUILDING SPECIFICATIONS CHART

Component	US	Metric
3.3L (VIN N)		
Main journal		
Diameter:	2.4988-2.4998 in.	63.47-63.495 mm
Taper:	0.0003 in.	0.008 mm
Out of round:	0.0003 in.	0.008 mm
Clearance:	0.0003-0.0018 in.	0.008-0.045 mm
End-play:	0.003-0.0011 in.	0.076-0.279 mm
Crankpin		
Diameter:	2.2487-2.2499 in.	57.117-57.147 mm
Taper:	0.0003 in.	0.008 mm
Out of round:	0.0003 in.	0.008 mm
Clearance		
Bearing:	0.0003-0.0026 in.	0.0076-0.071 mm
Side:	0.003-0.015 in.	0.076-0.381 mm
3.8L (VIN 3)		
Main journal		
Diameter:	2.4995 in.	63.4873 mm
Taper:	0.0002 in.	0.005 mm
Out of round:	0.0002 in.	0.005 mm
Clearance:	0.003-0.0018 in.	0.08-0.0457 mm
End-play:	0.003-0.0011 in.	0.08-0.2794 mm
Length		
Numbers 1, 3, 4:	0.864 in.	21.9456 mm
Number 2:	1.057 in.	28.8478 mm
Crankpin		
Diameter:	2.2487-2.2495 in.	57.1169-57.1373 mm
Taper:	0.0002 in.	0.005 mm
Out of round:	0.0002 in.	0.005 mm
Clearance:	0.0005-0.0026 in.	0.0127-0.066 mm
Bearing:	0.003-0.015 in.	0.0762-0.381 mm
Side:	0.654 in.	16.611 mm

91083C28

4

DRIVEABILITY AND EMISSIONS CONTROLS

EMISSION CONTROLS

You'll find emission controls, ignition controls and fuel system controls are interrelated systems on the newer cars. In this section of the manual you'll find emission components related to exhaust gas recirculation, crankcase fume venting, evaporative. The Electronic Engine Control portion of the section should be used in conjunction with the Fuel System section of the manual.

Crankcase Ventilation System

OPERATION

All these gasoline vehicles are equipped with a positive crankcase ventilation (PCV) system to control crankcase blow-by vapors. The system functions as follows:

When the engine is running, a small portion of the gases which are formed in the combustion chamber leak by the piston rings and enter the crankcase. Since these gases are under pressure, they tend to escape from the crankcase and enter the atmosphere. If these gases are allowed to remain in the crankcase for any period of time, they contaminate the engine oil and cause sludge to build up in the crankcase. If the gases are allowed to escape into the atmosphere, they pollute the air with unburned hydrocarbons.

The job of the crankcase emission control equipment is to recycle these gases back into the engine combustion chamber where they are reburned.

The crankcase (blow-by) gases are recycled in the following way: as the engine is running, clean, filtered air is drawn through the air filter and into the crankcase. As the air passes through the crankcase, it picks up the combustion gases and carries them out of the crankcase, through the oil separator, through the PCV valve, and into the induction system. As they enter the intake manifold, they are drawn into the combustion chamber where they are reburned.

The most critical component in the system is the PCV valve. This valve controls the amount of gases which are recycled into the combustion chamber. At low engine speeds, the valve is partially closed, limiting the flow of gases into the intake manifold. As engine speed increases, the valve opens to admit greater quantities of gases into the intake manifold. If the valve should become blocked or plugged, the gases will be prevented from escaping from the crankcase by the normal route. Since these gases are under pressure, they will find their own way out of the crankcase. This alternate route is usually a weak oil seal or gasket in the engine. As the gas escapes by the gasket, it also creates an oil leak. Besides causing oil leaks, a clogged PCV valve also allows these gases to remain in the crankcase for an extended period of time, promoting the formation of sludge in the engine.

SERVICE (COMPONENT TESTING)

Inspect the PCV system hose and connections at each tune-up and replace any deteriorated hoses. Check the PCV valve at every tune-up and replace it at 30,000 mile (48,900km) intervals.

1. Remove the PCV valve from the rocker arm cover.
2. Start engine, allow to reach normal temperature and idle speed.
3. Place your thumb over the end of the valve to check for vacuum. If no vacuum, check the valve and hose. Most likely the hose is plugged up.
4. Newer computer controlled vehicles may no show much of a change in engine rpm when the valve is blocked or removed due to the computer compensating almost instantly to the vacuum change.
5. Remove the valve from the engine and hose. Shake the valve; it should rattle. If not, it's plugged up with dirt and must be replaced.
6. When replacing a PCV valve, you MUST use the correct valve. Many valves look alike on the outside, but have different mechanical values. Putting an incorrect PCV valve on a vehicle can cause a great deal of driveability problems. The engine computer assumes the valve is the correct one and may overadjust ignition timing or fuel mixture.

REMOVAL & INSTALLATION

PCV Valve

▶ **See Figure 1**

The valve is located in a rubber grommet in the valve cover, connected to the air cleaner housing by a large diameter rubber hose. In replacing the PCV valve,

86811049

Fig. 1 Remove the PCV valve, inspect and replace it if necessary

make sure it is fully inserted in the hose, that the clamp is moved over the ridge on the valve so that the valve will not slip out of the hose, and that the valve is fully inserted into the grommet in the valve cover.

1. Pull the valve (with the hose attached) from the rubber grommet in the valve cover.
2. Remove the valve from the hose.
3. Inspect the rubber grommet that houses the valve for deterioration, and replace if necessary.

To install:

4. Install the new (or reusable) PCV valve into the hose.
5. Press the valve back into the rubber grommet in the valve cover.

PCV Filter

The PCV filter is located in the air cleaner housing and must be replaced every 50,000 miles (80,000 km).

1. Remove the air cleaner housing lid.
2. Slide back the filter retaining clip and remove the old filter.
3. Install the new filter, replace the retaining clip and replace the housing lid.

Evaporative Emission Control System

OPERATION

The basic Evaporative Emission Control (EEC) system used on all models is the carbon canister storage method. The system is used to reduce emissions of fuel vapors from the car's fuel system. Evaporated fuel vapors are stored for burning during combustion rather than being vented into the atmosphere when the engine is not running. To accomplish this, the fuel tank and the carburetor float bowl are vented through a vapor canister containing activated charcoal. The system utilizes a sealed fuel tank with a dome that collects fuel vapors and allows them to pass on into a line connected with the vapor canister. In addition, the vapors that form above the float chamber in the carburetor also pass into a line connected with the canister. The canister absorbs these vapors in a bed of activated charcoal and retains them until the canister is purged or cleared by air drawn through the filter at its bottom. The absorbing occurs when the car is not running, while the purging or cleaning occurs when the car is running. The amount of vapor being drawn into the engine at any given time is too small to have an effect on either fuel economy or engine performance.

The Computer Control Module (ECM/PCM) controls the vacuum to the canister purge valve by using an electrically operated solenoid valve. When the system is in the "Open Loop" mode, the solenoid valve is energized and blocks all vacuum to the canister purge valve. When the system is in the "Closed Loop" mode, the solenoid valve is de-energized and vacuum is then supplied to operate the purge valve. This releases the fuel vapors, collected in the canister, into the induction system.

It is extremely important that only vapors be transferred to the engine. To avoid the possibility of liquid fuel being drawn into the system, the following features are included as part of the total system:

- A fuel tank overfill protector is provided to assure adequate room for expansion of liquid fuel volume with temperature changes.
- A one point fuel tank venting system is provided on all models to assure that the tank will be vented under any normal car attitude. This is accomplished by the use of a domed tank.
- A pressure-vacuum relief valve is located in the fuel cap.

➡**Some canisters are of the closed design. They draw air from the air cleaner rather than the bottom of the canister.**

REMOVAL & INSTALLATION

Vapor Canister

▶ **See Figure 2**

1. Loosen the screw holding the canister retaining bracket.
2. If equipped with A/C, loosen the attachments holding the accumulator and pipe assembly.
3. Rotate the canister retaining bracket and remove the canister.
4. Tag and disconnect the hoses leading from the canister.

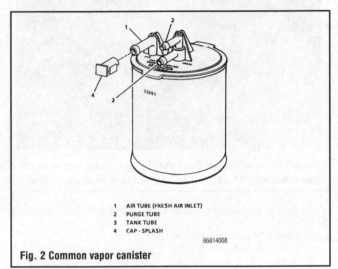

1 AIR TUBE (FRESH AIR INLET)
2 PURGE TUBE
3 TANK TUBE
4 CAP - SPLASH

86814008

Fig. 2 Common vapor canister

To install:
5. Connect the canister, attach with the mounting bolts.
6. Attach the tagged hoses leading to the canister. Make sure the connections are correct.

Filter

1. Remove the vapor canister.
2. Pull the filter out from the bottom of the canister.
To install:
3. Install a new filter and then replace the canister.

Evaporative Canister Purge Solenoid Valve

1. Disconnect the negative battery cable.
2. Some vehicles you will need to raise and support the vehicle.
3. Remove the electrical connection and vacuum line from the purge solenoid valve.
4. Some models will have the valve bolted in, remove the bolts to release the valve.
5. On other models, release the locking tab on the solenoid bracket, then remove the purge solenoid valve from the bracket.
To install:
6. Reinstall the valve by inserting the mounting bolts and tightening down, or install the valve to the bracket, then snap the valve down over the locking tabs of the bracket.
7. Connect the vacuum lines and electrical connection to the valve.
8. Lower the vehicle, if raised and supported.
9. Connect the negative battery cable.

Exhaust Gas Recirculation (EGR) System

OPERATION

➡**Not all vehicles are equipped with an EGR system.**

The EGR system is used to reduce oxides of nitrogen (NOx) emission levels caused by high combustion chamber temperatures. This is accomplished by the use of an EGR valve which opens, under specific engine operating conditions, to admit a small amount of exhaust gas into the intake manifold, below the throttle plate. The exhaust gas mixes with the incoming air charge and displaces a portion of the oxygen in the air/fuel mixture entering the combustion chamber. The exhaust gas does not support combustion of the air/fuel mixture but it takes up volume, the net effect of which is to lower the temperature of the combustion process. This lower temperature also helps control detonation.

The EGR valve is a mounted on the intake manifold and has an opening into the exhaust manifold. On some vehicles, the EGR valve is opened by manifold vacuum to permit exhaust gas to flow into the intake manifold. On others, the EGR valve is purely electrical and uses solenoid valves to open the flow passage. If too much exhaust gas enters, combustion will not occur. Because of this, very little exhaust gas is allowed to pass through the valve. The EGR system will be activated once the engine reaches normal operating temperature and the EGR valve will open when engine operating conditions are above idle speed and below Wide Open Throttle (WOT). On California vehicles equipped with a Vehicle Speed Sensor (VSS), the EGR valve opens when the VSS signal is greater than 2 mph. The EGR system is deactivated on vehicles equipped with a Torque Converter Clutch (TCC) when the TCC is engaged. There are three basic types of systems as described below, differing in the way EGR flow is modulated.

Positive Backpressure EGR Valve

▶ **See Figure 3**

An air bleed valve, located inside the EGR valve assembly acts as a vacuum regulator. The bleed valve controls the amount of vacuum in the vacuum chamber by bleeding vacuum to outside air during the open phase of the cycle. When the EGR valve receives enough backpressure through the hollow shaft, it closes the valve. At this point, maximum available vacuum is applied to the diaphragm and the EGR valve opens. If there is a small amount of vacuum or no vacuum in the vacuum chamber such as wide open throttle or at idle, the EGR valve will not open. The positive backpressure EGR valve also will not open if vacuum is applied to the valve with the engine stopped or idling.

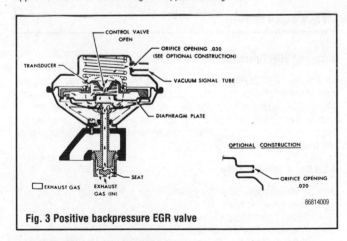

CONTROL VALVE OPEN
ORIFICE OPENING .030 (SEE OPTIONAL CONSTRUCTION)
TRANSDUCER
VACUUM SIGNAL TUBE
DIAPHRAGM PLATE
OPTIONAL CONSTRUCTION
ORIFICE OPENING .020
EXHAUST GAS
EXHAUST GAS (IN)
SEAT

86814009

Fig. 3 Positive backpressure EGR valve

Negative Backpressure EGR Valve

The negative backpressure EGR valve is similar to the positive backpressure EGR valve except that the bleed valve spring is moved from above the diaphragm to below and the bleed valve is normally closed. The negative backpressure EGR valve varies the amount of exhaust gas flow into the intake manifold depending on manifold vacuum and variations in exhaust backpressure. The diaphragm on the valve has an internal air bleed hole which is held closed by a small spring when there is no exhaust backpressure. Engine vacuum opens the EGR valve against the pressure of a spring. When manifold vacuum combines with negative exhaust backpressure, the vacuum bleed hole opens and the EGR valve closes. This valve will open if vacuum is applied with the engine not running.

Digital EGR Valve

▶ **See Figure 4**

The digital EGR valve, used on most of the newer engines such as the 3.1L (VIN T) and 3.1L (VIN M), it is designed to control the flow of EGR, independent of intake manifold vacuum. The valve controls EGR flow through 3 solenoid-opened orifices, which increase in size, to produce 7 possible combinations. When a solenoid is energized, the armature with attached shaft and swivel pintle, is lifted, opening the orifice.

The digital EGR valve is opened by the ECM/PCM, grounding each solenoid circuit individually. The flow of EGR is regulated by the ECM/PCM which uses information from the Engine Coolant Temperature Sensor (ECT), Throttle Position Sensor (TPS), Manifold Absolute Pressure (MAP) sensor and Mass Air Flow Sensor (MAF) to determine the appropriate rate of flow for a particular engine operating condition.

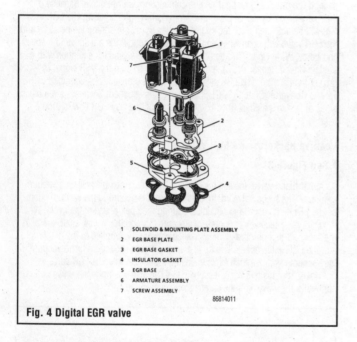

1	SOLENOID & MOUNTING PLATE ASSEMBLY
2	EGR BASE PLATE
3	EGR BASE GASKET
4	INSULATOR GASKET
5	EGR BASE
6	ARMATURE ASSEMBLY
7	SCREW ASSEMBLY

86814011

Fig. 4 Digital EGR valve

Incorrect EGR Operation

Too much EGR flow at idle, cruise, or during cold operation may result in the engine stalling after cold start, the engine stalling at idle after deceleration, vehicle surge during cruise and rough idle. If the EGR valve is always open, the vehicle may not idle. Too little or no EGR flow allows combustion temperatures to get too high which could result in spark knock (detonation), engine overheating and/or emission test failure.

EGR Valve Identification

- Positive backpressure EGR valves will have a "P" stamped on the top side of the valve below the date built.
- Negative backpressure EGR valves will have a "N" stamped on the top side of the valve below the date built.
- Port EGR valves have no identification stamped below the date built.

REMOVAL & INSTALLATION

▶ **See Figures 5 and 6**

Backpressure EGR valves

1. Disconnect the negative battery cable.
2. Remove the air cleaner assembly.

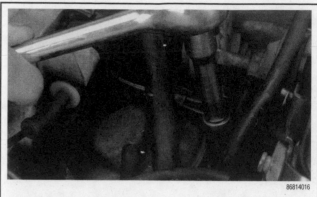

Fig. 5 Remove the EGR valve retaining bolts with a suitable wrench

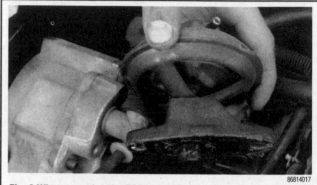

Fig. 6 When removing the EGR valve, be sure to also remove all old gasket material and clean off the engine's valve mounting surface

3. Tag and disconnect the necessary hoses and wiring to gain access to the EGR valve.
4. Remove the EGR valve retaining bolts.
5. Remove the EGR valve. Discard the gasket.
6. Buff the exhaust deposits from the mounting surface and around the valve using a wire wheel.
7. Remove deposits from the valve outlet.
8. Clean the mounting surfaces of the intake manifold and valve assembly.

To install:

9. Install a new EGR gasket.
10. Install the EGR valve to the manifold.
11. Install the retaining bolts and torque to 11–22 ft. lbs. (15–30 Nm).
12. Connect the wiring and hoses.
13. Install the air cleaner assembly.
14. Connect the negative battery cable.

Digital EGR Valves

1. Disconnect the negative battery cable.
2. Disengage the electrical connector at the solenoid.
3. Remove the 2 base-to-flange bolts.
4. Remove the digital EGR valve.

To install:

5. Install the digital EGR valve.
6. Install the 2 base-to-flange bolts. Tighten to 18–22 ft. lbs. (25–30 Nm).
7. Connect the negative battery cable.

EGR Solenoid

1. Disconnect the negative battery cable.
2. Remove the air cleaner, as required.
3. Some models require the MAP sensor to be removed.
4. Disengage the electrical connector at the solenoid.
5. Disconnect the vacuum hoses.
6. Remove the retaining bolts and the solenoid.
7. Remove the filter, as required.

To install:

8. If removed, install the filter.
9. Install the solenoid and retaining bolts, then tighten to 15–22 ft. lbs. (20–30 Nm).
10. Position and install the MAP sensor if removed.
11. Connect the vacuum hoses.
12. Connect the electrical connector.
13. If removed, install the air cleaner.
14. Connect the negative battery cable.

Emission Control Systems

Emission control system constitute the largest body of emission control devices installed on A-Body cars. Many of these systems are controlled by or engine control computer. Included in this category are: Thermostatic Air Cleaner (THERMAC); Air Management System; Early Fuel Evaporation System (EFE); Exhaust Gas Recirculation (EGR); Computer Command Control System (CCC); Throttle Body Injection (TBI); Multi-Port Fuel Injection (MFI); Deceleration Valve; Mixture Control Solenoid (M/C); Throttle Position Sensor (TPS); Idle Speed Control (ISC); Electronic Spark Timing (EST); Torque Converter Clutch (TCC); Catalytic Converter and the Oxygen Sensor System. A brief description of each system and any applicable service procedures follows.

Thermostatic Air Cleaner (THERMAC)

♦ See Figure 7

All Feedback Carbureted, and Throttle Body Injected engines use the THERMAC system. This system is designed to warm the air entering the carburetor when underhood temperatures are low, and to maintain a controlled air temperature into the carburetor at all times. By allowing preheated air to enter the carburetor, the amount of time the choke is on is reduced, resulting in better fuel economy and lower emissions. Engine warm-up time is a also reduced.

The THERMAC system is composed of the air cleaner body, a filter, sensor unit, vacuum diaphragm, damper door, and associated hoses and connections. Heat radiating from the exhaust manifold is trapped by a heat stove and is ducted to the air cleaner to supply heated air to the carburetor. A movable door in the air cleaner case snorkel allows air to be drawn in from the heat stove (cold operation). The door position is controlled by the vacuum motor, which receives intake manifold vacuum as modulated by the temperature sensor.

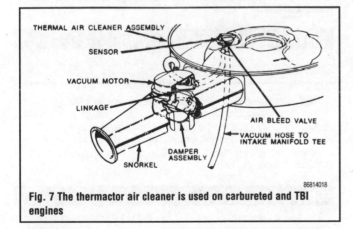

THERMAL AIR CLEANER ASSEMBLY
SENSOR
VACUUM MOTOR
LINKAGE
AIR BLEED VALVE
VACUUM HOSE TO INTAKE MANIFOLD TEE
DAMPER ASSEMBLY
SNORKEL

86814018

Fig. 7 The thermactor air cleaner is used on carbureted and TBI engines

SYSTEM CHECKS

1. Check the vacuum hoses for leaks, kinks, breaks, or improper connections and correct any defects.
2. With the engine off, check the position of the damper door within the snorkel. A mirror can be used to make this job easier. The damper door should be open to admit outside air.
3. Apply at least 7 in. Hg (24 kPa) of vacuum to the damper diaphragm unit. The door should close. If it doesn't, check the diaphragm linkage for binding and correct hookup.
4. With the vacuum still applied and the door closed, clamp the tube to trap

the vacuum. If the door doesn't remain closed, there is a leak in the diaphragm assembly.

Air Management System

The AIR management system, is used to provide additional oxygen to continue the combustion process after the exhaust gases leave the combustion chamber. Air is injected into either the exhaust port(s), the exhaust manifold(s) or the catalytic converter by an engine driven air pump. The system is in operation at all times and will bypass air only momentarily during deceleration and at high speeds. The bypass function is performed by the AIR Management Valve, while the check valve protects the air pump by preventing any backflow of exhaust gases.

The AIR management system helps reduce HC and CO content in the exhaust gases by injecting air into the exhaust ports during cold engine operation. This air injection also helps the catalytic converter to reach the proper temperature quicker during warm-up. When the engine is warm (Closed Loop), the AIR system injects air into the beds of a three-way converter to lower the HC and the CO content in the exhaust.

The Air Management system utilizes the following components:

- An engine driven AIR pump
- AIR management valves (Air Control, Air Switching)
- Air flow and control hoses
- Check valves
- A dual-bed, three-way catalytic converter

The belt driven, vane-type air pump is located at the front of the engine and supplies clean air to the AIR system for purposes already stated. When the engine is cold, the Electronic Control Module (ECM) energizes an AIR control solenoid. This allows air to flow to the AIR switching valve. The AIR switching valve is then energized to direct air to the exhaust ports.

When the engine is warm, the ECM/PCM de-energizes the AIR switching valve, thus directing the air between the beds of the catalytic converter. This provides additional oxygen for the oxidizing catalyst in the second bed to decrease HC and CO, while at the same time keeping oxygen levels low in the first bed, enabling the reducing catalyst to effectively decrease the levels of NOx.

If the AIR control valve detects a rapid increase in manifold vacuum (deceleration), certain operating modes (wide open throttle, etc.) or if the ECM/PCM self-diagnostic system detects any problem in the system, air is diverted to the air cleaner or directly into the atmosphere.

The primary purpose of the ECM/PCM's divert mode is to prevent backfiring. Throttle closure at the beginning of deceleration will temporarily create air/fuel mixtures which are too rich to burn completely. These mixtures become burnable when they reach the exhaust if combined with the injection air. The next firing of the engine will ignite this mixture causing an exhaust backfire. Momentary diverting of the injection air from the exhaust prevents this.

The AIR management system check valves and hoses should be checked periodically for any leaks, cracks or deterioration.

REMOVAL & INSTALLATION

Air Pump

♦ See Figures 8 and 9

1. Remove the AIR management valves and/or adapter at the pump.
2. Loosen the air pump adjustment bolt and remove the drive belt.
3. Remove the pump pulley.
4. Unscrew the pump mounting bolts and then remove the pump.

To install:

5. Install the pump with the mounting bolts loose.
6. Attach the pump pulley to the pump.
7. Install the pump belt, then adjust.
8. Install the AIR management valves and/or adapter at the pump.
9. Tighten the mounting bolts to 20–35 ft. lbs. (27–56 Nm).

Check Valve

1. Release the clamp and disconnect the air hoses from the valve.
2. Unscrew the check valve from the air injection pipe.

To install:

3. Install the check valve into the air injection pipe.
4. Connect the hoses and tighten with the clamps.

Fig. 8 Loosen the air pump adjustment bolt . . .

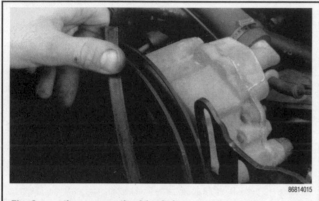

Fig. 9 . . . then remove the drive belt

Air Management Valve

1. Disconnect the negative battery cable.
2. Remove the air cleaner.
3. Tag and disconnect the vacuum hose from the valve.
4. Tag and disconnect the air outlet hoses from the valve.
5. Bend back the lock tabs and then remove the bolts holding the elbow to the valve.
6. Tag and disconnect any electrical connections at the valve and then remove the valve from the elbow.

To install:

7. Install the valve to the bracket or adapter and lock tabs if used, with a new gasket.
8. Tighten the attaching screws to 140 inch lbs. (16 Nm).
9. Bend the tab to hex flat against the bolt and screw heads.
10. Install the outlet and vacuum signal hoses and electrical connections, then check for leaks and correct operation.

Emission Service Light

An emissions indicator flag may appear in the odometer window of the speedometer on some vehicles. The flag could say "Sensor," "Emissions" or "Catalyst" depending on the part or assembly that is scheduled for regular emissions maintenance replacement. The word "Sensor" indicates a need for oxygen sensor replacement and the words "Emissions" or "Catalyst" indicate the need for catalytic converter catalyst replacement.

RESETTING

1. Remove the instrument panel trim plate.
2. Remove the instrument cluster lens.
3. Locate the flag indicator reset notches at the driver's side of the odometer.
4. Use a pointed tool to apply light downward pressure on the notches, until the indicator is reset.

5. When the indicator is reset an alignment mark will appear in the left center of the odometer window.

Service Interval Reminder Light

RESETTING

If equipped, the SERVICE REMINDER section of the Driver Information Center (DIC) display shows how many miles remain until service is needed. When the RESET button is pressed twice, a type of service and number of miles remaining until the service is needed will be displayed. Each time the RESET button is pressed, another type of service and mile remaining for it will be displayed.

With the ignition switch in the RUN, BULB, TEST or START position, voltage is applied from the ECM/PCM fuse through a pink/black wire to the ECM/PCM. As the vehicle moves the speed sensor sends pulses to the ECM/PCM. The ECM/PCM then sends signals to the speed input of the DIC module. The DIC module converts these pulses to miles. The module then subtracts the miles travelled from the distance on the DIC display. All four types of service can be displayed at the same time.

To reset the service light it will be necessary to subtract the mileage from the service interval light that is illuminated. The miles remaining for a certain type of service can be decreased by holding the RESET button, and the miles remaining will be decreased in steps of 500 miles (805 km) every 5 seconds. If the RESET button is held in and the miles remaining reach zero, the DIC display will show the service interval for the service selected. The service intervals are: oil filter and change 7500 miles (12,077 km), next oil filter 15,000 miles (24,155 km), tire rotation 7500 miles (12,077 km), next rotation 15,000 miles (24,155 km), tune-up 30,000 miles (48,309 km).

If the RESET button is still held down, the miles will decrease in steps of 500 miles (805 km) from the service interval. When the RESET button is released, the mileage display will be the new distance until the service should be performed.

When the service distance reaches zero, the service reminder item will be displayed. If the service interval is reset within 10 miles (16 km), the display will go out immediately. If more than 10 miles pass before the service interval is reset, the item will remain displayed for another 10 miles before going out.

➡**On some models it may be necessary to depress the SYSTEM RECALL button in order to display the service interval light on the driver information center.**

Service Engine Soon (SES) Light

RESETTING

The Service Engine Soon (SES) light or Check Engine light will light if an engine or emission problem is detected. If an emission problem is detected the computer will store a code for that fault. If the fault goes away or is repair the light will go out, but the code will remain in memory. If the problem returns or is not repair the light will not go out and can not be reset. When the problem goes away the light goes out.

Oxygen Sensor (O₂S)

The exhaust oxygen sensor or O_2S is mounted in the exhaust stream where it monitors oxygen content in the exhaust gas. The newer models have a heated oxygen sensor, which is slightly different from the conventional sensor. The oxygen content in the exhaust is a measure of the air/fuel mixture going into the engine. The oxygen in the exhaust reacts with the oxygen sensor to produce a voltage which is read by the ECM/PCM. The voltage output is very low, ranging from 0.1 volt in a high oxygen-lean mixture condition to 0.9 volt in a low oxygen-rich mixture condition.

Testing the oxygen sensor without the use of special scan tools to observe its operation is difficult. The oxygen sensor should not be condemned because of Codes 44, 45, or 131–134. These codes tell you the oxygen sensor is seeing a constant rich or leak mixture. This code is usually not due to a bad oxygen sensor. A rich mixture could be a dirty air filter, stuck choke, leaking injector, burn valve or other problems. A lean mixture could be a vacuum leak, low fuel pressure or even a bad spark plug wire. Follow the proper charts to test the components.

PRECAUTIONS

- Careful handling of the oxygen sensor is essential.
- The electrical pigtail and connector are permanently attached and should not be removed from the oxygen sensor.
- The in-line electrical connector and louvered end of the oxygen sensor must be kept free of grease, dirt and other contaminants.
- Avoid using cleaning solvents of any type on the oxygen sensor.
- Do not drop or roughly handle the oxygen sensor.
- The oxygen sensor may be difficult to remove if the engine temperature is below 120°F (48°C). Excessive force may damage the threads in the exhaust manifold or exhaust pipe.

REMOVAL & INSTALLATION

◆ See Figure 10

➡The oxygen sensor must be replaced every 30,000 miles (48,309 km). The sensor may be difficult to remove when the engine temperature is below 120°F (48°C). Excessive removal force may damage the threads in the exhaust manifold or pipe and result in injury; follow the removal procedure carefully.

1. Locate the oxygen sensor; it protrudes from the center of the exhaust manifold at the front of the engine compartment. (The sensor looks somewhat like a spark plug.)
2. Disengage the electrical connector from the oxygen sensor.
3. Spray a commercial heat riser solvent onto the sensor threads and allow it to soak in for at least five minutes.
4. **Carefully** unscrew and remove the sensor.

86814021

Fig. 10 The oxygen sensor protrudes from the center of the exhaust manifold at the front of the engine compartment and looks somewhat like a spark plug

To install:

5. Coat the new sensor's threads with GM anti-seize compound No. 5613695 or the equivalent. This is not a conventional anti-seize paste. The use of a regular compound may electrically insulate the sensor, rendering it inoperative. You must coat the threads with an electrically conductive anti-seize compound.
6. Tighten the sensor to 30 ft. lbs. (42 Nm). Do not overtighten.
7. Attach the electrical connector. Be careful not to damage the electrical pigtail. Check the sensor boot for proper fit and installation.

ELECTRONIC ENGINE CONTROL SYSTEMS

There are 3 basic fuel control systems used on these General Motors A-Body cars. The feedback carburetor vehicles use a system called Computer Command Control (CCC) System. The other two systems are fuel injection systems. One system is called Throttle Body Injection (TBI); this system uses an injector built into the throttle body. Throttle body injected vehicles appear very much like carbureted vehicles, but you'll notice there is no choke. The third system is Multi-Port Fuel Injection (MFI), or a variation known as Sequential Fuel Injection (SFI). This MFI/SFI system has an injector mounted in the intake manifold at each intake valve. There is one injector for each cylinder.

Feedback Carburetor and Computer Command Control (CCC) System

The CCC system monitors engine and vehicle operating conditions which it uses to control engine and emission control systems. This system controls engine operation and lowers the exhaust emissions while maintaining good fuel economy and driveability. The Computer Control Module (ECM/PCM) is the brain of the CCC system. The ECM/PCM controls engine related systems constantly adjusting the engine operation. In addition to maintaining the ideal air/fuel ratio for the catalytic converter and adjusting ignition timing, the CCC system also controls the Air Management System so that the catalytic converter can operate at the highest efficiency possible. The system also controls lock-up on the transaxle's torque converter clutch, adjusts idle speed over a wide range of conditions, purges the evaporative emissions charcoal canister, controls the EGR valve operation and operates the Early Fuel Evaporative (EFE) system. Not all engines use all of the above subsystems.

The CCC system is primarily an emission control system, designed to maintain a 14.7:1 air/fuel ratio under all operating conditions. When this ideal air/fuel ratio is maintained the catalytic converter can control oxides of nitrogen (NOx), hydrocarbon (HC) and carbon monoxide (CO) emissions.

There are 2 operation modes for CCC system: closed loop and open loop fuel control. Closed loop fuel control means the oxygen sensor is controlling the carburetor's air/fuel mixture ratio. Under open loop fuel control operating conditions (wide open throttle, engine and/or oxygen sensor cold), the oxygen sensor has no effect on the air/fuel mixture.

➡On some engines, the oxygen sensor will cool off while the engine is idling, putting the system into open loop operation. To restore closed loop operation, run the engine at part throttle and accelerate from idle to part throttle a few times.

The basic system block diagram shows the catalytic converter located in the exhaust system close to the engine. It is ahead of the muffler and tailpipe. If the converter is to do its job effectively, the engine must receive an air/fuel mixture of approximately 14.7:1.

The carburetor mixes air and gasoline into a combustible mixture before delivering it to the engine. However, carburetors have reached a point where they can no longer control the air/fuel mixture sufficiently close to the ideal 14.7:1 ratio for most operating conditions. Therefore, a different type of control must be used on the carburetor, something that has never been used before.

An electric solenoid in the carburetor controls the air/fuel ratio. The solenoid is connected to an electronic module (ECM/PCM) which is an on board computer. The ECM/PCM provides a controlling signal to the solenoid. The solenoid controls the metering rod(s) and an idle air bleed valve to closely control the air/fuel ration throughout the operating range of the engine. However, since the engine operates under a wide variety of conditions, the computer must be told what those conditions are. This is so that it will know what to tell the carburetor solenoid to do.

A sensor is located in the exhaust stream close to the engine. It's known as an oxygen sensor or usually refer to as the O_2S sensor. This sensor functions when the engine's exhaust temperature rises above 600°F (315°C). There is a direct relationship between the mixture delivered by the carburetor and the amount of oxygen left in the exhaust gases. The O_2S sensor can determine whether the exhaust is too rich or too lean. It sends a varying voltage signal to the ECM/PCM.

The ECM/PCM will then signal the mixture control solenoid to deliver richer or leaner mixture for the current engine operating conditions. As the carburetor makes a change, the O_2S sensor will sense that change and signal the ECM/PCM whether or not it's too rich or too lean. The ECM/PCM will then make a correction, if necessary. This goes on continually and is what we refer to as Closed Loop operation. Closed loop conditions deliver a 14.7:1 air/fuel mixture to the engine. This makes it possible for the converter to act upon all 3 of the major pollutants in an efficient and effective manner. consider, however, what happens in the morning when it's cold and the vehicle is started. If the system where to keep the air/fuel mixture to the 14.7:1 air/fuel ratio when it's cold the chances are that the engine wouldn't run very well. When the engine is cold, it has to have a richer mixture. An automatic choke is used to give the engine a richer mixture until it is up to normal operating temperature. during this time, the O_2S sensor signals are ignored by the ECM/PCM.

A temperature sensor is located in the water jacket of the engine and connected to the electronic control module. When the engine is cold, the temperature sensor will tell the ECM/PCM to ignore the oxygen sensor signal, since the sensor is too cold to operate. The electronic control module then tells the carburetor to deliver a richer mixture based upon what has already been programmed into the ECM/PCM. The ECM/PCM will also use information from other sensors during cold start operation.

After the engine has been running for some time and has reached normal operating temperature, the temperature sensor will signal the ECM/PCM that the engine is warm and it can accept the oxygen sensor signal. If other system requirements are met, closed loop operations begins. The oxygen sensor will then influence the ECM/PCM as to what mixture it should deliver to the engine. In addition to these 2 conditions, there are 3 other conditions which affect the air/fuel mixture delivered to the engine. First is the load that is placed upon the engine. When an engine is working hard, such as pulling a heavy load up a long grade, it requires a richer air/fuel mixture. This is different from a vehicle that is operating in a cruise condition on a level highway at a constant rate of speed.

Manifold vacuum is used to determine engine load. A manifold pressure sensor is connected to the intake manifold. It detects changes in the manifold pressure which are signalled to the ECM/PCM. As changes occur, the load placed upon the engine varies. The ECM/PCM takes this varying signal into account when determining what mixture the carburetor should be delivering to the engine. The next condition in determining what air/fuel mixture should be is the amount of throttle opening. The more throttle opening at any given time, the richer the mixture required by the engine. On most applications a Throttle Position Sensor (TPS) in the carburetor sends a signal to the ECM/PCM. It tells the ECM/PCM the position of the throttle, whether it is at idle, partial, or wide-open throttle.

The last condition, which has a bearing on the mixture that the engine would require, is the speed the engine is running. Certainly when an engine is operating at 600 rpm, it doesn't need as much gasoline as it does when it is operating at 4000 rpm. Therefore, a tachometer signal from the distributor is delivered to the ECM/PCM. This tells the ECM/PCM how fast the engine is running. This signal will also be taken into consideration when the ECM/PCM decides what mixture the carburetor should be delivering to the engine. In the typical CCC system, the ECM/PCM will use various inputs to make decisions that will best control the operation of the mixture control solenoid for maximum system efficiency.

CCC SYSTEM COMPONENTS

Computer Control Module

The Electronic Control Module (ECM) and the Powertrain Control Module (PCM) are one and the same. While older vehicles have the ECM name badge and newer vehicles the PCM, they are both computer control modules. The ECM/PCM is a reliable solid state computer, protected in a metal box. It is used to monitor and control all the functions of the CCC system and is located in on the passenger side kick panel. The ECM/PCM can perform several on-car functions at the same time and has the ability to diagnose itself as well as other CCC system circuits.

The ECM/PCM performs the functions of an on and off switch. It can send a voltage signal to a circuit or connect a circuit to ground at a precise time. Programmed into the ECM/PCM's memory are voltage and time values. These valves will differ from engine to engine. As an example then, if the ECM/PCM sees a proper voltage value for the correct length of time it will perform a certain function. This could be turning the EGR system on as the engine warms up. If however, the voltage or the time interval is not correct, the ECM/PCM will also recognize this. It will not perform its function and in most cases turn the "CHECK ENGINE" or "SERVICE ENGINE SOON" light on.

The other CCC components include the oxygen sensor, an electronically controlled variable-mixture carburetor, a 3-way catalytic converter, throttle position and coolant sensors, a Barometric Pressure (BARO) sensor, a Manifold Absolute Pressure (MAP) sensor, a "CHECK ENGINE" light on the instrument cluster and an Electronic Spark Timing (EST) distributor, which on some engines is equipped with an Electronic Spark Control (ESC) or Knock Sensor (KS), which retards ignition spark under some conditions (detonation, etc.).

Other components used by the CCC system include the Air Injection Reaction (AIR) Management System, charcoal canister purge solenoid, EGR valve control, vehicle speed sensor (located in the instrument cluster), transaxle torque converter clutch solenoid (automatic transaxle models only), idle speed control and Early Fuel Evaporative (EFE) system.

The CCC system ECM/PCM, in addition to monitoring sensors and sending a control signal to the carburetor, also controls the charcoal canister purge, AIR Management System, fuel control, idle speed control, idle air control, automatic transaxle converter clutch lock-up, distributor ignition timing, EGR valve control, EFE control, air conditioner compressor clutch operation, electric fuel pump and the "CHECK ENGINE" light.

The AIR Management System is an emission control which provides additional oxygen either to the catalyst or the exhaust manifold. An AIR Management System, composed of an air switching valve and/or an air control valve, controls the air pump flow and is itself controlled by the ECM/PCM. The AIR system uses vacuum operated, ECM/PCM controlled (grounds to complete the circuit and energize the solenoids) valves to control the AIR switching.

The charcoal canister purge control is an electrically operated solenoid valve controlled by the ECM/PCM. When energized, the purge control solenoid blocks vacuum from reaching the canister purge valve. When the ECM/PCM de-energizes the purge control solenoid, vacuum is allowed to reach the canister and operate the purge valve. This releases the fuel vapors collected in the canister into the induction system.

The EGR valve control solenoid is activated by the ECM/PCM in similar fashion to the canister purge solenoid. When the engine is cold, the ECM/PCM energizes the solenoid, which blocks the vacuum signal to the EGR valve. When the engine is warm, the ECM/PCM de-energizes the solenoid and the vacuum signal is allowed to reach and activate the EGR valve.

The Torque Converter Clutch (TCC) lock-up is controlled by the ECM/PCM through an electrical solenoid in the automatic transaxle. When the vehicle speed sensor in the instrument panel signals the ECM/PCM that the vehicle has reached the correct speed, the ECM/PCM energizes the solenoid which allows the torque converter to mechanically couple the engine to the transmission. When the brake pedal is pushed or during deceleration, passing, etc., the ECM/PCM returns the transaxle to fluid drive.

The idle speed control adjusts the idle speed to load conditions and will lower the idle speed under no-load or low-load conditions to conserve gasoline.

The Early Fuel Evaporative (EFE) system is used on most engines to provide rapid heat to the engine induction system to promote smooth start-up and operation. There are 2 types of system: vacuum servo and electrically heated. They use different means to achieve the same end, which is to pre-heat the incoming air/fuel mixture. They may or may not be controlled by the ECM/PCM.

A/C Wide Open Throttle (WOT) Control: on this system the ECM/PCM controls the A/C compressor clutch to disengage the clutch during hard acceleration. On some engines, the ECM/PCM disengages the clutch during the engine start-up on a warm engine. The WOT control is not installed on all engines.

Electronic Spark Control (ESC) or Knock Sensor (KS): on this system the ECM/PCM controls spark timing on certain engines to allow the engine to have maximum spark advance without spark knock. This improves the driveability and fuel economy. This system is not used on all engines.

Shift Light Control, as equipped on some vehicles, utilizes an ECM/PCM activated light to indicate the best manual transaxle shift point for maximum fuel economy. This control is not used on all engines.

Rochester Feedback Carburetors

The E2ME and E2MC are 2-barrel single stage design. All carburetors are used with the Computer Command Control (CCC) System of fuel control. All Rochester carburetors consist of 3 major assemblies: the air horn, the float bowl and the throttle body. They have 6 basic operating systems: float, idle, main metering, power, pump and choke.

A single float chamber supplies fuel to the carburetor bores. A closed-cell rubber float, brass needle seat and a rubber tipped float valve with pull clip, are used to control fuel level in the float chamber. An electrically operated mixture control solenoid, mounted in the float bowl, is used to control the air and fuel mixture in the primary bores of the carburetor. The plunger in the solenoid is controlled (or pulsed) by electrical signals received from the Computer Control Module (ECM/PCM).

The air valve and metering rods control the air/fuel metering in the secondary bores. A pair of tapered metering rods are attached to a hanger, which operates by cam action resulting from the air valve angle and provides the additional fuel flow necessary during increased engine air flow at wide open throttle.

General Motors Rochester carburetors are identified by their model code. The carburetor model identification number is stamped vertically on the float bowl, near the secondary throttle lever. The letters in the model name describe the specific features of the carburetor. For example: The first letter "E" indicates the carburetor is Electronically controlled. The second and third digits, "2S" indicates the carburetor is a member of the Varajet family. The last digit "E" indicates an integral Electric choke. The identification code is stamped on the float bowl.

➡ **If a carburetor number has an "E" at the end (such as E2ME), that carburetor has an integral Electric Choke.**

For Carburetor repair, overhaul or adjustment, refer to procedures covered in

DIAGNOSIS & TESTING

➡ **The following explains how to activate the trouble code signal light in the instrument cluster and gives an explanation of what each code means. This is not a full CCC system troubleshooting and isolation procedure.**

Before suspecting the CCC system or any of its components as faulty, check the ignition system including distributor, timing, spark plugs and wires. Check the engine compression, air cleaner and emission control components not controlled by the ECM/PCM. Also check the intake manifold, vacuum hoses and hose connectors for leaks and the carburetor bolts for tightness.

The following symptoms could indicate a possible problem with the CCC system.

- Detonation
- Stalls or idles rough when cold
- Stalls or idles rough when hot
- Missing
- Hesitation
- Surges
- Poor gasoline mileage
- Sluggish or spongy performance
- Hard starting—cold
- Objectionable exhaust odors (rotten egg smell)
- Cuts out
- Improper idle speed

As a bulb and system check, the "CHECK ENGINE" light will come on when the ignition switch is turned to the **ON** position but the engine is not started. The "CHECK ENGINE" light will also produce the trouble code or codes by a series of flashes which translate as follows. When the diagnostic test terminal under the dash is grounded, with the ignition in the **ON** position and the engine not running, the "CHECK ENGINE" light will flash once, pause, then flash twice in rapid succession. This is a code 12, which indicates that the diagnostic system is working. After a long pause, the code 12 will repeat itself 2 more times. The cycle will then repeat itself until the engine is **STARTED** or the ignition is turned **OFF**.

When the engine is started, the "CHECK ENGINE" light will remain on for a few seconds, then turn off. If the "CHECK ENGINE" light remains on, the self-diagnostic system has detected a problem. If the test terminal is then grounded, the trouble code will flash 3 times. If more than a single problem is found, each trouble code will flash 3 times. Trouble codes will flash in numerical order (lowest code number to highest). The trouble codes series will repeat as long as the test terminal is grounded.

A trouble code indicates a problem with a given circuit. For example, trouble code 14 indicates a problem in the cooling sensor circuit. This includes the coolant sensor, its electrical harness and the Electronic Control Module (ECM). Since the self-diagnostic system cannot diagnose every possible fault in the system, the absence of a trouble code does not mean the system is trouble-free. To determine problems within the system which do not activate a trouble code, a system performance check must be made.

In the case of an intermittent fault in the system, the "CHECK ENGINE" light

will go out when the fault goes away, but the trouble code will remain in the memory of the ECM. Therefore, it a trouble code can be obtained even though the "CHECK ENGINE" light is not on, the trouble code must be evaluated. It must be determined if the fault is intermittent or if the engine must be at certain operating conditions (under load, etc.) before the "CHECK ENGINE" light will come on. Some trouble codes will not be recorded in the ECM/PCM until the engine has been operated at part throttle for about 5–18 minutes. On the CCC system, a trouble code will be stored until terminal **R** of the ECM/PCM has been disconnected from the battery for 10 seconds.

An easy way to erase the computer memory on the CCC system is to disconnect the battery terminals from the battery. If this method is used, don't forget to reset clocks and electronic preprogrammable radios. Another method is to remove the fuse marked ECM/PCM in the fuse panel. Not all models have such a fuse.

CCC System Circuit Diagnosis

To diagnose CCC system circuits, use the same general troubleshooting approach that is used for other automotive electrical systems. Finding the fault in a CCC circuit will require the testing tools described in this section, along with the manufacturer's Diagnostic Trouble Codes (DTC'S). Always use a digital voltmeter, rather than an analog model, for precise readings.

Testing CCC System Performance

A dwellmeter is used to analyze operation of the M/C solenoid circuit. The operation of that circuit is controlled by the ECM/PCM, which used information from the sensors.

A chart called the "System Performance Check" is provided in the section. This chart provides step-by-step instructions to determine if the M/C control solenoid circuit, ECM/PCM and various sensors (M/C control system) are functioning properly. If they are not, the chart indicates the steps to take in order to locate and repair the source of the trouble.

Charts for the other systems, such as AIR, EST, EGR, EFE, TCC and canister purge are also provided in the section. Another chart called the "Diagnostic Circuit Check" follows the system performance check. This chart is the starting point for any diagnosis.

The dwellmeter is used to diagnose the M/C control system. Connect a dwellmeter to the pigtail connector in the M/C solenoid wiring harness. In the old contact point style ignition system, the dwellmeter read the period of time that the points were closed (dwell) and voltage flowed to the ignition coil.

In the CCC system the dwellmeter is used to read the time that the ECM/PCM closed the M/C solenoid circuit to ground, allowing voltage to operate the M/C solenoid. Dwell, as used in CCC system performance diagnosis, is the time that the M/C solenoid circuit is closed (or energized). The dwellmeter will translate this time into degrees. The 6-cylinder (0–60 degree) scale on the dwellmeter is used for this reading. The ability of the dwellmeter to perform this kind of conversion makes it an ideal tool to check the amount of time the ECM/PCM,'s internal switch is closed, thus energizing the M/C solenoid. The only difference is that the degree scale on the meter is more like the percent of solenoid ON time rather than actual degrees of dwell.

Connecting the Dwellmeter

First set the dwellmeter on the 6-cylinder position, then connect it to the Mixture Control (M/C) solenoid dwell lead to measure the output of the ECM/PCM. Do not allow the terminal to touch ground, including any hoses. The dwellmeter must be set to the 6-cylinder position when diagnosing all engines, whether working on a 4, 6, or 8-cylinder engine.

➡ **Some older dwellmeters may not work properly on CCC. Don't use any dwellmeter which causes a change in engine operation when it is connected to the solenoid lead.**

The 6-cylinder scale on the dwellmeter provides evenly divided points, for example:

- 15 degrees = 1/4 scale
- 30 degrees = midscale
- 45 degrees = 3/4 scale

Connect the positive clip lead of the dwellmeter to the M/C solenoid pigtail connector shown in. Attach the other dwellmeter clip lead to ground. Do not allow the clip leads to contact other conductive cables or hoses which could interfere with accurate readings.

After connecting the dwellmeter to a warm, operating engine, the dwell at idle and part throttle will vary between 5–55 degrees. That is, the needle will move continuously up and down the scale. Needle movement indicates that the engine is in closed loop and that the dwell is being varied by signals from the ECM/PCM. However, if the engine is cold, has just been restarted, or the throttle is wide open, the dwell will be fixed and the needle will be steady. Those are signs that the engine is in open loop.

Diagnostic checks to find a condition without a trouble code are usually made on a warm engine (in closed loop) as indicated by a hot upper radiator hose. There are 3 ways of distinguishing open from closed loop operation.

1. A variation in dwell will occur only in closed loop.

2. Test for closed loop operation. Cause the mixture to become richer, by restricting the air flow through into the carburetor or manually closing the choke. If the dwellmeter moves up scale, that indicates closed loop.

3. If a large vacuum leak is created and the dwell drops down, that also indicates closed loop.

Reading the Dwellmeter

The mixture control (M/C) solenoid moves the metering rods up and down 10 times per second. This frequency was chosen to be slow enough to allow full stop-to-stop M/C solenoid travel, but fast enough to prevent any undesirable influence on vehicle response.

The duration of the on period determines whether the mixture is rich (mostly up) or lean (mostly down). When the metering rods are down for a longer period (54 degrees) than they are up (6 degrees), a lean mixture results.

As the solenoid on-time changes, the up time and down time of the metering rods also changes. When a lean mixture is desired, the M/C solenoid will restrict fuel flow through the metering jet 90% of the time, or, in other words, a lean mixture will be provided to the engine.

This lean command will read as 54 degrees on the dwellmeter (54 degrees is 90% of 60 degrees). This means the M/C solenoid has restricted fuel flow 90% of the time. A rich mixture is provided when the M/C solenoid restricts fuel flow only 10% of the time and allows a rich mixture to flow to the engine. A rich command will have a dwellmeter reading of 6 degrees (10% of 60 degrees); the M/C solenoid has restricted fuel flow 10% of the time.

On some engines dwellmeter readings can vary between 5–55 degrees, rather than between 6–54 degrees. The ideal mixture would be shown on the dwellmeter with the needle varying or swinging back and forth, anywhere between 10–50 degrees. Varying means the needle continually moves up and down the scale. The amount it moves does not matter, only the fact that it does move. The dwell is being varied by the signal sent to the ECM by the oxygen sensor in the exhaust manifold.

Under certain operating conditions such as Wide Open Throttle (WOT), or a cold engine, the dwell will remain fixed and the needle will be steady. Remember, a low dwellmeter reading (5–10°) announces the ECM signal to the M/C control solenoid is a rich command, while 55° would indicate a lean command.

Open and Closed Loop Operation

Two terms are often used when referring to CCC system operation. They are closed loop and open loop.

Basically, closed loop indicates that the ECM/PCM is using information from the exhaust oxygen sensor to influence operation of the mixture control (M/C) solenoid. the ECM/PCM still considers other information, such as engine temperature, rpm, barometric and manifold pressure and throttle position, along with the exhaust oxygen sensor information.

During open loop, all information except the exhaust oxygen sensor input is considered by the ECM/PCM to control the M/C solenoid. The manufacturer's diagnostic charts are based on a warmed up engine (closed loop operation), and will generally say to run the engine at part throttle for 3 minutes or until there is a varying dwellmeter indication before beginning diagnosis.

It is important to note that the exhaust oxygen sensor may cool below its operational temperature during prolonged idling. This will cause an open loop condition and make diagnostic chart information unusable during diagnosis. Engine rpm must be increased to warm the exhaust oxygen sensor and re-establish a closed loop condition.

SYSTEM DIAGNOSTIC CIRCUIT CHECK

Begin the Diagnostic Circuit Check by making sure that the diagnostic system itself is working. Turn the ignition to **ON** with the engine stopped. If the

"CHECK ENGINE" or "SERVICE ENGINE SOON" light comes on, ground the diagnostic code terminal (test lead) under the dash. If the "CHECK ENGINE" or "SERVICE ENGINE SOON" light flashes Code 12, the self-diagnostic system is working and can detect a faulty circuit. If there is no Code 12, see the appropriate chart in this section. If any additional codes flash, record them for later use.

If a Code 51 flashes, use chart 51 to diagnose that condition before proceeding with the Diagnostic Circuit Check. A Code 51 means that the "CHECK ENGINE" or "SERVICE ENGINE SOON" light flashes 5 times, pauses, then flashes once. After a longer pause, code 51 will flash again twice in this same way. To find out what diagnostic step to follow, look up the chart for Code 51 in this section. If there is not a Code 51, follow the "No Code 51" branch of the chart.

Clear the ECM memory by disconnecting the voltage lead either at the fuse panel or the ECM letter connector for 10 seconds. This clears any codes remaining from previous repairs, or codes for troubles not present at this time. Remember, even though a code is stored, if the trouble is not present the diagnostic charts cannot be used. The charts are designed only to locate present faults.

➡ **When erasing the computer memory on the CCC system the ignition switch must be turned OFF before removing any fuses**, wire connectors or battery cables. If the battery cable is to disconnect from the battery, don't forget to reset clocks and electronic preprogrammable radios.

Next, remove the TEST terminal ground, set the parking brake and put the transaxle in **P**. Run the warm engine for several minutes, making sure it is run at the specified curb idle. Then, if the "CHECK ENGINE" or "SERVICE ENGINE SOON" light comes on while the engine is idling, ground the TEST lead again and observe (count) the flashing trouble code.

If the "CHECK ENGINE" or "SERVICE ENGINE SOON" light does not come on, check the codes which were recorded earlier. If there were no additional codes, road test the vehicle for the problem being diagnosed to make sure it still exists.

The purpose of the Diagnostic Circuit check is to make sure the "CHECK ENGINE" or "SERVICE SOON SOON" light works, that the ECM is operating and can recognize a fault and to determine if any trouble codes are stored in the ECM memory.

If trouble codes are stored, it also checks to see if they indicate an intermittent problem. This is the starting point of any diagnosis. If there are no codes stored, move on to the System Performance Check.

The codes obtained from the "CHECK ENGINE" or "SERVICE ENGINE SOON" light display method indicate which diagnostic charts provide in the section are to be used. For example, code 23 can be diagnosed by following the step-by-step procedures on chart 23.

➡ **If more than a single code is stored in the ECM/PCM, the lowest code number must be diagnosed first. then proceed to the next highest code. The only exception is when a 50 series flashes. 50 series code take precedence over all other trouble codes and must be dealt with first, since they point to a fault in the PROM unit or the ECM/PCM.**

SERVICE

Before suspecting the CCC system, or any of its components as being faulty, check the ignition system (distributor, timing, spark plugs and wires). Check the engine compression, the air cleaner and any of the emission control components that are not controlled by the ECM/PCM. Also check the intake manifold, the vacuum hoses and hose connectors for any leaks. Check the carburetor mounting bolts for tightness.

The following symptoms could indicate a possible problem area with the CCC system:

- Detonation
- Stalling or rough idling when the engine is cold
- Stalling or rough idling when the engine is hot
- Missing
- Hesitation
- Surging
- Poor gasoline mileage
- Sluggish or spongy performance
- Hard starting when engine is cold
- Hard starting when the engine is hot
- Objectionable exhaust odors

- Engine cuts out
- Improper idle speed

As a bulb and system check, the Check Engine light will come on when the ignition switch is turned to the ON position but the engine is not started.

The Check Engine light will also produce the trouble code/codes by a series of flashes which translate as follows: When the diagnostic test terminal under the instrument panel is grounded, with the ignition in the ON position and the engine not running, the Check Engine light will flash once, pause, and then flash twice in rapid succession. This is a Code 12, which indicates that the diagnostic system is working. After a long pause, the Code 12 will repeat itself two more times. This whole cycle will then repeat itself until the engine is started or the ignition switch is turned OFF.

When the engine is started, the Check Engine light will remain on for a few seconds and then turn off. If the Check Engine light remains on, the self-diagnostic system has detected a problem. If the test terminal is then grounded, the trouble code will flash (3) three times. If more than one problem is found to be in existence, each trouble code will flash (3) three times and then change to the next one. Trouble codes will flash in numerical order (lowest code number to highest). The trouble code series will repeat themselves for as long as the test terminal remains grounded.

A trouble code indicates a problem with a given circuit. For example, trouble code 14 indicates a problem in the coolant sensor circuit. This includes the coolant sensor, its electrical harness and the Computer Control Module (ECM/PCM).

Since the self-diagnostic system cannot diagnose every possible fault in the system, the absence of a trouble code does not necessarily mean that the system is trouble-free. To determine whether or not a problem with the system exists that does not activate a trouble code, a system performance check must be made. You can follow the symptom charts for the fuel system your car has. If the chart doesn't help you find the problem or instructs you to more involved testing using special tool you may wish to seek a qualified service technician. Guessing which component to test or testing a component incorrectly can be very expensive.

In the case of an intermittent fault in the system, the Check Engine light will go out when the fault goes away, but the trouble code will remain in the memory of the ECM/PCM. Therefore, if a trouble code can be obtained even though the Check Engine light is not on, it must still be evaluated. It must be determined if the fault is intermittent or if the engine must be operating under certain conditions (acceleration, deceleration, etc.) before the Check Engine light will come on. In some cases, certain trouble codes will not be recorded in the ECM/PCM until the engine has been operated at part throttle for at least 5 to 18 minutes.

On the CCC system, a trouble code will be stored until the terminal **R** at the ECM/PCM has been disconnected from the battery for at least 10 seconds, or the battery cable has be removed.

ACTIVATING THE TROUBLE CODE

On the CCC system, locate the test terminal under the instrument panel. Use a jumper wire and ground only the lead.

➡**Ground the test terminal according to the instructions given previously in the Basic Troubleshooting section.**

CARBURETOR COMPONENT TESTING

Electric Choke

Check the choke unloader and idle setting adjustments. The choke linkage and fast idle cam must operate freely. Bent, dirty or otherwise damaged linkage must be cleaned, repaired or replaced as necessary. Do not lubricate linkage since lubricant will collect dust and cause sticking.

1. Allow the choke to cool so that when the throttle is opened slightly, the choke blade fully closes.
2. Start the engine and determine the time for the choke blade to reach the full open position.
3. If the choke blade fails to open fully within 3½ minutes, proceed with Step 4 and 5 below.
4. Check the voltage at the choke heater connection (engine must be running):

a. If the voltage is approximately 12–15 volts, replace the electric choke unit.

b. If the voltage is low or zero, check all wires and connections. If any connections in the oil pressure switch circuitry are faulty, or if pressure switch is failed open, the oil warning light will be on with the engine running. Repair wires or connectors as required.

5. If Steps 4a and 4b do not correct the problem, replace oil pressure switch. No gasket is used between the choke cover and the choke housing due to grounding requirements.

Hot Air Choke

1. With the parking brake applied and the drive wheels blocked, place the transaxle in **P** or **N**, start the engine and allow it to warm up. Visually check to be sure the choke valve fully opens.
2. If the choke fails to open fully, momentarily touch the choke housing and the hot air inlet pipe or hose, to determine if sufficient heat is reaching the choke stat.

✳✳ CAUTION

The choke housing and hot air inlet pipe or hose will be HOT to the touch; use caution to prevent burns.

3. If the choke housing and or heat inlet are cool to the touch, check for a loss of vacuum to the housing, restricted heat inlet pipe in the choke housing or choke heat pipe, or restricted passages in the manifold choke heat stove.
4. Replace or correct as necessary.

Float Level

This is an external check procedure.
1. Remove the air horn vent stack.
2. With engine idling and choke wide open, insert gauge J–9789–135, or equivalent, in vent slot or vent hole. Allow the gauge to float freely.
3. Observe the mark on the gauge that lines up with the top of the casting.
4. Setting should be within ¹⁄₁₆ in. (2mm) of the specified float level setting.
5. If not within specified range, check fuel pressure.
6. If fuel pressure is correct, remove air horn and adjust float.

Mixture Control Solenoid

This is a mixture control solenoid travel test. Before checking the mixture control solenoid travel, it may be necessary to modify the float gauge J–9789–130 or equivalent (used to externally check the float level).

This should be done by filing or grinding the sufficient material off the gauge to allow for insertion down the vertical D-shaped hole in the air horn casting (located next to the idle air bleed valve cover).

Check that the gauge freely enters the D-shaped vent hole and does not bind. The gauge will also be used to determine the total mixture control solenoid travel.

With the engine off and the air cleaner removed, measure the control solenoid travel as follows:
1. Remove the air horn vent stack.
2. Insert a modified float gauge J–9789–130 or equivalent down the D-shaped vent hole. Press down on the gauge and release it.
3. Observe that the gauge moves freely and does not bind. With the gauge released (solenoid in the up position), be sure to read it at eye level and record the mark on the gauge that lines up with the top of the air horn casting (upper edge).
4. Lightly press down on the gauge until bottomed (solenoid in the down position). Record the mark on the gauge that lines up with the top of the air horn casting.
5. Subtract the gauge up dimension from gauge dimension. Record the difference. This difference is total solenoid travel.
6. If total solenoid travel is not ¹⁄₁₆–⅛ in. (2–3mm), perform the mixture control solenoid adjustments. If the difference is ¹⁄₁₆–⅛ in. (2–3mm), proceed to the idle air bleed valve adjustment.

➡**If adjustment is required, it will be necessary to remove the air horn and drive out the mixture control solenoid screw plug from the under side of the air horn.**

Idle Load Compensator (ILC)

1. Inspect the condition of the tube cap covering the access to plunger travel adjustment screw. If missing or damaged, the diaphragm chamber will lose vacuum.
2. Hold throttle lever half open, to allow ILC to extend fully.
3. Apply finger pressure to the ILC plunger.
4. Apply 20 in. Hg (68 kPa) of vacuum to the ILC, plunger should begin to retract. If not replace the ILC.
5. Observe vacuum gauge, vacuum should hold for at least 20 seconds, if not replace the ILC.
6. Release vacuum from the ILC. The plunger should extend, if not replace the ILC.

Pulse Air Injection (PULSAIR)

All engines use the Pulsair air injection system, which uses exhaust system air pulses to siphon fresh air into the exhaust manifold. The injected air supports continued combustion of the hot exhaust gases in the exhaust manifold, reducing exhaust emissions. A secondary purpose of the Pulsair system is to introduce more oxygen into the exhaust system upstream of the catalytic converter, to supply the converter with the oxygen required for the oxidation reaction.

Air is drawn into the Pulsair valve through a hose connected to the air cleaner. The air passes through a check valve (there is one check valve for each cylinder, all check valves are installed in the Pulsair valve), then through a manifold pipe to the exhaust manifold. All manifold pipes are the same length, to prevent uneven pulsation. The check valves open during pulses of negative exhaust back pressure, admitting air into the manifold pipe and the exhaust manifold. During pulses of positive exhaust back pressure, the check valves close, preventing backfiring into the Pulsair valve and air cleaner.

The Pulsair check valves, hoses and pipes should be checked occasionally for leaks, cracks, or breaks.

REMOVAL & INSTALLATION

1. Remove the air cleaner case. Disconnect the rubber hose(s) from the Pulsair valve(s).
2. Disconnect the support bracket, if present. Some V6 engines have a Pulsair solenoid and bracket, which must be removed.
3. Unscrew the attaching nuts and remove the Pulsair tubes from the exhaust manifold(s).
   To install:
4. First apply a light coat of clean oil to the ends of the Pulsair tubes.
5. Install the tubes to the exhaust manifold(s), tightening the nuts to 10–13 ft. lbs. (14–18 Nm). Connect the support bracket and, if applicable, the solenoid and bracket. Connect the rubber hose(s) and install the air cleaner.

Deceleration Valve

▶ See Figure 11

The purpose of the deceleration valve is to prevent backfiring in the exhaust system during deceleration. The normal position of the valve is closed. When

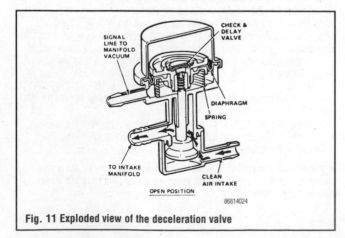

SIGNAL LINE TO MANIFOLD VACUUM
CHECK & DELAY VALVE
DIAPHRAGM
SPRING
TO INTAKE MANIFOLD
CLEAN AIR INTAKE
OPEN POSITION
86814024

Fig. 11 Exploded view of the deceleration valve

deceleration causes a sudden vacuum increase in the vacuum signal lines, the pressure differential on the diaphragm will overcome the closing force of the spring, opening the valve and bleeding air into the intake manifold.

Air trapped in the chamber above the vacuum diaphragm will bleed at a calibrated rate through the delay valve portion of the integral check and delay valve, reducing the vacuum acting on the diaphragm. When the vacuum load on the diaphragm and the spring load equalize, the valve assembly will close, shutting off the air flow into the intake manifold.

The check valve portion of the check and delay valve provides quick balancing of chamber pressure when a sudden decrease in vacuum is caused by acceleration rather than deceleration.

Mixture Control Solenoid (M/C)

The fuel flow through the carburetor idle main metering circuits is controlled by a mixture control (M/C) solenoid located in the carburetor. The M/C solenoid changes the air/fuel mixture to the engine by controlling the fuel flow through the carburetor. The ECM/PCM controls the solenoid by providing a ground. When the solenoid is energized, the fuel flow through the carburetor is reduced, providing a leaner mixture. When the ECM/PCM removes the ground, the solenoid is de-energized, increasing the fuel flow and providing a richer mixture. The M/C solenoid is energized and de-energized at a rate of 10 times per second.

Throttle Position Sensor (TPS)

▶ See Figure 12

The throttle position sensor is mounted in the carburetor body and is used to supply throttle position information to the ECM/PCM. The ECM/PCM memory stores an average of operating conditions with the ideal air/fuel ratios for each of those conditions. When the ECM/PCM receives a signal that indicates throttle position change, it immediately shifts to the last remembered set of operating conditions that resulted in an ideal air/fuel ratio control. The memory is continually being updated during normal operations.

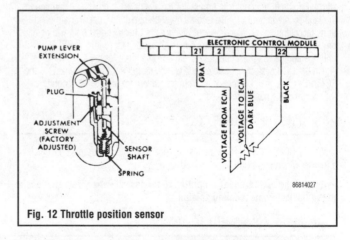

PUMP LEVER EXTENSION
PLUG
ADJUSTMENT SCREW (FACTORY ADJUSTED)
SENSOR SHAFT
SPRING
ELECTRONIC CONTROL MODULE
21 2 22
GRAY
VOLTAGE FROM ECM
VOLTAGE TO ECM
DARK BLUE
BLACK
86814027

Fig. 12 Throttle position sensor

Idle Speed Control (ISC)

▶ See Figure 13

The idle speed control does just what its name implies-it controls the idle. The ISC is used to maintain low engine speeds while at the same time preventing stalling due to engine load changes. The system consists of a motor assembly mounted on the carburetor which moves the throttle lever so as to open or close the throttle blades.

The whole operation is controlled by the ECM/PCM. The ECM/PCM monitors engine load to determine the proper idle speed. To prevent stalling, it monitors the air conditioning compressor switch, the transaxle, the park/neutral switch and the ISC throttle switch. The ECM/PCM processes all this information and then uses it to control the ISC motor which in turn will vary the idle speed as necessary.

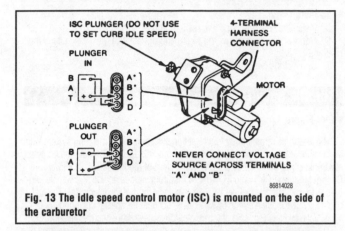

Fig. 13 The idle speed control motor (ISC) is mounted on the side of the carburetor

Electronic Spark Timing (EST)

All models use EST. The EST distributor, as described in an earlier section, contains no vacuum or centrifugal advance mechanism and uses a seven terminal HEI module. It has four wires going to a four terminal connector in addition to the connectors normally found on HEI distributors. A reference pulse, indicating engine rpm is sent to the ECM/PCM. The ECM/PCM determines the proper spark advance for the engine operating conditions and then sends an EST pulse back to the distributor.

Under most normal operating conditions, the ECM/PCM will control the spark advance. However, under certain operating conditions such as cranking or when setting base timing, the distributor is capable of operating without ECM/PCM control. This condition is called BYPASS and is determined by the BYPASS lead which runs from the ECM/PCM to the distributor. When the BYPASS lead is at the proper voltage (5), the ECM/PCM will control the spark. If the lead is grounded or open circuited, the HEI module itself will control the spark. Disconnecting the 4-terminal EST connector will also cause the engine to operate in the BYPASS mode.

Torque Converter Clutch (TCC)

All models with an automatic transaxle use a TCC. The ECM/PCM controls the converter by means of a solenoid mounted in the transaxle. When the vehicle speed reaches a certain level, the ECM energizes the solenoid and allows the torque converter to mechanically couple the transaxle to the engine. When the operating conditions indicate that the transaxle should operate as a normal fluid coupled transaxle, the ECM/PCM will de-energize the solenoid. Depressing the brake will also return the transaxle to normal automatic operation.

Catalytic Converter

▶ See Figure 14

The catalytic converter is a muffler-like container built into the exhaust system to aid in the reduction of exhaust emissions. The catalyst element consists of individual pellets or a honeycomb monolithic substrate coated with a noble metal such as platinum, palladium, rhodium or a combination. When the exhaust gases come into contact with the catalyst, a chemical reaction occurs which will reduce the pollutants into harmless substances including water and carbon dioxide.

There are essentially two types of catalytic converters: an oxidizing type and a three-way type. The oxidizing type requires the addition of oxygen to spur the catalyst into reducing the engine's HC and CO emissions into H_2O and CO_2. The oxidizing catalytic converter, while effectively reducing HC and CO emissions, does little, if anything in the way of reducing NOx emissions. Thus, the three-way catalytic converter.

The three-way converter, unlike the oxidizing type, is capable of reducing HC, CO and NOx emissions, all at the same time. In theory, it seems impossible to reduce all three pollutants in one system since the reduction of HC and CO requires the addition of oxygen, while the reduction of NOx calls for the removal of oxygen. In actuality, the three-way system really can reduce all three pollutants, but only if the amount of oxygen in the exhaust system is precisely con-

Fig. 14 The catalytic converter is a muffler-like device built into the exhaust system to aid in the reduction of exhaust emissions—1985 Celebrity wagon shown

trolled. Due to this precise oxygen control requirement, the three-way converter system is used only in conjunction with an oxygen sensor system.

There are no service procedures required for the catalytic converter, although the converter body should be inspected occasionally for damage.

PRECAUTIONS

- Use only unleaded fuel.
- Avoid prolonged idling; the engine should run no longer than 20 minutes at curb idle and no longer than 10 minutes at fast idle.
- Do not disconnect any of the spark plug leads while the engine is running.
- Make engine compression checks as quickly as possible.

TESTING

At the present time there is no known way to reliably test catalytic converter operation in the field. The only reliable test is a 12 hour and 40 minute soak test which must be done in a laboratory.

An infrared HC/CO tester is not sensitive enough to measure the higher tailpipe emissions from a failing converter. Thus, a bad converter may allow enough emissions to escape so that the car is no longer in compliance with Federal or state standards, but will still not cause the needle on a tester to move off zero.

The chemical reactions which occur inside a catalytic converter generate a great deal of heat. Most converter problems can be traced to fuel or ignition system problems which cause unusually high emissions. As a result of the increased intensity of the chemical reactions, the converter literally burns itself up.

A completely failed converter might cause a tester to show a slight reading. As a result, it is occasionally possible to detect one of these.

As long as you avoid severe overheating and the use of leaded fuels it is reasonably safe to assume that the converter is working properly. If you are in doubt, take the car to a diagnostic center that has a tester.

Early Fuel Evaporation (EFE)

All models are equipped with this system to reduce engine warm-up time, improve driveability and reduce emissions. The system is electric and uses a ceramic heater grid located underneath the primary bore of the carburetor as part of the carburetor insulator/gasket. When the ignition switch is turned on and the engine coolant temperature is low, voltage is applied to the EFE relay by the ECM/PCM. The EFE relay in turn energizes the heater grid. When the coolant temperature increases, the ECM/PCM de-energizes the relay which will then shut off the EFE heater.

REMOVAL & INSTALLATION

EFE Grid

▶ See Figure 15

1. Remove the air cleaner and disconnect the negative battery cable.
2. Tag and disconnect all electrical, vacuum connections from the carburetor.
3. Unattach the fuel lines and cap them to keep from fuel spilling out, make sure to have a rag handy for any messes.
4. Disconnect the EFE heater electrical lead.
5. Remove the carburetor.
6. Lift off the EFE heater grid.

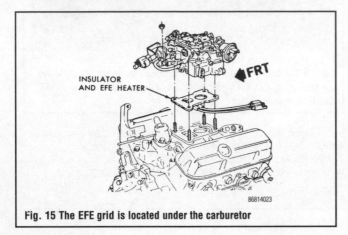

Fig. 15 The EFE grid is located under the carburetor

To install:

7. Clean the surface of the manifold where the grid is to lie, along with the bottom of the carburetor.
8. Install the new EFE grid to the intake manifold.
9. Mount the carburetor, then install all the tagged vacuum lines and electrical leads to the carburetor.
10. Connect the fuel lines.
11. Double check all the lines and hoses are properly connected, then install the air cleaner assembly.
12. Connect the negative battery cable.
13. Adjust the carburetor if needed.

EFE Heater Relay

▶ See Figure 16

1. Disconnect the negative battery cable.
2. Remove the retaining bracket.
3. Tag and disconnect all electrical connections.
4. Unscrew the retaining bolts and remove the relay.

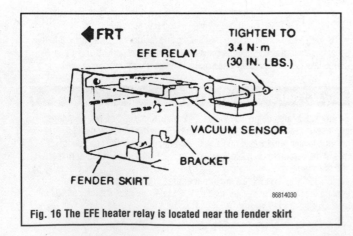

Fig. 16 The EFE heater relay is located near the fender skirt

To install:

5. Install the new relay with the retaining bolts, tighten the bolts.
6. Connect the electrical wiring to the appropriate locations, then attach the retaining bracket.
7. Connect the negative battery cable.

Throttle Body Fuel Injection (TBI)

▶ See Figure 17

The electronic throttle body fuel injection system is a fuel metering system with the amount of fuel delivered by the throttle body injector(s) (TBI) determined by an electronic signal supplied by the Electronic Control Module (ECM) or Powertrain Control Module (PCM). The ECM/PCM monitors various engine and vehicle conditions to calculate the fuel delivery time (pulse width) of the injector(s). The fuel pulse may be modified by the ECM/PCM to account for special operating conditions, such as cranking, cold starting, altitude, acceleration, and deceleration.

The Throttle Body Injection (TBI) system provides a means of fuel distribution for controlling exhaust emissions within legislated limits. The TBI system, by precisely controlling the air/fuel mixture under all operating conditions, provides as near as possible complete combustion.

This is accomplished by using a Computer Control Module (ECM/PCM), a small on-board microcomputer that receives electrical inputs from various sensors about engine operating conditions. An oxygen sensor in the main exhaust stream functions to provide feedback information to the ECM/PCM as to the oxygen content, lean or rich, in the exhaust. The ECM/PCM uses this information from the oxygen sensor, and other sensors, to modify fuel delivery to achieve, as near as possible, an ideal air/fuel ratio of 14.7:1. This air/fuel ratio allows the 3-way catalytic converter to be more efficient in the conversion process of reducing exhaust emissions while at the same time providing acceptable levels of driveability and fuel economy.

COMPUTER CONTROL MODULE

The ECM/PCM program electronically signals the fuel injector in the TBI assembly to provide the correct quantity of fuel for a wide range of operating conditions. Several sensors are used to determine existing operating conditions and the ECM/PCM then signals the injector to provide the precise amount of fuel required.

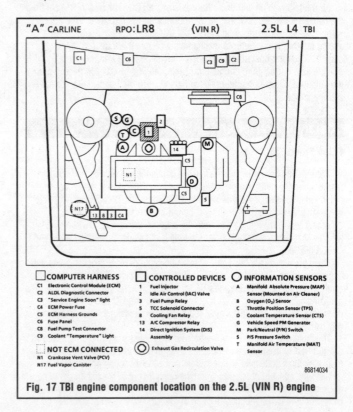

Fig. 17 TBI engine component location on the 2.5L (VIN R) engine

The ECM/PCM used on TBI vehicles has a learning capability. If the battery is disconnected to clear diagnostic codes, or for repair, the learning process has to begin all over again. A change may be noted in vehicle performance. To teach the vehicle, make sure the vehicle is at operating temperature and drive at part throttle, under moderate acceleration and idle conditions, until performance returns.

The TBI assembly is centrally located on the intake manifold where air and fuel are distributed through a single bore in the throttle body, similar to a carbureted engine. Air for combustion is controlled by a single throttle valve which is connected to the accelerator pedal linkage by a throttle shaft and lever assembly. A special plate is located directly beneath the throttle valve to aid in mixture distribution.

Fuel for combustion is supplied by 1 or 2 fuel injector(s), mounted on the TBI assembly, whose metering tip is located directly above the throttle valve. The injector is pulsed or timed open or closed by an electronic output signal received from the ECM/PCM. The ECM/PCM receives inputs concerning engine operating conditions from the various sensors (coolant temperature sensor, oxygen sensor, etc.). The ECM/PCM, using this information, performs high speed calculations of engine fuel requirements and pulses or times the injector, open or closed, thereby controlling fuel and air mixtures to achieve, as near as possible, ideal air/fuel mixture ratios.

When the ignition key is turned **ON**, the ECM/PCM will initialize (start program running) and energize the fuel pump relay. The fuel pump pressurizes the system to approximately 10 psi. If the ECM/PCM does not receive a distributor reference pulse (telling the ECM/PCM the engine is turning) within 2 seconds, the ECM/PCM will then de-energize the fuel pump relay, turning off the fuel pump. If a distributor reference pulse is later received, the ECM/PCM will turn the fuel pump back on.

The ECM/PCM controls the exhaust emissions by modifying fuel delivery to achieve, as near as possible, and air/fuel ratio of 14.7:1. The injector on-time is determined by various inputs to the ECM/PCM. By increasing the injector pulse, more fuel is delivered, enriching the air/fuel ratio. Decreasing the injector pulse, leans the air/fuel ratio. Pulses are sent to the injector in 2 different modes: synchronized and non-synchronized.

Synchronized Mode

In synchronized mode operation, the injector is pulsed once for each distributor reference pulse. In dual injector throttle body systems, the injectors are pulse alternately.

Non-synchronized Mode

In non-synchronized mode operation, the injector is pulsed once every 12.5 milliseconds or 6.25 milliseconds depending on calibration. This pulse time is totally independent of distributor reference pulses. Non-synchronized mode results only under the following conditions:
• The fuel pulse width is too small to be delivered accurately by the injector (approximately 1.5 milliseconds)
• During the delivery of prime pulses (prime pulses charge the intake manifold with fuel during or just prior to engine starting)
• During acceleration enrichment
• During deceleration leanout

The basic TBI unit is made up of 2 major casting assemblies: (1) a throttle body with a valve to control airflow and (2) a fuel body assembly with an integral pressure regulator and fuel injector to supply the required fuel. An electronically operated device to control the idle speed and a device to provide information regarding throttle valve position are included as part of the TBI unit.

The fuel injector(s) is a solenoid-operated device controlled by the ECM/PCM. The incoming fuel is directed to the lower end of the injector assembly which has a fine screen filter surrounding the injector inlet. The ECM/PCM actuates the solenoid, which lifts a normally closed ball valve off a seat. The fuel under pressure is injected in a conical spray pattern at the walls of the throttle body bore above the throttle valve. The excess fuel passes through a pressure regulator before being returned to the vehicle's fuel tank.

The pressure regulator is a diaphragm-operated relief valve with injector pressure on one side and air cleaner pressure on the other. The function of the regulator is to maintain a constant pressure drop across the injector throughout the operating load and speed range of the engine.

The throttle body portion of the TBI may contain ports located at, above, or below the throttle valve. These ports generate the vacuum signals for the EGR valve, MAP sensor, and the canister purge system.

The Throttle Position Sensor (TPS) is a variable resistor used to convert the degree of throttle plate opening to an electrical signal to the ECM/PCM. The ECM/PCM uses this signal as a reference point of throttle valve position. In addition, an Idle Air Control (IAC) assembly, mounted in the throttle body is used to control idle speeds. A cone-shaped valve in the IAC assembly is located in an air passage in the throttle body that leads from the point beneath the air cleaner to below the throttle valve. The ECM/PCM monitors idle speeds and, depending on engine load, moves the IAC cone in the air passage to increase or decrease air bypassing the throttle valve to the intake manifold for control of idle speeds.

Cranking Mode

During engine crank, for each distributor reference pulse the ECM/PCM will deliver an injector pulse (synchronized). The crank air/fuel ratio will be used if the throttle position is less than 80% open. Crank air fuel is determined by the ECM/PCM and ranges from 1.5:1 at 33°F (36°C) to 14.7:1 at 201°F (94°C).

The lower the coolant temperature, the longer the pulse width (injector on-time) or richer the air/fuel ratio. The higher the coolant temperature, the less pulse width (injector on-time) or the leaner the air/fuel ratio.

Clear Flood Mode

If for some reason the engine should become flooded, provisions have been made to clear this condition. To clear the flood, the driver must depress the accelerator pedal enough to open to wide-open throttle position. The ECM/PCM then issues injector pulses at a rate that would be equal to an air/fuel ratio of 20:1. The ECM/PCM maintains this injector rate as long as the throttle remains wide open and the engine rpm is below 600. If the throttle position becomes less than 80%, the ECM/PCM then would immediately start issuing crank pulses to the injector calculated by the ECM/PCM based on the coolant temperature.

Run Mode

There are 2 different run modes. When the engine rpm is above 400, the system goes into open loop operation. In open loop operation, the ECM/PCM will ignore the signal from the oxygen (O_2) sensor and calculate the injector on-time based upon inputs from the coolant and manifold absolute pressure sensors.

During open loop operation, the ECM/PCM analyzes the following items to determine when the system is ready to go to the closed loop mode:
1. The oxygen sensor varying voltage output. (This is dependent on temperature.)
2. The coolant sensor must be above the specified temperature.
3. A specific amount of time must elapse after starting the engine. These values are stored in the PROM.

When these conditions have been met, the system goes into closed loop operation In closed loop operation, the ECM/PCM will modify the pulse width (injector on-time) based upon the signal from the oxygen sensor. The ECM/PCM will decrease the on-time if the air/fuel ratio is too rich, and will increase the on-time if the air/fuel ratio is too lean.

The pulse width, thus the amount of enrichment, is determined by manifold pressure change, throttle angle change, and coolant temperature. The higher the manifold pressure and the wider the throttle opening, the wider the pulse width. The acceleration enrichment pulses are delivered non-synchronized. Any reduction in throttle angle will cancel the enrichment pulses. This way, quick movements of the accelerator will not over-enrich the mixture.

Acceleration Enrichment Mode

When the engine is required to accelerate, the opening of the throttle valve(s) causes a rapid increase in Manifold Absolute Pressure (MAP). This rapid increase in the manifold pressure causes fuel to condense on the manifold walls. The ECM/PCM senses this increase in throttle angle and MAP, then supplies additional fuel for a short period of time. This prevents the engine from stumbling due to too lean a mixture.

Deceleration Leanout Mode

Upon deceleration, a leaner fuel mixture is required to reduce emission of hydrocarbons (HC) and carbon monoxide (CO). To adjust the injection on-time, the ECM/PCM uses the decrease in manifold pressure and the decrease in throttle position to calculate a decrease in pulse width. To maintain an idle fuel ratio of 14.7:1, fuel output is momentarily reduced. This is done because of the fuel remaining in the intake manifold during deceleration.

Deceleration Fuel Cut-Off Mode

The purpose of deceleration fuel cut-off is to remove fuel from the engine during extreme deceleration conditions. Deceleration fuel cut-off is based on values of manifold pressure, throttle position, and engine rpm stored in the calibration PROM. Deceleration fuel cut-off overrides the deceleration enleanment mode.

Battery Voltage Correction Mode

The purpose of battery voltage correction is to compensate for variations in battery voltage to fuel pump and injector response. The ECM/PCM modifies the pulse width by a correction factor in the PROM. When battery voltage decreases, pulse width increases.

Battery voltage correction takes place in all operating modes. When battery voltage is low, the spark delivered by the distributor may be low. To correct this low battery voltage problem, the ECM/PCM can do any or all of the following:
- Increase injector pulse width (increase fuel)
- Increase idle rpm
- Increase ignition dwell time

Fuel Cut-Off Mode

When the ignition is **OFF**, the ECM/PCM will not energize the injector. Fuel will also be cut off if the ECM/PCM does not receive a reference pulse from the distributor. To prevent dieseling, fuel delivery is completely stopped as soon as the engine is stopped. The ECM/PCM will not allow any fuel supply until it receives distributor reference pulses which prevents flooding.

Backup Mode

When in this mode, the ECM/PCM is operating on the fuel backup logic calibrated by the Cal-Pak. The Cal-Pak is used to control the fuel delivery if the ECM/PCM fails. This mode verifies that the backup feature is working properly. The parameters that can be read on a scan tool in this mode are not much use for service.

Highway Mode

When driven at highway speeds the system may enter highway or semi-closed loop mode. This improves fuel economy by leaning out fuel mixture slightly. The ECM/PCM must see correct engine temperature, ignition timing, canister activity and a constant vehicle speed before if will enter this mode. The system will switch back to closed loop periodically to check all system functions.

A scan tool determines highway mode by looking at the integrator/block learn values and oxygen sensor voltage. Integrator and block learn will show very little change and the oxygen sensor voltage is be less than 100 millivolts.

DLC/ALCL/ALDL Connector

The Assembly Line Communication Link (ALCL) or Assembly Line Diagnostic Link (ALDL) is now called the Data Link Connector (DLC). The diagnostic connector is usually located in the passenger compartment. It has terminals which are used in the assembly plant to check that the engine is operating properly before it leaves the plant. This connector is a very useful tool in diagnosing fuel injected engines. Important information from the ECM/PCM is available at this terminal and can be read with one of the many popular scanner tools.

FUEL INJECTION SUBSYSTEMS

Electronic Fuel Injection (EFI) is the name given to the entire fuel injection system. Various subsystems are combined to form the overall system. These subsystems are:
- Fuel supply system
- Throttle Body Injector (TBI) assembly
- Idle Air Control (IAC)
- Computer Control Module (ECM/PCM)
- Data sensors
- Electronic Spark Timing (EST)
- Emission controls

Fuel Supply System

Fuel, supplied by an electric fuel pump mounted in the fuel tank, passes through an in-line fuel filter to the TBI assembly. To control fuel pump operation, a fuel pump relay is used.

When the ignition switch is turned to the **ON** position, the fuel pump relay activates the electric fuel pump for 1.5–2.0 seconds to prime the injector. If the ECM/PCM does not receive reference pulses from the distributor after this time, the ECM/PCM signals the relay to turn the fuel pump off. The relay will once again activate the fuel pump when the ECM/PCM receives distributor reference pulses.

The oil pressure sender is the backup for the fuel pump relay. The sender has 2 circuits, 1 for the instrument cluster light or gauge, the other to activate the fuel pump if the relay fails. If the fuse relay has failed, the sender activates the fuel pump when oil pressure reaches 4 psi. Thus a failed fuel pump relay would cause a longer crank, especially in cold weather. If the fuel pump fails, a no start condition exists.

Throttle Body Injector (TBI) Assembly

The basic TBI model 700 is used on 4-cylinder engines, is made up of 2 major casting assemblies: (1) a throttle body with a valve to control airflow and (2) a fuel body assembly with an integral pressure regulator and fuel injector to supply the required fuel. A device to control idle speed (IAC) and a device to provide information about throttle valve position (TPS) are included as part of the TBI unit.

The model 220 is used on V6 and V8 engines, consists of 3 major castings. (1) fuel meter cover with pressure regulator, (2) Fuel meter body with injectors and (3) throttle body with IAC valve and TPS sensor.

The throttle body portion of the TBI unit may contain ports located at, above, or below the throttle valve. These ports generate the vacuum signals for the EGR valve, MAP sensor, and the canister purge system.

The fuel injector is a solenoid-operated device controlled by the ECM/PCM. The incoming fuel is directed to the lower end of the injector assembly which has a fine screen filter surrounding the injector inlet. The ECM/PCM turns on the solenoid, which lifts a normally closed ball valve off a seat. The fuel, under pressure, is injected in a conical spray pattern at the walls of the throttle body bore above the throttle valve. The excess fuel passes through a pressure regulator before being returned to the vehicle fuel tank.

The pressure regulator is a diaphragm-operated relief valve with the injector pressure on one side, and the air cleaner pressure on the other. The function of the regulator is to maintain constant pressure (approximately 11 psi or 76 kPa) to the injector throughout the operating loads and speed ranges of the engine. If the regulator pressure is too low, below 9 psi (62 kPa), it can cause poor performance. Too high a pressure could cause detonation and a strong fuel odor.

Idle Air Control (IAC)

♦ See Figure 18

The purpose of the Idle Air Control (IAC) system is to control engine idle speed while preventing stalls due to changes in engine load. The IAC assembly, mounted on the throttle body, controls bypass air around the throttle plate. By extending or retracting a conical valve, a controlled amount of air can move around the throttle plate. If rpm is too low, more air is diverted around the throttle plate to increase rpm.

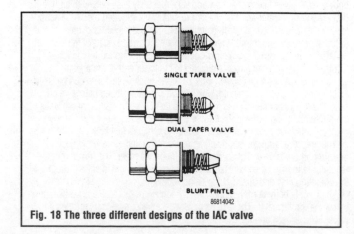

SINGLE TAPER VALVE

DUAL TAPER VALVE

BLUNT PINTLE

86814042

Fig. 18 The three different designs of the IAC valve

During idle, the proper position of the IAC valve is calculated by the ECM/PCM based on battery voltage, coolant temperature, engine load, and engine rpm. If the rpm drops below a specified rate, the throttle plate is closed. The ECM/PCM will then calculate a new valve position.

Three different designs are used for the IAC conical valve. The first design used is single 35 taper while the second design used is a dual taper. The third design is a blunt valve. Care should be taken to insure use of the correct design when service replacement is required.

The IAC motor has 255 different positions or steps. The zero, or reference position, is the fully extended position at which the pintle is seated in the air bypass seat and no air is allowed to bypass the throttle plate. When the motor is fully retracted, maximum air is allowed to bypass the throttle plate. When the motor is fully retracted, maximum air is allowed to bypass the throttle plate.

The ECM/PCM always monitors how many steps it has extended or retracted the pintle from the zero or reference position; thus, it always calculates the exact position of the motor. Once the engine has started and the vehicle has reached approximately 40 mph, the ECM/PCM will extend the motor 255 steps from whatever position it is in. This will bottom out the pintle against the seat. The ECM/PCM will call this position 0 and thus keep its zero reference updated.

The IAC only affects the engine's idle characteristics. If it is stuck fully open, idle speed is too high (too much air enters the throttle bore) If it is stuck closed, idle speed is too low (not enough air entering). If it is stuck somewhere in the middle, idle may be rough, and the engine won't respond to load changes.

Idle Speed Control (ISC)

Incorrect diagnosis and/or misunderstanding of the idle speed control systems used on fuel injected engines may lead to unnecessary replacement of the IAC valve. Engine idle speed is controlled by the ECM/PCM which changes the idle speed by moving the IAC valve. The ECM/PCM adjusts idle speed in response to fluctuations in engine load (A/C, power steering, electrical loads, etc.) to maintain acceptable idle quality and proper exhaust emission performance.

The following is provided to help you better understand the system. Asking yourself questions that a mechanic would ask will help you narrow down the problem area.

Rough Idle/Low Idle Speed

The ECM/PCM will respond to increases in engine load, which would cause a drop in idle speed, by moving the IAC valve to maintain proper idle speed. After the induced load is removed the ECM/PCM will return the idle speed to the proper level.

During A/C compressor operation (MAX, BI-LEVEL, NORM or DEFROST mode) the ECM/PCM will increase idle speed in response to an A/C-ON signal, thereby compensating for any drop in idle speed due to compressor load. On some vehicles, the ECM/PCM will also increase the idle speed in response to high power steering loads.

During periods of especially heavy loads (A/C-ON plus parking maneuvers) significant effects on idle quality may be experienced. These effects are more pronounced on 4-cylinder engines. Abnormally low idle, rough idle and idle shake may occur if the ECM/PCM does not receive the proper signals from the monitored systems.

High Idle Speed/Warm-Up Idle Speed (No Kickdown)

Engine idle speeds as high as 2100 rpm may be experienced during cold starts to quickly raise the catalytic converter to operating temperature for proper exhaust emissions performance. The idle speed attained after a cold start is ECM/PCM controlled and will not drop for 45 seconds regardless of driver attempts to kickdown.

It is important to note that fuel injected engines have no accelerator pump or choke. Idle speed during warm-up is entirely ECM/PCM controlled and cannot be changed by accelerator kickdown or pumping.

Abnormally low idle speeds are usually caused by an ECM/PCM system-controlled or monitored irregularity, while the most common cause for abnormally high idle speed is an induction (intake air) leak. The idle air control valve may occasionally lose its memory function, and it has an ECM/PCM pro-grammed method of relearning the correct idle position. This reset, when required, will occur the next time the car exceeds 35 mph (56 km/h). At that time, the ECM/PCM seats the pintle of the IAC valve in the throttle body to determine a reference point. Then it backs out a fixed distance to maintain proper idle speed.

SENSORS

A variety of sensors provide information to the ECM/PCM regarding engine operating characteristics. These sensors and their functions are described below. Be sure to take note that not every sensor described is used with every engine application.

Coolant Temperature (ECT)

The Engine Coolant Temperature Sensor (ECT) is a thermister (a resistor which changes value based on temperature) mounted on the engine coolant stream. As the temperature of the engine coolant changes, the resistance of the coolant sensor changes. Low coolant temperature produces a high resistance (100,000 ohms at 40°C/40°F), while high temperature causes low resistance (70 ohms at 130°C/266°F).

The ECM/PCM supplies a 5 volt signal to the coolant sensor and measures the voltage that returns. By measuring the voltage change, the ECM/PCM determines the engine coolant temperature. The voltage will be high when the engine is cold and low when the engine is hot. This information is used to control fuel management, IAC, spark timing, EGR, canister purge and other engine operating conditions.

A failure in the coolant sensor circuit should either set a Code 14 or 15. These codes indicate a failure in the coolant temperature sensor circuit.

Oxygen

The exhaust oxygen sensor is mounted in the exhaust system where it can monitor the oxygen content of the exhaust gas stream. The oxygen content in the exhaust reacts with the oxygen sensor to produce a voltage output. This voltage ranges from approximately 100 millivolts (high oxygen—lean mixture) to 900 millivolts (low oxygen—rich mixture).

By monitoring the voltage output of the oxygen sensor, the ECM/PCM will determine what fuel mixture command to give to the injector (lean mixture = low voltage and a rich command; rich mixture = high voltage and a lean command).

Remember that oxygen sensor indicates to the ECM/PCM what is happening in the exhaust. It does not cause things to happen. It is a type of gauge: high oxygen content = lean mixture; low oxygen content = rich mixture. The ECM/PCM adjusts fuel to keep the system working.

The oxygen sensor, if open should set a Code 13. A constant low voltage in the sensor circuit should set a Code 44 while a constant high voltage in the circuit should set a Code 45. Codes 44 and 45 could also be set as a result of fuel system problems.

Manifold Absolute Pressure

The Manifold Absolute Pressure (MAP) sensor measures the changes in the intake manifold pressure which result from engine load and speed changes. The pressure measured by the MAP sensor is the difference between barometric pressure (outside air) and manifold pressure (vacuum). A closed throttle engine coastdown would produce a relatively low MAP value (approximately 20–35 kPa), while wide-open throttle would produce a high value (100 kPa). This high value is produced when the pressure inside the manifold is the same as outside the manifold, and 100% of outside air (or 100 kPa) is being measured. This MAP output is the opposite of what you would measure on a vacuum gauge. The use of this sensor also allows the ECM/PCM to adjust automatically for different altitude.

The ECM/PCM sends a 5 volt reference signal to the MAP sensor. As the MAP changes, the electrical resistance of the sensor also changes. By monitoring the sensor output voltage the ECM/PCM can determine the manifold pressure. A higher pressure, lower vacuum (high voltage) requires more fuel, while a lower pressure, higher vacuum (low voltage) requires less fuel. The ECM/PCM uses the MAP sensor to control fuel delivery and ignition timing. A failure in the MAP sensor circuit should set a Code 33 or Code 34.

Intake Air Temperature

The Intake Air Temperature (IAT) and Manifold Air Temperature (MAT) are the same sensor. This sensor is a thermistor mounted in the intake manifold or air intake. A thermistor is a resistor which changes resistance based on temperature. Low manifold air temperature produces a high resistance (100,000 ohms at 40°F/40°C), while high temperature cause low resistance (70 ohms at 266°F/130°C).

The ECM/PCM supplies a 5 volt signal to the MAT/IAT sensor through a resistor in the ECM/PCM and monitors the voltage. The voltage will be high when the manifold air is cold and low when the air is hot. By monitoring the voltage, the ECM/PCM calculates the air temperature and uses this data to help determine the fuel delivery and spark advance. A failure in the MAT/IAT circuit should set either a Code 23 or Code 25.

Vehicle Speed

▶ See Figure 19

➡A vehicle equipped with a speed sensor, should not be driven without a the speed sensor connected, as idle quality may be affected. Also extreme poor gas mileage and a code will be stored in the computers memory.

The Vehicle Speed Sensor (VSS) is mounted behind the speedometer in the instrument cluster or on the transaxle/speedometer drive gear. It provides electrical pulses to the ECM/PCM from the speedometer head. The pulses indicate the road speed. The ECM/PCM uses this information to operate the IAC, canister purge, and TCC.

Some vehicles equipped with digital instrument clusters use a Permanent Magnet (PM) generator to provide the VSS signal. The PM generator is located in the transaxle and replaces the speedometer cable. The signal from the PM generator drives a stepper motor which drives the odometer. A failure in the VSS circuit should set a Code 24.

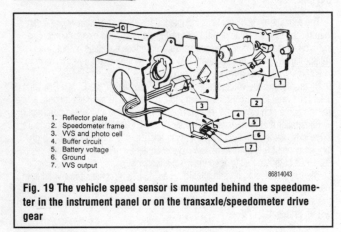

1. Reflector plate
2. Speedometer frame
3. VVS and photo cell
4. Buffer circuit
5. Battery voltage
6. Ground
7. VVS output

86814043

Fig. 19 The vehicle speed sensor is mounted behind the speedometer in the instrument panel or on the transaxle/speedometer drive gear

Throttle Position

▶ See Figure 20

The Throttle Position Sensor (TPS) is connected to the throttle shaft and is controlled by the throttle mechanism. A 5 volt reference signal is sent to the TPS from the ECM/PCM. As the throttle valve angle is changed (accelerator pedal moved), the resistance of the TPS also changes. At a closed throttle position, the resistance of the TPS is high, so the output voltage to the ECM/PCM will be low (approximately 0.5 volts). As the throttle plate opens, the resistance decreases so that, at wide open throttle, the output voltage should be approxi-

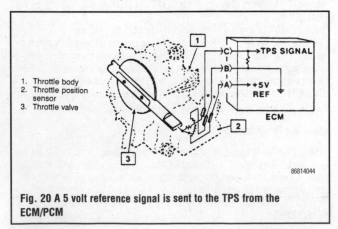

1. Throttle body
2. Throttle position sensor
3. Throttle valve

86814044

Fig. 20 A 5 volt reference signal is sent to the TPS from the ECM/PCM

mately 5 volts. At closed throttle position, the voltage at the TPS should be less than 1.25 volts.

By monitoring the output voltage from the TPS, the ECM/PCM can determine fuel delivery based on throttle valve angle (driver demand). The TPS can either be misadjusted, shorted, open or loose. Misadjustment might result in poor idle or poor wide-open throttle performance. An open TPS signals the ECM/PCM that the throttle is always closed, resulting in poor performance. This usually sets a Code 22. A shorted TPS gives the ECM/PCM a constant wide-open throttle signal and should set a Code 21. A loose TPS indicates to the ECM that the throttle is moving. This causes intermittent bursts of fuel from the injector and an unstable idle. On some vehicles, the TPS is adjustable and therefore can be adjusted to correct any complications caused by to high or to low of a voltage signal.

Crankshaft and Camshaft

▶ See Figures 21 and 22

These sensors are mounted on the engine block, near the engine crankshaft, and also near the camshaft on some engines. The sensors are used to send a signal through the Direct Ignition System (DIS) module to the ECM. The ECM uses this reference signal to calculate engine speed and crankshaft position. There are several names for these sensors, 3X and 24X Crankshaft Position Sensor (CPS).

In a typical 4 cylinder engine application, a sensor is mounted with the ignition module and 2 ignition coils to comprise the direct ignition assembly. When mounted on the engine block, the sensor tip is very close to a metal disk wheel with slots which is mounted on the crankshaft.

The sensor tip contains a small magnet and a small coil of wire. As the metal disk wheel with the slots rotates past the sensor tip, the magnetic field of the

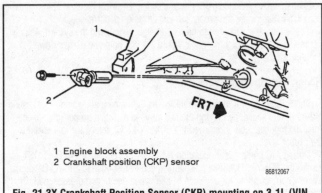

1 Engine block assembly
2 Crankshaft position (CKP) sensor

86812067

Fig. 21 3X Crankshaft Position Sensor (CKP) mounting on 3.1L (VIN M) engine

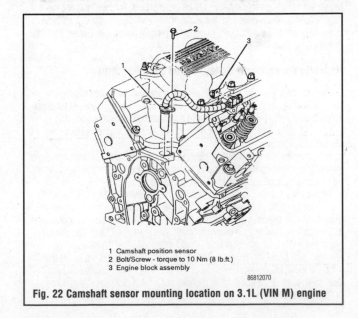

1 Camshaft position sensor
2 Bolt/Screw - torque to 10 Nm (8 lb.ft.)
3 Engine block assembly

86812070

Fig. 22 Camshaft sensor mounting location on 3.1L (VIN M) engine

permanent magnet is changed and a voltage is induced into the coil. This voltage signal is sent to the ignition module. The ignition module is able to determine engine speed from the frequency of the voltage curve, which changes with engine speed.

A 6-cylinder engine may use a different type of sensor called a hall effect switch. With the direct ignition connected to the vehicle electrical system, the system voltage is applied to the hall effect switch located near the tip of the sensor. A small permanent magnet creates a magnetic field in the hall effect switch circuit. As the disc wheel with the slots rotates past the sensor tip, the magnetic field in the hall effect switch changes and a change in the voltage occurs at the hall effect switch output terminal.

Since this terminal is connect to the ignition module, the module senses this change in voltage and correlates the frequency of the voltage curve to determine the engine speed. The ignition module then uses this voltage input to help determine when to close and open the ignition coil primary circuit and fire the spark plug.

SWITCHES

Park/Neutral Switch

➡ **Vehicle should not be driven with the park/neutral switch disconnected, as idle quality may be affected in PARK or NEUTRAL and a Code 24 (VSS) may be set.**

This switch indicates to the ECM/PCM when the transaxle is in **P** or **N**. The information is used by the ECM for control on the torque converter clutch, EGR, and the idle air control valve operation.

Air Conditioner Request Signal

This signal indicates to the ECM/PCM that an air conditioning mode is selected at the switch and that the A/C low pressure switch is closed. The ECM/PCM controls the A/C and adjusts the idle speed in response to this signal.

Torque Converter Clutch (TCC) Solenoid

The purpose of the Torque Converter Clutch (TCC) system is designed to eliminate power loss by the converter (slippage) to increase fuel economy. By locking the converter clutch, a more effective coupling to the flywheel is achieved. The converter clutch is operated by the ECM/PCM controlled torque converter clutch solenoid.

Power Steering Pressure (PSPS)

The Power Steering Pressure Switch (PSPS) is used so that the power steering oil pressure pump load will not effect the engine idle. Turning the steering wheel increase the power steering oil pressure and pump load on the engine. The power steering pressure switch will close before the load can cause an idle problem.

Oil Pressure

The oil pressure switch is usually mounted on the back of the engine, just below the intake manifold. Some vehicles use the oil pressure switch as a parallel power supply, with the fuel pump relay and will provide voltage to the fuel pump, after approximately 4 psi (28 kPa) of oil pressure is reached. This switch will also help prevent engine seizure by shutting off the power to the fuel pump and causing the engine to stop when the oil pressure is lower than 4 psi (28 kPa).

IGNITION

Various components are used in conjunction with the ignition system. Below are the basics for the TBI.

Electronic Spark Timing (EST)

Electronic Spark Timing (EST) is used on all engines. The EST distributor contains no vacuum or centrifugal advance and uses a 7-terminal distributor module. It also has 4 wires going to a 4-terminal connector in addition to the connectors normally found on HEI distributors. A reference pulse, indicating both engine rpm and crankshaft position, is sent to the ECM/PCM. The ECM/PCM determines the proper spark advance for the engine operating conditions and sends an EST pulse to the distributor.

The EST system is designed to optimize spark timing for better control of exhaust emissions and for fuel economy improvements. The ECM/PCM monitors information from various engine sensors, computes the desired spark timing and changes the timing accordingly. A backup spark advance system is incorporated in the module in case of EST failure.

Electronic Spark Control (ESC)

When engines are equipped with Electronic Spark Control (ESC) in conjunction with EST, ESC is used to reduce spark advance under conditions of detonation. A knock sensor signals a separate ESC controller to retard the timing when it senses engine knock. The ESC controller signals the ECM/PCM which reduces spark advance until no more signals are received from the knock sensor.

Direct Ignition System (DIS)

Components of the Direct Ignition System (DIS) are a coil pack, ignition module, crankshaft reluctor ring, magnetic sensor and the ECM/PCM. The coil pack consists of 2 separate, interchangeable, ignition coils. These coils operate in the same manner as previous coils. Two coils are needed because each coil fires for 2 cylinders. The ignition module is located under the coil pack and is connected to the ECM/PCM by a 6 pin connector. The ignition module controls the primary circuits to the coils, turning them on and off and controls spark timing below 400 rpm and if the ECM/PCM bypass circuit becomes open or grounded.

The magnetic pickup sensor inserts through the engine block, just above the pan rail in proximity to the crankshaft reluctor ring. Notches in the crankshaft reluctor ring trigger the magnetic pickup sensor to provide timing information to the ECM/PCM. The magnetic pickup sensor provides a cam signal to identify correct firing sequence and crank signals to trigger each coil at the proper time.

This system uses EST and control wires from the ECM/PCM, as with the distributor systems. The ECM/PCM controls the timing using crankshaft position, engine rpm, engine temperature and manifold absolute pressure sensing.

EMISSION CONTROL

Various components are used to control exhaust emissions from a vehicle. These components are controlled by the ECM based on different engine operating conditions. These components are described in the following paragraphs. Not all components are used on all engines.

Exhaust Gas Recirculation (EGR) System

EGR is a oxides of nitrogen (NOx) control which recycles exhaust gases through the combustion cycle by admitting exhaust gases into the intake manifold. The amount of exhaust gas admitted is adjusted by a vacuum controlled valve in response to engine operating conditions. If the valve is open, the recirculated exhaust gas is released into the intake manifold to be drawn into the combustion chamber.

The integral exhaust pressure modulated EGR valve uses a transducer responsive to exhaust pressure to modulate the vacuum signal to the EGR valve. The vacuum signal is provided by an EGR vacuum port in the throttle body valve. Under conditions when exhaust pressure is lower than the control pressure, the EGR signal is reduced by an air bleed within the transducer. Under conditions when exhaust pressure is higher than the control pressure, the air bleed is closed and the EGR valve responds to an unmodified vacuum signal. Physical arrangement of the valve components will vary depending on whether the control pressure is positive or negative.

Positive Crankcase Ventilation (PCV) System

A closed Positive Crankcase Ventilation (PCV) system is used to provide more complete scavenging of crankcase vapors. Fresh air from the air cleaner is supplied to the crankcase, mixed with blow-by gases and then passed through a PCV valve into the induction system.

The primary mode of crankcase ventilation control is through the PCV valve which meters the mixture of fresh air and blow-by gases into the induction system at a rate dependent upon manifold vacuum.

To maintain the idle quality, the PCV valve restricts the ventilation system flow whenever intake manifold vacuum is designed to allow excessive amounts of blow-by gases to backflow through the breather assembly into the air cleaner and through the throttle body to be consumed by normal combustion.

Thermostatic Air Cleaner (TAC) System

To assure optimum driveability under varying climatic conditions, a heated intake air system is used on engines. This system is designed to warm the air entering the TBI to insure uniform inlet air temperatures. Under this condition, the fuel injection system can be calibrated to efficiently reduce exhaust emission and to eliminate throttle blade icing. The Thermac system used on fuel injected vehicles operates identically to other Thermac systems.

Evaporative Emission Control (EEC) Systems

The basic evaporative emission control system used on all vehicles uses the carbon canister storage method. This method transfers fuel vapor to an activated carbon storage device for retention when the vehicle is not operating. A ported vacuum signal is used for purging vapors stored in the canister.

CONTROLLED CANISTER PURGE

The ECM/PCM controls a solenoid valve which controls vacuum to the purge valve in the charcoal canister. In open loop, before a specified time has expired and below a specified rpm, the solenoid valve is energized and blocks vacuum to the purge valve. When the system is in closed loop, after a specified time and above a specified rpm, the solenoid valve is de-energized and vacuum can be applied to the purge valve. This releases the collected vapors into the intake manifold. On systems not using an ECM/PCM controlled solenoid, a Thermo Vacuum Valve (TVV) is used to control purge. See the appropriate vehicle sections for checking procedures.

AIR MANAGEMENT CONTROL

The air management system aids in the reduction of exhaust emissions by supplying air to either the catalytic converter, engine exhaust manifold, or to the air cleaner. The ECM/PCM controls the air management system by energizing or de-energizing an air switching valve. Operation of the air switching valve is dependent upon such engine operating characteristics as coolant temperature, engine load, and acceleration (or deceleration), all of which are sensed by the ECM/PCM.

PULSAIR REACTOR SYSTEM

The Pulsair Injection Reactor (PAIR) system utilizes exhaust pressure pulsations to draw air into the exhaust system. Fresh air from the clean side of the air cleaner supplies filtered air to avoid dirt build-up on the check valve seat. The air cleaner also serves as a muffler for noise reduction. The internal mechanism of the Pulsair valve reacts to 3 distinct conditions.
- If the pressure is positive, the disc is forced to the closed position and no exhaust gas is allowed to flow past the valve and into the air supply line.
- If there is a negative pressure (vacuum) in the exhaust system at the valve, the disc will open, allowing fresh air to mix with the exhaust gases.
- Due to the inertia of the system, the disc ceases to follow the pressure pulsations at high engine rpm. At this point, the disc remains closed, preventing any further fresh air flow.

The firing of the engine creates a pulsating flow of exhaust gases which are of positive (+) or negative (-) pressure. This pressure or vacuum is transmitted through external tubes to the Pulsair valve.

CATALYTIC CONVERTER

Of all emission control devices available, the catalytic converter is the most effective in reducing tailpipe emissions. The major tailpipe pollutants are hydrocarbons (HC), carbon monoxide (CO), and oxides of nitrogen (NOx).

SERVICE PRECAUTIONS

When working around any part of the fuel system, take precautionary steps to prevent fire and/or explosion:
- Disconnect negative terminal from battery (except when testing with battery voltage is required).
- When possible, use a flashlight instead of a drop light.
- Keep all open flame and smoking material out of the area.

- Use a shop cloth or similar to catch fuel when opening a fuel system.
- Relieve fuel system pressure before servicing.
- Use eye protection.
- Always keep a dry chemical (class B) fire extinguisher near the area.

➡**Due to the amount of fuel pressure in the fuel lines, before doing any work to the fuel system, the fuel system should be depressurized.**

Electrostatic Discharge Damage

Electronic components used in the control system are often design to carry very low voltage and are very susceptible to damage caused by electrostatic discharge. It is possible for less than 100 volts of static electricity to cause damage to some electronic components. By comparison it takes as much as 4000 volts for a person to even feel the zap of a static discharge.

There are several ways for a person to become statically charged. The most common methods of charging are by friction and induction. An example of charging by friction is a person sliding across a car seat, in which a charge as much as 25,000 volts can build up. Charging by induction occurs when a person with well insulated shoes stands near a highly charged object and momentarily touches ground. Charges of the same polarity are drained off, leaving the person highly charged with the opposite polarity. Static charges of either type can cause damage, therefore, it is important to use care when handling and testing electronic components.

➡**To prevent possible electrostatic discharge damage to the ECM/PCM, do not touch the connector pins or soldered components on the circuit board. When handling a PROM, Mem-Cal or Cal-Pak, do not touch the component leads and remove the integrated circuit from the carrier.**

DIAGNOSTIC ENGINE COMPUTER CODES

Data Link Connector (DLC)

▶ See Figure 23

The Data Link Connector (DLC) is also known as the Assembly Line Communication Link (ALCL) and also known as the Assembly Line Diagnostic Link (ALDL). It is a diagnostic connector located in the passenger compartment usually under the instrument panel, and is sometimes called the DIAGNOSTIC CONNECTOR. The assembly plant were the vehicles originate use the connector to check the engine for proper operation before it leaves the plant. Terminal B is the diagnostic TEST terminal (lead) and it can be connected to terminal A, or ground, to enter the Diagnostic mode or the Field Service Mode.

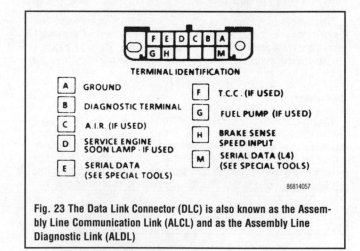

Fig. 23 The Data Link Connector (DLC) is also known as the Assembly Line Communication Link (ALCL) and as the Assembly Line Diagnostic Link (ALDL)

Reading Codes and Diagnostic Modes

This information is able to be read by putting the ECM/PCM into 1 of 4 different modes. These modes are entered by inserting a specific amount of resistance between the DLC connector terminals A and B. The modes and resistances needed to enter these modes are as follows:

DIAGNOSTIC MODES—0 OHMS

When 0 resistance is between terminals A and B of the DLC connector, the diagnostic mode is entered. There are 2 positions to this mode. One with the engine **OFF**, but the ignition **ON**; the other is when the engine is running called Field Service Mode.

If the diagnostic mode is entered with the engine in the **OFF** position, trouble codes will flash and the idle air control motor will pulsate in and out. Also, the relays and solenoids are energized with the exception of the fuel pump and injector.

As a bulb and system check, the SERVICE ENGINE SOON light will come on with the ignition switch **ON** and the engine not running. When the engine is started, the SERVICE ENGINE SOON light will turn off. If the SERVICE ENGINE SOON light remains on, the self-diagnostic system has detected a problem.

If the B terminal is then grounded with the ignition **ON**, engine not running, each trouble code will flash and repeat 3 times. If more than 1 problem has been detected, each trouble code will flash 3 times. Trouble codes will flash in numeric order (lowest number first). The trouble code series will repeat as long as the B terminal is grounded.

A trouble code indicates a problem in a given circuit (Code 14, for example, indicates a problem in the coolant sensor circuit; this includes the coolant sensor, connector harness, and ECM/PCM). The procedure for pinpointing the problem can be found in diagnosis. Similar charts are provided for each code.

Also in this mode all ECM/PCM controlled relays and solenoids except the fuel pump relay. This allows checking the circuits which may be difficult to energize without driving the vehicle and being under particular operating conditions. The IAC valve will move to its fully extended position on most models, block the idle air passage. This is useful in checking the minimum idle speed.

FIELD SERVICE MODE—0 OHMS

When the DLC connector terminal B is grounded with the engine running, the ECM/PCM goes into the field service mode. In this mode, the SERVICE ENGINE SOON light flashes closed or open loop and indicates the rich/lean status of the engine. The ECM/PCM runs the engine at a fixed ignition timing advanced above the base setting.

The SERVICE ENGINE SOON light will show whether the system is in Open loop or Closed loop. In Open loop the SERVICE ENGINE SOON light flashes 2 times and one half times per second. In Closed loop the light flashes once per second. Also in closed loop, the light will stay OUT most of the time if the system is too lean. It will stay ON most of the time if the system is too rich. In either case the Field Service mode check, which is part of the Diagnostic circuit check, will lead you into choosing the correct diagnostic chart to refer to.

BACKUP MODE—3.9 KILO-OHMS

The backup mode is entered by applying 3.9 kilo-ohms resistance between terminals A and B of the DLC connector with the ignition switch in the **ON** position. The DLC scanner tool can now read 5 of the 20 parameters on the data stream. These parameters are as mode status, oxygen sensor voltage, rpm, block learn and idle air control. There are 2 ways to enter the backup mode. Using a scan tool is one way of putting a 3.9 kilo-ohms resistor across terminals A and B of the DLC is another.

SPECIAL MODE—10 KILO-OHMS

This special mode is entered by applying a 10K ohms resistor across terminals A and B. When this happens the ECM does the following:
• Allows all of the serial data to be read.
• Bypasses all timers.
• Add a calibrated spark advance.
• Enables the canister purge solenoid on some engines.
• Idles at 950–1050 rpm fixed idle air control and fixed base pulse width on the injector.
• Forces the idle air control to reset at part throttle (approximately 2000 rpm).
• Disables the park/neutral restrict functions.

OPEN OR ROAD TEST MODE—20 KILO-OHMS

On engines that can be monitored in the Open mode, certain parameters can be observed without changing the engine operating characteristics. The parameters capable of being read vary with the engine families. Most Scan tools are programmed so that the system will go directly into the DLC mode if the Open mode is not available.

DLC SCAN TESTER INFORMATION

▶ **See Figure 24**

A DLC display unit (DLC tester, scanner, monitor, etc.), allows you to read the engine control system information from the DLC connector under the instrument panel. It can provide information faster than a digital voltmeter or ohmmeter can. The scan tool does not diagnose the exact location of the problem. The tool supplies information about the ECM/PCM, the information that it is receiving and the commands that it is sending plus special information such as integrator and block learn. To use a DLC display tool you should understand thoroughly how an engine control system operates.

A DLC scanner or monitor puts a fuel injection system into a special test mode. This mode commands an idle speed of 1000 rpm. The idle quality cannot be evaluated with a tester plugged in. Also the test mode commands a fixed spark with no advance. On vehicles with Electronic Spark Control (ECS) and its knock sensor, there will be a fixed spark, but it will be advanced. On vehicles with ESC, there might be a serious spark knock which is bad enough to prevent road testing the vehicle in the DLC test mode. Be sure to check the tool manufacturer for instructions on special test modes which should overcome these limitations.

When a tester is used with a fuel injected engine, it bypasses the timer that keeps the system in Open loop for a certain period of time. When all Closed loop conditions are met, the engine will go into Closed loop as soon as the vehicle is started. This means that the air management system will not function properly and air may go directly to the converter as soon as the engine is started.

These tools cannot diagnose everything. They do not tell where a problem is located in a circuit. The diagnostic charts to pinpoint the problems must still be used. These tester's do not let you know if a solenoid or relay has been turned on. They only tell the ECM/PCM command. To find out if a solenoid has been turned on, check it with a suitable test light or digital voltmeter, or see if vacuum through the solenoid changes.

SCAN TOOLS FOR INTERMITTENT PROBLEMS

In some scan tool applications, the data update rate may make the tool less effective than a voltmeter, such as when trying to detect an intermittent problem which lasts for a very short time. Some scan tools have a snapshot function which stores several seconds or even minutes of operation to located an intermittent problem. Scan tools allow one to manipulate the wiring harness or components under the hood with the engine not running while observing the scan tool's readout.

The scan tool can be plugged in and observed while driving the vehicle under the condition when the SERVICE ENGINE SOON light turns on momentarily or when the engine driveability is momentarily poor. If the problem seems to be related to certain parameters that can be checked on the scan tool, they should be checked while driving the vehicle. If there does not seem to be any correlation between the problem and any specific circuit, the scan tool can be checked on each position. Watching for a period of time to see if there is any change in the reading that indicates intermittent operation.

The scan tool is also an easy way to compare the operating parameters of a poorly operating engine with typical scan data for the vehicle being serviced or those of a known good engine. For example, a sensor may shift in value but not set a trouble code. Comparing the sensor's reading with those of a known good parameters may uncover the problem.

86814061

Fig. 24 The Data Link Connector (DLC) display unit (DLC tester, scanner, monitor, etc.) allows you to read the engine control system information from the DLC connector under the instrument panel. It can provide information faster than a digital voltmeter or ohmmeter

The scan tool has the ability to save time in diagnosis and prevent the replacement of good parts. The key to using the scan tool successfully for diagnosis lies in the ability to understand the system being diagnosed, as well as the scan tool's operation and limitations.

CLEARING TROUBLE CODES

When the ECM/PCM finds a problem with the system, the SERVICE ENGINE SOON light will come on and a trouble code will be recorded in the ECM/PCM memory. If the problem is intermittent, the SERVICE ENGINE SOON light will go out after 10 seconds, when the fault goes away. However the trouble code will stay in the ECM/PCM memory until the battery voltage to the ECM/PCM is removed. Removing the battery voltage for 10 seconds will clear all trouble codes. Do this by disconnecting the ECM/PCM harness from the positive battery terminal pigtail for 10 seconds with the key in the **OFF** position, or by removing the ECM/PCM fuse for 10 seconds with the key **OFF**.

➡ **To prevent ECM/PCM damage, the key must be OFF when disconnecting and reconnecting ECM/PCM power.**

INTEGRATOR AND BLOCK LEARN

The integrator and block learn functions of the ECM/PCM are responsible for making minor adjustments to the air/fuel ratio on the fuel injected GM vehicles. These small adjustments are necessary to compensate for pinpoint air leaks and normal wear.

The integrator and block learn are 2 separate ECM/PCM memory functions which control fuel delivery. The integrator makes a temporary change and the block learn makes a more permanent change. Both of these functions apply only while the engine is in CLOSED LOOP. They represent the on-time of the injector. Also, integrator and block learn controls fuel delivery on the fuel injected engines as does the MC solenoid dwell on the CCC carbureted engines.

Integrator

Integrator is the term applied to a means of temporary change in fuel delivery. Integrator is displayed through the DLC data line and monitored with a scanner as a number range between 0 and 255 with an average of 128. The integrator monitors the oxygen sensor output voltage (usually below 450 mV) and adds and subtracts fuel depending on the lean or rich condition of the oxygen sensor. When the integrator is displaying 128, it indicates a neutral condition. This means that the oxygen sensor is seeing results of the 14.7:1 air/fuel mixture burned in the cylinders.

➡ **An air leak in the system (a lean condition) would cause the oxygen sensor voltage to decrease while the integrator would increase (add more fuel) to temporarily correct for the lean condition. If this happened the injector pulse width would increase.**

Block Learn

Although the integrator can correct fuel delivery over a wide range, it is only for a temporary correction. Therefore, another control called block learn was added. Although it cannot make as many corrections as the integrator, it does so for a longer period of time. It gets its name from the fact that the operating range of the engine for any given combinations of rpm and load is divided into 16 cell or blocks.

The computer has a given fuel delivery stored in each block. As the operating range gets into a given block the fuel delivery will be based on what value is stored in the memory in that block. Again, just like the integrator, the number represents the on-time of the injector. Also, just like the integrator, the number 128 represents no correction to the value that is stored in the cell or block. When the integrator increases or decreases, block learn which is also watching the integrator will make corrections in the same direction. As the block learn makes corrections, the integrator correction will be reduced until finally the integrator will return to 128 if the block learn has corrected the fuel delivery.

Block Learn Memory

Block learn operates on 1 of 2 types of memories depending on application: non-volatile or volatile. The non-volatile memories retain the value in the block learn cells even when the ignition switch is turned **OFF**. When the engine is restarted, the fuel delivery for a given block will be based on information stored in memory.

The volatile memories lose the numbers stored in the block learn cells when the ignition is turned to the **OFF** position. Upon restarting, the block learn starts at 128 in every block and corrects from that point as necessary.

Integrator/Block Learn Limits

Both the integrator and block learn have limits which will vary from engine to engine. If the mixture is off enough so that the block learn reaches the limit of its control and still cannot correct the condition, the integrator would also go to it's limit of control in the same direction and the engine would then begin to run poorly. If the integrators and block learn are close to or at their limits of control, the engine hardware should be checked to determine the cause of the limits being reached, vacuum leaks, sticking injectors, etc.

If the integrator is lied to, for example, if the oxygen sensor lead was grounded (lean signal) the integrator and block learn would add fuel to the engine to cause it to run rich. However, with the oxygen sensor lead grounded, the ECM/PCM would continue seeing a lean condition eventually setting a Code 44 and the fuel control system would change to open loop operations.

Closed Loop Fuel Control

The purpose of closed loop fuel control is to precisely maintain an air/fuel mixture 14.7:1. When the air/fuel mixture is maintained at 14.7:1, the catalytic converter is able to operate at maximum efficiency which results in lower emission levels.

Since the ECM/PCM controls the air/fuel mixture, it needs to check its output and correct the fuel mixture for deviations from the ideal ratio. The oxygen sensor feeds this output information back to the ECM/PCM.

ENGINE PERFORMANCE DIAGNOSIS

Engine performance diagnostic procedures are guides that will lead to the most probable causes of engine performance complaints. They consider the components of the fuel, ignition, and mechanical systems that could cause a particular complaint, and then outline repairs in a logical sequence.

It is important to determine if the SERVICE ENGINE SOON light is on or has come on for a short interval while driving. If the SERVICE ENGINE SOON light has come on, the Computer Command Control System should be checked for stored **TROUBLE CODES** which may indicate the cause for the performance complaint.

All of the symptoms can be caused by worn out or defective parts such as spark plugs, ignition wiring, etc. If time and/or mileage indicate that parts should be replaced, it is recommended that it be done.

➡ **Before checking any system controlled by the Electronic Fuel Injection (EFI) system, the Diagnostic Circuit Check must be performed or misdiagnosis may occur. If the complaint involves the SERVICE ENGINE SOON light, go directly to the Diagnostic Circuit Check.**

Basic Troubleshooting

➡ **The following explains how to activate the trouble code signal light in the instrument cluster and gives an explanation of what each code means. This is not a full system troubleshooting and isolation procedure.**

Before suspecting the system or any of its components as faulty, check the ignition system including distributor, timing, spark plugs and wires. Check the engine compression, air cleaner, and emission control components not controlled by the ECM/PCM. Also check the intake manifold, vacuum hoses and hose connectors for leaks.

The following symptoms could indicate a possible problem with the system:
- Detonation
- Stalls or idles rough when cold
- Stalls or idles rough when hot
- Missing
- Hesitation
- Surges
- Poor gasoline mileage
- Sluggish or spongy performance
- Hard starting-cold

- Objectionable exhaust odors (that rotten egg smell)
- Cuts out
- Improper idle speed

As a bulb and system check, the SERVICE ENGINE SOON light will come on when the ignition switch is turned to the **ON** position but the engine is not started. The SERVICE ENGINE SOON light will also produce the trouble code or codes by a series of flashes which translate as follows. When the diagnostic test terminal under the dash is grounded, with the ignition in the **ON** position and the engine not running, the SERVICE ENGINE SOON light will flash once, pause, then flash twice in rapid succession. This is a Code 12, which indicates that the diagnostic system is working. After a long pause, the Code 12 will repeat itself 2 more times. The cycle will then repeat itself until the engine is started or the ignition is turned off.

When the engine is started, the SERVICE ENGINE SOON light will remain on for a few seconds, then turn off. If the SERVICE ENGINE SOON light remains on, the self-diagnostic system has detected a problem. If the test terminal is then grounded, the trouble code will flash 3 times. If more than 1 problem is found, each trouble code will flash 3 times. Trouble codes will flash in numerical order (lowest code number to highest). The trouble codes series will repeat as long as the test terminal is grounded.

A trouble code indicates a problem with a given circuit. For example, trouble Code 14 indicates a problem in the cooling sensor circuit. This includes the coolant sensor, its electrical harness, and the ECM/PCM. Since the self-diagnostic system cannot diagnose every possible fault in the system, the absence of a trouble code does not mean the system is trouble-free. To determine problems within the system which do not activate a trouble code, a system performance check must be made.

In the case of an intermittent fault in the system, the SERVICE ENGINE SOON light will go out when the fault goes away, but the trouble code will remain In the memory of the ECM/PCM. Therefore, if a trouble code can be obtained even though the SERVICE ENGINE SOON light is not on, the trouble code must be evaluated. It must be determined if the fault is intermittent or if the engine must be at certain operating conditions (under load, etc.) before the SERVICE ENGINE SOON light will come on. Some trouble codes will not be recorded in the ECM/PCM until the engine has been operated at part throttle for about 5–18 minutes.

Fuel System Pressure Testing

Due to the varied application of components, a general procedure is outlined. For the exact procedure for the vehicle being service use Chart A7 for the appropriate engine. A fuel system pressure test is part of several of the diagnostic charts and symptom checks.

1. Relieve the fuel pressure from the fuel system. Turn the ignition **OFF** and remove the air cleaner assembly (if necessary).
2. Plug the Thermac vacuum port if required on the TBI unit.
3. Uncouple the fuel supply flexible hose in the engine compartment and install fuel pressure gauge J–29658/BT–8205 or equivalent in the pressure line or install the fuel pressure gauge into the pressure line connector located near the left engine compartment frame rail. Connection of the fuel gauge will vary accordingly to all the different engine application.
4. Be sure to tighten the fuel line to the gauge to ensure that there no leaks during testing.
5. Start the engine and observe the fuel pressure reading. The fuel pressure should be 9–13 psi (62–90 kPa).
6. Relieve the fuel pressure. Remove the fuel pressure gauge and reinstall the fuel line. Be sure to install a new O-ring on the fuel feed line.
7. Start the engine and check for fuel leaks. Stop the engine and remove the plug covering the Thermac vacuum port on the TBI unit and install the air cleaner assembly.

➡ **Some vehicles will use more sensors than others. Also, a complete general diagnostic section is outlined. The steps and procedures can be altered as necessary according to the specific model being diagnosed and the sensors it is equipped with. If the battery power is disconnected for any reason, the volatile memory resets and the learning process begins again. A change may be noted in the performance of the vehicle. To teach the vehicle, ensure that the engine is at normal operating temperature. Then, the vehicle should be driven at part throttle, with moderate acceleration and idle conditions until normal performance returns.**

TBI SYSTEM DIAGNOSTIC CHARTS

To properly diagnose driveability problems, refer to the trouble code charts which appear later in this section. Make certain the charts cover the appropriate engine. If your check engine light is not lit, check for engine stored engine codes. If any codes are stored write them down for reference later. Clear the codes as described earlier. Road test the vehicle to see if any of the codes return. Never try to fix a code problem until you're sure that it comes back. It may have been an old code from years ago that was never cleared or a code that was set do to a rain storm, battery jump, etc.

After clearing any codes and checking that they do not return. If the car drives fine you're finished. But if there are no codes and the car runs poorly you'll need to check the symptoms charts. The problem is most likely not the computer or the devices it controls but the ignition system or engine mechanical.

If you do have a code(s) that returns start with the lowest code and follow the proper chart. You must follow every step of the chart and not jump from test to test or you'll never be certain to find and fix the real problem.

Start with the lowest to highest code chart, making sure to use the charts for your engine. If you have a 50 series code, like code 54. Always check those out first. They are rare but usually indicate a problem with the computer itself or its ability to test itself properly.

➡ **Whereas component repair and replacement are covered in Section 5 (Fuel System), this section only deals with testing the system for driveability and emission problems.**

Multi-Port Fuel Injection (MFI) and Sequential Fuel Injection (SFI)

Both the MFI and SFI systems are controlled by a Computer Control Module (ECM or PCM) which monitors engine operations and generates output signals to provide the correct air/fuel mixture, ignition timing and engine idle speed control. Input to the control unit is provided by an oxygen sensor, coolant temperature sensor, detonation sensor, hot film mass sensor and throttle position sensor. The ECM/PCM also receives information concerning engine rpm, road speed, transaxle gear position, power steering and air conditioning.

The injectors are located, one at each intake port, rather than the single injector found on the earlier throttle body system. The injectors are mounted on a fuel rail and are activated by a signal from the computer control module. The injector is a solenoid-operated valve which remains open depending on the width of the electronic pulses (length of the signal) from the ECM/PCM. The longer the open time, the more fuel is injected. In this manner, the air/fuel mixture can be precisely controlled for maximum performance with minimum emissions.

Fuel is pumped from the tank by a high pressure fuel pump, located inside the fuel tank. It is a positive displacement roller vane pump. The impeller serves as a vapor separator and pre-charges the high pressure assembly. A pressure regulator maintains 41–47 psi (282–324 kPa) in the fuel line to the injectors and the excess fuel is fed back to the tank. A fuel accumulator is used to dampen the hydraulic line hammer in the system created when all injectors open simultaneously.

The Mass Air Flow (MAF) Sensor is used to measure the mass of air that is drawn into the engine cylinders. It is located just ahead of the air throttle in the intake system and consists of a heated film which measures the mass of air, rather than just the volume. A resistor is used to measure the temperature of the film at 75°F (24°C) above ambient temperature. As the ambient (outside) air temperature rises, more energy is required to maintain the heated film at the higher temperature and the control unit used this difference in required energy to calculate the mass of the incoming air. The control unit uses this information to determine the duration of fuel injection pulse, timing and EGR.

The throttle body incorporates an Idle Air Control (IAC) that provides for a bypass channel through which air can flow. It consists of an orifice and pintle which is controlled by the ECM/PCM through a step motor. The IAC provides air flow for idle and allows additional air during cold start until the engine reaches operating temperature. As the engine temperature rises, the opening through which air passes is slowly closed.

The Throttle Position Sensor (TPS) provides the control unit with information on throttle position, in order to determine injector pulse width and hence correct mixture. The TPS is connected to the throttle shaft on the throttle body and consists of as potentiometer with on end connected to a 5 volt source from the ECM/PCM and the other to ground. A third wire is connected to the ECM/PCM to measure the voltage output from the TPS which changes as the throttle valve angle is changed (accelerator pedal moves). At the closed throttle position, the output is low (approximately 0.4 volts). As the throttle valve opens, the output increases to a maximum 5 volts at Wide Open Throttle (WOT). The TPS can be misadjusted open, shorted, or loose and if it is out of adjustment, the idle quality or WOT performance may be poor. A loose TPS can cause intermittent bursts of fuel from the injectors and an unstable idle because the ECM/PCM thinks the throttle is moving. This should cause a trouble code to be set. Once a trouble code is set, the ECM/PCM will use a preset value for the TPS and some vehicle performance may return. A small amount of engine coolant is routed through the throttle assembly to prevent freezing inside the throttle bore during cold operation.

COMPUTER CONTROL MODULE

The fuel injection system is controlled by an on-board computer, the Electronic Control Module/Powertrain Control Module (ECM/PCM), usually located in the passenger compartment. The ECM/PCM monitors engine operations and environmental conditions (ambient temperature, barometric pressure, etc.) needed to calculate the fuel delivery time (pulse width/injector on-time) of the fuel injector. The fuel pulse may be modified by the ECM/PCM to account for special operating conditions, such as cranking, cold starting, altitude, acceleration and deceleration.

The ECM/PCM controls the exhaust emissions by modifying fuel delivery to achieve, as nearly as possible an air/fuel ratio of 14.7:1. The injector on-time is determined by the various sensor inputs to the ECM/PCM. By increasing the injector pulse, more fuel is delivered, enriching the air/fuel ratio. Pulses are sent to the injector in 2 different modes, synchronized and non-synchronized.

In synchronized mode operation, the injector is pulsed once for each distributor reference pulse. In non-synchronized mode operation, the injector is pulsed once every 12.5 milliseconds or 6.25 milliseconds depending on calibration. This pulse time is totally independent of distributor reference.

The ECM/PCM constantly monitors the input information, processes this information from various sensors, and generates output commands to the various systems that affect vehicle performance.

The ability of the ECM/PCM to recognize and adjust for vehicle variations (engine, transaxle, vehicle weight, axle ratio, etc.) is provided by a removable calibration unit (PROM) that is programmed to tailor the ECM/PCM for the particular vehicle. There is a specific ECM/PCM—PROM combination for each specific vehicle, and the combinations are not interchangeable with those of other vehicles.

The ECM/PCM also performs the diagnostic function of the system. It can recognize operational problems, alert the driver through the SERVICE ENGINE SOON light, and store a code or codes which identify the problem areas to aid the in making repairs.

➡**Instead of an edgeboard connector, newer ECM/PCM's have a header connector which attaches solidly to the ECM/PCM case. Like the edgeboard connectors, the header connectors have a different pinout identification for different engine designs.**

The ECM/PCM consists of 3 parts, a Controller (the ECM/PCM without a PROM), a Calibrator called a PROM (Programmable Read Only Memory) and a Cal-Pak.

PROM

To allow 1 model of the ECM/PCM to be used for many different vehicles, a device called a Calibrator (or PROM) is used. The PROM is located inside the ECM/PCM and has information on the vehicle's weight, engine, transaxle, axle ratio and other components.

While one ECM/PCM part number can be used by many different vehicles, a PROM is very specific and must be used for the right vehicle. For this reason, it is very important to check the latest parts book and or service bulletin information for the correct PROM part number when replacing the PROM.

An ECM/PCM used for service (called a controller) comes without a PROM. The PROM from the old ECM/PCM must be carefully removed and installed in the new ECM/PCM.

Cal-Pak

▶ See Figure 25

A device called a Cal-Pak is added to allow fuel delivery if other parts of the ECM/PCM are damaged. It has an access door in the ECM/PCM, and removal

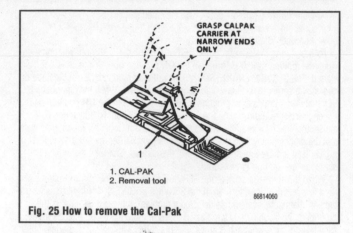

1. CAL-PAK
2. Removal tool

86814060

Fig. 25 How to remove the Cal-Pak

and replacement procedures are the same as with the PROM. If the Cal-Pak is missing, a Code 52 will be set. Not all vehicles with MFI/SFI are equipped with a Cal-Pak.

Mem-Cal

This assembly contains the functions of the PROM Cal-Pak and the ESC module used on other GM applications. Like the PROM, it contains the calibrations needed for a specific vehicle as well as the back-up fuel control circuitry required if the rest of the ECM becomes damaged or faulty.

Synchronized Mode

In synchronized mode operation, the injector is pulsed once for each distributor reference pulse.

Non-synchronized Mode

In non-synchronized mode operation, the injector is pulsed once every 12.5 milliseconds or 6.25 milliseconds depending on calibration. This pulse time is totally independent of distributor reference pulses. Non-synchronized mode results only under the following conditions:

1. The fuel pulse width is too small to be delivered accurately by the injector (approximately 1.5 milliseconds)
2. During the delivery of prime pulses (prime pulses charge the intake manifold with fuel during or just prior to engine starting)
3. During acceleration enrichment
4. During deceleration leanout

Starting Mode

When the engine is first turned **ON**, the ECM/PCM will turn on the fuel pump relay for 2 seconds and the fuel pump will build up pressure. The ECM/PCM then checks the coolant temperature sensor (ECT), throttle position sensor (TPS) and crank sensor, then the ECM/PCM determines the proper air/fuel ratio for starting. This ranges from 1.5:1 at −33°F (−36°C) to 14.7:1 at 201°F (94°C).

The ECM/PCM controls the amount of fuel that is delivered in the Starting Mode by changing how long the injectors are turned on and off. This is done by pulsing the injectors for very short times.

Clear Flood Mode

If for some reason the engine should become flooded, provisions have been made to clear this condition. To clear the flood, the driver must depress the accelerator pedal enough to position the throttle in its wide-open position. The ECM/PCM then issues a command to completely turn off the fuel flow. The ECM/PCM holds this operational mode as long as the throttle stays in the wide-open position and the engine rpm is below 600. If the throttle position becomes less than 62% (2.9mv) on MFI vehicles or 80% on SFI vehicles, the ECM/PCM returns to the starting mode.

Run Mode

There are 2 different run modes. When the engine is first started and the rpm is above 400, the system goes into Open Loop operation. In open loop operation, the ECM/PCM will ignore the signal from the oxygen sensor (O2S) and calculate the injector on-time based upon inputs from the coolant sensor (ECT), mass air flow (MAF) and mass air temperature (MAT) sensors.

During Open Loop operation, the ECM/PCM analyzes the following items to determine when the system is ready to go to the Closed Loop mode.

1. The oxygen sensor (O2S) varying voltage output showing that is hot enough to operate properly. This is dependent on temperature.

2. The coolant sensor (ECT) must be above specified temperature.

3. A specific amount of time must elapse after starting the engine. These values are stored in the PROM.

4. The engine speed is above 800 rpm since start up.

When these conditions have been met, the system goes into Closed Loop operation In Closed Loop operation, the ECM/PCM will calculate the air/fuel ratio (injector on time) based upon the signal from the oxygen sensor. The ECM/PCM will decrease the on-time if the air/fuel ratio is too rich, and will increase the on-time if the air/fuel ratio is too lean.

Acceleration Mode

When the engine is required to accelerate, the opening of the throttle valve(s) causes a rapid increase in Manifold Absolute Pressure (MAP). This rapid increase in MAP causes fuel to condense on the manifold walls. The ECM/PCM senses this increase in throttle angle and MAP, and supplies additional fuel for a short period of time. This prevents the engine from stumbling due to too lean a mixture.

Deceleration Mode

Upon deceleration, a leaner fuel mixture is required to reduce emission of hydrocarbons (HC) and carbon monoxide (CO). To adjust the injection on-time, the ECM/PCM uses the decrease in MAP and the decrease in throttle position to calculate a decrease in injector on time. To maintain an idle fuel ratio of 14.7:1, fuel output is momentarily reduced. This is done because of the fuel remaining in the intake manifold. The ECM/PCM can cut off the fuel completely for short periods of time.

Battery Voltage Correction Mode

The purpose of battery voltage correction is to compensate for variations in battery voltage to fuel pump and injector response. The ECM/PCM compensates by increasing the engine idle rpm.

Battery voltage correction takes place in all operating modes. When battery voltage is low, the spark delivered by the distributor may be low. To correct this low battery voltage problem, the ECM/PCM can do any or all of the following:

• Increase injector on time (increase fuel)
• Increase idle rpm
• Increase ignition dwell time

Fuel Cut-off Mode

When the ignition is **OFF**, no fuel will be delivered by the injectors. Fuel will also be cut off if the ECM/PCM does not receive a reference pulse from the distributor. To prevent dieseling, fuel delivery is completely stopped as soon as the engine is stopped. The ECM/PCM will not allow any fuel supply until it receives distributor reference pulses which prevents flooding.

Converter Protection Mode

In this mode the ECM/PCM estimates the temperature of the catalytic converter and then modifies fuel delivery to protect the converter from high temperatures. When the ECM/PCM has determined that the converter may overheat, it will cause open loop operation and will enrich the fuel delivery. A slightly richer mixture will then cause the converter temperature to be reduced.

Fuel Backup Mode

The ECM/PCM functions in the fuel backup circuit mode if any one, or any combination, of the following exist:

• The ECM/PCM voltage is lower than 9 volts.
• The cranking voltage is below 9 volts.
• The PROM is missing or not functioning.
• The ECM/PCM circuit fails to insure the computer operating pulse. The computer operating pulse (COP) is an internal ECM/PCM feature designed to inform the fuel backup circuit that the ECM/PCM is able to function.

Some engines run erratically in the fuel backup mode, while others seemed to run very well. Code 52 will be set to indicate a missing Cal-Pak. The fuel backup circuit is ignition fed and senses Throttle Position Sensor (TPS), Engine Coolant Temperature Sensor (ECT) and rpm. The fuel backup circuit controls the fuel pump relay and the pulse width of the injectors. Some vehicles have this mode, not all.

Data Link Connector (DLC/ALDL)

The Data Link Connector (DLC) or Assembly Line Data Link (ALDL), is a diagnostic connector located in the passenger compartment, usually under the instrument panel.

The assembly plant were the vehicles originate use these connectors to check the engine for proper operation before it leaves the plant. Vehicles with the ALDL system, enter the Diagnostic mode or the Field Service Mode by connecting or jumping terminal B, the diagnostic TEST terminal to terminal A, or ground circuit. Vehicles with the check connector, connect or jump terminal TE1, the diagnostic TEST terminal to terminal E1, or ground circuit. This connector is a very useful tool in diagnosing fuel injected engines. Important information from the ECM/PCM is available at this terminal and can be read with one of the many popular scanner tools.

FUEL CONTROL SYSTEM

The fuel control system is made up of the following components:
• Fuel supply system
• Throttle body assembly
• Fuel injectors
• Fuel rail
• Fuel pressure regulator
• Idle Air Control (IAC)
• Fuel pump
• Fuel pump relay
• Inline fuel filter

The fuel control system starts with the fuel in the fuel tank. An electric fuel pump, located in the fuel tank with the fuel gauge sending unit, pumps fuel to the fuel rail through an in-line fuel filter. The pump is designed to provide fuel at a pressure above the pressure needed by the injectors. A pressure regulator in the fuel rail keeps fuel available to the injectors at a constant pressure. Unused fuel is returned to the fuel tank by a separate line.

In order for the fuel injectors to supply a precise amount of fuel at the command of the ECM/PCM, the fuel supply system maintains a constant pressure drop of approximately 41–47 psi (284–325 kPa) across the injectors. As manifold vacuum changes, the fuel system pressure regulator controls the fuel supply pressure to compensate. On the MFI vehicles the fuel is supplied at the same time in a pulse injection timing, on the SFI vehicles the fuel is supplied in the order of the timing. The fuel pressure accumulator used on select models, isolates fuel line noise. The fuel rail is bolted rigidly to the engine and it provides the upper mount for the fuel injectors. It also contains a spring loaded pressure tap for testing the fuel system or relieving the fuel system pressure.

The injectors are controlled by the ECM/PCM. They deliver fuel in one of several modes as previously described. In order to properly control the fuel supply, the fuel pump is operated by the ECM/PCM through the fuel pump relay and oil pressure switch.

Throttle Body Unit

▶ See Figure 26

The throttle body unit has a throttle valve to control the amount of air delivered to the engine. The TPS and IAC valve are also mounted onto the throttle body. The throttle body contains vacuum ports located at, above or below the throttle valve. These vacuum ports generate the vacuum signals needed by various components.

On some vehicles, the engine coolant is directed through the coolant cavity at the bottom of the throttle body to warm the throttle valve and prevent icing.

Fuel Injector

▶ See Figure 27

A fuel injector is installed in the intake manifold at each cylinder. Mounting is approximately 3–4 in. (7.5–10mm) from the center line of the intake valve on

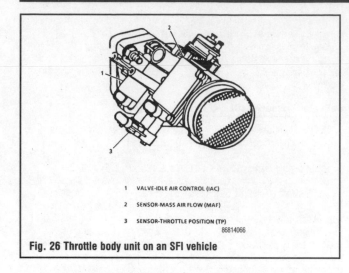

1 VALVE-IDLE AIR CONTROL (IAC)

2 SENSOR-MASS AIR FLOW (MAF)

3 SENSOR-THROTTLE POSITION (TP)

86814066

Fig. 26 Throttle body unit on an SFI vehicle

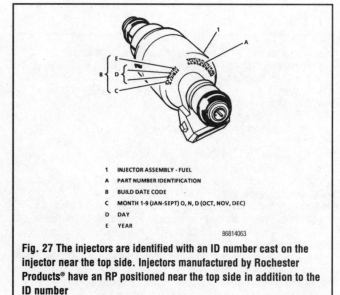

1 INJECTOR ASSEMBLY - FUEL

A PART NUMBER IDENTIFICATION

B BUILD DATE CODE

C MONTH 1-9 (JAN-SEPT) O, N, D (OCT, NOV, DEC)

D DAY

E YEAR

86814063

Fig. 27 The injectors are identified with an ID number cast on the injector near the top side. Injectors manufactured by Rochester Products® have an RP positioned near the top side in addition to the ID number

the V6 and the V8 engine applications. The nozzle spray pattern is on a 25 degree angle. The fuel injector is a solenoid operated device controlled by the ECM/PCM. The ECM/PCM turns on the solenoid, which opens the valve which allows fuel delivery. The fuel, under pressure, is injected in a conical spray pattern at the opening of the intake valve. The fuel, which is not used by the injectors, passes through the pressure regulator before returning to the fuel tank.

An injector that is partly open, will cause loss of fuel pressure after the engine is shut down, so long crank time would be noticed on some engines. Also, dieseling could occur because some fuel could be delivered after the ignition is turned to **OFF** position.

There are 2 O-ring seals used. The lower O-ring seals the injector at the intake manifold. The O-rings are lubricated and should be replaced whenever the injector is removed from the intake manifold. The O-rings provide thermal insulation, thus preventing the formation of vapor bubbles and promoting good hot start characteristics. The O-rings also prevent excess injector vibration.

Air leakage at the injector/intake area would create a lean cylinder and a possible driveability problem. A second seal is used to seal the fuel injector at the fuel rail connection. The injectors are identified with an ID number cast on the injector near the top side. Injectors manufactured by Rochester® Products have an **RP** positioned near the top side in addition to the ID number.

Fuel Rail

▶ See Figure 28

The fuel rail is bolted rigidly to the engine and it provides the upper mount for the fuel injectors. It distributes fuel to the individual injectors. Fuel is deliv-

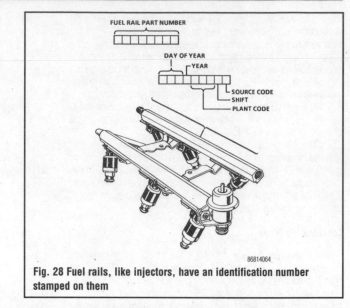

FUEL RAIL PART NUMBER

DAY OF YEAR

YEAR

SOURCE CODE

SHIFT

PLANT CODE

86814064

Fig. 28 Fuel rails, like injectors, have an identification number stamped on them

ered to the input end of the fuel rail by the fuel lines, goes through the rail, then to the fuel pressure regulator. The regulator keeps the fuel pressure to the injectors at a constant pressure. The remaining fuel is then returned to the fuel tank. The fuel rail also contains a spring loaded pressure tap for testing the fuel system or relieving the fuel system pressure.

Pressure Regulator

▶ See Figure 29

The fuel pressure regulator contains a pressure chamber separated by a diaphragm relief valve assembly with a calibrated spring in the vacuum chamber

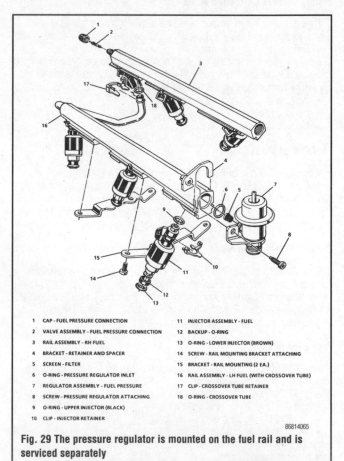

1 CAP - FUEL PRESSURE CONNECTION

2 VALVE ASSEMBLY - FUEL PRESSURE CONNECTION

3 RAIL ASSEMBLY - RH FUEL

4 BRACKET - RETAINER AND SPACER

5 SCREEN - FILTER

6 O-RING - PRESSURE REGULATOR INLET

7 REGULATOR ASSEMBLY - FUEL PRESSURE

8 SCREW - PRESSURE REGULATOR ATTACHING

9 O-RING - UPPER INJECTOR (BLACK)

10 CLIP - INJECTOR RETAINER

11 INJECTOR ASSEMBLY - FUEL

12 BACKUP - O-RING

13 O-RING - LOWER INJECTOR (BROWN)

14 SCREW - RAIL MOUNTING BRACKET ATTACHING

15 BRACKET - RAIL MOUNTING (2 EA.)

16 RAIL ASSEMBLY - LH FUEL (WITH CROSSOVER TUBE)

17 CLIP - CROSSOVER TUBE RETAINER

18 O-RING - CROSSOVER TUBE

86814065

Fig. 29 The pressure regulator is mounted on the fuel rail and is serviced separately

side. The fuel pressure is regulated when the pump pressure acting on the bottom spring of the diaphragm overcomes the force of the spring action on the top side.

The diaphragm relief valve moves, opening or closing an orifice in the fuel chamber to control the amount of fuel returned to the fuel tank. Vacuum acting on the top side of the diaphragm along with spring pressure controls the fuel pressure. A decrease in vacuum creates an increase in the fuel pressure. An increase in vacuum creates a decrease in fuel pressure.

An example of this is under heavy load conditions the engine requires more fuel flow. The vacuum decreases under a heavy load condition because of the throttle opening. A decrease in the vacuum allows more fuel pressure to the top side of the pressure relief valve, thus increasing the fuel pressure.

The pressure regulator is mounted on the fuel rail and serviced separately. If the pressure is too low, poor performance could result. If the pressure is too high, excessive odor and a Code 45 may result.

Idle Air Control (IAC)

The purpose of the Idle Air Control (IAC) system is to control engine idle speeds while preventing stalls due to changes in engine load. The IAC assembly, mounted on the throttle body, controls bypass air around the throttle plate. By extending or retracting a conical valve, a controlled amount of air can move around the throttle plate. If rpm is too low, more air is diverted around the throttle plate to increase rpm.

During idle, the proper position of the IAC valve is calculated by the ECM/PCM based on battery voltage, coolant temperature, engine load, and engine rpm. If the rpm drops below a specified rate, the throttle plate is closed. The ECM/PCM will then calculate a new valve position.

Three different designs are used for the IAC conical valve. The first design used is single taper while the second design used is a dual taper. The third design is a blunt valve. Care should be taken to insure use of the correct design when service replacement is required.

The IAC motor has 255 different positions or steps. The zero, or reference position, is the fully extended position at which the pintle is seated in the air bypass seat and no air is allowed to bypass the throttle plate. When the motor is fully retracted, maximum air is allowed to bypass the throttle plate. When the motor is fully retracted, maximum air is allowed to bypass the throttle plate.

The ECM/PCM always monitors how many steps it has extended or retracted the pintle from the zero or reference position thus, it always calculates the exact position of the motor. Once the engine has started and the vehicle has reached approximately 40 mph, the ECM/PCM will extend the motor 255 steps from whatever position it is in. This will bottom out the pintle against the seat. The ECM/PCM will call this position **0** and thus keep its zero reference updated.

The IAC only affects the engine's idle characteristics. If it is stuck fully open, idle speed is too high (too much air enters the throttle bore) If it is stuck closed, idle speed is too low (not enough air entering). If it is stuck somewhere in the middle, idle may be rough, and the engine won't respond to load changes.

Fuel Pump

The fuel is supplied to the system from an in-tank positive displacement roller vane pump. The pump supplies fuel through the in-line fuel filter to the fuel rail assembly. The pump is removed for service along with the fuel gauge sending unit. Once they are removed from the fuel tank, they pump and sending unit can be serviced separately.

Fuel pressure is achieved by rotation of the armature driving the roller vane components. The impeller at the inlet end serves as a vapor separator and a precharger for the roller vane assembly.

The fuel pump delivers more fuel than the engine can consume even under the most extreme conditions. Excess fuel flows through the pressure regulator and back to the tank via the return line. The constant flow of fuel means that the fuel system is always supplied with cool fuel, thereby preventing the formation of fuel-vapor bubbles (vapor lock).

Fuel Pump Relay Circuit

The fuel pump relay is usually located on the right or left front inner fender (or shock tower) or on the engine side of the firewall (center cowl). The fuel pump electrical system consists of the fuel pump relay, ignition circuit and the ECM/PCM circuits are protected by a fuse. The fuel pump relay contact switch is in the normally open (NO) position.

When the ignition is turned **ON** the ECM/PCM will for 2 seconds, supply voltage to the fuel pump relay coil, closing the open contact switch. The ignition circuit fuse can now supply ignition voltage to the circuit which feeds the relay contact switch. With the relay contacts closed, ignition voltage is supplied to the fuel pump. The ECM/PCM will continue to supply voltage to the relay coil circuit as long as the ECM/PCM receives the rpm reference pulses from the ignition module.

The fuel pump control circuit also includes an engine oil pressure switch with a set of normally open contacts. The switch closes at approximately 4 lbs. of oil pressure and provides a secondary battery feed path to the fuel pump. If the relay fails, the pump will continue to run using the battery feed supplied by the closed oil pressure switch. A failed fuel pump relay will result in extended engine crank times in order to build up enough oil pressure to close the switch and turn on the fuel pump.

In-Line Fuel Filter

The fuel filter is of a 10–20 micron size and is serviced only as a complete unit. O-rings are used at all threaded connections to prevent fuel leakage. The threaded flex hoses connect the filter to the fuel tank feed line.

SENSORS

A variety of sensors provide information to the ECM/PCM regarding engine operating characteristics. These sensors and their functions are described below. Be sure to take note that not every sensor described is used with every GM engine application.

Electronic Spark Timing (EST)

Electronic spark timing (EST) is used on all engines equipped with HEI distributors and direct ignition systems. The EST distributor contains no vacuum or centrifugal advance and uses a 7-terminal distributor module. It also has 4 wires going to a 4-terminal connector in addition to the connectors normally found on HEI distributors. A reference pulse, indicating both engine rpm and crankshaft position, is sent to the ECM/PCM. The ECM/PCM determines the proper spark advance for the engine operating conditions and sends an **EST** pulse to the distributor.

The EST system is designed to optimize spark timing for better control of exhaust emissions and for fuel economy improvements. The ECM/PCM monitors information from various engine sensors, computes the desired spark timing and changes the timing accordingly. A backup spark advance system is incorporated in the module in case of EST failure.

The basic function of the fuel control system is to control the fuel delivery to the engine. The fuel is delivered to the engine by individual fuel injectors mounted on the intake manifold near each cylinder.

The main control sensor is the oxygen sensor which is located in the exhaust manifold. The oxygen sensor tells the ECM/PCM how much oxygen is in the exhaust gas and the ECM/PCM changes the air/fuel ratio to the engine by controlling the fuel injectors. The best mixture (ratio) to minimize exhaust emissions is 14.7:1 which allows the catalytic converter to operate the most efficiently. Because of the constant measuring and adjusting of the air/fuel ratio, the fuel injection system is called a **CLOSED LOOP** system.

➡Whenever the term Electronic Control Module (ECM) is used in this manual, it refers to the engine control computer, regardless of whether it is a Powertrain Control Module (PCM) or Electronic Control Module (ECM).

Electronic Spark Control (ESC)

When engines are equipped with ESC in conjunction with EST, ESC is used to reduce spark advance under conditions of detonation. A knock sensor signals a separate ESC controller to retard the timing when it senses knock. The ESC controller signals the ECM/PCM which reduces spark advance until no more signals are received from the knock sensor.

Engine Coolant Temperature (ECT)

▶ See Figure 30

The coolant sensor is a thermister (a resistor which changes value based on temperature) mounted on the engine coolant stream. As the temperature of the engine coolant changes, the resistance of the coolant sensor changes. Low

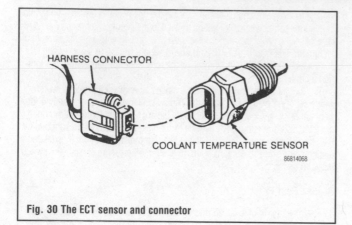

HARNESS CONNECTOR

COOLANT TEMPERATURE SENSOR

86814068

Fig. 30 The ECT sensor and connector

coolant temperature produces a high resistance (100,000 ohms at −40°C/−40°F), while high temperature causes low resistance (70 ohms at 130°C/266°F).

The ECM/PCM supplies a 5 volt signal to the coolant sensor and measures the voltage that returns. By measuring the voltage change, the ECM/PCM determines the engine coolant temperature. The voltage will be high when the engine is cold and low when the engine is hot. This information is used to control fuel management, IAC, spark timing, EGR, canister purge and other engine operating conditions.

A failure in the coolant sensor circuit should either set a Code 14 or 15 on MFI and P0117 or P0118 on SFI. These codes indicate a failure in the coolant temperature sensor circuit. Once the trouble code is set, the ECM/PCM will use a default valve for engine coolant temperature.

Intake Air Temperature (IAT)

The Intake Air Temperature Sensor (IAT) is a thermister which changes the value based on the temperature of air entering the engine. A low temperature produces a high resistance, while a low temperature causes a low resistance. The ECM/PCM supplies a 5 volt signal to the sensor through a resister in the ECM/PCM, then measures the voltage. A failure in the IAT sensor could result in a Code of P0112 or P0113 in the SFI and Codes 23 or 25 in the MFI. The Manifold Air Temperature (MAT) Sensor is another name for the IAT sensor.

Oxygen (O₂S)

◆ **See Figure 31**

The exhaust oxygen sensor is mounted in the exhaust system where it can monitor the oxygen content of the exhaust gas stream. The oxygen content in the exhaust reacts with the oxygen sensor to produce a voltage output. This voltage ranges from approximately 100 millivolts (high oxygen—lean mixture) to 900 millivolts (low oxygen—rich mixture).

By monitoring the voltage output of the oxygen sensor, the ECM/PCM will determine what fuel mixture command to give to the injector (lean mixture = low voltage and a rich command, rich mixture = high voltage and a lean command).

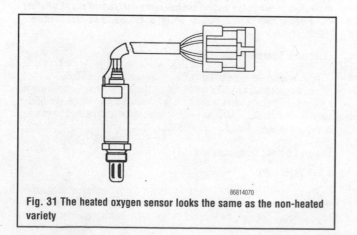

86814070

Fig. 31 The heated oxygen sensor looks the same as the non-heated variety

Remember that the oxygen sensor only indicates to the ECM/PCM what is happening in the exhaust. It does not cause things to happen. It is a type of gauge: high oxygen content = lean mixture; low oxygen content = rich mixture. The ECM/PCM adjusts fuel to keep the system working.

The oxygen sensor, if open, should set a Code 13. A constant low voltage in the sensor circuit should set a Code 44 in MFI and P0131 in SFI, while a constant high voltage in the circuit should set a Code 45 in MFI and P0132 or P0131 in SFI. Codes 44, 45, P0132 and P0131 could also be set as a result of fuel system problems. The oxygen sensor on MFI vehicles is not heated, but it is heated on SFI vehicles.

Manifold Absolute Pressure (MAP)

The Manifold Absolute Pressure (MAP) sensor measures the changes in the intake manifold pressure which result from engine load and speed changes. The pressure measured by the MAP sensor is the difference between barometric pressure (outside air) and manifold pressure (vacuum). A closed throttle engine coastdown would produce a relatively low MAP value (approximately 20–35 kPa), while wide-open throttle would produce a high value (100 kPa). This high value is produced when the pressure inside the manifold is the same as outside the manifold, and 100% of outside air (or 100 kPa) is being measured. This MAP output is the opposite of what you would measure on a vacuum gauge. The use of this sensor also allows the ECM/PCM to adjust automatically for different altitude.

The ECM/PCM sends a 5 volt reference signal to the MAP sensor. As the MAP changes, the electrical resistance of the sensor also changes. By monitoring the sensor output voltage the ECM/PCM can determine the manifold pressure. A higher pressure, lower vacuum (high voltage) requires more fuel, while a lower pressure, higher vacuum (low voltage) requires less fuel. The ECM/PCM uses the MAP sensor to control fuel delivery and ignition timing. A failure in the MAP sensor circuit should set a Code 33 or Code 34.

Manifold Air Temperature (MAT)

The Manifold Air Temperature (MAT) sensor also known as the IAT sensor, is a thermistor mounted in the intake manifold. A thermistor is a resistor which changes resistance based on temperature. Low manifold air temperature produces a high resistance (100,000 ohms at -40°F/-4°C), while high temperature cause low resistance (70 ohms at 266°F/130°C).

The ECM/PCM supplies a 5 volt signal to the MAT sensor through a resistor in the ECM/PCM and monitors the voltage. The voltage will be high when the manifold air is cold and low when the air is hot. By monitoring the voltage, the ECM calculates the air temperature and uses this data to help determine the fuel delivery and spark advance. A failure in the MAT or IAT sensor could result in Codes P0112 or P0113 for SFI vehicles and Codes 23 or 25 for MFI vehicles. Once the trouble code is set, the ECM/PCM will use an artificial default value for the MAT and some vehicle performance will return.

Mass Air Flow (MAF)

The Mass Air Flow (MAF) sensor measures the amount of air which passes through it. The ECM/PCM uses this information to determine the operating condition of the engine, to control fuel delivery. A large quantity of air indicates acceleration, while a small quantity indicates deceleration or idle.

This sensor produces a frequency output between 32 and 150 hertz. A scan tool will display air flow in terms of grams of air per second (gm/sec), with a range from 3gm/sec to 150 gm/sec. A failure in the MAF sensor could produce a Code of P0101 for SFI vehicles.

Vehicle Speed

➡**A vehicle equipped with a speed sensor, should not be driven without a the speed sensor connected, as idle quality may be affected.**

The Vehicle Speed Sensor (VSS) is mounted behind the speedometer in the instrument cluster or on the transaxle/speedometer drive gear. It provides electrical pulses to the ECM/PCM from the speedometer head. The pulses indicate the road speed. The ECM/PCM uses this information to operate the IAC, canister purge, and TCC.

Some vehicles equipped with digital instrument clusters use a Permanent Magnet (PM) generator to provide the VSS signal. The PM generator is located in the transaxle and replaces the speedometer cable. The signal from the PM generator drives a stepper motor which drives the odometer. A failure in the VSS circuit should set a Code 24 for MFI vehicles and Code P0502 for SFI vehicles.

Throttle Position (TPS)

The Throttle Position Sensor (TPS) is connected to the throttle shaft and is controlled by the throttle mechanism. A 5 volt reference signal is sent to the TPS from the ECM/PCM. As the throttle valve angle is changed (accelerator pedal moved), the resistance of the TPS also changes. At a closed throttle position, the resistance of the TPS is high, so the output voltage to the ECM/PCM will be low (approximately 0.5 volt). As the throttle plate opens, the resistance decreases so that, at wide open throttle, the output voltage should be approximately 5 volts. At closed throttle position, the voltage at the TPS should be less than 1.25 volts.

By monitoring the output voltage from the TPS, the ECM/PCM can determine fuel delivery based on throttle valve angle (driver demand). The TPS can either be misadjusted, shorted, open or loose. Misadjustment might result in poor idle or poor wide-open throttle performance. An open TPS signals the ECM/PCM that the throttle is always closed, resulting in poor performance. This usually sets a Code 22 for MFI vehicles. A shorted TPS gives the ECM/PCM a constant wide-open throttle signal and should set a Code 21 on MFI vehicles. A loose TPS on MFI vehicles indicates to the ECM/PCM that the throttle is moving. This causes intermittent bursts of fuel from the injector and an unstable idle. Once the trouble code is set, the ECM/PCM will use an artificial default value for the TBI and some vehicle performance will return.

A problem in the 5 volt circuit of SFI vehicles should set off Codes P0122 or P0123 and a problem with the TPS sensor ground circuit may set Codes P0123 and P0117. Once the DTC is set on SFI vehicles, the ECM/PCM will use an artificial default value based on the mass air flow for the TPS sensor and some vehicle performance will return. A high idle on SFI vehicles may result in Codes P0122 or P0123 to be set.

Crankshaft

Some systems use a magnetic crankshaft sensor, mounted remotely from the ignition module, which protrudes into the block within approximately 0.050 in. (0.127mm) of the crankshaft reluctor. The reluctor is a special wheel cast into the crankshaft with 7 slots machined into it, 6 of which are equally spaced (60 degrees apart). A seventh slot is spaced approximately 10 degrees from one of the other slots and severs to generate a **SYNC PULSE** signal. As the reluctor rotates as part of the crankshaft, the slots change the magnetic field of the sensor, creating an induced voltage pulse.

Based on the crank sensor pulses, the ignition module sends 2X reference signals to the ECM/PCM which are used to indicate crankshaft position and engine speed. The ignition module continues to send these reference pulses to the ECM at a rate of 1 per each 180 degrees of the crankshaft rotation. This signal is called the 2X reference because it occurs 2 times per crankshaft revolution.

The ignition also sends a second, 1X reference signal to the ECM/PCM which occurs at the same time as the **SYNC PULSE** from the crankshaft sensor. This signal is called the 1X reference because it occurs 1 time per crankshaft revolution. The 1X reference and the 2X reference signals are necessary for the ECM/PCM to determine when to activate the fuel injectors. Also known as the 3X Crankshaft Position Sensor.

By comparing the time between pulses, the ignition module can recognize the pulse representing the seventh slot (sync pulse) which starts the calculation of the ignition coil sequencing. The second crank pulse following the **SYNC PULSE** signals the ignition module to fire the No. 2–3 ignition coil and the fifth crank pulse signals the module to fire the No. 1–4 ignition coil.

24X Crankshaft Position Sensor

The 24X sensor is used to improve the idle spark control at engine speeds up to approximately 1200 rpm. Four 24X pulses to be seen between two 3X pulses. If the sequence of these pulses is not correct for 50 engine revolutions, the ECM/PCM will set off a Code of P0321.

Dual Crank/Combination

The dual crank sensor is mounted in a pedestal on the front of the engine near the harmonic balancer. The sensor consists of 2 Hall Effect switches, which depend on 2 metal interrupter rings mounted on the balancer to activate them. Windows in the interrupters activate the hall effect switches as they provide a patch for the magnetic field between the switches transducers and magnets.

When one of the hall effect switches is activated, it grounds the signal line to the C3I module, pulling that signal line's (Sync Pulse or Crank) applied voltage low, which is interpreted as a signal.

Because of the way the signal is created by the dual crank sensor, the signal circuit is always either at a high or low voltage (square wave signal). Three crank signal pulses and one **SYNC PULSE** are created during each crankshaft revolution. The crank signal is used by the C3I module to create a reference signal which is also a square wave signal similar to the crank signal. The reference signal is used to calculate the engine rpm and crankshaft position by the ECM/PCM. The **SYNC PULSE** is used by the C3I module to begin the ignition coil firing sequence starting with No. 3–6 coil. The firing sequence begins with this coil because either piston No. 3 or piston No. 6 is now at the correct position in compression stroke for the spark plugs to be fired. Both the crank sensor and the **SYNC PULSE** signals must be received by the ignition module for the engine to start. A misadjusted sensor or bent interrupter ring could cause rubbing of the sensor resulting in potential driveability problems, such as rough idle, poor performance, or a non start condition.

➡ **Failure to have the correct clearance will damage the crankshaft sensor.**

The dual crank sensor is not adjustable for ignition timing but positioning of the interrupter ring is very important. A clearance of 0.025 in. (0.635mm) is required on either side of the interrupter ring. A dual crank sensor that is damaged, due to mispositioning or a bent interrupter ring, can result in a hesitation, sag stumble or dieseling condition.

To determine if the dual crank sensor could be at fault, scan the engine rpm with a suitable scan tool, while driving the vehicle. An erratic display indicates that a proper reference pulse has not been received by the ECM/PCM, which may be the result of a malfunctioning dual crank sensor.

Air Conditioning Pressure

The air conditioning (A/C) pressure sensor provides a signal to the computer control module (ECM/PCM) which indicates varying high side refrigerant pressure between approximately 0–450 psi (0–3102 kPa). The ECM/PCM used this input to the A/C compressor load on the engine to help control the idle speed with the IAC valve.

The A/C pressure sensor electrical circuit consists of a 5 volt reference line and a ground line, both provided by the ECM/PCM and a signal line to the ECM/PCM. The signal is a voltage that varies approximately 0.1 volt at 0 psi (0 kPa), to 4.9 volts at 450 psi (3102 kPa) or more. A problem in the A/C pressure circuits or sensor should set a Code 66 on MFI vehicles and Code P1530 on SFI vehicles, then will make the A/C compressor inoperative.

Non-Air Conditioning Program Input

Vehicles not equipped with air conditioning (A/C) have a circuit connecting the ECM/PCM terminal BC3 to ground, to program to operate without A/C related components connected to it. Vehicles with A/C do not have a wire in ECM BC3 terminal. If this circuit is open on a non-A/C vehicle it may cause false Codes 26 and/or Code 66. If terminal BC3 is grounded on A/C equipped vehicles, it will cause the compressor relay to be on whenever the ignition is in the **ON** position.

Detonation (Knock)

◆ **See Figure 32**

This sensor is a piezoelectric sensor located near the back of the engine (transaxle end). It generates electrical impulses which are directly proportional to the frequency of the knock which is detected. A buffer then sorts these signals and eliminates all except for those frequency range of detonation. This information is passed to the ESC module and then to the ECM/PCM, so that the ignition timing advance can be retarded until the detonation stops.

SWITCHES

Park/Neutral Switch

➡ **Vehicle should not be driven with the park/neutral switch disconnected as idle quality may be affected in park or neutral and a Code 24 (VSS) may be set.**

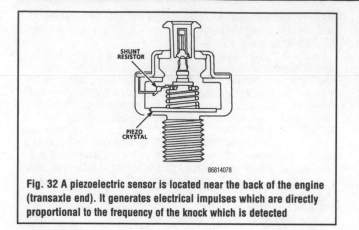

Fig. 32 A piezoelectric sensor is located near the back of the engine (transaxle end). It generates electrical impulses which are directly proportional to the frequency of the knock which is detected

This switch indicates to the ECM/PCM when the transaxle is in **P** or **N**. the information is used by the ECM/PCM for control on the torque converter clutch, EGR, and the idle air control valve operation.

Air Conditioning Request Signal

This signal indicates to the ECM/PCM that an air conditioning mode is selected at the switch and that the A/C low pressure switch is closed. The ECM/PCM controls the A/C and adjusts the idle speed in response to this signal.

Torque Converter Clutch Solenoid

◗ See Figure 33

The purpose of the torque converter clutch system is to eliminate power loss (slippage) by the converter and increase fuel economy. By locking the converter clutch, a more effective coupling to the flywheel is achieved. The converter clutch is operated by the ECM/PCM controlled torque converter clutch solenoid.

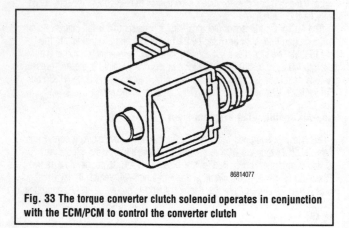

Fig. 33 The torque converter clutch solenoid operates in conjunction with the ECM/PCM to control the converter clutch

Power Steering Pressure Switch

The power steering pressure switch is used so that the power steering oil pressure pump load will not effect the engine idle. Turning the steering wheel increase the power steering oil pressure and pump load on the engine. The power steering pressure switch will close before the load can cause an idle problem. The ECM/PCM will also turn the A/C clutch off when high power steering pressure is detected.

Oil Pressure Switch

The oil pressure switch is usually mounted on the back of the engine, just below the intake manifold. Some vehicles use the oil pressure switch as a parallel power supply, with the fuel pump relay and will provide voltage to the fuel pump, after approximately 4 psi (28 kPa) of oil pressure is reached. This switch will also help prevent engine seizure by shutting off the power to the fuel pump and causing the engine to stop when the oil pressure is lower than 4 psi (28 kPa).

EMISSION CONTROL SYSTEMS

Various components are used to control exhaust emissions from a vehicle. These components are controlled by the ECM/PCM based on different engine operating conditions. These components are described in the following paragraphs. Not all components are used on all engines.

Exhaust Gas Recirculation (EGR) System

EGR is a oxides of nitrogen (NOx) control which recycles exhaust gases through the combustion cycle by admitting exhaust gases into the intake manifold. The amount of exhaust gas admitted is adjusted by a vacuum controlled valve in response to engine operating conditions. If the valve is open, the recirculated exhaust gas is released into the intake manifold to be drawn into the combustion chamber.

The integral exhaust pressure modulated EGR valve uses a transducer responsive to exhaust pressure to modulate the vacuum signal to the EGR valve. The vacuum signal is provided by an EGR vacuum port in the throttle body valve. Under conditions when exhaust pressure is lower than the control pressure, the EGR signal is reduced by an air bleed within the transducer. Under conditions when exhaust pressure is higher than the control pressure, the air bleed is closed and the EGR valve responds to an unmodified vacuum signal. Physical arrangement of the valve components will vary depending on whether the control pressure is positive or negative.

The newer models use what is called a digital EGR valve. The digital EGR valve is designed to accurately supply EGR to an engine, independently of the intake manifold vacuum. The valve controls EGR flow from the exhaust to the intake manifold through three orifices which increment in size to produce seven different combinations. When a solenoid is energized, the armature, with the attached shaft and swivel pintle is lifted, this opens the orifice. The flow accuracy is dependent on the metering orifice size only, which results in improved control.

The digital EGR is opened by the ECM/PCM QDM (quad driver), grounding each respective solenoid circuit. The EGR valve usually opens under certain conditions such as, a warm engine operation, and an above idle speed condition.

Positive Crankcase Ventilation (PCV) System

A closed Positive Crankcase Ventilation (PCV) system is used to provide more complete scavenging of crankcase vapors. Fresh air from the air cleaner is supplied to the crankcase, mixed with blow-by gases and then passed through a PCV valve into the induction system.

The primary mode of crankcase ventilation control is through the PCV valve, which meters the mixture of fresh air and blow-by gases into the induction system at a rate dependent upon manifold vacuum.

To maintain the idle quality, the PCV valve restricts the ventilation system flow whenever intake manifold vacuum is designed to allow excessive amounts of blow-by gases to backflow through the breather assembly into the air cleaner and through the throttle body to be consumed by normal combustion.

Evaporative Emission Control (EEC) Systems

The basic evaporative emission control system used on all vehicles uses the carbon canister storage method. This method transfers fuel vapor to an activated carbon storage device for retention when the vehicle is not operating. A ported vacuum signal is used for purging vapors stored in the canister.

CONTROLLED CANISTER PURGE

The ECM/PCM controls a solenoid valve which controls vacuum to the purge valve in the charcoal canister. In open loop, before a specified time has expired and below a specified rpm, the solenoid valve is energized and blocks vacuum to the purge valve. When the system is in closed loop, after a specified time and above a specified rpm, the solenoid valve is de-energized and vacuum can be applied to the purge valve. This releases the collected vapors into the intake manifold. On systems not using an ECM/PCM controlled solenoid, a Thermo Vacuum Valve (TVV) is used to control purge. See the appropriate vehicle sections for checking procedures.

Air Management Control

The air management system aids in the reduction of exhaust emissions by supplying air to either the catalytic converter, engine exhaust manifold, or to the air cleaner. The ECM/PCM controls the air management system by energizing or de-energizing an air switching valve. Operation of the air switching valve is dependent upon such engine operating characteristics as coolant temperature, engine load, and acceleration (or deceleration), all of which are sensed by the ECM/PCM.

PULSAIR REACTOR SYSTEM

The Pulsair Injection Reactor (PAIR) system utilizes exhaust pressure pulsations to draw air into the exhaust system. Fresh air from the clean side of the air cleaner supplies filtered air to avoid dirt build-up on the check valve seat. The air cleaner also serves as a muffler for noise reduction. The internal mechanism of the Pulsair valve reacts to 3 distinct conditions.

The firing of the engine creates a pulsating flow of exhaust gases which are of positive (+) or negative (-) pressure. This pressure or vacuum is transmitted through external tubes to the Pulsair valve.

1. If the pressure is positive, the disc is forced to the closed position and no exhaust gas is allowed to flow past the valve and into the air supply line.

2. If there is a negative pressure (vacuum) in the exhaust system at the valve, the disc will open, allowing fresh air to mix with the exhaust gases.

3. Due to the inertia of the system, the disc ceases to follow the pressure pulsations at high engine rpm. At this point, the disc remains closed, preventing any further fresh air flow.

Catalytic Convertor

Of all emission control devices available, the catalytic converter is the most effective in reducing tailpipe emissions. The major tailpipe pollutants are hydrocarbons (HC), carbon monoxide (CO), and oxides of nitrogen (NOx).

SERVICE PRECAUTIONS

When working around any part of the fuel system, take precautionary steps to prevent fire and/or explosion:
- Disconnect negative terminal from battery (except when testing with battery voltage is required).
- When ever possible, use a flashlight instead of a drop light.
- Keep all open flame and smoking material out of the area.
- Use a shop cloth or similar to catch fuel when opening a fuel system.
- Relieve fuel system pressure before servicing.
- Use eye protection.
- Always keep a dry chemical (class B) fire extinguisher near the area.

➡Due to the amount of fuel pressure in the fuel lines, before doing any work to the fuel system, the fuel system should be depressurized.

Electrostatic Discharge Damage

Electronic components used in the control system are often design to carry very low voltage and are very susceptible to damage caused by electrostatic discharge. It is possible for less than 100 volts of static electricity to cause damage to some electronic components. By comparison it takes as much as 4000 volts for a person to even feel the zap of a static discharge.

There are several ways for a person to become statically charged. The most common methods of charging are by friction and induction. An example of charging by friction is a person sliding across a car seat, in which a charge as much as 25,000 volts can build up. Charging by induction occurs when a person with well insulated shoes stands near a highly charged object and momentarily touches ground. Charges of the same polarity are drained off, leaving the person highly charged with the opposite polarity. Static charges of either type can cause damage, therefore, it is important to use care when handling and testing electronic components.

➡To prevent possible electrostatic discharge damage to the ECM/PCM, do not touch the connector pins or soldered components on the circuit board. When handling a PROM, Mem-Cal or Cal-Pak, do not touch the component leads and remove the integrated circuit from the carrier.

ECM/PCM LEARNING ABILITY

The ECM/PCM has a learning capability. If the battery is disconnected, the learning process has to begin all over again. A change may be noted in the vehicle's performance. To teach the ECM/PCM, insure the vehicle is at operating temperature and drive at part throttle, with moderate acceleration and idle conditions, until performance returns.

DLC/CHECK CONNECTOR

➧ See Figure 34

The Data Link Connector or Assembly Line Diagnostic Link (DLC/ALDL), is a diagnostic connector located usually under the instrument panel, it is sometimes covered by a plastic cover labeled "DIAGNOSTIC CONNECTOR." The assembly plant were the vehicles originate use these connectors to check the engine for proper operation before it leaves the plant. The connector can also be used by a technician to identify stored codes using different procedures and to read the ECM/PCM data using a hand held scan tool, such as TECH 1. Although it is recommended to use as hand held scan tool to read diagnostic trouble codes, it may be possible to flash codes on certain vehicle. These vehicles have a 12 pin DLC.

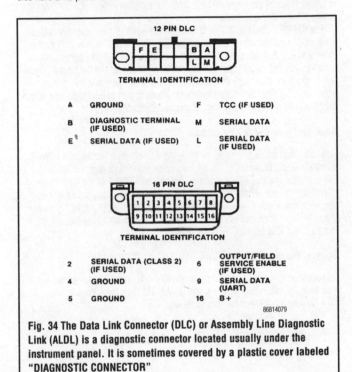

Fig. 34 The Data Link Connector (DLC) or Assembly Line Diagnostic Link (ALDL) is a diagnostic connector located usually under the instrument panel. It is sometimes covered by a plastic cover labeled "DIAGNOSTIC CONNECTOR"

READING CODES AND DIAGNOSTIC MODES

This information is able to be read by putting the ECM/PCM into 1 of 4 different modes. These modes are entered by inserting a specific amount of resistance between the DLC/ALDL connector terminals A and B. The modes and resistances needed to enter these modes are as follows:

Diagnostic Modes—0 Ohms

When 0 resistance is between terminals A and B of the DLC/ALDL connector, the diagnostic mode is entered. There are 2 positions to this mode. One with the engine OFF, but the ignition ON; the other is when the engine is running called Field Service Mode.

If the diagnostic mode is entered with the engine in the OFF position, trouble codes will flash and the idle air control motor will pulsate in and out. Also, the relays and solenoids are energized with the exception of the fuel pump and injector.

As a bulb and system check, the SERVICE ENGINE SOON light will come on with the ignition switch ON and the engine not running. When the engine is started, the SERVICE ENGINE SOON light will turn off. If the SERVICE ENGINE SOON light remains on, the self-diagnostic system has detected a problem.

If the B terminal is then grounded with the ignition ON, engine not running, each trouble code will flash and repeat 3 times. If more than 1 problem has been detected, each trouble code will flash 3 times. Trouble codes will flash in numeric order (lowest number first). The trouble code series will repeat as long as the B terminal is grounded.

A trouble code indicates a problem in a given circuit (Code 14, for example, indicates a problem in the coolant sensor circuit, this includes the coolant sensor, connector harness, and ECM/PCM). The procedure for pinpointing the problem can be found in diagnosis. Similar charts are provided for each code.

Also in this mode all ECM/PCM controlled relays and solenoids except the fuel pump relay. This allows checking the circuits which may be difficult to energize without driving the vehicle and being under particular operating conditions. The IAC valve will move to its fully extended position on most vehicles, block the idle air passage. This is useful in checking the minimum idle speed.

Field Service Mode—0 Ohms

When the DLC/ALDL connector terminal B is grounded with the engine running, the ECM/PCM goes into the field service mode. In this mode, the SERVICE ENGINE SOON light flashes closed or open loop and indicates the rich/lean status of the engine. The ECM/PCM runs the engine at a fixed ignition timing advanced above the base setting.

The SERVICE ENGINE SOON light will show whether the system is in Open Loop or Closed Loop. In Open Loop the SERVICE ENGINE SOON light flashes 2 times and one half times per second. In Closed Loop the light flashes once per second. Also in Closed Loop, the light will stay OUT most of the time if the system is too lean. It will stay ON most of the time if the system is too rich. In either case the Field Service mode check, which is part of the Diagnostic circuit check, will lead you into choosing the correct diagnostic chart to refer to.

Back-up Mode—3.9 Kilo-ohms

The backup mode is entered by applying 3.9 kilo-ohms resistance between terminals A and B of the DLC/ALDL connector with the ignition switch in the **ON** position. The DLC/ALDL scanner tool can now read 5 of the 20 parameters on the data stream. These parameters are as mode status, oxygen sensor voltage, rpm, block learn and idle air control. There are 2 ways to enter the backup mode. Using a scan tool is one way, putting a 3.9 kilo-ohms resistor across terminals A and B of the DLC/ALDL is another.

Special Mode—10 Kilo-ohms

This special mode is entered by applying a 10K ohms resistor across terminals A and B. When this happens, the ECM/PCM does the following:
- Allows all of the serial data to be read
- Bypasses all timers
- Adds a calibrated spark advance
- Enables the canister purge solenoid on some engines
- Idles at 1000 rpm fixed idle air control and fixed base pulse width on the injector
- Forces the idle air control to reset at part throttle (approximately 2000 rpm)
- Disables the Park/Neutral restriction functions

Open or Road Test Mode—20 Kilo-ohms

The system is in this mode during normal operation and is used by a scan tool to extract data while driving the vehicle.

DLC/ALDL Scan Tester Information

An DLC/ALDL display unit (DLC/ALDL tester, scanner, monitor, etc.), allows a you to read the engine control system information from the DLC/ALDL connector under the instrument panel. It can provide information faster than a digital voltmeter or ohmmeter can. The scan tool does not diagnose the exact location of the problem. The tool supplies information about the ECM/PCM, the information that it is receiving and the commands that it is sending plus special information such as integrator and block learn. To use an DLC/ALDL display tool you should understand thoroughly how an engine control system operates.

An DLC/ALDL scanner or monitor puts a fuel injection system into a special test mode. This mode commands an idle speed of 1000 rpm. The idle quality cannot be evaluated with a tester plugged in. When a scanner is in a special test mode it commands a fixed spark with no advance. On vehicles with Electronic Spark Control (ESC), there will be a fixed spark, but it will be advanced. On vehicles with ESC, there might be a serious spark knock, this spark knock could be bad enough so as not being able to road test the vehicle in the DLC/ALDL test mode. Be sure to check the tool manufacturer for instructions on special test modes which should overcome these limitations.

When a tester is used with a fuel injected engine, it bypasses the timer that keeps the system in Open Loop for a certain period of time. When all Closed Loop conditions are met, the engine will go into Closed Loop as soon as the vehicle is started. This means that the air management system will not function properly and air may go directly to the converter as soon as the engine is started.

These tools cannot diagnose everything. They do not tell where a problem is located in a circuit. The diagnostic charts to pinpoint the problems must still be used. These testers do not let you know if a solenoid or relay has been turned on. They only tell the you the ECM/PCM command. To find out if a solenoid has been turned on, check it with a suitable test light or digital voltmeter, or see if vacuum through the solenoid changes.

Scan Tools For Intermittents

In some scan tool applications, the data update rate may make the tool less effective than a voltmeter, such as when trying to detect an intermittent problem which lasts for a very short time. Some scan tools have a snapshot function which stores several seconds or even minutes of operation to located an intermittent problem. Scan tools allow one to manipulate the wiring harness or components under the hood with the engine not running while observing the scan tool's readout.

The scan tool can be plugged in and observed while driving the vehicle under the condition when the SERVICE ENGINE SOON light turns on momentarily or when the engine driveability is momentarily poor. If the problem seems to be related to certain parameters that can be checked on the scan tool, they should be checked while driving the vehicle. If there does not seem to be any correlation between the problem and any specific circuit, the scan tool can be checked on each position. Watching for a period of time to see if there is any change in the reading that indicates intermittent operation.

The scan tool is also an easy way to compare the operating parameters of a poorly operating engine with typical scan data for the vehicle being serviced or those of a known good engine. For example, a sensor may shift in value but not set a trouble code. Comparing the sensor's reading with those of a known good parameters may uncover the problem.

The scan tool has the ability to save time in diagnosis and prevent the replacement of good parts. The key to using the scan tool successfully for diagnosis lies in the ability to understand the system being diagnosed, as well as the scan tool's operation and limitations.

CLEARING TROUBLE CODES

When the ECM/PCM detects a problem with the system, the SERVICE ENGINE SOON light will come on and a trouble code will be recorded in the ECM/PCM memory. If the problem is intermittent, the SERVICE ENGINE SOON light will go out after 10 seconds, when the fault goes away. However the trouble code will stay in the ECM/PCM memory until the battery voltage to the ECM/PCM is removed. Removing the battery voltage for 10 seconds will clear all trouble codes. Do this by disconnecting the ECM/PCM harness from the positive battery terminal pigtail for 10 seconds with the key in the **OFF** position, or by removing the ECM/PCM fuse for 10 seconds with the key **OFF**.

➡**To prevent ECM/PCM damage, the key must be OFF when disconnecting and reconnecting ECM/PCM power.**

INTEGRATOR AND BLOCK LEARN

The integrator and block learn functions of the ECM/PCM are responsible for making minor adjustments to the air/fuel ratio on the fuel injected GM vehicles. These small adjustments are necessary to compensate for pinpoint air leaks and normal wear.

The integrator and block learn are 2 separate ECM/PCM memory functions which control fuel delivery. The integrator makes a temporary change and the block learn makes a more permanent change. Both of these functions apply only while the engine is in Closed Loop. They represent the on-time of the injector. Also, integrator and block learn controls fuel delivery on the fuel injected engines as does the MC solenoid dwell on the CCC carbureted engines.

Integrator

Integrator is the term applied to a means of temporary change in fuel delivery. Integrator is displayed through the DLC/ALDL data line and monitored with a scanner as a number between 0 and 255 with an average of 128. The integrator monitors the oxygen sensor output voltage and adds and subtracts fuel depending on the lean or rich condition of the oxygen sensor. When the integrator is displaying 128, it indicates a neutral condition. This means that the oxygen sensor is seeing results of the 14.7:1 air/fuel mixture burned in the cylinders.

→An air leak in the system (a lean condition) would cause the oxygen sensor voltage to decrease while the integrator would increase (add more fuel) to temporarily correct for the lean condition. If this happened the injector pulse width would increase.

Block Learn

Although the integrator can correct fuel delivery over a wide range, it is only for a temporary correction. Therefore, another control called block learn was added. Although it cannot make as many corrections as the integrator, it does so for a longer period of time. It gets its name from the fact that the operating range of the engine for any given combinations of rpm and load is divided into 16 cell or blocks.

The computer has a given fuel delivery stored in each block. As the operating range gets into a given block the fuel delivery will be based on what value is stored in the memory in that block. Again, just like the integrator, the number represents the on-time of the injector. Also, just like the integrator, the number 128 represents no correction to the value that is stored in the cell or block. When the integrator increases or decreases, block learn which is also watching the integrator will make corrections in the same direction. As the block learn makes corrections, the integrator correction will be reduced until finally the integrator will return to 128 if the block learn has corrected the fuel delivery.

Block Learn Memory

Block learn operates on 1 of 2 types of memories depending on application: non-volatile or volatile. The non-volatile memories retain the value in the block learn cells even when the ignition switch is turned **OFF**. When the engine is restarted, the fuel delivery for a given block will be based on information stored in memory.

The volatile memories lose the numbers stored in the block learn cells when the ignition is turned to the **OFF** position. Upon restarting, the block learn starts at 128 in every block and corrects from that point as necessary.

Integrator/Block Learn Limits

Both the integrator and block learn have limits which will vary from engine to engine. If the mixture is off enough so that the block learn reaches the limit of its control and still cannot correct the condition, the integrator would also go to its limit of control in the same direction and the engine would then begin to run poorly. If the integrators and block learn are close to or at their limits of control, the engine hardware should be checked to determine the cause of the limits being reached, vacuum leaks, sticking injectors, etc.

If the integrator is lied to, for example, if the oxygen sensor lead was grounded (lean signal) the integrator and block learn would add fuel to the engine to cause it to run rich. However, with the oxygen sensor lead grounded, the ECM/PCM would continue seeing a lean condition eventually setting a Code 44 and the fuel control system would change to open loop operations.

CLOSED LOOP FUEL CONTROL

The purpose of closed loop fuel control is to precisely maintain an air/fuel mixture 14.7:1. When the air/fuel mixture is maintained at 14.7:1, the catalytic converter is able to operate at maximum efficiency which results in lower emission levels.

Since the ECM/PCM controls the air/fuel mixture, it needs to check its output and correct the fuel mixture for deviations from the ideal ratio. The oxygen sensor feeds this output information back to the ECM/PCM.

ENGINE PERFORMANCE DIAGNOSIS

Engine performance diagnostic procedures are guides that will lead to the most probable causes of engine performance complaints. They consider the components of the fuel, ignition, and mechanical systems that could cause a particular complaint, and then outline repairs in a logical sequence.

It is important to determine if the SERVICE ENGINE SOON light is on or has come on for a short interval while driving. If the SERVICE ENGINE SOON light has come on, the Computer Command Control System should be checked for stored **TROUBLE CODES** which may indicate the cause for the performance complaint.

All of the symptoms can be caused by worn out or defective parts such as spark plugs, ignition wiring, etc. If time and/or mileage indicate that parts should be replaced, it is recommended that it be done.

→Before checking any system controlled by the Electronic Fuel Injection (EFI) system, the Diagnostic Circuit Check must be performed or misdiagnosis may occur. If the complaint involves the SERVICE ENGINE SOON light, go directly to the Diagnostic Circuit Check.

Basic Troubleshooting

→The following explains how to activate the trouble code signal light in the instrument cluster and gives an explanation of what each code means. This is not a full system troubleshooting and isolation procedure.

Before suspecting the system or any of its components as faulty, check the ignition system including distributor, timing, spark plugs and wires. Check the engine compression, air cleaner, and emission control components not controlled by the ECM/PCM. Also check the intake manifold, vacuum hoses and hose connectors for leaks.

The following symptoms could indicate a possible problem with the system:
- Detonation
- Stalls or rough idle-cold
- Stalls or rough idle-hot
- Missing
- Hesitation
- Surges
- Poor gasoline mileage
- Sluggish or spongy performance
- Hard starting-cold
- Objectionable exhaust odors (that rotten egg smell)
- Cuts out
- Improper idle speed

As a bulb and system check, the SERVICE ENGINE SOON light will come on when the ignition switch is turned to the **ON** position but the engine is not running. The SERVICE ENGINE SOON light will also produce the trouble code or codes by a series of flashes which translate as follows. When the diagnostic test terminal under the dash is grounded, with the ignition in the **ON** position and the engine not running, the SERVICE ENGINE SOON light will flash once, pause, then flash twice in rapid succession. This is a Code 12, which indicates that the diagnostic system is working. After a long pause, the Code 12 will repeat itself 2 more times. The cycle will then repeat itself until the engine is started or the ignition is turned **OFF**.

When the engine is started, the SERVICE ENGINE SOON light will remain on for a few seconds, then turn off. If the SERVICE ENGINE SOON light remains on, the self-diagnostic system has detected a problem. If the test terminal is then grounded, the trouble code will flash 3 times. If more than 1 problem is found, each trouble code will flash 3 times. Trouble codes will flash in numerical order (lowest code number to highest). The trouble codes series will repeat as long as the test terminal is grounded.

A trouble code indicates a problem with a given circuit. For example, trouble Code 14 indicates a problem in the cooling sensor circuit. This includes the coolant sensor, its electrical harness, and the ECM/PCM. Since the self-diagnostic system cannot diagnose every possible fault in the system, the absence of a trouble code does not mean the system is trouble-free. To determine problems within the system which do not activate a trouble code, a system performance check must be made.

In the case of an intermittent fault in the system, the SERVICE ENGINE SOON light will go out when the fault goes away, but the trouble code will remain in the memory of the ECM/PCM. Therefore, it a trouble code can be obtained even though the SERVICE ENGINE SOON light is not on, the trouble code must be evaluated. It must be determined if the fault is intermittent or if the engine must be at certain operating conditions (under load, etc.) before the SERVICE ENGINE SOON light will come on. Some trouble codes will not be recorded in the ECM/PCM until the engine has been operated at part throttle for about 5–18 minutes.

INTERMITTENT SERVICE ENGINE SOON LIGHT

An intermittent open in the ground circuit would cause loss of power through the ECM/PCM and intermittent SERVICE ENGINE SOON light operation. When the ECM/PCM loses ground, distributor ignition is lost. An intermittent open in the ground circuit would be described as an engine miss.

Therefore, an intermittent SERVICE ENGINE SOON light, no code stored and a driveability comment described as similar to a miss will require checking the grounding circuit and the Code 12 circuit as it originates at the ignition coil.

UNDERVOLTAGE TO THE ECM/PCM

An undervoltage condition below 9 volts will cause the SERVICE ENGINE SOON light to come on as long as the condition exist.

Therefore, an intermittent SERVICE ENGINE SOON light, no code stored and a driveability comment described as similar to a miss will require checking the grounding circuit, Code 12 circuit and the ignition feed circuit to terminal C of the ECM/PCM. This does nor eliminate the necessity of checking the normal vehicle electrical system for possible cause such as a loose battery cable.

OVERVOLTAGE TO THE ECM/PCM

The ECM/PCM will also shut off when the power supply rises above 16 volts. The overvoltage condition will also cause the SERVICE ENGINE SOON to come on as long as this condition exists.

A momentary voltage surge in a vehicle's electrical system is a common occurrence. These voltage surges have never presented any problems because the entire electrical system acted as a shock absorber until the surge dissipated. Voltage surges or spikes in the vehicle's electrical system have been known, on occasion, to exceed 100 volts.

The system is a low voltage (between 9 and 16 volts) system and will not tolerate these surges. The ECM/PCM will be shut off by any surge in excess of 16 volts and will come back on, only after the surge has dissipated sufficiently to bring the voltage under 16 volts.

A surge will usually occur when an accessory requiring a high voltage supply is turned off or down. The voltage regulator in the vehicle's charging system cannot react to the changes in the voltage demands quickly enough and surge occurs. The driver should be questioned to determine which accessory circuit was turned off that caused the SERVICE ENGINE SOON light to come on.

Therefore, intermittent SERVICE ENGINE SOON light operation, with no trouble code stored, will require installation of a diode in the appropriate accessory circuit.

TPS OUTPUT CHECK TEST

Due to the varied application of components, a general procedure is outlined. For the exact procedure for the vehicle being service use Code 21 or 22 chart the appropriate engine.

With Scan Tool

1. Use a suitable scan tool to read the TPS voltage.
2. With the ignition switch **ON** and the engine **OFF**, the TPS voltage should be less than 1.25 volts.
3. If the voltage reading is higher than specified, replace the throttle position sensor.

Without Scan Tool

1. Remove air cleaner. Disconnect the TPS harness from the TPS.
2. Using suitable jumper wires, connect a digital voltmeter J–29125–A or equivalent to the correct TPS terminals A and B.

3. With the ignition **ON** and the engine running, The TPS voltage should be 0.3–1.0 volts at base idle to approximately 4.5 volts at wide open throttle.
4. If the reading on the TPS is out of specification, check the minimum idle speed before replacing the TPS.
5. If the voltage reading is correct, remove the voltmeter and jumper wires and reconnect the TPS connector to the sensor.
6. Reinstall the air cleaner.

FUEL SYSTEM PRESSURE

Testing

When the ignition switch is turned **ON**, the in-tank fuel pump is energized for as long as the engine is cranking or running and the control unit is receiving signals from the HEI distributor or DIS. If there are no reference pulses, the control unit will shut off the fuel pump within 2 seconds. The pump will deliver fuel to the fuel rail and injectors and then to the pressure regulator, where the system pressure is controlled to maintain 26–46 psi (179–317 kPa). Each vehicle varies slightly in the amount of psi.

1. Connect pressure gauge J-34730-1, or equivalent, to fuel pressure test point on the fuel rail. Wrap a rag around the pressure tap to absorb any leakage that may occur when installing the gauge.
2. Turn the ignition **ON** and check that pump pressure is 24–40 psi (165–275 kPa). This pressure is controlled by spring pressure within the regulator assembly.
3. Start the engine and allow it to idle. The fuel pressure should drop to 28–32 psi (193–220 kPa) due to the lower manifold pressure.

➡ **The idle pressure will vary somewhat depending on barometric pressure. Check for a drop in pressure indicating regulator control, rather than specific values.**

4. On turbocharged vehicles, use a low pressure air pump to apply air pressure to the regulator to simulate turbocharger boost pressure. Boost pressure should increase fuel pressure by 1 lb. for every lb. of boost. Again, look for changes rather than specific pressures. The maximum fuel pressure should not exceed 46 psi (317 kPa).
5. If the fuel pressure drops, check the operation of the check valve, the pump coupling connection, fuel pressure regulator valve and the injectors. A restricted fuel line or filter may also cause a pressure drip. To check the fuel pump output, restrict the fuel return line and run 12 volts to the pump. The fuel pressure should rise to approximately 75 psi (517 kPa) with the return line restricted.

✳✳ CAUTION

Before attempting to remove or service any fuel system component, it is necessary to relieve the fuel system pressure.

CRANKSHAFT SENSOR

Inspection

1. Disconnect the negative battery cable.
2. Rotate the harmonic balancer using a 28mm socket and pull on the handle until the interrupter ring fills the sensor slots and edge of the interrupter window is aligned with the edge of the deflector on the pedestal.
3. Insert feeler gauge adjustment tool J-36179 or equivalent into the gap between the sensor and the interrupter on each side of the interrupter ring.
4. If the gauge will not slide past the sensor on either side of the interrupter ring, the sensor is out of adjustment or the interrupter ring is bent.
5. The clearance should be checked again, at 3 positions around the interrupter ring approximately 120° apart.
6. If found out of adjustment, the sensor should be removed and inspected for potential damage.

VACUUM DIAGRAMS

Following is a listing of vacuum diagrams for most of the engine and emissions package combinations covered by this manual. Because vacuum circuits will vary based on various engine and vehicle options, always refer first to the vehicle emission control information label, if present. Should the label be missing, or should the vehicle be equipped with a different engine than the car's original equipment, refer to the following diagrams for the same or similar configuration.

If you wish to obtain a replacement emissions label, most manufacturers make the labels available for purchase. The labels can usually be ordered from a local dealer.

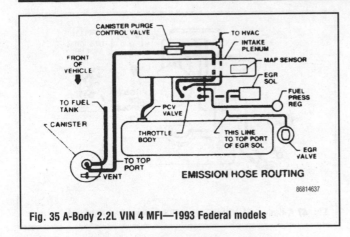

Fig. 35 A-Body 2.2L VIN 4 MFI—1993 Federal models

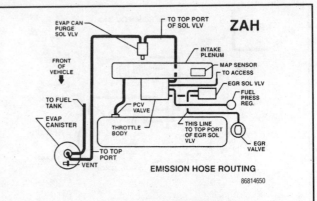

Fig. 39 A-Body 2.2L VIN 4 MFI—All 1994–96 models

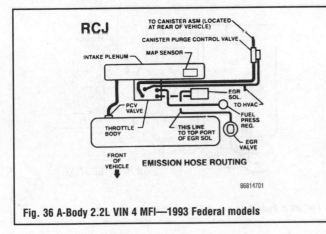

Fig. 36 A-Body 2.2L VIN 4 MFI—1993 Federal models

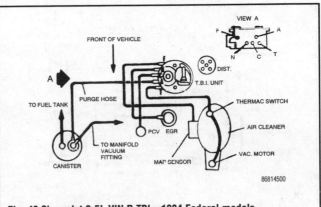

Fig. 40 Chevrolet 2.5L VIN R TBI—1984 Federal models

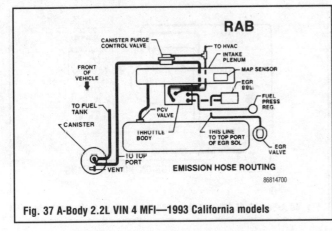

Fig. 37 A-Body 2.2L VIN 4 MFI—1993 California models

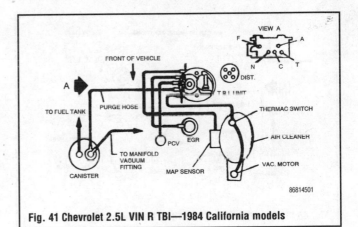

Fig. 41 Chevrolet 2.5L VIN R TBI—1984 California models

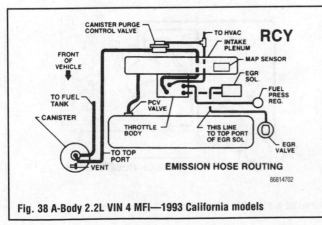

Fig. 38 A-Body 2.2L VIN 4 MFI—1993 California models

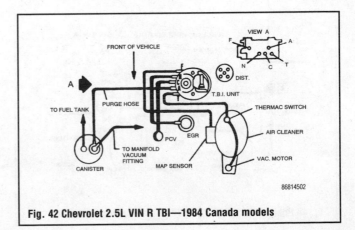

Fig. 42 Chevrolet 2.5L VIN R TBI—1984 Canada models

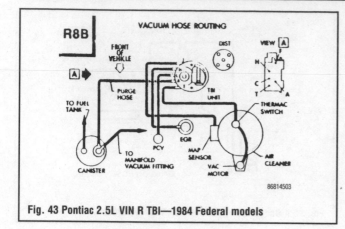

Fig. 43 Pontiac 2.5L VIN R TBI—1984 Federal models

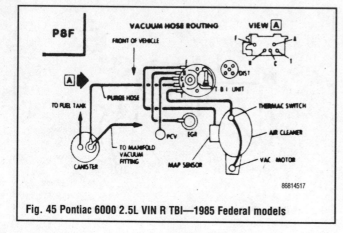

Fig. 44 Pontiac 2.5L VIN R TBI—1984 California models

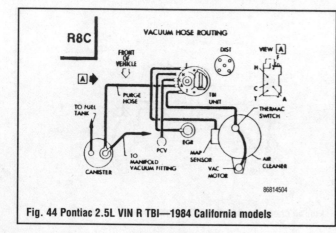

Fig. 45 Pontiac 6000 2.5L VIN R TBI—1985 Federal models

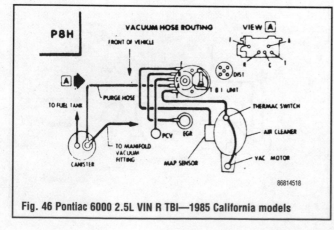

Fig. 46 Pontiac 6000 2.5L VIN R TBI—1985 California models

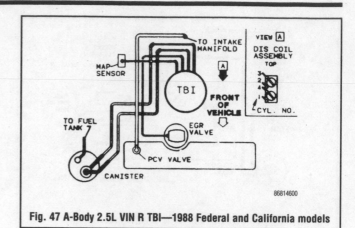

Fig. 47 A-Body 2.5L VIN R TBI—1988 Federal and California models

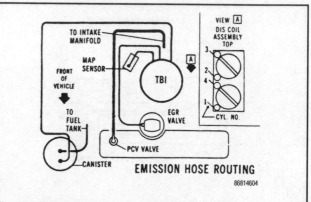

Fig. 48 A-Body 2.5L VIN R TBI—1989 Federal models

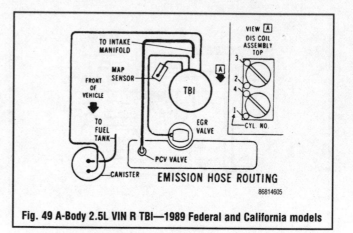

Fig. 49 A-Body 2.5L VIN R TBI—1989 Federal and California models

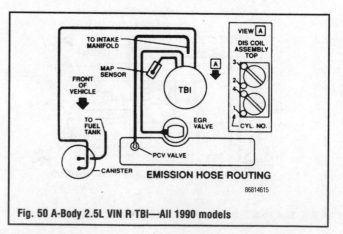

Fig. 50 A-Body 2.5L VIN R TBI—All 1990 models

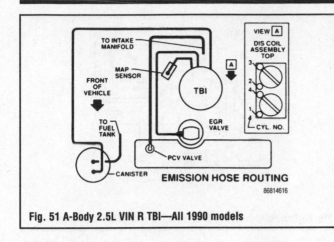

Fig. 51 A-Body 2.5L VIN R TBI—All 1990 models

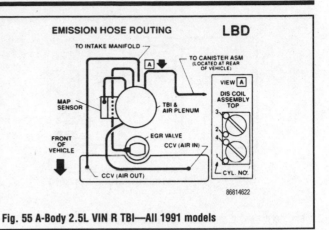

Fig. 55 A-Body 2.5L VIN R TBI—All 1991 models

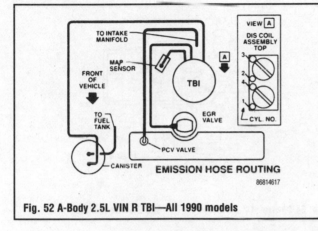

Fig. 52 A-Body 2.5L VIN R TBI—All 1990 models

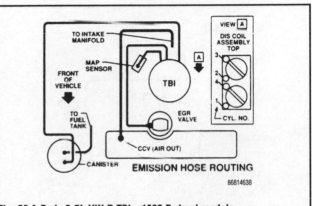

Fig. 56 A-Body 2.5L VIN R TBI—1992 Federal models

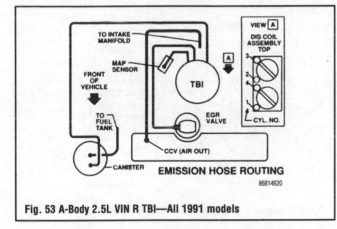

Fig. 53 A-Body 2.5L VIN R TBI—All 1991 models

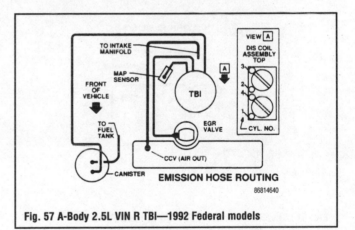

Fig. 57 A-Body 2.5L VIN R TBI—1992 Federal models

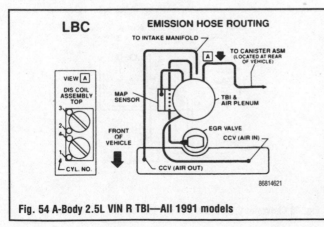

Fig. 54 A-Body 2.5L VIN R TBI—All 1991 models

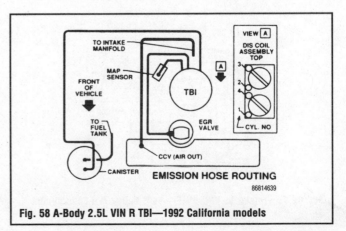

Fig. 58 A-Body 2.5L VIN R TBI—1992 California models

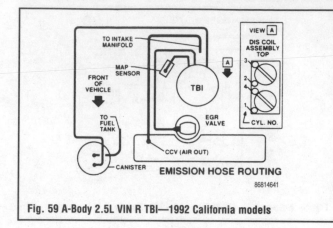

Fig. 59 A-Body 2.5L VIN R TBI—1992 California models

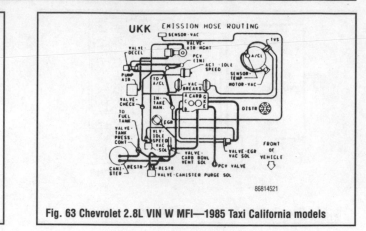

Fig. 63 Chevrolet 2.8L VIN W MFI—1985 Taxi California models

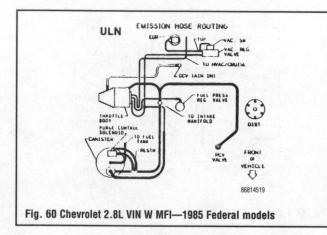

Fig. 60 Chevrolet 2.8L VIN W MFI—1985 Federal models

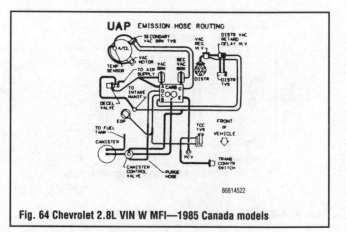

Fig. 64 Chevrolet 2.8L VIN W MFI—1985 Canada models

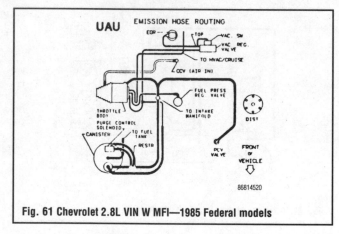

Fig. 61 Chevrolet 2.8L VIN W MFI—1985 Federal models

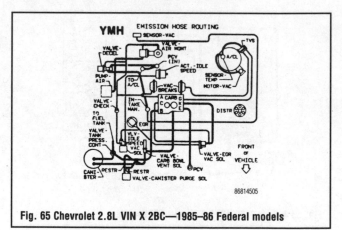

Fig. 65 Chevrolet 2.8L VIN X 2BC—1985–86 Federal models

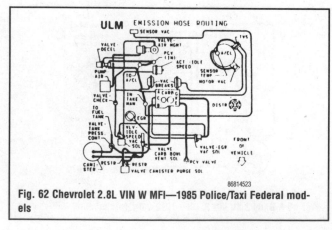

Fig. 62 Chevrolet 2.8L VIN W MFI—1985 Police/Taxi Federal models

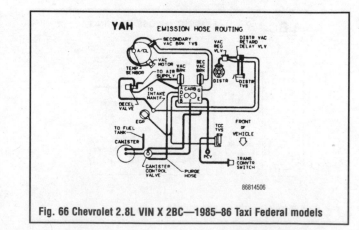

Fig. 66 Chevrolet 2.8L VIN X 2BC—1985–86 Taxi Federal models

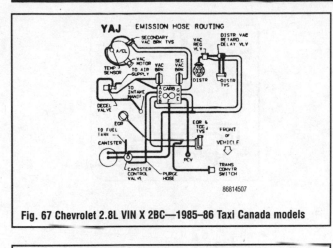

Fig. 67 Chevrolet 2.8L VIN X 2BC—1985–86 Taxi Canada models

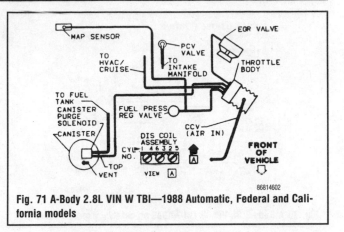

Fig. 71 A-Body 2.8L VIN W TBI—1988 Automatic, Federal and California models

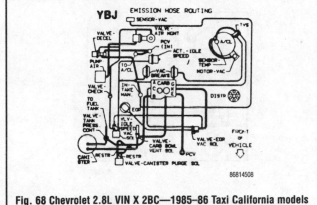

Fig. 68 Chevrolet 2.8L VIN X 2BC—1985–86 Taxi California models

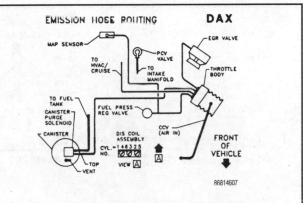

Fig. 72 A-Body 2.8L VIN W TBI—1989 Automatic, Federal models

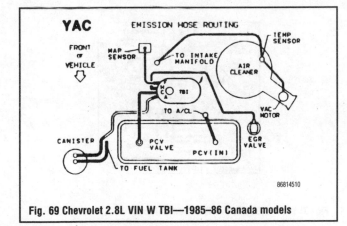

Fig. 69 Chevrolet 2.8L VIN W TBI—1985–86 Canada models

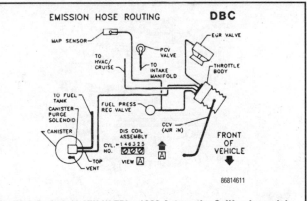

Fig. 73 A-Body 2.8L VIN W TBI—1989 Automatic, California models

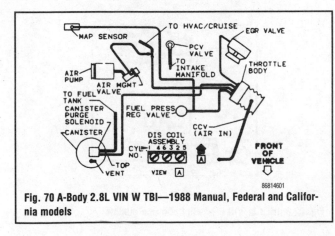

Fig. 70 A-Body 2.8L VIN W TBI—1988 Manual, Federal and California models

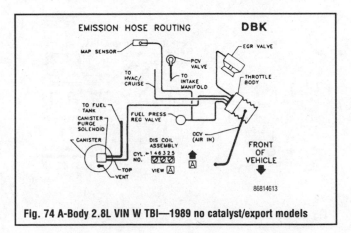

Fig. 74 A-Body 2.8L VIN W TBI—1989 no catalyst/export models

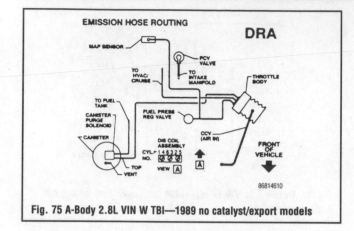

Fig. 75 A-Body 2.8L VIN W TBI—1989 no catalyst/export models

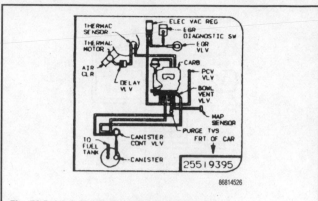

Fig. 79 Buick 3.0L VIN E—1985 Federal models

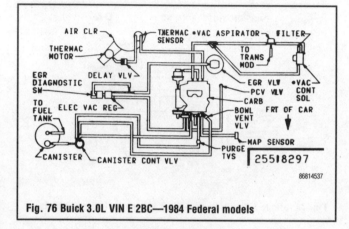

Fig. 76 Buick 3.0L VIN E 2BC—1984 Federal models

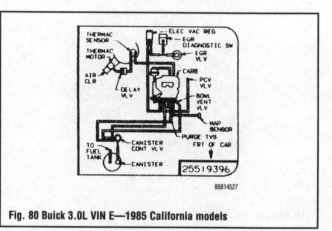

Fig. 80 Buick 3.0L VIN E—1985 California models

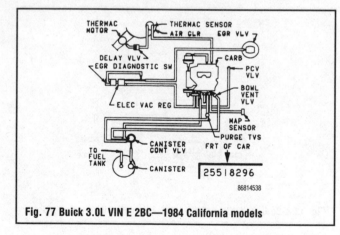

Fig. 77 Buick 3.0L VIN E 2BC—1984 California models

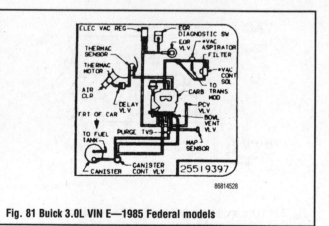

Fig. 81 Buick 3.0L VIN E—1985 Federal models

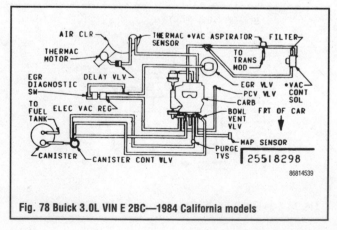

Fig. 78 Buick 3.0L VIN E 2BC—1984 California models

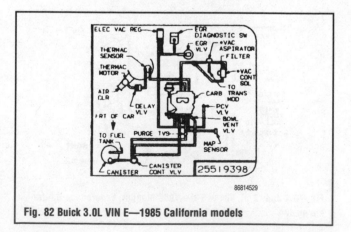

Fig. 82 Buick 3.0L VIN E—1985 California models

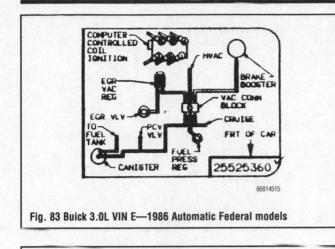

Fig. 83 Buick 3.0L VIN E—1986 Automatic Federal models

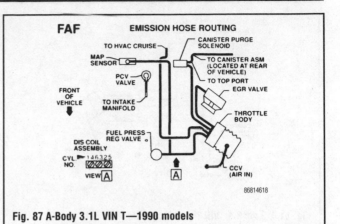

Fig. 87 A-Body 3.1L VIN T—1990 models

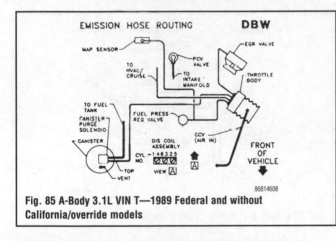

Fig. 84 Buick 3.0L VIN E—1986 Automatic California models

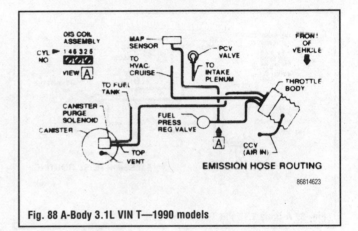

Fig. 88 A-Body 3.1L VIN T—1990 models

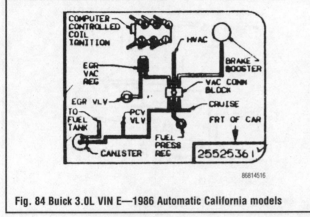

Fig. 85 A-Body 3.1L VIN T—1989 Federal and without California/override models

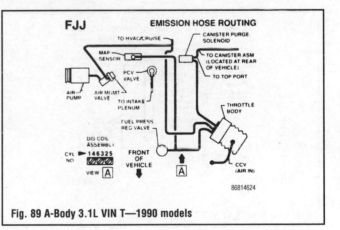

Fig. 89 A-Body 3.1L VIN T—1990 models

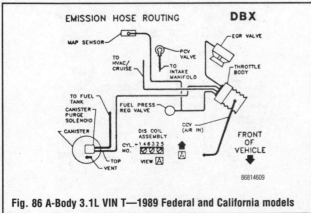

Fig. 86 A-Body 3.1L VIN T—1989 Federal and California models

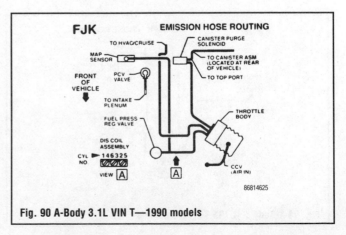

Fig. 90 A-Body 3.1L VIN T—1990 models

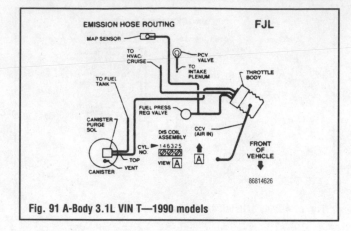

Fig. 91 A-Body 3.1L VIN T—1990 models

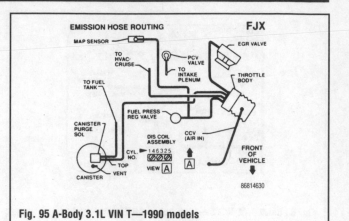

Fig. 95 A-Body 3.1L VIN T—1990 models

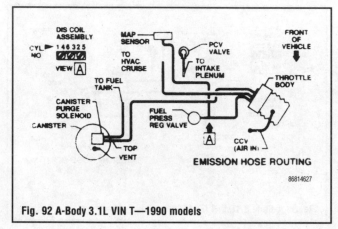

Fig. 92 A-Body 3.1L VIN T—1990 models

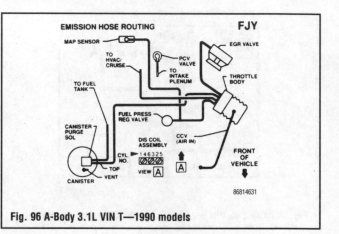

Fig. 96 A-Body 3.1L VIN T—1990 models

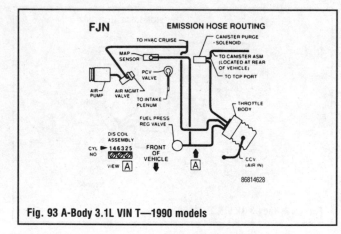

Fig. 93 A-Body 3.1L VIN T—1990 models

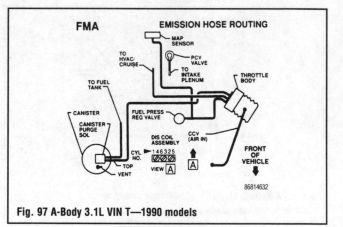

Fig. 97 A-Body 3.1L VIN T—1990 models

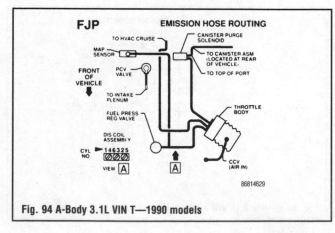

Fig. 94 A-Body 3.1L VIN T—1990 models

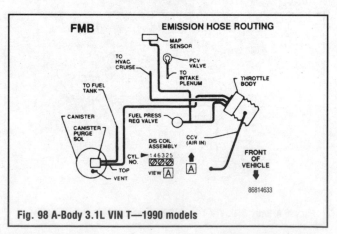

Fig. 98 A-Body 3.1L VIN T—1990 models

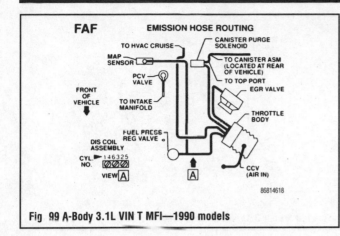

Fig. 99 A-Body 3.1L VIN T MFI—1990 models

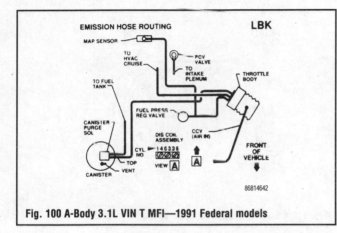

Fig. 100 A-Body 3.1L VIN T MFI—1991 Federal models

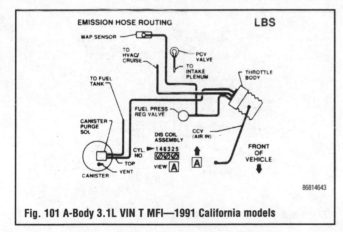

Fig. 101 A-Body 3.1L VIN T MFI—1991 California models

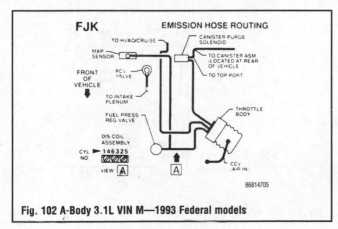

Fig. 102 A-Body 3.1L VIN M—1993 Federal models

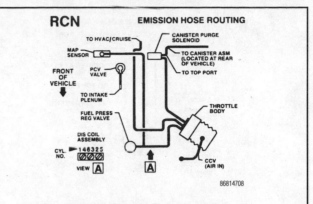

Fig. 103 A-Body 3.1L VIN M—1993 Federal models

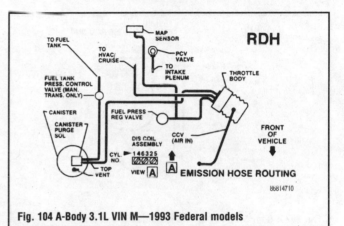

Fig. 104 A-Body 3.1L VIN M—1993 Federal models

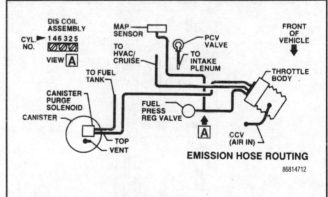

Fig. 105 A-Body 3.1L VIN M—1993 Federal models

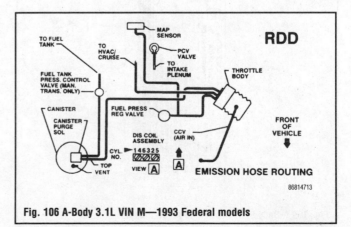

Fig. 106 A-Body 3.1L VIN M—1993 Federal models

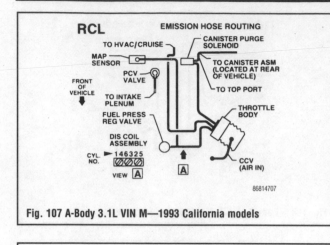

Fig. 107 A-Body 3.1L VIN M—1993 California models

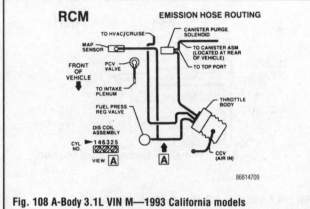

Fig. 108 A-Body 3.1L VIN M—1993 California models

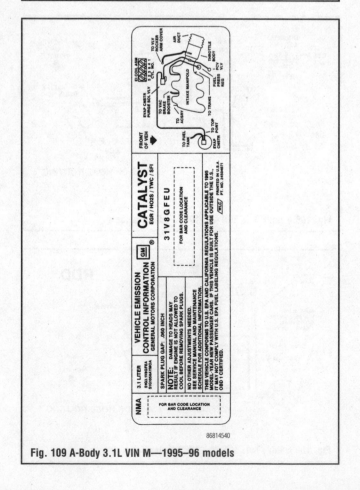

Fig. 109 A-Body 3.1L VIN M—1995-96 models

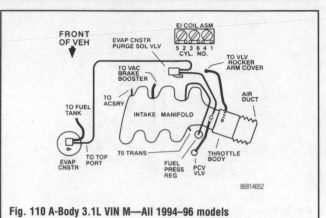

Fig. 110 A-Body 3.1L VIN M—All 1994-96 models

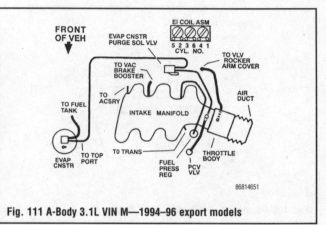

Fig. 111 A-Body 3.1L VIN M—1994-96 export models

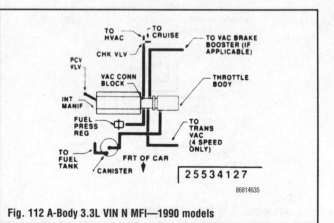

Fig. 112 A-Body 3.3L VIN N MFI—1990 models

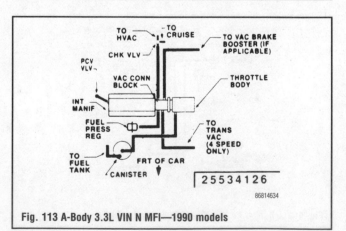

Fig. 113 A-Body 3.3L VIN N MFI—1990 models

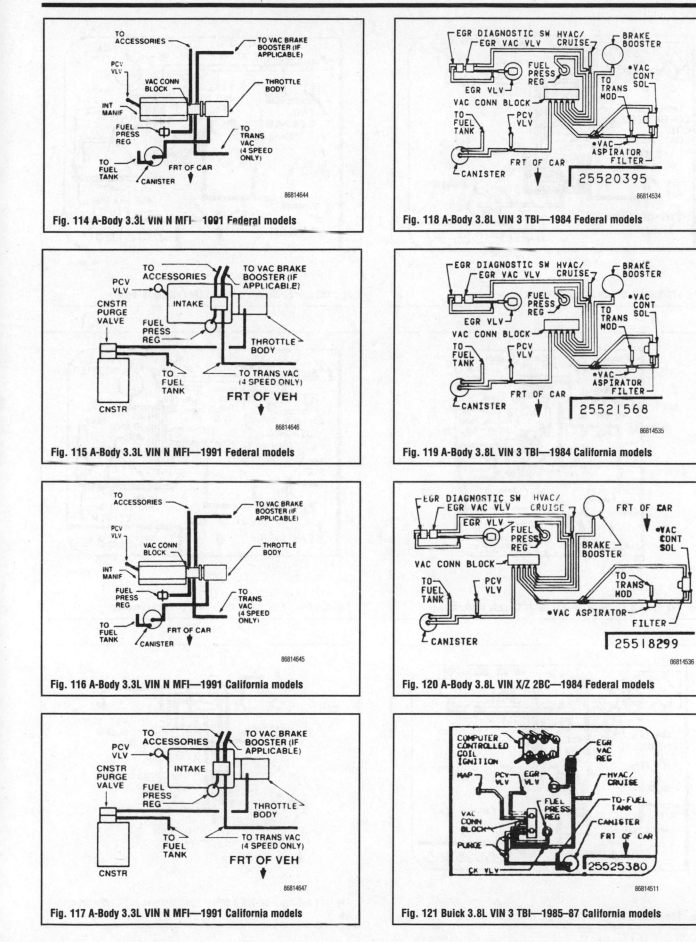

Fig. 114 A-Body 3.3L VIN N MFI—1991 Federal models

Fig. 115 A-Body 3.3L VIN N MFI—1991 Federal models

Fig. 116 A-Body 3.3L VIN N MFI—1991 California models

Fig. 117 A-Body 3.3L VIN N MFI—1991 California models

Fig. 118 A-Body 3.8L VIN 3 TBI—1984 Federal models

Fig. 119 A-Body 3.8L VIN 3 TBI—1984 California models

Fig. 120 A-Body 3.8L VIN X/Z 2BC—1984 Federal models

Fig. 121 Buick 3.8L VIN 3 TBI—1985–87 California models

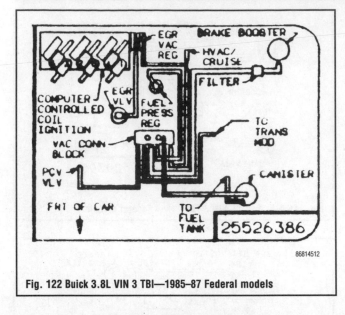

Fig. 122 Buick 3.8L VIN 3 TBI—1985–87 Federal models

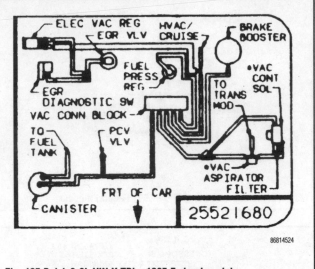

Fig. 125 Buick 3.8L VIN X TBI—1985 Federal models

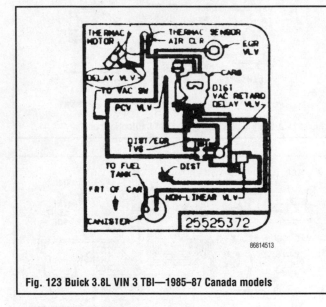

Fig. 123 Buick 3.8L VIN 3 TBI—1985–87 Canada models

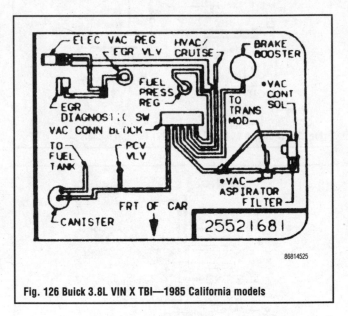

Fig. 126 Buick 3.8L VIN X TBI—1985 California models

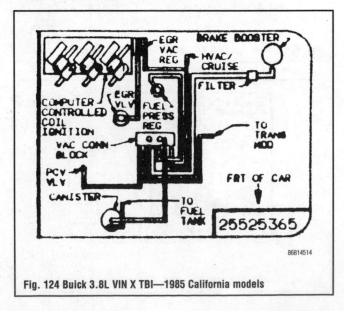

Fig. 124 Buick 3.8L VIN X TBI—1985 California models

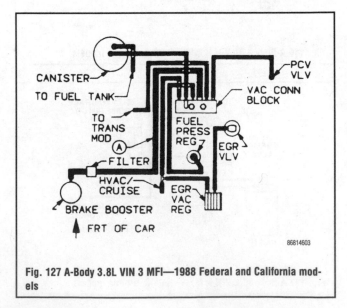

Fig. 127 A-Body 3.8L VIN 3 MFI—1988 Federal and California models

5

FUEL
SYSTEM

BASIC FUEL SYSTEM DIAGNOSIS

When there is a problem starting or driving a vehicle, two of the most important checks involve the ignition and the fuel systems. The questions most mechanics attempt to answer first, "is there spark?" and "is there fuel?" will often lead to solving most basic problems. For ignition system diagnosis and testing, please refer to Section 2 of this manual. If the ignition system checks out (there is spark), then you must determine if the fuel system is operating properly (is there fuel?).

CARBURETED FUEL SYSTEM

Mechanical Fuel Pump

Mechanical fuel pumps are used on 6-2.8L engines. The pump has a vapor return line for both emission control purposes and to reduce the likelihood of vapor lock. The fuel pump is located at the left side of the engine.

REMOVAL & INSTALLATION

▶ **See Figure 1**

1. Disconnect the negative cable at the battery. Raise and support the car.
2. Remove the pump shields and the oil filter, if so equipped.
3. With a shop towel handy, disconnect the inlet hose from the pump. Disconnect the vapor return hose, if equipped, then wrap the towel around the hose to catch any spilt fuel.
4. Loosen the fuel line at the carburetor, then disconnect the outlet pipe from the pump. Use another towel or the same one if possible for spilt fuel.
5. Remove the two mounting bolts and remove the pump from the engine.
   To install:
6. Place a new gasket on the pump and install the pump on the engine. Tighten the two mounting bolts alternately and evenly.
7. Install the pump outlet pipe. This is easier if the pipe is disconnected from the carburetor. Tighten the fitting while backing up the pump nut with another wrench. Install the pipe at the carburetor.
8. Install the inlet and vapor hoses. Install the shields (if equipped) and oil filter. Lower the car, connect the negative battery cable, start the engine, and check for leaks.

TESTING

To determine if the pump is in good condition, tests for both volume and pressure should be performed. The tests are made with the pump installed. Never replace a fuel pump without first performing these simple tests.

Be sure that the fuel filter has been changed at the specified interval. If in doubt, install a new filter first.

Pressure Test

1. Disconnect the fuel line at the carburetor and connect a fuel pump pressure gauge. Hold the gauge up so that it's approximately 16 inches above the pump. Pinch the fuel return line.
2. Start the engine and check the pressure with the engine at idle. If the pump has a vapor return hose, squeeze it off so that an accurate reading can be obtained. Pressure should measure 5.5–6.5 psi (38–45 kPa) consistently.
3. If the pressure is incorrect, replace the pump. If it is okay, go on to the volume test.

Volume Test

1. Disconnect the pressure gauge. Run the fuel line into a graduated container.
2. Run the engine at idle until one pint of gasoline has been pumped. One pint should be delivered in 30 seconds or less. There is normally enough fuel in the carburetor float bowl to perform this test, but refill it if necessary.
3. If the delivery rate is below the minimum, check the lines for restrictions or leaks, then replace the pump.

Carburetor

▶ **See Figures 2 and 3**

The Rochester E2SE is used on most 1982 and later A-body cars. It is a two barrel, two stage carburetor of downdraft design used in conjunction with the Computer Command Control system of fuel control. The carburetor has special design features for optimum air/fuel mixture control during all ranges of engine operation. In 1982 there was also the E2ME carburetor, it is a two barrel, single stage design carburetor.

A triple venturi arrangement with plain tube nozzle is used in each bore which results in precise fuel metering control during the off idle and part of the throttle ranges of the engine operation. The E2ME also uses the Computer Command Control system of fuel control. Like the E2SE the E2ME carburetor has special design features for optimum air/fuel mixture control during all periods of engine operation. All Rochester carburetors consist of 3 major assemblies: the air horn, the float bowl and the throttle body. They have 6 basic operating systems: float, idle, main metering, power, pump and choke.

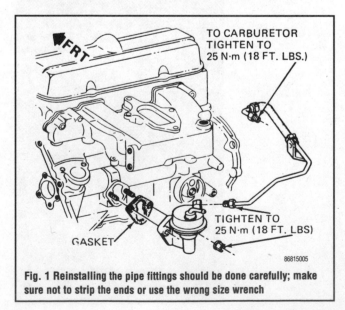

Fig. 1 Reinstalling the pipe fittings should be done carefully; make sure not to strip the ends or use the wrong size wrench

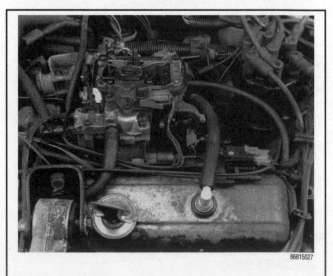

Fig. 2 Rochester E2SE carburetor assembly on the vehicle

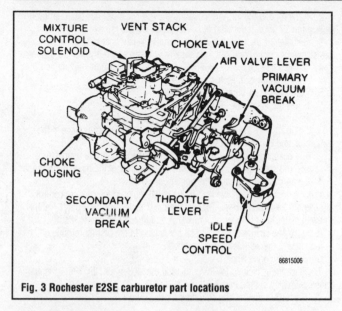

Fig. 3 Rochester E2SE carburetor part locations

MODEL IDENTIFICATION

▶ See Figure 4

General Motors Rochester carburetors are identified by their model code. The carburetor model identification number is stamped vertically on the float bowl, near the secondary throttle lever. The letters in the model name describe the specific features of the carburetor. For example: The first letter "E" indicates the carburetor is Electronically controlled. The second and third digits, "2S" indicates the carburetor is a member of the Varajet family. The last digit "E" indicates an integral Electric choke. The identification code is stamped on the float bowl.

ADJUSTMENTS

Fast Idle

▶ See Figure 5

1. Position the transaxle in the Park or Neutral position.
2. Set the ignition timing and curb idle speed, and disconnect and plug hoses as directed on the emission control decal.

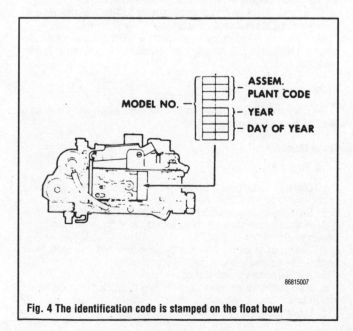

Fig. 4 The identification code is stamped on the float bowl

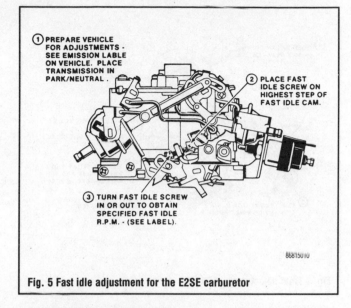

Fig. 5 Fast idle adjustment for the E2SE carburetor

3. Place the fast idle screw on the highest step of the cam, or what is specified on the emissions label.
4. Start the engine and adjust the engine speed to specification with the fast idle screw.

Choke Valve Angle Gauge

▶ See Figure 6

1. Attach the angle gauge magnet to the closed valve.
2. Rotator the degree scale until zero is opposite the pointer.
3. Center the leveling bubble, then rotate the scale to the specified angle.
4. Open the choke valve.
5. Adjust the linkage if the bubble is not recentered.

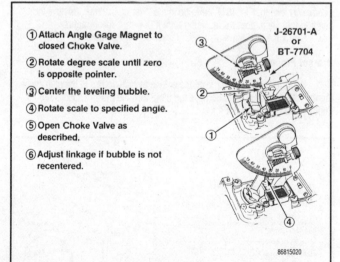

Fig. 6 A choke valve angle gauge is used often in adjustments

Float

1982–84 MODELS

▶ See Figure 7

1. Remove the air horn from the throttle body.
2. Use your fingers to hold the retainer in place, and to push the float down into light contact with the needle.

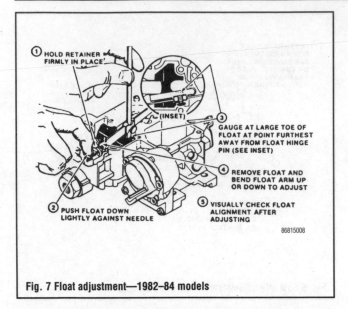

① HOLD RETAINER FIRMLY IN PLACE

③ GAUGE AT LARGE TOE OF FLOAT AT POINT FURTHEST AWAY FROM FLOAT HINGE PIN (SEE INSET)

④ REMOVE FLOAT AND BEND FLOAT ARM UP OR DOWN TO ADJUST

② PUSH FLOAT DOWN LIGHTLY AGAINST NEEDLE

⑤ VISUALLY CHECK FLOAT ALIGNMENT AFTER ADJUSTING

(INSET)

86815008

Fig. 7 Float adjustment—1982–84 models

3. Measure the distance from the toe of the float (furthest from the hinge) to the top of the carburetor (gasket removed).

4. To adjust, remove the float and gently bend the arm to specification. After adjustment, check the float alignment in the chamber.

1985–86 MODELS

♦ See Figure 8

1. Remove the air horn, horn gasket, and upper float bowl insert.
2. Attach special tool J-34817-1 to the float bowl.
3. Place the J-34817-3 in the base of the carburetor, with the contact pin resting on the outer edge of the float lever.
4. Measure the distance from the top of the casting to the top of the float, at the point farthest from the float hinge, use tool J-9789-90.
5. If the gap is 2/32 in. (1.59mm) or more different than specification (larger or smaller), use tool J-34817-20 to bend the lever up or down. Remove the bending tool, then measure repeating until it is within specification.
6. Check the float alignment, then reassemble the carburetor.

Pre-set Procedure

1. Remove the carburetor from the engine to gain access to the plug covering the idle mixture needle. Remove the plug, turn the mixture needle in until lightly seated and back out 4 turns.

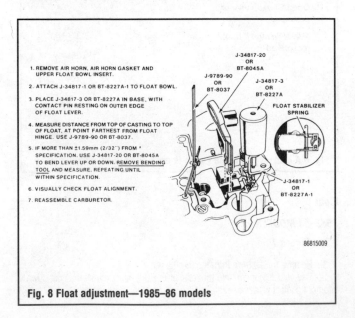

1. REMOVE AIR HORN, AIR HORN GASKET AND UPPER FLOAT BOWL INSERT.

2. ATTACH J-34817-1 OR BT-8227A-1 TO FLOAT BOWL.

3. PLACE J-34817-3 OR BT-8227 IN BASE, WITH CONTACT PIN RESTING ON OUTER EDGE OF FLOAT LEVER.

4. MEASURE DISTANCE FROM TOP OF CASTING TO TOP OF FLOAT, AT POINT FARTHEST FROM FLOAT HINGE. USE J-9789-90 OR BT-8037.

5. IF MORE THAN ±1.59mm (2/32″) FROM SPECIFICATION. USE J-34817-20 OR BT-8045A TO BEND LEVER UP OR DOWN. REMOVE BENDING TOOL AND MEASURE. REPEATING UNTIL WITHIN SPECIFICATION.

6. VISUALLY CHECK FLOAT ALIGNMENT.

7. REASSEMBLE CARBURETOR.

J-34817-20 OR BT-8045A

J-9789-90 OR BT-8037

J-34817-3 OR BT-8227A

FLOAT STABILIZER SPRING

J-34817-1 OR BT-8227A-1

86815009

Fig. 8 Float adjustment—1985–86 models

2. If the plug in the air horn covering the idle air bleed has been removed, replace the air horn. If the plug is still in place, do not remove it.

3. Remove the vent stack screen assembly to gain access to the lean mixture screw. Be sure to reinstall the vent stack screen assembly after adjustment.

4. Using a special tool J-28696-10 or equivalent, turn the mixture screw in until it lightly bottoms, then back out 2½ turns.

5. Reinstall the carburetor on the engine.
   a. Do not install the air cleaner and gasket.
   b. Disconnect the bowl vent line at the carburetor.
   c. Disconnect the EGR valve hose and the canister purge hose at the carburetor, and cap the ports.
   d. Locate hose on port "D" on the emissions label to the temperature sensor and secondary vacuum break TVS. Disconnect the hose at the sensor on the air cleaner, then plug the open hose.
   e. Connect the positive lead of the dwell meter to the mixture control solenoid test lead (green). Connect the other meter lead to ground. Set the dwell meter to 6-cylinder position. Connect the tachometer to distributor lead (brown). The tachometer should be connected to the distributor side of the tach filter if the vehicle has a tachometer.

6. Block the drive wheels.

7. Place the vehicle in PARK (automatic transaxles) or NEUTRAL (manual transaxles), then set the Parking brake.

8. Proceed to the mixture adjustment procedure.

Mixture Adjustment

1. Perform the carburetor pre-set procedure.

2. Run the engine on high step of the fast idle cam. until the engine cooling fan starts to cycle.

3. Run the engine at 3,000 rpm and adjust the lean mixture screw slowly in small increments allowing time for dwell to stabilize after turning the screw to obtain an average dwell of 35°. If the dwell is too low, back the screw out, if too high, turn it in. If you are unable to adjust it to specifications, inspect the main metering circuit for leaks or restrictions.

4. Return to idle.

5. Adjust the mixture screw to obtain the average dwell of 25° with the cooling fan in the off cycle. If the reading is too low, back the screw out. If the reading is too high, turn it in. Allow time for reading to stabilize after each adjustment. Adjustment is very sensitive. Make a final check with the adjusting tool removed.

6. If you are unable to adjust to specifications, inspect the idle system for leaks, or restrictions.

7. Disconnect the mixture control solenoid when the cooling fan is in the off cycle, then check for an rpm change of at least 50 rpm. If the rpm does not change enough, inspect the idle air bleed circuit for restrictions or leaks.

8. Run the engine at 3,000 rpm for a few moments, then note the dwell reading. Dwell should be varying with the average reading of 35°.

9. If the 35° is not the average dwell, reset the lean mixture screw per step 3. Then reset the idle mixture screw to obtain a 25° dwell per steps 5 and 6.

10. If you have an average dwell, reconnect the systems disconnected (purge and vent hoses, EGR valve etc.), then reinstall the vent screen and set the idle speed.

Pump

The E2ME and the E2SE carburetors have a non-adjustable pump lever. No adjustments are either necessary or possible.

Choke Unloader

♦ See Figure 9

1. Connect a rubber band to the intermediate choke lever, then open the throttle valve to allow the choke valve to close.

2. Set up the angle gauge and the angle to specifications.

3. Position the fast idle screw on the second step of the fast idle cam (against the rise of the high step).

4. Turn the choke lever shaft to open the choke valve and make contact with the black closing tang.

5. Hold the primary throttle wide open.

6. If the engine is warm, close the choke valve by pushing in on the intermediate choke lever.

7. Bend the unloader tang until the bubble is centered.

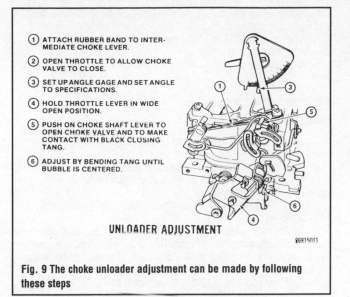

1. ATTACH RUBBER BAND TO INTERMEDIATE CHOKE LEVER.
2. OPEN THROTTLE TO ALLOW CHOKE VALVE TO CLOSE.
3. SET UP ANGLE GAGE AND SET ANGLE TO SPECIFICATIONS.
4. HOLD THROTTLE LEVER IN WIDE OPEN POSITION.
5. PUSH ON CHOKE SHAFT LEVER TO OPEN CHOKE VALVE AND TO MAKE CONTACT WITH BLACK CLOSING TANG.
6. ADJUST BY BENDING TANG UNTIL BUBBLE IS CENTERED.

UNLOADER ADJUSTMENT

86815011

Fig. 9 The choke unloader adjustment can be made by following these steps

Choke Coil Lever

▶ See Figure 10

1. Remove the three retaining screws and remove the choke cover and coil. On models with a riveted choke cover, drill out the three rivets and remove the cover and choke coil.

➡A choke stat cover retainer kit is required for reassembly.

2. Place the fast idle screw on the high step of the cam.
3. Close the choke by pushing in on the intermediate choke lever.
4. Insert a drill or gauge of the specified size into the hole in the choke housing. The choke lever in the housing should be up against the side of the gauge.
5. If the lever does not just touch the gauge, bend the intermediate choke rod to adjust.

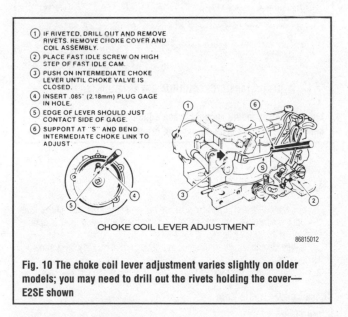

1. IF RIVETED, DRILL OUT AND REMOVE RIVETS. REMOVE CHOKE COVER AND COIL ASSEMBLY.
2. PLACE FAST IDLE SCREW ON HIGH STEP OF FAST IDLE CAM.
3. PUSH ON INTERMEDIATE CHOKE LEVER UNTIL CHOKE VALVE IS CLOSED.
4. INSERT .085" (2.18mm) PLUG GAGE IN HOLE.
5. EDGE OF LEVER SHOULD JUST CONTACT SIDE OF GAGE.
6. SUPPORT AT "S" AND BEND INTERMEDIATE CHOKE LINK TO ADJUST.

CHOKE COIL LEVER ADJUSTMENT

86815012

Fig. 10 The choke coil lever adjustment varies slightly on older models; you may need to drill out the rivets holding the cover—E2SE shown

Fast Idle Cam-Choke Rod

▶ See Figure 11

➡A special angle gauge should be used. If it is not available, an inch (millimeter) measurement can be made.

1. Adjust the choke coil lever and fast idle first.
2. Rotate the degree scale until it is zeroed.

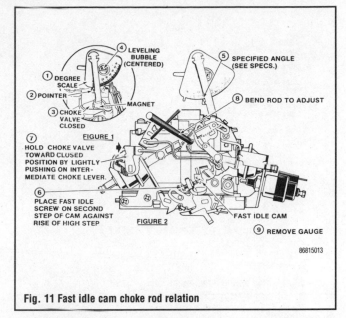

1. DEGREE SCALE
2. POINTER
3. CHOKE VALVE CLOSED
4. LEVELING BUBBLE (CENTERED)
5. SPECIFIED ANGLE (SEE SPECS.)
8. BEND ROD TO ADJUST

MAGNET

FIGURE 1

7. HOLD CHOKE VALVE TOWARD CLOSED POSITION BY LIGHTLY PUSHING ON INTERMEDIATE CHOKE LEVER.
6. PLACE FAST IDLE SCREW ON SECOND STEP OF CAM AGAINST RISE OF HIGH STEP

FIGURE 2

FAST IDLE CAM

9. REMOVE GAUGE

86815013

Fig. 11 Fast idle cam choke rod relation

3. Close the choke and install the degree scale onto the choke plate. Center the leveling bubble.
4. Rotate the scale so that the specified degree is opposite the scale pointer.
5. Place the fast idle screw on the second step of the cam (against the high step). Close the choke by pushing in the intermediate lever.
6. Bend the fast idle cam rod at the U to adjust the angle to specifications.

Air Valve Rod

▶ See Figure 12

1. Close the air valve.
2. Insert the specified gauge between the rod and the end of the slot in the plunger.
3. Seat the vacuum diaphragm with an outside vacuum source. Tape over the purge bleed hole if present.
4. Rotate the air valve in the direction of the open air valve by applying a light pressure to the air valve shaft.
5. Bend the rod to adjust the clearance, notice the location of the bubble.

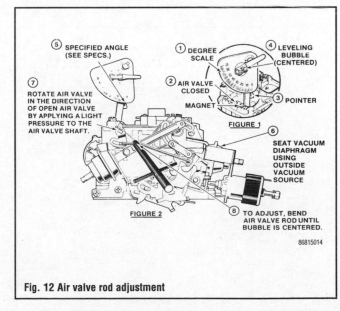

5. SPECIFIED ANGLE (SEE SPECS.)
1. DEGREE SCALE
4. LEVELING BUBBLE (CENTERED)
2. AIR VALVE CLOSED
3. POINTER
MAGNET

FIGURE 1

7. ROTATE AIR VALVE IN THE DIRECTION OF OPEN AIR VALVE BY APPLYING A LIGHT PRESSURE TO THE AIR VALVE SHAFT.

6. SEAT VACUUM DIAPHRAGM USING OUTSIDE VACUUM SOURCE

FIGURE 2

8. TO ADJUST, BEND AIR VALVE ROD UNTIL BUBBLE IS CENTERED.

86815014

Fig. 12 Air valve rod adjustment

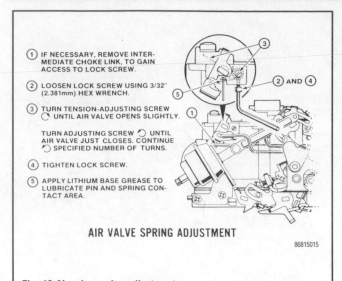

AIR VALVE SPRING ADJUSTMENT

① IF NECESSARY, REMOVE INTER-MEDIATE CHOKE LINK, TO GAIN ACCESS TO LOCK SCREW.

② LOOSEN LOCK SCREW USING 3/32" (2.381mm) HEX WRENCH.

③ TURN TENSION-ADJUSTING SCREW ↻ UNTIL AIR VALVE OPENS SLIGHTLY.

TURN ADJUSTING SCREW ↺ UNTIL AIR VALVE JUST CLOSES. CONTINUE ↺ SPECIFIED NUMBER OF TURNS.

④ TIGHTEN LOCK SCREW.

⑤ APPLY LITHIUM BASE GREASE TO LUBRICATE PIN AND SPRING CONTACT AREA.

86815015

Fig. 13 Air valve spring adjustment

Air Valve Spring

▶ See Figure 13

1. To gain access to the lock screw, remove the intermediate choke link.
2. Using a ³⁄₃₂ in. (2.34mm) hex wrench, loosen the lock screw.
3. Turn the adjusting screw clockwise until the air valve opens slightly, then turn the screw counterclockwise until the valve closes and continue the number of specified turns.
4. Tighten the lock screw and apply lithium grease to the pin and the spring contact area.

Primary Side Vacuum Break

▶ See Figure 14

1. Connect a rubber band to the intermediate choke lever, then open the throttle valve to allow the choke valve to close.
2. Set up the angle gauge and the angle to specifications.
3. Position the fast idle screw on the second step of the fast idle cam (against the rise of the high step).
4. Turn the choke lever shaft to open the choke valve and make contact with the black closing tang.
5. Seat the choke vacuum diaphragm with an outside vacuum source.

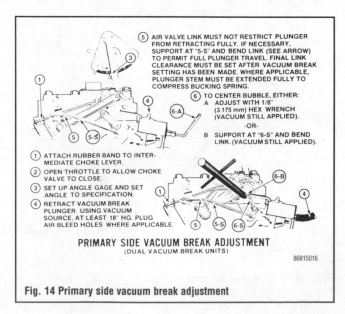

⑤ AIR VALVE LINK MUST NOT RESTRICT PLUNGER FROM RETRACTING FULLY. IF NECESSARY, SUPPORT AT "5-S" AND BEND LINK (SEE ARROW) TO PERMIT FULL PLUNGER TRAVEL. FINAL LINK CLEARANCE MUST BE SET AFTER VACUUM BREAK SETTING HAS BEEN MADE. WHERE APPLICABLE, PLUNGER STEM MUST BE EXTENDED FULLY TO COMPRESS BUCKING SPRING.

⑥ TO CENTER BUBBLE, EITHER:
A. ADJUST WITH 1/8" (3.175 mm) HEX WRENCH (VACUUM STILL APPLIED).
-OR-
B. SUPPORT AT "6-S" AND BEND LINK (VACUUM STILL APPLIED).

① ATTACH RUBBER BAND TO INTERMEDIATE CHOKE LEVER.

② OPEN THROTTLE TO ALLOW CHOKE VALVE TO CLOSE.

③ SET UP ANGLE GAGE AND SET ANGLE TO SPECIFICATION.

④ RETRACT VACUUM BREAK PLUNGER USING VACUUM SOURCE, AT LEAST 18" HG. PLUG AIR BLEED HOLES WHERE APPLICABLE.

PRIMARY SIDE VACUUM BREAK ADJUSTMENT
(DUAL VACUUM BREAK UNITS)

86815016

Fig. 14 Primary side vacuum break adjustment

6. Push in on the intermediate choke lever to close the choke valve, and hold closed during adjustment.
7. Adjust by using a ⅛ in. (3mm) hex wrench to turn the screw in the rear cover until the bubble is centered.
8. After adjusting, apply RTV silicone sealant over the screw to seal the setting.

Secondary Vacuum Break

▶ See Figure 15

1. Connect a rubber band to the intermediate choke lever, then open the throttle valve to allow the choke valve to close.
2. Set up the angle gauge and the angle to specifications.
3. Position the fast idle screw on the second step of the fast idle cam (against the rise of the high step).
4. Turn the choke lever shaft to open the choke valve and make contact with the black closing tang.
5. Seat the choke vacuum diaphragm with an outside vacuum source.
6. Push in on the intermediate choke lever to close the choke valve, and hold closed during adjustment. Make sure the plunger spring is compressed and seated, if present.
7. Adjust by using a ⅛ in. (3mm) hex wrench to turn the screw in the rear cover until the bubble is centered.
8. After adjusting, apply RTV silicone sealant over the screw to seal the setting.

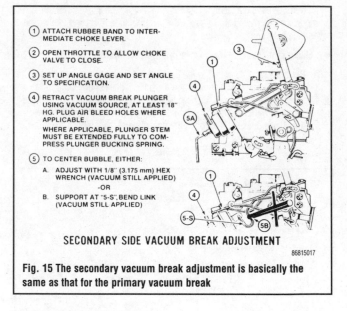

① ATTACH RUBBER BAND TO INTER-MEDIATE CHOKE LEVER.

② OPEN THROTTLE TO ALLOW CHOKE VALVE TO CLOSE.

③ SET UP ANGLE GAGE AND SET ANGLE TO SPECIFICATION.

④ RETRACT VACUUM BREAK PLUNGER USING VACUUM SOURCE, AT LEAST 18" HG. PLUG AIR BLEED HOLES WHERE APPLICABLE.
WHERE APPLICABLE, PLUNGER STEM MUST BE EXTENDED FULLY TO COMPRESS PLUNGER BUCKING SPRING.

⑤ TO CENTER BUBBLE, EITHER:
A. ADJUST WITH 1/8" (3.175 mm) HEX WRENCH (VACUUM STILL APPLIED)
-OR-
B. SUPPORT AT "5-S", BEND LINK (VACUUM STILL APPLIED)

SECONDARY SIDE VACUUM BREAK ADJUSTMENT

86815017

Fig. 15 The secondary vacuum break adjustment is basically the same as that for the primary vacuum break

Secondary Throttle Lockout

▶ See Figure 16

1. Pull the choke wide open by pushing out on the intermediate choke lever.
2. Open the throttle until the end of the secondary actuating lever is opposite the toe of the lockout lever.
3. Gauge clearance between the lockout lever and secondary lever should be as specified.
4. To adjust, bend the lockout lever where it contacts the fast idle cam.

Choke Link/Fast Idle Cam

▶ See Figure 17

1. Connect a rubber band to the intermediate choke lever, then open the throttle valve to allow the choke valve to close.
2. Set up the angle gauge and the angle to specifications.
3. Position the fast idle screw on the second step of the fast idle cam (against the rise of the high step).
4. Turn the choke lever shaft to open the choke valve and make contact with the black closing tang.

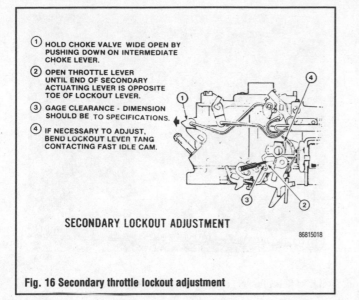

① HOLD CHOKE VALVE WIDE OPEN BY PUSHING DOWN ON INTERMEDIATE CHOKE LEVER.

② OPEN THROTTLE LEVER UNTIL END OF SECONDARY ACTUATING LEVER IS OPPOSITE TOE OF LOCKOUT LEVER.

③ GAGE CLEARANCE - DIMENSION SHOULD BE TO SPECIFICATIONS.

④ IF NECESSARY TO ADJUST, BEND LOCKOUT LEVER TANG CONTACTING FAST IDLE CAM.

SECONDARY LOCKOUT ADJUSTMENT

86815018

Fig. 16 Secondary throttle lockout adjustment

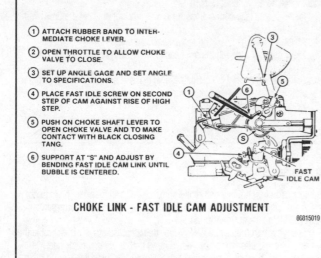

① ATTACH RUBBER BAND TO INTER-MEDIATE CHOKE LEVER.

② OPEN THROTTLE TO ALLOW CHOKE VALVE TO CLOSE.

③ SET UP ANGLE GAGE AND SET ANGLE TO SPECIFICATIONS.

④ PLACE FAST IDLE SCREW ON SECOND STEP OF CAM AGAINST RISE OF HIGH STEP.

⑤ PUSH ON CHOKE SHAFT LEVER TO OPEN CHOKE VALVE AND TO MAKE CONTACT WITH BLACK CLOSING TANG.

⑥ SUPPORT AT "S" AND ADJUST BY BENDING FAST IDLE CAM LINK UNTIL BUBBLE IS CENTERED.

FAST IDLE CAM

CHOKE LINK - FAST IDLE CAM ADJUSTMENT

86815019

Fig. 17 Fast idle cam choke link

5. Support at the **S** point and bend the fast idle cam link until the bubble is centered.

REMOVAL & INSTALLATION

▶ **See Figures 18 thru 24**

1. Raise the hood and apply a cover on the fender.
2. Disconnect the battery cables and remove the battery.
3. Remove the air cleaner and gasket.
4. Disconnect the accelerator linkage.
5. Tag then disconnect the fuel pipes and hoses, then all the vacuum lines to the carburetor.
6. Tag and disconnect all electrical connections.
7. If equipped with an Automatic Transaxle, disconnect the downshift cable.
8. If equipped with cruise control, disconnect the linkage.
9. Unscrew the carburetor mounting bolts and remove the carburetor from the manifold.
10. Remove the EFE heater, then cover the fuel opening so that dirt can not enter.

To install:

11. Inspect the EFE heater for damage. Be sure that the throttle body and EFE mating surfaces are clean.

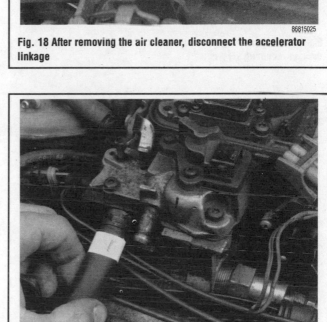

86815025

Fig. 18 After removing the air cleaner, disconnect the accelerator linkage

86815026

Fig. 19 Tag, then disconnect, the fuel lines and all vacuum lines to the carburetor

86815028

Fig. 20 Tag, then disconnect, all electrical connections to the carburetor, including the choke coil housing

Fig. 21 After removing all connections to the carburetor, unfasten the four mounting screws . . .

Fig. 22 . . . then remove the carburetor assembly from the manifold

Fig. 23 Remove the EFE heater

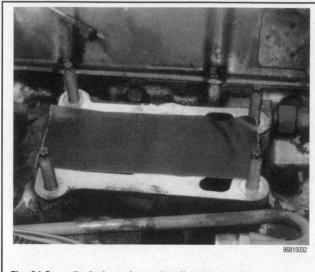

Fig. 24 Cover the fuel opening so that dirt cannot enter

12. Install the new or rebuilt carburetor onto the manifold, then tighten the nuts alternately to 13 ft. lbs. (18 Nm).

13. Install the linkage connections for cruise, accelerator and the downshift cable.

14. Attach all the fuel lines and tagged vacuum lines.

15. Make sure all connections are intact, then install the battery and cable connections.

16. Start the engine and check for any fuel leaks. If any are present, turn the engine off immediately, fix the leak. If none are present proceed.

17. Remove the fender covers and lower the hood.

OVERHAUL

E2SE Carburetor

Efficient carburetion depends greatly on careful cleaning and inspection during overhaul, since dirt, gum, water, or varnish in or on the carburetor parts are often responsible for poor performance.

Overhaul your carburetor in a clean, dust-free area. Carefully disassemble the carburetor, referring often to the exploded views and directions packaged with the rebuilding kit. Keep all similar and look-alike parts segregated during disassembly and cleaning to avoid accidental interchange during assembly. Make a note of all jet sizes.

When the carburetor is disassembled, wash all parts (except diaphragms, electric choke units, pump plunger, and any other plastic, fiber, or rubber parts) in clean carburetor solvent. Do not leave parts in the solvent any longer than is necessary to sufficiently loosen the deposits. Excessive cleaning may remove the special finish from the float bowl and choke valve bodies, leaving these parts unfit for service. Rinse all parts in clean solvent and blow them dry with compressed air or allow them to air dry. Wipe clean all cork, plastic, and fiber parts with a clean, lint-free cloth.

Blow out all passages and jets with compressed air and be sure that there are no restrictions or blockages. Never use wire or similar tools to clean jets, fuel passages, or air bleeds. Clean all jets and valves separately to avoid accidental interchange.

Check all parts for wear or damage. If wear or damage is found, replace the defective parts. Especially check the following:

1. Check the float needle and seat for wear. If wear is found, replace the complete assembly.

2. Check the float hinge pin for wear and the float(s) for dents or distortion. Replace the float if fuel has leaked into it.

3. Check the throttle and choke shaft bores for wear or an out-of-round condition. Damage or wear to the throttle arm, shaft, or shaft bore will often require replacement of the throttle body. These parts require a close tolerance of fit, wear may allow air leakage which could affect starting and idling.

E2SE CARBURETOR SPECIFICATIONS

Year	Carburetor Identification	Float Level (in.)	Fast Idle Cam (deg.)	Choke Coil lever (in.)	Air Valve Rod (deg.)	Primary Vacuum Break (deg.)	Secondary Vacuum Break (deg.)	Choke Unloader (deg.)
1984	17084431	11/32	15°	.085	1°	26°	38°	42°
	17084434	11/32	15°	.085	1°	26°	38°	42°
	17084435	11/32	15°	.085	1°	26°	38°	42°
	17084452	5/32	28°	.085	1°	25°	35°	45°
	17084453	5/32	28°	.085	1°	25°	35°	45°
	17084455	5/32	28°	.085	1°	25°	35°	45°
	17084456	5/32	28°	.085	1°	25°	35°	45°
	17084458	5/32	28°	.085	1°	25°	35°	45°
	17064532	5/32	28°	.085	1°	25°	35°	45°
	17064534	5/32	28°	.085	1°	25°	35°	45°
	17084535	5/32	28°	.085	1°	25°	35°	45°
	17084537	5/32	28°	.085	1°	25°	35°	45°
	17084538	5/32	28°	.085	1°	25°	35°	45°
	17084540	5/32	28°	.085	1°	25°	35°	45°
	17084542	1/8	28°	.085	1°	25°	35°	45°
	17084532	9/32	28°	.085	1°	25°	35°	45°
	17084633	9/32	28°	.085	1°	25°	35°	45°
	17084635	9/32	28°	.085	1°	25°	35°	45°
	17084636	9/32	28°	.085	1°	25°	35°	45°
1985	17084534	5/32	28°	.085	1°	25°	35°	45°
	17084535	5/32	28°	.085	1°	25°	35°	45°
	17034540	5/32	28°	.085	1°	25°	35°	45°
	17034542	1/8	22°	.085	1°	25°	35°	45°
	17085356	9/32	22°	.085	1°	25°	30°	30°
	17085357	1/8	22°	.085	1°	25°	30°	30°
	17085358	9/32	22°	.085	1°	25°	30°	30°
	17085359	9/32	22°	.085	1°	25°	30°	30°
	17085368	1/8	22°	.085	1°	25°	30°	30°
	17085369	9/32	22°	.085	1°	25°	30°	30°
	17085370	9/32	22°	.085	1°	25°	30°	30°
	17085371	9/32	22°	.085	1°	25°	30°	30°
	17085452	5/32	28°	.085	1°	28°	35°	45°
	17085453	5/32	28°	.085	1°	28°	35°	45°
	17085458	5/32	28°	.085	1°	28°	35°	45°
1986	17084534	5/32	28°	.085	1°	25°	35°	45°
	17084535	5/32	28°	.085	1°	25°	35°	45°
	17084540	5/32	28°	.085	1°	25°	35°	45°
	17084542	5/32	28°	.085	1°	25°	35°	45°

E2SE CARBURETOR SPECIFICATIONS

Year	Carburetor Identification	Float Level (in.)	Fast Idle Cam (deg.)	Choke Coil Lever (in.)	Air Valve Rod (deg.)	Primary Vacuum Break (deg.)	Secondary Vacuum Break (deg.)	Choke Unloader (deg.)
1982	17082196	5/16	18°	.096	—	21°	19°	27°
	17082316	1/4	17°	.090	10	26°	34°	35°
	17082317	1/4	17°	.090	10	29°	35°	35°
	17082320	1/4	25°	.142	10	30°	35°	33°
	17082321	1/4	25°	.142	10	29°	34°	35°
	17082640	1/4	17°	.090	10	26°	34°	35°
	17082641	1/4	17°	.090	10	29°	35°	35°
	17082642	1/4	25°	.142	10	30°	35°	33°
1983	17083356	13/32	22°	.085	1°	25°	35°	30°
	17083357	13/32	22°	.085	1°	25°	35°	30°
	17083358	13/32	22°	.085	1°	25°	35°	30°
	17083359	13/32	22°	.085	1°	25°	35°	30°
	17083368	1/8	22°	.085	1°	25°	35°	30°
	17083370	1/8	22°	.085	1°	25°	35°	45°
	17083450	1/8	28°	.085	1°	27°	35°	45°
	17083451	1/8	28°	.085	1°	27°	35°	45°
	17083452	1/8	28°	.085	1°	27°	35°	45°
	17083453	1/8	28°	.085	1°	27°	35°	45°
	17083454	1/8	28°	.085	1°	27°	35°	45°
	17083455	1/8	28°	.085	1°	27°	35°	45°
	17083456	1/8	28°	.085	1°	27°	35°	45°
	17083630	1/4	28°	.085	1°	27°	35°	45°
	17083631	1/4	28°	.085	1°	27°	35°	45°
	17083632	1/4	28°	.085	1°	27°	35°	45°
	17083633	1/4	28°	.085	1°	27°	35°	45°
	17083634	1/4	28°	.085	1°	27°	35°	45°
	17083635	1/4	28°	.085	1°	27°	35°	45°
	17083636	1/4	28°	.085	1°	27°	35°	45°
	17063650	1/8	28°	.085	1°	25°	35°	45°
1984	17072683	9/32	28°	.085	1°	25°	35°	45°
	17074812	9/32	28°	.085	1°	25°	35°	45°
	17084356	9/32	22°	.085	1°	25°	30°	30°
	17084357	9/32	22°	.085	1°	25°	30°	30°
	17084358	9/32	22°	.085	1°	25°	30°	30°
	17084359	9/32	22°	.085	1°	25°	30°	30°
	17084368	1/8	22°	.085	1°	25°	30°	30°
	17084370	1/8	22°	.085	1°	25°	30°	30°
	17034430	11/32	15°	.085	1°	26°	38°	42°

➡Throttle shafts and bushings are not included in overhaul kits. They can be purchases separately.

4. Inspect the idle mixture adjusting needles for burrs or grooves. Any such condition requires replacement of the needle, since you will not be able to obtain a satisfactory idle.

5. Check the bowl cover for warped surfaces with a straightedge.

6. Closely inspect the accelerator pump plunger for wear and damage, replacing as necessary.

7. After the carburetor is assembled, check the choke valve for freedom of operation.

Carburetor overhaul kits are recommended for each overhaul. These kits contain all gaskets and new parts to replace those which deteriorate most rapidly. Failure to replace all parts supplied with the kit (especially gaskets) can result in poor performance later.

Some carburetor manufacturers supply overhaul kits for three basic types: minor repair, major repair, and gasket kits. Basically, they contain the following:

Minor Repair Kits:
- All gaskets
- Float needle valve
- All diagrams
- Spring for the pump diaphragm

Major Repair Kits:
- All jets and gaskets
- All diaphragms
- Float needle valve
- Pump ball valve
- Float
- Complete intermediate rod
- Intermediate pump lever
- Some cover hold-down screws and washers

Gasket Kits:
- All gaskets

After cleaning and checking all components, reassemble the carburetor, using new parts and referring to the exploded view. When reassembling, make sure that all screws and jets are tight in their seats, but do not overtighten as the tips will be distorted. Tighten all screws gradually, in rotation. Do not tighten needle valves into their seats, uneven jetting will result. Always use new gaskets. Be sure to adjust the float level when reassembling.

Carburetor Adjustments

PRELIMINARY CHECKS

The following should be observed before attempting any adjustments.

1. Thoroughly warm the engine. If the engine is cold, be sure that it reaches operating temperature.

2. Check the torque of all carburetor mounting nuts and assembly screws. Also check the intake manifold-to-cylinder head bolts. If air is leaking at any of these points, any attempts at adjustment will inevitably lead to frustration.

3. Check the manifold heat control valve (if used) to be sure that it is free.

4. Check and adjust the choke as necessary.

5. Adjust the idle speed and mixture. If the mixture screws are capped, don't adjust them unless all other causes of rough idle have been eliminated. If any adjustments are performed that might possible change the idle speed or mixture, adjust the idle and mixture again when you are finished.

Before you make any carburetor adjustments make sure that the engine is in tune. Many problems which are thought to be carburetor related can be traced to an engine which is simply out-of-tune. Any trouble in these areas will have symptoms like those of carburetor problems.

THROTTLE BODY FUEL INJECTION (TBI) SYSTEM

General Information

The electronic throttle body fuel injection system is a fuel metering system with the amount of fuel delivered by the throttle body injector(s) determined by an electronic signal supplied by the Computer Control Module (ECM/PCM). The ECM/PCM monitors various engine and vehicle conditions to calculate the fuel delivery time (pulse width) of the injector(s). The fuel pulse may be modified by the ECM/PCM to account for special operating conditions, such as cranking, cold starting, altitude, acceleration, and deceleration.

The Throttle Body Injection (TBI) system provides a means of fuel distribution for controlling exhaust emissions within legislated limits. The TBI system, by precisely controlling the air/fuel mixture under all operating conditions, provides as near as possible complete combustion.

This is accomplished by using an Computer Control Module (ECM/PCM) (a small on-board microcomputer) that receives electrical inputs from various sensors about engine operating conditions. An oxygen sensor in the main exhaust stream functions to provide feedback information to the ECM/PCM as to the oxygen content, lean or rich, in the exhaust. The ECM/PCM uses this information from the oxygen sensor, and other sensors, to modify fuel delivery to achieve, as near as possible, an ideal air/fuel ratio of 14.7:1. This air/fuel ratio allows the 3-way catalytic converter to be more efficient in the conversion process of reducing exhaust emissions while at the same time providing acceptable levels of driveability and fuel economy.

Relieving Fuel System Pressure

✵ CAUTION

It is necessary to relieve the fuel system pressure to reduce the risk of fire or personal injury. Have a shop rag handy in case of any spilt fuel when disconnecting fuel lines.

1. Loosen the fuel filler cap on the vehicle.
2. Raise the vehicle, then disconnect the fuel pump electrical connector.
3. Lower the vehicle.

4. Start and run the engine until the fuel supply remaining in the fuel lines is consumed.

5. Engage the starter for three seconds to allow relief of any remaining pressure.

6. Disconnect the negative battery cable.

Electric Fuel Pump

REMOVAL & INSTALLATION

▶ **See Figure 25**

1. Relieve fuel system pressure.
2. Disconnect the negative battery cable.
3. Raise the vehicle and safely support.
4. Drain the fuel tank.
5. Disconnect wiring from the tank.
6. Remove the ground wire retaining screw from under the body.
7. Disconnect all hoses from the tank.
8. Support the tank on a jack and remove the retaining strap nuts.
9. Lower the tank and remove it.

10. Notice the position of the filter for replacement. Support the pump with one hand and grasp the filter with the other. Rotate the filter in one direction, then pull off of the pump. Discard the filter.

11. Disconnect the fuel pump connector, on wagons it will not be necessary.

12. On all models excluding wagons:
   a. Place the sending unit on a bench upside down, then pull the fuel pump downwards to remove from the mounting bracket. Tilt the pump outwards and remove from the pulsator.

13. On wagons proceed as follows:
   a. Disconnect the negative terminal nut and lead (black) from the pump.
   b. Disconnect the positive lead (gray) from the pump, then loosen the coupler clamps.

To install:

14. On all models excluding wagons:
   a. Assemble the rubber bumper and insulator onto the pump.

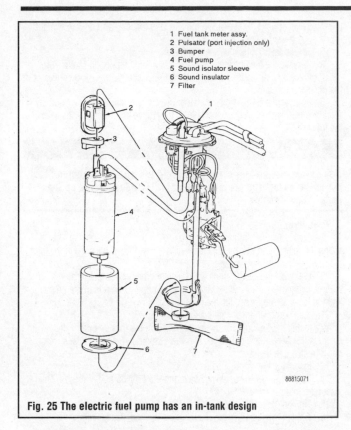

Fig. 25 The electric fuel pump has an in-tank design

1 Fuel tank meter assy.
2 Pulsator (port injection only)
3 Bumper
4 Fuel pump
5 Sound isolator sleeve
6 Sound insulator
7 Filter

b. Position the fuel sender assembly upside down and install the fuel pump between the pulsator and mounting bracket.

c. Connect the pump electrical connector.

15. On all wagon models:

a. Position the fuel sender assembly upside down and install the coupler and coupler clamps to the inlet tube, but do not tighten at this time.

b. Install the pump between the coupler and the mounting bracket, then tighten the clamps so that 5–8 teeth are engaged.

c. Attach the positive lead (gray) to its positive terminal with the nut, then attach the negative lead (black) to the negative terminal.

➡ **Always install a new filter when installing a new pump.**

16. Position the pump filter on the new pump and push the outer edge of the ferrule until it is fully seated.

17. Install the sending unit.

18. Install the gas tank and check for leaks.

19. Reconnect the battery cable.

Throttle Body

REMOVAL & INSTALLATION

1. Relieve the fuel system pressure as described above.
2. Disconnect the negative battery cable.
3. Remove the air cleaner.
4. Disconnect all wiring from the idle air control valve, throttle position sensor, and the fuel injector.
5. Remove the grommet with wires from the throttle body.
6. Disconnect the linkage from the unit.
7. Mark and disconnect the vacuum lines from the unit.
8. Follow the CAUTION under the fuel Pressure Test above, then disconnect the fuel feed and return lines from the unit. Discard the fuel line O-rings.
9. Unbolt and remove the unit and flange gasket, then discard the gasket.

To install:

10. Place a cover over the throttle body opening on the manifold to prevent dirt from entering the engine.

11. Clean the gasket surface on the throttle body and the intake manifold.

12. Install a new flange gasket, then mount the TBI unit to the manifold.

13. Tighten the TBI attaching bolts to 10–18 ft. lbs. (13–24 Nm).

14. Slip the new O-rings onto the fuel lines, then attach the fuel feed and return lines to the throttle body. The use of a fuel line wrench is needed for tightening the lines.

15. Tighten the line nuts to 18–20 ft. lbs. (24–27 Nm).

16. Attach the marked vacuum lines to there proper locations, then connect the linkages.

17. Install the grommet with the wires to the throttle body, along with any other electrical connections. Make sure all the connections are properly seated.

18. Tighten the fuel filler cap, then connect the negative battery cable.

19. Inspect with the engine **OFF** to see that the accelerator pedal is free, depress the pedal to the floor and release. Until this is the case then you can proceed.

20. Turn the ignition switch **ON** for two seconds, then turn the ignition **OFF** for ten seconds. Again turn the ignition **ON** and check for leaks.

21. Attach the air cleaner assembly and gasket.

22. Reset the Idle Air Control valve pintle position.

a. Block the drive wheels, then apply the Parking brake.

b. Start the engine, then hold the idle speed above 2000 rpm. Ground the diagnostic test terminal (ALDL) for ten seconds, then remove the ground.

c. Turn the ignition **OFF**, then restart the engine and check for proper idle operation.

Injector

REPLACEMENT

▶ **See Figures 26 thru 31**

1. Relieve fuel system pressure as described above.
2. Disconnect the negative battery cable.
3. Remove the air cleaner.
4. Remove the electrical connection to the injector. On Model 300, unfasten

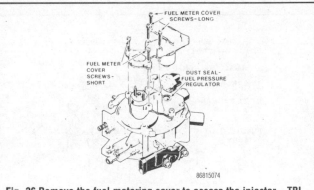

Fig. 26 Remove the fuel metering cover to access the injector—TBI Model 300

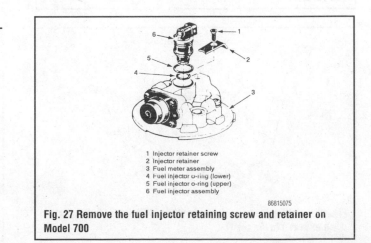

1 Injector retainer screw
2 Injector retainer
3 Fuel meter assembly
4 Fuel injector o-ring (lower)
5 Fuel injector o-ring (upper)
6 Fuel injector assembly

Fig. 27 Remove the fuel injector retaining screw and retainer on Model 700

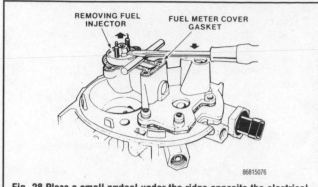

Fig. 28 Place a small prytool under the ridge opposite the electrical connector of the injector, and carefully pry it out—Model 300 shown

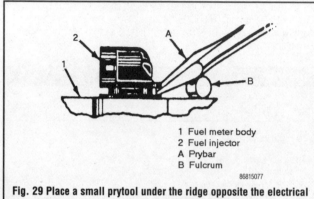

1 Fuel meter body
2 Fuel injector
A Prybar
B Fulcrum

Fig. 29 Place a small prytool under the ridge opposite the electrical connector of the injector, and carefully pry it out—Model 700 shown

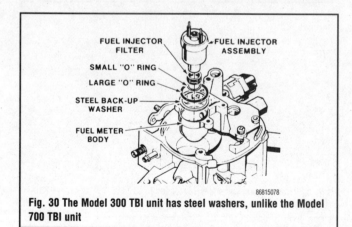

Fig. 30 The Model 300 TBI unit has steel washers, unlike the Model 700 TBI unit

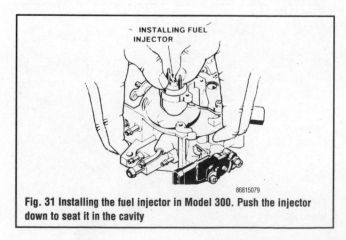

Fig. 31 Installing the fuel injector in Model 300. Push the injector down to seat it in the cavity

the injector connector by squeezing the two tabs together and pulling straight up.

5. On Model 300, remove the fuel metering cover.
6. Remove the fuel injector retaining screw and retainer on Model 700.
7. Place a small prytool under the ridge opposite the electrical connector of the injector, and carefully pry it out.
8. Remove the two O-rings from the injector and discard them. Carefully rotate the injector fuel filter back and forth to remove the filter from the base of the injector.

✳✳ CAUTION

Do not remove the four screws securing the pressure regulator to the meter cover. The pressure regulator includes a large spring under heavy tension.

To install:

9. Attach the filter to the injector, make sure the large end of the filter is facing the injector, so that the filter covers the raised rib at the base of the injector.
10. Lubricate the new O-rings with clean engine oil or transmission fluid, then place them on the injector. Make sure the upper O-ring is in the groove and the lower O-ring is up, flush against the filter.
11. If so equipped install the steel washer.
12. Install the fuel injector by positioning it in the throttle body with the electrical connector face cut-out for the wire grommet, then push the injector down to seat it in the cavity.
13. Install the injector retainer.
14. Apply Loctite®262 or an equivalent to the threads of the injector. Then install the injector retainer screw.
15. Tighten the retainer screw.
16. Tighten the fuel filler cap, the connect the negative battery cable.

Idle Air Control (IAC) Valve

◆ **See Figures 32 and 33**

REMOVAL & INSTALLATION

1. Remove the air cleaner.
2. Disconnect the electrical connection from the idle air control assembly (IAC).
3. Remove the idle air control assembly (IAC) from the throttle body.

➥Before installing a new idle air control valve, measure the distance that the valve is extended. This measurement should be made from motor housing to end of the cone. The distance should be no greater than 1⅛ in. (28mm). If the cone is extended too far damage to the valve may result. The IAC valve pintle may also be retracted by using IAC/ISC Motor Tester J-37027/BT-8256K. It is recommended not to push or pull on the IAC pintle. The force required to move the pintle of a new valve should not cause damage. Do not soak the IAC valve in any liquid cleaner or solvent as damage may result.

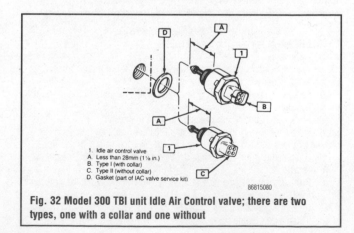

1. Idle air control valve
A. Less than 28mm (1⅛ in.)
B. Type I (with collar)
C. Type II (without collar)
D. Gasket (part of IAC valve service kit)

Fig. 32 Model 300 TBI unit Idle Air Control valve; there are two types, one with a collar and one without

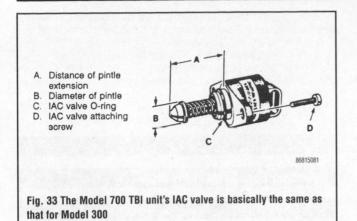

Fig. 33 The Model 700 TBI unit's IAC valve is basically the same as that for Model 300

A. Distance of pintle extension
B. Diameter of pintle
C. IAC valve O-ring
D. IAC valve attaching screw

4. Be sure to identify the replacement idle air control valve and replace with an identical part. The IAC valve pintle shape and diameter are designed for specific applications.

➡Shiny spots on the pintle or seat are normal and do not indicate misalignment or bend in the shaft.

To install:

5. Install a new O-ring and lubricate with engine oil onto the IAC valve.
6. Install the new idle air control valve with the attaching screws using a threadlocking material Loctite®262 or an equivalent.
7. Tighten the screws to 27 inch lbs. (3 Nm).
8. Reconnect all electrical connections.
9. Replace the air cleaner assembly.
10. The base idle will not be correct unit the ECM/PCM resets the IAC.

➡Be sure to clean the IAC valve O-ring sealing surface, pintle valve seat and air passage. Use a suitable carburetor cleaner (be sure it is safe to use on systems equipped with an oxygen sensor) and a parts cleaning brush to remove the carbon deposits. Do not use a cleaner that contains methyl ethyl ketone. It is an extremely strong solvent and not necessary for this type of deposits. Shiny spots on the pintle or on the seat are normal and do not indicate a misalignment or a bent pintle shaft. If the air passage has heavy deposits, remove the throttle body for a complete cleaning. Replace the IAC O-ring with a new one.

Resetting Procedure

1. If a repair has been made, reset the IAC before retesting.
2. Turn the ignition switch **OFF** for 10 seconds.
3. Start the engine for 5 seconds.
4. Turn the ignition switch **OFF** for 10 seconds.
5. Retest IAC system, as necessary.

Throttle Position Sensor

REMOVAL & INSTALLATION

▶ **See Figures 34 and 35**

1. Disconnect the negative battery cable. Remove the air cleaner assembly along with the necessary duct work.
2. Remove the TPS attaching screws. If the TPS is riveted to the throttle body, it will be necessary to drill out the rivets.
3. Remove the TPS from the throttle body assembly.

➡The throttle position sensor is an electrical component and should not be immersed in any type of liquid solvent or cleaner, as damage may result.

To install:

4. With the throttle valve closed, install the TPS onto the throttle shaft. Rotate the TPS counterclockwise to align the mounting holes. Install the retaining screws or rivets. Tighten the retaining screws to 18 inch lbs. (2 Nm).

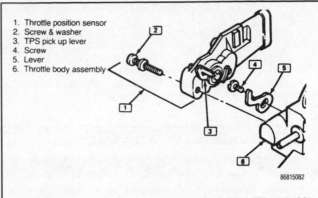

1. Throttle position sensor
2. Screw & washer
3. TPS pick up lever
4. Screw
5. Lever
6. Throttle body assembly

Fig. 34 Throttle Position Sensor (TPS) on a Model 300 TBI assembly

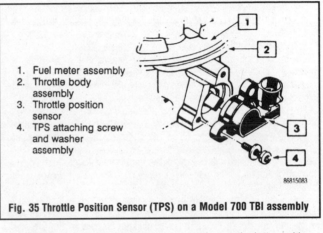

1. Fuel meter assembly
2. Throttle body assembly
3. Throttle position sensor
4. TPS attaching screw and washer assembly

Fig. 35 Throttle Position Sensor (TPS) on a Model 700 TBI assembly

5. Install the air cleaner assembly and connect the negative battery cable. Perform the TPS output check and adjust the TPS if applicable.

ADJUSTMENT

Not all vehicles provide for this adjustment. Generally, newer vehicles don't have adjustable throttle position sensors. If the sensor your car is equipped with does not have slots at the mounting screws, then it's not adjustable.

1. Remove air cleaner. Disconnect the TPS harness from the TPS.
2. Using suitable jumper wires, connect a digital voltmeter J-34029-A or equivalent from the TPS connector center terminal B to the outside terminal A. A suitable ALDL scanner can also be used to read the TPS output voltage.
3. With the ignition **ON** and the engine stopped, The TPS voltage should be less than 1.25 volts.
4. If the reading on the TPS is not within the specified range, rotate the TPS until 0.42–0.54 volts are obtained. If this specified voltage cannot be obtained, replace the TPS.
5. If the voltage reading is correct, remove the voltmeter and jumper wires and reconnect the TPS connector to the sensor. Re-install the air cleaner.

Idle Speed

ADJUSTMENT

This procedure should be performed only when the throttle body parts have been replaced. Newer models may not provide for this adjustment, as the computer is responsible for idle control.

➡**The following procedure requires the use of a special tool.**

1. Remove the air cleaner and gasket.
2. Plug the vacuum port on the TBI marked THERMAC.
3. If the car is equipped with a tamper resistant plug that covers the throttle

stop screw, the TBI unit must be removed as previously described in order to remove the plug.

4. Remove the throttle valve cable from the throttle control bracket to allow access to the throttle stop screw.

5. Connect a tachometer to the engine.

6. Start the engine and run it to normal operating temperature.

7. Install tool J-33047 into the idle air passage of the throttle body. Be sure that the tool is fully seated and that no air leaks exist.

8. Using a #20 Torx bit (0.16 in.–4mm), turn the minimum air screw until the engine rpm is 675–725 with auto. trans. or 725–825 with manual trans. The AT should be in Park, the MT in Neutral.

9. Stop the engine and remove the special tool.

10. Install the cable on the throttle body.

11. Use RTV sealant to cover the throttle stop screw.

MULTI-PORT/SEQUENTIAL FUEL INJECTION SYSTEMS

General Information

The Multi-Port Injection (MFI) and Sequential Fuel Injection (SFI) systems are controlled by an Computer Control Module (ECM/PCM) which monitors engine operations and generates output signals to provide the correct air/fuel mixture, ignition timing and engine idle speed control. Input to the control unit is provided by an oxygen sensor, (heated on the SFI) coolant temperature sensor, detonation sensor, mass air flow sensor and throttle position sensor. The ECM/PCM also receives information concerning engine rpm, road speed, transaxle gear position, power steering and air conditioning.

The injectors are located, one at each intake port, rather than the single injector found on the earlier throttle body system. The injectors are mounted on a fuel rail and are activated by a signal from the electronic control module. The injector is a solenoid-operated valve which remains open depending on the width of the electronic pulses (length of the signal) from the ECM/PCM; the longer the open time, the more fuel is injected. The MFI system has fuel flowing to the injectors at a pulse time and the SFI system has fuel flowing to the injectors in sequence of the firing order. In other words, if the firing order is 1–2–3–4–5–6 the fuel will be sent to the injectors in that order. In this manner, the air/fuel mixture can be precisely controlled for maximum performance with minimum emissions.

Fuel is pumped from the tank by a high pressure fuel pump, located inside the fuel tank. It is a positive displacement roller vane pump. The impeller serves as a vapor separator and pre-charges the high pressure assembly. A pressure regulator maintains 28–36 psi (179–248 kPa) in the fuel line to the injectors and the excess fuel is fed back to the tank. A fuel accumulator is used to dampen the hydraulic line hammer in the system created when all injectors open simultaneously.

The Mass Air Flow (MAF) Sensor is used to measure the mass of air that is drawn into the engine cylinders. It is located just ahead of the air throttle in the intake system and consists of a heated film which measures the mass of air, rather than just the volume. A resistor is used to measure the temperature of the film at 75° above ambient temperature. As the ambient (outside) air temperature rises, more energy is required to maintain the heated film at the higher temperature and the control unit used this difference in required energy to calculate the mass of the incoming air. The control unit uses this information to determine the duration of fuel injection pulse, timing and EGR.

The throttle body incorporates an Idle Air Control (IAC) that provides for a bypass channel through which air can flow. It consists of an orifice and pintle which is controlled by the ECM through a step motor. The IAC provides air flow for idle and allows additional air during cold start until the engine reaches operating temperature. As the engine temperature rises, the opening through which air passes is slowly closed.

The Throttle Position Sensor (TPS) provides the control unit with information on throttle position, in order to determine injector pulse width and hence correct mixture. The TPS is connected to the throttle shaft on the throttle body and consists of as potentiometer with on end connected to a 5 volt source from the ECM and the other to ground. A third wire is connected to the ECM/PCM to measure the voltage output from the TPS which changes as the throttle valve angle is changed (accelerator pedal moves). At the closed throttle position, the output is low (approximately 0.4 volts); as the throttle valve opens, the output increases to a maximum 5 volts at Wide Open Throttle (WOT). The TPS can be misadjusted open, shorted, or loose and if it is out of adjustment, the idle quality or WOT performance may be poor. A loose TPS can cause intermittent bursts of fuel from the injectors and an unstable idle because the ECM/PCM thinks the throttle is moving. This should cause a trouble code to be set. Once a trouble code is set, the ECM/PCM will use a preset value for TPS and some vehicle performance may return. A small amount of engine coolant is routed through the throttle assembly to prevent freezing inside the throttle bore during cold operation.

Relieving Fuel System Pressure

✳✳ CAUTION

Before opening any part of the fuel system, the pressure must be relieved. Follow the procedure below to relieve the pressure:

The fuel pressure release fitting is located at the top rear of the fuel injection rail. Use of a fuel pressure gauge, J-34730-1 or an equivalent.

1. Disconnect the negative battery cable to avoid possible fuel discharge.

2. Loosen the fuel filler cap to relieve the pressure.

3. Connect a fuel pressure gauge to the pressure valve, wrap a towel around the fitting while connecting a gauge to avoid spillage.

4. Install a bleed hose into an approved unbreakable container, then open the valve to bleed the pressure.

5. Drain any excess fuel in the gauge into the container.

Electric Fuel Pump

The electric fuel pumps are attached to the fuel sending unit, which is located in the fuel tank.

✳✳ CAUTION

Before opening any part of the fuel system, the pressure must be relieved. Follow the procedure below to relieve the pressure:

REMOVAL & INSTALLATION

1. Relieve fuel system pressure.

2. Disconnect the negative battery cable.

3. Raise the vehicle and safely support.

4. Drain the fuel tank.

5. Disconnect wiring from the tank.

6. Remove the ground wire retaining screw from under the body.

7. Disconnect all hoses from the tank.

8. Support the tank on a jack and remove the retaining strap nuts.

9. Lower the tank and remove it.

10. Notice the position of the filter for replacement. Support the pump with one hand and grasp the filter with the other. Rotate the filter in one direction, then pull off of the pump. Discard the filter.

11. Disconnect the fuel pump connector, on wagons it will not be necessary.

12. On all models excluding wagons:

a. Place the sending unit on a bench upside down, then pull the fuel pump downwards to remove from the mounting bracket. Tilt the pump outwards and remove from the pulsator.

13. On wagons proceed as follows:

a. Disconnect the negative terminal nut and lead (black) from the pump.

b. Disconnect the positive lead (gray) from the pump, then loosen the coupler clamps.

To install:

14. On all models excluding wagons:

a. Assemble the rubber bumper and insulator onto the pump.

b. Position the fuel sender assembly upside down and install the fuel pump between the pulsator and mounting bracket.

c. Connect the pump electrical connector.

15. On all wagon models:

a. Position the fuel sender assembly upside down and install the coupler and coupler clamps to the inlet tube, but do not tighten at this time.

b. Install the pump between the coupler and the mounting bracket, then tighten the clamps so that 5–8 teeth are engaged.

c. Attach the positive lead (gray) to its positive terminal with the nut, then attach the negative lead (black) to the negative terminal.

➡ **Always install a new filter when installing a new pump.**

16. Position the pump filter on the new pump and push the outer edge of the ferrule until it is fully seated.

17. Install the sending unit.

18. Install the gas tank and check for leaks.

19. Reconnect the battery cable.

TESTING

Pressure Test

1. Relive the fuel system pressure.

2. On MFI equipped engines, disconnect the fuel line from the EFI, then connect the fuel line to a pressure gauge.

➡ **If the system is equipped with a fuel return hose, squeeze it off so that an accurate reading can be obtained.**

3. On the MFI equipped engines, connect a jumper wire from the positive battery terminal to the **G** terminal of the ALCL unit or on the carbureted engines, start the engine, then check the fuel pressure.

4. The fuel pressure should be about 34–46 psi.

➡ **If the pressures do not indicate correctly, check the fuel line for restrictions or the pump for malfunctions.**

Volume Test

This test should be completed after the pressure test has been performed.

1. Disconnect the pressure gauge from the fuel line and connect a flexible tube from the fuel line to an unbreakable container.

➡ **If the engine is equipped with a fuel return line, squeeze off the line to obtain an accurate reading.**

2. Connect a jumper wire from the positive battery cable to the **G** terminal of the ALCL unit.

3. In 15 seconds, the fuel pump should supply ½ pint of fuel.

➡ **If the fuel volume is below minimum, check the fuel line for restrictions.**

4. After testing, reconnect the fuel line to the EFI unit.

Throttle Body

The throttle body is located at the front of the engine and is attached to the intake plenum.

REMOVAL & INSTALLATION

▶ **See Figure 36**

1. Disconnect the negative battery cable.

2. On MFI systems drain the coolant from the cooling system until the level is below the throttle body.

3. Remove the air inlet duct, the vacuum hoses and the coolant hoses from the throttle body.

4. Disconnect the accelerator and cruise control (if equipped) cables.

5. Remove the Idle Air Control (IAC) and the Throttle Position Sensor (TPS) electrical connectors from the throttle body.

6. Remove the nuts holding the throttle body to the upper intake manifold assembly.

7. Remove the throttle body and flange gasket, clean the gasket areas thoroughly.

To install:

8. Install a new flange gasket, then mount the throttle body assembly onto the intake manifold.

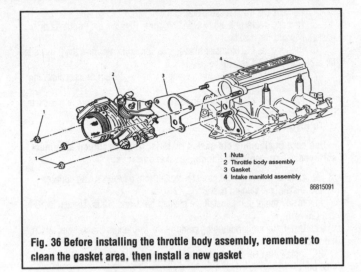

1 Nuts
2 Throttle body assembly
3 Gasket
4 Intake manifold assembly

86815091

Fig. 36 Before installing the throttle body assembly, remember to clean the gasket area, then install a new gasket

9. Install the retaining nuts, then tighten to 21 ft. lbs. (28 Nm).

10. Reinstall the coolant hose to the throttle body of the MFI system.

11. Attach all the control cables, then make adjustments accordingly.

12. Install the vacuum hoses and sensors, then attach the electrical connections to the sensors.

13. Install the air inlet duct. Connect the negative battery cable.

14. Add coolant to the system.

15. Reset the IAC pintle position:

a. Turn the ignition **ON**.

b. Ground the engine diagnostic lead for about five seconds.

16. Start the engine and check for proper idle and leaks.

Plenum/Upper Intake Manifold

The Plenum is the top portion of the intake manifold. This portion must be removed before servicing the injector system.

REMOVAL & INSTALLATION

MFI Engines—Except 3.1L (VIN T)

1. Disconnect the negative battery cable.

2. Tag and disconnect the vacuum lines.

3. Remove the EGR to plenum nuts.

4. Remove the two throttle body bolts.

5. Remove the throttle cable bracket bolts.

6. Remove the ignition wire plastic shield bolts.

7. Remove the plenum bolts.

8. Remove the plenum and gaskets from the engine.

To install:

9. Clean the gasket area, then install new gaskets.

10. Connect the plenum with the mounting bolts, then tighten them to 16 ft. lbs. (21 Nm).

11. Attach the ignition wire plastic shield bolts, then the throttle body bolts.

12. Tighten the throttle body bolts to 18 ft. lbs. (25 Nm).

13. Install the EGR to plenum nuts, then attach the throttle cable bracket bolts.

14. Hook up the vacuum lines, then connect the negative battery cable.

15. With the engine in the **OFF** position, make sure the accelerator pedal is free. Depress the pedal to the floor and release.

16. Reset the IAC pintle position:

a. Turn the ignition **ON**.

b. Ground the engine diagnostic lead for about five seconds.

3.1L Engine (VIN T)

1. Disconnect the negative battery cable.

2. Remove the air inlet duct at the throttle body and crankcase vent pipe at the valve cover grommet.

3. Disconnect the vacuum harness connector from the throttle body.

4. Remove the throttle cable bracket bolt.

5. Remove the throttle body attaching bolts. Remove the throttle body and gasket. Discard the gasket.

6. Remove the EGR transfer tube-to-plenum bolts. Remove the EGR transfer tube and gasket. Discard the gasket.

7. Remove the air conditioning compressor-to-plenum bracket attaching hardware. Remove the bracket.

8. Remove the plenum bolts and studs. Remove the plenum and gaskets. Discard the gaskets.

To install:

➡**Use care in cleaning old gasket material from machined aluminum surfaces. Sharp tool may damage gasket surfaces.**

9. Carefully, remove old gasket material from gasket sealing surfaces.

10. Install new plenum gaskets.

11. Install the plenum. Install the plenum bolts and studs. Tighten to 18 ft. lbs. (25 Nm).

12. Install the air conditioning compressor-to-plenum bracket and attaching hardware.

13. Install the EGR transfer tube with a new gasket. Install the EGR transfer tube bolts.

14. Install a new throttle body gasket. Install the throttle body and attaching bolts.

15. Install the throttle cable bracket bolt.

16. Connect the vacuum harness connector to the throttle body.

17. Connect the air inlet duct to the throttle body and crankcase vent pipe to the valve cover grommet.

18. Connect the negative battery cable.

19. With the ignition switch in the **OFF** position, ensure that the movement of the accelerator is free.

20. Perform the Idle Learn Procedure, as described in Section 1.

3.1 L Engine (VIN M)

1. Disconnect the negative battery cable.

2. Drain the coolant, then disconnect the air inlet duct.

3. Remove the accelerator and cruise control cables at the throttle body accelerator control cable bracket.

4. Disconnect the fuel pipe clip at the accelerator cable bracket, then remove the bracket.

5. Disconnect the vacuum lines, matchmarking them for installation.

6. Remove the EGR valve.

7. Unfasten the heater inlet hose clamps at the heater inlet pipe.

8. Remove the ignition coil front bolts, then loosen the rear bolts.

9. Remove the alternator braces.

10. Disconnect the electrical connections to the IAC valve, MAF and TPS sensors.

11. Remove the upper intake manifold bolts and studs, then remove the assembly. Discard of the gaskets.

12. Disassemble the throttle body from the upper intake manifold.

13. Remove the heater hoses from the upper intake manifold.

14. Disconnect the fuel pressure regulator vacuum line.

15. Clean the gasket surfaces.

To install:

16. Assemble the throttle body to the upper intake manifold.

17. Attach the heater hoses to the upper intake manifold.

18. Install new upper intake manifold gaskets, then connect the upper intake manifold by guiding the upper intake manifold heater hoses onto the heater inlet pipe.

19. Install the upper intake manifold bolts and studs, then tighten the bolts and studs to 18 ft. lbs. (25 Nm).

20. Attach the heater hose clamps at the heater inlet pipe.

21. Install the alternator braces.

22. Insert the ignition coil front and rear bolts, then tighten.

23. Install the EGR valve bolts.

24. Connect the vacuum lines previously matchmarked.

25. Connect the electrical connections to the sensors and valves.

26. Attach the alternator control cable bracket, then connect the fuel pipe clip at the accelerator control cable bracket. Attach all the control cables.

27. Adjust the accelerator cable and cruise cables.

28. Attach the air inlet duct.

29. Install the negative battery cable, then refill the coolant.

30. Start the engine and check the coolant level, fill if needed.

Fuel Rail

REMOVAL & INSTALLATION

▶ **See Figures 37 and 38**

Before removal you should clean the fuel rail assembly. Use a special cleaner such as GM X-30 or an equivalent. Do not soak the rails in the solvent, follow the manufacturer's instructions.

1. Disconnect the negative battery cable.

2. Relieve the fuel system pressure.

3. Remove the intake manifold plenum, as required.

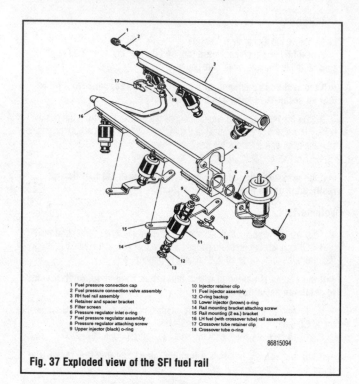

1 Fuel pressure connection cap	10 Injector retainer clip
2 Fuel pressure connection valve assembly	11 Fuel injector assembly
3 RH fuel rail assembly	12 O-ring backup
4 Retainer and spacer bracket	13 Lower injector (brown) o-ring
5 Filter screen	14 Rail mounting bracket attaching screw
6 Pressure regulator inlet o-ring	15 Rail mounting (2 ea.) bracket
7 Fuel pressure regulator assembly	16 LH fuel (with crossover tube) rail assembly
8 Pressure regulator attaching screw	17 Crossover tube retainer clip
9 Upper injector (black) o-ring	18 Crossover tube o-ring

86815094

Fig. 37 Exploded view of the SFI fuel rail

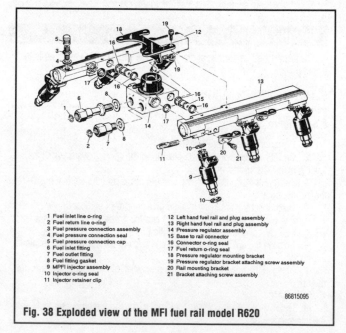

1 Fuel inlet line o-ring	12 Left hand fuel rail and plug assembly
2 Fuel return line o-ring	13 Right hand fuel rail and plug assembly
3 Fuel pressure connection assembly	14 Pressure regulator assembly
4 Fuel pressure connection seal	15 Base to rail connector
5 Fuel pressure connection cap	16 Connector o-ring seal
6 Fuel inlet fitting	17 Fuel return o-ring seal
7 Fuel outlet fitting	18 Pressure regulator mounting bracket
8 Fuel fitting gasket	19 Pressure regulator bracket attaching screw assembly
9 MPFI injector assembly	20 Rail mounting bracket
10 Injector o-ring seal	21 Bracket attaching screw assembly
11 Injector retainer clip	

86815095

Fig. 38 Exploded view of the MFI fuel rail model R620

4. Disconnect the fuel feed and return lines at the fuel rail. Use a backup wrench, as required, to support the fuel rail tube fittings.

5. Remove the fuel line O-rings and discard.

6. Disconnect the vacuum line at the pressure regulator, then remove the regulator (if needed).

7. Disconnect the fuel injector electrical connectors, then the coolant temperature sensor connector.

8. Remove the fuel rail attaching bolts. Remove the fuel rail assembly. Note the location and routing of vacuum hoses around the fuel rail before removing the rail.

9. Remove the injector O-ring seal from the spray tip end of each injector. Discard the O-rings.

To install:

10. Lubricate new injector O-ring seals with engine oil and install on the spray tip end of each injector.

11. Install the fuel rail assembly into the intake manifold. Tilt the rail assembly to install the injectors. Install the fuel rail attaching bolts and fuel rail bracket bolts. Tighten fuel rail attaching bolts.

12. Connect the electrical connection to the coolant temperature sensor, then the injector electrical connectors. Rotate the injectors, as required, to prevent stretching the wire harness.

13. Attach the main injector harness.

14. Install new O-rings on the fuel feed and return lines. Connect the fuel lines and tighten.

15. If removed, install the pressure regulator and connect the vacuum line.

16. Install the intake manifold plenum.

17. Connect the negative battery cable.

18. Tighten the fuel filler cap.

19. Turn the ignition switch to the **ON** position for 2 seconds, then turn to the **OFF** position for 10 seconds. Again, turn the ignition switch to the **ON** position and check for fuel leaks.

20. If equipped with the 3.1L (VIN T) engine, perform the Idle Learn Procedure, as described in Section 1.

Fuel Injectors

REMOVAL & INSTALLATION

♦ **See Figures 39 and 40**

1. Disconnect the negative battery cable.
2. Relieve fuel system pressure.
3. Remove the intake plenum and, if equipped, remove the runners.

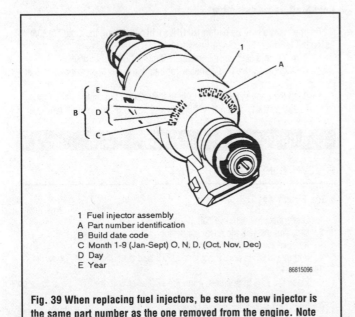

1 Fuel injector assembly
A Part number identification
B Build date code
C Month 1-9 (Jan-Sept) O, N, D, (Oct, Nov, Dec)
D Day
E Year

86815096

Fig. 39 When replacing fuel injectors, be sure the new injector is the same part number as the one removed from the engine. Note the location for identification

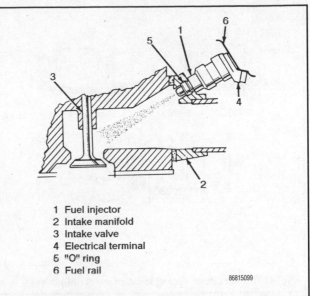

1 Fuel injector
2 Intake manifold
3 Intake valve
4 Electrical terminal
5 "O" ring
6 Fuel rail

86815099

Fig. 40 After the injector is installed, turn the ignition switch to the ON position for 2 seconds. Turn the ignition switch to the OFF position for 10 seconds. Again turn the ignition switch to the ON position and check for fuel leaks at the O-ring

4. Remove the fuel rail assembly.

5. Disconnect the injectors electrical connections.

6. Rotate the injector retaining clip to the release position, discard the clip.

7. Remove the injector from the fuel rail assembly.

8. Remove the O-rings from both ends of the injector and discard. Save the injector O-ring backups for use on assembly.

To install:

➡ **When replacing fuel injectors, be sure the new injector is the same part number as the one removed from the engine.**

To install:

9. Install the injector backups, then lubricate new injector O-rings with engine oil and install on the injectors.

10. Put the new injector retainer clip on the injector. Position the open end of the clip facing the injector electrical connector.

11. Install injector into fuel rail injector socket with the electrical connectors facing out.

12. Rotate the injector clip to the locked position.

13. Make sure all electrical connections are intact.

14. Install the fuel rail assembly.

15. Check for fuel leaks by performing the following:

a. Temporarily connect the negative battery cable.

b. Turn the ignition switch to the **ON** position for 2 seconds. Turn the ignition switch to the **OFF** position for 10 seconds. Again turn the ignition switch to the **ON** position and check for fuel leaks.

c. Disconnect the negative battery cable.

16. Install the plenum assembly.

17. Tighten the fuel filler cap.

18. Connect the negative battery cable.

Idle Air Control Valve

REMOVAL AND INSTALLATION

♦ **See Figures 41 and 42**

The idle air control valve is mounted to the throttle body and controls the bypass air around the throttle plate. It is used to control the engine idle speed, to prevent stalls due to changes in the engine load.

1. Remove the electrical connector from the Idle Air Control (IAC) valve assembly.

2. Unscrew the IAC from the throttle body and discard the gasket.

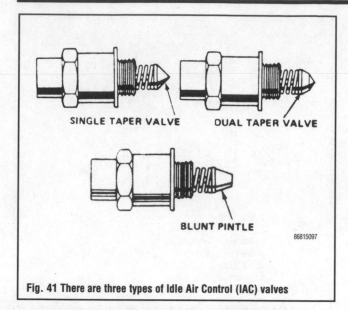

Fig. 41 There are three types of Idle Air Control (IAC) valves

➡Do not remove the thread locking compound from the threads.

To install:

3. Clean and inspect the IAC valve O-ring sealing surface, pintle seat and air passage. Do not soak the valve in any liquid cleaner or solvent, this will damage the valve. Use a carburetor cleaner and a parts cleaning brush to remove any carbon deposits. Shiny spots on the pintle or seat are normal and do not mean misalignment or a bent shaft.

4. If installing a new IAC valve, you will need to measure the distance between the tip of the pintle and the mounting flange. If it is greater than 1 inch (25mm), use finger pressure to slowly retract the pintle.

5. Lubricate the IAC valve O-ring with clean engine oil, then install the valve assembly.

6. Attach the IAC with the mounting screws, tighten them to 27 inch lbs. (3 Nm).

7. Connect the electrical connectors.

8. Reset the IAC valve pintle:
   a. Turn the ignition **ON** for five seconds.
   b. Turn the ignition **OFF** for ten seconds.
   c. Start the engine, then check for proper idle operation.

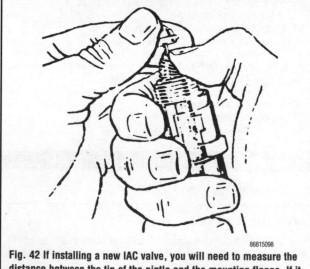

Fig. 42 If installing a new IAC valve, you will need to measure the distance between the tip of the pintle and the mounting flange. If it is greater than 1 inch (25mm), use finger pressure to slowly retract the pintle

Cold Start Valve

REMOVAL & INSTALLATION

▶ **See Figure 43**

The cold start valve (not controlled by the ECM/PCM) provides additional fuel during the starting mode to improve cold start ups.

1. Disconnect the negative battery cable.
2. Remove the IAC pipe and the engine mount strut brace.
3. Remove the fuel line from the fuel rail, the electrical connector from the valve and the valve retaining bolt.
4. Pull the cold start valve from the fuel rail.
5. Clean the areas around the valve and the connection with a suitable cleaner.
6. Remove the valve from the tube and body assembly, then bend the tab back to permit unscrewing of the valve.

To install:

7. Coat the O-ring seals with engine oil, then install the new valve O-ring seal and body O-ring seal on the cold start valve.
8. Install the tube O-ring seal on the tube and body assembly. Insert the cold start valve into the body assembly.

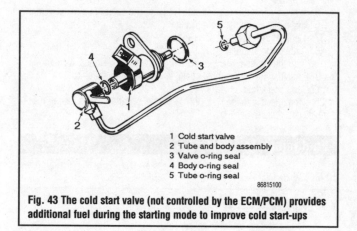

1 Cold start valve
2 Tube and body assembly
3 Valve o-ring seal
4 Body o-ring seal
5 Tube o-ring seal

Fig. 43 The cold start valve (not controlled by the ECM/PCM) provides additional fuel during the starting mode to improve cold start-ups

ADJUSTMENT

Cold Start Valve Assembly

This procedure is to be performed ONLY when installing the Cold Start Valve Assembly.

1. Turn the cold start valve completely into the body, until it seats.
2. Back out the valve one complete turn, until the electrical connector is at the top.
3. Bend the body tang forward to limit the rotation to less than a full turn.
4. Coat the new O-ring with engine oil and install it into the fuel rail.

Throttle Position Sensor (TPS)

REMOVAL & INSTALLATION

▶ **See Figure 44**

1. Disconnect the negative battery cable.
2. Unfasten the TPS electrical connector.
3. Remove the 2 mounting screws.
4. Remove the TPS and, if equipped, TPS seal from the throttle body.

To install:

5. Place the TPS in position. Align the TPS lever with the TPS drive lever on the throttle body.
6. Install the 2 TPS mounting screws.
7. Fasten the electrical connector.
8. Connect the negative battery cable.

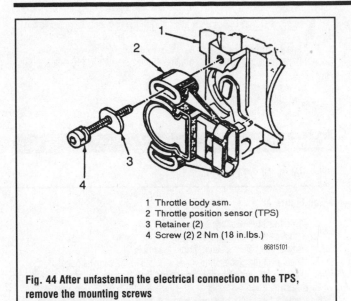

1 Throttle body asm.
2 Throttle position sensor (TPS)
3 Retainer (2)
4 Screw (2) 2 Nm (18 in.lbs.)

86815101

Fig. 44 After unfastening the electrical connection on the TPS, remove the mounting screws

Mass Air Flow (MAF) Sensor

REMOVAL & INSTALLATION

♦ **See Figure 45**

1. Disconnect the negative battery cable.
2. Detach the electrical connector, then remove the MAF sensor.
3. On some vehicles you will need to loosen the clamps on the air inlet ducts, then remove the air inlet ducts and remove the MAF sensor.
   To install:

➡ **Take note that this is an expensive and fragile sensor. If it was defective try and find the cause so the new one will not be damaged by the same problem, especially the air filter, broken screen, defective charging system, etc.**

4. If removed install the air duct setup, then install the MAF sensor.
5. Mount with the attaching screws, then install the electrical connection to the sensor.
6. Reconnect the negative battery cable.

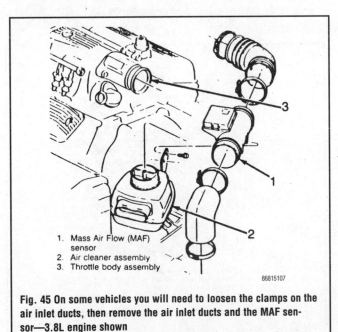

1. Mass Air Flow (MAF) sensor
2. Air cleaner assembly
3. Throttle body assembly

86815107

Fig. 45 On some vehicles you will need to loosen the clamps on the air inlet ducts, then remove the air inlet ducts and the MAF sensor—3.8L engine shown

Crankshaft Sensor

REMOVAL & INSTALLATION

3.8L Engine

On vehicles with a manual transaxles, the crankshaft position sensor is easily accessed from beneath the engine. On vehicles with automatic transaxles, the rack and pinion heat shield and the converter intermediate exhaust assembly must be removed first.

1. Disconnect the negative battery cable.
2. Disconnect the electrical connector at the sensor.
3. Using a 28mm socket and pull handle, rotate the harmonic balancer until any window in the interrupter is aligned with the crank sensor.
4. Loosen the pinch bolt on the sensor pedestal until the sensor is free to slide.
5. Remove the pedestal to the engine mounting bolts.
6. While manipulating the sensor within the pedestal, carefully remove the sensor and pedestal as a unit.
   To install:
7. Loosen the pinch bolt on the new sensor pedestal until the sensor is free to slide.
8. Verify that the window in the interrupter is still in the correct place.
9. Install the sensor and pedestal as a unit while making sure that the interrupter ring is aligned within the proper slot.
10. Install the pedestal and tighten the engine mounting bolts to 22 ft. lbs. (30 Nm).

3X Sensor

♦ **See Figure 46**

1. Disconnect the negative battery cable.
2. Remove the sensor harness connection to the sensor.
3. Unsecure the sensor block bolt.
4. Remove the Crankshaft Position (CKP) sensor from the vehicle. Inspect the O-ring for cracks and replace if needed.
   To install:
5. Install the new O-ring if needed and lubricate with engine oil.
6. Install the sensor into the hole in the block.
7. Install the mounting screw and tighten to 71–88 inch lbs. (8–10 Nm).
8. Attach the sensor harness connector, then connect the negative battery cable.

Dual Crank Sensor

Sections 3 and 4 of this manual also cover testing, removal and installation, and adjustment of many computer controlled components.

1. Disconnect the negative battery cable.
2. Remove the belt(s) from the crankshaft pulley.
3. Raise and support the vehicle safely.
4. Remove the right front wheel and inner fender access cover.

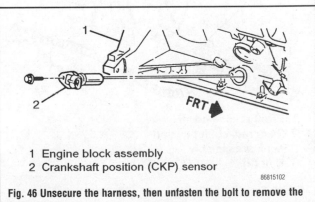

1 Engine block assembly
2 Crankshaft position (CKP) sensor

86815102

Fig. 46 Unsecure the harness, then unfasten the bolt to remove the CKP sensor

5. Remove the crankshaft harmonic balancer retaining bolt, then remove the harmonic balancer.

6. Disconnect the sensor electrical connector.

7. Remove the sensor and pedestal from the engine block, then separate the sensor from the pedestal.

To install:

8. Loosely install the crankshaft sensor to the pedestal.

9. Using tool J-37089 or equivalent, position the sensor with the pedestal attached, on the crankshaft.

10. Install the pedestal-to-block retaining bolts. Tighten to 14–28 ft. lbs. (20–40 Nm).

11. Tighten the pedestal pinch bolt 30–35 inch lbs. (3–4 Nm).

12. Remove tool J-37089 or equivalent.

13. Place tool J-37089 or equivalent, on the harmonic balancer and turn. If any vane of the harmonic balancer touches the tool, replace the balancer assembly.

➡**A clearance of 0.025 in. (0.635mm) is required on either side of the interrupter ring. Be certain to obtain the correct clearance. Failure to do so will damage the sensor. A misadjusted sensor of bent interrupter ring could cause rubbing of the sensor, resulting in potential driveability problems, such as rough idle, poor performance, or a no-start condition.**

14. Install the balancer on the crankshaft. Install the balancer retaining bolt. Tighten the retaining bolt to 200–239 ft. lbs. (270–325 Nm).

15. Install the inner fender shield.

16. Install the right front wheel assembly. Tighten the wheel nuts to 100 ft. lbs. (136 Nm).

17. Lower the vehicle.

18. Install the belt(s).

19. Reconnect the negative battery cable.

24X Crank Sensor

▸ **See Figure 47**

1. Disconnect the negative battery cable.

2. Remove the serpentine belt from the crankshaft pulley.

3. Raise and support the vehicle safely.

4. Remove the crankshaft harmonic balancer retaining bolt, then remove the harmonic balancer.

5. Disconnect the sensor electrical connector.

6. Unfasten the sensor bolts, then remove the sensor.

To install:

7. Install the crankshaft sensor to the engine with the two mounting bolts. Tighten the bolts to 8 ft. lbs. (10 Nm).

8. Attach the electrical harness to the sensor.

9. Using tool J-29113 or equivalent, install the harmonic balancer to the vehicle.

10. Apply a thread sealer such as GM 1052080 or an equivalent to the threads if the crankshaft balancer bolt, then tighten the bolt to 110 ft. lbs. (150 Nm).

11. Lower the vehicle.

12. Install the serpentine belt.

13. Reconnect the negative battery cable.

Camshaft Sensor

REMOVAL & INSTALLATION

▸ **See Figure 48**

1. Disconnect the negative battery cable.

2. Remove the serpentine drive belt.

3. Remove the power steering pump assembly.

4. Disconnect the electrical harness attached to the camshaft sensor.

5. Unfasten the bolt attaching the sensor, then remove the sensor.

To install:

6. Connect the camshaft sensor with the mounting bolt, then tighten the bolt to 8 ft. lbs. (10 Nm).

7. Attach the electrical harness to the sensor.

8. Install the power steering pump.

9. Install the serpentine drive belt, then connect the negative battery cable.

Minimum Idle Speed

ADJUSTMENTS

The engine should be at normal operating temperature before making this adjustment. Newer engines do not provide for this adjustment as the idle is completely computer controlled. If the computer cannot control the idle, the most likely cause a defective idle air control valve. Test the IAC valve, check the engine mechanical for basic tune-up, vacuum leaks, proper compression and the rest of the fuel control system. The least likely item bad is the computer itself, unless someone has recently working on the computer or the electrical system. For models that are adjustable following the following procedures:

1. Using an awl, pierce the idle stop screw plug (located on the side of the throttle body) and remove it by prying it from the housing.

2. Using a jumper wire, ground the diagnostic lead of the IAC motor.

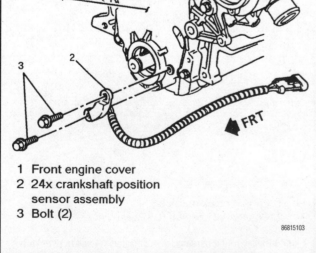

1 Front engine cover
2 24x crankshaft position sensor assembly
3 Bolt (2)

86815103

Fig. 47 The 24X crankshaft sensor is secured by two bolts

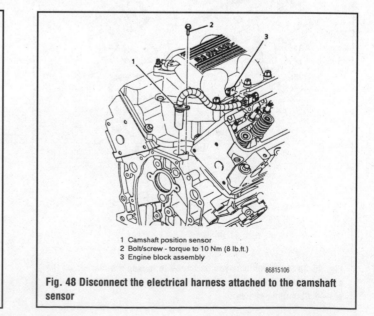

1 Camshaft position sensor
2 Bolt/screw - torque to 10 Nm (8 lb.ft.)
3 Engine block assembly

86815106

Fig. 48 Disconnect the electrical harness attached to the camshaft sensor

3. Turn on the ignition, DO NOT start the engine and wait for 30 seconds, then disconnect the IAC electrical connector. Remove the diagnostic lead ground lead and start the engine. Allow the system to go to closed loop.

4. Adjust the idle set screw to 550 rpm for the automatic transaxle (in Drive) or 650 rpm for the manual transaxle (in Neutral).

5. Turn the ignition **OFF** and reconnect the IAC motor lead.
6. Using a voltmeter, adjust the TPS to 0.45–0.65 volt and secure the TPS.
7. Recheck the setting, then start the engine and check for proper idle operation.
8. Seal the idle stop screw with silicone sealer.

FUEL TANK

Tank Assembly

REMOVAL & INSTALLATION

▶ **See Figures 49 and 50**

1. Relieve the fuel pressure from the vehicle, as is explained earlier in this section.
2. Disconnect the negative cable at the battery.
3. Raise and support the car.
4. Drain the tank. There is no drain plug, remaining fuel in the tank must be siphoned through the fuel feed line (the line to the fuel pump), because of the restrictor in the filler neck.
5. Disconnect the hose and the vapor return hose from the sending unit fittings.
6. Remove the ground wire screw.
7. Unplug the sending unit electrical connector.
8. Detach the vent hose. Disconnect any quick connect fittings.
9. If necessary, remove the exhaust pipe heat shield.
10. With an assistant supporting the tank, unbolt the retaining straps, and lower and remove the tank.
11. Remove the sending unit from the tank. Then remove the tank insulator pads, making note of where they are to be placed on the new tank.
    To install:
12. Attach the insulator pads to the new tank, then install the sending unit.
13. With an assistant, position the tank and support it while attaching the retaining strap mounting bolts.
14. Tighten the front retaining strap bolts to 25 ft. lbs. (34 Nm) and the rear to 17 ft. lbs. (23 Nm).
15. If applicable, install the exhaust pipe heat shield.
16. Attach any quick connect fittings and all the EVAP connecting hoses.
17. Connect the sending unit electrical harness. Install the fuel filler vent hose and clamp, tighten the clamp to 22 inch lbs. (3 Nm).
18. Lower the vehicle.
19. Add fuel to the tank and install the filler cap.
20. Check for leaks. If non are present, connect the negative battery cable.

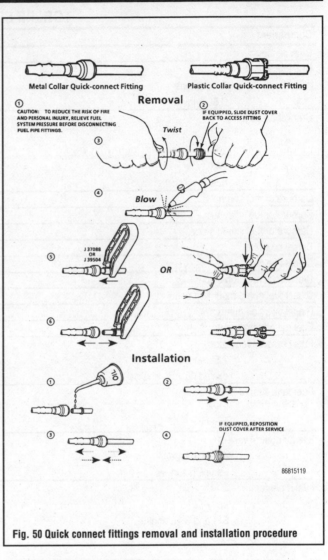

Fig. 50 Quick connect fittings removal and installation procedure

SENDING UNIT REPLACEMENT

The fuel gauge sending unit is attached to the fuel pump on cars with an electric in-tank pump. The following procedure is for pump and sending unit removal and installation. If the vehicle has a pump mounted on the engine, the basic steps will still lead you through sending unit replacement. Be extremely cautious of sparks or flame when working around the fuel pump. NEVER apply battery power to a used fuel pump out of the fuel tank.

1. Relieve the fuel system pressure, then disconnect the negative battery cable.
2. Raise and support the vehicle safely. Drain the fuel tank.
3. Disconnect wiring from the tank, then remove the ground wire retaining screw from under the body.
4. Disconnect all hoses from the tank.
5. Support the tank on a jack and remove the retaining strap nuts.
6. Lower the tank and remove it from the vehicle.
7. Remove the fuel gauge/pump retaining ring using a suitable spanner wrench.
8. Remove the gauge unit and the pump.

Fig. 49 After raising the car you will have a full view of the gas tank

To install:

9. Install the gauge unit and the pump.
10. Install the fuel gauge/pump retaining ring using a suitable spanner.
11. Raise the tank and install it to the vehicle.
12. Support the tank on a jackstand and install the retaining strap nuts.
13. Connect the hoses to the tank.

14. Connect the electrical connectors and the ground wire, if equipped.
15. Lower the vehicle.
16. Fill the fuel tank.
17. Turn the ignition switch to the **ON** position for 2 seconds, then turn to the **OFF** position for 10 seconds. Turn the ignition switch back to the **ON** position and check for fuel leaks.

TORQUE SPECIFICATIONS

Component	US	Metric
Cam sensor:	8 ft. lbs.	10 Nm
Crankshaft bolt:		
3.3L engine	220 ft. lbs.	300 Nm
3.8L engine	220 ft. lbs.	300 Nm
Crankshaft sensor:		
3.8L vin-3	22 ft. lbs.	30 Nm
3X	71-88 inch lbs.	8-10 Nm
24X	8 ft. lbs.	10 Nm
dual	14-28 ft. lbs.	20-40 Nm
Carburetor monting nuts:	13 ft. lbs.	18 Nm
Carburetor fuel inlet nut:	18 ft. lbs.	24 Nm
Carburetor fuel line fuittings:	22 ft. lbs.	30 Nm
Diesel nozzle:	25 ft. lbs.	34 Nm
Diesel line nut:	25 ft. lbs.	34 Nm
Diesel inlet and outlet line:	18 ft. lbs.	24 Nm
Diesel fuel pump mounting bolts:	18 ft. lbs.	24 Nm
Diesel injection pump:	35 ft. lbs.	47 Nm
Fuel rail attaching nuts:	20 ft. lbs.	27 Nm
Fuel pressure regulator:		
2.5L engine	22 inch lbs.	2.5 Nm
excluding 2.5L engine	102 inch lbs.	11.5 Nm
Fuel tank straps:		
front	25 ft. lbs.	34 Nm
rear	17 ft. lbs.	23 Nm
Idle air control valve:		
screw in type	13 ft. lbs.	18 Nm
retaining screws	27 inch lbs.	3 Nm
Intake plenum:		
early EFI	16 ft. lbs.	21 Nm
SFI and 3.1L engine	18 ft. lbs.	25 Nm
Throttle position sensor:	18 inch lbs.	2 Nm
TBI fuel line nuts:	18-20 ft. lbs.	24-27 Nm
TBI injector retainer:	27 inch lbs.	3 Nm
TBI pessure regulator cover:	21 inch lbs.	2 Nm
TBI body bolts:	10-21 ft. lbs.	13-28 Nm
TBI tube module assembly:	27 inch lbs.	3 Nm

86815130

6

CHASSIS ELECTRICAL

UNDERSTANDING AND TROUBLESHOOTING ELECTRICAL SYSTEMS

Over the years covered by this manual, import and domestic manufacturers began incorporating electronic control systems into their production lines. In fact, most (if not all) new vehicles sold today are equipped with one or more on-board computer. These electronic components (with no moving parts) should theoretically last the life of the vehicle, provided nothing external happens to damage the circuits or memory chips.

While it is true that electronic components should never wear out, in the real world malfunctions do occur. It is also true that any computer-based system is extremely sensitive to electrical voltages and cannot tolerate careless or haphazard testing/service procedures. An inexperienced individual can literally cause major damage looking for a minor problem by using the wrong kind of test equipment or connecting test leads/connectors with the ignition switch **ON**. When selecting test equipment, make sure the manufacturer's instructions state that the tester is compatible with whatever type of system is being serviced. Read all instructions carefully and double check all test points before installing probes or making any test connections.

The following section outlines basic diagnosis techniques for dealing with automotive electrical systems. Along with a general explanation of the various types of test equipment available to aid in servicing modern automotive systems, basic repair techniques for wiring harnesses and connectors are also given. Read the basic information before attempting any repairs or testing. This will provide the background of information necessary to avoid the most common and obvious mistakes that can cost both time and money. Although the replacement and testing procedures are simple in themselves, the systems are not, and unless one has a thorough understanding of all components and their function within a particular system, the logical test sequence these systems demand cannot be followed. Minor malfunctions can make a big difference, so it is important to know how each component affects the operation of the overall system to find the ultimate cause of a problem without replacing good components unnecessarily. It is not enough to use the correct test equipment; the test equipment must be used correctly.

Safety Precautions

❊❊ CAUTION

Whenever working on or around any electrical or electronic systems, always observe these general precautions to prevent the possibility of personal injury or damage to electronic components.

• Never install or remove battery cables with the key **ON** or the engine running. Jumper cables should be connected with the key **OFF** to avoid power surges that can damage electronic control units. Engines equipped with computer controlled systems should avoid both giving and getting jump starts due to the possibility of serious damage to components from arcing in the engine compartment when connections are made with the ignition **ON**.

• Always remove the battery cables before charging the battery. Never use a high output charger on an installed battery or attempt to use any type of "hot shot" (24 volt) starting aid.

• Exercise care when inserting test probes into connectors to insure good contact without damaging the connector or spreading the pins. Always probe connectors from the rear (wire) side, NOT the pin side, to avoid accidental shorting of terminals during test procedures.

• Never remove or attach wiring harness connectors with the ignition switch **ON**, especially to an electronic control unit.

• Do not drop any components during service procedures and never apply 12 volts directly to any component (like a solenoid or relay) unless instructed specifically to do so. Some component electrical windings are designed to safely handle only 4 or 5 volts and can be destroyed in seconds if 12 volts are applied directly to the connector.

• Remove the electronic control unit if the vehicle is to be placed in an environment where temperatures exceed approximately 176°F (80°C), such as a paint spray booth or when arc/gas welding near the control unit location.

Add-On Electrical Equipment

The electrical system in your car is designed to perform under reasonable operating conditions without interference between components. Before any additional electrical equipment is installed, it is recommended that you consult your dealer or a reputable repair facility familiar with the vehicle and its systems.

If the vehicle is equipped with mobile radio equipment and/or mobile telephone, it may have an effect upon the operation of the ECM. Radio Frequency Interference (RFI) from the communications system can be picked up by the car's wiring harnesses and conducted into the ECM, giving it the wrong messages at the wrong time. Although well shielded against RFI, the ECM should be further protected by taking the following measures:

• Install the antenna as far as possible from the ECM. Since the ECM is located behind the center console area, the antenna should be mounted at the rear of the car.

• Keep the antenna wiring a minimum of eight inches away from any wiring running to the ECM and from the ECM itself. NEVER wind the antenna wire around any other wiring.

• Mount the equipment as far from the ECM as possible. Be very careful during installation not to drill through any wires or short a wire harness with a mounting screw.

• Insure that the electrical feed wire(s) to the equipment are properly and tightly connected. Loose connectors can cause interference.

• Make certain that the equipment is properly grounded to the car. Poor grounding can damage expensive equipment.

Organized Troubleshooting

When diagnosing a specific problem, organized troubleshooting is a must. The complexity of a modern automobile demands that you approach any problem in a logical, organized manner. There are certain troubleshooting techniques that are standard:

1. Establish when the problem occurs. Does the problem appear only under certain conditions? Were there any noises, odors, or other unusual symptoms?

2. Isolate the problem area. To do this, make some simple tests and observations; then eliminate the systems that are working properly. Check for obvious problems such as broken wires, dirty connections or split/disconnected vacuum hoses. Always check the obvious before assuming something complicated is the cause.

3. Test for problems systematically to determine the cause once the problem area is isolated. Are all the components functioning properly? Is there power going to electrical switches and motors? Is there vacuum at vacuum switches and/or actuators? Is there a mechanical problem such as bent linkage or loose mounting screws? Performing careful, systematic checks will often turn up most causes on the first inspection without wasting time checking components that have little or no relationship to the problem.

4. Test all repairs after the work is done to make sure that the problem is fixed. Some causes can be traced to more than one component, so a careful verification of repair work is important to pick up additional malfunctions that may cause a problem to reappear or a different problem to arise. A blown fuse, for example, is a simple problem that may require more than another fuse to repair. If you don't look for a problem that caused a fuse to blow, a shorted wire for example, may go undetected.

Experience has shown that most problems tend to be the result of a fairly simple and obvious cause, such as loose or corroded connectors or air leaks in the intake system. This makes careful inspection of components during testing essential to quick and accurate troubleshooting.

TEST EQUIPMENT

➡**Pinpointing the exact cause of trouble in an electrical system can sometimes only be accomplished by the use of special test equipment. The following describes commonly used test equipment and explains how to put it to best use in diagnosis. In addition to the information covered below, the manufacturer's instructions booklet provided with the tester should be read and clearly understood before attempting any test procedures.**

Jumper Wires

Jumper wires are simple, yet extremely valuable, pieces of test equipment. They are basically test wires which are used to bypass sections of a circuit. The simplest type of jumper wire is a length of multi-strand wire with an alligator clip at each end. Jumper wires are usually fabricated from lengths of standard automotive wire and whatever type of connector (alligator clip, spade connector or pin connector) that is required for the particular vehicle being tested. The well equipped tool box will have several different styles of jumper wires in several different lengths. Some jumper wires are made with three or more terminals coming from a common splice for special purpose testing. In cramped, hard-to-reach areas it is advisable to have insulated boots over the jumper wire terminals in order to prevent accidental grounding, sparks, and possible fire, especially when testing fuel system components.

Jumper wires are used primarily to locate open electrical circuits, on either the ground (-) side of the circuit or on the hot (+) side. If an electrical component fails to operate, connect the jumper wire between the component and a good ground. If the component operates only with the jumper installed, the ground circuit is open. If the ground circuit is good, but the component does not operate, the circuit between the power feed and component may be open. By moving the jumper wire successively back from the lamp toward the power source, you can isolate the area of the circuit where the open is located. When the component stops functioning, or the power is cut off, the open is in the segment of wire between the jumper and the point previously tested.

You can sometimes connect the jumper wire directly from the battery to the hot terminal of the component, but first make sure the component uses 12 volts in operation. Some electrical components, such as fuel injectors, are designed to operate on about 4 volts and running 12 volts directly to the injector terminals can burn out the wiring.

By inserting an in-line fuse holder between a set of test leads, a fused jumper wire can be used for bypassing open circuits. Use a 5 amp fuse to provide protection against voltage spikes. When in doubt, use

a voltmeter to check the voltage input to the component and measure how much voltage is normally being applied.

✳✳ CAUTION

Never use jumpers made from wire that is of lighter gauge than used in the circuit under test. If the jumper wire is of too small gauge, it may overheat and possibly melt. Never use jumpers to bypass high resistance loads in a circuit. Bypassing resistances, in effect, creates a short circuit. This may, in turn, cause damage and fire. Jumper wires should only be used to bypass lengths of wire.

Unpowered Test Lights

The 12 volt test light is used to check circuits and components while electrical current is flowing through them. It is used for voltage and ground tests. Twelve volt test lights come in different styles but all have three main parts; a ground clip, a probe, and a light. The most commonly used 12 volt test lights have pick-type probes. To use a 12 volt test light, connect the ground clip to a good ground and probe wherever necessary with the pick. The pick should be sharp so that it can be probed into tight spaces.

✳✳ CAUTION

Do not use a test light to probe electronic ignition spark plug or coil wires. Never use a pick-type test light to probe wiring on computer controlled systems unless specifically instructed to do so. Any wire insulation that is pierced by the test light probe should be taped and sealed with silicone after testing.

Like the jumper wire, the 12 volt test light is used to isolate opens in circuits. But, whereas the jumper wire is used to bypass the open to operate the load, the 12 volt test light is used to locate the presence of voltage in a circuit. If the test light glows, you know that there is power up to that point; if the 12 volt test light does not glow when its probe is inserted into the wire or connector, you know that there is an open circuit (no power). Move the test light in successive steps back toward the power source until the light in the handle does glow. When it glows, the open is between the probe and point which was probed previously.

➡**The test light does not detect that 12 volts (or any particular amount of voltage) is present; it only detects that some voltage is present. It is advisable before using the test light to touch its terminals across the battery posts to make sure the light is operating properly.**

Self-Powered Test Lights

The self-powered test light usually contains a 1.5 volt penlight battery. One type of self-powered test light is similar in design to the 12 volt unit. This type has both the battery and the light in the handle, along with a pick-type probe tip. The second type has the light toward the open tip, so that the light illuminates the contact point. The self-powered test light is a dual purpose piece of test equipment. It can be used to test for either open or short circuits when power is isolated from the circuit (continuity test). A powered test light should not be used on any computer controlled system or component unless specifically instructed to do so. Many engine sensors can be destroyed by even this small amount of voltage applied directly to the terminals.

Voltmeters

A voltmeter is used to measure voltage at any point in a circuit, or to measure the voltage drop across any part of a circuit. It can also be used to check continuity in a wire or circuit by indicating current flow from one end to the other. Voltmeters usually have various scales on the meter dial and a selector switch to allow the selection of different voltages. The voltmeter has a positive and a negative lead. To avoid damage to the meter, always connect the negative lead to the negative (-) side of circuit (to ground or nearest the ground side of the circuit) and connect the positive lead to the positive (+) side of the circuit (to the power source or the nearest power source). Note that the negative voltmeter lead will always be black and that the positive voltmeter will always be some color other than black (usually red). Depending on how the voltmeter is connected into the circuit, it has several uses.

A voltmeter can be connected either in parallel or in series with a circuit and it has a very high resistance to current flow. When connected in parallel, only a small amount of current will flow through the voltmeter current path; the rest will flow through the normal circuit current path and the circuit will work normally. When the voltmeter is connected in series with a circuit, only a small amount of current can flow through the circuit. The circuit will not work properly, but the voltmeter reading will show if the circuit is complete or not.

Ohmmeters

The ohmmeter is designed to read resistance (Ω) in a circuit or component. Although there are several different styles of ohmmeters, all will usually have a selector switch which permits the measurement of different ranges of resistance (usually the selector switch allows the multiplication of the meter reading by 10, 100, 1,000, and 10,000). A calibration knob allows the meter to be set at zero for accurate measurement. Since all ohmmeters are powered by an internal battery (usually 9 volts), the ohmmeter can be used as a self-powered test light. When the ohmmeter is connected, current from the ohmmeter flows through the circuit or component being tested. Since the ohmmeter's internal resistance and voltage are known values, the amount of current flow through the meter depends on the resistance of the circuit or component being tested.

The ohmmeter can be used to perform a continuity test for opens or shorts (either by observation of the meter needle or as a self-powered test light), and to read actual resistance in a circuit. It should be noted that the ohmmeter is used to check the resistance of a component or wire while there is no voltage applied to the circuit. Current flow from an outside voltage source (such as the vehicle battery) can damage the ohmmeter, so the circuit or component should be isolated from the vehicle electrical system before any testing is done. Since the ohmmeter uses its own voltage source, either lead can be connected to any test point.

➡**When checking diodes or other solid state components, the ohmmeter leads can only be connected one way in order to measure current flow in a single direction. Make sure the positive (+) and negative (-) terminal connections are as described in the test procedures to verify the one-way diode operation.**

In using the meter for making continuity checks, do not be concerned with the actual resistance readings. Zero resistance, or any reading, indicates continuity in the circuit. Infinite resistance indicates an open in the circuit. A high resistance reading where there should be none indicates a problem in the circuit. Checks for short circuits are made in the same manner as checks for open circuits except that the circuit must be isolated from both power and normal ground. Infinite resistance indicates no continuity to ground, while zero resistance indicates a dead short to ground.

Ammeters

An ammeter measures the amount of current flowing through a circuit in units called amperes or amps. Amperes are units of electron flow which indicate how fast the electrons are flowing through the circuit. Since Ohms Law dictates that current flow in a circuit is equal to the circuit voltage divided by the total circuit resistance, increasing voltage also increases the current level (amps). Likewise, any decrease in resistance will increase the amount of amps in a circuit. At normal operating voltage, most circuits have a characteristic amount of amperes, called "current draw" which can be measured using an ammeter. By referring to a specified current draw rating, measuring the amperes, and comparing the two values, one can determine what is happening within the circuit to aid in diagnosis. An open circuit, for example, will not allow any current to flow so the ammeter reading will be zero. More current flows through a heavily loaded circuit or when the charging system is operating.

An ammeter is always connected in series with the circuit being tested. All of the current that normally flows through the circuit must also flow through the ammeter; if there is any other path for the current to follow, the ammeter reading will not be accurate. The ammeter itself has very little resistance to current flow and therefore will not affect the circuit, but it will measure current draw only when the circuit is closed and electricity is flowing. Excessive current draw can blow fuses and drain the battery, while a reduced current draw can cause motors to run slowly, lights to dim and other components to not operate properly. The ammeter can help diagnose these conditions by locating the cause of the high or low reading.

Multimeters

Different combinations of test meters can be built into a single unit designed for specific tests. Some of the more common combination test devices are known as Volt/Amp testers, Tach/Dwell meters, or Digital Multimeters. The Volt/Amp tester is used for charging system, starting system or battery tests and consists of a voltmeter, an ammeter and a variable resistance carbon pile. The voltmeter will usually have at least two ranges for use with 6, 12 and/or 24 volt systems. The ammeter also has more than one range for testing various levels of battery loads and starter current draw. The carbon pile can be adjusted to offer different amounts of resistance. The Volt/Amp tester has heavy leads to carry large amounts of current and many later models have an inductive ammeter pickup that clamps around the wire to simplify test connections. On some models, the ammeter also has a zero-center scale to allow testing of charging and starting systems without switching leads or polarity. A digital multimeter is a voltmeter, ammeter and ohmmeter combined in an instrument which gives a digital readout. These are often used when testing solid state circuits because of their high input impedance (usually 10 megohms or more).

The tach/dwell meter that combines a tachometer and a dwell (cam angle) meter is a specialized kind of voltmeter. The tachometer scale is marked to show engine speed in rpm and the dwell scale is marked to show degrees of distributor shaft rotation. In most electronic ignition systems, dwell is determined by the control unit, but the dwell meter can also be used to check the duty cycle (operation) of some electronic engine control systems. Some tach/dwell meters are powered by an internal battery, while others take their power from the car battery in use. The battery powered testers usually require calibration much like an ohmmeter before testing.

TESTING

Open Circuits

To use the self-powered test light to check for open circuits, first isolate the circuit from the vehicle's 12 volt power source by disconnecting the battery or wiring harness connector. Connect the test light ground clip to a good ground and probe sections of the circuit sequentially with the test light. (start from either end of the circuit). If the light is out, the open is between the probe and the circuit ground. If the light is on, the open is between the probe and end of the circuit toward the power source.

Short Circuits

By isolating the circuit both from power and from ground, and using a self-powered test light, you can check for shorts to ground in the circuit. Isolate the circuit from power and ground. Connect the test light ground clip to a good ground and probe any easy-to-reach test point in the circuit. If the light comes on, there is a short somewhere in the circuit. To isolate the short, probe a test point at either end of the isolated circuit (the light should be on). Leave the test light probe engaged and open connectors, switches, remove parts, etc., sequentially, until the light goes out. When the light goes out, the short is between the last circuit component opened and the previous circuit opened.

➡**The 1.5 volt battery in the test light does not provide much current. A weak battery may not provide enough power to illuminate the test light even when a complete circuit is made (especially if there are high resistances in the circuit). Always make sure that the test battery is strong. To check the battery, briefly touch the ground clip to the probe; if the light glows brightly the battery is strong enough for testing. Never use a self-powered test light to perform checks for opens or shorts when power is applied to the electrical system under test. The 12 volt vehicle power will quickly burn out the 1.5 volt light bulb in the test light.**

Available Voltage Measurement

Set the voltmeter selector switch to the 20V position and connect the meter negative lead to the negative post of the battery. Connect the positive meter lead to the positive post of the battery and turn the ignition switch **ON** to provide a load. Read the voltage on the meter or digital display. A well charged battery should register over 12 volts. If the meter reads below 11.5 volts, the battery power may be insufficient to operate the electrical system properly. This test determines voltage available from the battery and should be the first step in any electrical trouble diagnosis procedure. Many electrical problems, especially on computer controlled systems, can be caused by a low state of charge in the battery. Excessive corrosion at the battery cable terminals can cause a poor contact that will prevent proper charging and full battery current flow.

Normal battery voltage is 12 volts when fully charged. When the battery is supplying current to one or more circuits it is said to be "under load". When everything is off the electrical system is under a "no-load" condition. A fully charged battery may show about 12.5 volts at no load; will drop to 12 volts under medium load; and will drop even lower under heavy load. If the battery is partially discharged the voltage decrease under heavy load may be excessive, even though the battery shows 12 volts or more at no load. When allowed to discharge further, the battery's available voltage under load will decrease more severely. For this reason, it is important that the battery be fully charged during all testing procedures to avoid errors in diagnosis and incorrect test results.

Voltage Drop

When current flows through a resistance, the voltage beyond the resistance is reduced (the larger the current, the greater the reduction in voltage). When no current is flowing, there is no voltage drop because there is no current flow. All points in the circuit which are connected to the power source are at the same voltage as the power source. The total voltage drop always equals the total source voltage. In a long circuit with many connectors, a series of small, unwanted voltage drops due to corrosion at the connectors can add up to a total loss of voltage which impairs the operation of the normal loads in the circuit.

INDIRECT COMPUTATION OF VOLTAGE DROPS

1. Set the voltmeter selector switch to the 20 volt position.
2. Connect the meter negative lead to a good ground.
3. While operating the circuit, probe all resistances loads in the circuit with the positive meter lead and observe the voltage readings. There should be little or no voltage drop before the first load.

DIRECT MEASUREMENT OF VOLTAGE DROPS

1. Set the voltmeter switch to the 20 volt position.
2. Connect the voltmeter negative lead to the ground side of the resistance load to be measured.
3. Connect the positive lead to the positive side of the resistance or load to be measured.
4. Read the voltage drop directly on the 20 volt scale.

Too high a voltage indicates too high a resistance. If, for example, a blower motor runs too slowly, you can determine if there is too high a resistance in the resistor pack. By taking voltage drop readings in all parts of the circuit, you can isolate the problem. Too low a voltage drop indicates too low a resistance. Take the blower motor for example again. If a blower motor runs too fast in the MED and/or LOW position, the problem can be isolated in the resistor pack by taking voltage drop readings in all parts of the circuit to locate a possibly shorted resistor. The maximum allowable voltage drop under load is critical, especially if there is more than one high resistance problem in a circuit because all voltage drops are cumulative. A small drop is normal due to the resistance of the conductors.

HIGH RESISTANCE TESTING

1. Set the voltmeter selector switch to the 4 volt position.
2. Connect the voltmeter positive lead to the positive post of the battery.
3. Turn on the headlights and heater blower to provide a load.
4. Probe various points in the circuit with the negative voltmeter lead.
5. Read the voltage drop on the 4 volt scale. Some average maximum allowable voltage drops are:
- FUSE PANEL: 0.7 volts
- IGNITION SWITCH: 0.5 volts
- HEADLIGHT SWITCH: 0.7 volts
- IGNITION COIL (+): 0.5 volts
- ANY OTHER LOAD: 1.3 volts

➡**Voltage drops are all measured while a load is operating; without current flow, there will be no voltage drop.**

Resistance Measurement

The batteries in an ohmmeter will weaken with age and temperature, so the ohmmeter must be calibrated or "zeroed" before taking measurements. To zero the meter, place the selector switch in its lowest range and touch the two ohmmeter leads together. Turn the calibration knob until the meter needle is exactly on zero.

➡**All analog (needle) type ohmmeters must be zeroed before use, but some digital ohmmeter models are automatically calibrated when the switch is turned on. Self-calibrating digital ohmmeters do not have an adjusting knob, but it's a good idea to check for a zero readout before use by touching the leads together. All computer controlled systems require the use of a digital ohmmeter with at least 10 megohms impedance for testing. Before any test procedures are attempted, make sure the ohmmeter used is compatible with the electrical system or damage to the on-board computer could result.**

To measure resistance, first isolate the circuit from the vehicle power source by disconnecting the battery cables or the harness connector. Make sure the key is **OFF** when disconnecting any components or the battery. Where necessary, also isolate at least one side of the circuit to be checked in order to avoid reading parallel resistances. Parallel circuit resistances will always give a lower reading than the actual resistance of either of the branches. When measuring the resistance of parallel circuits, the total resistance will always be lower than the smallest resistance in the circuit. Connect the meter leads to both sides of the circuit (wire or component) and read the actual measured ohms on the meter scale. Make sure the selector switch is set to the proper ohm scale for the circuit being tested to avoid misreading the ohmmeter test value.

☀ WARNING

Never use an ohmmeter with power applied to the circuit. Like the self-powered test light, the ohmmeter is designed to operate on its own power supply. The normal 12 volt automotive electrical system current could damage the meter!

Wiring Harnesses

The average automobile contains about ½ mile of wiring, with hundreds of individual connections. To protect the many wires from damage and to keep them from becoming a confusing tangle, they are organized into bundles, enclosed in plastic or taped together and called wiring harnesses. Different harnesses serve different parts of the vehicle. Individual wires are color coded to help trace them through a harness where sections are hidden from view.

Automotive wiring or circuit conductors can be in any one of three forms:
1. Single strand wire
2. Multi-strand wire
3. Printed circuitry

Single strand wire has a solid metal core and is usually used inside such components as alternators, motors, relays and other devices. Multi-strand wire has a core made of many small strands of wire twisted together into a single

conductor. Most of the wiring in an automotive electrical system is made up of multi-strand wire, either as a single conductor or grouped together in a harness. All wiring is color coded on the insulator, either as a solid color or as a colored wire with an identification stripe. A printed circuit is a thin film of copper or other conductor that is printed on an insulator backing. Occasionally, a printed circuit is sandwiched between two sheets of plastic for more protection and flexibility. A complete printed circuit, consisting of conductors, insulating material and connectors for lamps or other components is called a printed circuit board. Printed circuitry is used in place of individual wires or harnesses in places where space is limited, such as behind instrument panels.

Since automotive electrical systems are very sensitive to changes in resistance, the selection of properly sized wires is critical when systems are repaired. A loose or corroded connection or a replacement wire that is too small for the circuit will add extra resistance and an additional voltage drop to the circuit. A ten percent voltage drop can result in slow or erratic motor operation, for example, even though the circuit is complete. The wire gauge number is an expression of the cross-section area of the conductor. The most common system for expressing wire size is the American Wire Gauge (AWG) system.

Gauge numbers are assigned to conductors of various cross-section areas. As gauge number increases, area decreases and the conductor becomes smaller. A 5 gauge conductor is smaller than a 1 gauge conductor and a 10 gauge is smaller than a 5 gauge. As the cross-section area of a conductor decreases, resistance increases and so does the gauge number. A conductor with a higher gauge number will carry less current than a conductor with a lower gauge number.

➡**Gauge wire size refers to the size of the conductor, not the size of the complete wire. It is possible to have two wires of the same gauge with different diameters because one may have thicker insulation than the other.**

12 volt automotive electrical systems generally use 10, 12, 14, 16 and 18 gauge wire. Main power distribution circuits and larger accessories usually use 10 and 12 gauge wire. Battery cables are usually 4 or 6 gauge, although 1 and 2 gauge wires are occasionally used. Wire length must also be considered when making repairs to a circuit. As conductor length increases, so does resistance. An 18 gauge wire, for example, can carry a 10 amp load for 10 feet without excessive voltage drop; however if a 15 foot wire is required for the same 10 amp load, it must be a 16 gauge wire.

An electrical schematic shows the electrical current paths when a circuit is operating properly. It is essential to understand how a circuit works before trying to figure out why it doesn't. Schematics break the entire electrical system down into individual circuits and show only one particular circuit. In a schematic, no attempt is made to represent wiring and components as they physically appear on the vehicle; switches and other components are shown as simply as possible. Face views of harness connectors show the cavity or terminal locations in all multi-pin connectors to help locate test points.

If you need to backprobe a connector while it is on the component, the order of the terminals must be mentally reversed. The wire color code can help in this situation, as well as a keyway, lock tab or other reference mark.

WIRING REPAIR

Soldering is a quick, efficient method of joining metals permanently. Everyone who has the occasion to make wiring repairs should know how to solder. Electrical connections that are soldered are far less likely to come apart and will conduct electricity much better than connections that are only "pig-tailed" together. The most popular (and preferred) method of soldering is with an electrical soldering gun. Soldering irons are available in many sizes and wattage ratings. Irons with higher wattage ratings deliver higher temperatures and recover lost heat faster. A small soldering iron rated for no more than 50 watts is recommended, especially on electrical systems where excess heat can damage the components being soldered.

There are three ingredients necessary for successful soldering; proper flux, good solder and sufficient heat. A soldering flux is necessary to clean the metal of tarnish, prepare it for soldering and to enable the solder to spread into tiny crevices. When soldering, always use a rosin core solder which is non-corrosive and will not attract moisture once the job is finished. Other types of flux (acid core) will leave a residue that will attract moisture and cause the wires to corrode. Tin is a unique metal with a low melting point. In a molten state, it dissolves and alloys easily with many metals. Solder is made by mixing tin with lead. The most common proportions are 40/60, 50/50 and 60/40, with the percentage of tin listed first. Low priced solders usually contain less tin, making them very difficult for a beginner to use because more heat is required to melt the solder. A common solder is 40/60 which is well suited for all-around general use, but 60/40 melts easier and is preferred for electrical work.

Soldering Techniques

Successful soldering requires that the metals to be joined be heated to a temperature that will melt the solder, usually 360–460°F (182–238°C). Contrary to popular belief, the purpose of the soldering iron is not to melt the solder itself, but to heat the parts being soldered to a temperature high enough to melt the solder when it is touched to the work. Melting flux-cored solder on the soldering iron will usually destroy the effectiveness of the flux.

➡**Soldering tips are made of copper for good heat conductivity, but must be "tinned" regularly for quick transference of heat to the project and to prevent the solder from sticking to the iron. To "tin" the iron, simply heat it and touch the flux-cored solder to the tip; the solder will flow over the hot tip. Wipe the excess off with a clean rag, but be careful as the iron will be hot.**

After some use, the tip may become pitted. If so, simply dress the tip smooth with a smooth file and "tin" the tip again. Flux-cored solder will remove oxides but rust, bits of insulation and oil or grease must be removed with a wire brush or emery cloth. For maximum strength in soldered parts, the joint must start off clean and tight. Weak joints will result in gaps too wide for the solder to bridge.

If a separate soldering flux is used, it should be brushed or swabbed on only those areas that are to be soldered. Most solders contain a core of flux and separate fluxing is unnecessary. Hold the work to be soldered firmly. It is best to solder on a wooden board, because a metal vise will only rob the piece to be soldered of heat and make it difficult to melt the solder. Hold the soldering tip with the broadest face against the work to be soldered. Apply solder under the tip close to the work, using enough solder to give a heavy film between the iron and the piece being soldered, while moving slowly and making sure the solder melts properly. Keep the work level or the solder will run to the lowest part and favor the thicker parts, because these require more heat to melt the solder. If the soldering tip overheats (the solder coating on the face of the tip burns up), it should be retinned. Once the soldering is completed, let the soldered joint stand until cool. Tape and seal all soldered wire splices after the repair has cooled.

Wire Harness Connectors

Most connectors in the engine compartment or otherwise exposed to the elements are protected against moisture and dirt which could create oxidation and deposits on the terminals.

These special connectors are weatherproof. All repairs require the use of a special terminal and the tool required to service it. This tool is used to remove the pin and sleeve terminals. If removal is attempted with an ordinary pick, there is a good chance that the terminal will be bent or deformed. Unlike standard blade type terminals, these weatherproof terminals cannot be straightened once they are bent. Make certain that the connectors are properly seated and all of the sealing rings are in place when connecting leads. On some models, a hinge-type flap provides a backup or secondary locking feature for the terminals. Most secondary locks are used to improve connector reliability by retaining the terminals if the small terminal lock tangs are not positioned properly.

Molded-on connectors require complete replacement of the connection. This means splicing a new connector assembly into the harness. All splices should be soldered to insure proper contact. Use care when probing the connections or replacing terminals in them as it is possible to short between opposite terminals. If this happens to the wrong terminal pair, it is possible to damage certain components. Always use jumper wires between connectors for circuit checking and never probe through weatherproof seals.

Open circuits are often difficult to locate by sight because corrosion or terminal misalignment are hidden by the connectors. Merely wiggling a connector on a sensor or in the wiring harness may correct the open circuit condition. This should always be considered when an open circuit or a failed sensor is indicated. Intermittent problems may also be caused by oxidized or loose connections. When using a circuit tester for diagnosis, always probe connections from the wire side. Be careful not to damage sealed connectors with test probes.

All wiring harnesses should be replaced with identical parts, using the same gauge wire and connectors. When signal wires are spliced into a harness, use wire with high temperature insulation only. It is seldom necessary to replace a complete harness. If replacement is necessary, pay close attention to insure proper harness routing. Secure the harness with suitable plastic wire clamps to prevent vibrations from causing the harness to wear in spots or contact any hot components.

➡**Weatherproof connectors cannot be replaced with standard connectors. Instructions are provided with replacement connector and terminal packages. Some wire harnesses have mounting indicators (usually pieces of colored tape) to mark where the harness is to be secured.**

In making wiring repairs, its important that you always replace damaged wires with wires that are the same gauge as the wire being replaced. The heavier the wire, the smaller the gauge number. Wires are color-coded to aid in identification and whenever possible the same color coded wire should be used for replacement. A wire stripping and crimping tool is necessary to install solderless terminal connectors. Test all crimps by pulling on the wires; it should not be possible to pull the wires out of a good crimp.

Wires which are open, exposed or otherwise damaged are repaired by simple splicing. Where possible, if the wiring harness is accessible and the damaged place in the wire can be located, it is best to open the harness and check for all possible damage. In an inaccessible harness, the wire must be bypassed with a new insert, usually taped to the outside of the old harness.

When replacing fusible links, be sure to use fusible link wire, NOT ordinary automotive wire. Make sure the fusible segment is of the same gauge and construction as the one being replaced and double the stripped end when crimping the terminal connector for a good contact. The melted (open) fusible link segment of the wiring harness should be cut off as close to the harness as possible, then a new segment spliced in as described. In the case of a damaged fusible link that feeds two harness wires, the harness connections should be replaced with two fusible link wires so that each circuit will have its own separate protection.

➡**Most of the problems caused in the wiring harness are due to bad ground connections. Always check all vehicle ground connections for corrosion or looseness before performing any power feed checks to eliminate the chance of a bad ground affecting the circuit.**

Hard Shell Connectors

Unlike molded connectors, the terminal contacts in hard shell connectors can be replaced. Weatherproof hard-shell connectors with the leads molded into the shell have non-replaceable terminal ends. Replacement usually involves the use of a special terminal removal tool that depresses the locking tangs (barbs) on the connector terminal and allows the connector to be removed from the rear of the shell. The connector shell should be replaced if it shows any evidence of burning, melting, cracks, or breaks. Replace individual terminals that are burnt, corroded, distorted or loose.

➡**The insulation crimp must be tight to prevent the insulation from sliding back on the wire when the wire is pulled. The insulation must be visibly compressed under the crimp tabs, and the ends of the crimp should be turned in for a firm grip on the insulation.**

The wire crimp must be made with all wire strands inside the crimp. The terminal must be fully compressed on the wire strands with the ends of the crimp tabs turned in to make a firm grip on the wire. Check all connections with an ohmmeter to insure a good contact. There should be no measurable resistance between the wire and the terminal when connected.

Fusible Links

◊ See Figures 1 and 2

The fuse link is a short length of special, Hypalon (high temperature) insulated wire, integral with the engine compartment wiring harness and should not be confused with standard wire. It is several wire gauges smaller than the circuit which it protects. Under no circumstances should a fuse link replacement repair be made using a length of standard wire cut from bulk stock or from another wiring harness.

To repair any blown fuse link use the following procedure:
1. Determine which circuit is damaged, its location and the cause of the open fuse link. If the damaged fuse link is one of three fed by a common No. 10 or 12 gauge feed wire, determine the specific affected circuit.
2. Disconnect the negative battery cable.

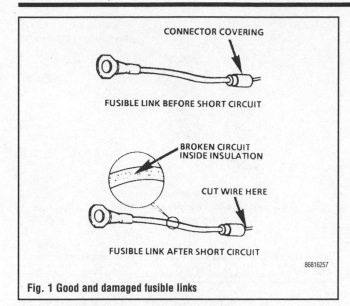

Fig. 1 Good and damaged fusible links

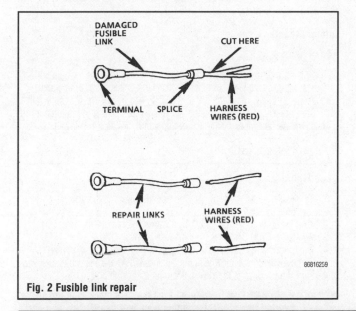

Fig. 2 Fusible link repair

3. Cut the damaged fuse link from the wiring harness and discard it. If the fuse link is one of three circuits fed by a single feed wire, cut it out of the harness at each splice end and discard it.

4. Identify and procure the proper fuse link with butt connectors for attaching the fuse link to the harness.

➡ **Heat shrink tubing must be slipped over the wire before crimping and soldering the connection.**

5. To repair any fuse link in a 3-link group with one feed:

a. After cutting the open link out of the harness, cut each of the remaining undamaged fuse links close to the feed wire weld.

b. Strip approximately ½ in. (13mm) of insulation from the detached ends of the two good fuse links. Insert two wire ends into one end of a butt connector, then carefully push one stripped end of the replacement fuse link into the same end of the butt connector and crimp all three firmly together.

➡ **Care must be taken when fitting the three fuse links into the butt connector as the internal diameter is a snug fit for three wires. Make sure to use a proper crimping tool. Pliers, side cutter, etc. will not apply the proper crimp to retain the wires and withstand a pull test.**

c. After crimping the butt connector to the three fuse links, cut the weld portion from the feed wire and strip approximately ½ in. (13mm) of insulation from the cut end. Insert the stripped end into the open end of the butt connector and crimp very firmly.

d. To attach the remaining end of the replacement fuse link, strip approximately ½ in. (13mm) of insulation from the wire end of the circuit from which the blown fuse link was removed, and firmly crimp a butt connector or equivalent to the stripped wire. Then, insert the end of the replacement link into the other end of the butt connector and crimp firmly.

e. Using rosin core solder with a consistency of 60 percent tin and 40 percent lead, solder the connectors and the wires at the repairs then insulate.

6. To replace any fuse link on a single circuit in a harness, cut out the damaged portion, strip approximately ½ in. (13mm) of insulation from the two wire ends and attach the appropriate replacement fuse link to the stripped wire ends with two proper size butt connectors. Solder the connectors and wires, then insulate.

7. To repair any fuse link which has an eyelet terminal on one end such as the charging circuit, cut off the open fuse link behind the weld, strip approximately ½ in. (13mm) of insulation from the cut end and attach the appropriate new eyelet fuse link to the cut stripped wire with an appropriate size butt connector. Solder the connectors and wires at the repair, then insulate.

➡ **When attaching a single No. 16, 17, 18 or 20 gauge fuse link to a heavy gauge wire, always double the stripped wire end of the fuse link before inserting and crimping it into the butt connector for positive wire retention.**

SUPPLEMENTAL INFLATABLE RESTRAINT SYSTEM (AIR BAG)

General Information

The Supplemental Inflatable Restraint (SIR) system helps supplement the protection offered by the driver's seat belt by deploying an air bag from the center of the steering wheel during certain front end collisions. The bag deploys when the vehicle is involved in a frontal crash of a sufficient force within 30 degrees of the centerline of the vehicle. Testing and any needed repairs should only be performed by a professional. Take cautions seriously when working near this system. Lack of care could result in possible air bag deployment, personal injury, or other needed repairs to the SIR system.

❋❋ CAUTION

Whenever carrying a live inflator module, make sure that the bag and opening is pointed away from you. Never carry the module by the wires or connector on the under side of the module. When placing the live inflator on a bench or any other surface, always face the bag and trim cover up, away from the surface. Never rest a steering column assembly on the steering wheel with the inflator module face down.

SYSTEM OPERATION

The main portions of the SIR system are the deployment loop and the Diagnostic Energy Reserve Module (DERM). The main function of the deployment loop is to supply current through the inflator module in the steering wheel. This will allow deployment of the air bag in the event of a frontal crash.

The arming sensor, SIR coil assembly, inflator module, and discriminating sensors make up the deployment loop. The arming sensor switches power to the inflator module on the high side of the loop. Either of the sensors can supply ground to the inflator module on the low side of the loop. The module is only supplied sufficient current to deploy when the arming sensor and at least one of the two discriminating sensors are closed simultaneously.

SYSTEM COMPONENTS

Diagnostic Energy Reserve Module (DERM)

❋❋ WARNING

Do not open the DERM case for any reason. Touching the connector pins or soldered components may cause electrostatic discharge

damage. Repair of a malfunctioning DERM is by the replacement only.

The DERM is designed to perform the following functions in the SIR system:

1. Energy Reserve—The DERM maintains a 36 Volt Loop Reserve (36 VLR) energy supply to provide deployment energy when the cars voltage is low or lost in a frontal collision.

2. Malfunction Detection—The DERM performs diagnostic monitoring of the SIR system electrical components.

3. Malfunction Recording—The DERM provides the SIR system diagnostic trouble code information through a scan tool.

4. Driver Notification—The DERM warns the driver of SIR malfunction by controlling the AIR BAG warning lamp.

5. Frontal Crash Recording—The DERM records the SIR system status during a frontal crash.

The DERM is connected to the SIR wiring harness by a 24-way connector. The harness connector uses a shorting bar across certain terminals in the contact area. The shorting bar connects the AIR BAG warning lamp to ground when the DERM harness connector is unplugged. This will cause the AIR BAG lamp to come on steadily whenever the ignition is in the **RUN** or **START** position with the DERM disconnected.

Air Bag Warning Lamp

Ignition voltage is applied to the AIR BAG warning lamp when the ignition switch is at the **RUN** or **START** positions. The DERM controls the lamp by providing ground with a lamp driver. The lamp is used in the SIR system to do the following:

1. Verify the lamp and DERM operation by flashing seven times when the ignition switch is **ON**.

2. Warn the driver of SIR electrical systems malfunctions which could potentially affect the operation of the SIR system. These malfunctions could cause a non-deployment of the air bag in a frontal crash, or deployment in cases less severe than intended.

Arming Sensor

The arming sensor is a protective switch that is located in the high side of the deployment loop. The sensor is calibrated to close at low level velocity changes, lower than the discriminating sensors. This will ensure that the inflator module is connected directly to the 36 VLR output of the DERM or **ignition 1** voltage when either of the sensors closes.

The arming sensor consists of a sensing element, normally open switch contacts, two diagnostic resistors, and two diodes. These sensing elements close the switch contacts when the velocity of the vehicle changes at a rate that indicates a potential need for deployment.

The 51K ohm diagnostic resistor is connected in parallel with the switch contacts allowing a small amount of voltage to pass operation. This current flow results in voltage drops across each component within the deployment loop. The DERM monitors these drops to detect circuit or component malfunctions. The 2.49K ohm diagnostic resistor is connected in parallel with the diodes allowing the DERM to monitor the voltage applied to the high side of the deployment loop. These two diodes in the arming sensor provide an isolation between the 36 VLR output of the DERM and IGNITION 1 voltage.

SIR Coil Assembly

▶ **See Figure 3**

The SIR coil assembly consists of two current carrying coils, which are attached to the steering column. The coils allow the rotation of the steering

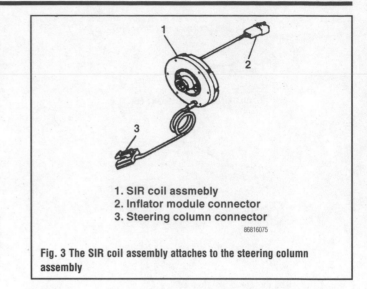

1. SIR coil assmebly
2. Inflator module connector
3. Steering column connector

86816075

Fig. 3 The SIR coil assembly attaches to the steering column assembly

wheel while maintaining continuous contact of the deployment loop to the inflator module.

Inflator Module

▶ **See Figure 4**

The inflator module is located on the steering wheel hub. The module consists of an inflatable bag and an inflator which is a canister of gas generating material and an initiating device. When the car is in a frontal crash of sufficient force. Current passing through the initiator ignites the material in the inflator module. The gas produced from this reaction quickly inflates the air bag.

DISARMING THE SYSTEM

▶ **See Figure 5**

1. To disable the SIR system, turn the steering wheel so that the vehicles wheels are pointing straight ahead.

2. Turn the ignition key to the **LOCK** position and remove the key.

3. Remove the AIR BAG fuse from the fuse block.

4. Unsecure the left sound insulator by removing the screws and nuts.

5. Remove the Connector Position Assurance (CPA) and the yellow two-way connector from the base of the steering column.

➡ **When the AIR BAG fuse is removed from the fuse block, and the key is in the ON position, the AIR BAG warning lamp will be ON. This is a normal condition and does not mean that the SIR system is malfunctioning.**

ENABLING THE SYSTEM

1. Engage the yellow two-way connector to the base of the steering column and the Connect Position Assurance (CPA).

2. Install the left sound insulator with the mounting screws and nuts.

3. Insert the AIR BAG fuse in the fuse block.

4. Turn the ignition switch to the **RUN** position and verify that the AIR BAG warning lamp flashes 7 times and then turns off. If it does not turn off have your SIR system checked by an authorized service center.

HEATER

The heating system provides heating, ventilation and defrosting for the windshield and side windows. The heater core is a heat exchanger supplied with coolant from the engine cooling system. Temperature is controlled by the temperature valve which moves an air door that directs air flow through the heater core for more heat or bypasses the heater core for less heat.

Vacuum actuators control the mode doors which direct air flow to the outlet ducts. The mode selector on the control panel directs engine vacuum to the actuators. The position of the mode doors determines whether air flows from the floor, panel, defrost or panel and defrost ducts (bi-level mode).

Blower Motor

REMOVAL & INSTALLATION

▶ **See Figures 6, 7 and 8**

➡ **This procedure is applicable for vehicles, with or without air conditioning.**

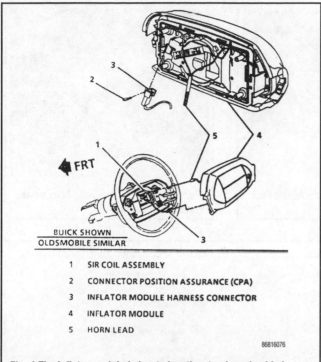

1 SIR COIL ASSEMBLY

2 CONNECTOR POSITION ASSURANCE (CPA)

3 INFLATOR MODULE HARNESS CONNECTOR

4 INFLATOR MODULE

5 HORN LEAD

86816076

Fig. 4 The inflator module is located on the steering wheel hub

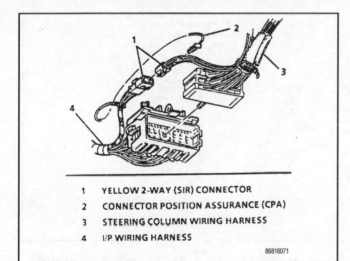

1 YELLOW 2-WAY (SIR) CONNECTOR

2 CONNECTOR POSITION ASSURANCE (CPA)

3 STEERING COLUMN WIRING HARNESS

4 I/P WIRING HARNESS

86816071

Fig. 5 Unplug the Connector Position Assurance (CPA) and the yellow two-way connector from the base of the steering column

1. Disconnect the negative cable at the battery.

2. On the 3.1L (VIN M) you will need to remove the serpentine belt and move the alternator aside. See Section 3 for removal and installation.

3. For the 2.2L (VIN 4), disconnect the air inlet resonator, then remove the torque strut from the engine. Rotate the engine slightly forward.

4. Working inside the engine compartment, disconnect the blower motor electrical leads.

5. Remove the motor retaining bolts. If there is a hose disconnect it, then remove the blower motor.

To install:

6. Position the blower motor on it's mount.

7. Install the mounting bolts and tighten until snug.

8. Attach the drain hose if removed, then engage the electrical connection to the motor.

9. On the 2.2L (VIN 4), properly position the engine and install the torque strut to the engine. Connect the air inlet resonator.

10. On the 3.1L (VIN M), install the alternator, if removed. Install the serpentine belt.

11. Connect the negative battery cable, tighten the cable bolt to 11 ft. lbs. (15 Nm).

12. Reset the radio, clock and any other applicable electronic devices.

Heater Core

REMOVAL & INSTALLATION

Air Conditioned Models

♦ See Figures 9, 10, 11 and 12

❄ CAUTION

When draining the coolant, keep in mind that cats and dogs are attracted by ethylene glycol antifreeze, and are quite likely to drink any that is left in an uncovered container or in puddles on the ground. This will prove fatal in sufficient quantity. Always drain the coolant into a sealable container. Coolant should be reused unless it is contaminated or several years old.

1. Disconnect the negative battery cable and drain the cooling system.

2. Disconnect the heater hoses from the heater core inlet and outlet connections in the engine compartment.

3. Allowing residual coolant from the heater core to drain. Cap the openings.

4. Working inside the vehicle, remove the lower instrument panel sound insulator.

5. Remove the heater floor outlet duct screws or clips and remove the duct.

6. Remove the heater core cover by removing the attaching screws and clips.

7. Remove the heater core cover.

8. Remove the heater core retainers and remove the heater core.

To install:

9. Position the heater core in the housing and install the retaining straps.

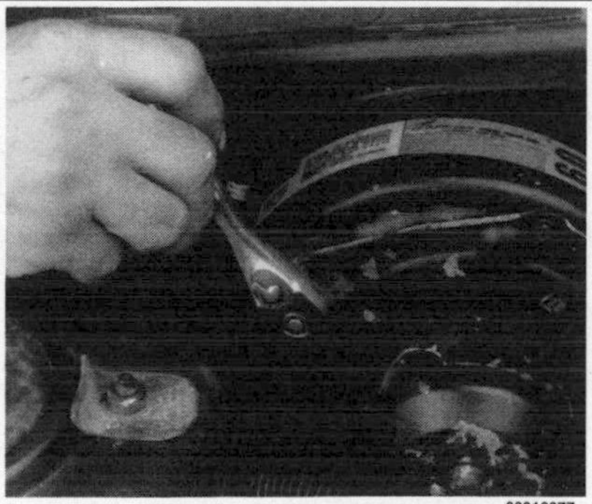

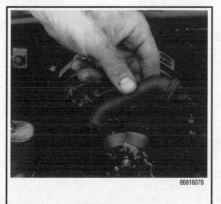

86816077

Fig. 6 Remove the blower motor retaining bolts . . .

86816078

Fig. 7 . . . then disconnect the hose

86816079

Fig. 8 The blower motor can now be removed

Fig. 9 Remove the heater floor outlet duct screws or clips . . .

Fig. 10 . . . then remove the heater floor outlet duct

Fig. 11 Remove the mounting bolts which retain the heater core

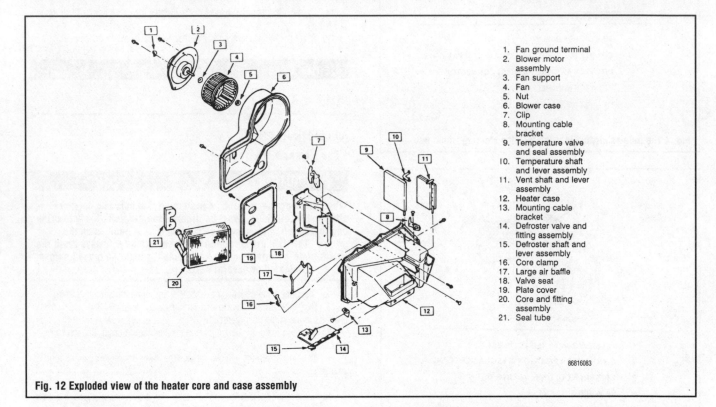

1. Fan ground terminal
2. Blower motor assembly
3. Fan support
4. Fan
5. Nut
6. Blower case
7. Clip
8. Mounting cable bracket
9. Temperature valve and seal assembly
10. Temperature shaft and lever assembly
11. Vent shaft and lever assembly
12. Heater case
13. Mounting cable bracket
14. Defroster valve and fitting assembly
15. Defroster shaft and lever assembly
16. Core clamp
17. Large air baffle
18. Valve seat
19. Plate cover
20. Core and fitting assembly
21. Seal tube

Fig. 12 Exploded view of the heater core and case assembly

10. Position the heater core cover on the housing and install the attaching screws and clips.
11. Install the floor outlet duct and attaching screws or clips.
12. Install the lower instrument panel sound insulator.
13. Working in the engine compartment, connect the heater core inlet and outlet hoses.
14. Fill the cooling system.
15. Start the engine and check for coolant leaks. Allow the engine to warm up sufficiently to confirm the proper operation of the heater.
16. Recheck for leaks. Check the cooling system level.

Air Conditioned Models

▶ See Figure 13

1. Drain the cooling system.

❋❋ CAUTION

When draining the coolant, keep in mind that cats and dogs are attracted by the ethylene glycol antifreeze, and are quite likely to drink any that is left in an uncovered container or in puddles on the ground. This will prove fatal in sufficient quantity. Always drain the

coolant into a sealable container. Coolant should be reused unless it is contaminated or several years old.

2. Disconnect the hoses at the core.
3. Remove the heater duct and lower side covers.
4. Remove the lower heater outlet.
5. Remove the two housing cover-to-air valve housing clips.
6. Remove the housing cover.
7. Remove the core restraining straps.
8. Remove the core tubing retainers and lift out the core.

To install:

9. Install the core, then attach the core tubing retainers.
10. Attach the core restraining straps.
11. Install the housing cover, then install the two housing cover-to-air valve housing clips.
12. Install the lower heater outlet, then attach the heater duct and lower side covers.
13. Connect the hoses at the core.
14. Fill the cooling system.
15. Start the engine and check for coolant leaks. Allow the engine to warm up sufficiently to confirm the proper operation of the heater.
16. Recheck for leaks. Check the cooling system level.

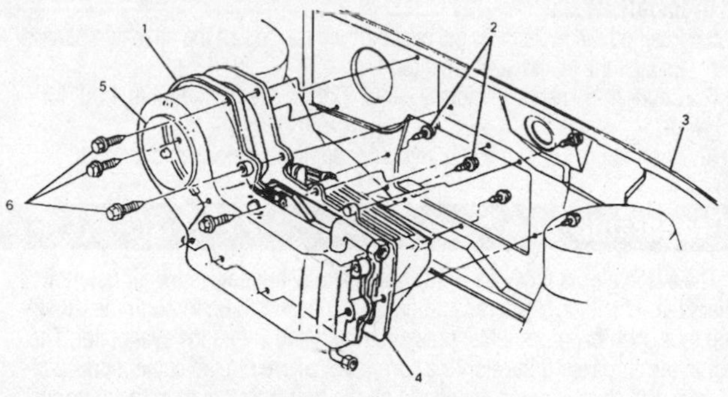

1   MODULE ASSEMBLY, HEATER AND AIR CONDITIONING
    EVAPORATOR AND BLOWER
2   BOLT/SCREW, HEATER AND AIR CONDITIONING EVAPORATOR AND
    BLOWER MODULE
3   DASH PANEL
4   GASKET, HEATER AND AIR CONDITIONING EVAPORATOR AND
    BLOWER MODULE
5   MOTOR ASSEMBLY, BLOWER
6   BOLT/SCREW, BLOWER MOTOR

86816084

Fig. 13 Heater and air conditioning module assembly

Control Cables

REMOVAL & INSTALLATION

1. Disconnect the negative battery cable.
2. Remove the temperature control assembly from the dash.
3. Remove the lower instrument panel sound insulator.
4. Tag and disconnect the cable(s) at the module and control.
5. Remove the cables.
To install:
6. Attach the cables in there proper locations, make sure any retaining clips are seated properly.
7. Install the lower instrument panel sound insulator.
8. Install the control assembly.
9. Adjust the cables as needed. Vehicles with sliding clips, proceed as follows:
   a. Place the control lever in the Cold position.
   b. Place the clip of the cable on the heater case temperature door post.
   c. Push the control head lever towards the Hot, until the temperature door seats and the spring back is out of the cable and control.
10. Connect the negative battery cable, tighten the cable bolt to 11 ft. lbs. (15 Nm).
11. Reset the radio, clock and any other electronic devises in need.

Control Panel

REMOVAL & INSTALLATION

1. Disconnect the negative battery cable.
2. Remove the radio knobs (if equipped) and the clock set knob (if equipped).

AIR CONDITIONER

General Information

❄ CAUTION

Some vehicles are equipped with the Supplemental Inflatable Restraint (SIR) system. This system must be disabled before performing service on or around the air bag, instrument panel components, wiring and sensors. Failure to follow safety and disabling procedures could result in accidental air bag deployment, possible personal injury and unnecessary air bag system repairs.

3. Remove the instrument bezel retaining screws.
4. Pull the bezel out to disconnect the rear defogger switch and the remote mirror control (if equipped).
5. Remove the instrument panel.
6. Remove the control head to dash screws and pull the head out.
7. Disconnect the electrical connectors and/or control cable(s) (if equipped), then remove the control head.
To install:
8. Attach the control head, then connect the electrical connectors and/or control cable(s) (if equipped).
9. Replace the control head in the dash and tighten down the dash screws.
10. Install the instrument panel.
11. Connect the rear defogger switch and the remote mirror control (if equipped).
12. Install the instrument bezel attaching it with the retaining screws.
13. Reinstall the radio knobs (if equipped) and the clock set knob (if equipped).
14. Connect the negative battery cable, tighten the cable bolt to 11 ft. lbs. (15 Nm).

Defroster Vacuum Actuator

REMOVAL & INSTALLATION

1. Remove the instrument panel.
2. Disconnect the defroster nozzle. Remove the two clips securing mode valve and the housing assembly-to-case, then disconnect the vacuum hose connections at the defroster actuator and mode actuator.
3. Remove the mode valve housing assembly.
4. Remove the two defroster actuator retaining screws.
5. Release the actuator rod and remove the actuator assembly.
To install:
6. Install the defroster actuator with the retaining screws and connecting actuator rod.
7. Install the mode valve and housing assembly.
8. Connect the vacuum lines at the defroster actuator and the mode valve actuator.
9. Connect the defroster nozzle, then install the instrument panel assembly.

Temperature Valve

REMOVAL & INSTALLATION

1. Disassemble the mode valve housing.
2. Remove the temperature control cable and slide the valve pivot rod towards the passenger side of the vehicle.
3. Remove the valve.
To install:
4. Position the temperature valve in the case and slide the pivot rod back in place.
5. Connect the temperature control cable.
6. Install the mode valve housing, then adjust the temperature cable.

The heater and air conditioning systems are controlled manually or electronically. The systems differ mainly in the way air temperature and the routing of air flow are controlled. The manual system controls air temperature through a cable-actuated lever and air flow through a vacuum switching valve and vacuum actuators. With Electronic Climate Control (ECC) systems, both temperature and air flow are controlled by the Body Control Module (BCM) through the Climate Control Panel (CCP). There are 2 types of compressors used. The HR-6 compressor, used on Cycling Clutch Orifice Tube (CCOT) systems, is a 6-cylinder axial compressor consisting of 3 double-ended pistons actuated by a swash plate shaft assembly. The compressor cycles on and off according to system demands. The compressor driveshaft is driven by the serpentine belt when the electromagnetic clutch is engaged.

The V-5 compressor, used on Variable Displacement Orifice Tube (VDOT) systems, is designed to meet the demands of the air conditioning system without cycling. The compressor employs a variable angle wobble plate controlling the displacement of 5 axially oriented cylinders. Displacement is controlled by a bellows actuated control valve located in the rear head of the compressor. The electromagnetic compressor clutch connects the compressor shaft to the serpentine drive belt when the coil is energized.

Service Valve Locations

Refer to Section 1 for discharging and charging of the air conditioning system.

The high-side service valve is normally located in the refrigerant line near the discharge fitting of the compressor.

The low-side service valve is normally located on the accumulator or in the condenser-to-evaporator refrigerant line.

Blower Motor Resistor

REMOVAL & INSTALLATION

◆ **See Figures 14 and 15**

1. Disconnect the negative battery cable.
2. Unplug the electrical connector at the resistor.
3. Remove the resistor attaching screws.
4. Remove the resistor from the evaporator case.

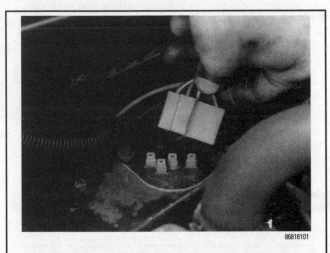

86816101

Fig. 14 Unplug the electrical connector from the resistor

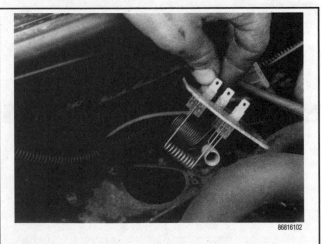

86816102

Fig. 15 After removing the attaching screws, pull the resistor from the case

To install:

5. Position the resistor in the evaporator case. Install the attaching screws.
6. Engage the electrical connector.
7. Connect the negative battery cable. Tighten the cable bolt to 11 ft. lbs. (15 Nm).
8. Reset the radio, clock and any other applicable electronic devices.

Evaporator

The evaporator is a device which cools and dehumidifies the air before it enters the vehicle. A high pressure liquid refrigerant flows through the expansion tube, then becomes a low pressure liquid and enters the evaporator. The heat in the air passing through the core is transferred to the cooler surface of the core. Which then cools the air. As all the heat transfers from the air to the evaporator core surface, any moisture in the air is condensed on the outside surface of the core and drained off as condensate.

REMOVAL & INSTALLATION

➡**Procedures for discharging and servicing the air conditioning system is described in Section 1. If a refrigerant recovery/recycling machine is not available, this job should be performed at a dealer or a shop that has the equipment.**

✳ CAUTION

Some vehicles are equipped with the Supplemental Inflatable Restraint (SIR) system. This system must be disabled before performing service on or around the air bag, instrument panel components, wiring and sensors. Failure to follow safety and disabling procedures could result in accidental air bag deployment, possible personal injury and unnecessary air bag system repairs.

1. Disconnect the negative battery cable.
2. Remove the air cleaner.
3. Properly discharge the air conditioning system into a recovery/recycling machine.
4. Unplug the module electrical connectors, disconnect the harness straps and move the harness aside.
5. On the 3.1L (VIN M) engine, remove the throttle modulator assembly.
6. Remove the heater hose routing bracket from the back of the cover.
7. Disconnect the liquid line at the evaporator inlet and low pressure line at the evaporator outlet.

➡**Cap the refrigerant lines when opening the system to prevent the entry of dirt and moisture and the loss of refrigerant lubricant.**

8. Remove the blower motor resistor from the top of the cover.
9. Unplug the blower motor electrical connector.
10. If equipped with the 2.8L MFI engine, remove the alternator bracket bolts, alternator rear brace bolt, alternator pivot bolt and move the alternator away from the module.
11. Remove the cover from the module.
12. Remove the evaporator core.
To install:

➡**If replacing the evaporator or if the original evaporator was flushed during service, add 2–3 fluid oz. (60–90ml) of refrigerant lubricant to the system.**

13. Clean the old gasket material from the cowl.
14. Install the evaporator core in the module.
15. Apply permagum sealer to the case, then install the cover using a new gasket.
16. Install the cover attaching screws.
17. If equipped with the 2.8L MFI engine, position the alternator and install the pivot bolts, rear brace bolt and alternator bracket bolts.
18. Engage the blower motor electrical connector.
19. Install the resistor to the top of the cover.
20. Install new O-rings to the liquid and low pressure lines. Lubricate O-rings with refrigerant oil.
21. Connect the liquid line at the evaporator inlet and low pressure line at the evaporator outlet.

22. Install the heater hose routing bracket to the cover.
23. On the 3.1L (VIN M) install the throttle modulator assembly.
24. Route the cowl harness in the straps and connect the module electrical connectors.
25. Connect the negative battery cable. Tighten the cable bolt to 11 ft. lbs. (15 Nm).
26. Evacuate, recharge and leak test the system.
27. Reset the radio, clock and any other applicable electronic devices.

Manual Control Head

REMOVAL & INSTALLATION

1. Disconnect the negative battery cable.
2. Remove the hush panel, as required.
3. Remove the instrument panel trim plate.
4. Remove the control head attaching screws and pull the control head out.
5. Unplug the electrical and vacuum connectors at the back of the control head. Disconnect the temperature control cable.
6. Remove the control head.
To install:
7. Position the control head near the mounting location. Engage the electrical and vacuum connectors and cables to the back of the control head. Connect the temperature control cable.
8. Install the control head and attaching screws.
9. Install the instrument panel trim plate.
10. Install the hush panel, if removed.
11. Connect the negative battery cable. Tighten the cable bolt to 11 ft. lbs. (15 Nm).
12. Reset the radio, clock and any other applicable electronic devices.

Manual Control Cables

REMOVAL & INSTALLATION

▶ **See Figure 16**

1. Disconnect the negative battery cable.
2. Remove the temperature control assembly from the dash.
3. Remove the lower instrument panel sound insulator.
4. Tag and disconnect the cable(s) at the module.
5. Remove the cables.

To install:
6. Attach the cables in there proper locations, make sure any retaining clips are seated properly.
7. Install the lower instrument panel sound insulator.
8. Install the control assembly.
9. Adjust the cables as needed.
10. Connect the negative battery cable, tighten the cable bolt to 11 ft. lbs. (15 Nm).
11. Reset the radio, clock and any other applicable electronic devices.

ADJUSTMENT

Without Sliding Clips

1. Attach the cable to the control assembly.
2. Place the control lever in the **OFF** position.
3. Place the opposite loop of cable on the lever or actuator post.
4. Push the sheath toward the lever until the lever or actuator seats and the lash is out of the cable and control.
5. Tighten the screw to secure the cable.

With Sliding Clips

1. Place the control lever in the **COLD** position.
2. Place the clip of the cable on the heater case temperature door post.
3. Push the control head lever towards the **HOT** position, until the temperature door seats and the spring back is out of the cable and control.

Electronic Climate Control Panel

REMOVAL & INSTALLATION

▶ **See Figure 17**

1. Disconnect the negative battery cable.
2. Remove the instrument panel trim plate(s) to gain access to the electronic control panel.
3. Remove the control panel attaching screws.
4. Pull the control panel out far enough to unplug the electrical connector. Remove control panel.
To install:
5. Engage the control panel electrical connector
6. Install control panel attaching screws.
7. Install the instrument panel trim plate(s).

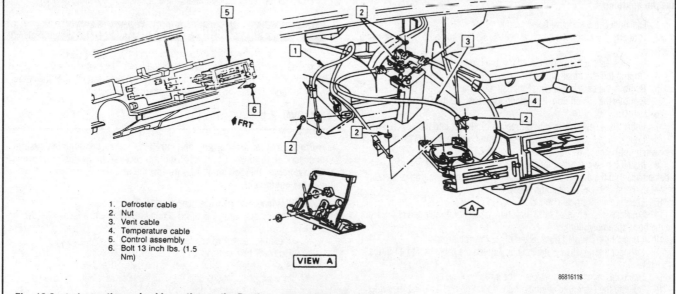

1. Defroster cable
2. Nut
3. Vent cable
4. Temperature cable
5. Control assembly
6. Bolt 13 inch lbs. (1.5 Nm)

FRT

VIEW A

86816118

Fig. 16 Control mounting and cable routing on the Pontiac wagon; others are similar

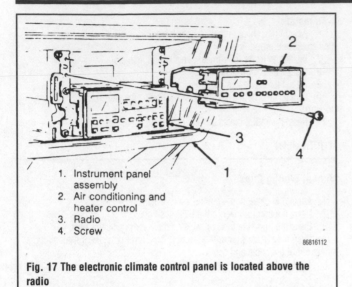

1. Instrument panel assembly
2. Air conditioning and heater control
3. Radio
4. Screw

86816112

Fig. 17 The electronic climate control panel is located above the radio

8. Connect the negative battery cable. Tighten the cable bolt to 11 ft. lbs. (15 Nm).
9. Reset the radio, clock and any other applicable electronic devices.

High-Pressure Compressor Cut-Off Switch

The function of the switch is to protect the engine from overheating in the event of excessively high compressor head pressure and to de-energize the compressor clutch before the high pressure relief valve discharge pressure is reached. The switch is mounted on the back of the compressor or on the refrigerant hose assembly near the back of the compressor. Servicing a switch mounted on the back of the compressor requires that the system be discharged. Switches mounted on the coupled hose assembly are mounted on Schrader-type valves and do not require discharging the system to be serviced.

REMOVAL & INSTALLATION

Compressor Mounted Switch

▶ **See Figure 18**

➡**Procedures for discharging and servicing the air conditioning system is described in Section 1. If a refrigerant recovery/recycling machine is not available, this job should be performed at a dealer or a shop that has the equipment.**

1. Disconnect the negative battery cable.
2. Properly discharge the air conditioning system into a recovery/recycling machine.
3. Remove the coupled hose assembly at the rear of the compressor.
4. Unplug the electrical connector.
5. Remove the switch retaining ring using internal snapring pliers.
6. Remove the switch from the compressor. Discard the O-ring.
To install:
7. Lubricate a new O-ring with refrigerant oil. Insert into the switch cavity.
8. Lubricate the control switch housing with clean refrigerant oil and insert the switch until it bottoms in the cavity.
9. Install the switch retaining snapring with the high point of the curved sides adjacent to the switch housing. Ensure that the retaining ring is properly seated in the switch cavity retaining groove.
10. Engage the electrical connector.
11. Lubricate new coupled hose assembly O-rings with refrigerant oil. Install on the hose assembly fittings.
12. Connect the coupled hose assembly to the compressor.
13. Connect the negative battery cable. Tighten the cable bolt to 11 ft. lbs. (15 Nm).
14. Evacuate, recharge and leak test the system.
15. Operate the system to ensure proper operation and leak test the switch.
16. Reset the radio, clock and any other applicable electronic devices.

1	A/C COMPRESSOR
2	A/C HIGH PRESSURE CUT-OUT SWITCH CONNECTOR
3	HARNESS RETAINER
4	BOLT/SCREW
5	POWER STEERING PIPES
6	RETAINER
7	BOLT/SCREW 10 N·m (88 LB. IN.)
8	A/C COMPRESSOR CLUTCH CONNECTOR

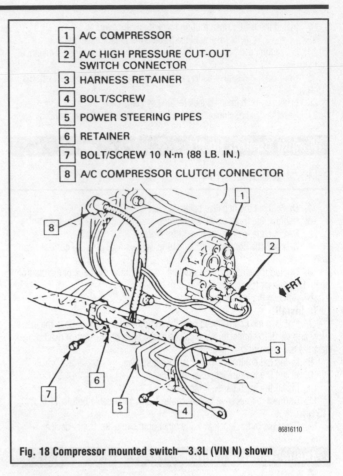

86816110

Fig. 18 Compressor mounted switch—3.3L (VIN N) shown

Refrigerant Line Mounted Switch

1. Disconnect the negative battery cable.
2. Unplug the electrical connector.
3. Remove the switch from the coupled hose assembly. Discard the O-ring.
To install:
4. Lubricate a new O-ring with refrigerant oil.
5. Install the O-ring on the switch and install the switch.
6. Engage the electrical connector.
7. Connect the negative battery cable. Tighten the cable bolt to 11 ft. lbs. (15 Nm).
8. Reset the radio, clock and any other applicable electronic devices.

Low-Pressure Compressor Cut-Off Switch

The function of the switch is to protect the compressor by de-energizing the compressor in the event of a low-charge condition. The switch may be mounted at the back of the compressor or on the coupled hose assembly near the compressor. Servicing the valve requires discharging the system.

REMOVAL & INSTALLATION

➡**Procedures for discharging and servicing the air conditioning system is described in Section 1. If a refrigerant recovery/recycling machine is not available, this job should be performed at a dealer or a shop that has the equipment.**

1. Disconnect the negative battery cable.
2. Properly discharge the air conditioning system into a recovery/recycling machine.
3. Unplug the electrical connector(s).
4. If the switch is mounted to the rear head of the compressor, remove the coupled hose assembly to gain access to the switch. Remove the switch.
5. If the switch is mounted to the coupled hose assembly, remove the switch from its mounting position.

To install:

6. Install the switch.
7. Lubricate new O-rings with refrigerant oil.
8. If the switch is mounted to the rear head of the compressor, install the switch. Install new O-rings on the coupled hose assembly and install the assembly to the back of the compressor.
9. If the switch is mounted on the coupled hose assembly, install the switch.
10. Engage the electrical connector(s).
11. Connect the negative battery cable. Tighten the cable bolt to 11 ft. lbs. (15 Nm).
12. Evacuate, charge and leak test the system.
13. Reset the radio, clock and any other applicable electronic devices.

Idle Speed Power Steering Pressure Switch

Engine idle speed is maintained by cutting off the compressor when high power steering loads are imposed at idle. The switch is located on the pinion housing portion of the steering rack.

REMOVAL & INSTALLATION

1. Disconnect the negative battery cable.
2. Unplug the electrical connector.
3. Unscrew the switch.
To install:
4. Install the switch.
5. Engage the electrical connector.
6. Connect the negative battery cable. Tighten the cable bolt to 11 ft. lbs. (15 Nm).
7. Allow the engine to reach normal operating temperature and confirm the proper operation of the switch.
8. Reset the radio, clock and any other applicable electronic devices.

Pressure Cycling Switch

The pressure cycling switch controls the refrigeration cycle by sensing low-side pressure as an indicator of evaporator temperature. The pressure cycling switch is the freeze-protection device in the system. The switch is mounted on a Schrader valve on the accumulator.

REMOVAL & INSTALLATION

▶ See Figure 19

➡**The system need not be discharged to remove the pressure cycling switch.**

1. Disconnect the negative battery cable.
2. Unplug the electrical connector.
3. Remove the switch and O-ring seal. Discard the O-ring.
To install:
4. Install a new O-ring. Lubricate with refrigerant oil.
5. Install the switch to the accumulator.
6. Engage the electrical connector.
7. Connect the negative battery cable. Tighten the cable bolt to 11 ft. lbs. (15 Nm).
8. Reset the radio, clock and any other applicable electronic devices.

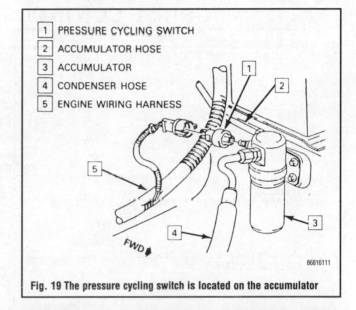

1	PRESSURE CYCLING SWITCH
2	ACCUMULATOR HOSE
3	ACCUMULATOR
4	CONDENSER HOSE
5	ENGINE WIRING HARNESS

FWD

86816111

Fig. 19 The pressure cycling switch is located on the accumulator

CRUISE CONTROL SYSTEMS

General Description

Cruise control is a speed control system which maintains a desired vehicle speed under normal driving conditions. Steep grades either up or down, may cause some variation in the set speed. Speed is maintained only by mechanically holding the throttle open or releasing it. The system cannot apply braking to slow the vehicle.

Most systems use vacuum to operate a throttle servo unit. The servo unit maintains a desired speed by trapping vacuum when the servo is at the desired position. The position of the servo and the vehicle speed are overseen by the controller or Cruise Control Module (CCM), this unit controls the input or release of vacuum within the servo, thus adjusting the throttle to maintain speed.

Some models may use an ElectroMotor Cruise (EMC) system. The EMC uses an electric motor and connecting strap to vary the throttle angle according to directions from the CCM. The system is completely independent of vacuum and allows smoother throttle transitions.

Although the systems vary widely across GM's model line (component location, circuitry, interaction of computers, etc.) all cruise control units share certain common traits:

• The system will not engage until the vehicle exceeds a minimum speed, usually 25 mph (40 kph).

• The system provides several modes of operation including cruise, coast, resume/accelerate, most allow "tap up" and "tap down", an incremental increase or decrease in set speed.

• All have a system **ON/OFF** switch, the system must be turned **ON** before it will engage. Many have a pilot light on the dash which illuminates when the cruise control is engaged.

• All systems will disconnect if the brake and/or clutch pedal is depressed when the system is engaged. The vacuum sustained systems release vacuum as well as interrupting the electrical signal to the controller.

• The accelerator may be depressed at any time to override the chosen cruising speed. If the system receives no new orders, it will remember the previous cruising speed and return to it when the driver finishes accelerating.

• Failures in the cruise control may stem from electrical, mechanical and/or vacuum problems within the cruise control system or any combination of these.

➡**The use of the speed control is not recommended when driving conditions do not permit maintaining a constant speed. These conditions may include heavy or varying traffic, winding roads or slippery surfaces.**

The main parts of the vacuum systems are the:
• Mode control switches
• Cruise Control Module (CCM)
• Servo unit
• Vehicle Speed Sensor (VSS)
• Vacuum supply
• Electrical and vacuum release switches
• Electrical harness

System Service Precautions

✳✳ CAUTION

Some vehicles are equipped with the Supplemental Inflatable Restraint (SIR) system. This system must be disabled before performing service on or around the air bag, instrument panel components, wiring and sensors. Failure to follow safety and disabling procedures could result in accidental air bag deployment, possible personal injury and unnecessary air bag system repairs.

- Never unplug any electrical connection with the ignition switch **ON**.
- Always wear a grounded wrist static strap when servicing any control

module or component labeled with a Electrostatic Discharge (ESD) sensitive device symbol.
  - Avoid touching module connector pins.
  - Leave new components and modules in the shipping package until ready to install them.
  - Always touch a vehicle ground after sliding across a vehicle seat or walking across vinyl or carpeted floors to avoid static charge damage.
  - Never allow welding cables to lie on, near or across any vehicle electrical wiring.
  - Do not allow extension cords for power tools or droplights to lie on, near or across any vehicle electrical wiring.
  - Do not operate the cruise control or the engine with the drive wheels off the ground.

CRUISE CONTROL TROUBLESHOOTING

Problem	Possible Cause
Will not hold proper speed	Incorrect cable adjustment
	Binding throttle linkage
	Leaking vacuum servo diaphragm
	Leaking vacuum tank
	Faulty vacuum or vent valve
	Faulty stepper motor
	Faulty transducer
	Faulty speed sensor
	Faulty cruise control module
Cruise intermittently cuts out	Clutch or brake switch adjustment too tight
	Short or open in the cruise control circuit
	Faulty transducer
	Faulty cruise control module
Vehicle surges	Kinked speedometer cable or casing
	Binding throttle linkage
	Faulty speed sensor
	Faulty cruise control module
Cruise control inoperative	Blown fuse
	Short or open in the cruise control circuit
	Faulty brake or clutch switch
	Leaking vacuum circuit
	Faulty cruise control switch
	Faulty stepper motor
	Faulty transducer
	Faulty speed sensor
	Faulty cruise control module

Note: Use this chart as a guide. Not all systems will use the components listed.

TCCA6C01

ENTERTAINMENT SYSTEM

Radio Receiver/Tape Player/CD Player

♦ **See Figure 20**

※ WARNING

Some vehicles are equipped with an anti-theft radio system. Please refer to your owner's manual or consult a dealer about any special procedures applicable to your system.

1. Disconnect the negative battery cable.
2. Remove the instrument panel insulator mounting screws enough to remove the steering column trim cover.
3. On some models it will be necessary to:
   a. Remove the ash tray, then the ash tray/fuse block assembly. Separate the fuse block and the ash tray. Push forward to access the cigarette lighter and the rear defogger switch.
   b. Disconnect the lighter and the defogger switch connectors.
   c. Remove the cigarette lighter, the glove box.
4. Remove the instrument panel center trim mounting nuts and the trim panel enough to unplug the radio.
5. Remove the radio mounting screws from the bracket(s), then pull the radio out enough to remove the electrical harness and the antenna lead.

To install:

6. Connect the electrical harness and the antenna lead.

7. Slide the radio into the mounting area, then install the radio attaching bolts to the bracket(s).
8. Install the instrument cluster trim plate.
9. Install the accessory trim plate.
10. Connect the negative battery cable. Tighten the cable bolt to 11 ft. lbs. (15 Nm).
11. Reset the radio, clock and any other applicable electronic devices.

Fixed Antenna

REMOVAL & INSTALLATION

Fender Mounted

♦ **See Figures 21 and 22**

1. Remove the steel mast from the antenna base.
2. Loosen the antenna escutcheon nut on top of the fender using a special tool J-28641 or an equivalent.
3. Remove the two side mounting bolts through the engine compartment.
4. On some models you will need to remove the right sound insulator and shroud panel to access the antenna cable.
5. Disconnect the antenna lead in the cable.
6. On some models you will need to:

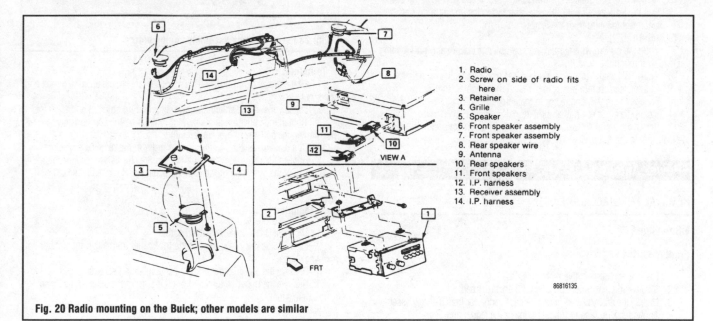

1. Radio
2. Screw on side of radio fits here
3. Retainer
4. Grille
5. Speaker
6. Front speaker assembly
7. Front speaker assembly
8. Rear speaker wire
9. Antenna
10. Rear speakers
11. Front speakers
12. I.P. harness
13. Receiver assembly
14. I.P. harness

86816135

Fig. 20 Radio mounting on the Buick; other models are similar

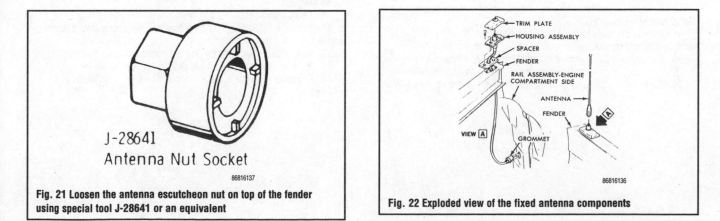

J-28641
Antenna Nut Socket

86816137

Fig. 21 Loosen the antenna escutcheon nut on top of the fender using special tool J-28641 or an equivalent

86816136

Fig. 22 Exploded view of the fixed antenna components

a. Raise and support the car, to remove the inner fender clips and screws.

b. Pull back the inner fender strip and remove the escutcheon nut. Remove the antenna base assembly.

7. Inspect the grommet in the fender wheel for cracks or distortion of any kind.

To install:

8. Replace the grommet if needed.

9. Slide the new antenna into place, with the antenna lead attached.

10. Install the escutcheon nut. Attach the inner fender clips and screws, then lower the vehicle.

11. Tighten the two mounting bolts in the engine compartment, then tighten the antenna escutcheon nut.

12. Install the antenna mast to the base.

13. Reinstall the right shroud panel and sound insulator.

Windshield Mounted

The pigtail from the glass to the lead-in can be replaced by carefully cutting away the sealer, removing the pigtail and soldering a new pigtail to the copper plate. Use a rosin core solder and only enough heat to obtain a good solder joint. Reseal with RTV. Body sealer should not be used. To replace the lead-in:

1. Disconnect the lead-in from the radio.

2. Connect a 3 ft. length of wire to the lead-in connector to aid in pulling the new lead-in into place.

3. Remove the lower windshield reveal molding and the air inlet grille.

4. Unplug the pigtail connector from the antenna lead-in connector at the cowl.

5. Remove the two attaching screws and the antenna lead-in to the cowl.

6. Pull the lead-in out until the wire attached in the previous step is accessible. Disconnect the wire from the lead-in.

To install:

7. Wrap the pull-in wire around the new antenna lead-in and start feeding the lead-in through the cowl.

8. Apply RTV sealer to the cowl where the lead-in attaches to the cowl.

9. Pull the lead-in into place, then install the attaching screws.

10. Engage the pigtail connector to the antenna lead-in.

11. Install the air inlet grille and the reveal molding.

12. Remove the pull-in wire from the antenna lead-in connector, then plug the lead-in into the radio.

Power Antenna

REMOVAL & INSTALLATION

▶ **See Figure 23**

Front Mounted

1. Disconnect the negative battery cable.

2. Remove the instrument panel sound absorber pad.

3. Unplug the antenna lead-in and harness connector from the relay assembly.

4. Apply masking tape to the rear edge of the fender and door.

5. If required, remove the inner to outer fender retaining screws.

6. If required, raise the vehicle and support it safely, then remove the associated front wheel assembly.

7. Remove the lower rocker panel retaining screws, lower fender-to-body retaining bolt and remove the lower rocker panel, as required.

8. Remove the inner splash shield from the fender, as required.

9. Remove the upper antenna retaining nut, using an appropriately tool.

10. Remove the antenna-to-bracket retaining bolts, then remove the antenna.

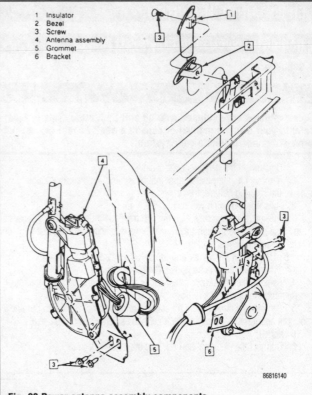

1	Insulator
2	Bezel
3	Screw
4	Antenna assembly
5	Grommet
6	Bracket

86816140

Fig. 23 Power antenna assembly components

To install:

11. Fit the antenna into position, then loosely install the antenna gasket and upper nut.

12. Loosely install the antenna to bracket retaining bolts.

13. Tighten the upper antenna retaining nut, using the appropriately tool, then tighten the antenna to bracket retaining bolts.

14. Complete installation in the reverse order of the removal procedure.

15. Apply silicone grease to the harness connector before reconnecting.

16. Check the operation of the antenna mast. Reset the radio and clock, if required.

Rear Mounted

1. Disconnect the negative battery cable.

2. From inside the trunk, remove the trim panel from either the right or left rear wheel area.

3. Remove the antenna mounting bracket retaining screws.

4. Remove the upper antenna nut and bezel from the antenna, using an appropriately tool.

5. Remove the lead-in cable and wiring connector.

6. Remove the antenna assembly from the vehicle.

To install:

7. Fit the antenna to the vehicle, then connect the lead-in cable.

8. Install the nut and bezel to the antenna and mounting bracket retaining screws.

9. Apply silicone grease to the harness connector before reconnecting.

10. Install the trim panel and reconnect the negative battery cable.

11. Check the operation of the antenna mast. Reset the radio and clock, if required.

WINDSHIELD WIPERS

Windshield Wiper Blade and Arm

REMOVAL & INSTALLATION

▶ **See Figure 24**

Wiper blade insert replacement procedures are detailed in Section 1.
Removal of the wiper arms requires the use of a special tool, GM J-8966 or its equivalent prytool. Versions of this tool are generally available in auto parts stores.

1. With the wipers on, turn the ignition **OFF** when the blades get to the mid-wipe position.
2. Mark the position of the arms on the windshield.
3. Lift the wiper arm from the windshield, then insert the tool under the wiper arm. Pry the arm off the upper transmission drive shaft.
4. Disconnect the washer hose from the arm (if so equipped).
5. Remove the wiper blade assembly from the arm.

To install:

6. Install the wiper blade on the arm. Align the arm with the mark made on the windshield.
7. Attach the wiper arm assembly to the transmission drive shaft, then push in the arm retaining latch, and return the wiper arm assembly to the windshield.
8. Turn the ignition in the **ON** position, then park the wipers.

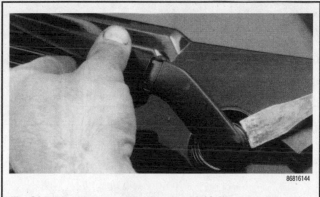

Fig. 24 Lift the wiper arm from the windshield, then insert the tool under the wiper arm

ADJUSTMENT

The only adjustment for the wiper arms is to remove an arm from the transmission shaft, rotate the arm the required distance and direction and then install the arm back in position so it is in line with the blackout line on the glass. The wiper motor must be in the park position.

The correct blade-out wipe position on the driver's side is $1\frac{1}{32}$ in. (28mm) for 1982–85 models and $1\frac{1}{16}$ in. (18mm) for 1986–96 models, from the tip of the blade to the left windshield pillar molding. The correct blade-down wipe position on the passenger side of the car is in line with the blackout line at the bottom of the glass.

Rear Wiper Arm and Blade

REMOVAL & INSTALLATION

▶ **See Figure 25**

Removal of the wiper arms requires the use of special tool, GM J-8966 or its equivalent prytool. Versions of this tool are generally available in auto parts stores.

1. Lift the wiper arm from the window, then insert the tool under the wiper arm. Lever the arm off the transmission drive shaft. Use care not to damage the paint on the vehicle.
2. Remove the wiper blade from the arm.

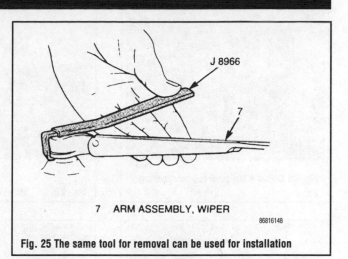

7 ARM ASSEMBLY, WIPER

Fig. 25 The same tool for removal can be used for installation

To install:

3. Install the wiper blade onto the arm.
4. Position the wiper arm on the wiper motor drive shaft so that the blade assembly rests in the proper park position.
5. Press down on the wiper arm until it is fully seated on the drive shaft. The same special tool for removal can be used for installation.

Wiper Motor

REMOVAL & INSTALLATION

▶ **See Figures 26 thru 31**

1. Disconnect the negative battery cable.
2. Remove the wiper arms.
3. Remove the cowl cover.
4. When lifting the cowl up disconnect the washer nozzle hoses.
5. Loosen (but do not remove) the drive link-to-crank arm attaching nuts and detach the drive link from the motor crank arm.
6. Unplug the wiper motor electrical connector.
7. Remove the wiper motor attaching bolts.
8. Remove the wiper motor, guiding the crank arm through the hole.

To install:

9. Insert the wiper motor, guiding the crank arm through the hole.
10. Guide the crank arm through the opening in the body and then tighten the mounting bolts to 4–6 ft. lbs. (5–8 Nm).
11. Install the drive link to the crank arm with the motor in the park position.
12. Install the wiper motor attaching bolts.
13. Engage the electrical connectors.
14. Connect the wiper arm drive link to the crank arm.
15. Install the cowl cover.
16. Install the wiper arms.
17. Connect the negative battery cable. Tighten the cable bolt to 11 ft. lbs. (15 Nm).
18. Reset the radio, clock and any other applicable electronic devices.

Rear Wiper Motor

REMOVAL & INSTALLATION

1. Disconnect the negative battery cable.
2. Remove the wiper arm assembly from the wiper motor drive shaft.
3. Remove the nut and washer from the wiper motor drive shaft.
4. Unfasten the liftgate glass opening upper finish molding.
5. Remove the electrical harness from the motor.
6. Remove the two screws, then guide the motor out of the tailgate recess.

Fig. 26 Remove the cowl lower attaching bolts . . .

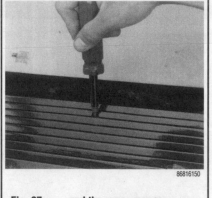

Fig. 27 . . . and the upper screws

Fig. 28 Disconnect the washer nozzle hoses from the cowl

Fig. 29 Unplug the wiper motor electrical connector

Fig. 30 Unfasten the wiper motor attaching bolts . . .

Fig. 31 . . . then remove the wiper motor, guiding the crank arm through the hole

To install:

➡When fasteners are removed always reinstall them at the same location from which they were removed. If a fastener need replacing, always use the same fastener, or one of equal size and/or stronger that the original. If these conditions are not followed, parts or system damage could occur.

   7. Install the wiper motor in the recess of the tailgate.
   8. Tighten the two screws to 53 inch lbs. (6 Nm).
   9. Apply the washer and nut to the wiper shaft, then tighten to 62 inch lbs. (7 Nm).
   10. Connect the electrical harness to the motor assembly.
   11. Install the liftgate glass upper molding.
   12. Connect the negative battery cable. Tighten the cable bolt to 11 ft. lbs. (15 Nm).
   13. Attach the wiper arm to the motor drive shaft.
   14. Reset the radio, clock, etc. as necessary.

Wiper Linkage

REMOVAL & INSTALLATION

▸ **See Figures 32 and 33**

   1. Disconnect the negative battery cable.
   2. Remove the wiper arms.
   3. Remove the shroud top vent grille.
   4. Loosen (but do not remove) the drive link-to-crank arm attaching nuts.
   5. Loosen the two nuts, then separate the transmission drive link from the wiper motor crank arm using tool J-39232 or equivalent.
   6. Unscrew the linkage-to-cowl panel retaining screws and remove the linkage by guiding it through the access hole in the shroud upper panel.
   7. Some models you will need to unsnap the two water deflectors from the transmission assembly.

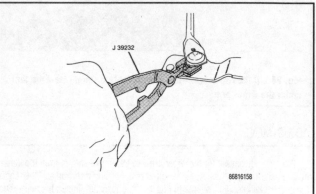

Fig. 32 Separate the transmission drive link from the wiper motor crank arm using tool J-39232 or equivalent

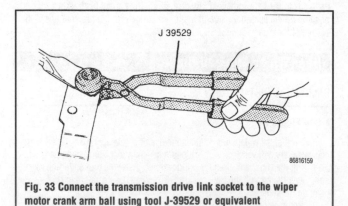

Fig. 33 Connect the transmission drive link socket to the wiper motor crank arm ball using tool J-39529 or equivalent

To install:

8. Attach the two water deflectors over the position marks on the transmission, then snap closed to secure.

9. Insert the transmission assembly by positioning it in the plenum chamber through the panel openings.

10. Install the screws loosely.

11. Connect the transmission drive link socket to the wiper motor crank arm ball using tool J-39529 or equivalent. Tighten the nuts to 62 inch lbs. (7 Nm).

12. Align the transmission assembly, then tighten the screws to 71 inch lbs. (8 Nm).

13. Attach the cowl panel.

14. Connect the negative battery cable. Tighten the cable bolt to 11 ft. lbs. (15 Nm).

15. Install the wiper arm assembly, check for operation, adjust the blades if needed.

16. Reset the radio and clock.

INSTRUMENTS AND SWITCHES

Instrument Cluster

REMOVAL & INSTALLATION

✽✽ CAUTION

The instrument cluster contains all of the displays, lamps and indicators which provide the operating information to the driver. Be extra careful when working around electrical items in your vehicle, many solid state components can be damaged by electrostatic discharge. If you are working around the SIR system remember to disarm the system. Otherwise air bag deployment could occur and cause personal injury.

You may want to place a clean cloth over the steering column to prevent scratches. On vehicles with tilt steering, it will help to lower the wheel all the way then unscrew the tilt wheel lever.

Century

✽✽ CAUTION

Some vehicles are equipped with the Supplemental Inflatable Restraint (SIR) system. This system must be disabled before performing service on or around the air bag, instrument panel components, wiring and sensors. Failure to follow safety and disabling procedures could result in accidental air bag deployment, possible personal injury and unnecessary air bag system repairs.

1. Disconnect the negative battery cable.
2. Disable the SIR, if equipped.
3. Disconnect the speedometer cable and pull it through the firewall.
4. Remove the left side hush panel retaining screws and nut.
5. Remove the right side hush panel retaining screws and nut.
6. Remove the shift indicator cable clip.
7. Remove the steering column trim plate.
8. Put the gear selector in **L** or **1**. Remove the retaining screws and gently pull out the instrument panel trim plate.
9. Disconnect the parking brake cable at the lever by pushing it forward and sliding it from its slot.
10. Unbolt and lower the steering column.
11. Remove the gauge cluster retaining screws. Pull the cluster out far enough to disconnect any wires, then remove the instrument cluster.

To install:

12. Install the gauge cluster, then attach the electrical wires and install the retaining screws.

13. Position the steering column, then install the retaining bolts.

14. Connect the parking brake cable at the lever.

15. Put the gear selector in **L** or **P**. Install the instrument panel trim plate.

16. Install the steering column trim plate.

17. Install the shift indicator cable clip.

Washer Pump

REMOVAL & INSTALLATION

1. Disconnect the negative battery cable.
2. Disconnect the electrical harness on the pump.
3. Drain the washer solvent from the fluid reservoir.
4. Remove screws mounting the reservoir, then disconnect the fluid hoses.
5. Pull the reservoir from the engine compartment, then remove the pump from the reservoir.
6. Inspect the grommet which the pump is mounted into for dry-rot or any other deterioration.
7. Installation is the reverse of removal.

18. Install the right side hush panel retaining screws and nut.

19. Install the left side hush panel retaining screws and nut.

20. Pull the speedometer cable through the firewall and connect to the speedometer.

21. Connect the negative battery cable. Tighten the cable bolt to 11 ft. lbs. (15 Nm).

22. Enable the SIR, if equipped.

23. Reset the radio, clock and any other applicable electronic devices.

Celebrity

1. Disconnect the negative battery cable.
2. Remove instrument panel hush trim.
3. Remove vent control housing, as required.
4. On non-air conditioning vehicles, remove steering column trim cover screws and lower cover with vent cables attached. On air conditioning vehicles, remove trim cover attaching screws and remove cover.
5. Remove instrument cluster trim pad.
6. Remove ash tray, retainer and fuse block, disconnecting wires as necessary.
7. Remove headlight switch knob and instrument panel trim plate. Unplug electrical connectors of any accessory switches in trim plate.
8. Remove cluster assembly and disconnect speedometer cable, **PRNDL** and cluster electrical connectors.

To install:

9. Install cluster assembly and connect speedometer cable, **PRNDL** and cluster electrical connectors.

10. Install headlight switch knob and instrument panel trim plate. Engage electrical connectors of any accessory switches in trim plate.

11. Install the ash tray, retainer and fuse block. Engage the electrical connectors.

12. Install instrument cluster trim pad.

13. On non-air conditioned vehicles, raise the cover with vent cables attached and install steering column trim cover screws. On air conditioned vehicles, install trim cover and attaching screws.

14. If removed, install vent control housing.

15. Install instrument panel hush panel.

16. Connect the negative battery cable. Tighten the cable bolt to 11 ft. lbs. (15 Nm).

17. Reset the radio, clock and any other applicable electronic devices.

Ciera and Cruiser

▶ **See Figures 34 and 35**

✽✽ CAUTION

Some vehicles are equipped with the Supplemental Inflatable Restraint (SIR) system. This system must be disabled before performing service on or around the air bag, instrument panel components, wiring and sensors. Failure to follow safety and disabling procedures could result in accidental air bag deployment, possible personal injury and unnecessary air bag system repairs.

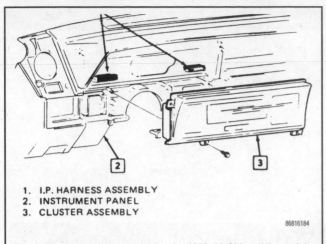

1. I.P. HARNESS ASSEMBLY
2. INSTRUMENT PANEL
3. CLUSTER ASSEMBLY

86816184

Fig. 34 Instrument cluster mounting for 1992–96 Oldsmobile models

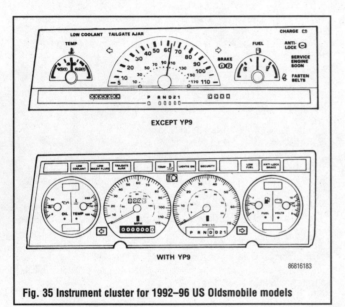

86816183

Fig. 35 Instrument cluster for 1992–96 US Oldsmobile models

1. Disconnect the negative battery cable.
2. Disable the SIR, if equipped.
3. Remove left instrument panel trim pad.
4. Remove instrument panel cluster trim cover.
5. Disconnect speedometer cable at transaxle or cruise control transducer, if equipped.
6. Remove steering column trim cover.
7. Disconnect shift indicator clip from steering column shift bowl.
8. Remove 4 screws attaching cluster assembly to instrument panel.
9. Pull assembly out far enough to reach behind cluster and disconnect speedometer cable.
10. Remove cluster assembly.
To install:
11. Install the cluster assembly.
12. Connect the speedometer cable.
13. Install the 4 screws attaching cluster assembly to instrument panel.
14. Connect shift indicator clip to steering column shift bowl.
15. Install the steering column trim cover.
16. Connect the speedometer cable at the transaxle or cruise control transducer, if equipped.
17. Install the instrument panel cluster trim cover.
18. Install the left instrument panel trim pad.
19. Connect the negative battery cable. Tighten the cable bolt to 11 ft. lbs. (15 Nm).
20. Reset the radio, clock and any other applicable electronic devices.

6000

1. On the electronic instrument cluster you will need to call up and record the maintenance reminder mileages (DIC) before proceeding.

➡ **The service button is located on the instrument panel, the mileages will display and pushing the system recall button momentarily.**

2. Disconnect the negative battery cable, and remove the center and left side lower instrument panel trim plate.
3. Remove the screws securing the instrument cluster to the instrument panel carrier.
4. Remove the instrument cluster lens to gain access to the speedometer head and gauges.
5. Remove right side and left side hush panels and steering column trim cover. Disconnect the parking brake cable and vent cables, if equipped.
6. Remove steering column retaining bolts and lower the steering column.
7. Disconnect temperature control cable, inner-to-outer air conditioning wire harness and inner-to-outer air conditioning vacuum harness, if equipped.
8. Disconnect the chassis harness behind the left lower instrument panel and ECM/PCM connectors behind glove box. Disconnect instrument panel harness at cowl.
9. Remove center instrument panel trim plate, radio, (if equipped) and disconnect the neutral switch and brake light switch.
10. Remove upper and lower instrument panel retaining screws, nuts and bolts.
11. Pull instrument panel assembly out far enough to disconnect ignition switch, headlight dimmer switch and turn signal switch. Disconnect all other accessory wiring and vacuum lines necessary to remove instrument panel assembly.
12. Remove instrument panel assembly with wiring harness.
To install:
13. Install instrument panel assembly with wiring harness.
14. Connect ignition switch, headlight dimmer switch and turn signal switch. Connect all other accessory wiring and vacuum lines.
15. Install upper and lower instrument panel retaining screws, nuts and bolts.
16. Connect neutral switch and brake light switch. Install the radio, if equipped, and install center instrument panel trim plate.
17. Connect chassis harness behind left lower instrument panel and ECM/PCM connectors behind glove box. Connect instrument panel harness at cowl.
18. Connect temperature control cable, inner-to-outer air conditioning wire harness and inner-to-outer air conditioning vacuum harness, if equipped.
19. Raise the steering column and install retaining bolts.
20. Install right side and left side hush panels, steering column trim cover and connect parking brake cable and vent cables, if equipped.
21. Install the instrument cluster lens.
22. Install the screws securing the instrument cluster to the instrument panel carrier.
23. Install the center and left side lower instrument panel trim plate.
24. Connect the negative battery cable. Tighten the cable bolt to 11 ft. lbs. (15 Nm).
25. Reset the radio, clock and any other applicable electronic devices.
26. Reset the service reminder:
   a. Sequence through the service items by momentarily depressing and releasing the button until the desired service item is displayed. When the desired item is displayed DO NOT release the button.
   b. After the button is held for 5–10 seconds, the service interval miles displayed will count down in 500 mile intervals. When the desired interval is reached, release the button.

Speedometer

REMOVAL & INSTALLATION

➡ **When replacing a speedometer head Federal law requires the odometer reading of the replacement unit be set to the reading of the unit being replaced. If this is not possible, it is required by law to apply a label in the drivers door stating the previous odometer reading and the date of replacement. The replacement reading must be set to zero.**

Century

1. Disconnect the negative battery cable and disable the SIR system.
2. Remove the left side trim plate.
3. Remove the instrument cluster housing screws. Remove the instrument cluster. If the vehicle is equipped with tilt-wheel steering, working room can be gained by removing the tilt-wheel cover.
4. Remove the speedometer lens screws and remove the speedometer lens.
5. Disconnect the speedometer cable by pushing in on the retaining clip and pulling back on the cable.
6. Remove the screws securing the speedometer to the instrument panel, then remove the speedometer assembly.

To install:

7. Install the speedometer assembly and the screws securing the speedometer assembly to the instrument panel.
8. Connect the speedometer cable.
9. Install the speedometer lens and retaining screws.
10. Install the instrument cluster housing and retaining screws. If equipped with tilt-wheel steering and the tilt-wheel cover was removed, replace the cover.
11. Install the left side trim plate.
12. Connect the negative battery cable. Tighten the cable bolt to 11 ft. lbs. (15 Nm).
13. Enable the SIR system.
14. Reset the radio, clock and any other applicable electronic devices.

Celebrity

1. Disconnect the negative battery cable.
2. Remove the cluster trim panel.
3. Remove the cluster lens screws. Remove the cluster lens.
4. Remove the speedometer-to-cluster attaching screws. Remove the speedometer from the instrument cluster.
5. Disconnect the speedometer cable and remove the speedometer assembly.

To install:

6. Position the speedometer assembly and connect the speedometer cable.
7. Install the speedometer-to-instrument cluster and install the attaching screws.
8. Install the cluster lens and attaching screws.
9. Install the cluster trim panel.
10. Connect the negative battery cable. Tighten the cable bolt to 11 ft. lbs. (15 Nm).
11. Reset the radio, clock and any other applicable electronic devices.

Ciera and Cruiser

1. Disconnect the negative battery cable and disable the SIR system.
2. Remove the instrument cluster assembly.
3. Remove the vehicle speed sensor screw from the rear of the speedometer. Remove the vehicle speed sensor, if equipped.
4. Remove the speedometer lens screws and remove the speedometer lens. Remove the bezel.
5. Remove the screw that holds the speedometer to the instrument cluster.
6. Remove the speedometer head by pulling forward. Disconnect the speedometer cable by prying gently on the retainer and pulling the speedometer cable from the speedometer head.

To install:

7. Position the speedometer head and connect the speedometer cable.
8. Install the screw that holds the speedometer to the instrument cluster.
9. Install the speedometer lens and attaching screws. Install the bezel.
10. Install the vehicle speed sensor and the attaching screw at the rear of the speedometer.
11. Install the instrument cluster assembly.
12. Connect the negative battery cable. Tighten the cable bolt to 11 ft. lbs. (15 Nm).
13. Enable the SIR system.
14. Reset the radio, clock and any other applicable electronic devices.

6000

1. Disconnect the negative battery cable.
2. Remove the center and left lower trim plates.
3. Remove the screws securing the instrument cluster assembly to the dash assembly. Remove the instrument cluster.
4. Remove the instrument cluster lens screws. Remove the instrument cluster lens.
5. Remove the screws securing the speedometer to the instrument cluster. Remove the speedometer.
6. Disconnect the speedometer cable from the rear of the speedometer.

To install:

7. Connect the speedometer cable at the rear of the speedometer.
8. Install speedometer and the screws securing the speedometer to the instrument cluster.
9. Install the instrument cluster lens and attaching screws.
10. Install the instrument cluster and the screws securing the instrument cluster assembly to the dash assembly.
11. Install the center and left lower trim plates.
12. Connect the negative battery cable. Tighten the cable bolt to 11 ft. lbs. (15 Nm).
13. Reset the radio, clock and any other applicable electronic devices.

Tachometer

REMOVAL & INSTALLATION

▶ **See Figure 36**

1. Remove the shift indicator.
2. Unfasten the retainers securing the tachometer to the cluster, then remove the tachometer by pulling it out.

To install:

3. Insert the tachometer into the cluster. Using the screws attach the tachometer to the cluster assembly.
4. Install the shift indicator.

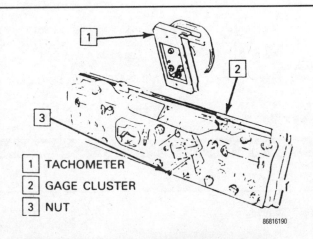

1	TACHOMETER
2	GAGE CLUSTER
3	NUT

86816190

Fig. 36 The tachometer is secured to the back of the cluster

Speedometer Cable

REMOVAL & INSTALLATION

▶ See Figure 37

➡**Removing the instrument cluster will give better access to the speedometer cable.**

1. Remove the instrument cluster.
2. Slide the cable out from the casing. If the cable is broken, the casing will have to be unscrewed from the transaxle and the broken piece removed from that end.
3. Before installing a new cable, slip a piece of cable into the speedometer and spin it between your fingers in the direction of normal rotation. If the mechanism sticks or binds, the speedometer should be repaired or replaced.

To install:

4. Inspect the casing. If it is cracked, kinked, or broken, the casing should be replaced.
5. Slide a new cable into the casing, engaging the transaxle end securely. Sometimes it is easier to unscrew the casing at the transaxle end, install the cable into the transaxle fitting, then screw the casing back into place. Install the instrument cluster.

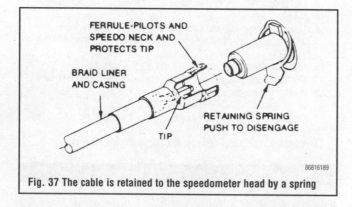

FERRULE-PILOTS AND SPEEDO NECK AND PROTECTS TIP

BRAID LINER AND CASING

RETAINING SPRING PUSH TO DISENGAGE

TIP

86816189

Fig. 37 The cable is retained to the speedometer head by a spring

Gauges

REMOVAL & INSTALLATION

1. Disconnect the negative battery cable.
2. Remove the instrument panel cluster trim pad.
3. Unfasten the cluster lens, then put aside on a clean cloth so not to scratch the lens.
4. The gauge can be taken off the cluster by removing the attaching screws.

To install:

5. Attach the new gauge on the cluster with the screws removed previously.
6. Attach the cluster lens with the mounting screws, then install the cluster trim pad.
7. Connect the negative battery cable. Tighten the cable bolt to 11 ft. lbs. (15 Nm).
8. Reset the radio, clock or any components which lost power while the battery cable was disconnected.

Windshield Wiper Switch

REMOVAL & INSTALLATION

1982–86 Models

1. Disconnect the negative battery cable.
2. Remove the steering wheel, the cover and the lock plate assembly.

3. Remove the turn signal actuator arm, the lever and the hazard flasher button.
4. Remove the turn signal switch screws, the lower steering column trim panel and the steering column bracket bolts.
5. Unplug the turn signal switch and the wiper switch connectors.
6. Pull the turn signal rearward 6–8 in. (15–20mm), then remove the key buzzer switch and the cylinder lock.
7. Remove and pull the steering column housing rearward, then remove the housing cover screw.
8. Remove the wiper switch pivot and the switch.
9. To install, reverse the removal procedures.

1987–96 Models

✳✳ CAUTION

Some vehicles are equipped with the Supplemental Inflatable Restraint (SIR) system. This system must be disabled before performing service on or around the air bag, instrument panel components, wiring and sensors. Failure to follow safety and disabling procedures could result in accidental air bag deployment, possible personal injury and unnecessary air bag system repairs.

1. Disconnect the negative battery cable and disable the SIR system.
2. Remove the steering wheel and turn signal switch. It may be necessary to first remove the column mounting nuts and remove the bracket-to-mast jacket screws, then separate the bracket from the mast jacket to allow the connector clip on the ignition switch to be pulled from the column assembly.
3. Tag and unplug the washer/wiper switch lower connector.
4. Remove the screws attaching the column housing to the mast jacket. Be sure to note the position of the dimmer switch actuator rod for reassembly in the same position. Remove the column housing and switch as an assembly.

➡**Certain tilt columns are equipped with a removable plastic cover on the column housing. This provides access to the wiper switch without removing the entire column housing.**

5. Turn the assembly over and use a drift to remove the pivot pin from the washer/wiper switch. Remove the switch.

To install:

6. Place the switch into position in the housing. Install the pivot pin.
7. Position the housing onto the mast jacket and attach by installing the screws. Install the dimmer switch actuator rod in the same position as noted when removed. Check switch operation.
8. Reconnect lower end of the switch assembly.
9. Install the ignition switch connector clip to the column assembly.
10. Install the mast jacket to the bracket.
11. If removed, install the column mounting nuts and the retaining bolts.
12. Install the turn signal switch and steering wheel.
13. Connect the negative battery cable. Tighten the cable bolt to 11 ft. lbs. (15 Nm).
14. Enable the SIR system.
15. Reset the radio, clock and any other applicable electronic devices.

Headlight Switch

REMOVAL & INSTALLATION

Century

1. Disconnect the negative battery cable.
2. Remove the instrument panel trim plate.
3. Remove the left side instrument panel switch trim panel by removing the attaching screws. Gently rock the panel out.
4. Remove the switch screws, then pull the switch straight out.

To install:

5. Install the switch and the attaching screws.
6. Install the left side instrument panel switch trim panel and it's attaching screws.

7. Install the instrument panel trim plate.

8. Connect the negative battery cable. Tighten the cable bolt to 11 ft. lbs. (15 Nm).

9. Reset the radio, clock and any other applicable electronic devices.

Celebrity

1. Disconnect the negative battery cable.
2. Remove the headlight switch knob.
3. Remove the instrument panel trim pad.
4. Unbolt the switch mounting plate from the instrument panel carrier.
5. Disconnect the wiring from the switch.
6. Remove the switch.

To install:

7. Install the switch.
8. Connect the wiring to the switch.
9. Install the bolts attaching the switch mounting plate to the instrument panel carrier.
10. Install the instrument panel trim pad.
11. Install the headlight switch knob.
12. Connect the negative battery cable. Tighten the cable bolt to 11 ft. lbs. (15 Nm).
13. Reset the radio, clock and any other applicable electronic devices.

Ciera and Cruiser

1. Disconnect the negative battery cable.
2. Remove the left side instrument panel trim pad.
3. Unbolt the switch from the instrument panel.
4. Pull the switch rearward and remove it.

To install:

5. Install the switch and engage the electrical connectors.
6. Install the bolts attaching the switch to the instrument panel.
7. Install the left side instrument panel trim pad.
8. Connect the negative battery cable. Tighten the cable bolt to 11 ft. lbs. (15 Nm).
9. Reset the radio, clock and any other applicable electronic devices.

6000

1. Disconnect the negative battery cable.
2. Remove the steering column trim cover and headlight rod and knob by reaching behind the instrument panel and depressing the lock tab.
3. Remove the left instrument panel trim plate.
4. Unbolt and remove the switch and bracket assembly from the instrument panel.
5. Loosen the bezel and remove the switch from the bracket.

To install:

6. Install the switch to the bracket and install the bezel.
7. Install the switch and bracket assembly to the instrument panel and install the attaching bolts.
8. Install the left instrument panel trim plate.
9. Install the headlight rod and knob. Install the steering column trim cover.
10. Connect the negative battery cable. Tighten the cable bolt to 11 ft. lbs. (15 Nm).
11. Reset the radio, clock and any other applicable electronic devices.

Dimmer Switch

REMOVAL & INSTALLATION

✳✳ CAUTION

Some vehicles are equipped with the Supplemental Inflatable Restraint (SIR) system. This system must be disabled before performing service on or around the air bag, instrument panel components, wiring and sensors. Failure to follow safety and disabling procedures could result in accidental air bag deployment, possible personal injury and unnecessary air bag system repairs.

1. Disable the SIR system if equipped.
2. Disconnect the negative battery cable.
3. Remove the steering wheel. Remove the trim cover.
4. Remove the turn signal switch assembly.
5. Remove the ignition switch stud and screw. Remove the ignition switch.
6. Remove the dimmer switch actuator rod by sliding it from the switch assembly.
7. Remove the dimmer switch bolts and remove the dimmer switch.

To install:

8. Install the dimmer switch and attaching bolts.
9. Install the dimmer switch actuator rod by sliding it into the switch assembly.
10. Adjust the dimmer switch by depressing the switch slightly and inserting a ^{3}⁄$_{32}$ in. (2mm) drill bit into the adjusting hole. Push the switch up to remove any play and tighten the dimmer switch adjusting screw.
11. Install the ignition switch, stud and screw.
12. Install the turn signal switch assembly.
13. Install the trim cover. Install the steering wheel.
14. Connect the battery negative cable.
15. Enable the SIR system.
16. Reset the radio, clock and any other accessories.

Combination Switch

REMOVAL & INSTALLATION

▶ See Figures 38, 39 and 40

✳✳ CAUTION

Some vehicles are equipped with the Supplemental Inflatable Restraint (SIR) system. This system must be disabled before performing service on or around the air bag, instrument panel components, wiring and sensors. Failure to follow safety and disabling procedures could result in accidental air bag deployment, possible personal injury and unnecessary air bag system repairs.

1. Disable the SIR system, if equipped.
2. Disconnect the negative battery cable.
3. Remove the steering wheel. Remove the trim cover.
4. Loosen the cover screws. Pry the cover off with a flat bladed tool, then lift the cover off the shaft.
5. Position the U-shaped lockplate compressing tool on the end of the steering shaft and compress the lock plate by turning the shaft nut clockwise. Pry the wire snapring out of the shaft groove.
6. Remove the tool and lift the lock plate off the shaft.
7. Slip the canceling cam, upper bearing preload spring, and thrust washer off the shaft.

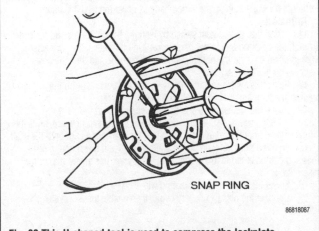

SNAP RING

86818087

Fig. 38 This U-shaped tool is used to compress the lockplate

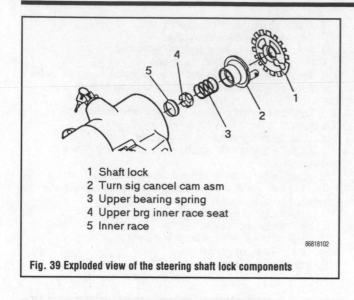

1 Shaft lock
2 Turn sig cancel cam asm
3 Upper bearing spring
4 Upper brg inner race seat
5 Inner race

86818102

Fig. 39 Exploded view of the steering shaft lock components

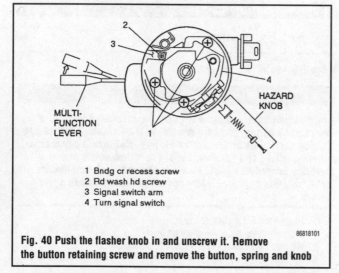

MULTI-
FUNCTION
LEVER

HAZARD
KNOB

1 Bndg cr recess screw
2 Rd wash hd screw
3 Signal switch arm
4 Turn signal switch

86818101

Fig. 40 Push the flasher knob in and unscrew it. Remove the button retaining screw and remove the button, spring and knob

8. Remove the turn signal lever. Push the flasher knob in and unscrew it. Remove the button retaining screw and remove the button, spring and knob.

9. Pull the switch connector out the mast jacket and tape the upper part to facilitate switch removal. Attach a long piece of wire to the turn signal switch connector. When installing the turn signal switch, feed this wire through the column first, then use this wire to pull the switch connector into position. On tilt wheels, place the turn signal and shifter housing in low position and remove the harness cover.

10. Remove the three switch mounting screws. Remove the switch by pulling it straight up while guiding the wiring harness cover through the column.

To install:

11. Install the replacement switch by working the connector and cover down through the housing and under the bracket. On tilt models, the connector is worked down through the housing, under the bracket, and then the cover is installed on the harness.

12. Install the switch mounting screws and the connector on the mast jacket bracket. Install the column-to-dash trim plate.

13. Install the flasher knob and the turn signal lever.

14. With the turn signal lever in neutral and the flasher now out, slide the thrust washer, upper bearing preload spring, and canceling cam onto the shaft.

15. Position the lock plate on the shaft and press it down until a new snapring can be inserted in the shaft groove. Always use a new snapring when assembling.

16. Install the cover and the steering wheel.

17. Connect the negative battery cable, then enable the SIR system, if equipped.

Clock

REMOVAL & INSTALLATION

1. Remove the instrument panel cluster bezel.
2. Unfasten the clock retaining screws and remove the clock.

Back-up Light Switch

REMOVAL & INSTALLATION

1. Working from underneath the dashboard, locate the back-up light switch on the steering column and remove the wiring harness.
2. Pull downward and remove the switch from the steering column.

To install:

3. Apply the parking brake and place the gear select lever in **N**.
4. Align the actuator on the switch with the hole in the shift tube.
5. Position the rearward portion of the switch (connector side) to fit into the cutout in the lower jacket.
6. Push up on the front of the switch, the two tangs on the housing back will snap into place in the rectangular holes in the jacket.
7. Adjust the switch by moving the gear selector to **P**. The main housing and the back should ratchet, providing proper switch adjustment.

Rear Defogger System

All systems operate on 12 volts. An instrument panel mounted switch with an integral indicator lamp is used to turn the system on.

Certain conditions such as outside temperature, vehicle speed, atmospheric pressure and even the number of passengers inside the vehicle affects the length of time required to remove fog from the glass.

The defogger is designed to turn off after approximately 10 minutes of operation. If the defogger is turn on again, it will only operate for approximately 5 minutes. You can however, turn the system off before the time is up by turning the defogger switch or ignition switch **OFF**.

REMOVAL & INSTALLATION

1. Disconnect the negative battery cable.
2. Remove the left side instrument panel or accessory trim plate, as required.
3. On some vehicles, it may be necessary to remove the steering column collar, steering column opening filler and cluster trim plate.
4. Remove the ash tray and sound insulator, as required.
5. On some vehicles, it may be necessary to remove the radio control knobs, air conditioning/heater control and/or cables.
6. Remove the rear defogger control retaining screws or clip and remove the switch.
7. Unplug the switch electrical connector.

To install:

8. Engage the electrical connector to the switch.
9. Fit the switch to the instrument panel and install the retaining screws.
10. Install the instrument panel or trim plate.
11. Reconnect the negative battery cable.
12. Reset the radio, clock and any other applicable accessories.

TESTING

▶ **See Figure 41**

1. Start the engine and pull out the defogger switch knob.
2. Using a test light, ground the end and touch the probe to each grid line. The test light should operate as indicated in the illustration.
3. If the test light remains bright at both ends of the grid lines, check for a loose ground.

➡The range zones may vary slightly from 1 glass to another. But, the test light brilliance will decrease proportionately as it is moved from left to right on the grid line.

4. If an abnormal reading is observed by the test light on any grid line, place the test light probe on the left of that bus bar and move the probe toward the right until the test lamp goes out. This will indicate a break in the continuity on that grid line.

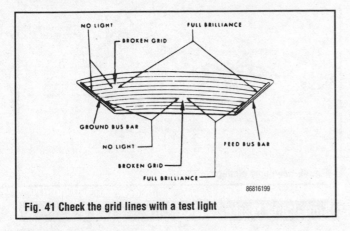

Fig. 41 Check the grid lines with a test light

REPAIR

♦ See Figure 42

1. Locate the break(s) on the grid line(s) and mark the outside of the glass, using a grease pencil.

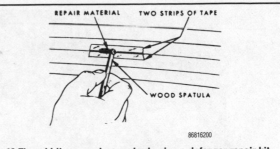

Fig. 42 The grid lines can be repaired using a defogger repair kit (GM part 1052858 or equivalent)

2. Disconnect the negative battery cable.
3. Clean the area to be repaired. Buff with fine steel wool and wipe clean with a damped cloth with alcohol.
4. Position a strip of tape above and below the grid line area to be repair.
5. Repair the grid line break using a defogger repair kit (GM part 1052858 or equivalent) and follow the manufacturer's instructions.
6. After the grid line has been repaired, carefully remove the strips of tape.
7. Apply heat, (using a heat gun or blow dryer) to the repaired area for approximately 1–2 minutes. A minimum temperature of 300°F (149°C) is required.

➡ **To avoid damage to the interior trim, protect the trim near the area to be repair. Allow the repair materials to cure for at least 24 hours. Do not operate the unit until such time has passed.**

8. Test the rear defogger operation to verify proper operation.

LIGHTING

❋ CAUTION

Take care not to squeeze the bulbs too tightly, they can break in you hand and causes injury. If the bulbs are stuck, spray them with penetrating oil and allow them to soak for a few minutes. There are also tools on the market for gripping and removing bulbs.

Headlights

REMOVAL & INSTALLATION

Non-European Style

♦ See Figures 43, 44, 45, 46 and 47

1. Remove the headlamp trim panel attaching screws.
2. Remove the headlamp bulb retaining screws. Do not touch the two headlamp aiming screws, (at the top and side of the retaining ring), or the headlamp aim will have to be readjusted.
3. Using a screwdriver, remove the retaining ring screws.

4. Pull the bulb and ring forward then separate them. Unplug the electrical connector from the rear of the bulb.
To install:
5. Plug the new bulb into the electrical connector.
6. Install the bulb into the retaining ring and install the ring and bulb.
7. Install the trim panel.

European Style

1. Open the hood.
2. Turn the bulb assembly counterclockwise ⅛ turn, pressing in firmly, until the flanges align with the slots in the retainer ring.
3. Pull out the bulb assembly. You may have to rock it up and down slightly to loosen it.
4. Disconnect the bulb base from the harness by lifting the plastic locking tab.
To install:
5. Snap a new bulb into the wiring harness. Make sure the locking tab is over the lock.
6. Install the bulb assembly by putting the small tab in the small notch in the retainer ring.
7. Turn the bulb assembly ⅛ turn clockwise to lock it in place.

Fig. 43 Remove the headlamp trim panel attaching screws

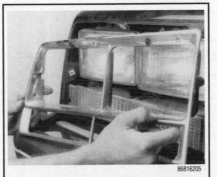

Fig. 44 Remove the headlamp trim panel assembly from its mounting location

Fig. 45 Using a screwdriver, remove the retaining ring screws

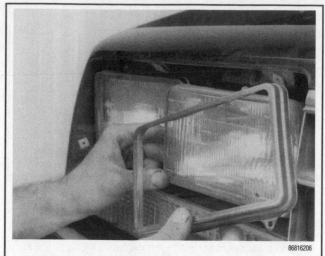

Fig. 46 Once the retaining ring screws are removed, the ring can be pulled away

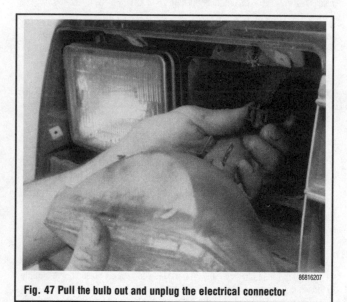

Fig. 47 Pull the bulb out and unplug the electrical connector

AIMING

♦ See Figure 48

The head lamps should be aimed using a special alignment tool, however this procedure may be used for temporary adjustment. Local regulations may vary regarding head lamp aiming, consult with your local authorities.

1. Verify the tires are at their proper inflation pressure. Clean the head lamp lenses and make sure there are no heavy loads in the trunk. The gas tank should be filled.
2. Position the vehicle on a level surface facing a flat wall 25 ft. (7.7 m) away.
3. Measure and record the distance from the floor to the center of the head lamp. Place a strip of tape across the wall at this same height.
4. Place strips of tape on the wall, perpendicular to the first measurement, indicating the vehicle centerline and the centerline of both head lamps.
5. Rock the vehicle side-to-side a few times to allow the suspension to stabilize.
6. Turn the lights on, adjust the head lamps to achieve a high intensity pattern.

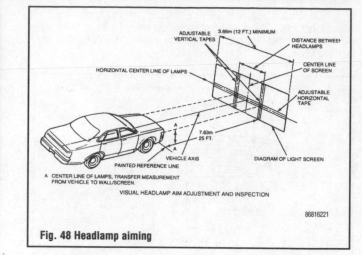

Fig. 48 Headlamp aiming

Signal and Marker Lights

REMOVAL & INSTALLATION

Front Turn Signal and Parking Lights

♦ See Figures 49, 50, 51, 52 and 53

1. On some models you will need to remove the headlight bezel mounting screws and the bezel.
2. Remove the mounting screws for the lamp assembly.
3. After the screws are removed, pull the assembly from the vehicle.
4. Disconnect the twist lock socket from the lens housing.

➡ **To remove the bulb, turn the twist lock socket (at the rear of the housing) counterclockwise ¼ turn, then remove the socket with the bulb; replace the bulb if defective.**

To install:
5. Install the electrical harness to the back of the unit.
6. Position the signal assembly, then attach to the vehicle with the mounting screws. Tighten the screws to 54 inch lbs. (6 Nm).
7. Insert the socket to the back of the unit, then attach the headlamp bezel if removed.

Side Marker Lights

♦ See Figure 54

1. Remove the marker light housing screws and the housing.
2. Disconnect the twist lock socket from the lens housing.

➡ **To remove the bulb, turn the twist lock socket (at the rear of the housing) counterclockwise ¼ turn, then remove the socket with the bulb; replace the bulb if defective.**

To install:
3. Connect the socket to the back of the lamp assembly.
4. Position the lamp housing to the vehicle, then attach with the mounting screws.

Rear Turn Signal, Brake and Parking Lights

♦ See Figures 55, 56 and 57

1. Remove the tail light assembly screws, then the assembly.
2. Disconnect the twist lock socket from the lens housing.

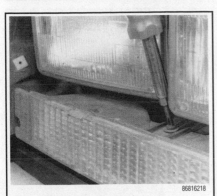

Fig. 49 Remove the mounting screws securing the lamp assembly

Fig. 50 After the screws are removed, pull the assembly from the vehicle

Fig. 51 Disconnect the twist lock socket from the lens housing

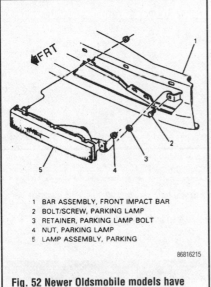

1 BAR ASSEMBLY, FRONT IMPACT BAR
2 BOLT/SCREW, PARKING LAMP
3 RETAINER, PARKING LAMP BOLT
4 NUT, PARKING LAMP
5 LAMP ASSEMBLY, PARKING

Fig. 52 Newer Oldsmobile models have the turn signal separate from the head-lamp assembly . . .

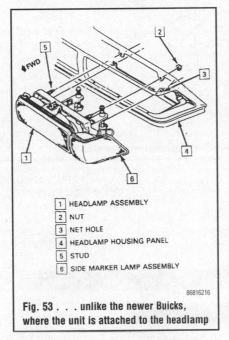

1 HEADLAMP ASSEMBLY
2 NUT
3 NET HOLE
4 HEADLAMP HOUSING PANEL
5 STUD
6 SIDE MARKER LAMP ASSEMBLY

Fig. 53 . . . unlike the newer Buicks, where the unit is attached to the headlamp

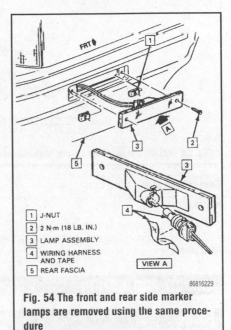

1 J-NUT
2 2 N·m (18 LB. IN.)
3 LAMP ASSEMBLY
4 WIRING HARNESS AND TAPE
5 REAR FASCIA

VIEW A

Fig. 54 The front and rear side marker lamps are removed using the same procedure

Fig. 55 Remove the tail light assembly screws, then the assembly—wagon shown

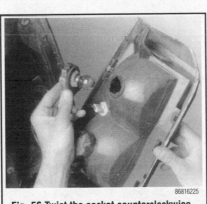

Fig. 56 Twist the socket counterclockwise to remove from the housing

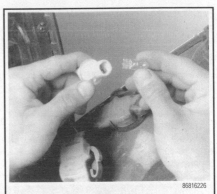

Fig. 57 This type of bulb simply can be pulled out of the socket for replacement

➡To remove the bulb, turn the twist lock socket (at the rear of the housing) counterclockwise ¼ turn, then remove the socket with the bulb; replace the bulb if defective.

To install:
3. Attach the socket assemblies to the back of the lamp unit.
4. Install the lamp assembly to the vehicle with the mounting screws.

License Plate Light

1. Remove the lens screws.
2. Once the lens is removed you, can access the bulb and replace if needed.

To install:
3. Install the new bulb, then attach the lens to the body of the vehicle.

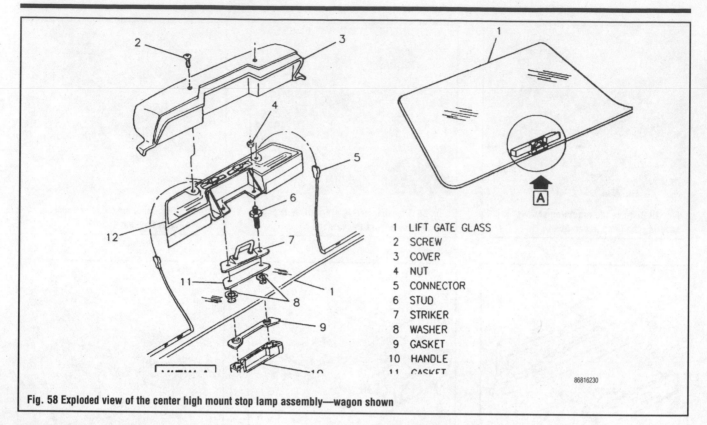

1	LIFT GATE GLASS
2	SCREW
3	COVER
4	NUT
5	CONNECTOR
6	STUD
7	STRIKER
8	WASHER
9	GASKET
10	HANDLE
11	GASKET

86816230

Fig. 58 Exploded view of the center high mount stop lamp assembly—wagon shown

Center High Mount Stop Lamp

▶ **See Figure 58**

1. Remove the screws securing the lamp cover.
2. Remove the mounting nuts, then unplug the electrical harness to the lamp assembly.

3. The lamp now should come out.

To install:

4. Position the lamp assembly to the vehicle, then attach the electrical harness to the lamp.
5. Install the mounting nut, tighten to 62 inch lbs. (7 Nm).
6. Attach the lamp cover.

CIRCUIT PROTECTION

Fuses

▶ **See Figure 59**

REPLACEMENT

Fuses protect all the major electrical systems in the car. In case of an electrical overload, the fuse melts, breaking the circuit and stopping the flow of electricity.

If a fuse blows, the cause should be investigated and corrected before the installation of a new fuse. This, however, is easier to say than to do. Because each fuse protects a limited number of components, your job is narrowed down somewhat.

The amperage of each fuse and the circuit it protects are marked on the fuse box, which is located under the left side (driver's side) of the instrument panel and pulls down for easy access. To replace a fuse, simply pull it from the panel. Insert a new (same amp rating) fuse in its place.

Circuit Breakers

The headlights are protected by a circuit breaker in the headlamp switch. If the circuit breaker trips, the headlights will either flash on and off, or stay off altogether. The circuit breaker rests automatically after the overload is removed.

The windshield wipers are also protected by a circuit breaker. If the motor overheats, the circuit breaker will trip, remaining off until the motor cools or the overload is removed. One common cause of overheating is operation of the wipers in heavy snow.

The circuit breakers for the power door locks and power windows are located in the fuse box.

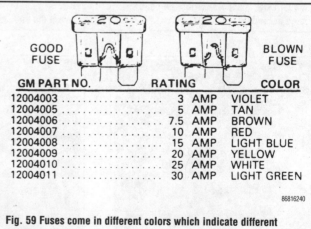

GM PART NO.	RATING	COLOR
12004003	3 AMP	VIOLET
12004005	5 AMP	TAN
12004006	7.5 AMP	BROWN
12004007	10 AMP	RED
12004008	15 AMP	LIGHT BLUE
12004009	20 AMP	YELLOW
12004010	25 AMP	WHITE
12004011	30 AMP	LIGHT GREEN

86816240

Fig. 59 Fuses come in different colors which indicate different amperage ratings

Flashers

REPLACEMENT

The hazard flasher is located in the convenience center, under the dash, on the left side kick panel. The turn signal flasher is installed in a clamp attached to the base of the steering column support inside the car. In all cases, replacement is made by unplugging the old unit and plugging in a new one.

WIRING DIAGRAMS

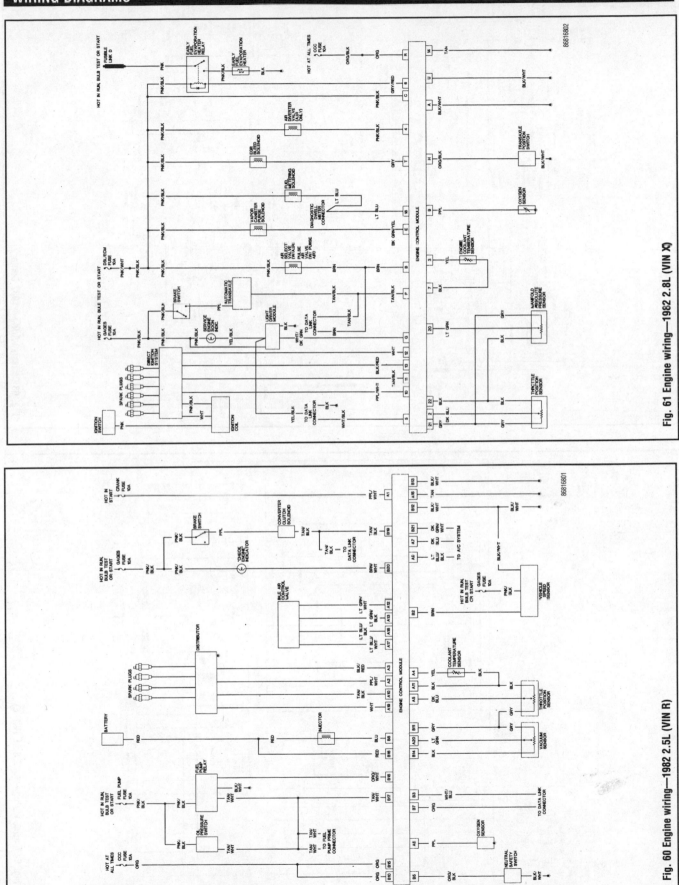

Fig. 61 Engine wiring—1982 2.8L (VIN X)

Fig. 60 Engine wiring—1982 2.5L (VIN R)

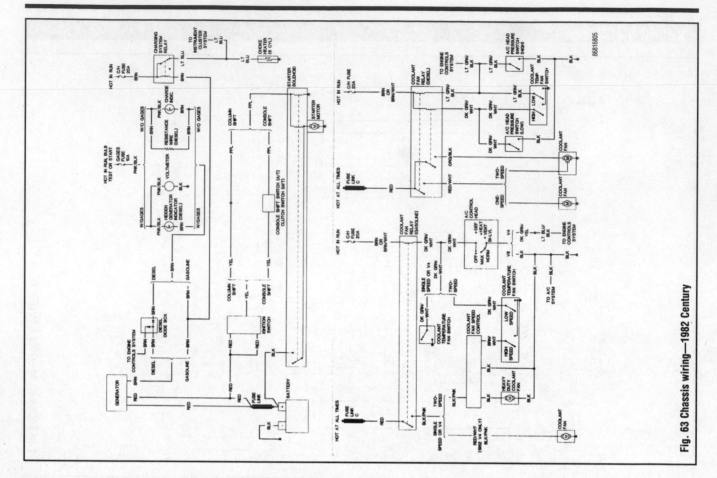

Fig. 63 Chassis wiring—1982 Century

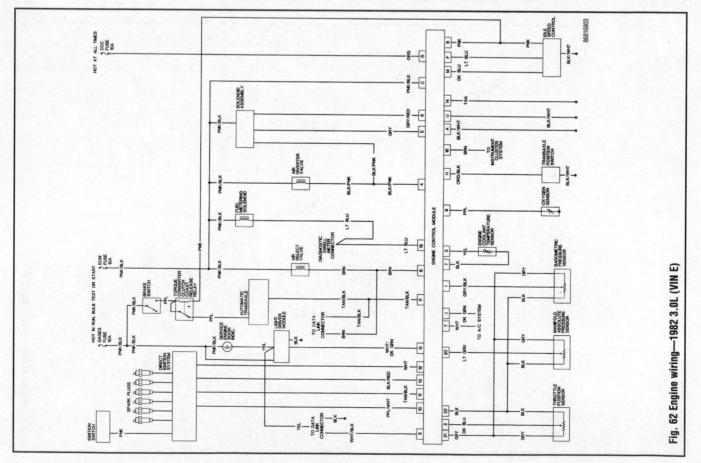

Fig. 62 Engine wiring—1982 3.0L (VIN E)

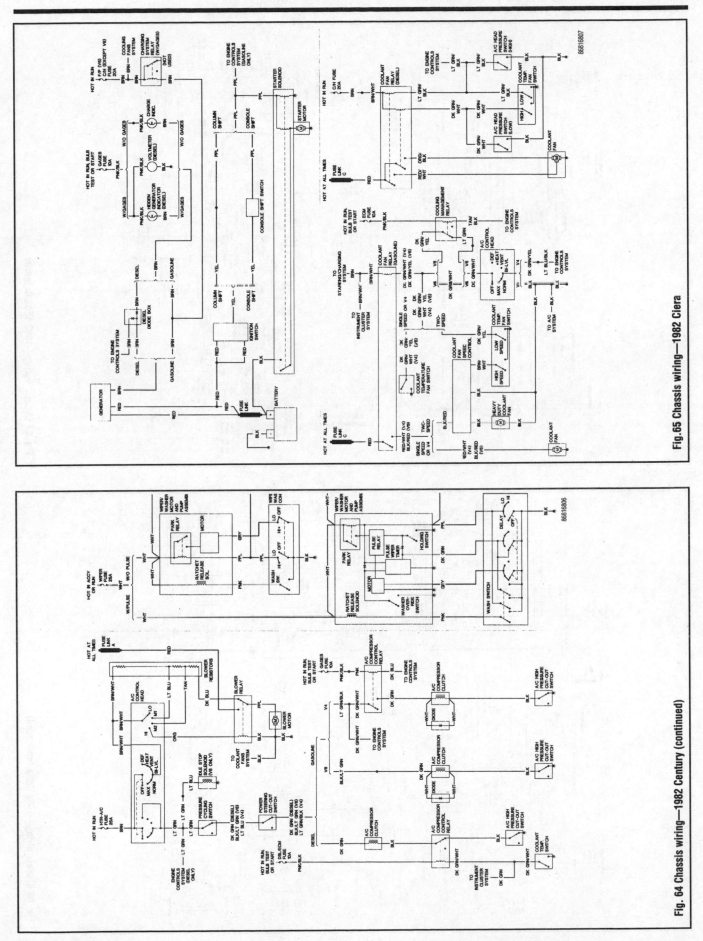

Fig.65 Chassis wiring—1982 Ciera

Fig. 64 Chassis wiring—1982 Century (continued)

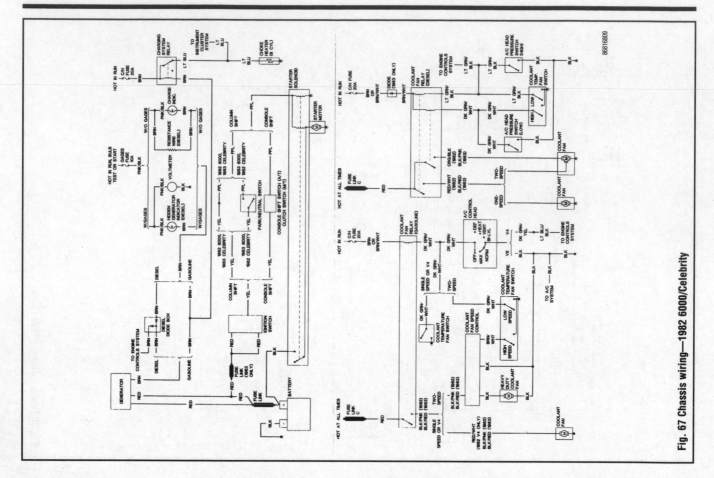

Fig. 67 Chassis wiring—1982 6000/Celebrity

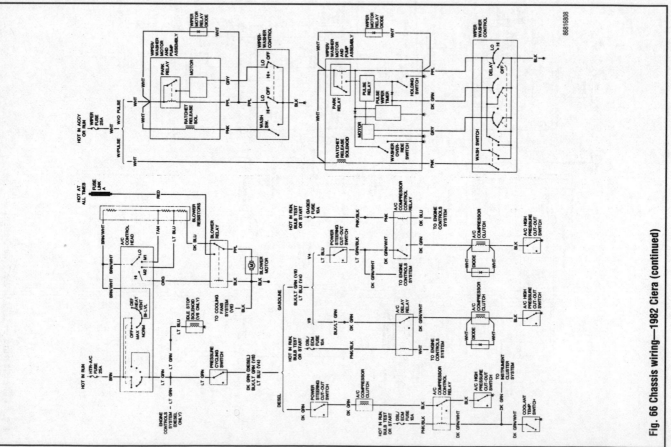

Fig. 66 Chassis wiring—1982 Ciera (continued)

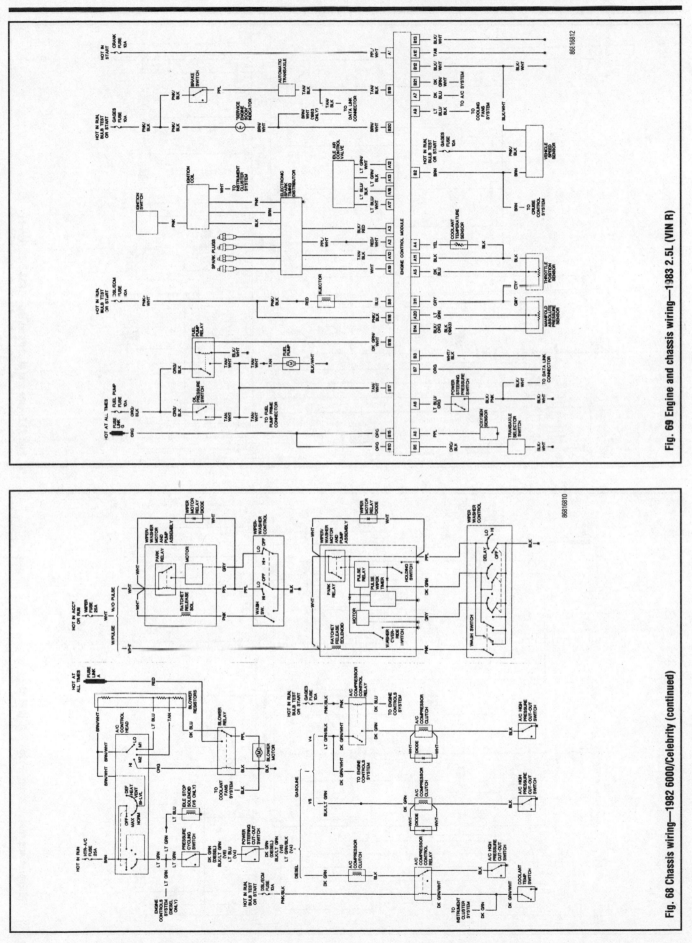

Fig. 69 Engine and chassis wiring—1983 2.5L (VIN R)

Fig. 68 Chassis wiring—1982 6000/Celebrity (continued)

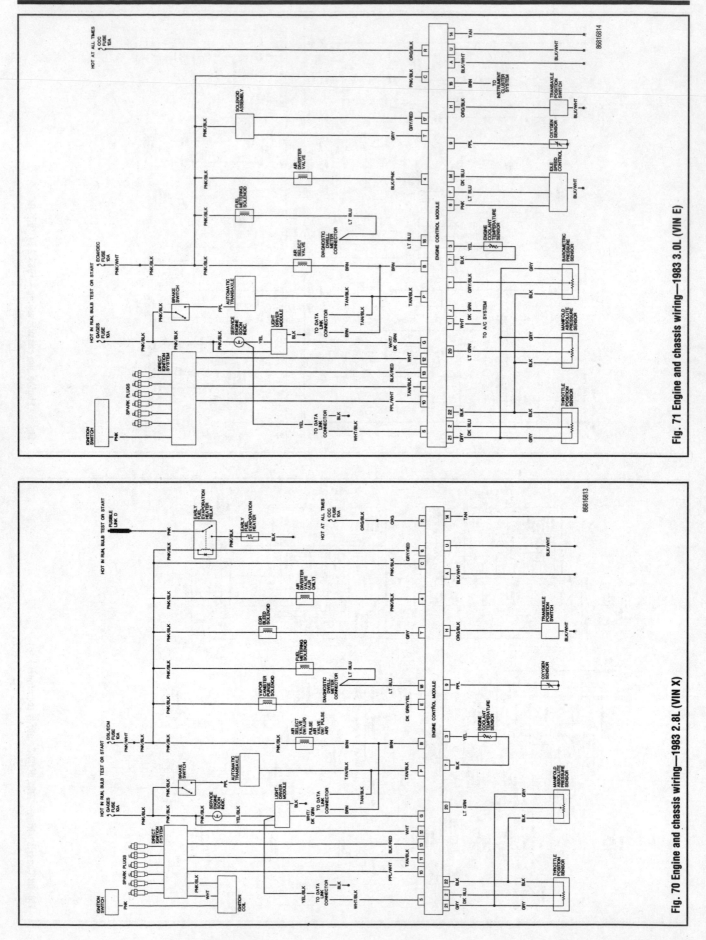

Fig. 71 Engine and chassis wiring—1983 3.0L (VIN E)

Fig. 70 Engine and chassis wiring—1983 2.8L (VIN X)

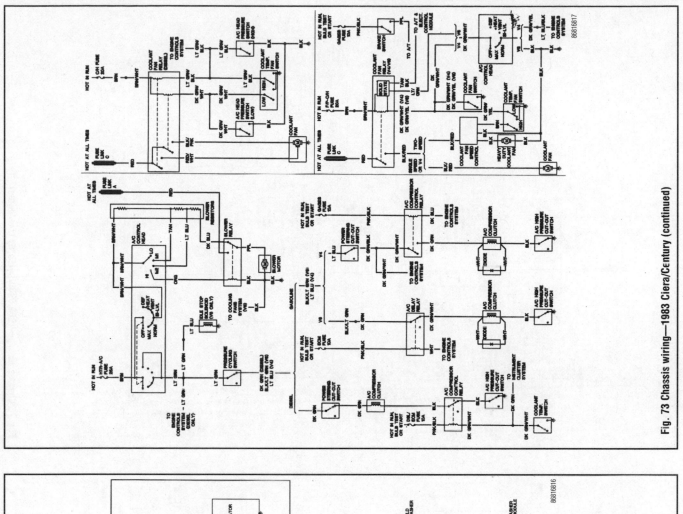

Fig. 73 Chassis wiring—1983 Ciera/Century (continued)

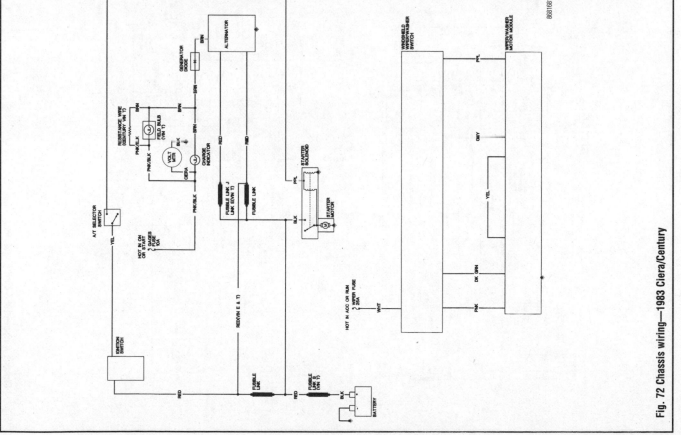

Fig. 72 Chassis wiring—1983 Ciera/Century

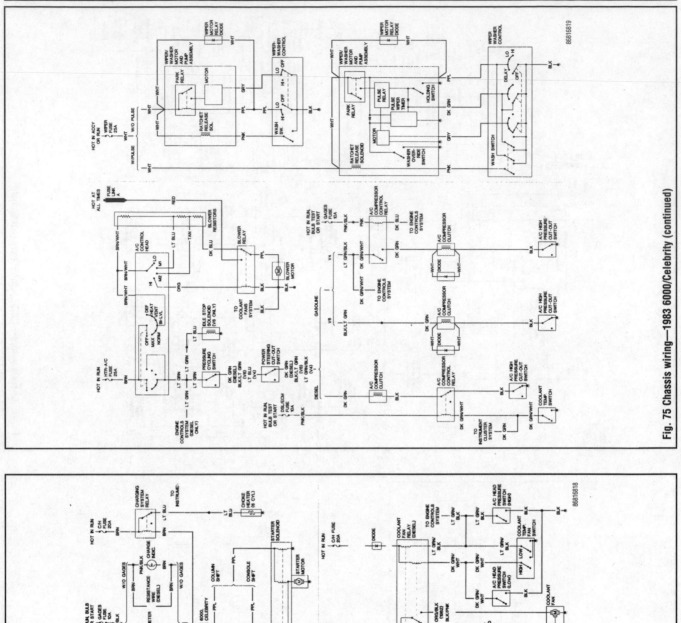

Fig. 75 Chassis wiring—1983 6000/Celebrity (continued)

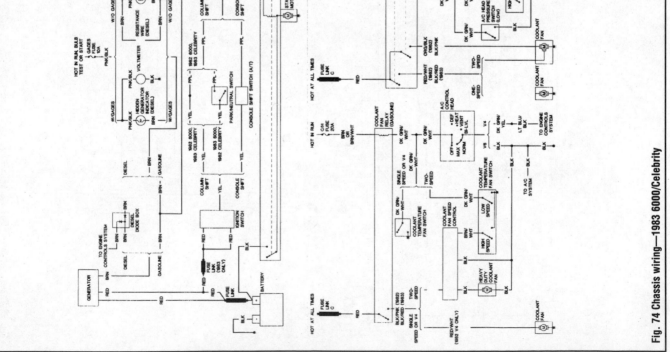

Fig. 74 Chassis wiring—1983 6000/Celebrity

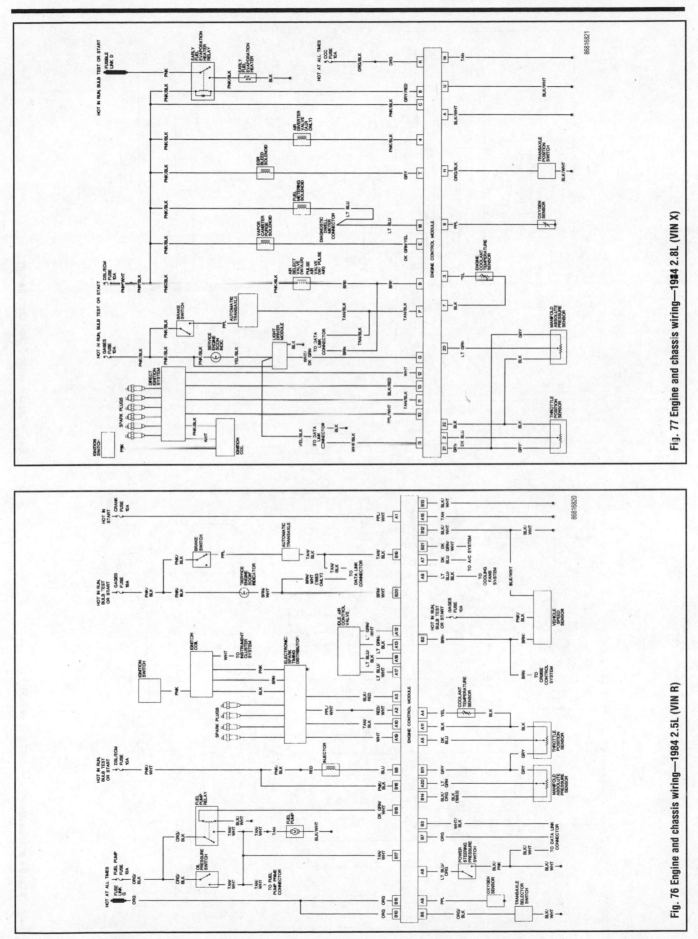

Fig. 77 Engine and chassis wiring—1984 2.8L (VIN X)

Fig. 76 Engine and chassis wiring—1984 2.5L (VIN R)

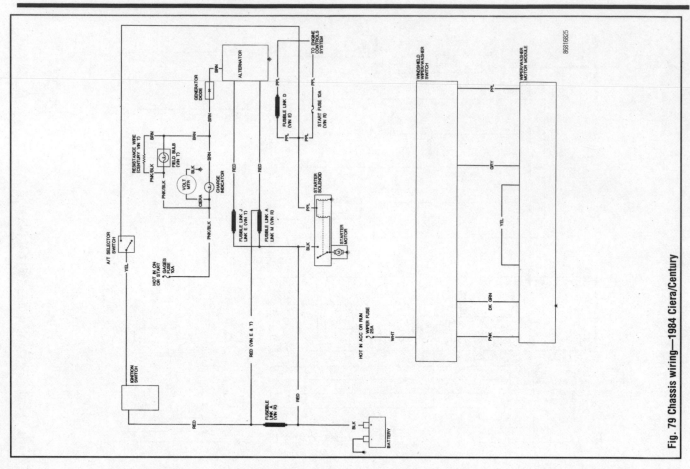

Fig. 79 Chassis wiring—1984 Ciera/Century

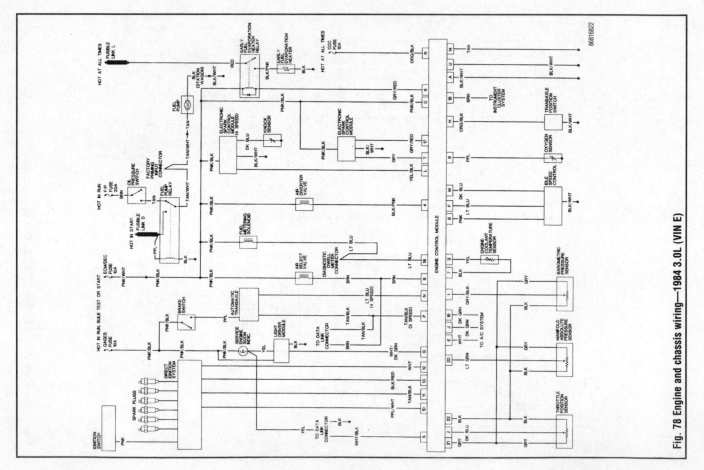

Fig. 78 Engine and chassis wiring—1984 3.0L (VIN E)

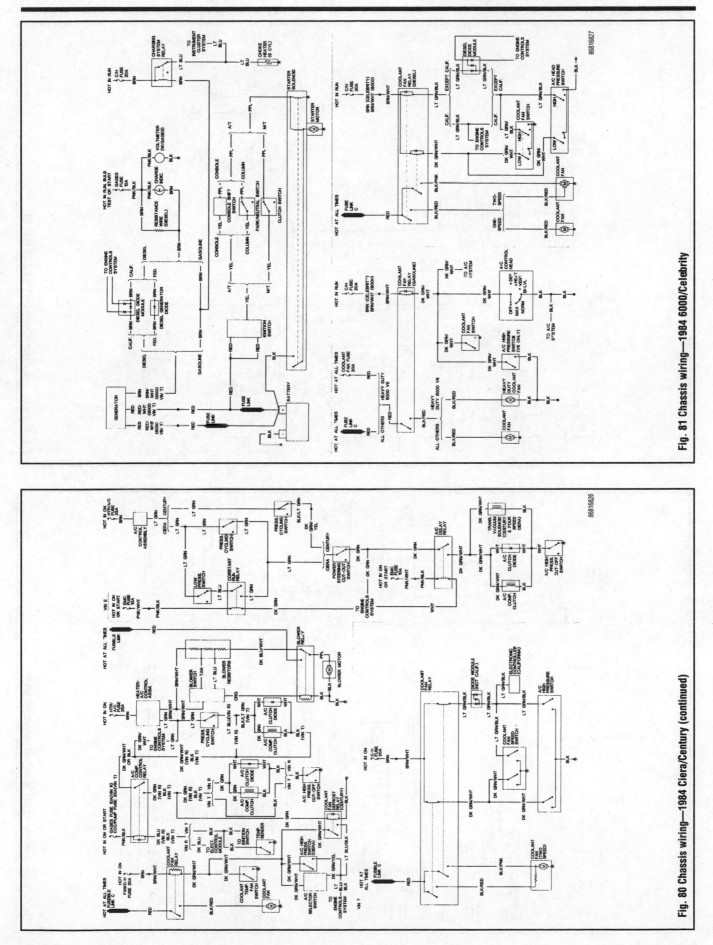

Fig. 81 Chassis wiring—1984 6000/Celebrity

Fig. 80 Chassis wiring—1984 Ciera/Century (continued)

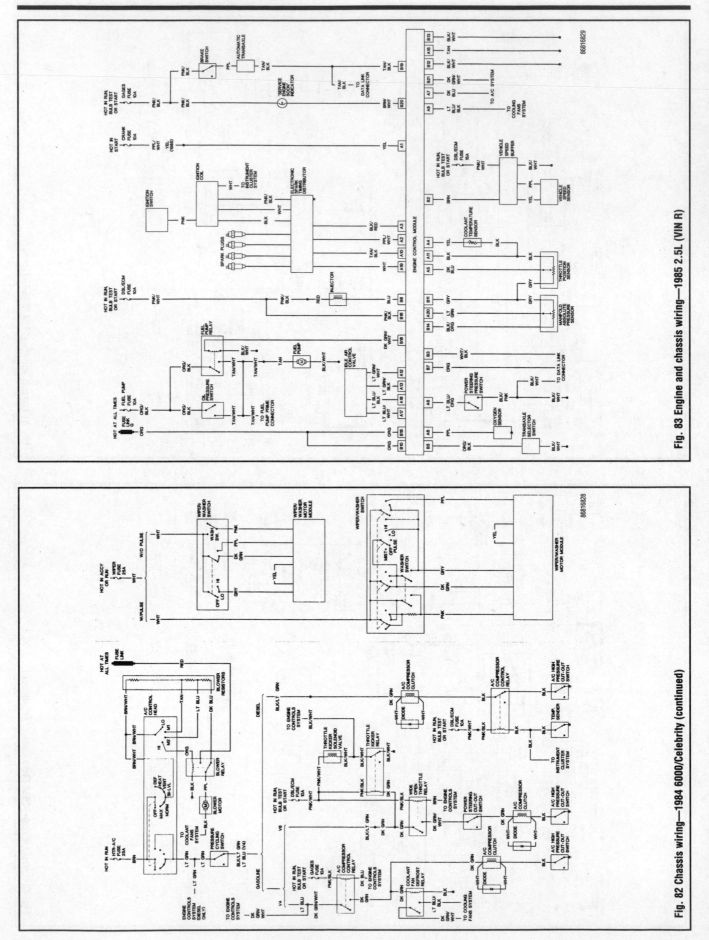

Fig. 83 Engine and chassis wiring—1985 2.5L (VIN R)

Fig. 82 Chassis wiring—1984 6000/Celebrity (continued)

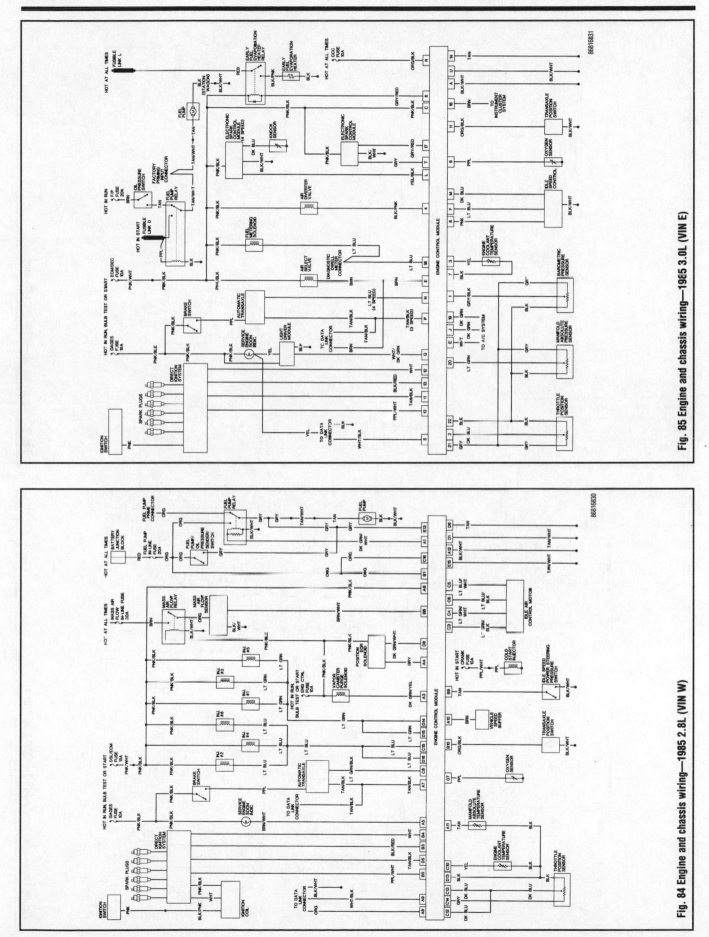

Fig. 85 Engine and chassis wiring—1985 3.0L (VIN E)

Fig. 84 Engine and chassis wiring—1985 2.8L (VIN W)

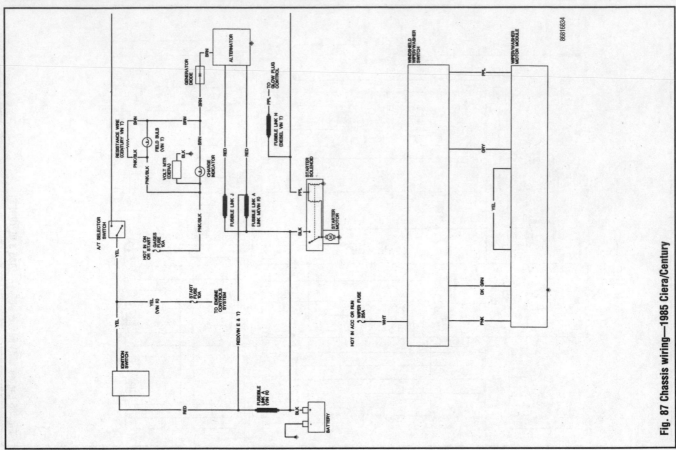

Fig. 87 Chassis wiring—1985 Ciera/Century

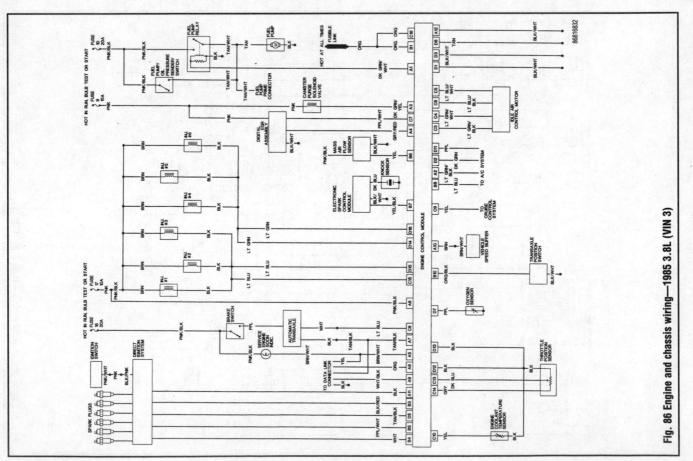

Fig. 86 Engine and chassis wiring—1985 3.8L (VIN 3)

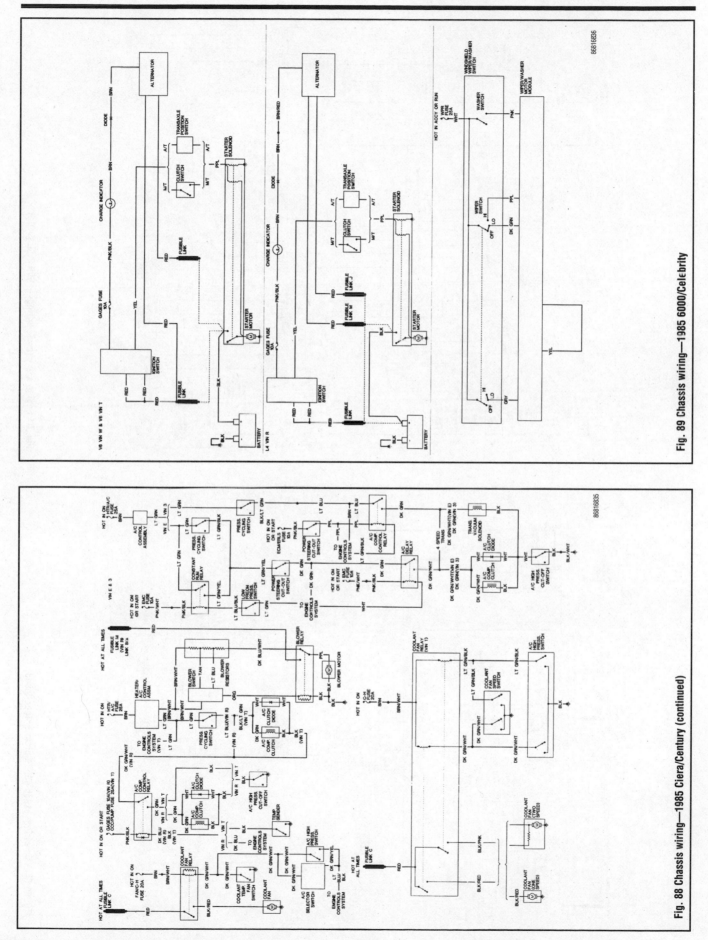

Fig. 89 Chassis wiring—1985 6000/Celebrity

Fig. 88 Chassis wiring—1985 Ciera/Century (continued)

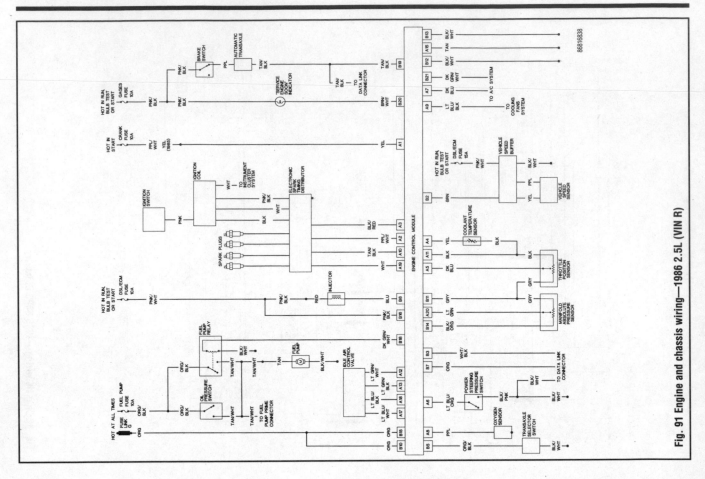

Fig. 91 Engine and chassis wiring—1986 2.5L (VIN R)

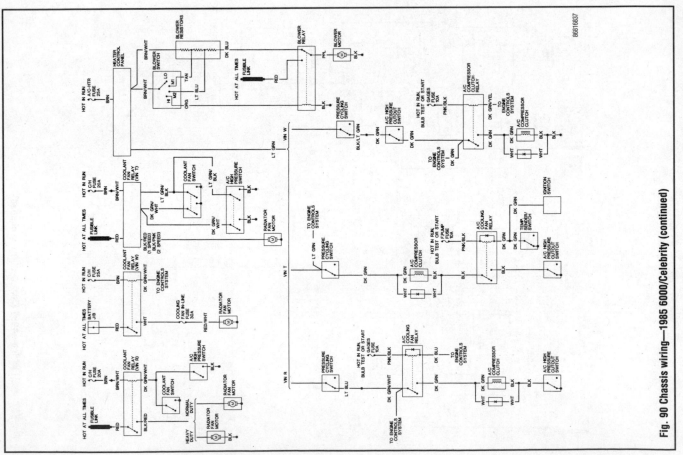

Fig. 90 Chassis wiring—1985 6000/Celebrity (continued)

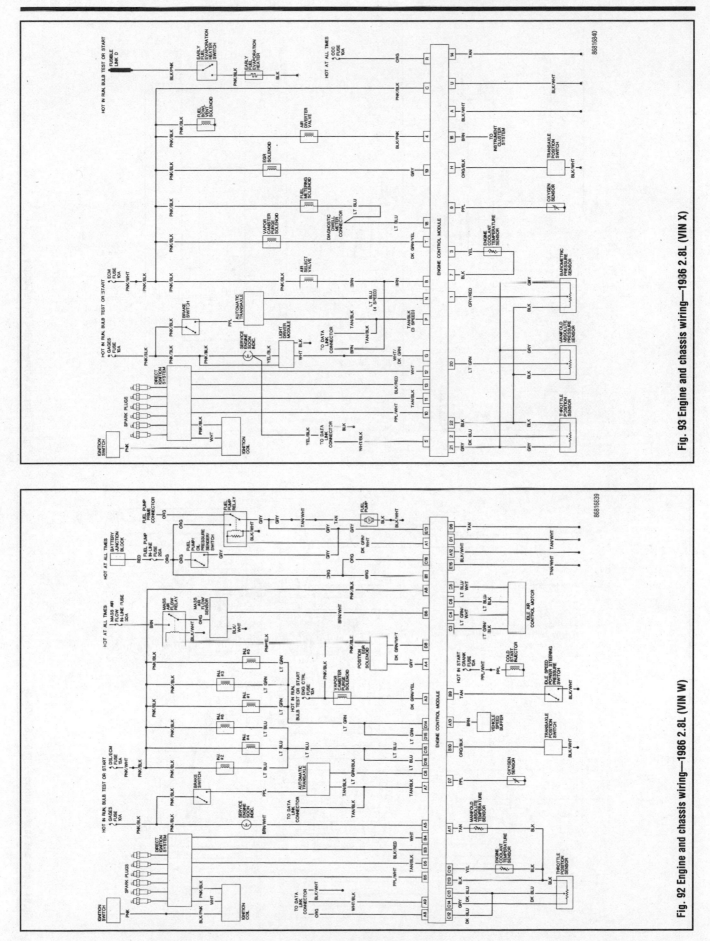

Fig. 93 Engine and chassis wiring—1936 2.8L (VIN X)

Fig. 92 Engine and chassis wiring—1986 2.8L (VIN W)

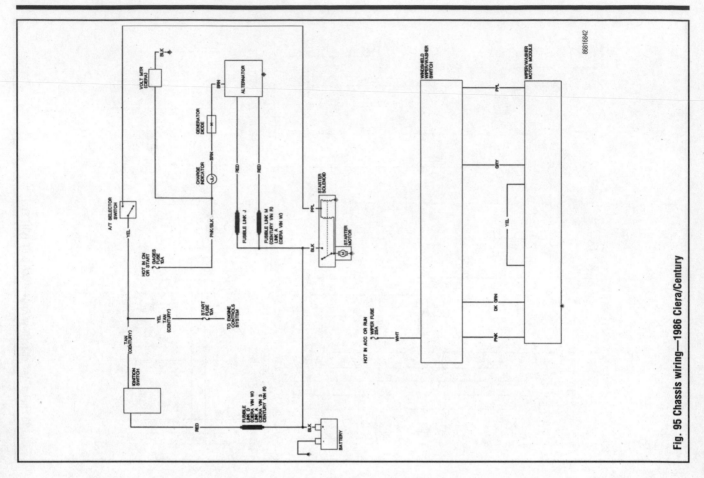

Fig. 95 Chassis wiring—1986 Ciera/Century

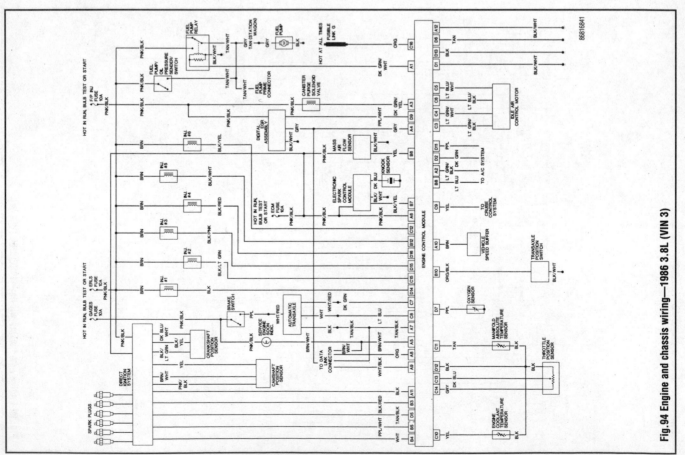

Fig. 94 Engine and chassis wiring—1986 3.8L (VIN 3)

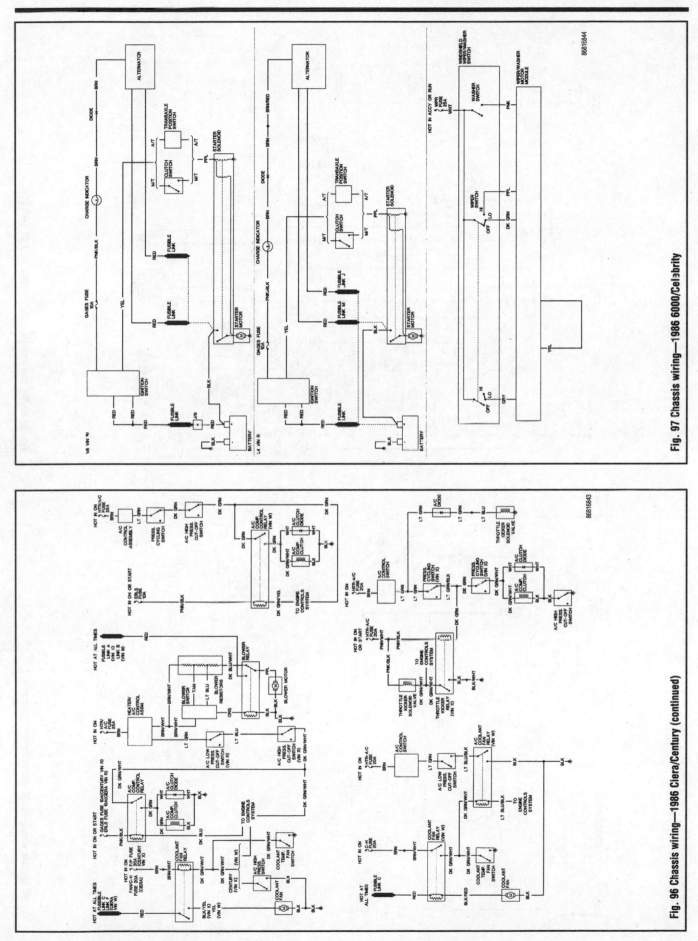

Fig. 97 Chassis wiring—1986 6000/Celebrity

Fig. 96 Chassis wiring—1986 Ciera/Century (continued)

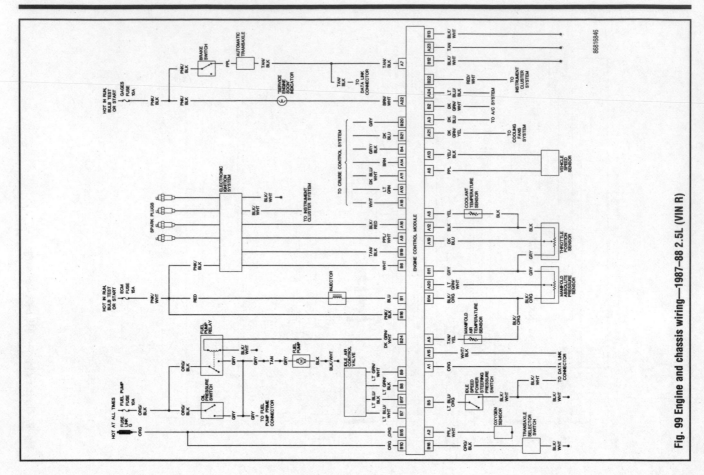

Fig. 99 Engine and chassis wiring—1987-88 2.5L (VIN R)

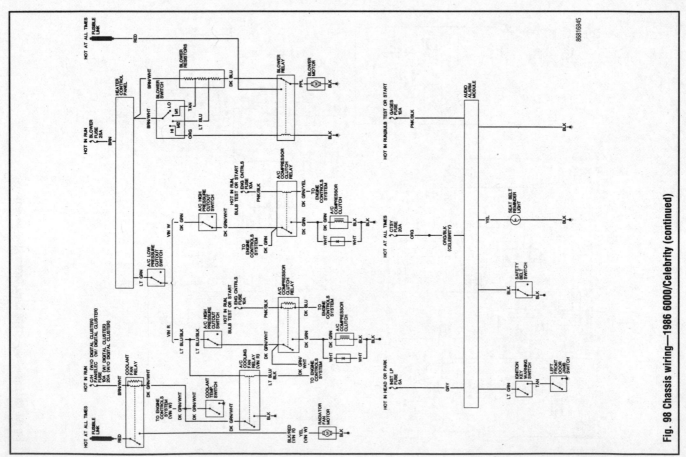

Fig. 98 Chassis wiring—1986 6000/Celebrity (continued)

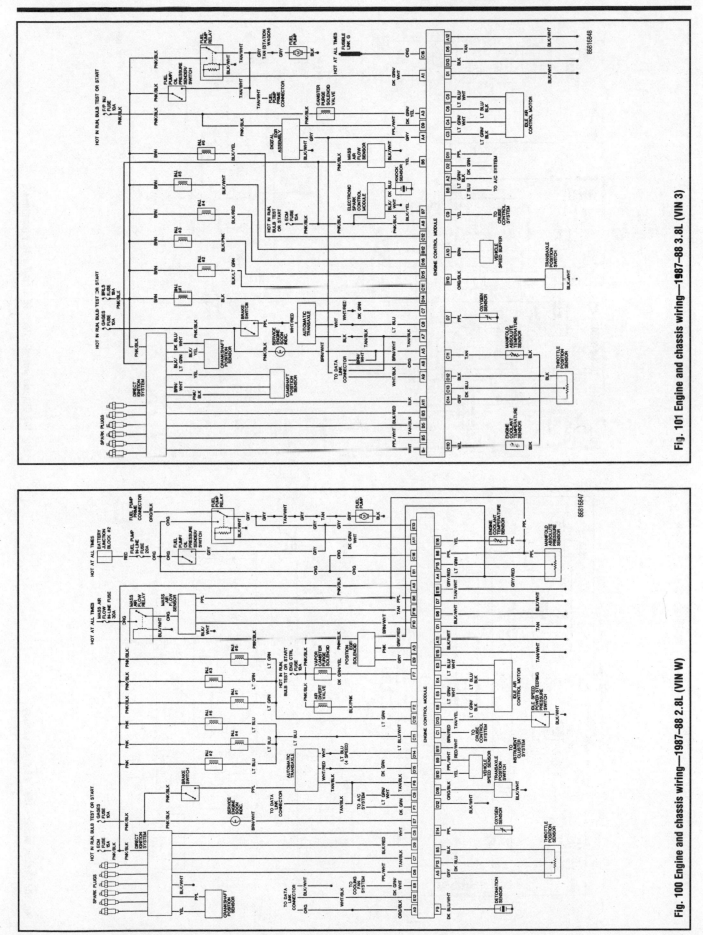

Fig. 101 Engine and chassis wiring—1987–88 3.8L (VIN 3)

Fig. 100 Engine and chassis wiring—1987–88 2.8L (VIN W)

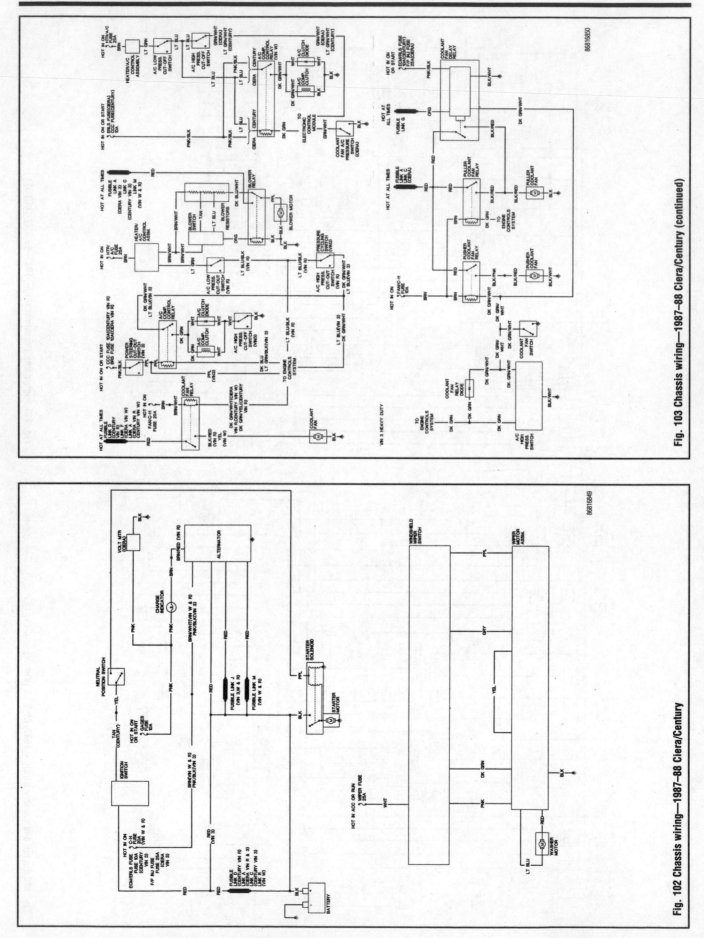

Fig. 103 Chassis wiring—1987–88 Ciera/Century (continued)

Fig. 102 Chassis wiring—1987–88 Ciera/Century

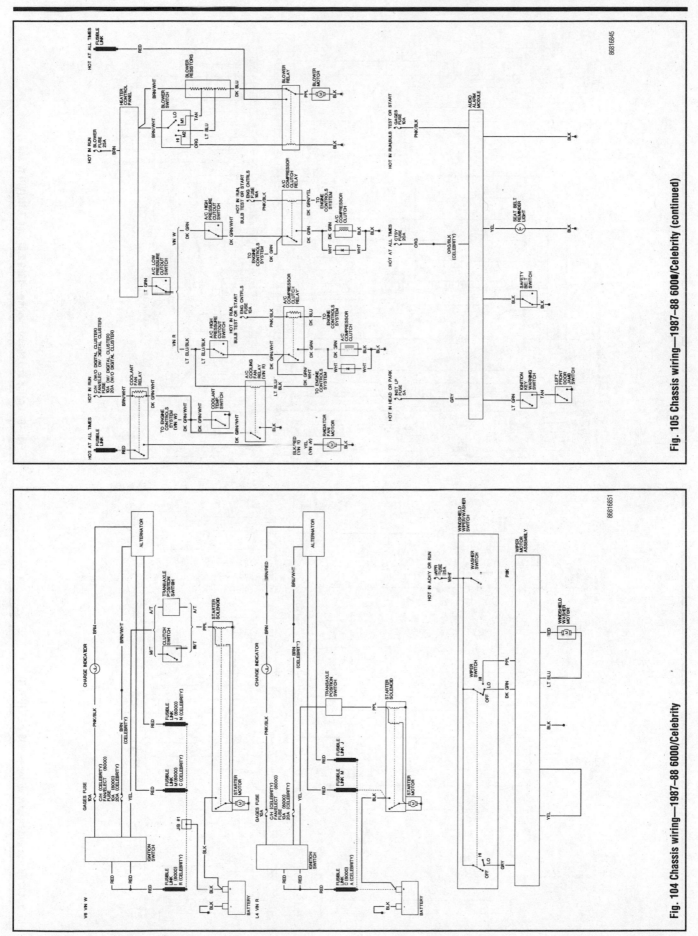

Fig. 105 Chassis wiring—1987–88 6000/Celebrity (continued)

Fig. 104 Chassis wiring—1987–88 6000/Celebrity

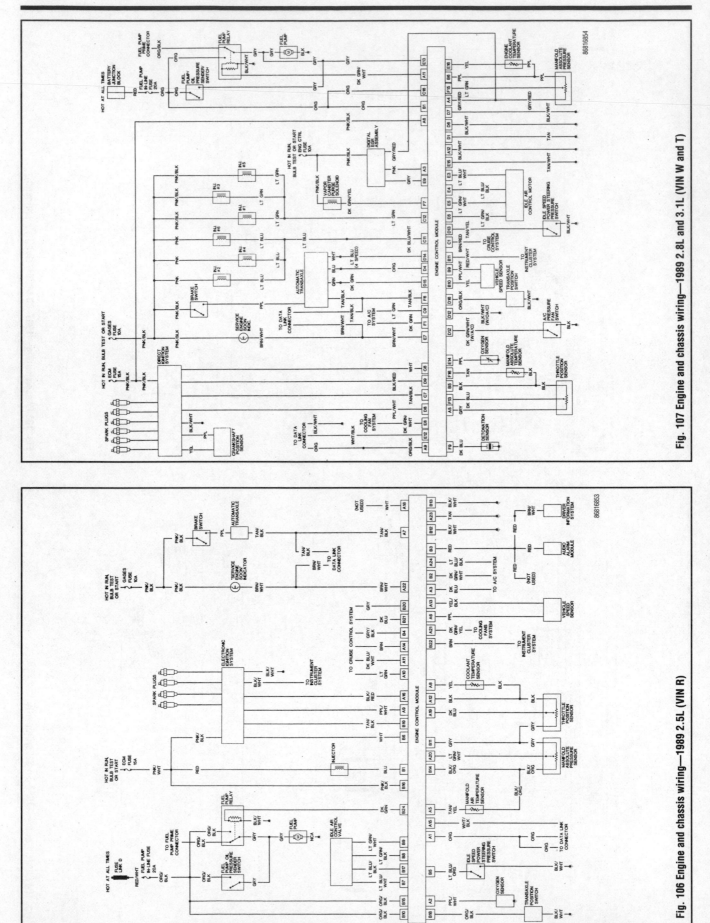

Fig. 107 Engine and chassis wiring—1989 2.8L and 3.1L (VIN W and T)

Fig. 106 Engine and chassis wiring—1989 2.5L (VIN R)

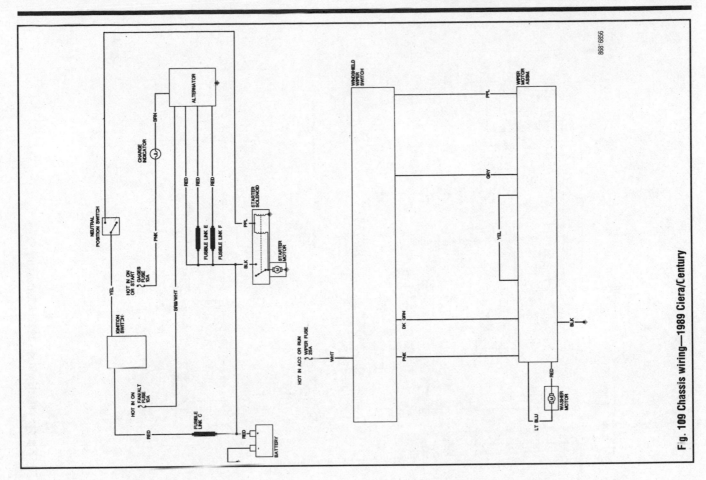

Fig. 109 Chassis wiring—1989 Ciera/Century

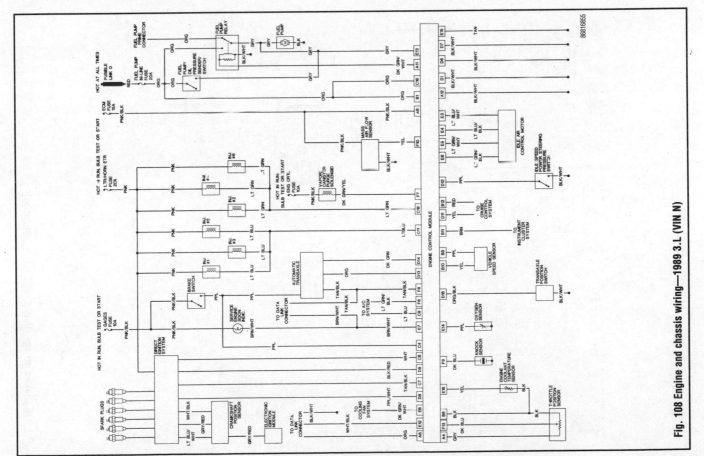

Fig. 108 Engine and chassis wiring—1989 3.L (VIN N)

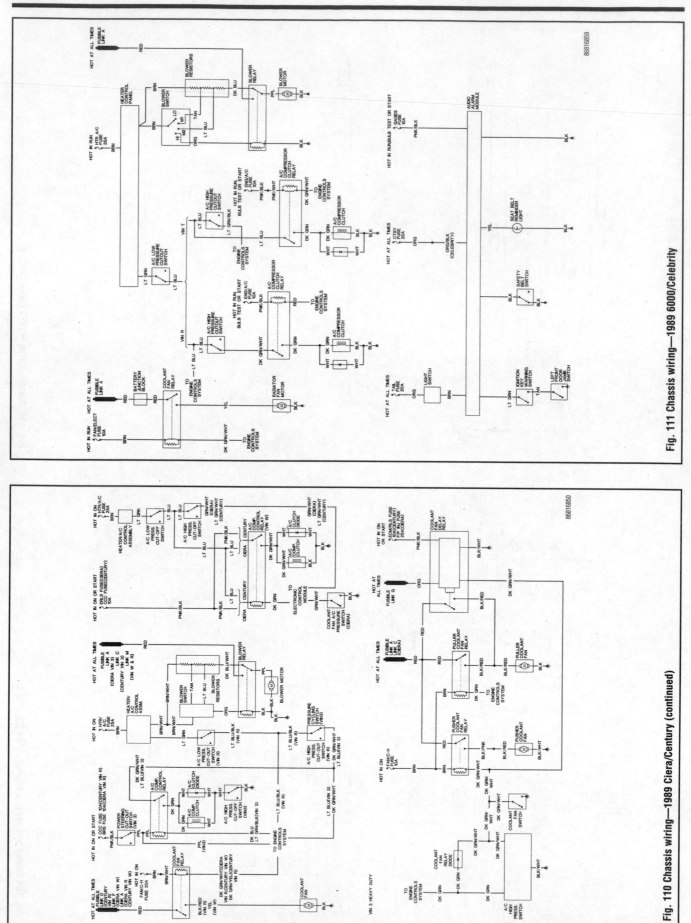

Fig. 111 Chassis wiring—1989 6000/Celebrity

Fig. 110 Chassis wiring—1989 Ciera/Century (continued)

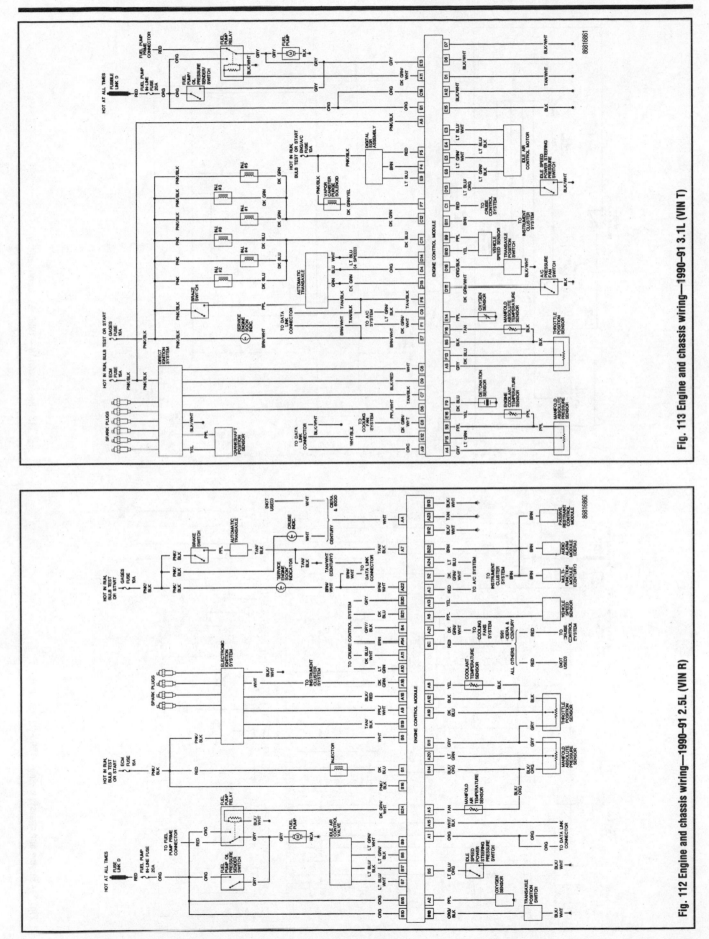

Fig. 113 Engine and chassis wiring—1990-91 3.1L (VIN T)

Fig. 112 Engine and chassis wiring—1990-91 2.5L (VIN R)

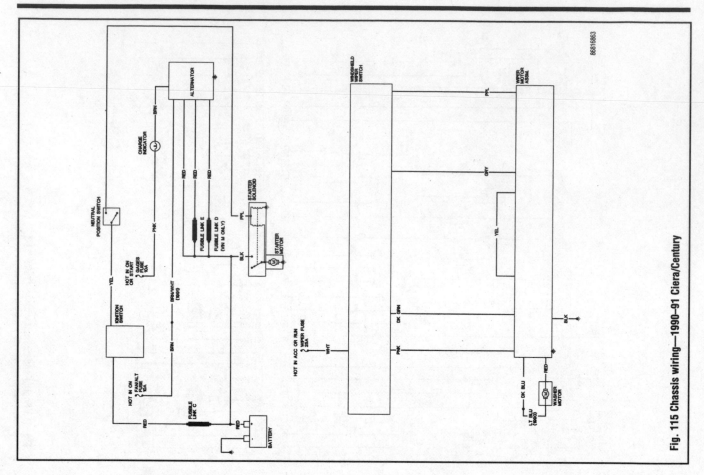

Fig. 115 Chassis wiring—1990-91 Ciera/Century

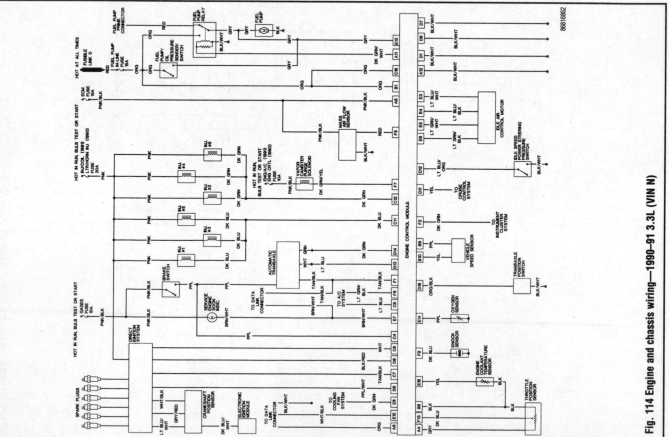

Fig. 114 Engine and chassis wiring—1990-91 3.3L (VIN N)

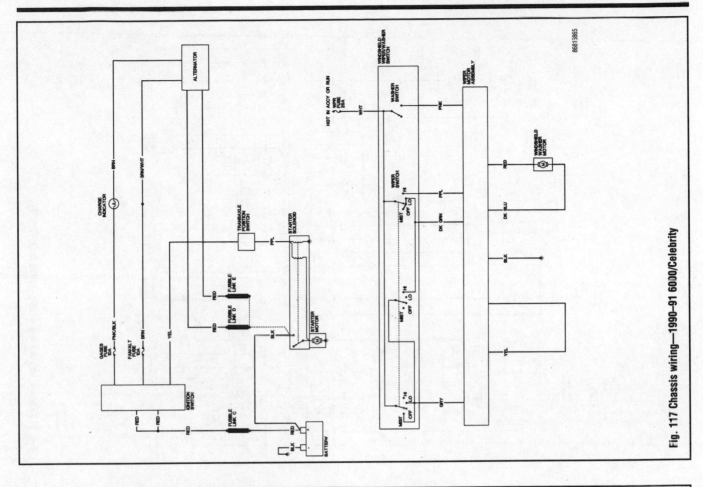

Fig. 117 Chassis wiring—1990–91 6000/Celebrity

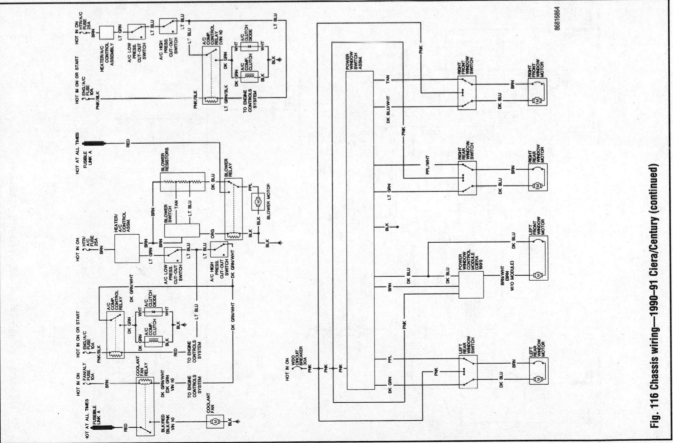

Fig. 116 Chassis wiring—1990–91 Ciera/Century (continued)

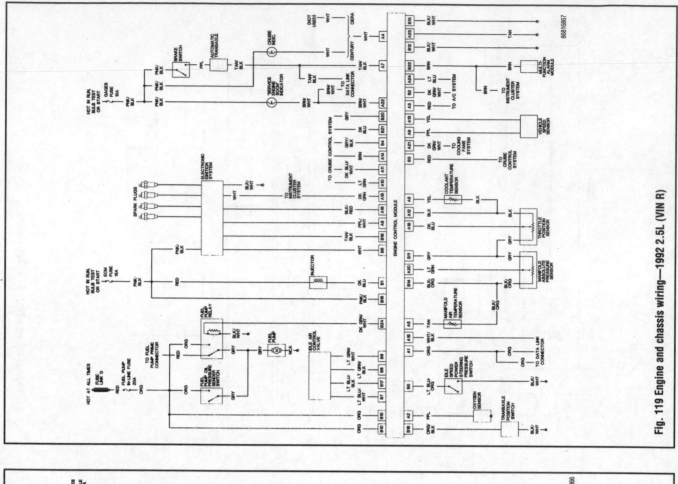

Fig. 119 Engine and chassis wiring—1992 2.5L (VIN R)

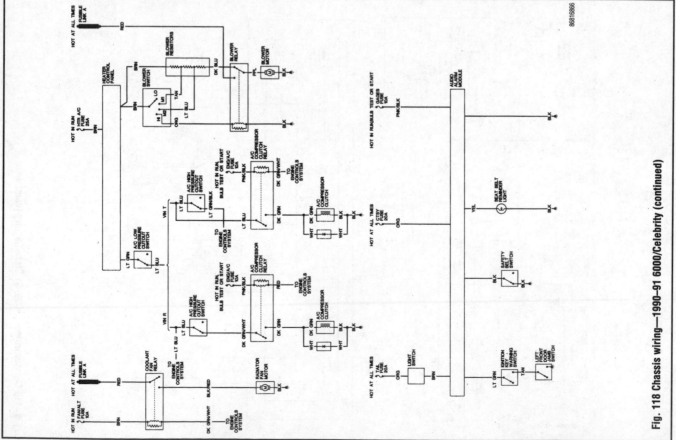

Fig. 118 Chassis wiring—1990–91 6000/Celebrity (continued)

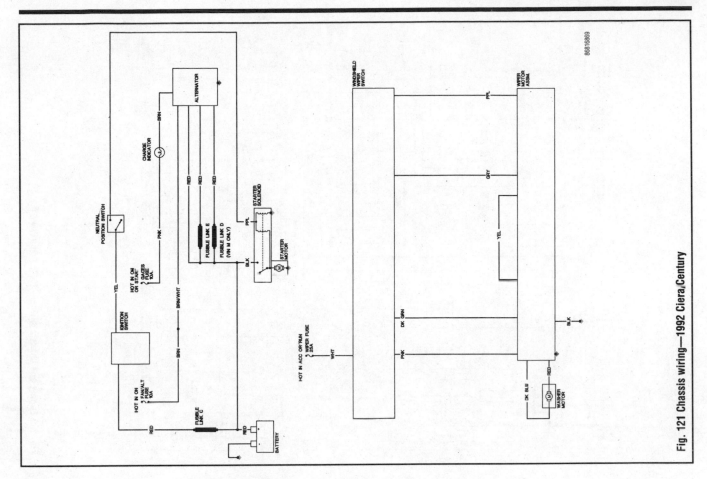

Fig. 121 Chassis wiring—1992 Ciera/Century

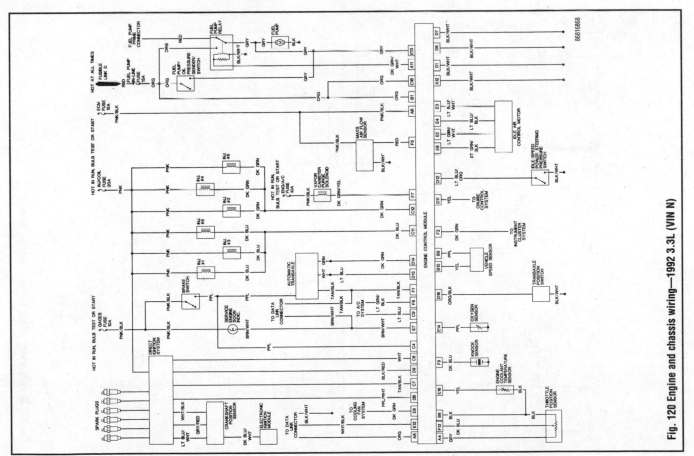

Fig. 120 Engine and chassis wiring—1992 3.3L (VIN N)

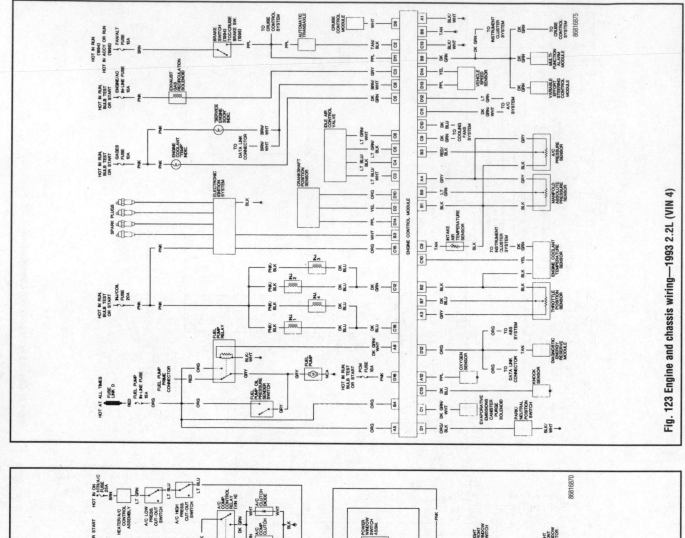

Fig. 123 Engine and chassis wiring—1993 2.2L (VIN 4)

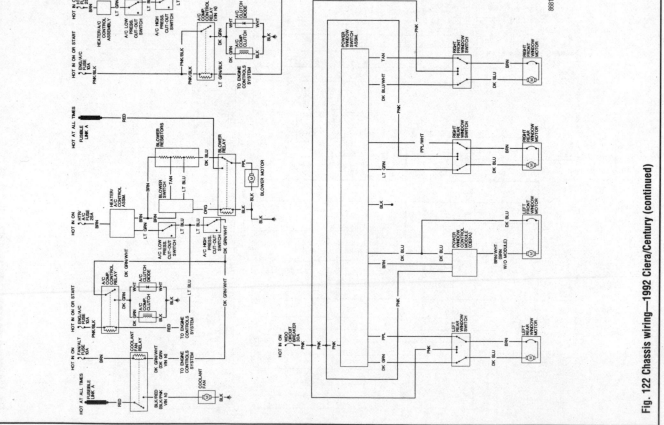

Fig. 122 Chassis wiring—1992 Ciera/Century (continued)

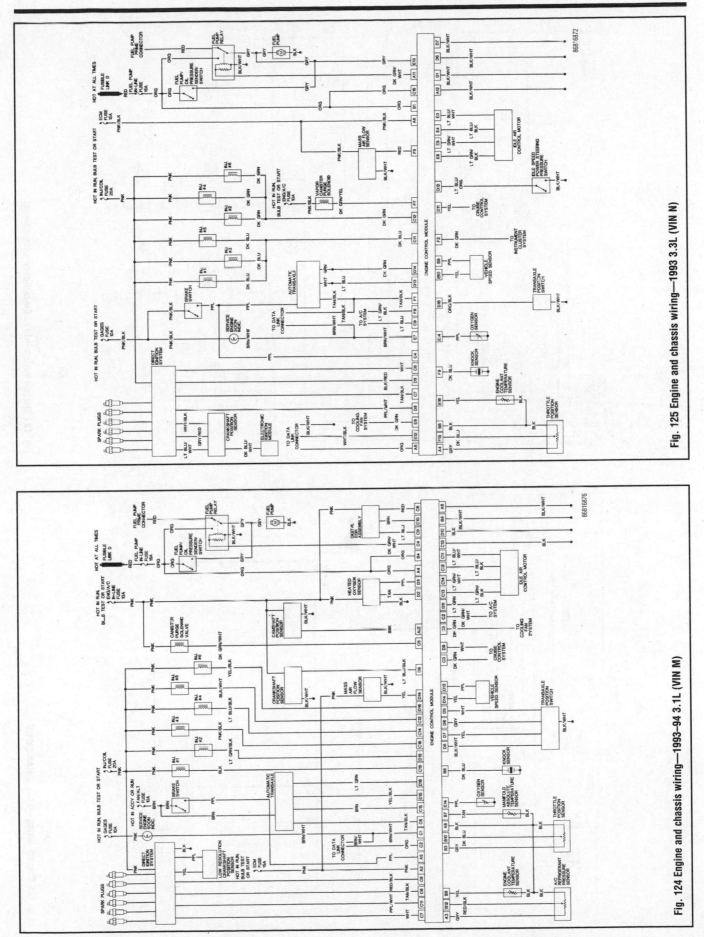

Fig. 125 Engine and chassis wiring—1993 3.3L (VIN N)

Fig. 124 Engine and chassis wiring—1993-94 3.1L (VIN M)

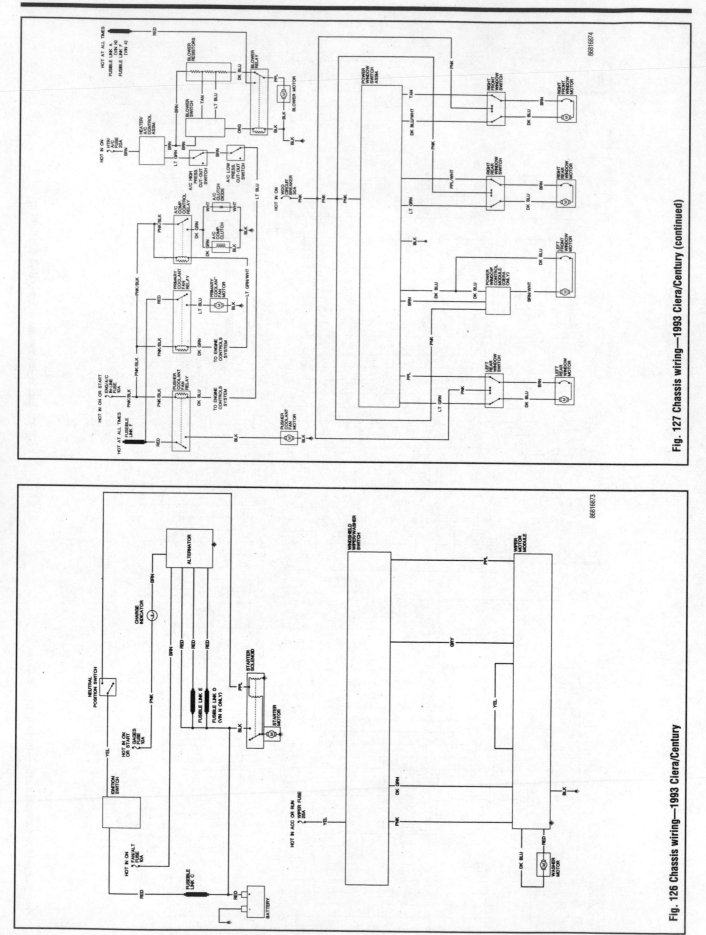

Fig. 127 Chassis wiring—1993 Ciera/Century (continued)

Fig. 126 Chassis wiring—1993 Ciera/Century

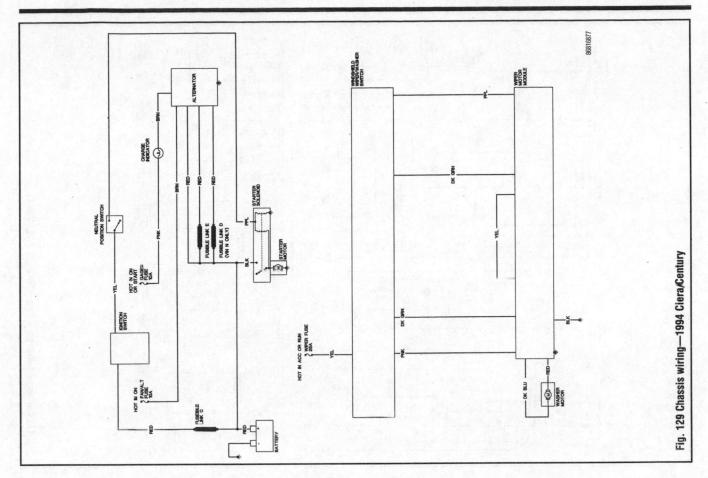

Fig. 129 Chassis wiring—1994 Ciera/Century

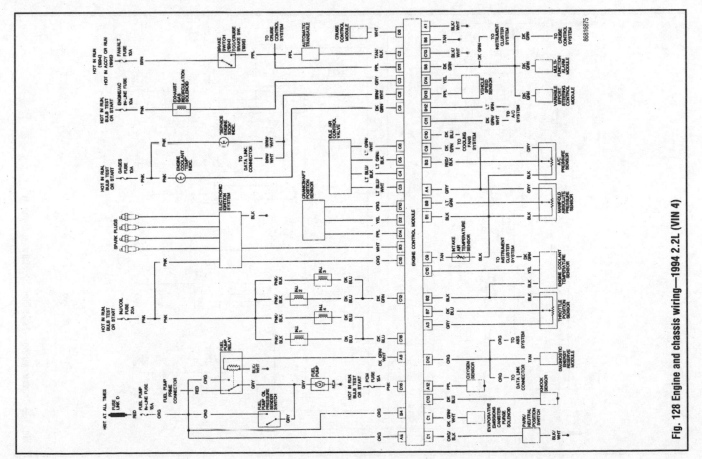

Fig. 128 Engine and chassis wiring—1994 2.2L (VIN 4)

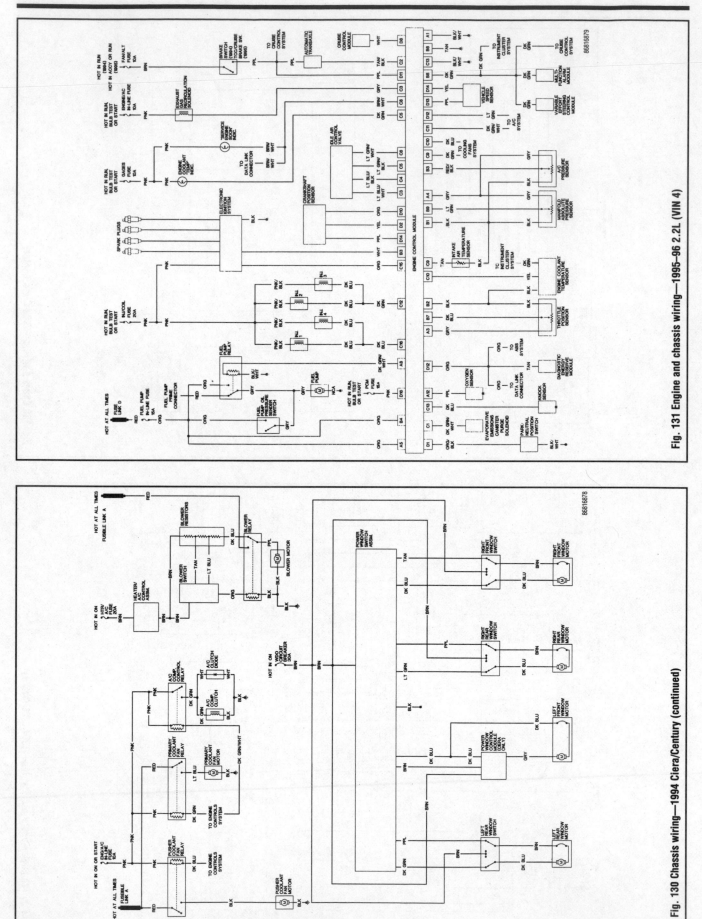

Fig. 131 Engine and chassis wiring—1995–96 2.2L (VIN 4)

Fig. 130 Chassis wiring—1994 Ciera/Century (continued)

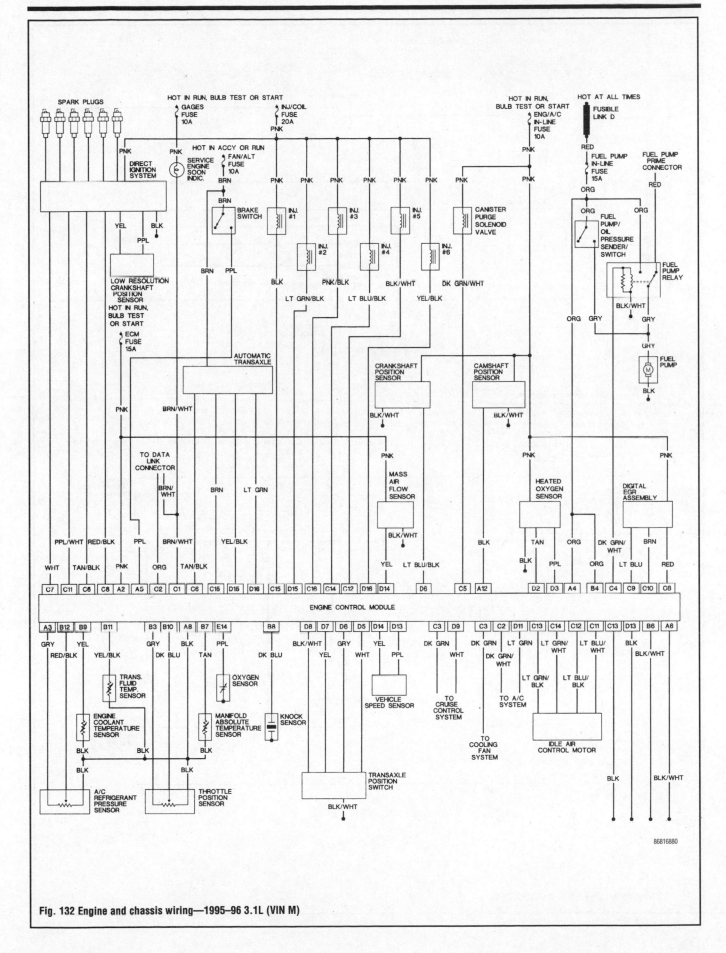

Fig. 132 Engine and chassis wiring—1995–96 3.1L (VIN M)

86816880

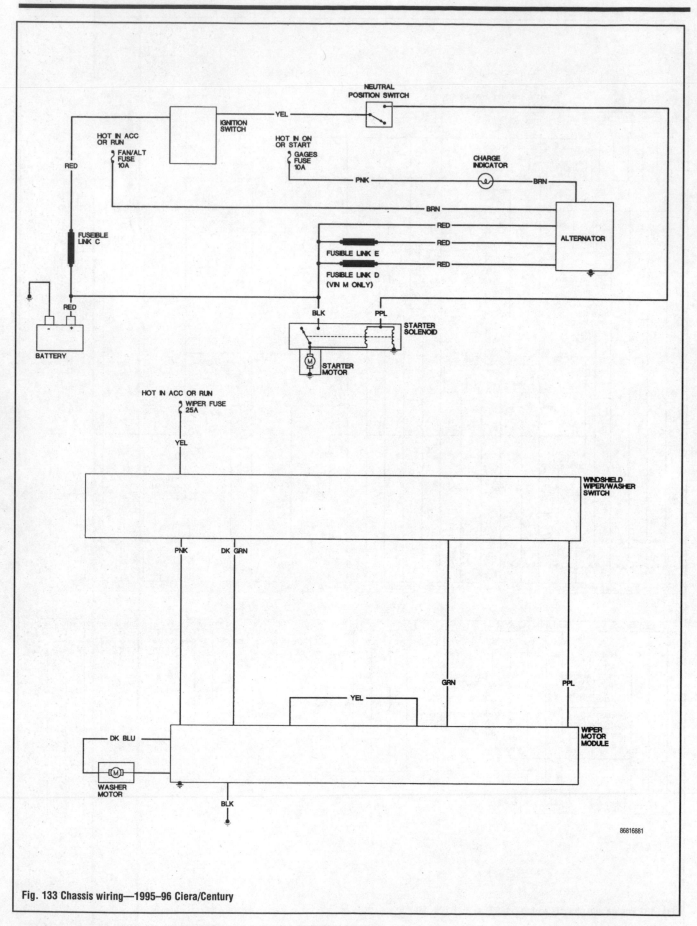

Fig. 133 Chassis wiring—1995–96 Ciera/Century

7

DRIVE TRAIN

MANUAL TRANSAXLE

General Information

Transaxle is the term used to identify a unit which combines the transmission and drive axle into one component. All 1982–86 models were equipped with MT-125 manual four speed transaxles. In 1987–88 Muncie five speed transaxles were used. The 4-speed transaxles use cable actuated clutches while the five speed clutches are hydraulically controlled utilizing a clutch master and slave cylinder.

All forward gears in this design are in constant mesh. Final drive from the transaxle is taken from the output gear, which is an integral part of the output shaft; the output gear transfers power to the differential ring gear and differential assembly. The differential is of conventional design.

The 4-speed transaxle assembly is a constant mesh design, combined with a differential unit and assembled in a single case, the forward gears are in constant mesh. For ease of shifting and gear selecting, synchronizers with blocker rings are controlled by shifting forks. A sliding idler gear arrangement is used for reverse gear.

The components consists of: an aluminum transaxle case, an aluminum clutch cover, input gear (shaft), output gear (shaft) and the differential assembly. Preloaded tapered roller bearings support the input gear, output gear and differential. Selective shims, used to establish the correct preload, are located beneath the right hand bearing cups.

The halfshafts which are attached to the front wheels, are turned by the differential and ring gear which are controlled by the final output gear.

The differential, consisting of a set of 4 gears, is a conventional arrangement that divides the torque between the halfshafts, allowing them to rotate at different speeds. Of the 4 gear set, 2 are known as differential side gears and the others are differential pinion gears.

The differential pinion gears, mounted on a differential pinion shaft, are free to rotate on the shaft. The pinion shaft, placed in the differential case bore, is at a right angle to the drive axle shaft. The Hydra-Matic Muncie 282 (HM-282) transaxle is a 5-speed unit. The gearing provides for 5 synchronized forward speeds, a reverse speed, a final drive with differential output and speedometer drive.

The input and output gear clusters are nested very close together, requiring extremely tight tolerances of shafts, gears and synchronizers.

The input shaft is supported by a roller bearing in the clutch and differential housing and a ball bearing in the transaxle case.

The output shaft is supported by a roller bearing in the clutch and differential housing and a combination ball-and-roller bearing in the transaxle case.

The differential case is supported by opposed tapered roller bearings which are under preload.

The speed gears are supported by roller bearings. A bushing supports the reverse idler gear.

Transaxle Identification

The transaxle identification stamp is located at the center top of the case. The transaxle identification tag is located on the left side near the left side cover.

Adjustments

LINKAGE

MT-125

1. Disconnect the negative battery cable.
2. Remove the shifter boot, the console and retainer inside the car. Shift into first gear, then loosen the shift cable mounting nuts E at the transaxle D and F.
3. With the shift lever in first gear, position (pulled to the left and held against the stop) insert a yoke clip to hold the lever hard against the reverse lockout stop as shown in view D. Install two No. 22 drill bits, or two 5/32in. (4mm) rods, into the two alignment holes in the shifter assembly to hold it in first gear. This is shown in view C.
4. Remove the lash from the transaxle by rotating the lever D in the direction of the arrow while tightening nut E. Tighten nut E on lever F.
5. Remove the two drill bits or pins from the shifter.

SHIM PART NO.	DIM C (MM)	COLOR & NO OF STRIPES
14008235	1.8	3 WHITE
476709	2.1	1 ORANGE
476710	2.4	2 ORANGE
476711	2.7	3 ORANGE
476712	3.0	1 BLUE
476713	3.3	2 BLUE
476714	3.6	3 BLUE
476715	3.9	1 WHITE
476716	4.2	2 WHITE

86817007

Fig. 1 Selective washer chart

6. Connect the negative battery cable. Road test the vehicle to check for a good neutral gate feel during shifting. It may be necessary to fine tune the adjustment after road testing.

SHIFTER SHAFT WASHER

▶ **See Figure 1**

If a hang-up is experienced in the 1–2 gear range and the shift cables are properly adjusted, it may be necessary to change the shift selector washer.

1. From the end of the housing, remove the reverse inhibitor fitting spring and washer.
2. Position the shifter shaft into the **2nd** gear position.
3. Measure the end of housing-to-end of shifter shaft (dimension **A**).
4. On the opposite end of the shaft, apply a load of 8.8–13.3 lbs. (4–6 kg) and measure the end of housing-to-end of shifter shaft (dimension **B**).
5. Subtract dimension **B** from dimension **A** and secure dimension **C**.
6. Using the dimension **C** and shifter shaft selective washer chart, select the correct shim washer to be used on the reinstallation.

Back-up Light Switch

REMOVAL & INSTALLATION

1. Remove the shifter knob from the shifter by removing the retaining screw at the back of the knob.
2. Remove the screws at the sides and front of the console.
3. Open the console box, then remove the retaining screw inside the box.
4. Remove the ashtray at the rear of the console, then remove the retaining screw behind the ashtray.
5. Slide the console rearward slightly, then lift it over the shifter.
6. Disconnect the wiring harness at the back-up light switch.
7. Remove the switch from the base of the shifter.
8. Reverse steps to install the switch.

Shift Cable

REMOVAL & INSTALLATION

4-Speed Transaxle

1. Disconnect the negative battery cable.
2. At the transaxle, disconnect the shift cables, then remove the retaining clamp.
3. At the shift control, remove the knob, the control cover and the boot or console (if equipped).
4. Disconnect the shift cables from the shift control.

5. Remove the front sill plate and pull the carpet back to gain access to the cables.

6. Remove the cable grommet cover screws, the floor pan cover and cables.

To install:

7. Route the cables into the vehicle, then install the cable cover and screws (at floor pan).

8. At the shift control assembly, connect the shift cables. Reposition carpet and install the sill plate.

9. Raise and safely support the vehicle.

10. At the transaxle, position the cables and install the retaining clamps.

11. Lower the vehicle.

12. Connect and adjust the cables at the shift lever assembly.

13. Install the console, if equipped, the boot, the control cover and the knob.

14. Attach the negative battery cable.

5-Speed Transaxle

♦ See Figure 2

1. Disconnect the negative battery cable.

2. Disconnect the shift cables from the transaxle by removing the cable clamp at the transaxle.

3. Remove the cable ends from the ball studs at the shift levers by twisting a large flat blade tool between the nylon socket and the lever.

4. Remove the knob, console and shift boot.

5. Remove the cable ends from the ball studs of the shifter by twisting a large flat blade tool between the nylon socket and the shifter lever. Do not pry the socket off the stud using the cable end for leverage.

6. Remove the spring clip holding the cables to the shifter base and remove the cables from the shifter.

7. Remove the right front sill plate and pull the carpet back to gain access to the cables.

8. Remove the cable grommet cover screws and cover at the floor pan and remove the cables.

To install:

9. Route the cables, then install the cable grommet cover and attaching screws at the floor pan.

10. Install the shift cables at the control assembly. Snap the cable ends onto the ball studs using the channel locks.

11. Reposition the carpet and install the sill plate.

12. Raise and support the vehicle safely.

13. Route the cables to the transaxle.

14. Lower the vehicle.

15. Position the cables and install the retaining clamps at the transaxle. Connect the cables to the shift levers.

16. Install the shift boot, console and knob.

17. Connect the negative battery cable.

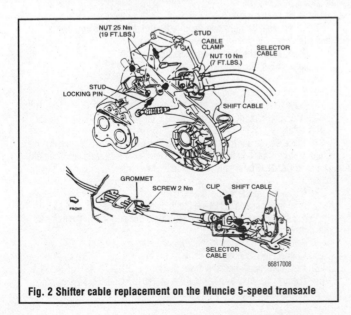

Fig. 2 Shifter cable replacement on the Muncie 5-speed transaxle

Manual Transaxle Assembly

REMOVAL & INSTALLATION

When removing and installing a transaxle, special tools may be required for the job. Read the procedure completely before actually working on the vehicle.

1982–83 Models

MT-125

1. Disconnect the negative battery cable from the transaxle case.

2. Remove the two transaxle strut bracket bolts on the left side of the engine compartment, if equipped.

3. Remove the top four engine-to-transaxle bolts, and the one at the rear near the firewall. The one at the rear is installed from the engine side.

4. Loosen the engine-to-transaxle bolt near the starter, but do not remove.

5. Disconnect the speedometer cable at the transaxle, or at the speed control transducer on cars so equipped.

6. Remove the retaining clip and washer from the shift linkage at the transaxle. Remove the clips holding the cables to the mounting bosses on the case.

7. Support the engine with a lifting chain.

8. Unlock the steering column and raise and support the car. Drain the transaxle. Remove the two nuts attaching the stabilizer bar to the left lower control arm. Remove the four bolts which attach the left retaining plate to the engine cradle. The retaining plate covers and holds the stabilizer bar.

9. Loosen the four bolts holding the right stabilizer bracket.

10. Disconnect and remove the exhaust pipe and crossover if necessary.

11. Pull the stabilizer bar down on the left side.

12. Remove the four nuts and disconnect the front and rear transaxle mounts from the engine cradle. Remove the two rear center crossmember bolts.

13. Remove the three right side front cradle attaching bolts. They are accessible under the splash shield.

14. Remove the top bolt from the lower front transaxle shock absorber if equipped.

15. Remove the left front wheel. Remove the front cradle-to-body bolts on the left side, and the rear cradle-to-body bolts.

16. Pull the left side driveshaft from the transaxle using G. M. special tool J-28468 or the equivalent. The right side axle shaft will simply disconnect from the cage. When the transaxle is removed, the right shaft can be swung out of the way. A boot protector should be used when disconnecting the driveshafts.

17. Swing the cradle to the left side. Secure out of the way, outboard of the fender well.

18. Remove the flywheel and starter shield bolts, then remove the shields.

19. Remove the two transaxle extension bolts from the engine-to-transaxle bracket, if equipped.

20. Place a jack under the transaxle case. Remove the last engine-to-transaxle bolt. Pull the transaxle to the left, away from the engine, then down and out from under the car.

To install:

21. Place the transaxle on a jack and raise it into position. Position the right axle shaft into its bore as the transaxle is bolted to the engine.

22. Swing the cradle into position and install the cradle-to-body bolts immediately. Be sure to guide the left axle shaft into place as the cradle is moved back into position.

23. Install the two transaxle extension bolts into the engine-to-transaxle bracket.

24. Install the lower engine-to-transaxle bolts.

25. Install the flywheel to starter shield and retaining bolts.

26. Remove the boot protectors from the driveshafts.

27. Attach the top bolt to the lower front transaxle shock absorber.

28. Install the four nuts and connect the front and rear transaxle mounts to the engine cradle. Install the two rear center crossmember bolts.

29. Attach the stabilizer bar.

30. Install the exhaust pipe and crossover.

31. Secure the four bolts holding the right stabilizer bracket.

32. Install the two nuts attaching the stabilizer bar to the left lower control arm. Install the four bolts which attach the left retaining plate to the engine cradle.

33. Remove the transaxle jack, then disconnect the engine lifting chain and lower the vehicle.

34. Fill the transaxle with the recommended fluid.

35. Install the retaining clip and washer to the shift linkage at the transaxle. Install the clips holding the cables to the mounting bosses on the case.

36. Connect the speedometer cable at the transaxle, or at the speed control transducer on cars so equipped.

37. Tighten the engine-to-transaxle bolt near the starter.

38. Install the top four engine-to-transaxle bolts, and the one at the rear near the firewall. The one at the rear is installed from the engine side.

39. Remove the two transaxle strut bracket bolts on the left side of the engine compartment, if equipped.

40. Connect the negative battery cable to the transaxle case.

1984–86 Models

MT-125

1. Disconnect the battery ground cable from the transaxle and support it with a wire.

2. Disconnect the horn's electrical lead and remove the horn's mounting bolt. Remove the air cleaner.

3. Support the clutch pedal upward against the bumper stop to release the pawl from the quadrant. Disconnect the clutch cable from the release lever at the transaxle.

✳✳ WARNING

DO NOT allow the clutch cable to snap rapidly toward the rear of the vehicle, for the quadrant in the adjusting mechanism can be damaged.

4. Lift the locking pawl away from the quadrant, then slide the cable out to the right side of the quadrant.

5. At the right side of the cowl, disconnect the cable retainer-to-upper stud nuts. Disconnect the cable from the transaxle bracket and remove the cable.

6. If equipped with a V6 engine, disconnect the fuel lines and clamps from the clutch cable bracket, then remove the exhaust crossover pipe.

7. At the transaxle, remove the shift linkage retaining clips and the shift cable retaining clips from the transaxle bosses.

8. Disconnect the speedometer cable at the transaxle. Remove the top engine-to-transaxle bolts.

9. Install and support the engine with tool J-22825-1. Raise the vehicle and drain the transaxle fluid.

10. Install the drive axle boot protector tool J-33162 to the drive axle boot. Remove the left front wheel and tire assembly.

11. Turn the steering wheel so that the intermediate shaft-to-steering gear stub shaft is in the upward position, then remove the bolt.

12. Position a floor jack under the engine to act as a support. Remove the power steering pressure line brackets.

13. Remove the steering gear mounting bolts, then support the steering gear. Disconnect the drive line vibration absorber, the front stabilizer from the left side lower control arm and the left side lower ball joint from the steering knuckle.

14. Remove both sides of the stabilizer bar reinforcements.

15. Using a ½ in. drill bit, drill through the spot weld (located between the rear holes of the left side front stabilizer bar mounting).

16. Disconnect the engine/transaxle mounts from the cradle. Remove the crossmember side bolts and the left side body bolts.

17. Remove the left side and the front crossmember assembly.

18. Using tools J-33008, J-29794 and J-261901, remove the left drive axle from the transaxle and the support.

➡**The right drive axle can be removed when the transaxle is removed from the vehicle.**

19. Remove the flywheel/starter shield bolts. Connect a transaxle jack to the transaxle, then remove the last engine-to-transaxle bolt.

20. Slide the transaxle away from the engine, lower the jack and move the transaxle away from the vehicle.

To install:

21. Place the transaxle on a jack and raise it into position. Position the right axle shaft into its bore as the transaxle is bolted to the engine.

22. Swing the cradle into position, then install the cradle-to-body bolts immediately. Be sure to guide the left axle shaft into place as the cradle is moved back into position.

23. Secure the flywheel/starter shield and bolts.

24. Attach the left side and front crossmember assembly.

25. Install the crossmember side bolts and the left side body bolts.

26. Connect the engine/transaxle mounts to the cradle.

27. Connect the left side lower ball joint to the steering knuckle.

28. Connect the front stabilizer to the left lower control arm.

29. Connect the drive line vibration absorber.

30. Install the stabilizer bar reinforcements, and the steering gear.

31. Install the power steering pressure line brackets.

32. Turn the steering wheel so that the intermediate shaft-to-steering gear stub shaft is in the upward position, then install the bolt.

33. Remove the drive axle boot protector tool J-33162 from the drive axle boot. Install the left front wheel and tire assembly.

34. Remove the engine support tool J-22825-1. Lower the vehicle and fill the transaxle with fluid.

35. Connect the speedometer cable at the transaxle. Install the top engine-to-transaxle bolts.

36. Install the shift linkage retaining clips and the shift cable retaining clips to the transaxle bosses.

37. If equipped with a V6 engine, connect the fuel lines and clamps to the clutch cable bracket, then install the exhaust crossover pipe.

38. At the right side of the cowl, connect the cable retainer-to-upper stud nuts. Install the cable to the transaxle bracket.

39. Lift the locking pawl away from the quadrant and slide the cable into the right side of the quadrant.

40. Connect the clutch cable to the release lever at the transaxle. Return the clutch pedal to its normal position.

41. Connect the horn's electrical lead and install the mounting bolt. Install the air cleaner.

42. Connect the battery ground cable to the transaxle.

1987–89 Models

MUNCIE

1. Disconnect the negative battery cable.

2. Remove the air cleaner and air intake duct assembly.

3. Detach the sound insulator from inside the car.

4. Remove the clutch master cylinder pushrod from the clutch pedal.

5. Remove the clutch slave cylinder from the transaxle.

6. Disconnect the exhaust crossover pipe.

7. Disconnect the shift cables at the transaxle.

8. Install the engine support fixture J-28467.

9. Remove the top engine to transaxle bolts.

10. Raise the car and suitably support it.

11. Remove the left-hand and right-hand front wheel and tire.

12. Install the drive axle boot seal protectors, Tool J-34754.

13. Remove the left-hand side frame and disconnect the rear transaxle mount from the bracket.

14. Drain the transaxle.

15. Disengage the right-hand and left-hand drive axles from the transaxle.

16. Remove the clutch housing cover bolts.

17. Disconnect the speedometer cable.

18. Attach a jack to the transaxle case.

19. Remove the remaining transaxle to engine bolts.

20. Slide the transaxle away from the engine. Carefully lower the jack while guiding the right-hand drive axle out of the transaxle.

To install:

21. Place the transaxle on a jack and guide it into the vehicle, position the right drive axle shaft into its bore as the transaxle is being installed. The right-hand shaft CANNOT be readily installed after the transaxle is connected to the engine.

22. Install the transaxle to engine bolts.

23. After the transaxle is fastened to the engine and the left drive axle is installed at the transaxle, position the left side frame and install the frame to body bolts.

24. Connect the transaxle to the front and rear mounts.

25. Connect the speedometer cable.

26. Install the clutch housing cover bolts.

27. Remove the drive axle boot seal protectors, Tool J-34754.

28. Fill the transaxle with the proper fluid.

29. Install the left side frame, then connect the rear transaxle mount to the bracket (if not already done).
30. Install the left and right front wheel and tire.
31. Remove the jack and safety supports and lower the car.
32. Install the top engine to transaxle bolts.
33. Remove the engine support fixture J-28467.
34. Connect the shift cables at the transaxle.
35. Connect the exhaust crossover pipe.
36. Install the clutch slave cylinder to the transaxle.
37. Install the clutch master cylinder pushrod from the clutch pedal.
38. Install the sound insulator inside the car.
39. Install the air intake duct assembly and the air cleaner.
40. Connect the negative battery cable.

Halfshafts

REMOVAL & INSTALLATION

▶ **See Figure 3**

✲✲ WARNING

Use care when removing the drive axle. Tri-pots can be damaged if the drive axle is overextended.

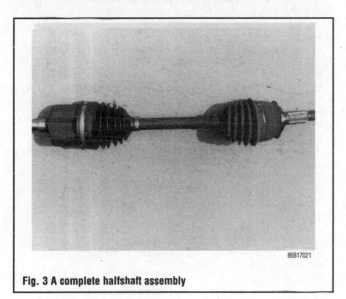

Fig. 3 A complete halfshaft assembly

Except Rear Axle—6000 STE AWD

▶ **See Figures 4, 5, 6 and 7**

1. Remove the hub nut and discard. A new hub nut must be used for reassembly.
2. Raise and safely support the vehicle. Remove the wheel and tire assembly.
3. Install an halfshaft boot seal protector onto the seal. The use of protector J-34754 or an equivalent is advised.
4. Disconnect the brake hose clip from the strut, but do not disconnect the hose from the caliper. Remove the brake caliper from the spindle and support the caliper with a length of wire. Do not allow the caliper to hang by the brake hose unsupported.
5. Mark the camber alignment cam bolt for reassembly. Remove the cam bolt and the upper attaching bolt from the strut and spindle.
6. Pull the steering knuckle assembly from the strut bracket.
7. Remove the halfshaft from the transaxle.
8. Using spindle remover tool J-28733 or equivalent, remove the halfshaft from the hub and bearing assembly. Do not allow the halfshaft to hang unsup-

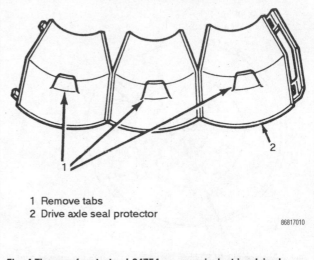

1 Remove tabs
2 Drive axle seal protector

Fig. 4 The use of protector J-34754 or an equivalent is advised

Fig. 5 Apply the protector as shown on the shaft

Fig. 6 With the other components disconnected from the axle shaft, it will slide out

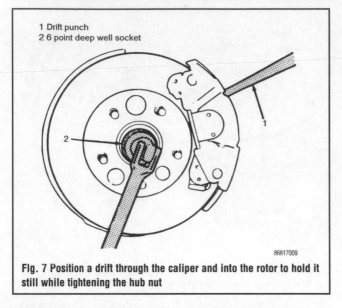

1 Drift punch
2 6 point deep well socket

Fig. 7 Position a drift through the caliper and into the rotor to hold it still while tightening the hub nut

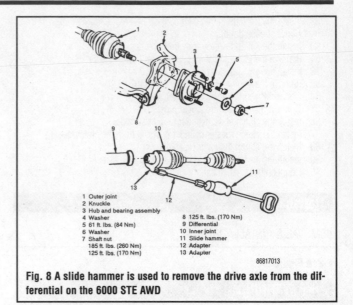

1 Outer joint
2 Knuckle
3 Hub and bearing assembly
4 Washer
5 61 ft. lbs. (84 Nm)
6 Washer
7 Shaft nut
   185 ft. lbs. (260 Nm)
   125 ft. lbs. (170 Nm)
8 125 ft. lbs. (170 Nm)
9 Differential
10 Inner joint
11 Slide hammer
12 Adapter
13 Adapter

Fig. 8 A slide hammer is used to remove the drive axle from the differential on the 6000 STE AWD

ported. If necessary, support using a length of wire in order to prevent component damage.

To install:

9. If a new halfshaft is to be installed, a new knuckle seal should be installed first along with a boot seal protector when necessary.

10. Loosely install the halfshaft into the transaxle and steering knuckle.

11. Loosely attach the steering knuckle to the suspension strut.

12. The halfshaft is an interference fit in the steering knuckle. Press the axle into place, then install the hub nut. When the shaft begins to turn with the hub, insert a drift through the caliper into one of the cooling slots in the rotor to keep it from turning.

➡️**On some vehicles, the hub flange has a notch in it which can be used to prevent the hub and the shaft from turning, when one of the hub bearing retainer bolts is removed, by placing a longer bolt put in its place through the notch.**

13. Tighten the hub nut to 70–75 ft. lbs. (95–103 Nm) to completely seat the shaft.

14. Install the brake caliper. Tighten the caliper mounting bolts to 30 ft. lbs. (41 Nm).

15. Load the hub assembly by lowering it onto a jackstand. Align the camber cam bolt marks made during removal, install the bolt and tighten to 140 ft. lbs. (190 Nm). Tighten the upper nut to the same value.

16. Install the halfshaft all the way into the transaxle using a suitable tool inserted into the groove provided on the inner retainer. Tap the tool until the shaft seats in the transaxle. Remove the boot seal protector.

17. Connect the brake hose clip the strut. Install the tire and wheel, lower the vehicle and tighten the hub nut to 192 ft. lbs. (260 Nm).

Rear Axle—6000 STE AWD

♦ **See Figure 8**

1. Raise and safely support the vehicle.

2. Remove the tire and wheel assembly.

3. Disconnect the parking brake cable end from the bracket.

4. Remove the bolts securing the brake line and the Electronic Ride Control (ERC) sensor bracket to the control arm. Loosen the anti-lock brake sensor bolt and mover the sensor out of the way.

5. Insert a suitable tool through the caliper into the rotor to prevent the rotor from turning.

6. Remove the shaft nut and washer using special tool J-34826. Discard the shaft nut.

7. Remove the 2 brake caliper bolts and remove the caliper. Support the caliper using a length of wire.

➡️**Do not allow the caliper to hang by the brake hose unsupported.**

8. Remove the rotor from the hub and bearing assembly.

9. Install leaf spring compression tool J-33432 or equivalent.

10. Remove the 3 bolts mounting the hub and bearing to the knuckle.

11. Remove the hub and bearing assembly from the knuckle using special tool J-28733-A or equivalent.

12. Remove the bolts and nut plate attaching the lower strut mount to the knuckle. Scribe the position of the upper bolt prior removing.

13. Install a suitable CV-boot protector to prevent damage to the boot.

14. Swing the knuckle downward and away from the driveshaft.

15. Remove the drive axle from the differential using a suitable slide hammer.

To install:

16. Install the drive axle to the differential. Ensure positive engagement by pulling outward on the inner axle end. Grasp the housing only. Do not grasp and pull on the axle shaft.

17. Swing the knuckle up to the lower strut mount.

18. Position the nut plate and install the lower strut mount bolts to the knuckle. Align the top bolt with scribe marks before tightening the bolts. Tighten the bolts to 148 ft. lbs. (200 Nm).

19. Remove the CV-boot protector.

20. Secure the hub and bearing assembly to the knuckle and axle spline.

21. Install the hub and bearing attaching bolts. Tighten to 61 ft. lbs. (84 Nm).

22. Remove the leaf spring compression tool.

23. Install the rotor to hub and bearing assembly.

24. Install the brake caliper to the rotor and install the retaining bolts. Tighten the bolts to 38 ft. lbs. (51 Nm).

25. Install the anti-lock brake sensor to the knuckle and install the retaining bolt. Using a non-ferrous feeler gauge, adjust the sensor gap to 0.028 in. (0.7mm). Tighten the adjustment screw to 19 inch lbs. (2.2 Nm).

26. Connect the parking brake cable end into the bracket.

27. Install the shaft washer and new torque prevailing nut. Hold the rotor with a suitable to prevent the axle from turning while tightening. Tighten to 192 ft. lbs. (260 Nm).

28. Install the tire and wheel assembly.

29. Check the rear wheel camber. Adjust as necessary.

➡️**If the lower strut to knuckle bolts are properly aligned with the scribe marks, no camber adjustment should be necessary.**

30. Lower the vehicle.

31. Tighten the lug nuts.

OVERHAUL

Outer Joint

♦ **See Figures 9 thru 15**

1. Remove the axle shaft.

2. Cut off the seal retaining clamp. Using a brass drift and a hammer,

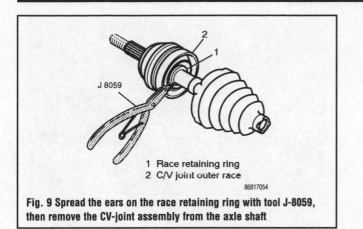

Fig. 9 Spread the ears on the race retaining ring with tool J-8059, then remove the CV-joint assembly from the axle shaft

1 Race retaining ring
2 C/V joint outer race

Fig. 10 Using a brass drift and a hammer, lightly tap on the inner race cage until it has tilted sufficiently to remove one of the balls. Tilt the cage in the opposite direction to remove the opposing ball. Remove the other balls in the same manner

1 Chrome alloy ball
2 C/V joint inner race
3 C/V joint cage
4 C/V joint outer race

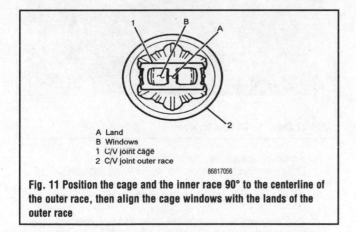

Fig. 11 Position the cage and the inner race 90° to the centerline of the outer race, then align the cage windows with the lands of the outer race

A Land
B Windows
1 C/V joint cage
2 C/V joint outer race

lightly tap the seal retainer from the outside toward the inside of the shaft to remove from the joint.

3. Use a pair of snapring pliers to spread the retaining ring apart. Pull the axle shaft from the joint.

4. Using a brass drift and a hammer, lightly tap on the inner race cage until it has tilted sufficiently to remove one of the balls. Tilt the cage in the opposite direction to remove the opposing ball. Remove the other balls in the same manner.

5. Position the cage and the inner race 90° to the centerline of the outer race, then align the cage windows with the lands of the outer race.

6. Rotate the inner race 90° to the centerline of the cage with the lands of the inner race aligned with the windows of the cage.

7. Pivot the inner race into the cage window and remove the inner race.

8. Clean all parts thoroughly and inspect for wear, make sure all parts are dry.

To install:

9. Assemble the new swage ring on the neck of the seal. DO NOT SWAGE.

10. Slide the swage ring onto the axle shaft, then position the neck of the seal in the seal groove on the axle shaft.

11. For the swage ring, mount the swage clamp tool, J-41048 in a vise and proceed:

a. Position the outboard end of the shaft assembly in the tool.
b. Align the top of the seal neck on the bottom die using the indicator line.
c. Place the top half of the tool on the lower half of the tool.
d. Make sure there are no pinch points on the seal before proceeding. This could cause damage to the seal.
e. Insert the bolts, then tighten by hand until snug.
f. Make sure that the seal, housing and swage ring all remain in alignment.
g. Continue to tighten each of the bolts 180° at a time, alternating until; both of the sides are bottomed.

12. Put a light coat of the grease provided in the rebuilding kit onto the ball grooves of the inner race and outer joint.

13. Hold the inner race 90° centerline of the cage with the lands of the inner race aligned with the windows of the cage and insert the inner race into the cage.

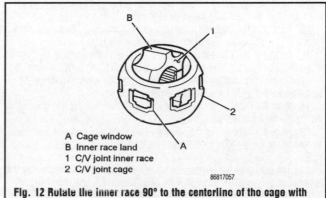

Fig. 12 Rotate the inner race 90° to the centerline of the cage with the lands of the inner race aligned with the windows of the cage

A Cage window
B Inner race land
1 C/V joint inner race
2 C/V joint cage

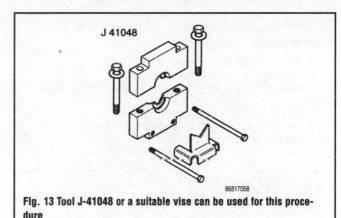

Fig. 13 Tool J-41048 or a suitable vise can be used for this procedure

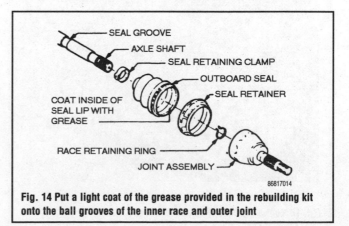

Fig. 14 Put a light coat of the grease provided in the rebuilding kit onto the ball grooves of the inner race and outer joint

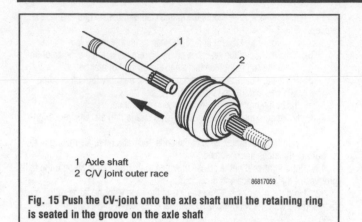

1 Axle shaft
2 C/V joint outer race

86817059

Fig. 15 Push the CV-joint onto the axle shaft until the retaining ring is seated in the groove on the axle shaft

14. Hold the cage and inner race 90° to centerline of the outer race, then align the cage windows with the lands of the outer race.

15. Assemble the cage and inner race into the outer race. Be sure that the retaining ring side of the inner race faces the axle shaft.

16. Insert the first chrome ball, then tilt the cage in the opposite direction to insert the opposing ball. Repeat this process until all of the balls are inserted.

17. Place approximately half of the grease from the service kit inside the seal, then pack the CV-joint with the remaining grease.

18. Push the CV-joint onto the axle shaft until the retaining ring is seated in the groove on the axle shaft.

19. Slide the large end of the seal with the a large seal clamp in place over the outside of the CV-joint race, then locate the seal lip in the groove on the race.

20. The seal must not be dimpled, stretched or out of shape in any way. If it is not in shape, equally pressurize the seal and shape it properly by hand.

21. Crimp the retaining ring clamp with tool J-35910 to 130 ft. lbs. (176 Nm).

22. Check the crimp profile for correct shape and ear gap.

Outer Boot

▶ **See Figures 16, 17 and 18**

1. Raise and support the vehicle safely.
2. Remove the front tire and wheel assembly.
3. Remove the caliper bolts. Remove the caliper and support using a length of wire.
4. Remove the hub nut, washer and wheel bearing.
5. Using a brass drift, lightly tap around the seal retainer to loosen it. Remove the seal retainer.

TCCS7031

Fig. 16 Removing the outer band from the CV-boot

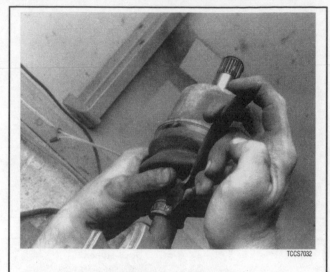

TCCS7032

Fig. 17 Removing the inner band from the CV-boot

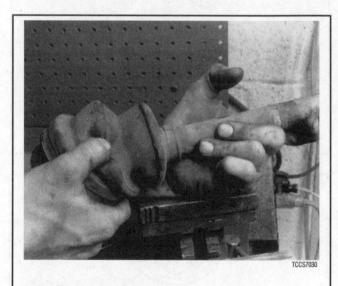

TCCS7030

Fig. 18 Check the CV-boot for wear

6. Remove the seal retaining clamp or ring and discard.
7. Using snapring pliers, remove the race retaining ring from the half-shaft.
8. Pull the outer joint assembly and the outboard seal away from the half-shaft.
9. Flush the grease from the joint and repack with half of the grease provided. Put the remainder of the grease in the seal.

To install:

10. Check the boots for wear.
11. Assemble the inner seal retainer, outboard seal and outer seal retainer to the halfshaft. Push the joint assembly onto the shaft until the retaining ring is seated in the groove.
12. Slide the outboard seal onto the joint assembly and secure using the outer seal retainer. Using seal clamp tool J-35910 or equivalent, tighten the outer clamp to 130 ft. lbs. (176 Nm) and the inner clamp to 100 ft. lbs. (136 Nm).
13. Install the wheel bearing, washer and hub nut. Tighten the hub nut to 192 ft. lbs. (260 Nm).
14. Secure the caliper with the caliper attaching bolts.
15. Install the front tire and wheel assembly.
16. Lower the vehicle.
17. Tighten the lug nuts.

Inner Joint

♦ **See Figures 19, 20, 21, 22 and 23**

1. Remove the axle shaft.

2. For swag ring removal use a hand grinder to cut through the ring.

3. Remove the larger seal retaining ring from the tri-pot joint with a side cutter and dispose.

4. Separate the seal from the trilobal tri-pot bushing at the large diameter, then slide the seal away from the joint along the axle shaft.

5. Remove the housing from the spider and shaft.

6. Spread the spacer ring with tool J-8059, then slide the spacer ring and spider back on the axle shaft.

7. Remove the shaft retaining ring from the groove on the axle shaft and slide the spider assembly off the shaft.

8. Clean the tri-pot balls, needle rollers and housing with clean solvent.

9. Remove the trilobal tri-pot bushing from the housing.

10. Remove the spacer ring and seal from the axle shaft.

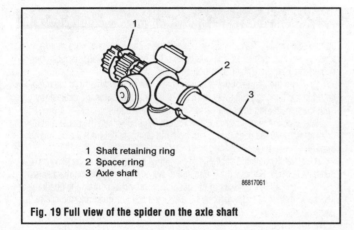

1 Shaft retaining ring
2 Spacer ring
3 Axle shaft

86817061

Fig. 19 Full view of the spider on the axle shaft

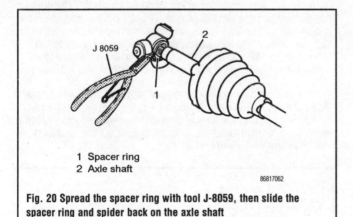

1 Spacer ring
2 Axle shaft

86817062

Fig. 20 Spread the spacer ring with tool J-8059, then slide the spacer ring and spider back on the axle shaft

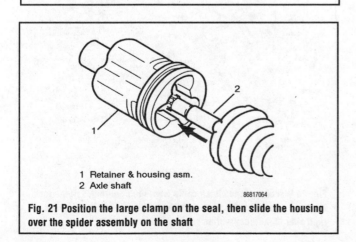

1 Retainer & housing asm.
2 Axle shaft

86817064

Fig. 21 Position the large clamp on the seal, then slide the housing over the spider assembly on the shaft

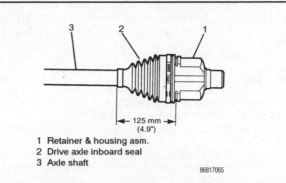

1 Retainer & housing asm.
2 Drive axle inboard seal
3 Axle shaft

125 mm (4.9")

86817065

Fig. 22 Position the joint assembly 4.9 in. (125mm) from the inner boot band

11. Inspect all parts for wear.

To install:

12. Connect the new ring on the neck of the seal. DO NOT SWAGE.

13. Slide the seal on the shaft, then position the neck of the seal in the groove on the axle shaft.

14. For the swag ring, mount the clamp tool in a vise, then proceed:

    a. Position the outboard end of the shaft assembly in the tool.

    b. Align the top of the seal neck on the bottom die using the indicator line.

    c. Place the top half of the tool on the lower half of the tool.

    d. Make sure there are no pinch points on the seal before proceeding. This could cause damage to the seal.

    e. Insert the bolts, then tighten by hand until snug.

    f. Make sure that the seal, housing and swage ring all remain in alignment.

    g. Continue to tighten each of the bolts 180° at a time, alternating until both of the sides are bottomed.

15. Install the spacer ring on the axle shaft and beyond the second groove.

16. Slide the spider assembly against the spacer ring on the shaft.

17. Be sure that the counterbored face of the spider faces the end of the shaft.

18. Install the shaft seating ring in the groove of the axle shaft with tool J-8059.

19. Slide the spider towards the end of the shaft, then reseat the spacer ring in the groove on the shaft.

20. Place approximately half of the grease from the service kit in the seal and use the remaining grease to repack the housing.

21. Install the trilobal tri-pot bushing to the housing.

22. Position the large clamp on the seal, then slide the housing over spider assembly on the shaft.

23. Slide the large diameter of the seal, with the large clamp in place, over the outside of the trilobal tri-pot bushing, then locate the lip of the seal in the groove.

24. Position the joint assembly at the correct distance, as illustrated.

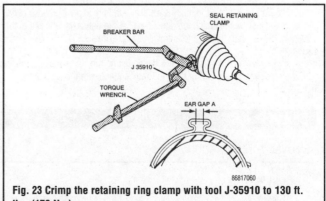

SEAL RETAINING CLAMP
BREAKER BAR
J 35910
TORQUE WRENCH
EAR GAP A

86817060

Fig. 23 Crimp the retaining ring clamp with tool J-35910 to 130 ft. lbs. (176 Nm)

25. The seal must not be dimpled, stretched or out of shape in any way. If it is not in shape, equally pressurize the seal and shape it properly by hand.

26. Crimp the retaining ring clamp with tool J-35910 to 130 ft. lbs. (176 Nm).

27. Check the crimp profile for correct shape and ear gap.

Inner Boot

1. Raise and safely support the vehicle.
2. Remove the front tire and wheel assembly.
3. Unsecure the caliper bolts, then remove the caliper and support it using a length of wire.
4. Remove the hub nut, washer and wheel bearing.
5. Remove the halfshaft. Place in a suitable holding fixture being careful not place undue pressure on the halfshaft.
6. Remove the joint assembly retaining ring. Remove the joint assembly.
7. Remove the race retaining ring and remove the seal retainer.

8. Remove the inner seal retaining clamp. Remove the inner joint seal.

9. Flush the grease from the joint and repack with half of the grease provided. Put the remainder of the grease in the seal.

To install:

10. Assemble the inner seal retainer, outboard seal and outer seal retainer to the halfshaft. Push the joint assembly onto the shaft until the retaining ring is seated in the groove.

11. Slide the outboard seal onto the joint assembly and secure using the outer seal retainer. Using seal clamp tool J-35910 or equivalent, tighten the outer clamp to 130 ft. lbs. (176 Nm) and the inner clamp to 100 ft. lbs. (136 Nm).

12. Insert the halfshaft assembly.

13. Secure the wheel bearing, washer and hub nut. Tighten the hub nut to 192 ft. lbs. (260 Nm).

14. Install the caliper and caliper attaching bolts.

15. Install the front tire and wheel assembly.

16. Lower the vehicle.

CLUTCH

❊❊ CAUTION

The clutch driven disc may contain asbestos, which has been determined to be a cancer causing agent. Never clean clutch surfaces with compressed air! Avoid inhaling any dust from any clutch surface! When cleaning clutch surfaces, use a commercially available brake cleaning fluid.

Adjustments

On 1982–86 models the only service adjustment necessary on the clutch is to maintain the correct pedal free play. Clutch pedal free play, or throwout bearing lash, decreases with driven disc wear. On 1987 and newer models a hydraulic clutch system provides automatic clutch adjustment.

LINKAGE AND PEDAL HEIGHT/FREE-PLAY

1982–86 Models

All cars use a self-adjusting clutch mechanism which may be checked as follows:

As the clutch friction material wears, the cable must be lengthened. This is accomplished by simply pulling the clutch pedal up to its rubber bumper. This action forces the pawl against its stop and rotates it out of mesh with the quadrant teeth, allowing the cable to play out until the quadrant spring load is balanced against the load applied by the release bearing. This adjustment procedure is required every 5,000 miles or less.

1. With engine running and brake on, hold the clutch pedal approximately ½ in. (13mm) from floor mat and move shift lever between first and reverse several times. If this can be done smoothly without clashing into reverse, the clutch is fully releasing. If shift is not smooth, clutch is not fully releasing and linkage should be inspected and corrected as necessary.

2. Check clutch pedal bushings for sticking or excessive wear.

3. Have an assistant sit in the driver's seat and fully apply the clutch pedal to the floor. Observe the clutch fork lever travel at the transaxle. The end of the clutch fork lever should have a total travel of approximately 1.5–1.7 in. (38–43mm).

4. If fork lever is not correct, check the adjusting mechanism by depressing the clutch pedal and looking for pawl to firmly engage with the teeth in the quadrant.

Clutch Pedal

REMOVAL & INSTALLATION

♦ See Figure 24

1. Support the clutch pedal upwards against the bumper stop to release the pawl from the quadrant. Disconnect the clutch cable from the release lever at the

transaxle assembly. Be careful and prevent the cable from snapping rapidly towards the rear of the car. The quadrant in the adjusting mechanism can be damaged by allowing the cable to snap back.

2. From the inside of the car, disconnect the clutch cable from the quadrant. Lift the locking pawl away from the quadrant, then slide the cable away from the pedal along the right hand side of the quadrant.

3. Remove the neutral start switch from the pedal, then the pedal mounting bracket. Remove the pedal pivot nut, bolt and clutch pedal from the mounting bracket.

4. Carefully note the positions of the adjusting mechanism, the pawl and quadrant springs. Remove the E ring and disassemble the adjusting mechanism.

5. Clean all the surfaces of the pedal assembly that contact the quadrant and pawl. If there is tooth damage on either the pawl or quadrant, replace both parts.

To install:

6. Position the quadrant spring into the pocket and assemble the quadrant part-way onto the pedal with the spring tang inserted into the upper hole at the pedal. Rotate the quadrant 90° to wind up the spring and allow the quadrant to stop clear from the side of the pedal. Push the quadrant and pedal together hooking the quadrant stop on front of the pedal. Surfaces of the pedal and quadrant should be in contact with the spring load holding stop and pedal in contact.

7. Position the pawl spring over the pawl ends, then install onto the stud at the top of the pedal. The wide hook end of the spring must be assembled over the front of the pedal as the pawl is pushed onto the pedal stud with the teeth in mesh. The spring must force the pawl teeth into the teeth of the quadrant to prevent the forward rotation of the quadrant.

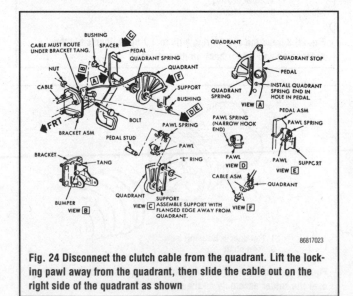

86817023

Fig. 24 Disconnect the clutch cable from the quadrant. Lift the locking pawl away from the quadrant, then slide the cable out on the right side of the quadrant as shown

8. Position the support on the pedal stud and rotate clockwise to engage the narrow hook end of the pawl spring, loading the outer end of the pawl spring until the large hole in the support fits onto the large hub of the pedal groove. Look at the picture view C and E.

9. Lubricate only the inner and outer diameter surfaces of each bushing, then install the bushing and spacer into the pedal assembly.

10. Check the bracket to insure that the bumper is in place on the pedal stop. Position the pedal to the mounting bracket, then install the pivot bolt and nut. Tighten the nut to 35 ft. lbs. (50 Nm) Check the pedal to ensure it swings freely on its pivot bolt.

11. Check the operation of the pawl and quadrant, making sure the pawl disengages from the quadrant when the pedal is pulled to its upper position, and the quadrant rotates freely in both directions.

12. Route the cable end back on the right side between the quadrant and pedal. Lift the pawl and raise the cable into the quadrant groove and connect the cable to the quadrant as in F.

13. Support the pedal upwards against the bumper stop to release the pawl from the quadrant. Attach the other end of the cable to the clutch release lever.

14. Connect the neutral start switch to the pedal and bracket.

15. Check the clutch operation, then adjust by lifting the pedal up to allow the mechanism to adjust the cable length. Depress the pedal slowly several times to set the pawl into mesh with the quadrant teeth.

Clutch Cable

REMOVAL & INSTALLATION

♦ **See Figures 24 and 25**

1. Support the clutch pedal upward against the bumper stop to release the pawl from the quadrant. Disconnect the end of the cable from the clutch release lever at the transaxle. Be careful to prevent the cable from snapping rapidly toward the rear of the car. The quadrant in the adjusting mechanism can be damaged by allowing the cable to snap back.

2. Disconnect the clutch cable from the quadrant. Lift the locking pawl away from the quadrant, then slide the cable out on the right side of the quadrant.

3. From the engine side of the cowl disconnect the two upper nuts holding the cable retainer to the upper studs. Disconnect the cable from the bracket mounted to the transaxle, and remove the cable.

4. Inspect the clutch cable for frayed wires, kinks, worn ends and excessive friction. If any of these conditions exist, replace the cable.

5. Inspect the clutch cable. Replace the cable if any of the conditions are found, frayed wires, kinked cable, worn end and excessive cable friction.

To install:

6. With the gasket in position on the two upper studs, position a new cable with the retaining flange against the bracket.

7. Attach the end of the cable to the quadrant, being sure to route the cable underneath the pawl.

8. Attach the two upper nuts to the retainer mounting studs, and tighten to specifications.

9. Attach the cable to the bracket mounted to the transaxle.

10. Support the clutch pedal upward against the bumper stop to release the pawl from the quadrant. Attach the outer end of the cable to the clutch release lever. Be sure not to yank on the cable, since overloading the cable could damage the quadrant.

11. Check clutch operation and adjust by lifting the clutch pedal up to allow the mechanism to adjust the cable length. Depress the pedal slowly several times to set the pawl into mesh with the quadrant teeth.

Driven Disc and Pressure Plate

REMOVAL & INSTALLATION

♦ **See Figures 26 thru 37**

1. On 1987 and newer models, disconnect the negative battery cable, remove the hush panel from inside the vehicle, then disconnect the clutch master cylinder pushrod from the clutch pedal.

2. Remove the transaxle.

3. Mark the pressure plate assembly and the flywheel so that they can be assembled in the same position. They were balanced as an assembly at the factory.

4. Loosen the attaching bolts one turn at a time until spring tension is relieved.

5. Support the pressure plate and remove the bolts. Remove the pressure plate and clutch disc. Do not disassemble the pressure plate assembly, replace it if defective.

6. Inspect the flywheel, clutch disc, pressure plate, throwout bearing and the clutch fork and pivot shaft assembly for wear. Replace the parts as required. If the flywheel shows any signs of overheating, or if it is badly grooved or scored, it should be replaced.

To install:

7. Clean the pressure plate and flywheel mating surfaces thoroughly. Position the clutch disc and pressure plate into the installed position, and support with a dummy shaft or clutch aligning tool. The clutch plate is assembled with the damper springs offset toward the transaxle. One side of the factory supplied clutch disc is stamped "Flywheel side" on some vehicles.

8. Install the pressure plate-to-flywheel bolts. Tighten them gradually in a crisscross pattern.

9. Lubricate the outside groove and the inside recess of the release bearing with high temperature grease. Wipe off any excess. Install the release bearing.

10. Install the transaxle.

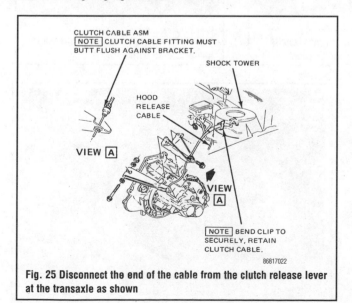

Fig. 25 Disconnect the end of the cable from the clutch release lever at the transaxle as shown

Fig. 26 View of the clutch and pressure plate assembly

Fig. 27 Removing the clutch and pressure plate bolts

Fig. 28 Removing the clutch and pressure plate assembly

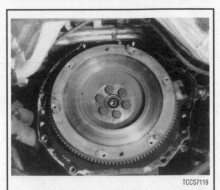

Fig. 29 View of the flywheel once the clutch assembly is removed

Fig. 30 Be sure that the flywheel surface is clean, before installing the clutch

Fig. 31 Check across the flywheel surface; it should be flat

Fig. 32 Checking the pressure plate for excessive wear

Fig. 33 Apply locking agent to clutch assembly bolts

Fig. 34 Install the clutch assembly bolts and tighten in steps, in an X pattern

Fig. 35 Be sure to use a torque wrench to tighten all the bolts

Fig. 36 Grease the throwout bearing assembly at the outer contact points

Fig. 37 Grease the throwout bearing assembly at the inner contact points

11. On 1987 and newer models connect the clutch master cylinder pushrod to the clutch pedal and install the retaining clip.

12. On 1987 and newer models, if equipped with cruise control, check the switch adjustment at the clutch pedal bracket.

13. Attach the clutch cable on older vehicles at the transaxle and clutch release lever.

➡ **When adjusting the cruise control switch, do not exert an upward force on the clutch pedal pad of more than 20 lbs. (9 kg) or damage to the master cylinder pushrod retaining ring may result.**

14. On 1987 and newer models, install the hush panel and reconnect the negative battery cable.

15. Check the clutch operation. Adjust and add fluid as necessary.

Clutch Master and Slave Cylinder

➡ **The clutch hydraulic system is removed and serviced as a complete assembly.**

REMOVAL & INSTALLATION

◆ **See Figure 38**

1. Disconnect the negative battery cable.
2. Remove the hush panel from inside the vehicle.
3. Remove the clutch master cylinder retaining nuts at the front of the dash.
4. Remove the slave cylinder retaining nuts at the transaxle.
5. Remove the hydraulic system as a unit from the vehicle.

To install:

6. Install the slave cylinder to the transaxle support bracket aligning the pushrod into the pocket on the clutch fork outer lever. Tighten the retaining nuts evenly to prevent damage to the slave cylinder. Tighten the nuts to 40 ft. lbs. (54 Nm).

➡ **Do not remove the plastic pushrod retainer from the slave cylinder. The straps will break on the first clutch pedal application.**

7. Position the clutch master cylinder to the front of the dash. Tighten the nuts evenly to 20 ft. lbs. (27 Nm).

8. Remove the pedal restrictor from the pushrod. Lube the pushrod bushing on the clutch pedal. Connect the pushrod to the clutch pedal and install the retaining clip.

9. If equipped with cruise control, check the switch adjustment at the clutch pedal bracket.

➡ **When adjusting the cruise control switch, do not exert an upward force on the clutch pedal pad of more than 20 lbs. or damage to the master cylinder pushrod retaining ring may result.**

10. Install the hush panel.

11. Press the clutch pedal down several times. This will break the plastic retaining straps on the slave cylinder pushrod. Do not remove the plastic button on the end of the pushrod.

12. Connect the negative battery cable.

OVERHAUL

This is a tedious, time consuming job. You can save yourself a lot of trouble by buying a rebuilt master cylinder from your dealer or parts supply house. The small difference in price between a rebuilding kit and a rebuilt part usually makes it more economical, in terms of time and work, to buy the rebuilt part.

1. Remove the master cylinder.
2. Remove the reservoir cover and drain the fluid.
3. Remove the pushrod and the rubber boot on non-power models.
4. Unbolt the proportioners and the failure warning switch from the side of the master cylinder body. Discard the O-rings found under the proportioners. Use new ones on installation. There may or may not be an O-ring under the original equipment failure warning switch. If there is, discard it. In either case, use a new O-ring upon assembly.
5. Clamp the master cylinder body in a vise, taking care not to crush it. Depress the primary piston with a wooden dowel and remove the lock ring with a pair of snapring pliers.
6. The primary and secondary pistons can be removed by applying compressed air into one of the outlets at the end of the cylinder and plugging the other three outlets. The primary piston must be replaced as an assembly if the seals are bad. The secondary piston seals are replaceable. Install these new seals with the lips facing outwards.
7. Inspect the bore for corrosion. If any corrosion is evident, the master cylinder body must be replaced. Do not attempt to polish the bore with crocus cloth, sandpaper or anything else. The body is aluminum, polishing the bore won't work.
8. To remove the failure warning switch piston assembly, remove the Allen head plug from the end of the bore and withdraw the assembly with a pair of needlenose pliers. The switch piston assembly seals are replaceable.
9. The reservoir can be removed from the master cylinder if necessary. Clamp the body in a vise by its mounting flange. Use a pry bar to remove the reservoir. If the reservoir is removed, remove the reservoir grommets and discard them. The quick take-up valves under the grommets are accessible after the retaining snaprings are removed. Use snapring pliers, no other tool will work.

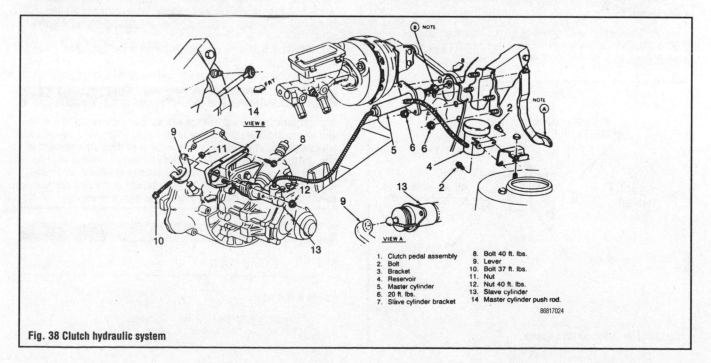

1. Clutch pedal assembly	8. Bolt 40 ft. lbs.
2. Bolt	9. Lever
3. Bracket	10. Bolt 37 ft. lbs.
4. Reservoir	11. Nut
5. Master cylinder	12. Nut 40 ft. lbs.
6. 20 ft. lbs.	13. Slave cylinder
7. Slave cylinder bracket	14. Master cylinder push rod.

86817024

Fig. 38 Clutch hydraulic system

10. Clean all parts in denatured alcohol and allow to air dry. Do not use anything else to clean and do not wipe dry with a rag, which will leaves bits of lint behind. Inspect all parts for corrosion or wear. Generally, it is best to replace all rubber parts whenever the master cylinder is disassembled and replace any metal part which shows any sign of wear or corrosion.

11. Lubricate all parts with fresh brake fluid before assembly.

12. Install the quick take-up valves into the master cylinder body and secure with the snaprings. Make sure the snaprings are properly seated in their grooves. Lubricate the new reservoir grommets with fresh brake fluid and press them into the master cylinder.

13. Install the reservoir into the grommets by placing the reservoir on its lid and pressing the master cylinder body down onto it with a rocking motion.

14. Lubricate the switch piston assembly. Install new O-rings and retainers on the piston. Install the piston assembly into the master cylinder and secure with the plug, using a new O-ring on the plug. Tighten to 40–140 inch lbs. (5–16 Nm).

15. Assemble the new secondary piston seals onto the piston. Lubricate the parts, then install the spring, spring retainer and secondary piston into the cylinder. Install the primary piston, depress and install the lock ring.

16. Install new O-rings on the proportioners and the failure warning switch. Install the proportioners and tighten to 18–30 ft. lbs. (25–40 Nm). Install the failure warning switch and tighten to 15–50 inch lbs. (2–6 Nm).

17. Clamp the master cylinder body upright into a vise by one of the mounting flanges. Fill the reservoir with fresh fluid. Pump the piston with a dowel until fluid squirts from the outlet ports. Continue pumping until the expelled fluid is free of air bubbles.

18. Install the master cylinder and bleed the clutch. Check the clutch system for proper operation.

AUTOMATIC TRANSAXLE

Identification

All automatic transaxles have a metal identification nameplate attached to the case exterior. The information on the nameplate will help in the servicing and determination of replacement parts when ordered through your dealer or local parts house.

Adjustments

THROTTLE VALVE (TV) CABLE

▶ **See Figure 39**

1. Check to see that the cable is in the full non-adjustment position.
2. Without twisting or kinking the cable, insert the cable slug into the idler pulley (cam) slot.

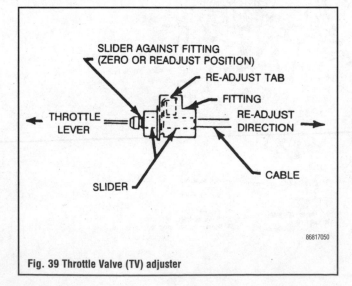

Fig. 39 Throttle Valve (TV) adjuster

SLIDER AGAINST FITTING
(ZERO OR READJUST POSITION)
RE-ADJUST TAB
FITTING
THROTTLE LEVER
RE-ADJUST DIRECTION
SLIDER
CABLE

86817050

HYDRAULIC SYSTEM BLEEDING

Bleeding air from the system is necessary any time part of the system has been disconnected, or the fluid level in the reservoir has been allowed to fall so low that air has been drawn into the master cylinder.

✳✳ WARNING

Never under any circumstance use fluid that has been bled from the system as it could be contaminated with air or moisture.

1. Clean the cap then remove the cap and diaphragm and fill the reservoir to the top with certified DOT 3 brake fluid.
2. Fully loosen the bleed screw which is in the slave cylinder body next to the inlet connection. Fluid will now begin to move from the master cylinder down the tube to the slave. It is important that for efficient gravity fill, the reservoir must be filled at all times.
3. At this point bubbles will be noticeable at the bleed screw outlet showing air is being expelled. When the slave is full, a steady stream of fluid will come from the slave outlet. At this point, tighten the bleed screw to 18 inch lbs. (2 Nm).
4. Install the diaphragm and cap to the reservoir. The fluid in the reservoir should be level with the step.
5. The hydraulic system should now be fully bled and should release the clutch. Check the vehicle by starting, then push the clutch pedal to the floor and selecting reverse gear. There should be no grinding of gears, if there is, the hydraulic system still contains air. If so, bleed the system again.

3. The accelerator cable must be installed before adjustment.
4. Rotate the idler pulley (cam) in a counter clockwise direction to 65 inch lbs. (7.3 Nm).
5. Check that the cable is moving freely. The cable may appear to function properly with the engine stopped or cold. Recheck after the engine is hot.
6. Road test the vehicle.

SHIFT LINKAGE

1. On some models you will need to lift up the locking button.
2. Place the shift lever into Neutral.
3. Disconnect the shift cable from the transaxle lever. Place the transaxle lever in Neutral, by moving the lever clockwise to the Low (L) detent, then counterclockwise through the Second (S) and Drive (D) detents to the Neutral detent.
4. Attach and tighten the shift cable to the pin on the transaxle lever. Check the shift operation.
5. On some models you will need to push down on the locking button.

✳✳ CAUTION

Any inaccuracies in shift linkage adjustments may result in premature failure of the transaxle due to operation without the controls in full detent. Such operation results in reduced fluid pressure and in turn, partial engagement of the affected clutches. Partial engagement of the clutches, with sufficient pressure to permit apparently normal vehicle operation will result in failure of the clutches and/or other internal parts after only a few miles of operation.

Neutral Safety/Back-Up Light Switch

REMOVAL & INSTALLATION

Shifter Mounted

1. Apply the parking brake and block the wheels.
2. Place the vehicle in the neutral position.

3. Remove the shifter knob from the shifter by removing the retaining screw at the back of the knob.

4. Remove the screws at the sides and front of the console.

5. Open the console box and remove the retaining screw inside the box.

6. Remove the ashtray at the rear of the console and remove the retaining screw behind the ashtray.

7. Slide the console rearward slightly, then lift it over the shifter.

8. Disconnect the wiring harness at the back-up light switch.

9. Remove the switch from the base of the shifter.

10. Reverse to install the switch.

11. Adjust if needed, unblock the wheels.

Transaxle Mounted

▶ **See Figure 40**

1. Apply the parking brake and block the wheels.

2. Place the vehicle in the neutral position.

3. Remove the shifter linkage

4. Disconnect the electrical harness to the switch.

5. Unfasten the switch, then lower from the vehicle.

To install:

6. Place the shift shaft in Neutral.

7. Align the flats of the shift shaft to flats in the switch.

8. Install the switch assembly.

➡ **If the bolt holes do not align with the mounting boss on the transaxle, verify the sift shaft DO NOT ROTATE THE SWITCH. The switch is pinned in the neutral position. If the switch has been rotated and the pin broken or when using an old switch, adjust it.**

9. Tighten the switch screw to 18 ft. lbs. (25 Nm).

10. Remove the gauge pin.

11. Attach the electrical connection, then connect the shifter linkage.

ADJUSTMENT

1. Place the transaxle control shifter in the neutral notch on the detent plate.

2. Loosen the switch attaching screws.

3. Rotate the switch on the shifter assembly to align the service adjustment hole with the carrier tang hole.

4. Insert a 3/32 in. (2.34mm) maximum diameter gauge pin to a depth of 5/8 in. (15mm).

5. Tighten the attaching screws.

6. Remove the gauge pin.

Automatic Transaxle Assembly

REMOVAL & INSTALLATION

✷✷ WARNING

Do not use air powered tools to dissemble or assemble a transaxle. Such tools will negate the diagnostic value of precision torquing, and improper bolt tightness can contribute to transaxle problems.

THM 125C

➡**Around September 1, 1991, the manufacturer changed the name of its THM 125C automatic transaxle to Hydra-Matic 3T40. However, 1989 and 1990 served as transitional years during which both names were in effect.**

1. Disconnect the negative battery cable from the transaxle. Tape the wire to the upper radiator hose to keep it out of the way.

2. Remove the air cleaner and disconnect the detent cable. Slide the detent cable in the opposite direction of the cable to remove it from the carburetor.

3. Unbolt the detent cable attaching bracket at the transaxle.

4. Pull up on the detent cable cover at the transaxle until the cable is exposed. Disconnect the cable from the rod.

5. Detach the electrical connectors at the neutral safety switch, Torque Converter Clutch (TCC) and Vehicle Speed Sensor (VSS).

6. Remove the two transaxle strut bracket bolts at the transaxle, if equipped.

7. Remove all the engine-to-transaxle bolts except the one near the starter. The one nearest the firewall is installed from the engine side; you will need a short handled box wrench or ratchet to reach it.

8. Loosen, but do not remove the engine-to-transaxle bolt near the starter.

9. Disconnect the speedometer cable at the upper and lower coupling. On cars with cruise control, remove the speedometer cable at the transducer.

10. Remove the retaining clip and washer from the shift linkage at the transaxle. Remove the two shift linkage at the transaxle. Remove the two shift linkage bracket bolts.

11. Disconnect and plug the two fluid cooler lines at the transaxle. These are inch-size fittings; use a back-up wrench to avoid twisting the lines.

12. Install an engine holding chain or hoist. Raise the engine enough to take its weight off the mounts.

13. Unlock the steering column and raise the car.

14. Remove the two nuts holding the anti-sway (stabilizer) bar to the left lower control arm (driver's side).

15. Remove the four bolts attaching the covering plate over the stabilizer bar to the engine cradle on the left side (driver's side).

16. Loosen but do not remove the four bolts holding the stabilizer bar bracket to the right side (passenger's side) of the engine cradle. Pull the bar down on the driver's side.

17. Disconnect the front and rear transaxle mounts at the engine cradle.

18. Remove the two rear center crossmember bolts.

19. Remove the three right (passenger) side front engine cradle attaching bolts. The nuts are accessible under the splash shield next to the frame rail.

20. Remove the top bolt from the lower front transaxle shock absorber, if equipped (V6 engine only).

21. Remove the left (driver) side front and rear cradle-to-body bolts.

22. Remove the left front wheel. Attach an axle shaft removing tool (GM part no. J-28468 or the equivalent) to a slide hammer. Place the tool behind the axle shaft cones and pull the cones out away from the transaxle. Remove the right shaft in the same manner. Set the shafts out of the way. Plug the openings in the transaxle to prevent fluid leakage and the entry of dirt.

23. Swing the partial engine cradle to the left (driver) side and wire it out of the way outboard of the fender well.

24. Remove the four torque converter and starter shield bolts. Remove the two transaxle extension bolts from the engine-to-transaxle bracket.

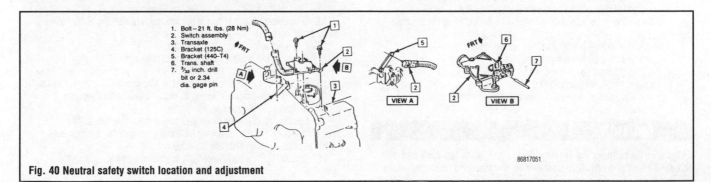

1. Bolt – 21 ft. lbs. (28 Nm)
2. Switch assembly
3. Transaxle
4. Bracket (125C)
5. Bracket (440-T4)
6. Trans. shaft
7. 3/32 inch. drill bit or 2.34 dia. gage pin

VIEW A   VIEW B

86817051

Fig. 40 Neutral safety switch location and adjustment

25. Attach a transaxle jack to the case.
26. Use a felt pen to matchmark the torque converter and flywheel. Remove the three torque converter-to-flywheel bolts.
27. Remove the transaxle-to-engine bolt near the starter. Remove the transaxle by sliding it to the left, away from the engine.

To install:

28. Place the transaxle on a jack and raise it into the vehicle. As the transaxle is installed, slide the right axle shaft into the case.
29. Align the matchmarks and connect the torque converter to the flywheel. Install the transaxle-to-engine bolt near the starter.
30. Install the engine-to-transaxle bracket extension bolts. Install the torque converter and starter shield bolts.
31. Install the partial engine cradle.
32. Install the left axle shaft.
33. Install the drivers side front and rear cradle to body bolts.
34. Install the top bolt to the lower front transaxle shock absorber, if equipped (V6 engine only).
35. Install the three right (passenger) side front engine cradle attaching bolts.
36. Install the two rear center crossmember bolts.
37. Connect the front and rear transaxle mounts at the engine cradle.
38. Install the stabilizer bar. Tighten the four bolts holding the stabilizer bar bracket to the right side (passenger's side) of the engine cradle.

➡ **To aid in stabilizer bar installation, a pry hole has been provided in the engine cradle.**

39. Install the four bolts attaching the covering plate over the stabilizer bar to the engine cradle on the left side (driver's side).
40. Install the two nuts holding the anti-sway (stabilizer) bar to the left lower control arm (driver's side).
41. Lower the vehicle and remove the engine support device.
42. Connect the two fluid cooler lines at the transaxle.
43. Install the two shift linkage bracket bolts.
44. Connect the two shift linkages at the transaxle and install the retaining clips and washers.
45. Connect the speedometer cable at the upper and lower coupling. On cars with cruise control, connect the speedometer cable at the transducer.
46. Tighten the engine-to-transaxle bolt near the starter.
47. Install all remaining engine-to-transaxle bolts. The one nearest the firewall is installed from the engine side, you will need a short handled box wrench or ratchet to reach it.
48. Install the two transaxle strut bracket bolts at the transaxle, if equipped.
49. Install the detent cable and air cleaner.
50. Connect the negative battery cable to the transaxle.
51. Fill the transaxle with fresh DEXRON III, then test drive.

Hydra-Matic 3T40

➡ **Around September 1, 1991, the manufacturer changed the name of its THM 125C automatic transaxle to Hydra-Matic 3T40. However, 1989 and 1990 served as transitional years during which both names were in effect.**

1. Remove the air cleaner assembly from the vehicle.
2. Disconnect the shift cable from the lever and bracket at the transaxle.
3. Detach the TV cable at the transaxle and throttle bracket.
4. Detach the electrical connections at the neutral safety switch, Torque Converter Clutch (TCC), and Vehicle Speed Sensor (VSS).
5. Remove the upper transaxle-to-engine bolts, including the electrical grounds.
6. Install tool J-28467-A the engine support fixture.
7. Raise and support the vehicle safely.
8. Remove the left front tire and wheel assembly.
9. Remove the left engine splash shield.
10. Raise and support the vehicle, remove the left splash shield.
11. Remove the left lower pinch bolt.

✳✳ CAUTION

Failure to disconnect the intermediate shaft from the rack and pinion stub shaft can result in damage to the steering gear and or the

intermediate shaft. This damage can cause loss of steering control, which could result in personal injury.

12. Unsecure and remove the intermediate shaft-to-steering stub shaft retaining bolt.
13. Remove the stabilizer shaft bracket nuts and brackets from the left control arm.
14. Unfasten and remove the left and right stabilizer reinforcement bolts and reinforcement to frame.
15. Remove the center punch 2 spot welds at the frame crossmember near the left stabilizer bar-to-frame mount. Drill out the spot welds enough to separate the frame and crossmember.
16. Remove the left steering gear to frame bolt, then detach the left-to-right frame section retaining bolts.
17. Support the frame on jackstands, remove the left frame-to-body bolts.
18. Unfasten the transaxle mount nuts from the frame.
19. Remove the jackstand and frame assembly.
20. Disconnect and remove the starter and converter shield screws and the shield.
21. Unbolt there three flywheel-to-converter bolts.
22. Remove the transaxle oil cooler lines.
23. Detach the transaxle support bracket-to-transaxle bolt.
24. Attach the transaxle jack to the transaxle case.
25. Remove the left drive axle from the transaxle, then remove the remaining transaxle bolts.
26. Lower the transaxle with an assistant, including the right drive axle from the unit.
27. Clean and flush the cooler lines with J-35944-A or an equivalent whenever the transaxle has been removed.
28. Install the transaxle with the help of an assistant, make sure the case is fully engaged on both locating dowels.
29. Reverse to install. Tighten the flywheel bolts to 47 ft. lbs. (63 Nm), the converter cover screws to 89 inch lbs. (10 Nm).
30. Fill the transaxle with fresh DEXRON III, then test drive.

Hydra-Matic 440-T4

➡ **Around September 1, 1991, the manufacturer changed the name of its Hydra-Matic 440-T4 automatic transaxle to Hydra-Matic 4T60-E. However, 1989 and 1990 served as transitional years during which both names were in effect.**

1. Disconnect the negative battery cable.
2. Remove the air cleaner and disconnect the TV cable at the throttle body.
3. Disconnect the shift linkage at the transaxle.
4. Remove the engine support fixture tool J-28467 or equivalent.
5. Unfasten all electrical connectors.
6. Remove the 3 bolts from the transaxle to the engine.
7. Disconnect the vacuum line at the modulator.
8. Raise and safely support the vehicle.
9. Remove the left front wheel and tire assembly.
10. Detach the left side ball joint from the steering knuckle.
11. Disconnect the brake line bracket at the strut.

➡ **A halfshaft seal protector tool J-34754 should be modified and installed on any halfshaft prior to service procedures on or near the halfshaft. Failure to do so could result in seal damage or joint failure.**

12. Remove the halfshafts from the transaxle.
13. Disconnect the pinch bolt at the intermediate steering shaft. Failure to do so could cause damage to the steering gear.
14. Remove the frame to stabilizer bolts.
15. Unsecure the stabilizer bolts at the control arm.
16. Remove the left front frame assembly.
17. Disconnect the speedometer cable or wire connector from the transaxle.
18. Detach the extension housing to engine block support bracket.
19. Disconnect the cooler pipes.
20. Remove the converter cover and converter-to-flywheel bolts.
21. Remove all of the remaining transaxle-to-engine bolts except one.
22. Position a jack under the transaxle.
23. Remove the remaining transaxle-to-engine bolt and remove the transaxle.

To install:

24. Install the transaxle in the vehicle. Install the engine-to-transaxle bolt accessible from under the vehicle. Tighten to 55 ft. lbs. (75 Nm).
25. Insert all of the remaining transaxle-to-engine bolts. Tighten to 55 ft. lbs. (75 Nm).
26. Remove the jack.
27. Install the converter-to-flywheel bolts and the converter cover.
28. Connect the cooler pipes.
29. Install the extension housing to engine block support bracket.
30. Connect the speedometer cable or wire connector to the transaxle.
31. Install the left front frame assembly.
32. Attach the stabilizer bolts at the control arm.
33. Install the frame-to-stabilizer bolts.
34. Connect the pinch bolt at the intermediate steering shaft.
35. Install the halfshafts to the transaxle.
36. Connect the brake line bracket at the strut.
37. Install the left side ball joint to the steering knuckle.
38. Install the left front wheel and tire assembly.
39. Lower the vehicle.
40. Connect the vacuum line at the modulator.
41. Install the 3 bolts from the transaxle to the engine.
42. Connect all electrical connectors.
43. Remove the engine support tool.
44. Attach the shift linkage to the transaxle.
45. Connect the TV cable at the throttle body and adjust as necessary. Install the air cleaner.
46. Connect the negative battery cable.
47. Fill the transaxle with fresh DEXRON III, test drive.

Hydra-Matic 4T60-E

➡ **Around September 1, 1991, the manufacturer changed the name of its Hydra-Matic 440-T4 automatic transaxle to Hydra-Matic 4T60-E. However, 1989 and 1990 served as transitional years during which both names were in effect.**

1. Remove the air cleaner assembly.
2. Remove the engine torque strut from the engine.
3. Disconnect the shift control cable bracket from the transaxle case.
4. Detach the Torque Converter Clutch (TCC) electrical connection from the unit.
5. Remove the vacuum hose form the modulator.
6. Unbolt the upper transaxle including grounds.
7. Install tool J-28467-A engine support.
8. Remove the engine splash shields.
9. Remove both front tires and wheels
10. Remove the pinch bolts from the control arms.
11. Unbolt the stabilizer shaft bolts and the reinforcement plates from the frame.

12. Unfasten the stabilizer shaft nuts and bracket from the control arm.
13. Using a 7/16 in. drill bit, drill through the two spot welds located between the front and rear holes of the left front stabilizer shaft mounting.
14. Remove the front and rear transaxle mounting nuts.
15. Disconnect the power steering cooler line bolts.
16. Disconnect the electrical harness from the frame.
17. Detach the right frame-to-left frame retaining bolt, then position a jackstand under the frame for support.
18. Loosen the two frame bolts from the frame.
19. Remove the left frame assembly with help from an assistant.
20. Unfasten the right lower ball joint from the knuckle, then remove the bolts from the transaxle support bracket.
21. Disconnect the power steering cooler line support from the transaxle.
22. Remove the transaxle converter cover.
23. Remove the starter assembly from the engine, then remove the torque converter bolts.
24. Unsecure the transaxle mount bolts from the case, then remove the mount.
25. Disconnect the neutral safety switch connection.
26. Slide both drive axles from the vehicle.
27. Remove the Vehicle Speed Sensor (VSS) connection from the transaxle.
28. Install a transaxle jack.
29. Remove the oil cooler lines and plug the openings.
30. Remove the remaining bolts at the transaxle, then with help from an assistant, lower the transaxle.
31. Clean and flush the cooler lines with J-35944-A or an equivalent. This should be done whenever the transaxle has been removed.
32. Install the transaxle with the help of an assistant.
33. Reverse to install, tightening the transaxle mounting bolts-to-case 41 ft. lbs. (55 Nm), converter bolts 47 ft. lbs. (63 Nm), converter cover bolts 89 inch lbs. (10 Nm), transaxle support bracket and bolts-to-transaxle 32 ft. lbs. (43 Nm), left/right frame-to-body bolts 40 ft. lbs. (54 Nm), and transaxle rear mount-to-frame bolts 24 ft. lbs. (33 Nm).
34. Fill the transaxle with fresh DEXRON III, then test drive.

Halfshafts

REMOVAL & INSTALLATION

Refer to the Halfshaft removal and installation procedure in the Manual Transaxle portion of this section.

OVERHAUL

Refer to the Halfshaft overhaul procedure in the Manual Transaxle portion of this section.

DRIVELINE

Replacement of the driveshaft on the Pontiac 6000 AWD is covered in detail under the Automatic Transaxle Driveshaft removal and installation procedure.

Driveshaft and U-Joint

REMOVAL & INSTALLATION

Original Driveshaft

▶ **See Figure 41**

1. Raise and safely support the vehicle.

➡ **The relationship between the center bearing support and the floor pan must be maintained. Established at the assembly plant, the relationship has an influence on the front joint stoke capacity and remains constant for the vehicle, regardless of the driveshaft installed.**

2. Scribe the transaxle output shaft flange opposite the "painted" marking on the front driveshaft. The rear pinion flange must be scribed opposite the "painted" marking on the rear driveshaft. Scribe the center support mounting plate to floor pan of the vehicle.

3. Remove the 4 bolts connecting the rear driveshaft to the rear axle pinion flange. Be sure to support the rear of the rear driveshaft while removing the remainder of the driveshaft.

➡ **Do not loosen, remove or disconnect the 4 bolts adjacent to the center double cardan joint. Disturbing these fasteners may result in a vibration.**

4. With the aid of an assistant, support the driveshaft while performing the following:
   a. Remove the 3 nuts retaining the center bearing support to the underbody of the vehicle.
   b. Remove the 4 bolts connecting the front driveshaft to the transaxle output shaft flange.
   c. Remove the driveshaft from the vehicle.

To install:

5. With the aid of an assistant, perform the following:
   a. Install the driveshaft to the vehicle.

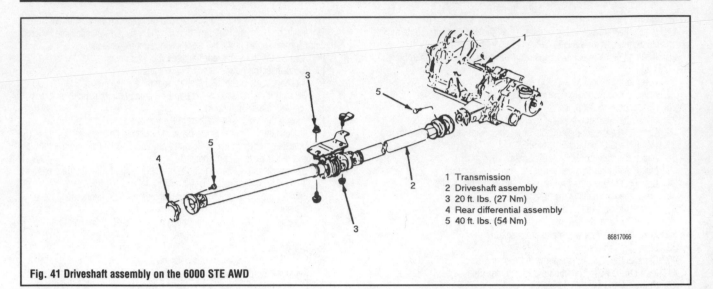

1 Transmission
2 Driveshaft assembly
3 20 ft. lbs. (27 Nm)
4 Rear differential assembly
5 40 ft. lbs. (54 Nm)

86817066

Fig. 41 Driveshaft assembly on the 6000 STE AWD

b. Align the rear driveshaft flange to the rear axle pinion flange, aligning the scribe marks.

c. Loosely install the nuts to the center bearing support and bolts to the rear axle pinion flange. Tighten the rear driveshaft flange to the rear axle pinion flange bolts to 40 ft. lbs. (54 Nm).

d. Install the bolts to the front driveshaft-to-transaxle output flange, using the reference marks to align the front flange position and center bracket location. Tighten the center bearing support bolts using the scribed reference marks to 25 ft. lbs. (34 Nm); nuts to 20 ft. lbs. (27 Nm). Tighten the front propeller shaft-to-transaxle output flange bolts to 40 ft. lbs. (54 Nm).

➡The center mount plate must be reinstalled at the scribed position so that the front CV-joint is correctly located within its travel limits.

6. Remove the support and lower the vehicle.
7. Road test the vehicle.

New Driveshaft

1. Remove the original driveshaft from the vehicle.
To install:
2. Using a dial indicator, measure and mark the bolt hole corresponding to the high point of radial run-out on both the transaxle output flange and rear axle pinion flange.
3. Transfer the center bearing bracket from the old driveshaft to the new driveshaft assembly.
4. With the aid of an assistant, perform the following:
a. Install the driveshaft to the vehicle.
b. Align the point marks supplied on the flanges of the propeller shaft to the scribe marks made during removal.
c. Loosely install the nuts to the center bearing support and bolts to the rear axle pinion flange. Tighten the rear driveshaft flange to the rear axle pinion flange bolts to 40 ft. lbs. (54 Nm).
d. Push the propeller shaft forward until a click is heard. Temporarily install a 0.9 in. (23mm) thick spacer between the output flange and the front driveshaft flange. Clamp in this position.
5. Install the remaining center bracket nuts. Tighten to 20 ft. lbs. (27 Nm).
6. Remove the spacer, extend the front CV-joint to meet the output flange and tighten the bolts. Tighten the front propeller shaft-to-transaxle output flange bolts to 40 ft. lbs. (54 Nm).
7. Verify correct location of the front CV-joint plunge.
8. Remove the supports. Lower the vehicle.

U-JOINT REPLACEMENT

♦ **See Figure 42**

A universal joint is two Y-shaped yokes connected by a crossmember called a spider. The spider is shaped like a cross having arms of equal length called trunnions. These U-joints are designed to handle the effects of various loadings

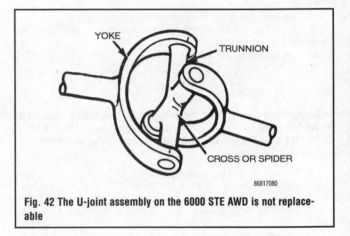

86817080

Fig. 42 The U-joint assembly on the 6000 STE AWD is not replaceable

and the rear axle windup during acceleration. Unfortunately these U-joints are not replaceable in the driveshaft unit. If you have any U-joint problems, the driveshaft unit must be replaced.

CENTER BEARING

♦ **See Figure 43**

A center support bearing is used to support the driveline at the connection of the driveshafts. The center bearing is a ball-type bearing mounted in a rubber cushion that is attached to the under body of the vehicle. The bearing is pre-lubricated and is sealed during manufacture.

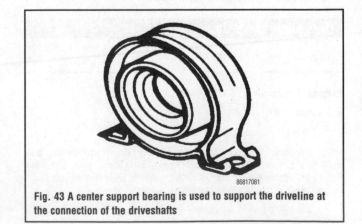

86817081

Fig. 43 A center support bearing is used to support the driveline at the connection of the driveshafts

REAR AXLE

Hub and Bearing Assembly

REMOVAL & INSTALLATION

6000 STE AWD

▶ **See Figure 44**

1. Raise and support the car on a hoist.
2. Remove the wheel.
3. Remove the brake caliper assembly and suspend on a wire.

✳✳ CAUTION

Do not hammer on the caliper, as damage to the bearing could result.

4. Remove the hub and bearing assembly to rear axle attaching bolts and remove the hub and bearing assembly.

➡**The bolts which attach the hub and bearing assembly also support the brake assembly. When removing these bolts, support the brake assembly with a wire or other means. Do not let the brake line support the brake assembly.**

To install:

5. Install the hub and bearing assembly to the rear axle, then tighten the hub and bearing bolts to 61 ft. lbs. (83 Nm).
6. Install the brake caliper.
7. Install the tire and wheel assembly, then lower the car.
8. Tighten the lug nuts.

Axle Assembly

REMOVAL & INSTALLATION

6000 STE AWD

1. Open the rear decklid.
2. Raise and safely support the vehicle.

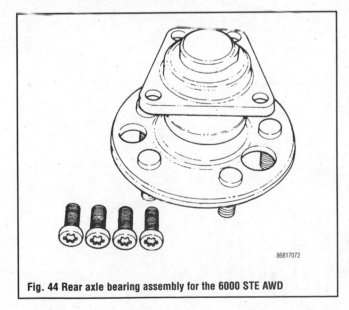

Fig. 44 Rear axle bearing assembly for the 6000 STE AWD

86817072

3. Remove both tire and wheel assemblies.
4. Disconnect the parking brake cable end from the bracket.
5. Insert a suitable tool through the caliper into the rotor to prevent the rotor from turning.
6. Remove the shaft nut and washer using special tool J-34826.
7. Discard the shaft nut.
8. Remove the anti-lock brake sensor bolt and move the sensor aside.
9. Unfasten the Electronic Ride Control (ERC) electrical connections and air lines, and disconnect the height sensor arm from the bracket stud.
10. Detach the brake line/ERC sensor bracket to the left control arm.
11. Disconnect the exhaust support bolt (above the cradle).
12. Scribe the relationship of the propeller shaft to the rear axle pinion flange, then remove the four shaft-to-differential bolts and suspend the propeller shaft with wire.
13. Remove the cradle-to-underbody bracket bolts, 4 on each side.
14. Install a spring compressor tool J-33432 or an equivalent onto the leaf spring.
15. Disconnect the strut upper mount bolts and nuts.
16. Lower the vehicle slightly to gain access to the luggage compartment nuts.
17. Raise the vehicle to the previous position, then release the spring tension and remove the spring compression tool.
18. Install a transaxle jack under the jacking plate, then remove the 4 cradle mount bolts.
19. Lower the axle assembly slightly, then disconnect the differential vent tube, then lower completely.

To install:

20. Raise the axle enough to connect the differential vent tube, then raise completely to align the cradle mount bores.
21. Attach the four cradle mount bolts and tighten to 103 ft. lbs. (140 Nm).
22. Remove the transaxle jack.
23. Install the spring compression tool, then tighten it to compress the spring.
24. The strut upper mount bolts and nuts need to be tightened to 28 ft. lbs. (38 Nm). Then lower the vehicle and install the mount nuts in the luggage compartment.
25. Raise the vehicle again, then remove the spring compression tool.
26. Attach the cradle brace-to-underbody bracket bolts, then tighten to 28 ft. lbs. (38 Nm).
27. Connect the four propeller shaft-to-differential bolts, and tighten to 40 ft. lbs. (54 Nm).
28. Install the exhaust support bolt above the cradle, then tighten to 11 ft. lbs. (15 Nm).
29. Attach the bolt securing the brake line/ERC sensor bracket to the left control arm, then tighten to 18 ft. lbs. (24 Nm).
30. Attach the ERC electrical connection, air lines and the height sensor arm to the bracket stud.
31. Connect the anti-lock brake sensors using one bolt each.
32. Attach the brake calipers and attach the Torx® bolts.
33. Connect the parking brake cable at the tensioner.
34. Connect the parking brake brackets, bolts and springs.
35. Connect the parking brake cables at both ends.
36. Tighten the cables at the tensioner.
37. Install both of the wheels, then lower the vehicle.
38. Close the decklid.

Disconnecting Air Lines

The Electronic Ride Control (ERC) system air lines use a spring clip connection with mounted sealing shoulders in the retainer and on the end of the air line with double "O" ring seals. Before disconnecting any air line, clean the connector and surrounding area. Squeeze the spring clip to release the connector. To reassemble, lubricate the "O" rings with petroleum jelly or an equivalent, then push the air line and the connector fully into the fitting.

TORQUE SPECIFICATIONS

Component	US	Metric
Clutch assembly:		
Clutch master cylinder	15-25 ft. lbs.	20-34 Nm
Clutch pedal-to-bracket	20-25 ft. lbs.	28-34 Nm
Clutch release lever	30-45 ft. lbs.	40-60 Nm
Clutch slave cylinder bleeder screw	18 inch lbs.	2 Nm
Clutch slave cylinder	14-20 ft. lbs.	18-26 Nm
Pressure plate-to-flywheel	12-18 ft. lbs.	16-24 Nm
4 Speed Transaxle:		
Case-to-cover bolts	16 ft. lbs.	21 Nm
Front support strut	48 ft. lbs.	65 Nm
Input shaft right bearing retainer	7 ft. lbs.	9 Nm
Pinion shaft lock bolt	7 ft. lbs.	9 Nm
Output shaft left bearing retainer	45 ft. lbs.	65 Nm
Rear mount through bolt nut	80 ft. lbs.	108 Nm
Reverse idler shaft lock bolt	16 ft. lbs.	21 Nm
Shift control mount nuts	18 ft. lbs.	24 Nm
Transaxle-to-engine	47-62 ft. lbs.	65-86 Nm
5 Speed Transaxle:		
Clutch housing-to-gear housing	15 ft. lbs	21 Nm
Control box-to-case	11-16 ft. lbs.	15-22 Nm
Differential gear	61 ft. lbs.	83 Nm
Differential pin	84 inch lbs.	9 Nm
End plate-to-gear housing	15 ft. lbs.	21 Nm
Drain plug	18 ft. lbs.	24 Nm
Flywheel	44-60 ft. lbs.	60-80 Nm
Front strut-to-frame	50 ft. lbs.	68 Nm
Front strut-to-transaxle	40 ft. lbs.	54 Nm
Interlock plate	15 ft. lbs.	21 Nm
Neutral saftey switch	3 ft. lbs.	4-5 Nm
Output bearing race	15 ft. lbs.	21 Nm
Output shaft bearing support	50 ft. lbs.	70 Nm
Pressure plate-to-flywheel	14-18 ft. lbs.	18-24 Nm
Rear cover	11-16 ft. lbs.	15-22 Nm
Rear mount through bolt nut	80 ft. lbs.	108 Nm
Reverse idler shaft bolt	22-33 ft. lbs.	30-45 Nm
Reverse shift bracket	11-16 ft. lbs.	15-22 Nm
Ring gear bolts	73-79 ft. lbs.	98-107 Nm
Shift contol mount nuts	18 ft. lbs.	24 Nm
Transaxle case-to-clutch housing	22-33 ft. lbs.	30-45 Nm
Transaxle-to-engine	60 ft. lbs.	75 Nm

86817089

TORQUE SPECIFICATIONS

Component	US	Metric
3T40 Automatic Transaxle:		
Case-to-cover	18 ft. lbs.	24 Nm
Oil pan-to-valve body cover	8 ft. lbs.	11 Nm
Manual detent spring-to-case	8 ft. lbs.	11 Nm
Cooler connector	23 ft. lbs.	38 Nm
Parking lock bracket-to-case	18 ft. lbs.	24 Nm
Pipe retainer-to-case	18 ft. lbs.	24 Nm
Govener cover-to-case	8 ft. lbs.	11 Nm
TV cable-to-case	75 inch lbs.	9 Nm
Pressure switch	8 ft. lbs.	11 Nm
4T60-E Automatic Transaxle:		
Case extension-to-case	22-30 ft. lbs.	30-41 Nm
Speed sensor retainer-to-case	71-124 inch lbs.	8-14 Nm
Special trans oil pan-to-case	80-115 inch lbs.	9-13 Nm
Channel plate-to-case	15-20 ft. lbs.	20-27 Nm
Temperature sensor	58-66 inch lbs.	6.5-7.5 Nm
Hub nut:		
Final	70-75 ft. lbs.	95-103 Nm
	192 ft. lbs.	260 Nm
Failure warning switch:		
	15-50 inch lbs.	2-6 Nm

86817090

8

SUSPENSION AND STEERING

WHEELS

Wheels

REMOVAL & INSTALLATION

▶ **See Figure 1**

There are many different aftermarket wheels that can be installed on your car. The procedures given in this manual are for the factory original wheels. If your vehicle is equipped with aftermarket wheels, follow any special instructions given by that manufacturer. Pay attention to any special washers, spacers or adapters that may have come with aftermarket wheels.

1. When removing a wheel, loosen all the lug nuts at least one full turn, before jacking up the car.
2. Raise and safely support the car.
3. Finish removing the already loosened lug nuts. Sometimes applying slight pressure on wheel toward car will make it easy to screw them off by hand.
4. Remove the wheel.
5. If the wheel is stuck on the hub place at least two lug nuts back on. Only screw them on two or three turns, don't allow them to touch the wheel.
6. Lower the vehicle back on the ground and rock it side to side. This is safer than shaking a vehicle that is on a jack. After the wheel pops loose, repeat the steps after raise and support the vehicle.

To install:

7. Place the wheel on the vehicle, hand-tighten all of the lug nuts. If the studs or nuts are rusty, now is a good time to place some light lubricate on them.
8. After all of the nuts are hand-tightened, lower the vehicle.
9. Further tighten the nuts with a lug wrench until they are all snug. Use the "star pattern" method of skipping every other nut in the tightening sequence until all 5 lug nuts have been tightened.
10. Finally, using a torque wrench, tighten the lug nuts to specification. Although 100 ft. lbs. (136 Nm) may be suitable for factory-equipped steel wheels, aftermarket wheels may require a different amount. Be careful to observe the recommended torque value.

➡ **Uneven tightening of wheel lug nuts can cause early disc brake pad and rotor wear.**

Inspection

Wheels can be distorted or bent and not effect dry road handling to a noticeable degree. Out of round wheels will show up as uneven tire wear, or make it

difficult to balance the tires. Without special tools it is difficult to check wheel radial run-out. It would be best to ask the shop that balances the tires for you to do this. But a good visual inspection will usually reveal any problems.

Look for any bends or cracks. Not all repairs can be made to a wheel. If a wheel has any repair marks like welds or patches it should be discarded. Steel wheels that have slight bends where the tire meets the wheel doesn't mean the wheel is bad. Many times this is cause by the tire changing machine and can be hammered back into shape. This will only work on steel wheels not alloy or aluminum. If a wheel had a little bend in this area and had been repair it should be rebalanced and placed in a tank of water to check for leaks.

Another way to check for leaks where the wheel and tire meet is to lay the wheel flat on the ground. Place dish detergent and water solution around the wheel and wait a few minutes. If there is a slow leak you will see suds. Flip the tire over and repeat this procedure. If a leak is found the tire must be removed from the wheel. Then the tire bead and wheel rim must be cleaned, lubricated and reassembled. Always recheck to make sure the leak is fixed.

Wheel Lug Studs

REPLACEMENT

▶ **See Figures 2 and 3**

1. To remove the wheel, loosen all the lug nuts at least one full turn, before jacking up the car.
2. Raise and safely support the car.
3. Remove the wheel and tire assembly.
4. Remove the brake assembly components.
5. Remove the hub assembly.
6. Remove the damaged stud using a C-clamp and pressing it out the back.

To install:

7. Install the new stud by inserting the stud into the hole.
8. Place washers on the stud, then install a lug nut and tighten evenly to pull stud into place.
9. Make certain stud doesn't turn in the hub or it will strip out the hole. If stud doesn't fit very tight you'll need to replace the hub, too.
10. Remove the nut and washers after the stud is seated.
11. Reinstall the hub and brake components.
12. Install the wheel, then hand-tighten the lug nuts.
13. Lower the vehicle and tighten the lug nuts to 100 ft. lbs. (136 Nm).

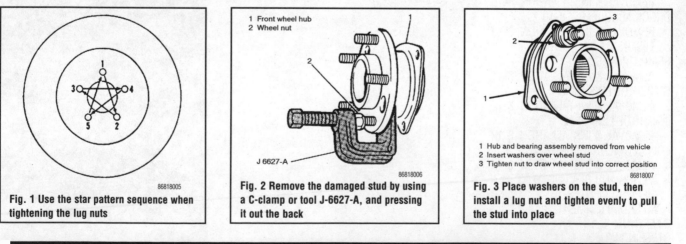

Fig. 1 Use the star pattern sequence when tightening the lug nuts

1 Front wheel hub
2 Wheel nut

J 6627-A

Fig. 2 Remove the damaged stud by using a C-clamp or tool J-6627-A, and pressing it out the back

1 Hub and bearing assembly removed from vehicle
2 Insert washers over wheel stud
3 Tighten nut to draw wheel stud into correct position

Fig. 3 Place washers on the stud, then install a lug nut and tighten evenly to pull the stud into place

FRONT SUSPENSION

▶ **See Figures 4, 5 and 6**

The A-Bodies uses a MacPherson strut front suspension design. The MacPherson strut combines the functions of a shock absorber and an upper

suspension member (upper arm) into one unit. The strut is surrounded by a coil spring, which provides normal front suspension functions.

The strut bolts to the body shell at its upper end, and to the steering knuckle at the lower end. The strut pivots with the steering knuckle by means of a sealed

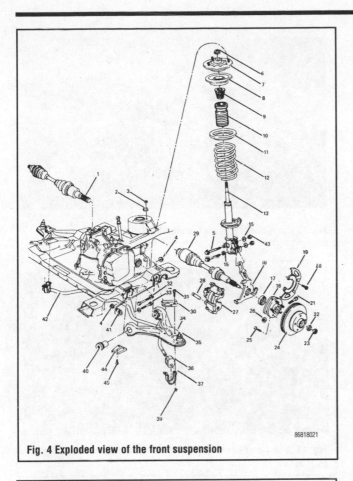

Fig. 4 Exploded view of the front suspension

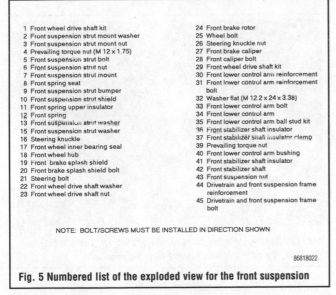

1 Front wheel drive shaft kit	24 Front brake rotor
2 Front suspension strut mount washer	25 Wheel bolt
3 Front suspension strut mount nut	26 Steering knuckle nut
4 Prevailing torque nut (M 12 x 1.75)	27 Front brake caliper
5 Front suspension strut bolt	28 Front caliper bolt
6 Front suspension strut nut	29 Front wheel drive shaft kit
7 Front suspension strut mount	30 Front lower control arm reinforcement
8 Front spring seat	31 Front lower control arm reinforcement
9 Front suspension strut bumper	bolt
10 Front suspension strut shield	32 Washer flat (M 12.2 x 24 x 3.38)
11 Front spring upper insulator	33 Front lower control arm bolt
12 Front spring	34 Front lower control arm
13 Front suspension strut washer	35 Front lower control arm ball stud kit
15 Front suspension strut washer	36 Front stabilizer shaft insulator
16 Steering knuckle	37 Front stabilizer shaft insulator clamp
17 Front wheel inner bearing seal	39 Prevailing torque nut
18 Front wheel hub	40 Front lower control arm bushing
19 Front brake splash shield	41 Front stabilizer shaft insulator
20 Front brake splash shield bolt	42 Front stabilizer shaft
21 Steering bolt	43 Front suspension nut
22 Front wheel drive shaft washer	44 Drivetrain and front suspension frame
23 Front wheel drive shaft nut	reinforcement
	45 Drivetrain and front suspension frame
	bolt

NOTE: BOLT/SCREWS MUST BE INSTALLED IN DIRECTION SHOWN

86818022

Fig. 5 Numbered list of the exploded view for the front suspension

mounting assembly at the upper end which contains a preloaded, non-adjustable bearing.

The steering knuckle is connected to the chassis at the lower end by a conventional lower control arm, and pivots in the arm in a preloaded ball joint of standard design. The knuckle is fastened to the ball joint stud by means of a castellated nut and cotter pin.

Advantages of the MacPherson strut design, aside from its relative simplicity, include reduced weight and friction, minimal intrusion into the engine and passenger compartments, and ease of service.

➡**When removing any steering components, it is advisable to matchmark (scribe) the locations of the components**

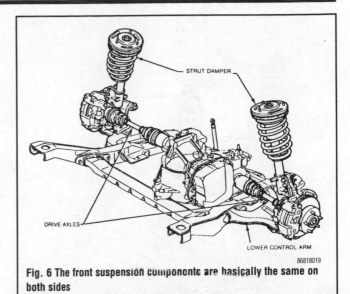

Fig. 6 The front suspension components are basically the same on both sides

MacPherson Struts and Coil Springs

TESTING

The purpose of a MacPherson strut, much like a shock absorber, is to dampen harsh spring movement and provide a means of dissipating the motion of the wheels. As a result, shocks encountered by the wheels are not totally transmitted to the body and, therefore, to you and your passengers. As the wheel moves up and down, the strut shortens and lengthens, thereby imposing a restraint on movement by its hydraulic action.

A good way to see if your struts are functioning correctly is to push one corner of the car until it is moving up and down for almost the full suspension travel, then release it and watch its recovery. If the car bounces slightly about one more time and comes to a rest, the strut is all right. If the car continues to bounce excessively, the struts will probably require replacement.

REMOVAL & INSTALLATION

◆ **See Figures 7 thru 13**

1. Remove the top strut-to-body mounting nuts.
2. Loosen the wheel nuts, then raise and support the vehicle on jackstands. Make sure the weight of the vehicle is not on the control arm.
3. Remove the wheel and tire assembly.
4. Remove the brake line bracket from the strut assembly.
5. Install the boot protector tool J-28712 (Double-Offset joint) or J-33162 (Tri-Pot joint) over the drive axle boot.

➡**If equipped with a Tri-Pot joint, disconnect the drive axle from the transaxle before separating the strut from the steering knuckle.**

6. If equipped, separate the ABS front brake sensor connection. These are on the 6000 STE models.
7. Before separating the strut from the steering knuckle, matchmark components by performing the following, as illustrated:
   a. Using a sharp tool, scribe the knuckle along the lower outboard strut radius.
   b. Scribe the strut flange on the inboard side, along the curve of the steering knuckle.
   c. Using a chisel, mark the strut-to-steering knuckle interface.
8. Remove the steering knuckle-to-strut bolts.

➡**The steering knuckle should be supported after removing the bolts to prevent axle joint overextension.**

9. Remove the strut.

To install:

10. Install the strut to the body, then secure with the mounting nuts. Hand-tighten the nuts.

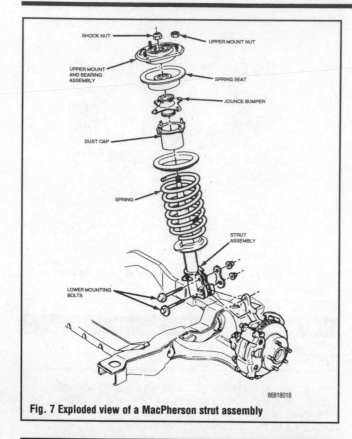

Fig. 7 Exploded view of a MacPherson strut assembly

Labels: SHOCK NUT, UPPER MOUNT NUT, UPPER MOUNT AND BEARING ASSEMBLY, SPRING SEAT, JOUNCE BUMPER, DUST CAP, SPRING, STRUT ASSEMBLY, LOWER MOUNTING BOLTS

Fig. 8 Using a ratchet, remove the top strut-to-body mounting nuts

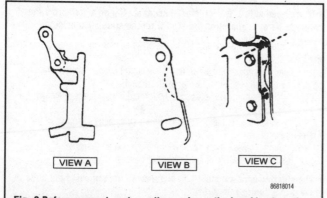

Fig. 9 Before removal, make scribe marks on the knuckle along the lower outboard strut radius (view A), the strut flange on the inboard side, along the curve of the steering knuckle (view B), and across the strut-to-steering knuckle interface (view C)

VIEW A   VIEW B   VIEW C

Fig. 10 Use a chisel to mark the strut-to-steering knuckle interface

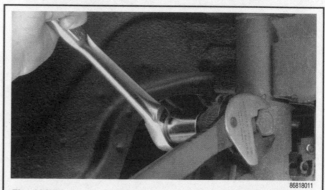

Fig. 11 With the use of two tools, remove the steering knuckle-to-strut bolts

Fig. 12 After removing the bolts connecting the steering knuckle to the strut, the strut can be extracted from the vehicle

11. Place a jack under the lower arm. Raise the arm and install the lower strut-to-knuckle bolts. Align the strut-to-steering knuckle marks made during removal. Tighten the strut-to-knuckle bolts to 122–140 ft. lbs. (165–190 Nm), and the strut-to-body nuts to 16–18 ft. lbs. (22–24 Nm).

12. Reconnect the ABS sensor wiring.

13. Install the brake hose bracket to the strut.

14. Install the wheel, hand-tighten the lug nuts. Raise the vehicle slightly to allow removal of the jackstands.

15. Remove the jackstands and lower the car. Tighten the lug nuts to 100 ft. lbs. (136 Nm).

➡️If a new strut dampener has been installed, the front end will have to be realigned.

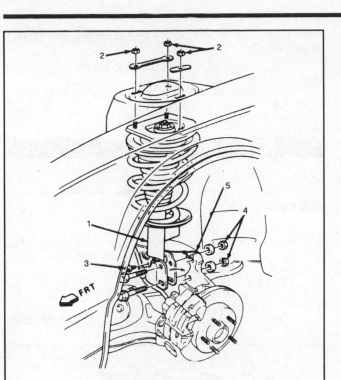

1 Strut assembly
2 Strut to body nuts 25 Nm (18 lbs. ft.)
3 Brake line bracket bolt 17 Nm (13 lbs.ft.)
4 Strut to steering knuckle nuts 190 Nm
  (140 lbs.ft.)
5 Retain steering knuckle with wire once
  strut assembly is removed

86818059

Fig. 13 Pontiac 6000 STE AWD strut mounting is slightly different than that of front wheel drive models

DISASSEMBLY & ASSEMBLY

A MacPherson strut compressor tool J-34013-B or the equivalent must be used.

1. Mount the compressor tool J-34013-B in the holder J-3289-20.
2. Install the strut in the compressor J-34013-B, then install the compressor adapters, if used.
3. Compress the spring approximately ½ its height after initial contact with the top cap. **Do not bottom the spring or the dampener rod**.
4. Remove the nut from the strut dampener shaft and place the J-34013-27 on top of the dampener shaft. Using this alignment rod J-34013-27 guide the dampener shaft straight down through the bearing cap while decompressing the spring.
5. Remove the components.
Assembly:
6. Install the bearing cap into J-34013-B if previously removed. Mount the strut into J-34013-B using the bottom locking pin only, then extend the dampener shaft and install J-34013-20 on the shaft.
7. Install the spring over the dampener and swing the assembly up so that the locking pin can be installed. Install the upper insulator, shield, bumper, and upper spring seat. Make sure that the flat on the upper spring seat is facing in the proper direction. The spring should seat flat at 10° forward of the centerline of the strut assembly spindle.
8. Install tool J-34013-13 and turn, forcing the screw while J-34013-27 centers the assembly. When the threads on the dampener shaft are visible, remove tool J-34013-27, then install the nut.
9. Tighten the nut, using a crow's foot line wrench while holding the dampener shaft with a socket.
10. Remove tool J-34013-20.

Lower Ball Joints

INSPECTION

1. Raise and safely support the car.
2. Grasp the tire at top and bottom and move the top to the tire in and out.
3. Observe for any horizontal movement of the knuckle relative to the control arm.
4. Ball joints must be replaced if there is any looseness in the ball joint and should be replaced if the seal is damaged. The ball joint may check good with a bad seal, but will not last long due to dirt and water entering the joint.

REMOVAL & INSTALLATION

◆ See Figures 14 and 15

Only one ball joint is used in each lower arm. The MacPherson strut design does not use an upper ball joint.

➡ Care must be exercised to prevent the halfshafts from being overextended. Support the lower arm.

1. Loosen the wheel nuts, raise the car.
2. Place a jackstand under the vehicles frame or suspension support.
3. Lower the vehicle slightly, so that the weight of the vehicle rest on the jackstands and not on the control arms.
4. Remove the tire and wheel assembly.
5. Install a CV-boot protector.
6. Remove the steering knuckle bolts, then remove the ball joint nut and cotter pin from the steering knuckle.

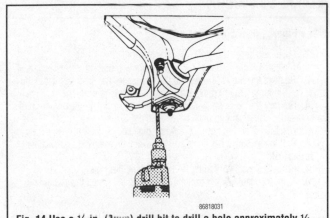

86818031

Fig. 14 Use a ⅛ in. (3mm) drill bit to drill a hole approximately ¼ in. (6mm) deep in the center of each of the three ball joint rivets

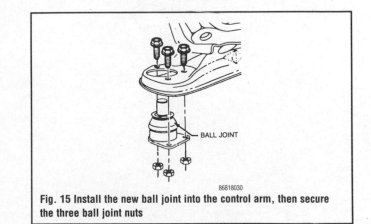

BALL JOINT

86818030

Fig. 15 Install the new ball joint into the control arm, then secure the three ball joint nuts

7. Use a ⅛ in. (3mm) drill bit to drill a hole approximately ¼ in. (6mm) deep in the center of each of the three ball joint rivets.

8. Use a ½ in. (13mm) drill bit to drill off the rivet heads. Drill only enough to remove the rivet head.

✳✷ WARNING

Take care not to drill through the halfshaft dust boots.

9. Use a hammer and punch to remove the rivets. Drive them out from the bottom.

10. Loosen the stabilizer shaft insulator nuts, then remove the ball joint assembly.

To install:

11. Install the new ball joint into the control arm. Secure the three ball joint nuts, see your instructions supplied by the part supplier for tightening specifications.

12. Install the ball joint into the knuckle pinch bolt fitting. It should go in easily if not, check the stud alignment. Install the pinch bolt from the rear to the front. Tighten to 40 ft. lbs. (50 Nm) for 1982–84 models, 33 ft. lbs. (45 Nm) for 1985–93 models, or 38 ft. lbs. (52 Nm) for 1994–96 models.

13. Remove the CV-boot protector.

14. Tighten the stabilizer shaft clamp insulator bolts to 32 ft. lbs. (43 Nm).

15. Install the wheel, hand-tighten the lug nuts.

16. Raise the vehicle slightly to allow removal of the jackstands.

17. Remove the jackstands, then lower the vehicle, tighten the lug nuts to 100 ft. lbs. (136 Nm).

Stabilizer Bar

REMOVAL & INSTALLATION

▶ **See Figure 16**

1. Raise and support the vehicle on jackstands.

2. Matchmark the stabilizer bar to the mounting bracket for installation.

3. Remove the two nuts attaching the clamps for the stabilizer bar to the lower control arms. Do not remove the studs from the control arm.

4. Remove the bolts which attach the retaining plates to the engine cradle on both sides. The retaining plate covers and holds the stabilizer bar.

5. Disconnect and remove the exhaust pipe and crossover if necessary.

6. Pull the stabilizer bar down and remove, then remove the insulators.

To install:

7. Install the insulators to the ends of the stabilizer bar.

8. Align the stabilizer bar to the matchmarks and attach the stabilizer to the frame.

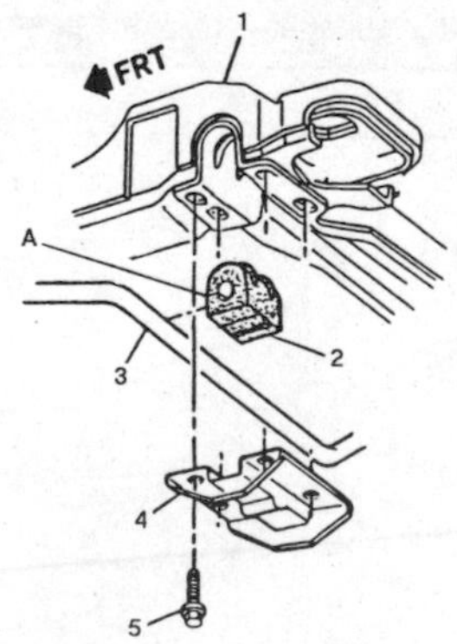

➡To aid in stabilizer bar installation, a pry hole has been provided in the engine cradle.

9. Install the reinforcements to each side at the frame, then tighten the reinforcement bolts to 40 ft. lbs. (55 Nm).

10. Secure the insulator clamps to the control arms and tighten the attaching nuts to 32 ft. lbs. (43 Nm).

11. Lower the vehicle.

Lower Control Arm

REMOVAL & INSTALLATION

▶ **See Figures 17 and 18**

1. Loosen the wheel nuts, raise the car.

2. Place jackstands under the frame, then lower the vehicle slightly so that the weight of the vehicle rests on the jackstands and not on the control arms.

3. Remove the tire and wheel assembly.

4. Place a boot protector over the axle boot.

5. Remove the stabilizer shaft to the control arm bolt.

6. Remove the steering knuckle pinch bolt.

7. Remove the control arm pivot bolts and the control arm from the vehicle.

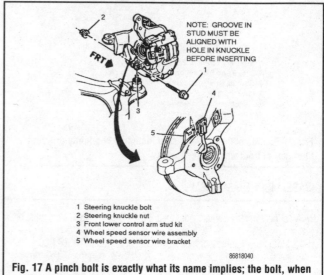

NOTE: GROOVE IN STUD MUST BE ALIGNED WITH HOLE IN KNUCKLE BEFORE INSERTING

1 Steering knuckle bolt
2 Steering knuckle nut
3 Front lower control arm stud kit
4 Wheel speed sensor wire assembly
5 Wheel speed sensor wire bracket

86818040

Fig. 17 A pinch bolt is exactly what its name implies; the bolt, when tightened, literally pinches the knuckle to the ball joint end

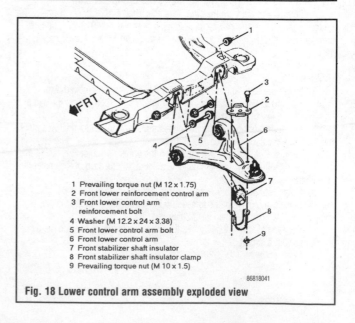

1 Prevailing torque nut (M 12 x 1.75)
2 Front lower reinforcement control arm
3 Front lower control arm reinforcement bolt
4 Washer (M 12.2 x 24 x 3.38)
5 Front lower control arm bolt
6 Front lower control arm
7 Front stabilizer shaft insulator
8 Front stabilizer shaft insulator clamp
9 Prevailing torque nut (M 10 x 1.5)

86818041

Fig. 18 Lower control arm assembly exploded view

A Install insulator with slit toward front of vehicles as shown
1 Frame
2 Stabilizer shaft frame bushing
3 Stabilizer shaft
4 Reinforcement plate
5 55 Nm (40 lbs.ft.)

86818060

Fig. 16 Front stabilizer bar mounting

8. If removal of the control arm bushings is required, refer to the accompanying illustration.

To install:

9. Insert the control arm to the frame. Install the control arm bolts and nuts, but do not tighten the nuts yet.

10. Install the stabilizer shaft insulators, then secure the steering knuckle in place with new nuts and bolts.

11. Raise the vehicle slightly so that the weight is supported by the control arms while tightening the mounting nuts.

12. Install the stabilizer bar clamp. Tighten to 33 ft. lbs. (45 Nm).

13. Tighten the control arm nut to 61 ft. lbs. (83 Nm).

14. Tighten the pinch bolt nut to 40 ft. lbs. (50 Nm) for 1982–84 models, 33 ft. lbs. (45 Nm) for 1985–94 models, or 38 ft. lbs. (52 Nm) for 1995–96 models.

15. Remove the boot protector.

16. Install the wheel and lug nuts. Raise the vehicle slightly to remove the jackstands from under the frame.

17. Lower the car, and tighten the lug nuts to 100 ft. lbs. (136 Nm).

CONTROL ARM BUSHING REPLACEMENT

♦ See Figure 19

Refer to the accompanying graphic for removal and installation of control arm bushings.

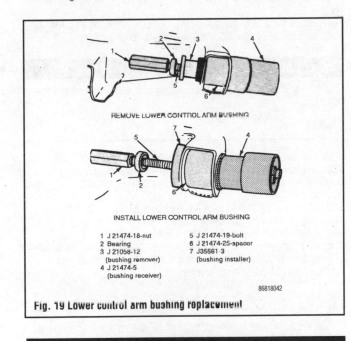

REMOVE LOWER CONTROL ARM BUSHING

INSTALL LOWER CONTROL ARM BUSHING

1 J 21474-18-nut	5 J 21474-19-bolt
2 Bearing	6 J 21474-25-spacer
3 J 21058-12 (bushing remover)	7 J35561-3 (bushing installer)
4 J 21474-5 (bushing receiver)	

86818042

Fig. 19 Lower control arm bushing replacement

Knuckle

REMOVAL & INSTALLATION

1982–89 Models

1. Remove the hub nut.
2. Raise the front of the car. Remove the wheel and tire.
3. Install an axle shaft boot seal protector, GM special tool J-28712 or equivalent, onto the seal.
4. Disconnect the brake hose clip from the MacPherson strut, but do not disconnect the hose from the caliper. Remove the brake caliper, rotor and shield from the spindle, and hang the caliper out of the way by a length of wire. Do not allow the caliper to hang by the brake hose.
5. Matchmark the camber alignment cam bolt for reassembly. Remove the cam bolt and the upper attaching bolt from the strut and spindle.
6. Pull the steering knuckle assembly from the strut bracket.

To install:

Prior to installation, a new knuckle seal should be installed on the steering knuckle.

7. Loosely attach the steering knuckle to the suspension strut, then install the rotor and the hub nut. When the shaft begins to turn with the hub, insert a drift through the caliper into one of the cooling slots in the rotor to keep it from turning. Insert a long bolt in the hub flange to prevent the shaft from turning. Tighten the hub nut to 70 ft. lbs. (95 Nm).

8. Tighten the brake caliper bolts to 30 ft. lbs. (41 Nm).

9. Load the hub assembly by lowering it onto a jackstand. Align the camber cam bolt marks made during removal, then install the bolt and tighten to 140 ft. lbs. (190 Nm). Tighten the upper nut to the same value.

10. Remove the boot seal protector.

11. Connect the brake hose clip to the strut. Install the tire and wheel, lower the car, and tighten the hub nut to 225 ft. lbs. (305 Nm) for 1981–82 models, or 185 ft. lbs. (251 Nm) for 1983–89 models.

1990–96 Models

1. Loosen the lug nuts on the side of the vehicle from which you will be removing the knuckle.

2. Raise and support the vehicle, then remove the lug nuts.

3. Remove and discard the hub nut, then disconnect the drive axle.

4. Disconnect the outer tie rod from the end of the steering knuckle. Scribe the strut to the knuckle, then remove the strut to knuckle bolts.

5. Loosen and remove the steering knuckle bolt and nut, then remove the knuckle. Disassemble the bearing hub and rotor splash shield. Using a prytool, dislodge the inner dust seal.

To install:

6. Install a new inner dust seal, then reconnect the bearing hub and rotor splash shield.

7. Attach the knuckle assembly with its mounting nut and bolt, tighten the nut to 38 ft. lbs. (52 Nm).

8. Install the strut bolts, then tighten them to 122 ft. lbs. (165 Nm).

9. Reconnect the drive axle. Install the hub nut, wheel and lug nuts.

10. Lower the vehicle, tighten the lug nuts to 100 ft. lbs. (136 Nm). Inspect the wheel alignment.

Front Hub and Bearing

REPLACEMENT

♦ See Figures 20, 21, 22, 23 and 24

The front wheel bearings are sealed, non-adjustable units which require no periodic attention. They are bolted to the steering knuckle by means of an integral flange.

You will need a special tool to pull the bearing free of the halfshaft: tool J-28733 or equivalent. You should also use a halfshaft boot protector tool such as J-28712 (Double-Offset joint) or J-33162 (Tri-Pot joint) to protect the parts from damage.

1. Raise and support the vehicle on jackstands. Remove the wheel and tire assembly.

2. Install a drive axle boot protector over the inboard CV-joint, tools J-28712 (Double-Offset Joint) or J-33162 (Tri-Pot Joint) can be used.

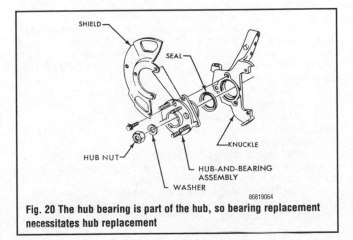

86819064

Fig. 20 The hub bearing is part of the hub, so bearing replacement necessitates hub replacement

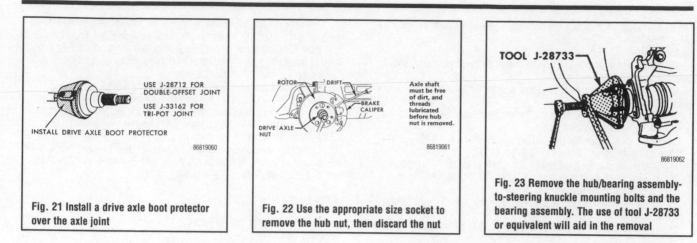

Fig. 21 Install a drive axle boot protector over the axle joint

Fig. 22 Use the appropriate size socket to remove the hub nut, then discard the nut

Fig. 23 Remove the hub/bearing assembly-to-steering knuckle mounting bolts and the bearing assembly. The use of tool J-28733 or equivalent will aid in the removal

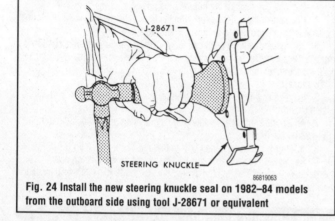

Fig. 24 Install the new steering knuckle seal on 1982–84 models from the outboard side using tool J-28671 or equivalent

3. Insert a drift punch through the caliper and into the brake rotor cooling fins. Clean the drive axle threads of all dirt and lubricant.

4. Remove the hub nut and washer, then discard the nut. Remove the drift punch. Remove the caliper and support it on a wire, then remove the rotor.

5. On ABS vehicles, disconnect the ABS sensor from the hub bearing.

6. Remove the hub bearing-to-steering knuckle mounting bolts, remove the backing plate. Separate the halfshaft from the hub bearing assembly using tool J-28733. Remove the hub and bearing assembly, retaining bolts, shield and O-ring.

➡️If the bearing assembly is to be reused, mark the assembly and the steering knuckle so that the assembly can be reinstalled in the same position. To prevent damage to the bearing, DO NOT use heat or a hammer.

7. Using a punch, tap the seal towards the engine. When the seal is removed from the steering knuckle, cut it off the drive axle using side cutters.
To install:

8. Clean the gasket and the seal mounting surfaces.

9. Depending on the application, use tool J-28671 on 1982–84 models or J-34657 on 1985–88 heavy duty models to install the new steering knuckle seal from the outboard side. On 1985–96 standard duty models, use tool J-34658 to install the seal from the inboard side. Be sure to grease the lip of the seal with wheel bearing grease.

10. Route the ABS sensor wire through the steering knuckle and connect it to the ABS harness.

11. Install a new O-ring around the hub bearing.

12. Guide the halfshaft spines into the hub bearing splines and make sure they engage properly.

13. Install the hub bearing onto the steering knuckle, install the backing plate and the bearing retaining bolts, then tighten the bolts to 63 ft. lbs. (85 Nm) standard duty or 77 ft. lbs. (104 Nm) for heavy duty.

14. Install the rotor and place the caliper assembly into position on the rotor, then tighten the caliper mounting bolts to 28 ft. lbs. (38 Nm) for 1982–84 models, or 38 ft. lbs. (51 Nm) for 1985–96 models.

15. Install the washer and new hub nut, then tighten the hub nut on the half-shaft partially to 74 ft. lbs. (100 Nm). If the rotor and hub starts to rotate as the hub nut is tightened, insert a drift through the caliper and into the rotor cooling fins to prevent rotation. Do not apply full torque to the hub nut at this time, just seat the bearing.

16. Remove the drive axle boot protector. Install the tire and wheel assembly.

17. Lower the vehicle, then tighten the hub nut to 225 ft. lbs. (305 Nm) for 1982 models or 185 ft. lbs. (251 Nm) for 1983–96 models.

Wheel Alignment

Only camber and toe are adjustable on these cars, caster is preset and non-adjustable.

CAMBER

Camber is the inward or outward tilt from the vertical, measured in degrees, of the front wheels at the top. An outward tilt gives the wheel positive camber, an inward tilt is called negative camber. Proper camber is critical to assure even tire wear.

Camber angle is adjusted on the A-Bodies by loosening the through bolts which attach the MacPherson strut to the steering knuckle in or out. The bolts must be tightened afterwards. The bolts must be seated properly between the inner and outer guide surfaces on the strut flange. Measurement of the camber angle requires special alignment equipment, thus the adjustment of camber is not a do-it-yourself job, and not covered here.

CASTER

Caster is the forward or rearward tilting of the steering axis from the vertical. A rearward tilt (at the top) is called positive, and the forward tilt is negative. Zero caster indicates that the strut is directly above the ball joint. Caster influences the directional control of the steering but does not affect the tire wear. If you have weak springs or you overload your vehicle this will effect the caster. Caster affects the vehicles directional stability and steering effort.

Caster is measured in degrees like camber. If one wheel has more positive caster than the other, this will cause the wheel to pull towards the center of the vehicle, causing the vehicle to move or lead toward the side with the least amount of positive caster. Caster is not adjustable.

TOE-IN

♦ See Figure 25

Toe is the amount, measured in a fraction of a millimeter, that the wheels are closer together at one end than the other. Toe-in means that the front wheels are closer together at the front than the rear. Toe-out means the rear of the front wheels are closer together than the front. A-Body cars are designed to have a slight amount of toe-in.

Toe is adjusted by turning the tie rods. It must be checked after camber has been adjusted, but it can be adjusted without disturbing the camber setting. You can make this adjustment without special equipment if you make very careful measurements. The wheels must be straight ahead.

1. Toe can be determined by measuring the distance between the centers of the tire treads, at the front of the tire and at the rear. If the tread pattern makes this impossible, you can measure between the edges of the wheel rims, but make sure to move the car forward and measure in a couple of places to avoid errors caused by bent rims or wheel run-out.

2. If the measurement is not within specifications, loosen the nuts at the steering knuckle end of the tie rod, and remove the tie rod boot clamps. Rotate the tie rods to align the toe to specifications. Rotate the tie rods evenly, or the steering wheel will be crooked when you're done.

3. When the adjustment is correct, tighten the nuts to 44 ft. lbs. (60 Nm). Adjust the boots and tighten the clamps.

✳✳ WARNING

If severely out of adjustment, a tire can wear out quite prematurely. It is advisable to have a front end alignment professionally done after replacing steering or suspension components to avoid costly tire wear.

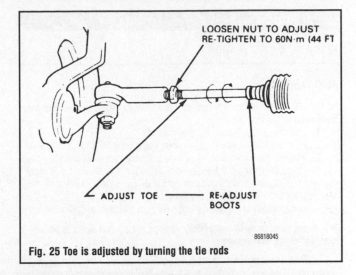

Fig. 25 Toe is adjusted by turning the tie rods

REAR SUSPENSION

A Front Wheel Drive (FWD) rear suspension consists of a solid rear axle tube containing an integral, welded-in stabilizer bar, coil springs, shock absorbers, a lateral track bar, and trailing arms. The trailing arms (control arms) are welded to the axle, and pivot at the frame. Fore-and-aft movement is controlled by the trailing arms; lateral movement is controlled by the track bar. A permanently lubricated and sealed hub and bearing assembly is bolted to each end of the axle tube, it is a non-adjustable unit which must be replaced as an assembly if defective.

The All Wheel Drive (AWD) rear suspension features a lightweight fiberglass transverse leaf spring which is mounted to the rear of the cradle. Other rear suspension components include struts, control arms, toe links, and a stabilizer bar. These components are all serviceable. The control arms, leaf springs and struts oppose the torque reaction on acceleration and braking and provides optimum handling. Each rear wheel has a spindle, a hub and bearing assembly, along with a knuckle which attaches to the outboard end of the control arm.

Coil Springs

REMOVAL & INSTALLATION

▶ See Figures 26 and 27

FWD Vehicles

✳✳ CAUTION

The coil springs are under a considerable amount of tension. Be extremely careful when removing or installing them, since they can exert enough force to cause very serious injuries.

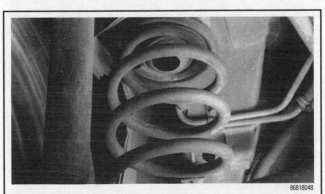

Fig. 26 With the vehicle in the air, access to the spring and shock absorber is much simpler

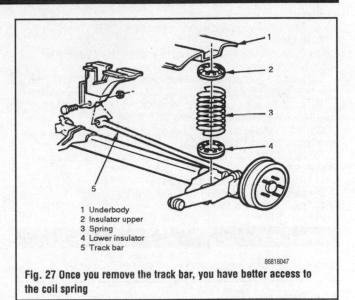

1 Underbody
2 Insulator upper
3 Spring
4 Lower insulator
5 Track bar

Fig. 27 Once you remove the track bar, you have better access to the coil spring

1. Raise and support the car on a hoist. Do not use twin-post hoist. The swing arc of the axle may cause it to slip from the hoist when the bolts are removed. If a suitable hoist is not available, raise and support the car on jackstands, and use a jack under the axle.

2. Support the rear axle with a jack that can be raised and lowered.

3. Remove the brake hose attaching brackets (right and left), allowing the hoses to hang freely. Do not disconnect the hoses.

4. Remove the track bar attaching bolts from the rear axle.

5. Remove both shock absorber lower attaching bolts from the axle.

6. Lower the axle. Remove the coil spring and insulator.

To install:

7. Position the spring and insulator on the axle. The leg on the upper coil of the spring must be parallel to the axle, facing the left hand side of the car.

8. Install the shock absorber and lower mounting bolts, then tighten to 43 ft. lbs. (58 Nm) for 1982–84 models, 35 ft. lbs. (47 Nm) for 1985–86 models, 44 ft. lbs. (59 Nm) for 1987–92 models, or 53 ft. lbs. (72 Nm) for 1993–96 models.

9. Install the track bar and tighten to 44 ft. lbs. (60 Nm) for 1982–92 models or 53 ft. lbs. (72 Nm) for 1993–96 models.

10. Install the brake line brackets to the frame, then tighten to 8 ft. lbs. (11 Nm).

11. Remove the axle support and lower the vehicle.

Leaf Spring

REMOVAL & INSTALLATION

AWD Vehicles

The 6000 STE AWD vehicle has rear leaf spring suspension rather than the common coil spring.

1. Loosen the lug nuts from the rear wheels.
2. Raise the vehicle with a suitable hoist. Remove the tire and wheel assembly.
3. Remove the 4 bolts from the jacking plate, then remove the jacking plate.
4. Install the spring compression tool J-33432. Unfasten the 1 bolt securing the brake line at the electronic ride control (ERC) sensor bracket to the left hand control arm, then move the bracket out of the way.
5. Remove both of the control arm outer nuts and bolts at the knuckles.

➡**It is not necessary to completely remove the control arms to permit removal of the leaf spring.**

6. Disconnect and remove the outer stabilizer bar brackets, then loosen the spring compression tool J-33432 to allow the control arm to drop, then remove the tool.
7. Unsecure the 4 bolts (2 on each side) from the left and right spring-to-cradle brackets, then remove the brackets.
8. Remove the leaf spring by sliding it outwards.

To install:

9. Position the leaf spring to the cradle assembly. Make sure that the spring is properly seated in the control arms.
10. Insert the 2 leaf spring-to-cradle brackets, use the 4 bolts and tighten them to 61 ft. lbs. (83 Nm).
11. Attach the spring compression tool J-33432 on the spring and tighten to draw the outer control arm bolt bores up to the knuckle bores.
12. Install the outer stabilizer bar brackets. Fasten the bolts and nuts to the outer control arms and tighten the nuts to 125 ft. lbs. (170 Nm).
13. Reinstall the 1 bolt on the left control arm which secures the brake line/ERC sensor bracket, then tighten to 18 ft. lbs. (24 Nm).
14. Remove the spring compressor tool.
15. Install the tire and wheel, then hand-tighten the lug nuts.
16. Lower the vehicle, then tighten the lug nuts to 100 ft. lbs. (136 Nm).

Track Bar

REMOVAL & INSTALLATION

♦ **See Figure 28**

1. Raise the vehicle on a hoist and support the rear axle.
2. On some models it may be necessary to remove the right hand lower shock bolt, then swing the shock aside.
3. On wagons it will be necessary to remove the track bar brace.
4. Remove the nut and bolt from both the axle and body attachments, then remove the bar.

To install:

5. Position the track bar at the axle mounting bracket and loosely install the bolt and nut.
6. Place the other end of the track bar into the body reinforcement and install the bolt and nut. Tighten the nut at the axle bracket to 44 ft. lbs. (60 Nm) for 1982–92 models or 53 ft. lbs. (72 Nm) for 1993–96 models. Tighten the nut at the body reinforcement to 35 ft. lbs. (47 Nm) for 1982–92 models, or 53 ft. lbs. (72 Nm) for 1993–96 models.
7. Remove the rear axle support and lower the vehicle.

Stabilizer Bar

REMOVAL & INSTALLATION

1. Loosen the rear lug nuts.
2. Raise and support the vehicle.

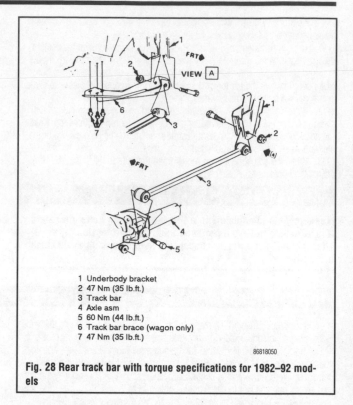

1 Underbody bracket
2 47 Nm (35 lb.ft.)
3 Track bar
4 Axle asm
5 60 Nm (44 lb.ft.)
6 Track bar brace (wagon only)
7 47 Nm (35 lb.ft.)

86818050

Fig. 28 Rear track bar with torque specifications for 1982–92 models

3. Remove the wheel and tire.
4. Unsecure the bolts and nuts attaching the outer stabilizer bar bracket to the control arm.
5. Remove the bolts attaching the inner stabilizer bar brackets to the cradle bracket.
6. Pull the stabilizer bar from the vehicle.

To install:

7. Position the stabilizer bar in the rear of the vehicle. Connect the stabilizer bar bracket to the cradle bracket with the bolts (on each side), then tighten them to 26 ft. lbs. (35 Nm).
8. Using the 3 bolts and nuts attach the outer stabilizer bar brackets (on each side) to the control arms, then tighten the bolts to 26 ft. lbs. (36 Nm).
9. Install the wheel and tire, then hand-tighten the lug nuts.
10. Lower the vehicle, then tighten the lug nuts to 100 ft. lbs. (136 Nm).

Shock Absorbers

REMOVAL & INSTALLATION

FWD Vehicles

♦ **See Figures 29, 30 and 31**

➡**If your vehicle is equipped with Electronic Ride Control (ERC) or super lift air shocks, you must bleed the system of air before disconnecting the hoses.**

1. Open the hatch or trunk lid, remove the trim cover if present, and remove the upper shock absorber nut.
2. Raise and support the car at a convenient working height if you desire. It is not necessary to remove the weight of the car from the shock absorbers, however, so you can leave the car on the ground if you prefer.
3. If the car is equipped with ERC or the superlift shock absorbers, disconnect the air line.
4. Remove the lower attaching bolt, then remove the shock.

To install:

5. If new shock absorbers are being installed, repeatedly compress them while inverted and extend them in their normal upright position. This will purge them of air.

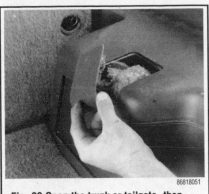

Fig. 29 Open the trunk or tailgate, then remove the shock absorber trim cover

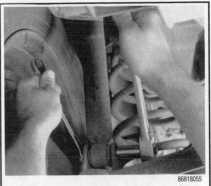

Fig. 30 Once the trim is removed, push the insulation aside and remove the shock nut cap. This will give you access to the upper shock nut

Fig. 31 Unfasten the lower attaching bolt, then remove the shock absorber

6. Insert the shock into position, then install the bolt and nut but do not tighten yet.

7. If super lift shocks are being installed, then connect the air hose to the shocks.

8. Lower the vehicle enough to guide the upper stud through the body opening, then install the upper nut loosely.

9. Tighten the lower mount nut and bolt to 43 ft. lbs. (58 Nm) for 1982–84 models, 38 ft. lbs. (51 Nm) for 1985–92 models, or 50 ft. lbs. (72 Nm) for 1993–96 models. Tighten the upper nut to 13 ft. lbs. (17 Nm) for 1982–83 models, 28 ft. lbs. (37 Nm) for 1984–92 models, or 18 ft. lbs. (25 Nm) for 1993–96 models.

10. Replace the upper nut cap, then the inner trim piece. Lower the vehicle the rest of the way, then close the trunk/liftgate.

11. Add air to the super lift shocks, approximately 80 kPa (12 psi), or see your owner's manual.

12. In the case of the ERC system, it automatically levels itself when the vehicle is on the ground and the key is turned on.

TESTING

Visually inspect the shock absorber. If there is evidence of leakage and the shock absorber is covered with oil, the shock is defective and should be replaced.

If there is no sign of excessive leakage (a small amount of weeping is normal) bounce the car at one corner by pressing down on the fender or bumper and releasing. When you have the car bouncing as much as you can, release the fender or bumper. The car should stop bouncing after the first rebound. If the bouncing continues past the center point of the bounce more than once, the shock absorbers are worn and should be replaced.

Rear Strut

REMOVAL & INSTALLATION

AWD Vehicles

▶ See Figures 32 and 33

The following tools or equivalent will be needed to do this repair: J-33432 leaf spring compressor and J-37619 ball joint stud remover.

1. Loosen the lug nuts on the rear wheels.
2. Open the decklid and raise the vehicle securely.
3. Remove the wheel and tire assembly, then remove the lug nuts.
4. Support the lower control arm with a suitable stand or install the leaf spring compressor tool J-33432.
5. Remove the outer toe link cotter pin and the castellated nut at the strut.
6. Disconnect the toe link end from the lower strut mount assembly using tool J-37619.
7. Remove the parking brake cable from the strut mount bracket and move it out of the way.
8. Remove the bolts from the parking brake cable bracket and remove the bracket.

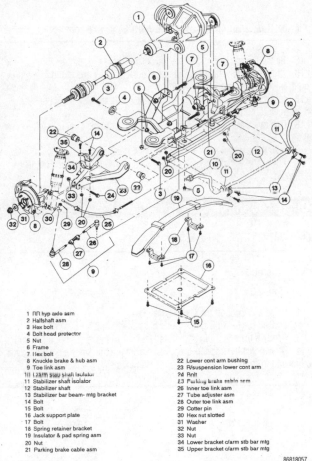

1	RR hyp axle asm
2	Halfshaft asm
3	Hex bolt
4	Bolt head protector
5	Nut
6	Frame
7	Hex bolt
8	Knuckle brake & hub asm
9	Toe link asm
10	C/arm stab shaft isolator
11	Stabilizer shaft isolator
12	Stabilizer shaft
13	Stabilizer bar beam- mtg bracket
14	Bolt
15	Bolt
16	Jack support plate
17	Bolt
18	Spring retainer bracket
19	Insulator & pad spring asm
20	Nut
21	Parking brake cable asm
22	Lower cont arm bushing
23	R/suspension lower cont arm
24	Bolt
25	Parking brake cable asm
26	Inner toe link asm
27	Tube adjuster asm
28	Outer toe link asm
29	Cotter pin
30	Hex nut slotted
31	Washer
32	Nut
33	Nut
34	Lower bracket c/arm stb bar mtg
35	Upper bracket c/arm stb bar mtg

Fig. 32 The AWD rear suspension utilizes one leaf spring and two strut assemblies, rather than shock absorbers

9. Loosen and remove the lower strut mount bolts that attach to the spindle, make sure to retain the nut plate for installation.

10. Disconnect the upper strut mount by removing the attaching bolts, then pull the strut assembly from the vehicle.

To install:

11. Position the strut to the upper strut mounting flange, install the upper strut mounting bolts and hand-tighten them.

12. Position the lower strut mount to the spindle assembly. Position the nut plate into place, then install the 2 bolts into the lower strut mount assembly.

13. Tighten the lower mount bolts to 148 ft. lbs. (200 Nm).

14. Install the brake cable bracket to the lower strut mount and install the 2 attaching bolts. Connect the parking brake cable into the cable bracket.

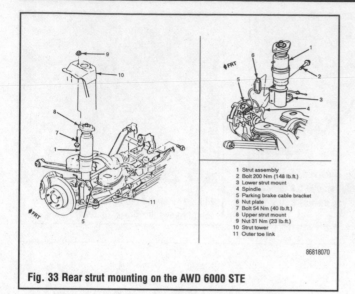

Fig. 33 Rear strut mounting on the AWD 6000 STE

1 Strut assembly
2 Bolt 200 Nm (148 lb.ft.)
3 Lower strut mount
4 Spindle
5 Parking brake cable bracket
6 Nut plate
7 Bolt 54 Nm (40 lb.ft.)
8 Upper strut mount
9 Nut 31 Nm (23 lb.ft.)
10 Strut tower
11 Outer toe link

86818070

15. Install the toe link end to the lower strut mount assembly.
16. Mount the castellated nut onto the outer toe link end at the lower strut mount, then tighten to 46 ft. lbs. (62 Nm).
17. Insert a new cotter pin at the castellated nut, tighten the upper strut mount bolts to 40 ft. lbs. (54 Nm).
18. Remove the leaf spring compression tool or stand supporting the control arm.
19. Install the wheel and tire, hand-tighten the lug nuts.
20. Lower the vehicle, tighten the lug nuts to 100 ft. lbs. (136 Nm). Close the decklid.

Outer Toe Link

REMOVAL & INSTALLATION

AWD Vehicles

▶ See Figure 34

1. Raise and support the vehicle.
2. Loosen the toe link sleeve outer tab nut and bolt.
3. Remove the cotter pin and castellated nut from the outer toe link end.
4. Disconnect the parking brake cable from the bracket. Remove the outer toe link end from the lower strut mount assembly using the ball joint stud

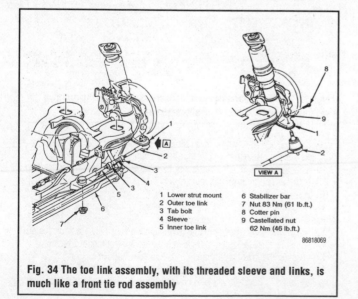

1 Lower strut mount
2 Outer toe link
3 Tab bolt
4 Sleeve
5 Inner toe link
6 Stabilizer bar
7 Nut 83 Nm (61 lb.ft.)
8 Cotter pin
9 Castellated nut
62 Nm (46 lb.ft.)

VIEW A

86818069

Fig. 34 The toe link assembly, with its threaded sleeve and links, is much like a front tie rod assembly

remover J-37619 or an equivalent. Remove one parking brake bracket bolt and loosen the other. Swing the bracket out of the way to allow installation of tool J-37619.
5. Remove the outer toe link from the toe link sleeve.

To install:
6. Insert the outer toe link to the toe link sleeve. Install the outer end into the lower strut mount.
7. Put the castellated nut onto the outer toe link end at the lower strut mount, then tighten the nut to 46 ft. lbs. (62 Nm). Insert a new cotter pin to the outer toe link end.
8. Tighten the parking brake bracket bolts and route the cable into the bracket.
9. Adjust the rear wheel alignment as necessary, then tighten the tow link sleeve outer tab nut and bolt to 14 ft. lbs. (19 Nm).
10. Lower the vehicle.

Inner Toe Link

REMOVAL & INSTALLATION

AWD Vehicles

▶ See Figure 34

1. Raise and support the vehicle.
2. Loosen the toe link sleeve inner tab nut and bolt.
3. Remove the nut from the inner toe link end.
4. Disconnect the inner toe link end from the rear crossmember assembly using the ball joint stud remover J-37619 or an equivalent.
5. Remove the inner toe link from the sleeve.

To install:
6. Install the toe link to the sleeve, then position the inner toe link end to the rear crossmember support bar.
7. Connect with the nut to the inner toe link end, then tighten the nut to 61 ft. lbs. (83 Nm).
8. Adjust the rear wheel alignment as needed.
9. Tighten the toe link sleeve inner tab nut and bolt to 14 ft. lbs. (19 Nm).
10. Lower the vehicle.

Lower Control Arm

REMOVAL & INSTALLATION

AWD Vehicles

1. Loosen the lug nuts on the rear wheels.
2. Raise and support the vehicle.
3. Support the control arm with a suitable stand or install tool J-33432 to neutralize the spring tension.
4. Remove the tire and wheel assembly.
5. Disconnect the 2 outer stabilizer bar bracket-to-control arm bolts and nuts.
6. Remove the one bolt connecting the brake line/ERC sensor bracket to the control arm (LH only), then move the bracket out of the way.
7. Remove the control arm-to-knuckle attaching bolt and nut.
8. Disconnect the lower control arm by slowly lowering the stand or loosening the spring compressing tool.
9. Unfasten the 2 control arm-to-cradle bolts and nuts.
10. Slide the control arm from the leaf spring.

To install:
11. Connect the control arm on the leaf spring, ensure that the leaf spring is in the correct position.
12. Attach the 2 control arm-to-cradle bolts and nuts, hand-tighten them only.
13. Raise the control arm or tighten the spring compressor to align the outer control arm bolt bore with the knuckle bore.
14. Install the control arm to knuckle with the attaching nuts and bolts.
15. Tighten the control arm nut at the knuckle to 125 ft. lbs. then the control arm at the cradle to 61 ft. lbs. (83 Nm).

16. Install the 1 bolt securing the brake line to the ERC sensor bracket to the control arm (LH only), then tighten the bolt to 18 ft. lbs. (24 Nm).

17. Connect the 2 outer stabilizer bar bracket to control arm bolts and nuts, then tighten them to 26 ft. lbs. (354 Nm).

18. Remove the stand or spring compressing tool that was used to support the arm.

19. Install the tire and wheel, hand-tighten the lug nuts.

20. Lower the vehicle, then tighten the lug nuts to 100 ft. lbs. (136 Nm).

Rear Hub and Bearing

REPLACEMENT

FWD Vehicles

1. Loosen the wheel lug nuts. Raise and support the car and remove the wheel.

2. Remove the brake drum. Removal procedures are covered in the next section, if needed.

➡ **Do not hammer on the brake drum to remove, as damage to the bearing may result.**

3. Remove the four hub and bearing retaining bolts, then remove the assembly from the axle.

➡ **The bolts which attach the hub and bearing assembly also support the brake assembly. When removing these bolts, be sure to support the brake assembly with a wire or something comparable. Do not allow the brake line to support the brake assembly.**

4. If equipped, disconnect the rear ABS wheel speed sensor.

To install:

5. Connect the ABS wheel speed sensor.

6. Install the hub and bearing assembly to the rear axle. Tighten the bolts to 45 ft. lbs. (60 Nm) for 1982–92 vehicles or 60 ft. lbs. (82 Nm) for 1983–96 vehicles.

7. Install the rear brake drum, then adjust the brakes. Install the wheel and lug nuts.

8. Lower the vehicle, then tighten the lug nuts to 100 ft. lbs. (136 Nm).

AWD Vehicles

◆ **See Figures 35 and 36**

1. Loosen the lug nuts, then raise and support the vehicle. Remove the wheel and tire assembly.

2. Disconnect the caliper assembly and suspend on a wire. Do not allow it to hang from the brake hose.

➡ **Do not hammer on the brake caliper, as this could cause damage to the bearing.**

3. Remove the hub and bearing assembly from the axle. If necessary, use a special tool such as J-28733-A or equivalent.

➡ **The bolts which attach the hub and bearing assembly also support the brake assembly. When removing these bolts, be sure to support the brake assembly with a wire or something comparable. Do not allow the brake line to support the brake assembly.**

To install:

4. Install the hub and bearing assembly into the rear axle. Tighten the hub and bearing bolts to 61 ft. lbs. (83 Nm).

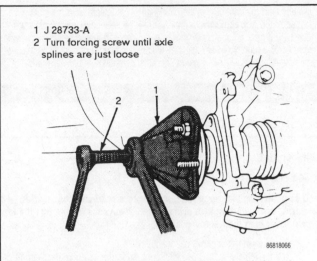

1 J 28733-A
2 Turn forcing screw until axle splines are just loose

Fig. 35 In order to remove the hub and bearing assembly from the axle, a special tool may be necessary

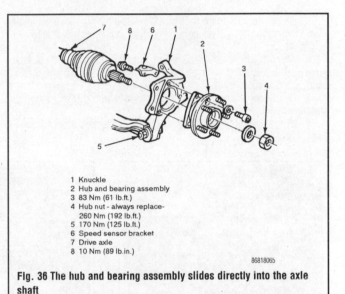

1 Knuckle
2 Hub and bearing assembly
3 83 Nm (61 lb.ft.)
4 Hub nut - always replace-
  260 Nm (192 lb.ft.)
5 170 Nm (125 lb.ft.)
6 Speed sensor bracket
7 Drive axle
8 10 Nm (89 lb.in.)

Fig. 36 The hub and bearing assembly slides directly into the axle shaft

5. Attach the brake caliper to the rear rotor.

6. Install the rear wheel, then hand-tighten the lug nuts.

7. Lower the car, then tighten the lug nuts to 100 ft. lbs. (136 Nm).

Rear End Alignment

When checking the rear alignment, the ELC system must have the superlift struts inflated with residual pressure only. Always install the alignment equipment following the manufactures instructions. Measure the alignment angles and record the readings. If adjustments are needed, make them in the camber toe order. Camber is adjusted by moving the top of the rotor in or out. Toe-in can be increased or decreased by changing the length of the tie rods. A threaded sleeve is provided for this purpose.

STEERING

The A-Body cars use an aluminum-housed Saginaw manual rack and pinion steering gear as standard equipment. The pinion is supported by and turns in a sealed ball bearing at the top and a pressed-in roller bearing at the bottom. The rack moves in bushings pressed into each end of the rack housing.

Wear compensation occurs through the action of an adjuster spring which forces the rack against the pinion teeth. This adjuster eliminates the need for periodic pinion preload adjustments. Preload is adjustable only at overhaul.

The inner tie rod assemblies are both threaded and staked to the rack. A special joint is used, allowing both rocking and rotating motion of the tie rods. The inner tie rod assemblies are lubricated for life and require no periodic attention.

Any service other than replacement of the outer tie rods or the boots requires removal of the unit from the car.

The optional power rack and pinion steering gear is an integral unit, and shares most features with the manual gear. A rotary control valve directs the hydraulic fluid to either side of the rack piston. The integral rack piston is attached to the rack and converts the hydraulic pressure into left or right linear motion. A vane-type constant displacement pump with integral reservoir provides hydraulic pressure. No in-car adjustments are necessary or possible on the system, except for periodic belt tension checks and adjustments for the pump.

Steering Wheel

REMOVAL & INSTALLATION

Without Air Bag

♦ **See Figures 37 thru 43**

➡**Disconnect the battery ground cable before removing the steering wheel. When installing a steering wheel, always make sure that the turn signal lever is in the neutral position.**

1. Disconnect the negative battery cable.
2. If your vehicle is equipped with controls for the radio on the steering wheel proceed as follows:
    a. Pry out the control button assembly with a thin bladed tool along the top of the edge of the assembly.
    b. Disconnect the steering wheel control.
3. On vehicles without the radio controls on the steering pad, take a thin-bladed tool and pry the pad off the steering wheel. On wheels with a center cap, pull off the cap.
4. After lifting the trim off, pry the horn wires from the back of the pad. On some models gently push down on the horn lead and turn left, the wire and spring will then come out of the canceling cam tower.
5. Remove the retainer ring with a pair of ring expanders, then remove the steering wheel nut.
6. Mark the wheel-to-shaft relationship, and then remove the wheel with a threaded puller.

➡**When removing a steering wheel with electronic accessory controls in the hub, take care to avoid damaging the electronic circuits. Wheel puller bolts used with the puller should be turned no more than 5 complete turns, in order to avoid contact with the sensitive circuits.**

7. Now the steering wheel will slide off the shaft quite easily.
To install:
8. Install the wheel on the shaft aligning the previously made marks.
9. Install the steering wheel nut, then tighten to 30 ft. lbs. (41 Nm).
10. Insert the retaining ring onto the steering shaft. Connect the horn wires into the canceling cam, pushing down and turning to the right into the lock position.
11. Install the center trim pad and reconnect the battery cable.

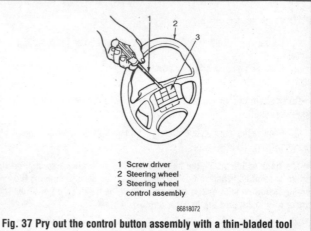

1 Screw driver
2 Steering wheel
3 Steering wheel control assembly

86818072

Fig. 37 Pry out the control button assembly with a thin-bladed tool along the top of the edge, being careful not to damage the control assembly

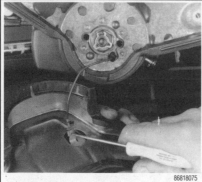

86818075

Fig. 38 Carefully pry the lead wire for the horn off of the horn pad

86818076

Fig. 39 Remove the retainer ring with a pair of retaining ring expanders

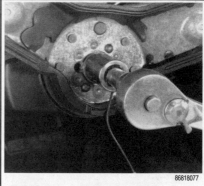

86818077

Fig. 40 Use a ratchet and socket to remove the steering wheel nut

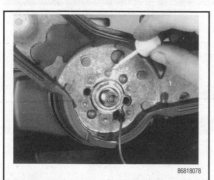

86818078

Fig. 41 Mark the wheel-to-shaft relationship with some correction fluid or white paint

86818079

Fig. 42 Install a universal threaded puller to remove the steering wheel . . .

86818080

Fig. 43 . . . and the steering wheel will slide off the shaft quite easily

With Air Bag

Whenever you are working on a vehicle with the Supplemental Inflatable Restraint (SIR) System, it is recommended that an authorized service center do the work. This system can cause serious injury to one's self if the air bag deploys.

1. Disable the SIR system as follows:

a. Turn the steering wheel so that the vehicles wheels are pointing straight ahead.

b. Turn the ignition key to the **LOCK** position and remove the key.

c. Remove the air bag fuse from the fuse block.

d. Unsecure the left sound insulator by removing the screws and nuts.

e. Remove the Connector Position Assurance (CPA) and the yellow two-way connector from the base of the steering column.

➡**When the "AIR BAG" fuse is removed from the fuse block, and the key is in the ON position the "AIR BAG" warning lamp will be ON. This is a normal condition and does not mean that the SIR system is malfunctioning.**

2. Loosen the screws in the back of the steering wheel using a T-30 Torx® driver or an equivalent until the inflator module can be released from the steering wheel.

✳✳ CAUTION

Whenever carrying a live inflator module, make sure that the bag and opening are pointed away from you. Never carry the module by the wires or connector on the underside of the module. In case of an accidental deployment, the bag will deploy with minimal amount of injury. When placing the live inflator on a bench or any other surface, always face the bag and trim cover up, away from the surface. Never rest a steering column assembly on the steering wheel with the inflator module face down on the column vertical. This will allow free space for the bag to expand in case of accidental deployment. Otherwise, personal injury could result.

3. Disconnect the coil assembly and the Connector Position Assurance (CPA) from the inflator module.

4. Using a thin bladed tool gently pry the top of the pad away from the steering wheel.

5. Disconnect the horn lead from the steering column by gently pushing down on the lead and turning left. The wire and spring will come out of the cancelling cam.

6. Remove the retainer ring with a pair of retaining ring expanders, then remove the nut from the steering shaft.

7. Mark the wheel-to-shaft relationship.

8. Attach a threaded universal puller to the steering wheel, do not screw the bolts in all the way this could cause damage to the coil assembly.

9. Remove the steering wheel assembly.

To install:

10. Install the steering wheel by aligning the mark on the steering wheel with the mark on the shaft.

11. Install the steering wheel nut, then tighten to 30 ft. lbs. (41 Nm). Install the retaining ring.

12. Connect the horn lead to the canceling cam tower by pushing down and turning right into the lock position.

13. Install the inflator module,

a. Attach the coil assembly connector and connector position assurance (CPA) to the inflator module.

b. Route the coil assembly lead around the mounting post and secure it under the clip.

c. Attach the inflator module to the steering wheel. DO NOT use the module if it has been dropped from a height of 8.2 ft. (2.5m) or more.

d. Ensure the wiring is not exposed or trapped between the inflator module and the steering wheel assembly on installation.

e. Tighten the inflator module screws to 25 inch lbs. (3 Nm).

14. Enable the SIR system,

a. Connect the yellow two-way connector to the base of the steering column and the connect position assurance (CPA).

b. Install the left sound insulator with the mounting screws.

c. Insert the AIR BAG fuse in the fuse block.

d. Turn the ignition switch to the **RUN** position and verify that the "AIR

BAG" warning lamp flashes 7 times and then turns OFF. If it does not turn off, have your SIR system checked by an authorized service center.

Turn Signal Switch

✳✳ CAUTION

On vehicles equipped with an SIR (air bag) system, disable the system before proceeding, by following the instructions at the beginning of this section. Failure to do so could result in accidental inflation of the air bag and personal injury.

REMOVAL & INSTALLATION

▶ See Figures 44, 45 and 46

1. Disable the SIR system if equipped with an air bag.

2. Disconnect the negative battery cable.

3. On vehicles equipped with an air bag, follow the special instructions in this section on steering wheel removal.

✳✳ CAUTION

Whenever carrying a live inflator module, make sure that the bag and opening are pointed away from you. Never carry the module by the wires or connector on the underside of the module. In case of an accidental deployment, the bag will deploy with minimal amount of injury. When placing the live inflator on a bench or any other surface, always face the bag and trim cover up, away from the surface. Never rest a steering column assembly on the steering wheel with the inflator module face down on the column vertical. This will allow free space for the bag to expand in case of accidental deployment. Otherwise, personal injury could result.

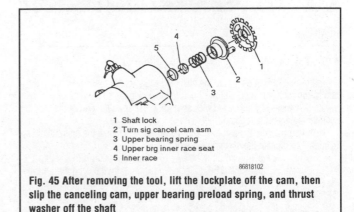

SNAP RING

86818087

Fig. 44 Position the U-shaped lockplate compressing tool on the end of the steering shaft and compress the lockplate by turning the shaft nut clockwise, then pry the wire snapring out of the shaft groove

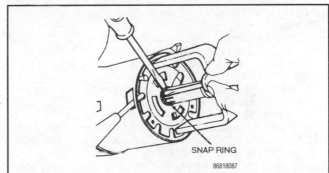

1 Shaft lock
2 Turn sig cancel cam asm
3 Upper bearing spring
4 Upper brg inner race seat
5 Inner race

86818102

Fig. 45 After removing the tool, lift the lockplate off the cam, then slip the canceling cam, upper bearing preload spring, and thrust washer off the shaft

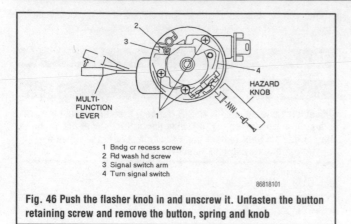

1 Bndg cr recess screw
2 Rd wash hd screw
3 Signal switch arm
4 Turn signal switch

86818101

Fig. 46 Push the flasher knob in and unscrew it. Unfasten the button retaining screw and remove the button, spring and knob

4. Remove the steering wheel as previously outlined. Remove the trim cover.
5. Loosen the cover screws. Pry the cover off with a flat-bladed tool, then lift the cover off the shaft.
6. Position the U-shaped lockplate compressing tool on the end of the steering shaft and compress the lock plate by turning the shaft nut clockwise, then pry the wire snapring out of the shaft groove.
7. Remove the tool and lift the lockplate off the shaft.
8. Slip the canceling cam, upper bearing preload spring, and thrust washer off the shaft.
9. Remove the turn signal lever. Push the flasher knob in and unscrew it. Remove the button retaining screw and remove the button, spring and knob.
10. Pull the switch connector out the mast jacket and tape the upper part to facilitate switch removal. Attach a long piece of wire to the turn signal switch connector. When installing the turn signal switch, feed this wire through the column first, and then use this wire to pull the switch connector into position. On tilt wheels, place the turn signal and shifter housing in low position and remove the harness cover.
11. Remove the three switch mounting screws. Remove the switch by pulling it straight up while guiding the wiring harness cover through the column.
To install:
12. Install the replacement switch by working the connector and cover down through the housing and under the bracket. On tilt models, the connector is worked down through the housing, under the bracket, and then the cover is installed on the harness.
13. Install the switch mounting screws and the connector on the mast jacket bracket. Install the column-to-dash trim plate.
14. Install the flasher knob and the turn signal lever.
15. With the turn signal lever in neutral and the flasher know out, slide the thrust washer, upper bearing preload spring, and canceling cam onto the shaft.
16. Position the lock plate on the shaft and press it down until a new snapring can be inserted in the shaft groove. Always use a new snapring when assembling.
17. Install the cover and the steering wheel.
18. Enable the SIR system if an air bag is present.

Ignition Switch

REMOVAL & INSTALLATION

▶ **See Figure 47**

The switch is located inside the channel section of the brake pedal support and is completely inaccessible without first lowering the steering column. The switch is actuated by a rod and rack assembly. A gear on the end of the lock cylinder engages the toothed upper end of the rod.

1. If your vehicle is equipped with the SIR system follow the instructions in Section 6 to disable the system before proceeding.
2. Lower the steering column, be sure to properly support it.
3. Put the switch in the **OFF**, unlocked position. With the cylinder removed, the rod is in the lock position when it is in the next to the uppermost detent. The **OFF**, unlocked position is two detents from the top.
4. Remove the two switch screws and remove the switch assembly.

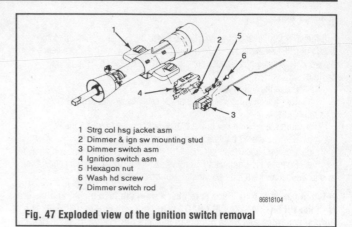

1 Strg col hsg jacket asm
2 Dimmer & ign sw mounting stud
3 Dimmer switch asm
4 Ignition switch asm
5 Hexagon nut
6 Wash hd screw
7 Dimmer switch rod

86818104

Fig. 47 Exploded view of the ignition switch removal

To install:
5. Before installing, place the new switch in the **OFF**, unlocked position and make sure the lock cylinder and actuating rod are in the **OFF**, unlocked (third detent from the top) position.
6. Install the activating rod into the switch, then assemble the switch onto the column. Tighten the mounting screws. Use only the specified screws since overlength screws could impair the collapsibility of the column.
7. Reinstall the steering column.
8. Enable the SIR system.

Ignition Lock Cylinder

✳✳ CAUTION

If the car is equipped with an air bag, do not service the steering column or dashboard components. Extreme danger of air bag deployment exists even with the battery removed! Serious injury could occur.

REMOVAL & INSTALLATION

Without Air Bag

1. Place the ignition switch in the **RUN** position.
2. Remove the lockplate, turn signal switch and buzzer switch.
3. Remove the screw and lock cylinder.

➡ **If the screw is dropped on removal, it could fall into the column, requiring complete disassembly to retrieve the screw.**

To install:
4. Rotate the cylinder clockwise to align cylinder key with the keyway in the housing.
5. Push the lock all the way in.
6. Install the screw. Tighten the screw to 14 inch lbs. (2 Nm) for adjustable columns and 25 inch lbs. (3 Nm) for standard columns.

With Air Bag

▶ **See Figure 48**

✳✳ CAUTION

Before proceeding, refer to Section 6 for information on disabling and enabling the SIR (air bag) system; otherwise, serious injury could occur.

1. Turn the steering wheel so the vehicles wheels are pointed straight ahead.
2. Place the ignition switch into the **LOCK** position to prevent undercentering of the coil assembly.
3. Disable the SIR system. Disconnect the negative battery cable.

4. Remove the coil assembly retaining ring, then disconnect the inflatable restraint coil assembly. Let the switch hang freely if removal is not needed. To remove the coil assembly proceed.

5. Remove the wave washer, then the shaft retaining lock ring with tool J-23653-SIR to push down on the shaft lock. Dispose of the ring, it is not reusable.

6. Remove the shaft lock, then disconnect the canceling cam assembly.

7. Remove the upper bearing spring, race seat and race.

8. Position the turn signal to the right turn (up) position.

9. Remove the multi-function lever and hazard knob assembly. Unfasten the round washer head screw and signal switch arm, along with the turn signal switch screws.

10. Remove the turn signal switch assembly by unfastening the connector from the bulkhead connector. Gently pull on the harness through the column and disconnect.

11. Make sure the coil assembly does not become uncentered, this could happen if the centering spring is pushed down letting the hub rotate while the coil is removed from the steering column

12. Remove the inflatable restraint coil assembly with the wiring harness from the column assembly.

13. Remove the wire protector, then attach a length of mechanics wire to the coil terminal connector to aid in reassembly. Then gently pull the wire through the column.

14. Remove the key from the steering column lock cylinder set, then remove the buzzer switch assembly.

15. Reinsert the key into the lock cylinder, turn it to the **LOCK** position.

16. Remove the lock retaining screw, then the cylinder.

To install:

➡**Make sure all fasteners are securely seated before applying the necessary torque. If you fail to do so, component damage or malfunctioning of the steering column may occur.**

17. Install the lock cylinder assembly, insert the retaining screw, then tighten to 22 inch lbs. (2.5 Nm).

18. Insert the key into the lock cylinder. Install the buzzer switch assembly. Turn the key to the **LOCK** position.

19. Install the turn signal switch assembly wiring harness through the column, let the switch hang freely. Connect the wiring to the bulkhead.

20. Insert the coil assembly wiring harness through the column letting the coil hang freely. Attach the turn signal assembly with the binding head screws. Tighten the screws to 30 inch lbs. (3 Nm).

21. Attach the signal switch arm with the round washer head screw, tighten the screw to 20 inch lbs. (2 Nm).

22. Install the hazard knob assembly and the multi-function lever.

23. Install the inner race, upper bearing race seat and spring. Attach the turn signal cancelling cam assembly, apply grease for lubrication.

24. Replace the shaft lock and install a new shaft lock retaining ring. Use tool J-23653-SIR or equivalent to push down on the shaft lock. The ring must be firmly seated in the groove on the shaft.

➡**Set the steering shaft so that the block tooth on the race and upper shaft is at the 12 o'clock position. The wheel on the car should be straight ahead. Set the ignition switch to the LOCK position, as this will ensure no damage to the coil assembly.**

25. Install the wave washer, then attach the coil assembly, make sure it is centered correctly.

26. Attach the coil assembly retaining ring, the ring must be firmly seated in the groove on the shaft.

27. Gently pull the lower coil assembly, turn signal, and pivot (pulse) wires to remove any kinks that may be inside the steering column assembly. If you fail to do this you can damage the wiring.

28. Complete assembling the steering column assembly.

29. Attach the negative battery cable.

30. Check the functions of the turn signal, make sure it cancels when turned on and the steering wheel is turned.

31. Enable the SIR system.

Steering Linkage

REMOVAL & INSTALLATION

Tie Rod Ends

INNER

▶ **See Figures 49, 50 and 51**

1. Loosen the lug nuts.
2. Raise and support the vehicle safely.

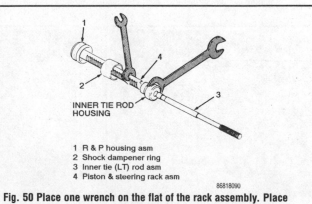

Fig. 49 Loosen the jam nut on the steering rack (inner tie rod)

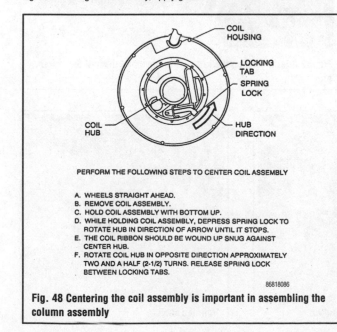

PERFORM THE FOLLOWING STEPS TO CENTER COIL ASSEMBLY

A. WHEELS STRAIGHT AHEAD.
B. REMOVE COIL ASSEMBLY.
C. HOLD COIL ASSEMBLY WITH BOTTOM UP.
D. WHILE HOLDING COIL ASSEMBLY, DEPRESS SPRING LOCK TO ROTATE HUB IN DIRECTION OF ARROW UNTIL IT STOPS.
E. THE COIL RIBBON SHOULD BE WOUND UP SNUG AGAINST CENTER HUB.
F. ROTATE COIL HUB IN OPPOSITE DIRECTION APPROXIMATELY TWO AND A HALF (2-1/2) TURNS. RELEASE SPRING LOCK BETWEEN LOCKING TABS.

Fig. 48 Centering the coil assembly is important in assembling the column assembly

1 R & P housing asm
2 Shock dampener ring
3 Inner tie (LT) rod asm
4 Piston & steering rack asm

Fig. 50 Place one wrench on the flat of the rack assembly. Place another wrench on the flats of the inner tie rod housing. Rotate the housing counter-clockwise until the tie rod separates from the rack

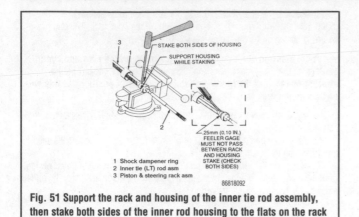

1 Shock dampener ring
2 Inner tie (LT) rod asm
3 Piston & steering rack asm

Fig. 51 Support the rack and housing of the inner tie rod assembly, then stake both sides of the inner rod housing to the flats on the rack

3. Remove the tire and wheel assembly.
4. Remove the rack and pinion assembly from the vehicle.
5. Disconnect and remove the outer tie rod from the inner tie rod assembly.
6. Loosen the jam nut on the steering rack (inner tie rod).
7. Remove the tie rod end nut and the end clamp. Disconnect the boot clamp with side cutters and discard the boot.
8. Slide the shock dampener from the inner tie rod assembly and the other side of the rack.
9. Make sure you hold on to the rack during the inner tie rod removal to prevent rack damage.

➡**In order to maintain proper front end alignment after installation, be sure to count the number of turns while removing the tie rod.**

10. Separate the inner tie rod end from the rack. Place one wrench on the flat of the rack assembly. Then, place a wrench on the flats of the inner tie rod housing. Rotate the housing counterclockwise until the tie rod separates from the rack.
To install:
11. The rack must be held during the inner tie rod installation to prevent internal gear damage.
12. Install the rack and pinion assembly, then slide the shock dampener on top the rack.
13. Screw the tie rod end onto the steering rack (inner tie rod) the same number of turns as counted for removal. This will give approximately correct toe. Tighten the nut approximately 70 ft. lbs. (95 Nm).
14. Make sure that the tie rod rocks freely in the housing before staking the inner tie rod assembly or the rack.
15. Support the rack and housing of the inner tie rod assembly, then stake both sides of the inner rod housing to the flats on the rack.
16. Check both stakes by inserting a (0.25mm) 0.010 inch feeler gauge between the rack and the tie rod housing as shown in the picture. The feeler must not pass between the rack and the housing stake.
17. Slide the shock dampener over the housing until it engages, then install a new boot clamp onto the rack and pinion boot.
18. Apply grease to the inner tie rod and housing. Insert the elbow of the boot into the breather tube. Install the boot onto the housing until it seats in the housing groove.

➡**Do not twist or pucker the boot after installation.**

19. Position a new boot clamp on the boot and crimp, then position the tie rod end clamp with a pair of pliers on the boot.
20. Install a hex jam nut to the inner tie rod assembly and tighten, then install the outer tie rod.
21. Install the tie and wheel assembly, hand-tighten the lug nuts.
22. Lower the vehicle, then tighten the lug nuts to 100 ft. lbs. (136 Nm).

OUTER

◆ **See Figures 52, 53, 54 and 55**

1. Loosen the lug nuts, then raise and support the vehicle.
2. Remove the tire and wheel assembly.
3. Loosen the jam nut.
4. Remove and discard the cotter pin.
5. Using a suitable tool remove the hex nut holding the tie rod in place.
6. With a tie rod puller, the tie rod can be separated from the knuckle.
7. After separation, unscrew the end from the shaft.
To install:
8. Connect the new outer tie rod end onto the inner shaft, then connect the tie rod end to the knuckle.
9. Tighten the hex slotted nut to 31–52 ft. lbs. (42–70 Nm) and align the cotter pin with the slot, (⅙ turn maximum). Do not back off the nut to install the cotter pin.
10. Insert a new cotter pin into the tie rod stud.
11. Adjust the toe, then tighten the jam nut to 52 ft. lbs. (70 Nm).

Fig. 52 After loosening the jam nut, remove and discard the cotter pin

Fig. 53 Using a suitable tool, remove the hex nut holding the tie rod in place

Fig. 54 The tie rod can be separated from the knuckle with a tie rod puller

Fig. 55 After separation, unscrew the end from the shaft

Rack Bearing Preload

ADJUSTMENT

1. Make the adjustment with the front wheels raised and the steering wheel centered. Be sure to check the returnability of the steering wheel to the center after adjustment.
2. Loosen the adjuster plug locknut and turn the adjuster plug clockwise until it bottoms in the gear assembly, then back off 50°–70° (approximately ⅙ revolution).
3. Install the lock to the adjusting nut, then tighten the adjusting nut to 50 ft. lbs. (70 Nm) while holding the adjuster plug stationary.

Manual Rack and Pinion

REMOVAL & INSTALLATION

▶ **See Figure 56**

1. Raise the intermediate shaft seal and remove intermediate shaft-to-stub shaft pinch bolt.
2. Raise and support the vehicle on jackstands, then remove both front wheel and tire assemblies.
3. Remove the cotter pins and nuts from both tie rod ends. Using tool J-6627 or BT-7101, press the tie rod ends from the steering knuckle.
4. If equipped with an Air Management pipe, remove the bracket bolt from the crossmember.
5. Remove the 2 rear cradle mounting bolts and lower the rear of the cradle about 4–5 in. (102–127mm).

❊❊ **WARNING**

If the rear of the cradle is lowered too far, the engine components nearest the cowl may be damaged.

6. If equipped, remove the rack and pinion heat shield.
7. Remove the rack and pinion mounting bolts, then the gear assembly through the left wheel opening.
To install:
8. Install the gear assembly through the left wheel opening and install the mounting bolts.
9. Install the heat shield.
10. Raise the rear of the cradle and install the mounting bolts.
11. Install the bracket bolt to the crossmember under the air management pipe.
12. Install the tie rod ends to the steering knuckles, install the retaining nuts and insert new cotter pins.
13. Install the front wheels and lower the vehicle.

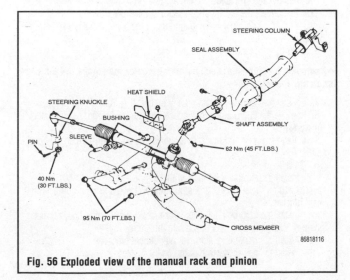

Fig. 56 Exploded view of the manual rack and pinion

14. Install the intermediate shaft seal and the intermediate shaft-to-stub shaft pinch bolt.
15. Check and adjust the toe-in as necessary.

Power Rack and Pinion

REMOVAL & INSTALLATION

Except 2.2L and 1993–96 3.1L Engines

▶ **See Figure 57**

1. Raise the intermediate shaft seal and remove intermediate shaft-to-stub shaft pinch bolt.
2. Remove the air cleaner and disconnect the pressure hoses from the steering gear.
3. Raise and support the vehicle on jackstands, then remove both front wheel and tire assemblies.
4. Remove the cotter pins and nuts from both tie rod ends. Using tool J-6627 or BT-7101, press the tie rod ends from the steering knuckle.
5. If equipped with an Air Management pipe, remove the bracket bolt from the crossmember.
6. Remove the 2 rear cradle mounting bolts and lower the rear of the cradle about 4–5 in. (102–127mm).

❊❊ **WARNING**

If the rear of the cradle is lowered too far, the engine components nearest the cowl may be damaged.

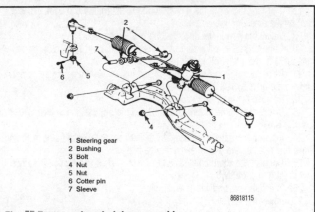

1 Steering gear
2 Bushing
3 Bolt
4 Nut
5 Nut
6 Cotter pin
7 Sleeve

Fig. 57 Power rack and pinion assembly

7. If equipped, remove the rack and pinion heat shield.
8. Remove the rack and pinion mounting bolts, then the gear assembly through the left wheel opening.
To install:
9. Install the gear assembly through the left wheel opening and install the mounting bolts.
10. Install the heat shield.
11. Raise the rear of the cradle and install the mounting bolts.
12. Install the bracket bolt to the crossmember under the air management pipe.
13. Install the tie rod ends to the steering knuckles, install the retaining nuts and insert new cotter pins.
14. Install the front wheels and lower the vehicle.
15. Install the high pressure hoses to the steering gear and install the air cleaner.
16. Install the intermediate shaft seal and the intermediate shaft-to-stub shaft pinch bolt.

2.2L Engine

1. Disconnect the negative battery cable.
2. Install an engine support fixture J-28467-A, or the equivalent.

3. Raise and safely support the vehicle.
4. Remove the tire and wheel assembly.
5. Remove the intermediate shaft lower pinch bolt.
6. Disconnect the intermediate shaft from stub shaft.

✳✳ CAUTION

Failure to disconnect the intermediate shaft from the rack and pinion stub shaft can result in damage to the steering gear and/or intermediate shaft. This damage can cause loss of steering control which could result in personal injury.

7. Remove the exhaust pipe hanger bracket near rear of frame including the brake line retainer and rubber exhaust pipe hangers.
8. Remove the engine and transaxle mount nuts at the subframe.
9. Support the rear of the subframe with jack stands.
10. Remove the rear subframe bolts and discard.
11. Lower the subframe for access to rack and pinion.

➡Do not lower the rear of the cradle too far, as damage to engine components nearest the cowl may result.

12. Remove the cotter pins and castle nuts from the outer tie rod ends and separate the tie rod ends from the steering knuckles using a suitable puller.
13. Disconnect the power steering lines from the steering gear.
14. Remove the rack and pinion mounting bolts and nuts.
15. Remove the rack and pinion through left wheel opening.
To Install:
16. Install the rack and pinion through left wheel opening.
17. Install the rack and pinion mounting bolts and nuts and tighten to 66 ft. lbs. (90 Nm).
18. Connect the power steering lines to the rack using new O-rings and tighten the fittings to 13 ft. lbs. (17 Nm) on the return line and 21 ft. lbs. (28 Nm) on the pressure line.
19. Install the power steering line clip to steering gear.
20. Connect the tie rod ends to the steering knuckles. Tighten the castle nuts to 31 ft. lbs. (42 Nm). Install new cotter pins.
21. Raise the subframe into position and install new frame mounting bolts. Tighten the bolts to 103 ft. lbs. (140 Nm).
22. Remove the jack.
23. Install the engine mount and transaxle mount nuts and tighten to 39 ft. lbs. (53 Nm).
24. Install the exhaust pipe hanger bracket near the rear of frame including brake line retainer and rubber exhaust pipe hanger.
25. Connect the intermediate shaft to the stub shaft and tighten the pinch bolt to 29 ft. lbs. (40 Nm).
26. Install the tire and wheel assembly.
27. Lower the vehicle.
28. Remove the support fixture.
29. Connect the negative battery cable.
30. Refill the power steering reservoir and bleed the system.
31. Check the front end alignment and adjust as necessary.

3.1L Engine (VIN M)

1. Disconnect the negative battery cable.
2. Remove engine torque strut from engine.
3. Install an engine support fixture J-28467-A, or the equivalent.
4. Raise and safely support the vehicle.
5. Remove the tire and wheel assembly.
6. Remove the cotter pins and castle nuts from the outer tie rod ends and separate the tie rod ends from the steering knuckles using a suitable puller.
7. Remove the center engine and rear transaxle mounts from the frame.
8. Remove the intermediate shaft lower pinch bolt.
9. Disconnect the intermediate shaft from stub shaft.

✳✳ CAUTION

Failure to disconnect the intermediate shaft from the rack and pinion stub shaft can result in damage to the steering gear and/or intermediate shaft. This damage can cause loss of steering control which could result in personal injury.

10. Remove the brace bolts and brace, including brake line brace.
11. Support the rear of the subframe with jack stands.
12. Remove the rear subframe bolts and discard.
13. Lower the subframe for access to rack and pinion.
14. Remove the steering gear heat shield.
15. Remove the clip holding lines at rack assembly.
16. Disconnect the power steering lines and O-rings.
17. Remove the rack and pinion mounting bolts and nuts.
18. Remove the rack and pinion unit through the left wheel well.
To Install:
19. Install the rack and pinion through left wheel opening.
20. Install the rack and pinion mounting bolts and nuts and tighten the mounting bolts to 66 ft. lbs. (90 Nm).
21. Connect the power steering lines to the rack using new O-rings and tighten the fittings to 13 ft. lbs. (17 Nm) on the return line and 21 ft. lbs. (28 Nm). on the pressure line.
22. Install the power steering line clip to steering gear.
23. Install the steering gear heat shield.
24. Raise the subframe into position and install new frame mounting bolts. Tighten the bolts to 103 ft. lbs. (140 Nm).
25. Remove the jack.
26. Install the engine mount and transaxle mount nuts and tighten to 39 ft. lbs. (53 Nm).
27. Install the brace and bolts including brake line brace.
28. Connect the intermediate shaft to the stub shaft and tighten the pinch bolt to 29 ft. lbs. (40 Nm).
29. Connect the tie rod ends to the steering knuckles. Tighten the castle nuts to 31 ft. lbs. (42 Nm). Install new cotter pins.
30. Install the tire and wheel assembly.
31. Lower the vehicle.
32. Remove the support fixture.
33. Connect the negative battery cable.
34. Refill the power steering reservoir and bleed the system.
35. Check the front end alignment and adjust as necessary.

Power Steering Pump

REMOVAL & INSTALLATION

1. Disconnect the negative battery cable.
2. Remove the hoses at the pump and tape the openings shut to prevent contamination. Position the disconnected lines in a raised position to prevent leakage.
3. Remove the pump belt.
4. On some 4-cylinder models it may be necessary to:
   a. Remove the radiator hose clamp bolt.
   b. Remove the right side fender splash shield.
5. On 2.8L models:
   a. Remove the air cleaner assembly.
   b. Disconnect the electrical connector at the blower motor.
   c. Drain the cooling system, then remove the heater hose at the water pump.
6. On 3.0L models, remove the alternator.

➡Removing a component such as the alternator may make the job easier on any model.

7. Loosen the retaining bolts and any braces, then remove the pump.
8. Remove the pump pulley and attach it to the new pump, as illustrated.
To install:
9. Install the pump and brackets to the engine and hand-tighten the retaining bolts.
10. On 3.0L models:
   a. Install the alternator support to the engine.
   b. Position the alternator adjustment bracket over the front pump adjustment bracket.
   c. Install the long bolt and alternator bracket, front pump bracket, rear pump bracket, and alternator support to the engine.
   d. Attach the remaining alternator adjustment bracket bolt.
   e. Install the power steering pump belt.

f. Raise the car, then install the rear pump adjustment bracket-to-pump nut.

11. Connect and tighten the hose fittings.

12. On 3.0L models, lower the vehicle, then install the alternator and belt.

13. On some 4-cylinder models, you will need to install the radiator hose clamp bolt.

14. On 2.8L models:

  a. Connect the water hose to the water pump.

  b. Install and connect the blower motor.

15. Refill the pump with fluid and bleed the system.

16. Install the pump belt and adjust the tension.

17. On 3.0L models, install the air cleaner assembly.

18. Connect the negative battery cable.

BLEEDING

1. Turn the ignition switch to the **OFF** position.

2. Raise the front of the vehicle enough to get the wheels off the ground.

3. Turn the steering wheel completely to the left.

4. Fill the fluid reservoir to the FULL COLD level, make sure to leave the cap off.

5. Let the fluid stand undisturbed for two minutes, then crank the engine for about two seconds. Refill the reservoir if necessary.

6. With an assistant checking the fluid level and condition, turn the steering wheel lock-to-lock at least 20 times, while the engine remains off.

7. Start the engine, then while idling maintain the fluid level. Install the cap.

8. Return the wheels to the center, then lower the front end to the ground.

9. Turn the wheels to the left and right, checking the fluid level and refilling if necessary.

TORQUE SPECIFICATIONS

Component		US	Metric
Brake line brackets:		8 ft. lbs.	11 Nm
Caliper retaining bolts:		38 ft. lbs.	51 Nm
Front crossmwmber-to-body bolts:		103 ft. lbs.	140 Nm
Halfshaft end nuts:		184-192 ft. lbs.	250-260 Nm
Knuckle camber cam bolt:		140 ft. lbs.	190 Nm
Knuckle attaching bolts:		38 ft. lbs.	52 Nm
Lower ball jopint pinch bolt:			
	1982-84	40 ft. lbs.	50 Nm
	1985-93	33 ft. lbs.	45 Nm
	1994-96	38 ft. lbs.	52 Nm
Lower control arm bolts:		61 ft. lbs.	83 Nm
MacPherson strut shaft nut:		65 ft. lbs.	85 Nm
MacPherson strut to fender:		18 ft. lbs.	24 Nm
MacPherson strut to knuckle:		122-140 ft. lbs.	165-190 Nm
Rear shock to lower mount:			
	1982-84	43 ft. lbs.	58 Nm
	1985-86	35 ft. lbs.	47 Nm
	1987-92	44 ft. lbs.	59 Nm
	1993-96	53 ft. lbs.	72 Nm
Rear shock to upper mount:		16 ft. lbs.	22 Nm
Rear axle top bolt 6000 AWD:		148 ft. lbs.	200 Nm
Rear control arm-to-bracket:		84 ft. lbs.	115 Nm
Rear control bracket-to-underbody:		28 ft. lbs.	38 Nm
Rear hub and bearing assembly:		44 ft. lbs.	60 Nm
Rear jack pad mounting bolts:		18 ft. lbs.	25 Nm
Rear track bar at brace or underebody:		35 ft. lbs.	47 Nm
Rear coil spring track bolt:			
	1982-92	44 ft. lbs.	60 Nm
	1993-96	53 ft. lbs.	72 Nm
Rear leaf spring-to-cradle bolts:		61 ft. lbs.	83 Nm
Rear strut lower mount bolts:		148 ft. lbs.	200 Nm
Spring retention plate bolts:		15 ft. lbs.	20 Nm
Stabilizer insulator clamps-to-control arms:		32 ft. lbs.	43 Nm
Steering column mounting bolts:		18 ft. lbs.	25 Nm
Steering rack mounting bolts:		59 ft. lbs.	80 Nm
Steering wheel retaining nut:		30 ft. lbs.	41 Nm
Tie rod adjustment jam nut:		52 ft. lbs.	70 Nm
Tie rod nut:		31-52 ft. lbs.	42-70 Nm
Toe link sleeve tab bolt:		14 ft. lbs.	19 Nm
Toe link inner nut:		61 ft. lbs.	83 Nm
Wheel lug nuts:		100 ft. lbs.	136 Nm

91088C01

9

BRAKES

BRAKE OPERATING SYSTEM

The A-Body cars have a diagonally split hydraulic system. This differs from conventional practice in that the left front and right rear brakes are on one hydraulic circuit, and the right front and left rear are on the other.

A diagonally split system necessitates the use of a special master cylinder design. The A-Body master cylinder incorporates the functions of a standard tandem master cylinder, plus a warning light switch and proportioning valves. Additionally, the master cylinder is designed with a quick take-up feature which provides a large volume of fluid to the brakes at low pressure when the brakes are initially applied. The lower pressure fluid acts to quickly fill the large displacement requirements of the system.

The front disc brakes are single piston sliding caliper units. Fluid pressure acts equally against the piston and the bottom of the piston bore in the caliper. This forces the piston outward until the pad contacts the caliper to slide over, carrying the other pad into contact with the other side of the rotor. The disc brakes are self-adjusting.

Rear drum brakes are conventional duo-servo units. A dual piston wheel cylinder mounted to the top of the backing plate, actuates both brake shoes. Wheel cylinder force to the shoes is supplemented by the tendency of the shoes to wrap into the drum (servo action). An actuating link, pivot and lever serve to automatically engage the adjuster as the brakes are applied when the car is moving in reverse. Provisions for manual adjustment are also provided. The rear brakes also serve as the parking brakes; linkage is mechanical. Vacuum boost is an option. The booster is a conventional tandem vacuum unit.

Adjustments

DISC BRAKES

The front disc brakes are self-adjusting. No adjustments are necessary or possible.

DRUM BRAKES

The drum brakes are designed to self-adjust when applied with the car moving in reverse. However, they can also be adjusted manually. This manual adjustment should also be performed whenever the linings are replaced.

➡Never adjust the parking brake cable, until after the regular service brakes have been adjusted.

Adjustment Through Drum

1. To remove the wheel, loosen all the lug nuts at least one full turn, before raising the car.
2. Raise and support the vehicle.
3. Remove the lug nuts and the wheel.
4. Use a punch to knock out the stamped area on the brake drum. If this is done with the drum installed on the car, the drum must then be removed to clean out all metal pieces. After adjustments are complete, obtain a hole cover from your dealer (part no. 4874119 or the equivalent) to prevent entry of dirt and water into the brakes.
5. Use an adjusting tool especially made for the purpose to turn the brake adjusting screw star wheel.

➡Keep turning the drum as you are adjusting it or you may overtighten the shoes against the drum.

6. Expand the shoes until there is a slight drag.
7. Back off the adjusting screw a few notches, if too tight. If the shoes still are dragging lightly, back off the adjusting screw one or two additional notches. If the brakes still drag, the parking brake adjustment is incorrect or the parking brake is applied. Disengage the parking brake or loosen the adjusting nut as necessary.
8. Install the hole cover into the drum.
9. Check the parking brake adjustment.
10. Install the wheel, hand-tighten the lug nuts. Lower the vehicle, then tighten the lug nuts to 100 ft. lbs. (136 Nm).

Adjustment Through Backing Plate

On some models, no marked area or stamped area is present on the drum. In this case, a hole must be drilled in the backing plate:

1. To remove the wheel, loosen all the lug nuts at least one full turn, before raising the car.
2. Raise and support the vehicle.
3. Remove the lug nuts and the wheel.
4. These backing plates have two round flat areas in the lower half through which the parking brake cable is installed. Drill a ½ in. (13mm) hole into the round flat area on the backing plate opposite the parking brake cable. This will allow access to the star wheel.
5. After drilling the hole, remove the drum and remove all metal particles. Install a hole plug (part no. 4874119 or the equivalent) to prevent the entry of water or dirt.
6. Use an adjusting tool especially made for the purpose to turn the brake adjusting screw star wheel.

➡Keep turning the drum as you are adjusting it or you may overtighten the shoes against the drum.

7. Expand the shoes until there is a slight drag.
8. Back off the adjusting screw a few notches, if too tight. If the shoes still are dragging lightly, back off the adjusting screw one or two additional notches. If the brakes still drag, the parking brake adjustment is incorrect or the parking brake is applied. Disengage the parking brake or loosen the adjusting nut as necessary.
9. Install the hole cover into the drum.
10. Check the parking brake adjustment.

➡Another option on these models is simply to remove the drum, adjust the shoe and try the drum on. If the drum fit is still loose, adjust the shoes out slightly more and repeat. Using this method may prove to be difficult, due to a ridge that forms on the outer edge of the drum.

11. Install the wheel, hand-tighten the lug nuts. Lower the vehicle, then tighten the lug nuts to 100 ft. lbs. (136 Nm).

Brake Light Switch

REMOVAL & INSTALLATION

▶ See Figure 1

1. Disconnect the negative battery cable.
2. On some models you may need to remove the sound insulator on the left side.
3. Unplug the wiring connectors from the brake light switch.

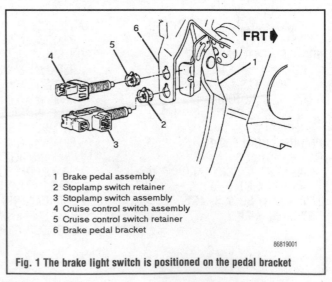

1 Brake pedal assembly
2 Stoplamp switch retainer
3 Stoplamp switch assembly
4 Cruise control switch assembly
5 Cruise control switch retainer
6 Brake pedal bracket

86819001

Fig. 1 The brake light switch is positioned on the pedal bracket

4. Unscrew the brake light switch from the tubular retaining clip.
To install:
5. Insert the new switch into the retainer until the switch body seats against the clip.
6. Engage the wiring connectors.
7. Pull the brake pedal rearward against the pedal stop. The switch will be moved in the tubular clip providing proper adjustment.
8. Reinstall the left sound insulator. Connect the negative battery cable and reset the clock and radio.

Brake Pedal

REMOVAL & INSTALLATION

1. Remove the lower steering column panel, if needed.
2. Unfasten the pushrod from the brake pedal.
3. Remove the hinge bolt and bushing from the unit, then remove the pedal.
To install:
4. Attach the brake pedal with the bushing and hinge bolt.
5. Tighten the bolt to 25 ft. lbs. (34 Nm).
6. Install the pushrod to the pedal.
7. Attach the lower steering column panel, if removed.

Master Cylinder

REMOVAL & INSTALLATION

▶ **See Figures 2 and 3**

1. For manual brakes, disconnect the master cylinder pushrod at the brake pedal inside the car. The pushrod is retained to the brake pedal by a clip. There is a washer under the clip, and a spring washer on the other side of the pushrod.

2. Unplug the electrical connector from the master cylinder.
3. Place a number of cloths or a container under the master cylinder to catch the brake fluid. Disconnect the brake tubes from the master cylinder, using a flare nut wrench, if one is available. Tape over or plug the open ends of the tubes.

➡**Brake fluid eats paint. Wipe up any spilled fluid immediately, then flush the area with clean water.**

4. Remove the two nuts attaching the master cylinder to the booster or firewall.
5. Remove the master cylinder.

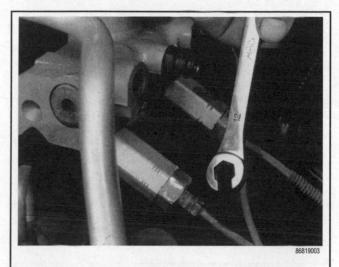

Fig. 3 Disconnect the brake tubes from the master cylinder with a flare nut wrench

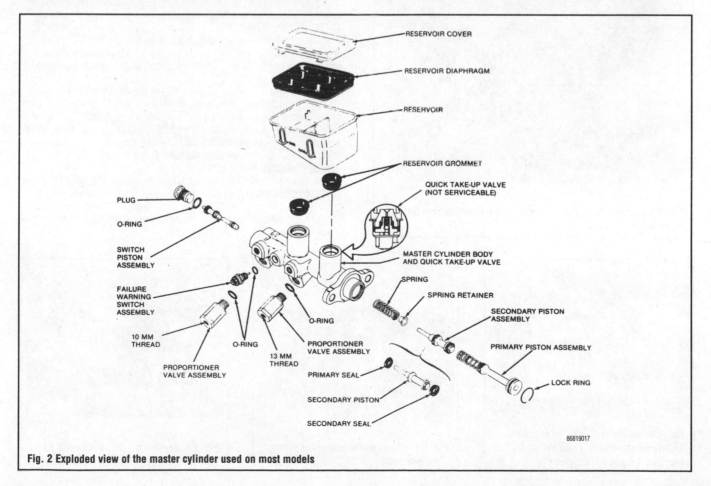

Fig. 2 Exploded view of the master cylinder used on most models

To install:

6. Attach the master cylinder to the firewall or the booster with the nuts. Tighten to 29 ft. lbs. (40 Nm) for 1982–84 models, 22 ft. lbs. (27 Nm) for 1985–88 models, and 20 ft. lbs. (27 Nm) 1989–96 models.

7. Reconnect the pushrod to the brake pedal.

8. Remove the tape from the lines and connect the lines to the master cylinder. Tighten to 12 ft. lbs. (17 Nm) for 1982–84 models, 18 ft. lbs. (24 Nm) for 1985–88 models, 24 ft. lbs. (32 Nm) for 1989–96 models. Connect the electrical lead.

9. Fill the master cylinder to the proper level with clean fresh brake fluid.

10. Bleed the brakes.

11. Recheck the fluid level and add fluid if needed.

OVERHAUL

♦ **See Figures 4, 5, 6 and 7**

This is a tedious, time consuming job. You can save yourself a lot of trouble by buying a rebuilt master cylinder from your dealer or parts supply house. The small difference in price between a rebuilding kit and a rebuilt part usually makes it more economical, in terms of time and work, to buy the rebuilt part.

1. Remove the master cylinder from the vehicle.

2. Remove the reservoir cover and drain the fluid, inspect the cap for any cuts, cracks, nicks or deterioration.

3. Remove the pushrod and the rubber boot on non-power models.

4. Unbolt the proportioners and the failure warning switch from the side of the master cylinder body. Discard the O-rings found under the proportioners. Use new ones on installation. There may or may not be an O-ring under the original equipment failure warning switch. If there is, discard it. In either case, use a new O-ring upon assembly.

Fig. 4 A seal pick can be used to remove the snapring from the master cylinder

5. Clamp the master cylinder body in a vise, taking care not to crush it. Remove the snapring with a pair of snapring pliers or suitable tool.

6. The primary and secondary pistons can be removed by applying compressed air into one of the outlets at the end of the cylinder and plugging the other three outlets. The primary piston must be replaced as an assembly if the seals are bad. The secondary piston seals are replaceable. Install these new seals with the lips facing outwards.

7. Inspect the cylinder bore for scoring or corrosion. If any corrosion is evident, the master cylinder body must be replaced. Do not attempt to polish the bore with crocus cloth, sandpaper or anything else. The body is aluminum, polishing the bore won't work.

8. To remove the failure warning switch piston assembly, unfasten the Allen head plug from the end of the bore and withdraw the assembly with a pair of needlenose pliers. The switch piston assembly seals are replaceable.

9. The reservoir can be removed from the master cylinder if necessary. Clamp the body in a vise by its mounting flange. Use a prytool to remove the reservoir. When the reservoir is removed, remove the reservoir grommets and discard them. The quick take-up valves under the grommets are accessible after the retaining snaprings are removed. Use snapring pliers, no other tool will work without damaging the component.

To assemble:

10. Clean all parts in denatured alcohol and allow to air dry. Do not use anything else to clean them, and do not wipe them dry with a rag, (which will leave bits of lint behind). Inspect all parts for corrosion or wear. Generally, it is best to replace all rubber parts whenever the master cylinder is disassembled and replace any metal part which shows any sign of wear or corrosion.

11. Lubricate all parts with clean brake fluid before assembly.

12. Install the quick take-up valves into the master cylinder body and secure with the snaprings. Make sure the snaprings are properly seated in their grooves. Lubricate the new reservoir grommets with clean brake fluid and press them into the master cylinder.

13. Install the reservoir into the grommets by placing the reservoir on its lid and pressing the master cylinder body down onto it with a rocking motion.

14. Lubricate the switch piston assembly with clean brake fluid. Install new O-rings and retainers on the piston. Install the piston assembly into the master cylinder and secure with the plug, using a new O-ring on the plug. Tighten to 40–140 inch lbs. (5–16 Nm).

15. Assemble the new secondary piston seals onto the piston. Lubricate the parts with clean brake fluid, then install the spring, spring retainer and secondary piston into the cylinder. Install the primary piston, depress and install the lockring.

16. Install new O-rings on the proportioners and the failure warning switch. Install the proportioners and tighten to 18–30 ft. lbs. (25–40 Nm). Install the failure warning switch, then tighten to 15–50 inch lbs. (2–6 Nm).

17. Clamp the master cylinder body upright into a vise by one of the mounting flanges. Fill the reservoir with fresh brake fluid. Pump the piston with a dowel until fluid squirts from the outlet ports. Continue pumping until the expelled fluid is free of air bubbles.

18. Install the master cylinder, then tighten the nuts to 29 ft. lbs. (40 Nm) for 1982–84 models or 20–22 ft. lbs. (28–30 Nm) for 1985–96 models. Bleed the brake system, then check the system for proper operation. Do not move the car until a "hard" brake pedal is obtained and the brake system has been thoroughly checked for soundness.

Fig. 5 When the master cylinder is completely disassembled, place the components on a clean workspace

Fig. 6 The seals on the secondary piston are replaceable

Fig. 7 Always install the components by hand before tightening them with a wrench

Power Brake Booster

REMOVAL & INSTALLATION

▶ **See Figures 8 and 9**

1. Remove the master cylinder from the booster. It is not necessary to disconnect the lines from the master cylinder. Just move the cylinder aside, make sure not to bend or distort any of the brake pipes.
2. Disconnect the vacuum booster pushrod from the brake pedal inside the car. It is retained by a bolt. A spring washer lies under the bolt head, and a flat washer goes on the other side of the pushrod eye, next to the pedal arm.
3. Remove the vacuum hose connected from the booster to the check valve.
4. Remove the four attaching nuts from inside the car. Remove the booster.
To install:
5. Install the booster on the firewall.
6. Connect the pushrod to the brake pedal. You may need to tilt the entire booster slightly to work the booster pushrod onto the pedal clevis pin without forcing unneeded side pressure on the pushrod.
7. Tighten the mounting nuts for the brake booster to 15–20 ft. lbs. (21–30 Nm).
8. Install the check valve and hose.

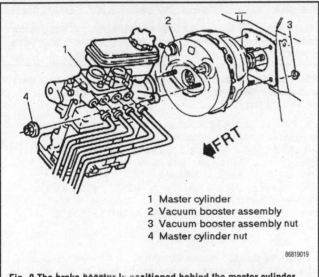

1 Master cylinder
2 Vacuum booster assembly
3 Vacuum booster assembly nut
4 Master cylinder nut

Fig. 8 The brake booster is positioned behind the master cylinder

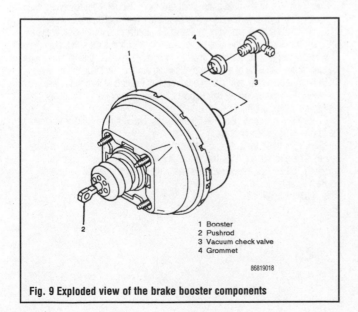

1 Booster
2 Pushrod
3 Vacuum check valve
4 Grommet

Fig. 9 Exploded view of the brake booster components

9. Install the master cylinder, then tighten the nuts to 29 ft. lbs. (40 Nm) for 1982–84 models or 20–22 ft. lbs. (28–30 Nm) for 1985–96 models. Bleed the brake system, then check the system for proper operation. Do not move the car until a "hard" brake pedal is obtained and the brake system has been thoroughly checked for soundness.

OVERHAUL

This job can be difficult, and requires a number of special tools which are expensive, (especially if they're to be used only once). Generally, it's better to leave this job to your dealer, or buy a rebuilt vacuum booster and install it yourself.

Proportioning Valves

REMOVAL & INSTALLATION

External Type

The external valves are used on 1982–86 models.
1. Disconnect and cap the brake line from the proportioning valve(s).
2. Using a suitable wrench remove the proportioning valve(s) from the master cylinder.

➡If both proportioning valves are removed at the same time, make sure the proportioning valves are installed in the correct places. The threads on the two valves differ slightly and installation in the wrong port can damage the master cylinder or proportioning valves. If the valves are replaced both valves must be the same color code.

3. Remove the old O-rings and discard.
To install:
4. Install new O-rings on the proportioning valve(s).
5. Install the proportioning valve(s) and tighten to 24 ft. lbs. (32 Nm).
6. Connect the brake line(s) to the proportioning valve(s) and tighten the fittings to 24 ft. lbs. (32 Nm).
7. Bleed the brake system.

Internal Type

The internal proportioning valves are used on 1987–96 models.
1. Remove the master cylinder from the vehicle.
2. Remove the brake master cylinder reservoir.
3. Remove the proportioning valve cap assemblies.
4. Remove the O-rings from the caps and discard of them.
5. Remove the springs, then use needle nose pliers to remove the proportioning valve pistons. If you are not careful you could damage the piston stems.
6. Remove the piston seals and pistons from the cylinder.
To install:
7. Inspect the pistons for any corrosion or deformation, replace them if needed.
8. Clean all the parts in denatured alcohol, then dry with compressed air.
9. Lubricate the new O-rings, valve seals, stem, and valve pistons with silicone grease.
10. Install the new seals on the valve pistons with the seal lips facing upward toward the cap assembly.
11. Install the pistons and seals in the master cylinder body. Insert new O-rings in the grooves of the proportioning valve cap assemblies. Install the caps to the cylinder body.
12. Tighten the caps to 20 ft. lbs. (27 Nm). Install the reservoir assembly.
13. Bleed the brake system, then check the system for proper operation. Do not move the car until a hard brake pedal is obtained.
14. Close the hood.

Fluid Level Sensor

REMOVAL & INSTALLATION

▶ **See Figures 10 and 11**

1. Unplug the electrical connection on the fluid level sensor located on the master cylinder.

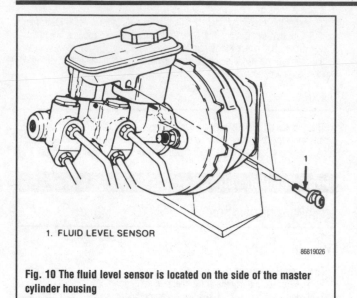

1. FLUID LEVEL SENSOR

86819026

Fig. 10 The fluid level sensor is located on the side of the master cylinder housing

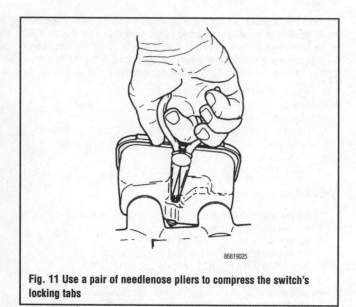

86819025

Fig. 11 Use a pair of needlenose pliers to compress the switch's locking tabs

2. Remove the level sensor by using a pair of needle nose pliers to compress the locking tabs on the inboard side of the master cylinder.

To install:

3. Insert the fluid level sensor into position until the locking tabs snap into place.

4. Install the electrical connection to the sensor.

Bleeding the Brakes

▶ See Figure 12

The purpose of bleeding the brakes is to expel air trapped in the hydraulic system. The system must be bled whenever the pedal feels spongy, indicating that compressible air has entered the system. It must also be bled whenever the system has been opened or repaired. You will need an assistant for this procedure.

86819039

Fig. 12 An assistant can be helpful in bleeding the brake system

※ CAUTION

Never reuse brake fluid which has been bled from the brake system. Brake fluid should be changed every few years. It deteriotates due to moisture being absorbed which lowers the boiling point.

➡Old brake fluid is often the cause of spongy brakes returning a week or so after bleeding the system. If all parts are OK, change the fluid by repeated bleeding.

1. Raise and support the vehicle securely. Your assistant should remain in the vehicle to apply the brake pedal when needed.

2. The sequence for bleeding is right rear, left front, left rear and right front. If the car has power brakes, bleed the vacuum by applying the brakes several times. Do not run the engine while bleeding the brakes.

3. Clean all the bleeder screws. You may want to give each one a shot of penetrating solvent to loosen it up. Seizure is a common problem with bleeder screws. They can break off, usually requiring replacement of the part to which they are attached.

4. Fill the master cylinder with DOT 3 brake fluid.

➡Brake fluid absorbs moisture from the air. Don't leave the master cylinder or the fluid container uncovered any longer than necessary. Be careful handling the fluid, it eats paint.

Check the level of the fluid often when bleeding, and refill the reservoirs as necessary. Don't let them run dry, or you will have to repeat the process.

5. Attach a length of clear vinyl tubing to the bleeder screw on the wheel cylinder. Insert the other end of the tube into a clear, clean jar half filled with brake fluid.

6. Have your assistant slowly depress the brake pedal. As this is done, open the bleeder screw 1/3–1/2 of a turn and allow the fluid to run through the tube. Close the bleeder screw before the pedal reaches the end of its travel. Have your assistant slowly release the pedal. Repeat this process until no air bubbles appear in the expelled fluid.

7. Repeat the procedure on the other brakes, checking the level of fluid in the master cylinder reservoir often.

After you're done, there should be no sponginess in the brake pedal. If there is, either there is still air in the line, (in which case the process should be repeated) or there is a leak somewhere, (which of course must be corrected before the car is moved).

8. Lower the vehicle.

FRONT DISC BRAKES

✳✳ CAUTION

Brake shoes may contain asbestos, which has been determined to be a cancer causing agent. Never clean the brake surfaces with compressed air! Avoid inhaling any dust from any brake surface! When cleaning brake surfaces, use a commercially available brake cleaning fluid.

Brake Pads

REMOVAL & INSTALLATION

Light Duty

▶ See Figures 13, 14, 15 and 16

1. Siphon ⅔ of the brake fluid out of the master cylinder reservoir.
2. To remove the wheels, loosen all the lug nuts at least one full turn, before raising the car.
3. Raise and safely support the vehicle.
4. Remove the tire and wheel assembly.
5. Install two wheel nuts to secure the rotor in place.
6. Unstake the outboard pads using a hammer and chisel.
7. Remove the caliper mounting bolts.
8. Remove the caliper from the steering knuckle and support on a wire. DO NOT disconnect the brake hose or allow the brake hose to support the weight of the caliper.
9. Remove the outboard pad from the caliper.
10. Pull the top of the inboard pad out from the caliper to disengage the spring clip securing the inboard pad and remove the pad.
11. Using a suitable C-clamp compress the caliper piston fully into the caliper bore.

To install:

12. Install a new spring clip on the back of the inboard pad. Make sure that the top tab in engaged in the pad before hooking the lower end.
13. Install the inboard pad with a new spring clip into the caliper piston. This can be done by locking the bottom edge of the spring clip into the piston and pushing the top of the pad back.
14. Install the outboard pad into the caliper.
15. Install the caliper on the steering knuckle and tighten the mounting bolts to 28 ft. lbs. (38 Nm) for 1982–84 models and 38 ft. lbs. (51 Nm) for 1985–96 models.

16. Pump up the brake pedal until the pads seat against the rotor. Using a suitable tool, secure the brake pedal in the down position keeping the front wheels locked.

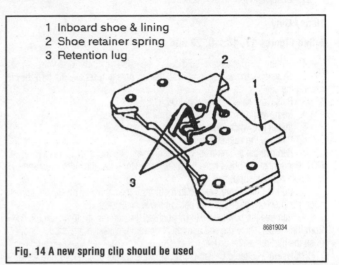

1 Inboard shoe & lining
2 Shoe retainer spring
3 Retention lug

Fig. 14 A new spring clip should be used

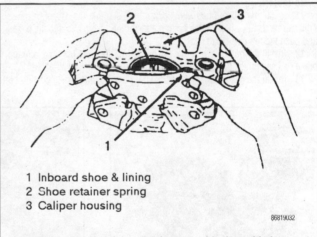

1 Inboard shoe & lining
2 Shoe retainer spring
3 Caliper housing

Fig. 15 Make sure that the top tab in engaged in the pad before hooking the lower end

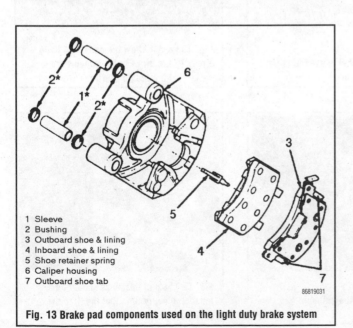

1 Sleeve
2 Bushing
3 Outboard shoe & lining
4 Inboard shoe & lining
5 Shoe retainer spring
6 Caliper housing
7 Outboard shoe tab

Fig. 13 Brake pad components used on the light duty brake system

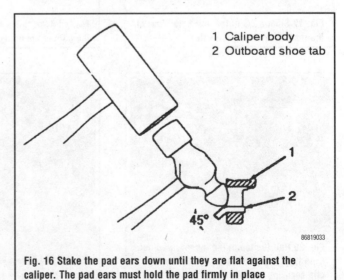

1 Caliper body
2 Outboard shoe tab

45°

Fig. 16 Stake the pad ears down until they are flat against the caliper. The pad ears must hold the pad firmly in place

17. Stake the pad ears down until they are flat against the caliper. The pad ears must secure the pad firmly in place.
18. Remove the two wheel nuts.
19. Install the tire and wheel assembly and tighten the lug nuts by hand.
20. Lower the vehicle. Then tighten the lug nuts to 100 ft. lbs. (136 Nm).
21. Check and top off the master cylinder.

Heavy Duty

▶ **See Figures 17, 18, 19, 20 and 21**

1. Siphon ⅔ of the brake fluid out of the master cylinder reservoir.
2. To remove the wheel, loosen all the lug nuts at least one full turn, before raising the car.
3. Raise and safely support the vehicle.
4. Remove the tire and wheel assembly.
5. Install two wheel nuts to secure the rotor in place.
6. Remove the caliper mounting bolts.
7. Remove the caliper from the steering knuckle and support on a wire. DO NOT disconnect the brake hose from the caliper or allow the caliper to hang by the brake hose unsupported.
8. Pull the top of the inboard pad out from the caliper to disengage the spring clip securing the inboard pad. Remove the pad.
9. Remove the outboard pad by pushing the pad inward to unseat the pad from the caliper. Once the pad alignment dowels are clear of the caliper body push the pad out of the caliper.
10. Using a suitable C-clamp compress the caliper piston fully into the caliper bore.

To install:

11. Install the inboard pad with a new spring clip into the caliper piston. This can be done by locking the bottom edge of the spring clip into the piston and push the top of the pad back.
12. Install the outboard pad into the caliper making sure the dowels in the brake pad seat in the holes in the caliper.
13. Install the caliper on the steering knuckle and tighten the mounting bolts to 28 ft. lbs. (38 Nm) for 1982–84 models and 38 ft. lbs. (51 Nm) for 1985–96 models.
14. Remove the two wheel nuts.
15. Install the tire and wheel assembly and tighten the lug nuts by hand.
16. Lower the vehicle. Tighten the lug nuts to 100 ft. lbs. (136 Nm).
17. Pump the brake pedal several times to seat the pads against the rotor.
18. Check and top off the master cylinder.

INSPECTION

▶ **See Figure 22**

The pad thickness should be inspected every time that the tires are removed for rotation. The outer pad can be checked by looking in at each end, which is the point at which the highest rate of wear occurs. The inner pad can be checked by looking down through the inspection hole in the top of the caliper. If the thickness of the pad is worn to within 0.030 in. (0.76mm) of the rivet at either end of the pad, all the pads should be replaced. This is the factory recommended measurement, your state's automobile inspection laws may not agree with this.

➡**Always replace all pads on both front wheels at the same time. Failure to do so will result in uneven braking action and premature wear.**

Brake Caliper

REMOVAL & INSTALLATION

▶ **See Figures 23, 24 and 25**

1. Siphon ⅔ of the brake fluid out of the master cylinder reservoir.
2. Release the parking brake.
3. Loosen the lug nuts, then raise and safely support the vehicle.
4. Remove the tire and wheel assembly.

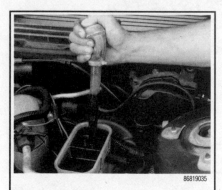

Fig. 17 Siphon 2/3 of the brake fluid out of the master cylinder reservoir

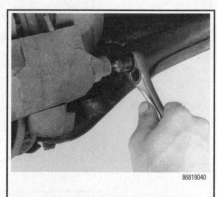

Fig. 18 A special socket is used to remove the caliper mounting bolts

Fig. 19 Do not allow the caliper to hang freely by the brake hose. Support the caliper with a length of wire

Fig. 20 Pull the top of the inboard pad out from the caliper to disengage the spring clip securing the inboard pad

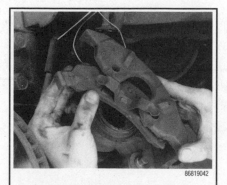

Fig. 21 Now remove the outboard pad from the caliper

Fig. 22 The pad thickness should be inspected every time that the tires are removed for rotation

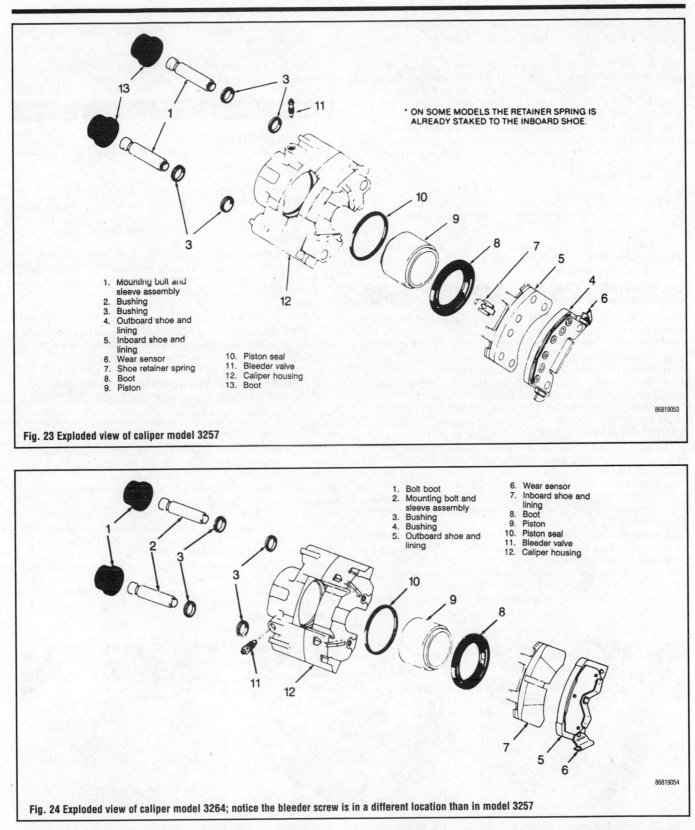

* ON SOME MODELS THE RETAINER SPRING IS
ALREADY STAKED TO THE INBOARD SHOE.

1. Mounting bolt and
   sleeve assembly
2. Bushing
3. Bushing
4. Outboard shoe and
   lining
5. Inboard shoe and
   lining
6. Wear sensor
7. Shoe retainer spring
8. Boot
9. Piston
10. Piston seal
11. Bleeder valve
12. Caliper housing
13. Boot

86819053

Fig. 23 Exploded view of caliper model 3257

1. Bolt boot
2. Mounting bolt and
   sleeve assembly
3. Bushing
4. Bushing
5. Outboard shoe and
   lining
6. Wear sensor
7. Inboard shoe and
   lining
8. Boot
9. Piston
10. Piston seal
11. Bleeder valve
12. Caliper housing

86819054

Fig. 24 Exploded view of caliper model 3264; notice the bleeder screw is in a different location than in model 3257

5. Install two wheel nuts to secure the rotor in place.

6. Using a large C-clamp, position the clamp on the caliper housing and against the back of the outboard pad and lining. Tighten the clamp slowly to press the piston into the caliper bore.

7. Remove the bolt attaching the hose fitting, only if the caliper is to be removed for overhaul. If only the pads are to be replaced, there is no need to disconnect the hose fitting.

8. Plug the opening in the caliper and the pipe to prevent fluid from seeping out and contamination.

9. Remove the Allen head caliper mounting bolts. Inspect them for corrosion and replace them if necessary.

To install:

10. Coat the bushings with silicone or grease.

11. Install the caliper and brake pads over the rotor, in the mounting bracket.

12. Install the mounting bolt and sleeve assembly, then tighten the mounting bolt to 28 ft. lbs. (38 Nm) for 1982–84 models and 38 ft. lbs. (51 Nm) for 1985–96 models.

13. Measure the clearance between the caliper and the bracket stops. If needed, remove the caliper and file down the ends of the bracket stops to provide clearance. The caliper may appear to be touching the lower abutment and still not be interfering. The caliper should slide freely on the mounting bolt and sleeve assemblies.

14. Install the brake hose to the caliper. The brake hose fitting should be tightened to 33 ft. lbs. (45 Nm). Always use new fasteners.

15. Install the wheel and tire, hand-tighten the lug nuts. Lower the vehicle, then tighten the lug nuts to 100 ft. lbs. (136 Nm).

16. Top off the brake fluid.

OVERHAUL

1. Remove the calipers.

2. Place some cloths or a slat of wood in front of the piston. Remove the piston by applying compressed air to the fluid inlet fitting. Use just enough air pressure to ease the piston from the bore.

✳✳ CAUTION

Do not try to catch the piston with your fingers, which can result in serious injury.

3. Remove the piston dust boot.

4. Remove the bleeder screw and cap from the caliper.

5. Inspect the piston for scoring, nicks, corrosion, wear, and damaged or worn chrome plating. Replace the piston if any defects are found.

6. Remove the piston seal from the caliper bore groove using a pick. Do not use a screwdriver, which will damage the bore. Inspect the caliper bore for nicks, corrosion and so on. Very light wear can be cleaned up with crocus cloth. Use finger pressure to rub the crocus cloth around the circumference of the bore, do not slide it in and out. More extensive wear or corrosion warrants replacement of the part.

To assemble:

7. Clean any parts which are to be reused in denatured alcohol. Dry them with compressed or allow to air dry. Don't wipe the parts dry with a cloth, which will leave behind bits of lint.

8. Install the bleeder screw, tightening it to 110–120 inch lbs. (13–14 Nm)

9. Lubricate a new seal, with clean brake fluid. Install the seal in its groove, making sure it is fully seated and not twisted.

10. Install the new dust boot on the piston. Lubricate the bore of the caliper with clean brake fluid and insert the piston into its bore. Position the boot in the caliper housing and seat it with a seal driver of the appropriate size, or tool No. J-29077.

11. Install the caliper bushings. Lubricate the beveled end that is flush with the caliper, with silicone.

12. Install the pads, the caliper and bleed the brakes.

13. Install the wheel and tire assembly. Hand-tighten the lug nuts.

14. Lower the vehicle, then tighten the lug nuts to 100 ft. lbs. (136 Nm).

Brake Disc (Rotor)

REMOVAL & INSTALLATION

▶ **See Figures 26 and 27**

1. Remove the wheel cover.

2. To remove the wheel, loosen all the lug nuts at least one full turn, before raising the car.

3. Raise and support the car, then remove the front wheel.

To assemble:

4. Remove the Allen head caliper mounting bolts and remove the brake caliper.

5. Remove the caliper from the knuckle and suspend from a length of wire. Do not allow the caliper to hang from the brake hose.

6. Pull the rotor from the knuckle.

To install:

7. Place the rotor onto the steering knuckle.

8. Place the caliper assembly into position on the rotor, then tighten the mounting bolt to 28 ft. lbs. (38 Nm) for 1982–84 models and 38 ft. lbs. (51 Nm) for 1985–96 models.

9. Install the tire and wheel, then tighten the lug nuts by hand.

10. Lower the car and tighten the lug nuts to 100 ft. lbs. (136 Nm).

11. Pump the brake pedal several times to seat the pads against the rotor.

INSPECTION

1. Check the rotor surface for wear or scoring. Deep scoring, grooves or rust pitting can be removed by refacing. This can be performed by your local machine shop or garage. Minimum thickness is stamped on the rotor, or see the brake specifications chart in this section. If the rotor is thinner than specifications after refinishing, it must be replaced.

2. Check the rotor parallelism with a micrometer. It must vary less than 0.0005 in. (0.0127mm) measured at four or more points around the circumference. Make all measurements at the same distance in from the edge of the rotor. Refinish the rotor if it fails to meet this specification.

3. Measure the disc run-out with a dial indicator. If run-out exceeds 0.002 in. (0.051mm) for 1982–85 models, 0.004 in. (0.10mm) for 1985–87 models, and 0.002 in. (0.051mm) for 1988–96 models and the wheel bearings are OK (if run-out is being measured with the disc on the car), the rotor must be refaced or replaced as necessary.

Fig. 25 A large C-clamp can be used to seat the piston in the caliper

86819050

Fig. 26 It is necessary to remove the caliper in order to remove the rotor

86819055

Fig. 27 With the caliper out of the way, the rotor can be removed from the hub

86819057

REAR DRUM BRAKES

✳✳ CAUTION

Brake shoes may contain asbestos, which has been determined to be a cancer causing agent. Never clean the brake surfaces with compressed air! Avoid inhaling any dust from any brake surface! When cleaning brake surfaces, use a commercially available brake cleaning fluid.

Brake Drums

REMOVAL & INSTALLATION

▶ **See Figures 28 and 29**

1. Loosen the wheel lug nuts. Raise and support the car, then remove the wheel

2. Clean the brake drum surface with a commercially available cleaning product, to remove the brake dust.

3. Remove the drum. If it cannot be slipped off easily, check to see that the parking brake is fully released. If so, the brake shoes are probably locked against

Fig. 28 Gently rock the drum side-to-side while pulling on it

Fig. 29 If the drum will not come off, spray some penetrating lubricant where the drum meets the hub

the drum. If the drum will still not come off, spray some penetrating lubricant where the drum meets the hub. If necessary, tap gently using a rubber mallet on the outer rim of the drum and/or around the inner drum diameter by the hub.

To install:

4. After removing the brake drum, wipe out the accumulated dust with a cloth saturated with brake cleaning fluid.

✳✳ WARNING

Do not blow the brake dust out of the drums with compressed air or lung-power. Brake linings may contain asbestos, a known cancer causing substance. Dispose of the cloth used to clean the parts after use.

5. Inspect the drums for cracks, deep grooves, roughness, scoring, or out-of-roundness. Replace any drum which is cracked.

6. Install the drum. Install the wheel and hand-tighten the lug nuts.

7. Lower the vehicle, then tighten the lug nuts to 100 ft. lbs. (140 Nm).

INSPECTION

1. After removing the brake drum, wipe out the accumulated dust with a cloth saturated with brake cleaning fluid.

✳✳ WARNING

Do not blow the brake dust out of the drums with compressed air or lung-power. Brake linings may contain asbestos, a known cancer causing substance. Dispose of the cloth used to clean the parts after use.

2. Inspect the drums for cracks, deep grooves, roughness, scoring, or out-of-roundness. Replace any drum which is cracked.

3. Smooth any slight scores by polishing the friction surface with fine emery cloth. Heavy or extensive scoring will cause excessive lining wear and should be removed from the drum through resurfacing. This can be performed by your local machine shop or garage. The maximum finished diameter of the drums is 7.899 in. (200.6mm) for 1982–83 models, 8.920 in. (226.56mm) for 1984–85 models, 8.877 in. (25.47mm) for 1986–87 models, 8.880 in. (225.55mm) for 1988–96 models.

Brake Shoes

INSPECTION

After removing the brake drum, inspect the brake shoes. If the lining is worn down to within 0.030 in. (0.8mm) of a rivet, the shoes must be replaced.

➡**This figure may disagree with your state's automobile inspection laws. If the brake lining is soaked with brake fluid or grease, it must be replaced. If this is the case, the brake drum should be sanded with crocus cloth to remove all traces of brake fluid, and the wheel cylinders should be overhauled or replaced.**

If the lining is chipped, cracked or otherwise damaged, it must be replaced with a new lining.

➡**Always replace the brake linings in sets of two on both ends of the axle. Never replace just one shoe or both shoes on only one side.**

Check the condition of the shoes, retracting springs and hold-down springs for signs of overheating. If the shoes or springs have a slight blue color, this indicates overheating. Replacement of the shoes and springs is recommended.

REMOVAL & INSTALLATION

1. Loosen the lug nuts on the wheel to be serviced, raise and support the car, and remove the wheel and brake drum.

2. Remove the hub and bearing assembly retaining bolts and remove the assembly from the axle. Reinstall two of the bolts to secure the backing plate.

➡️It is not necessary to remove the hub and wheel bearing assembly from the axle, but it does make the job easier. If you can work with the hub and bearing assembly in place, skip the step.

3. Remove the return springs from the shoes. There are special brake spring pliers available for this job.

4. Remove the hold-down springs by pressing them down and turning 90 degrees. There are special tools available to grab and turn these parts, but pliers work fairly well.

5. Remove the shoe hold-down pins from behind the brake backing plate. They will simply slide out once the hold-down spring tension is relieved.

6. Lift up the actuator lever for the self-adjusting mechanism and remove the actuating link. Remove the actuator lever, pivot and the pivot return spring.

7. Spread the shoes apart to clear the wheel cylinder pistons, then remove the parking brake strut and spring.

8. If the hub and bearing assembly is still in place, spread the shoes far enough apart to clear it.

9. Remove the shoes, with the adjusting screw and spring. Disconnect the parking brake cable from the lever.

10. With the shoes removed, note the position of the adjusting spring, then remove the spring and screw.

11. Remove the C-clip from the parking brake lever and the lever from the secondary shoe.

Inspection:

12. Use a damp cloth to remove all dirt and dust from the backing plate and brake parts.

13. Check the wheel cylinder by carefully pulling the lower edges of the wheel cylinder boots away from the cylinders. The inside of the cylinder may be moist with fluid. If excessive leakage exists, a wheel cylinder overhaul or replacement is in order. Do not delay, because brake failure could result.

➡️A small amount of fluid will be present to act as a lubricant for the wheel cylinder pistons. Fluid spilling from the boot, indicates excessive leakage and the necessity for cylinder overhaul or replacement.

14. Use fine emery cloth to clean all rust and dirt from the shoe contact surfaces on the backing plate.

To install:

15. Lubricate the fulcrum end of the parking brake lever with brake grease. Install the lever on the secondary shoe and secure with the C-clip.

16. Install the adjusting screw and spring on the shoes, connecting them together. The coils of the spring must not interfere with the star wheel on the adjuster. The left and right hand springs are not interchangeable. Do not mix them up.

17. Lubricate the shoe contact surfaces on the backing plate with the brake grease. Be certain that none of it actually gets on the linings or drums. Apply the same grease to the point where the parking brake cable contacts the plate. Use the grease sparingly.

18. Spread the shoe assemblies apart and connect the parking brake cable. Install the shoes on the backing plate, engaging the shoes at the top temporarily with the wheel cylinder pistons. Make sure that the star wheel on the adjuster is lined up with the adjusting hole in the backing plate, if back there.

19. Spread the shoes apart slightly and install the parking brake strut and spring. Make sure that the end of the strut without the spring engages the parking brake lever. The end with the spring engages the primary shoe (the one with the shorter lining).

20. Install the actuator pivot, lever and return spring. Install the actuating link in the shoe retainer. Lift up the actuator lever and hook the link into the lever.

21. Insert the hold-down pins through the back of the plate. Install the lever pivots and hold-down springs. Install the shoe return springs, careful not to stretch or otherwise distort these springs.

22. Take a look at everything. Make sure the linings are in the right place, the self-adjusting mechanism is correctly installed and the parking brake cable is secured. If in doubt, remove the other wheel and take a look at that one for comparison.

23. Measure the width of the linings, then measure the inside width of the drum. Adjust the linings by means of the adjuster so that the drum will fit onto the linings.

24. Install the hub and bearing assembly onto the axle, if removed. Tighten the retaining bolts to 45 ft. lbs. (60 Nm) without ABS, 60 ft. lbs. (82 Nm) with ABS.

25. Install the drum, adjust the brakes. Adjust the parking brake.

26. Install the wheel and hand-tighten the lug nuts.

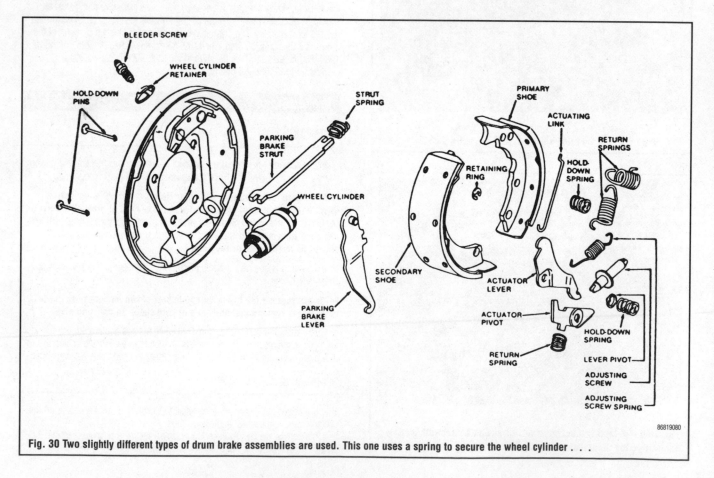

Fig. 30 Two slightly different types of drum brake assemblies are used. This one uses a spring to secure the wheel cylinder . . .

86819080

27. Lower the car. Tighten lug nuts to 100 ft. lbs. (136 Nm).

28. Check the pedal for any sponginess or lack of a hard feel. Check the braking action and the parking brake.

Wheel Cylinders

REMOVAL & INSTALLATION

◆ **See Figures 30 thru 40**

1. Loosen the wheel lug nuts. Raise and support the car, and remove the wheel. Remove the drum and brake shoes.

2. Remove any dirt from around the brake line fitting. Disconnect the brake line, then plug the opening to prevent fluid loss and contamination.

3. If the wheel cylinder is retained with bolts, simply remove the bolts. If retained with clips, remove the wheel cylinder retainer by using two awls or punches with a tip diameter of ⅛ in. (3mm) or less. Insert the awls or punches into the access slots between the wheel cylinder pilot and retainer locking tabs. Bend both tabs away simultaneously. Remove the wheel cylinder from the backing plate.

To install:

4. If retained with bolts, simply install wheel cylinder and tighten the bolts to 9–15 ft. lbs. (12–20 Nm). If retained with clips, position the wheel cylinder against the backing plate, then hold it in place with a wooden block between the wheel cylinder and the hub and bearing assembly.

5. Install a new retainer over the wheel cylinder abutment on the rear of the backing plate by pressing it into place with a 1⅛ in. (1mm) 12-point socket and an extension.

6. Install a new bleeder screw into the wheel cylinder. Tighten the bleeder screw to 89 inch lbs. (10 Nm). Attach the brake line, then tighten to 10–15 ft. lbs. (14–20 Nm).

7. Install the brake shoes and drum. Adjust the brakes.

8. Install the tire and wheel assembly. Install the lug nuts hand-tight.

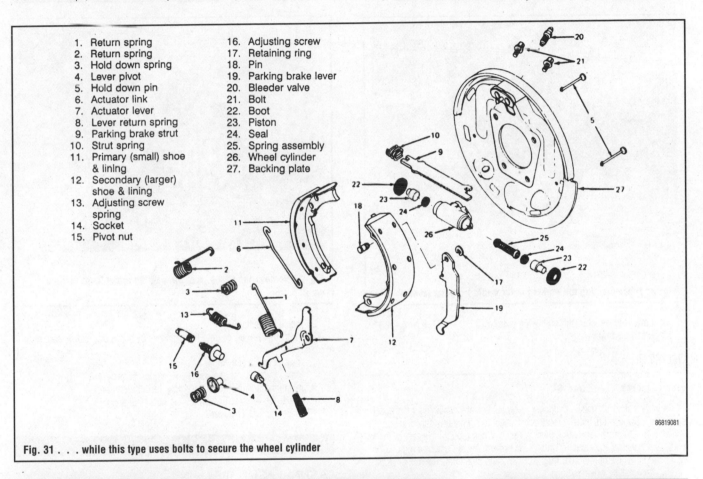

1. Return spring
2. Return spring
3. Hold down spring
4. Lever pivot
5. Hold down pin
6. Actuator link
7. Actuator lever
8. Lever return spring
9. Parking brake strut
10. Strut spring
11. Primary (small) shoe & lining
12. Secondary (larger) shoe & lining
13. Adjusting screw spring
14. Socket
15. Pivot nut
16. Adjusting screw
17. Retaining ring
18. Pin
19. Parking brake lever
20. Bleeder valve
21. Bolt
22. Boot
23. Piston
24. Seal
25. Spring assembly
26. Wheel cylinder
27. Backing plate

Fig. 31 . . . while this type uses bolts to secure the wheel cylinder

Fig. 32 If you remove the hub, install two of the bolts to secure the backing plate

Fig. 33 Special tools are available for disengaging the return springs

Fig. 34 Remove the hold-down springs by pressing down and turning 90 degrees

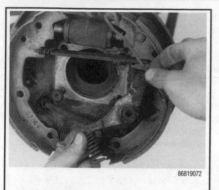

Fig. 35 Removing the actuator lever, pivot and the pivot return spring

Fig. 36 Spread the shoes apart to clear the wheel cylinder pistons, then remove the parking brake strut and spring

Fig. 37 Remove the brake shoes. Note the parking brake cable is still attached to the lever

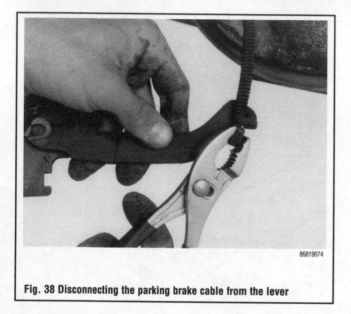

Fig. 38 Disconnecting the parking brake cable from the lever

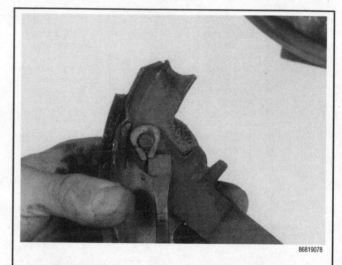

Fig. 39 Remove the C-clip from the parking brake lever using a small prytool

9. Lower the vehicle. Tighten the lug nuts to 100 ft. lbs. (136 Nm).
10. Bleed the brake system.

OVERHAUL

◆ **See Figures 41, 42 and 43**

As is the case with master cylinders, overhaul kits are available for the wheel cylinders, however it is usually more economical to simply buy new or rebuilt wheel cylinders rather rebuilding them yourself. When rebuilding wheel cylinders, avoid getting any contaminants in the system. Always use new high quality brake fluid; the use of improper fluid will swell and deteriorate the rubber parts.

1. Remove the wheel cylinders.
2. Remove the rubber boots from the cylinder ends. Discard the boots.
3. Remove the pistons and cups. Discard the cups.
4. Wash the cylinder and metal parts in denatured alcohol.

✳✳ WARNING

Never use mineral based solvents to clean the brake parts.

5. Allow the parts to air dry and inspect the cylinder bore for corrosion or wear. Light corrosion can be cleaned up with crocus cloth. Use finger pressure and rotate the cloth around the circumference of the bore. Do not move the cloth in and out. Any deep corrosion, pitting or wear warrants replacement of the part(s).
6. Rinse the parts and allow to dry. Do not dry with a rag, which will leave bits of line behind.
7. Lubricate the cylinder bore with clean brake fluid. Insert the spring assembly.
8. Install new cups. Do not lubricate prior to assembly.

9. Install the pistons.
10. Press the new boots onto the cylinders by hand. Do not lubricate prior to assembly.
11. Install the wheel cylinder.
12. Install the brake shoes and drum. Adjust the brakes.
13. Install the tire and wheel assembly. Install the lug nuts.
14. Lower the vehicle. Tighten the lug nuts until snug.
15. Bleed the brake system.

Brake Backing Plate

REMOVAL & INSTALLATION

1. Disconnect the negative battery cable.
2. To remove the wheel, loosen all the lug nuts at least one full turn, before raising the car.
3. Raise and safely support the car.
4. Remove the wheel and tire assembly.
5. Remove the brake drum, shoes and springs as previously described.
6. Unsecure the brake line from the wheel cylinder, then remove the wheel cylinder.
7. Remove the parking brake cable.
8. Remove the hub and bearing assembly.
9. Remove the backing plate.
To install:
10. Install the backing plate to axle.
11. Install the hub and bearing assembly.
12. Connect the parking brake cable to the backing plate.

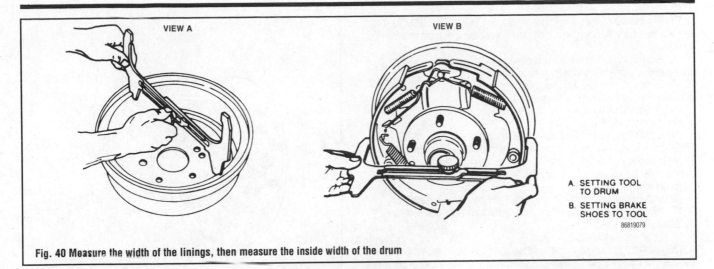

VIEW A

VIEW B

A. SETTING TOOL
   TO DRUM

B. SETTING BRAKE
   SHOES TO TOOL

86819079

Fig. 40 Measure the width of the linings, then measure the inside width of the drum

86819083

Fig. 41 Remove the wheel cylinders, then remove the rubber boots from the cylinder ends

86819084

Fig. 42 After the pistons are removed, the cup seals and spring can be removed

86819085

Fig. 43 Inspect the wheel cylinder for scoring, nicks, corrosion, and wear

13. Install the wheel cylinder, following the procedures outlined.
14. Install the brake components.
15. Adjust and bleed the rear brakes.
16. Adjust the parking brake cables.
17. Install the wheel and tire assembly, hand-tighten the lug nuts.
18. Lower the vehicle, then tighten the lug nuts to 100 ft. lbs. (136 Nm).

REAR DISC BRAKES

✳✳ CAUTION

Brake pads may contain asbestos, which has been determined to a cancer causing agent. Never clean the brake surfaces with compressed air! Avoid inhaling any dust from any brake surface! When cleaning brake surfaces, use a commercially available brake cleaning fluid.

Brake Pads

REMOVAL & INSTALLATION

▶ See Figures 44, 45, 46, 47 and 48

1. Siphon ⅔ of the brake fluid out of the master cylinder reservoir.
2. Release the parking brake, then raise and safely support the vehicle.
3. Remove the tire and wheel assembly.
4. Install two wheel nuts to secure the rotor in place.

✳✳ CAUTION

Be prepared to catch the springs when you are removing the spring pins. The springs may fly out and can cause personal injury

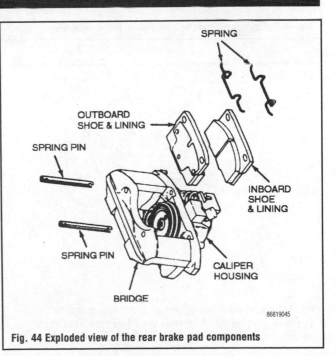

SPRING

OUTBOARD
SHOE & LINING

SPRING PIN

INBOARD
SHOE
& LINING

SPRING PIN

CALIPER
HOUSING

BRIDGE

86819045

Fig. 44 Exploded view of the rear brake pad components

5. Remove the spring pins using removal tool J 6125-1B and J 36620. The tool will thread into the spring pin. Using the tool remove the spring pins from the caliper.

6. Remove the outboard brake pad from the caliper. Loosen the parking brake cable adjustment if necessary to remove the pad.

7. Remove the inboard pad from the caliper. It may be necessary to slide the caliper in slightly to remove the pad.

8. Remove the two check valves from the end of the piston assembly, using a small flat bladed tool.

9. Bottom the piston in the caliper bore using a caliper spin back tool or tool J-36621. Turn the left caliper piston assembly counterclockwise and the right piston assembly clockwise. This is done to move the piston assembly back into the bore. Make sure the two notches in the caliper piston are at the 6 and 12 o'clock positions.

To install:

10. Install a new lubricated two way check valve into the piston assembly.

11. Install the inboard pad so the dowels on the back of the pad seat into the piston notches.

12. Install the outboard pad.

13. Install the pad spring over the outboard pad with the spring center section over the top of the pad. Slide the second spring pin into the caliper until the pad spring can be hooked under it.

14. Install the pad spring over the inboard pad with the spring center section over the top of the pad. Slide the second spring pin into the caliper until the pad spring can be hooked under it.

15. With both pad springs in place, drive the spring pins to the fully seated position in the caliper.

16. Install the tire and wheel. Hand-tighten the lug nuts.

17. Lower the vehicle, then tighten the lug nuts to 100 ft. lbs. (136 Nm).

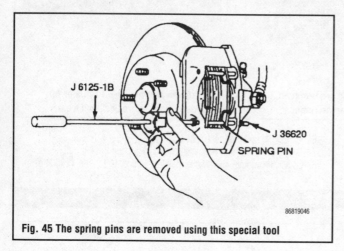

Fig. 45 The spring pins are removed using this special tool

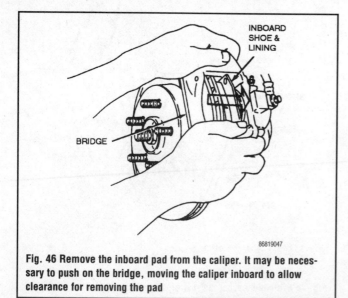

Fig. 46 Remove the inboard pad from the caliper. It may be necessary to push on the bridge, moving the caliper inboard to allow clearance for removing the pad

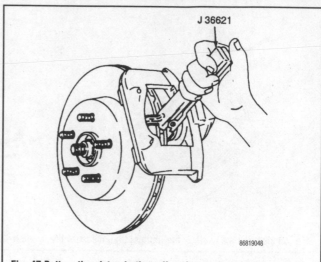

Fig. 47 Bottom the piston in the caliper bore using a caliper spin back tool

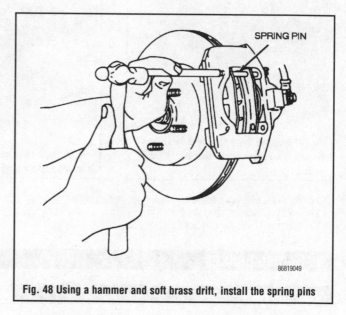

Fig. 48 Using a hammer and soft brass drift, install the spring pins

18. Pump the brake several times to seat the pads against the rotor. Top off the brake fluid.

INSPECTION

The pad thickness should be inspected every time that the tires are removed for rotation. The outer pad can be checked by looking in at each end, which is the point at which the highest rate of wear occurs. The inner pad can be checked by looking down through the inspection hole in the top of the caliper. If the thickness of the pad is worn to within 0.030 in. (0.76mm) of the rivet at either end of the pad, all the pads should be replaced. This is the factory recommended measurement, your state's automobile inspection laws may not agree with this.

➡**Always replace all pads on both wheels at the same time. Failure to do so will result in uneven braking action and premature wear.**

Brake Caliper

REMOVAL & INSTALLATION

1. To remove the wheel, loosen all the lug nuts at least one full turn, before raising the vehicle.

2. Raise and safely support the vehicle.
3. Remove the tire and wheel assembly.
4. Disconnect and cap the brake hose from the caliper.
5. Remove the brake pads.
6. Disconnect the parking brake cable from the parking brake lever and remove the return spring.
7. Remove the parking brake cable from the parking brake cable bracket. This can be done easily by inserting a ½ in. (13mm) wrench over the cable end lock tabs and pulling the cable out.
8. Remove the two caliper mounting bolts and remove the caliper from the vehicle.

To install:

9. Install the caliper over the rotor and install the caliper mounting bolts.
10. Tighten the mounting bolts to 74 ft. lbs. (100 Nm).
11. Install the parking brake cable into the cable mounting bracket.
12. Install the return spring and connect the cable end to the parking brake lever.
13. Install the brake pads.
14. Connect the brake hose to the caliper and tighten the mounting bolt to 33 ft. lbs. (45 Nm).
15. Bleed the brake system.
16. Install the tire and wheel. Hand-tighten the lug nuts.
17. Lower the vehicle, tighten the lug nuts to 100 ft. lbs. (136 Nm).

OVERHAUL

▶ **See Figures 49 and 50**

1. Raise and support the vehicle. Remove the wheel and tire assembly.
2. Remove the caliper.
3. Remove the parking brake lever and lever seal nut.
4. Inspect the bracket and bridge for cracks or distortion.
5. Disassemble the bridge bolts, bracket, and bridge, only if the bridge or bracket is suspected of being cracked or damaged in any way. The caliper can be overhauled without removing the bridge.
6. Inspect the piston for scoring, nicks, corrosion, wear and damaged or worn chrome plating. Replace the piston if any defects are found.
7. Remove the actuator screw by pressing on the threaded end. Inspect the actuator screw for cracks and thread damage.
8. Remove the balance spring, then unsecure the shaft seal and thrust washer from the actuator screw.
9. Remove the piston boot with a flat bladed tool, working carefully so that the piston bore is not scratched.
10. Remove the piston seal from the caliper bore groove using a piece of pointed wood or plastic. Do not use a metal tool, which will damage the bore. Inspect the caliper bore for nicks, corrosion and so on. Very light wear can be cleaned up with crocus cloth. Use finger pressure to rub the crocus cloth

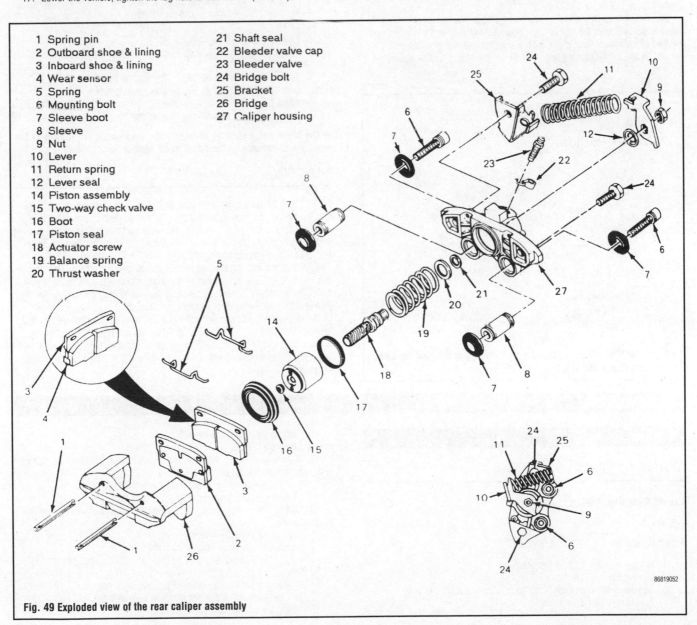

Fig. 49 Exploded view of the rear caliper assembly

1 Spring pin
2 Outboard shoe & lining
3 Inboard shoe & lining
4 Wear sensor
5 Spring
6 Mounting bolt
7 Sleeve boot
8 Sleeve
9 Nut
10 Lever
11 Return spring
12 Lever seal
14 Piston assembly
15 Two-way check valve
16 Boot
17 Piston seal
18 Actuator screw
19 Balance spring
20 Thrust washer
21 Shaft seal
22 Bleeder valve cap
23 Bleeder valve
24 Bridge bolt
25 Bracket
26 Bridge
27 Caliper housing

86819052

around the circumference of the bore, do not slide it in and out. More extensive wear or corrosion warrants replacement of the part.

11. Remove the bleeder screw and cap from the caliper.

To assemble:

12. Clean any parts which are to be reused in denatured alcohol. Dry them with compressed or allow to air dry. Don't wipe the parts dry with a cloth, which will leave behind bits of lint.

13. Assemble the bracket, bridge and bridge bolts, if they were removed. Tighten the bridge bolts to 74 ft. lbs. (100 Nm).

14. Install the bleeder screw, tightening to 110–120 inch lbs. (13–14 Nm).

15. Lubricate the new seal (provided in a repair kit), with clean brake fluid. Install the seal in its groove, making sure it is fully seated and not twisted.

16. Mount the thrust washer onto the actuator screw, then install the copper side of the thrust washer toward the piston and the grayish side toward the housing.

17. Lubricate the shaft seal and insert on the actuator screw.

18. Install the new dust boot on the piston. Insert the lubricated screw with the shaft seal and thrust washer into the caliper housing. Install the balancer spring into the housing bore, with the end of the spring in recess at the bottom of the bore.

19. Lubricate the bore of the caliper with clean brake fluid and insert the piston into its bore. Make sure the piston is well lubricated before insertion. Position the boot in the caliper housing and seat with a seal driver of the appropriate size, or tool No. J-36623.

20. Turn the actuator screw as necessary to allow the piston assembly to move to the bottom of the caliper bore. Lubricate the lever seal and install over the end of the actuator screw. The rubber sealing bead over the lever seal should be against the parking lever, and the copper end should be against the housing.

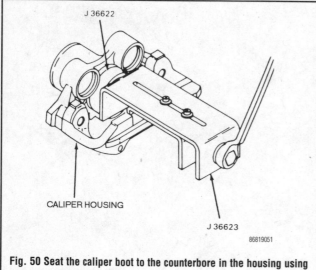

Fig. 50 Seat the caliper boot to the counterbore in the housing using tool No. J-36622 and J-36623

J 36622

CALIPER HOUSING

J 36623

86819051

21. Hold the parking lever back against the stop on the caliper housing while tightening the nut. This will prevent any accidental application of the parking brake mechanism.

22. Insert the lever and nut, the hex hole in the lever must engage the hex hole in the actuator screw. Tighten the nut to 35 ft. lbs. (47 Nm).

23. Seat the caliper boot to the counterbore in the housing using tool No. J-36622 and J-36623.

24. Install the pads and the caliper, then bleed the brakes.

25. Lower the vehicle.

Brake Disc (Rotor)

REMOVAL & INSTALLATION

1. To remove the wheel, loosen all the lug nuts at least one full turn, before raising the car.

2. Raise and safely support the vehicle.

3. Remove the tire and wheel assembly.

4. Remove the two caliper mounting bolts and remove the caliper from the knuckle.

5. Using a piece of wire, support the caliper out of the way. DO NOT disconnect the brake hose or allow the caliper to hang from the brake hose.

6. Remove the brake rotor from the vehicle.

To install:

7. Install the rotor on the vehicle.

8. Install the caliper onto the steering knuckle. Make sure the brake hose is not twisted.

9. Tighten the mounting bolts to 74 ft. lbs. (100 Nm).

10. Install the tire and wheel. Hand-tighten the lug nuts.

11. Lower the vehicle, then tighten the lug nuts to 100 ft. lbs. (136 Nm).

12. Pump the brake pedal several times to seat the pads against the rotor.

➡**The brake pedal must be pumped prior to operating the vehicle or the vehicle will not stop on the initial pedal application.**

INSPECTION

1. Check the rotor surface for wear or scoring. Deep scoring, grooves or rust pitting can be removed by refacing. This can be performed by your local machine shop or garage. Minimum thickness is stamped on the rotor, or see the brake specifications chart in this section. If the rotor is thinner than specification, after refinishing, it must be replaced.

2. Check the rotor parallelism using a micrometer. It must vary less than 0.0005 in. (0.0127mm) measured at four or more points around the circumference. Make all measurements at the same distance in from the edge of the rotor. Refinish the rotor if it fails to meet this specification.

3. Measure the disc run-out with a dial indicator. If run-out exceeds 0.002 in. (0.051mm) for 1982–85 models, 0.004 in. (0.10mm) for 1985–87 models, and 0.002 in. (0.051mm) for 1988–96 models and the wheel bearings are OK (if run-out is being measured with the disc on the car), the rotor must be refaced or replaced as necessary.

PARKING BRAKE

Cables

REMOVAL & INSTALLATION

Except Rear Disc Brakes

FRONT

♦ **See Figure 51**

1. Raise and safely support the vehicle.

2. Loosen the equalizer nut.

3. Disengage the front cable from the connector and equalizer.

4. Remove the clip at the frame.

5. Remove the cable from the hanger.

6. Lower the vehicle.

7. To remove the driver's side sound insulator panel, unsecure the screws and nuts. Remove the panel.

8. Remove the carpet finish molding, then lift the carpet.

9. Remove the cable retaining clip at the lever assembly.

10. Depress the retaining tangs and remove the cable and casing from the lever assembly.

11. Remove the cable from the retaining clips.

12. Remove the grommet retainer from the floor pan.

13. Unseat the grommet and pull the cable through the floor pan.

To install:

14. Insert the cable through the floor pan and grommet.

15. Seat the grommet. Install the grommet retainer to the floor pan.

16. Fasten the cable in the retaining clips.

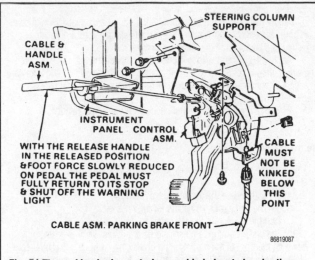

STEERING COLUMN
SUPPORT

CABLE &
HANDLE
ASM.

INSTRUMENT
PANEL   CONTROL
ASM.

WITH THE RELEASE HANDLE
IN THE RELEASED POSITION
&FOOT FORCE SLOWLY REDUCED
ON PEDAL THE PEDAL MUST
FULLY RETURN TO ITS STOP
& SHUT OFF THE WARNING
LIGHT

CABLE
MUST
NOT BE
KINKED
BELOW
THIS
POINT

CABLE ASM. PARKING BRAKE FRONT

86819087

Fig. 51 The parking brake control assembly is located under the dashboard on the driver's side

17. Connect the cable and casing to the lever assembly. Seat the retaining tangs.
18. Install the cable retaining clip at the lever assembly.
19. Place the carpet into position, then install the carpet finish molding.
20. Install the driver's side sound insulator panel with the attaching screws and nuts.
21. Raise and safely support the vehicle.
22. Fasten the cable to the hanger.
23. Install the clip to the frame.
24. Engage the front cable to the equalizer and connector.
25. Adjust the parking brake cable.
26. Lower the vehicle.

LEFT REAR

1. To remove the wheel, loosen all the lug nuts at least one full turn, before raising the car.
2. Raise and support the rear of the vehicle on jackstands.
3. Loosen the equalizer nut to relieve the cable tension, then remove the wheel and tire assembly.
4. Remove the brake drum, then insert a flat bladed tool between the brake shoe and the top of the brake adjuster bracket.
5. Push the bracket forward and release the top adjuster bracket rod. Remove the rear hold-down spring, the actuator lever and the lever return spring.
6. Remove the adjuster screw, spring and the top rear brake shoe return spring.
7. Remove the parking brake cable from the parking brake lever.
8. Depress the conduit fitting retaining tangs and remove the fitting from the backing plate.
9. Back off the equalizer nut and remove the left cable from the equalizer.
10. Depress the conduit fitting retaining tangs and remove the fitting from the axle bracket.
To install:
11. Install the cable through the rear of the backing plate. Seat the retaining tangs in the backing plate.
12. Connect the cable to the parking brake lever.
13. Install the brake drum, tire, wheel and lug nuts.
14. Engage the cable at the equalizer and connector.
15. Adjust the service brake shoes, then adjust the parking brake cable.
16. Install the wheel and tire, then hand-tighten the lug nuts.
17. Lower the vehicle, and tighten the lug nuts to 100 ft. lbs. (136 Nm).

RIGHT REAR

1. To remove the wheel, loosen all the lug nuts at least one full turn, before raising the car.
2. Raise and support the rear of the vehicle on jackstands.
3. Loosen the equalizer nut to relieve the cable tension, then remove the wheel and tire assembly.

4. Remove the brake drum, then insert a screwdriver between the brake shoe and the top of the brake adjuster bracket.
5. Push the bracket forward and release the top adjuster bracket rod. Remove the rear hold-down spring, the actuator lever and the lever return spring.
6. Remove the adjuster screw, spring and the top rear brake shoe return spring.
7. Remove the parking brake cable from the parking brake lever.
8. Depress the conduit fitting retaining tangs and remove the fitting from the backing plate.
9. Remove the cable button end from the connector.
10. Depress the conduit fitting retaining tangs and remove the fitting from the axle bracket.
To install:
11. Install the cable through the rear of the backing plate. Seat the retaining tangs in the backing plate.
12. Connect the cable to the parking brake lever.
13. Install the brake drum, wheel and hand-tighten the lug nuts.
14. Engage the cable at the equalizer and connector.
15. Adjust the regular service brake, then adjust the parking brake cable.
16. Lower the vehicle, then tighten the lug nuts to 100 ft. lbs. (136 Nm).

Rear Disc Brakes

FRONT

1. Raise and safely support the vehicle.
2. On the rear suspension member, loosen the nut on the parking brake cable equalizer.
3. Disconnect the front parking brake cable from the equalizer assembly.
4. Disconnect the parking brake cable from the frame clip at the left rear of the vehicle.
5. Pull the parking brake cable through the cable hanger in front of the clip mounting point.
6. Lower the vehicle.
7. Remove the drivers side sound insulator panel.
8. Remove the carpet finish molding.
9. Pull the carpet back to uncover the parking brake cable.
10. Remove the cable retaining clip at the parking brake lever assembly.
11. Disengage the parking brake cable housing locking fingers from the parking brake assembly.
12. Disconnect the cable end from the parking brake lever assembly.
13. Remove the grommet retainer from the floor pan.
14. Pull the cable through the floor pan and remove.
To install:
15. Pull the cable through the floor pan until the grommet can be seated in the hole in the floor.
16. Install the grommet retainer on the floor pan.
17. Connect the cable end to the parking brake assembly lever.
18. Seat the parking brake cable housing into the parking brake assembly until the locking fingers engage.
19. Install the cable retaining clip at the parking brake assembly.
20. Place the carpet back in place and install the carpet finish molding.
21. Install the drivers side sound insulator cable.
22. Raise and safely support the vehicle.
23. Route the cable through the cable hanger at the rear of the vehicle.
24. Install the cable mounting clip at the left rear of the vehicle.
25. Connect the cable to the parking brake equalizer on the rear suspension member.
26. Adjust the parking brake.
27. Lower the vehicle.

REAR

1. Raise and safely support the vehicle.
2. On the rear suspension member, loosen the nut on the parking brake cable equalizer.
3. Disconnect the front parking brake cable from the equalizer assembly.
4. Disconnect the cable from the mounting bracket on the rear axle assembly.
5. Remove the tire and wheel assembly.
6. Disconnect the parking brake cable end from the parking brake lever on the caliper and remove the return spring.

7. Disconnect the cable guide from the strut mounting bracket.

To install:

8. Connect the cable to the mounting bracket on the rear axle assembly.
9. Connect the cable end to the equalizer assembly.
10. Connect the cable to the cable guide on the strut.
11. Connect the cable to the bracket at the caliper, seat the locking fingers completely.
12. Install the return spring on the cable and connect the cable end to the caliper lever.
13. Install the tire and wheel assembly.
14. Adjust the parking brake cable.
15. Lower the vehicle.

ADJUSTMENT

Except ABS and Rear Disc Brakes

1. Adjust the brakes as described earlier.
2. Depress the parking brake pedal exactly three ratchet clicks.
3. Raise and support the car with both rear wheels off the ground.
4. Tighten the adjusting nut until the right rear wheel can just be turned backward using two hands, but cannot be turned forward.
5. Release the parking brake. Rotate the rear wheels, there should be no drag.
6. Lower the car.

ABS Models

1. Adjust the rear brakes. Apply the parking brake to 10 clicks and release. Repeat this process 5 times.
2. Check the parking brake pedal for a full release.
   a. Turn the ignition to the **ON** position and note if the brake indicator light is off.
   b. If the light is on and the brake seems to be released, then operate the parking brake pedal lever and pull downwards on the front of the cable to remove any slack.

3. Raise and support the vehicle.
4. Adjust the parking brake by turning the nut on the equalizer while spinning both rear wheels. When either the rear wheels develops a drag, stop adjusting and back off the equalizer nut one full turn.
5. Apply the parking brake to 4 clicks, then check the rear wheel rotation. The wheel should not move when you attempt to rotate it by hand, in a forward direction. There should be wheel drag or no movement at all when you rotate the wheel in the rearward direction.
6. Release the parking brake and check for a free wheel rotation.
7. Lower the vehicle. Test drive the vehicle.

Rear Disc Brakes

1. Press the brake pedal 3 times with the force of approximately 175 ft. lbs. (237 Nm).
2. Apply and release the parking brake 3 times.
3. Check the parking brake pedals for full release.
   a. Turn the ignition to the **ON** position.
   b. The brake warning lamp should be off. If this is not the case, pull down on the front of the front parking brake cable with the hand lever completely released. This will remove any slack from the lever assembly.
4. Raise and support the vehicle.
5. Check that the parking brake levers on both of the calipers are against the lever stops on the housings. If the levers are not against the stops, then check for binding in the rear cables, and/or loosen the cable at each adjuster until both of the left and right levers are against there stops.
6. If the cables are binding, replace them.
7. Tighten the cable at the adjuster until either the left or right lever begins to move off the stop, then loosen the adjustment until the lever moves back to barely touch the stop.
8. Lower the vehicle.
9. Operate the parking brake several times to check the adjustment. After the cable adjustment, the brake parking brake pedal should not travel more than 16 ratchet clicks. The rear wheels should not rotate forward when the lever is applied 14 to 16 ratchet clicks.

TEVES ANTI-LOCK BRAKE SYSTEM

General Description

The Teves Anti-Lock Brake System used on the General Motors A-Body cars is manufactured by Alfred Teves Technologies of West Germany. The 4-wheel system uses a combination of wheel speed sensors and a microprocessor to determine impending wheel lock-up and adjust the brake pressure to maintain the best braking. This system helps the driver maintain the control of the vehicle under heavy braking conditions.

❉❉ CAUTION

Some procedures in this section require that hydraulic lines, hoses and fitting be disconnected for inspection or testing purposes. Before disconnecting any hydraulic lines, hoses or fittings, be sure that the accumulator is fully depressurized. Failure to depressurize the hydraulic accumulator may result in personal injury.

➡**The use of rubber hoses or parts other than those specified for the ABS system may lead to functional problems and/or impaired braking or ABS function. Install all components included in repair kits for this system. Lubricate rubber pats with clean fresh brake fluid to ease assembly.**

SYSTEM OPERATION

Under normal driving conditions the Anti-lock system functions the same as a standard brake system. The primary difference is that the power assist for normal braking is provided by the booster portion of the hydraulic unit through the use of pressurized brake fluid.

If a wheel locking tendency is noted during a brake application, the ABS system will modulate hydraulic pressure in the individual wheel circuits to prevent any wheel from locking. A separate hydraulic line and 2 specific solenoid valves

are provided for each front wheel; both rear wheels share a set of solenoid valves and a single pipe from the master cylinder to the proportioner valve or tee. The proportioner valve splits the right and left rear brake circuits to the wheels.

➡**The Pontiac 6000 AWD incorporates a differential lock mounted on the transaxle transfer case. The lock is engaged when the vehicle is in all wheel drive and the transfer case differential is locked. Due to the rigid coupling of the front and rear axles through the drive train, the wheel speed sensors cannot relay accurate data to the controller. The differential lock disables the ABS system when the vehicle is in all wheel drive.**

The ABS system can increase, decrease or hold pressure in each hydraulic circuit depending on signals from the wheel speed sensors and the electronic brake control module.

During an ABS stop, a slight bump or a kick-back will be felt in the brake pedal. This bump will be followed by a series of short pulsations which occur in rapid succession. The brake pedal pulsations will continue until there is no longer a need for the anti-lock function or until the vehicle is stopped. A slight ticking or popping noise may be heard during brake applications with anti-lock. This noise is normal and indicates that the anti-lock system is being used.

During anti-lock stops on dry pavement, the tires may make intermittent chirping noises as they approach lock-up. These noises are considered normal as long as the wheel does not truly lock or skid. When the anti-lock system is being used, the brake pedal may rise even as the brakes are being applied. This is normal. Maintaining a constant force on the pedal will provide the shortest stopping distance.

Anti-Lock Warning Light

Vehicles equipped with the ABS have an amber warning light in the instrument panel marked ANTILOCK. Additionally, some models using this system will flash other ABS related messages on the Graphic Control Center or other message panels. The warning light will illuminate if a malfunction in the anti-lock brake system is detected by the electronic controller. In case of an electronic malfunction, the controller will turn on the ANTILOCK warning light and disable some or all of the anti-lock system. If only the ANTILOCK light is on, normal braking with full assist is operational but there may be reduced or no anti-lock function. If the ANTILOCK warning light and the red BRAKE warning light come on at the same time, there may be a fault in the hydraulic brake system.

The ANTILOCK light will turn on during the starting of the engine and will usually stay on for approximately 3 seconds after the ignition switch is returned to the RUN position.

➡**Due to system de-pressurization over time, a vehicle not started in several hours may have the BRAKE and ANTILOCK warning lights stay on up to 30 seconds when started. This is normal and occurs because the ABS pump must restore the correct pressure within the hydraulic accumulator. Both lamps will remain on while this recharging is completed.**

Brake System Warning Light

The Anti-lock Brake System uses a 2 circuit design so that some braking capacity is still available if hydraulic pressure is lost in 1 circuit. A BRAKE warning light is located on the instrument cluster and is designed to alert the driver of conditions that could result in reduced braking ability. Certain models may display brake related messages on screens or other panels, these messages supplement the brake warning light.

The BRAKE warning light should turn on briefly during engine starting and should remain on whenever the parking brake is not fully released. Additionally, the BRAKE warning lamp will illuminate if a sensor detects low brake fluid, if the pressure switch detects low accumulator pressure or if certain on-board computers run a self-check of the dashboard and instruments.

If the BRAKE warning light stays on longer than 30 seconds after starting the engine, or comes on and stays on while driving, there may be a malfunction in the brake hydraulic system.

SYSTEM COMPONENTS

Electronic Brake Control Module (EBCM)

The Electronic Brake Control Module (EBCM) monitors the speed of each wheel and the electrical status of the hydraulic unit. The EBCM's primary functions are to detect wheel lockup, control the brake system while in anti-lock mode and monitor the system for proper electrical operation. When 1 or more wheels approach lockup during a stop, the EBCM will command appropriate valve positions to modulate brake fluid pressure and provide optimum braking. It will continue to command pressure changes in the system until a locking tendency is no longer noted.

The EBCM is a separate computer used exclusively for control of the anti-lock brake system. The unit also controls the retention and display of the ABS trouble codes when in the diagnostic mode. As the EBCM monitors the system or performs a self-check, it can react to a fault by disabling the ABS system and illuminating the amber ANTILOCK warning light. The EBCM is located on the right side of the dashboard, generally behind the glove box.

Wheel Speed Sensors

A wheel speed sensor at each wheel transmits speed information to the EBCM by generating a small AC voltage relative to the wheel speed. The voltage is generated by magnetic induction caused by passing a toothed sensor ring past a stationary sensor. The signals are transmitted through a pair of wires which are shielded against interference. The EBCM then calculates wheel speed for each wheel based on the frequency of the AC voltage received from the sensor.

Hydraulic Components

The ABS uses an integrated hydraulic unit mounted on the firewall or cowl. This unit functions as a brake master cylinder and brake booster. Additionally, the hydraulic unit provides brake fluid pressure modulation for each of the individual wheel circuits as required during braking. The hydraulic unit consists of several individual components:

MASTER CYLINDER/BOOSTER ASSEMBLY

This portion of the hydraulic unit contains the valves and pistons necessary to develop hydraulic pressure within the brake lines. Pressure in the booster servo circuit is controlled by a spool valve which opens in response to the amount of force applied to the brake pedal. The rate at which the vehicle decelerates depends on the type of road surface and the pressure applied to the brake pedal.

The master cylinder portion uses a 3-circuit configuration during normal braking; individual circuits are provided for each front wheel while a shared circuit is used for the rear wheels. The 3 circuits are isolated so that a leak or malfunction in one will allow continued braking on the others.

The master cylinder/booster is a non-serviceable component and should never be disassembled.

VALVE BLOCK

The valve block is attached to the right side of the hydraulic unit and includes the 6 solenoid valves used to modulate pressures in the 3 circuits during anti-lock braking. Each circuit is equipped with an inlet and outlet valve.

During normal braking, the inlet valves are open and the outlet valves are closed. When anti-lock control begins, the EBCM switches 12 volts to the appropriate valve circuit. This allows the fluid pressure in each circuit to be increased, decreased or hold constant as the situation dictates. The position of the valves can be changed as quickly as 15 times per second when ABS is engaged.

The valve block may be serviced separately from the master cylinder/booster assembly but should never be disassembled.

MAIN VALVE

The main valve is a 2-position valve controlled by the Electronic Brake Control Module (EBCM). Except for testing, the valve is open only during ABS stops. When open, the valve allows pressurized brake fluid from the booster servo into the master cylinder front brake circuits to prevent excessive pedal travel.

The main valve is not serviceable as a component; the master cylinder/booster assembly must be replaced.

ACCUMULATOR

The hydraulic accumulator is used to store brake fluid at high pressure so that a supply of pressurized fluid is available for ABS operation and to provide power assist. The accumulator uses a rubber diaphragm to separate high-pressure nitrogen gas from the brake fluid.

Nitrogen in the accumulator is pre-charged to approximately 870 psi (6000 kPa). During normal operation, the pump and motor assembly charges the accumulator with brake fluid to an operation range of 2000–2600 psi (13,800–18,000 kPa).

Because of the high pressures in the system, it is extremely important to observe all safety and pressure reduction precautions before performing repairs or diagnosis.

PUMP/MOTOR ASSEMBLY

The ABS system uses a pump and motor assembly located on the left side of the hydraulic unit to pressurize fluid from the reservoir and store it in the accumulator. When pressure within the system drops, the pressure switch on the hydraulic unit grounds the pump motor relay which energizes the pump motor and pump.

The pump/motor assembly is serviceable only as an assembly; the pump must never be disconnected from the motor.

FLUID LEVEL SENSOR

Found in the fluid reservoir, this sensor is a float which operates 2 reed switches when low fluid level is detected. One switch will cause the red BRAKE warning light to illuminate; the other signals the EBCM and possibly other computers of the low fluid situation. Depending on model and equipment, other messages may be displayed to the driver. The Electronic Brake Control Module (EBCM) will engage the amber ANTILOCK warning light and disable the ABS function.

PRESSURE SWITCH

The pressure switch is mounted on the pump/motor assembly and serves 2 major functions, controlling the pump/motor and providing low pressure warning to the Electronic Brake Control Module (EBCM).

The switch will allow the pump/motor to run when system pressure drops below approximately 2030 psi (14,000 kPa) and will shut the pump/motor off when pressure in the accumulator is approximately 2610 psi (18,000 kPa).

Should pressure within the accumulator drop below approximately 1500 psi (10,300 kPa), internal switches will both signal the EBCM and turn on the red BRAKE warning lamp. If the system re-pressurizes and reaches at least 1900 psi (13,100 kPa), the switches will reset.

PROPORTIONER VALVE

Included in the rear brake circuit is a proportioner valve or tee assembly which limits brake pressure build-up at the rear brake calipers. Since the front brakes do the majority of the braking, less pressure is required for the rear brakes under certain conditions. The proportioner valve improves front-to-rear brake balance during normal braking.

Troubleshooting

SERVICE PRECAUTIONS

✳✳ CAUTION

This brake system uses a hydraulic accumulator which, when fully charged, contains brake fluid at very high pressure. Before disconnecting any hydraulic lines, hoses or fittings be certain that the accumulator pressure is completely relieved. Failure to depressurize the accumulator may result in personal injury and/or vehicle damage.

• If the vehicle is equipped with air bag (SIR) system, always properly disable the system before commencing work on the ABS system.
• Certain components within the ABS system are not intended to be serviced or repaired individually. Only those components with removal and installation procedures should be serviced.
• Do not use rubber hoses or other parts not specifically specified for the Teves ABS system. When using repair kits, replace all parts included in the kit. Partial or incorrect repair may lead to functional problems and require the replacement of the hydraulic unit.
• Lubricate rubber parts with clean, fresh brake fluid to ease assembly. Do not use lubricated shop air to clean parts, damage to rubber components may result.
• Use only brake fluid from an unopened container. Use of suspect or contaminated brake fluid can reduce system performance and/or durability.
• When any hydraulic component or line is removed or replaced, it may be necessary to bleed the entire system.
• A clean repair area is essential. Perform repairs after components have been thoroughly cleaned, then use only denatured alcohol to clean components. Do not allow ABS components to come into contact with any substance containing mineral oil, this includes used shop rags.
• Remove the lock pin before disconnecting Connector Position Assurance (CPA) connectors in the harnesses.
• The EBCM is a microprocessor similar to other computer units in the vehicle. Insure that the ignition switch is **OFF** before removing or installing controller harnesses. Avoid static electricity discharge at or near the Controller.
• Never disconnect any electrical connection with the ignition switch **ON** unless instructed to do so in a test.
• Always wear a grounded wrist strap when servicing any control module or component labeled with a Electrostatic Discharge (ESD) symbol.
• Avoid touching module connector pins.
• Leave new components and modules in the shipping package until ready to install them.
• To avoid static discharge, always touch a vehicle ground after sliding across a vehicle seat or walking across carpeted or vinyl floors.
• Never allow welding cables to lie on, near or across any vehicle electrical wiring.
• Do not allow extension cords for power tools or droplights to lie on, near or across any vehicle electrical wiring.

DEPRESSURIZING THE HYDRAULIC UNIT

The ABS pump motor assembly will keep the accumulator charged to a pressure between approximately 2000 psi (13,800 kPa) and 2600 psi (18,000 kPa) any time the ignition is in the **ON** or **RUN** position. The pump/motor cannot operate if the ignition is **OFF** or if a battery cable is disconnected.

1. With the ignition **OFF** and the negative battery cable disconnected, pump the brake pedal a minimum of 20 times using at least 50 ft. lbs. (68 Nm) of pedal force each time.
2. A definite increase in pedal effort will be felt as the accumulator becomes discharged.
3. After the increased pedal effort occurs, continue with 5–10 additional brake applications to release any remaining pressure.

VISUAL INSPECTION

Before any system diagnosis is begun, the brake system should be inspected visually for common faults which could disable the ABS or cause a code to set. Check the vehicle carefully for any sign of:
• Binding parking brake or faulty parking brake switch
• Low brake fluid
• System fluid leaks including pump/motor area
• Failed fuses or fusible links
• Failed ABS relay
• Loose or damaged wiring including connectors, harnesses, and insulation wear. Check the mounting and function of the brake calipers at each wheel
Carefully inspect the multi-pin connectors at the EBCM for pushouts or poor connections.

FUNCTIONAL CHECK

Once the visual check has been performed, perform the functional check (found in the diagnostic charts) to determine if the problem is truly ABS related or arising from common faults.

DISPLAYING ABS TROUBLE CODES

♦ See Figure 52

➥The 1st generation system found on the 6000 AWD does not display trouble codes; diagnosis is performed through symptom analysis and circuit testing.

Only certain ABS malfunctions will cause the EBCM to store diagnostic trouble codes. Failures causing a code will generally involve wheel speed sensors, main valve or the inlet and outlet valves. Conditions affecting the pump/motor assembly, the accumulator, pressure switch or fluid level sensor usually do not cause a code to set.

The EBCM will store trouble codes in a non-volatile memory. These codes remain in memory until erased through use of the correct procedure. The codes are NOT erased by disconnecting the EBCM, disconnecting the battery cable or turning off the ignition. Always be sure to clear the codes from the memory after repairs are made. To read stored ABS trouble codes:

1. Turn ignition switch to **ON**. Allow the pump to charge the accumulator. If fully discharged, the dash warning lights may stay on up to 30 seconds. If the ANTI-LOCK warning light does not go off within 30 seconds, make a note of it.
2. Turn ignition switch to **OFF**.
3. Remove the cover from the Assembly Line Diagnostic Link (ALDL) connector. Enter the diagnostic mode by using a jumper wire to connect pins H and A or to connect pin H to body ground.

➥On 1993 and later models the ALDL is also known as the Diagnostic Link Connector (DLC).

4. Turn the ignition switch to **ON** and count the light flashes for the first digit of the first code. The ANTI-LOCK light should illuminate for 4 seconds before beginning to flash. If, after 4 seconds, the light turns off and stays off, no codes are stored.
5. The light will pause for 3 seconds between the first and second digits of the first code and then continue flashing. When counting flashes, count only the ON pulses.
6. When the EBCM is finished transmitting the second digit of the first code, the ANTI-LOCK light will remain on. This last, constant ON should not be counted as a flash. Record the 2-digit code.
7. Without turning the ignition switch **OFF**, disconnect the jumper from pin H and reconnect it. If an additional code is present, it will be displayed in similar fashion to the first. Record the second code.

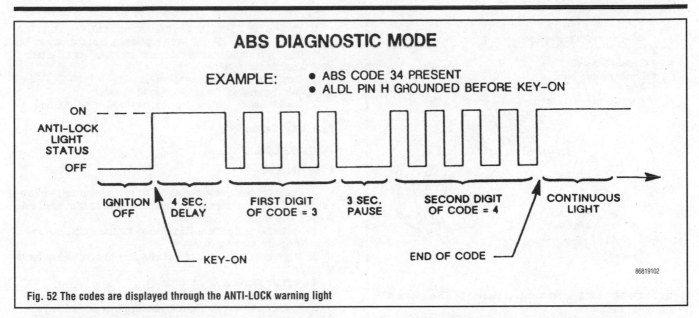

ABS DIAGNOSTIC MODE

EXAMPLE:
- ABS CODE 34 PRESENT
- ALDL PIN H GROUNDED BEFORE KEY-ON

ANTI-LOCK LIGHT STATUS — ON / OFF

IGNITION OFF | 4 SEC. DELAY | FIRST DIGIT OF CODE = 3 | 3 SEC. PAUSE | SECOND DIGIT OF CODE = 4 | CONTINUOUS LIGHT

KEY-ON

END OF CODE

86819102

Fig. 52 The codes are displayed through the ANTI-LOCK warning light

8. Repeat the disconnection and reconnection of pin H without changing the ignition switch position until no more codes are displayed. The system is capable of storing and displaying 7 codes, the ANTI-LOCK warning light will stay on continuously when all codes have been displayed.

9. After recording each code, remove the jumper from the ALDL and replace the cover.

➡**The ABS trouble codes are not specifically designated current or history codes. If the ANTI-LOCK light is on before entering the ABS diagnostic mode, at least 1 of the stored codes is current. It is impossible to tell which code is current. If the ANTI-LOCK light is off before entering the diagnostic mode, none of the codes are current.**

INTERMITTENTS

Although the ABS trouble codes stored by the EBCM are not identified as current or history codes, these codes may still be useful in diagnosing intermittent conditions.

If an intermittent condition is being diagnosed:

1. Obtain an accurate description of the circumstances in which the failure occurs.

2. Display and clear any ABS trouble codes which may be present in the EBCM.

3. Test drive the vehicle, attempting to duplicate the failure condition exactly.

4. After duplicating the condition(s), stop the vehicle and display any ABS codes which have set.

5. If no codes have been stored, refer to the Symptom Diagnosis Charts. A good description of vehicle behavior can be helpful in determining a most likely circuit.

Most intermittent problems are caused by faulty electrical connections or wiring. Always check for poor mating of connector halves or terminals not fully seated in connector bodies, deformed or damaged terminals and poor terminal to wire connections.

Most failures within the ABS will disable the anti-lock function for the entire ignition cycle, even if the fault clears before the next key–off occurrence. There are 3 situations which will allow the ABS to re–engage if the condition corrects during the ignition cycle. Each of these will illuminate 1 or both dash warning lights.

- Low system voltage: If the EBCM detects low voltage, the ANTI-LOCK warning lamp is illuminated. If the correct minimum voltage is restored to the EBCM, normal ABS function resumes.

- Low brake fluid level: Once detected by the fluid level sensor, this condition illuminates both the BRAKE and ANTI-LOCK warning lights; when the sensor indicates acceptable fluid level, the normal ABS function resumes.

- Low accumulator pressure: Should the accumulator lose or not develop correct pressure, both the BRAKE and ANTI-LOCK warning lights will illuminate.

Full function is restored when the correct pressure is achieved.

- Any condition interrupting power to either the EBCM or hydraulic unit may cause the warning lights to come on intermittently. These circuits include the main relay, main relay fuse, EBCM fuse, pump motor relay and all related wiring.

CLEARING TROUBLE CODES

Stored ABS trouble codes should not be cleared until all repairs are completed. The control module will not allow any codes to be cleared until all have been read. After reading each stored code, drive the vehicle at a speed over 18 mph. (31 km/h).

Re-read the system, if codes are still present, then not all the codes were read previously or additional repair is needed.

➡**In the following diagnostic charts, certain special tools may be required. Use of the J-35592 pinout box or equivalent, is required to avoid damage to the connectors at the EBCM. Use of J-35604 pressure gauge and J-35604-88 adapter (or equivalents) will be required to measure accumulator pressure. The use of a high-impedance Digital Volt/Ohmmeter (DVM or DVOM) is required at all times.**

Speed Sensors

REMOVAL & INSTALLATION

Front Speed Sensor

PONTIAC 6000 AWD

▶ See Figures 53 and 54

1. To remove the wheel, loosen all the lug nuts at least one full turn, before raising the car.

2. Raise and safely support the vehicle.

3. Remove the tire and wheel.

4. Unplug the wheel sensor connector from the wiring harness.

5. Remove the sensor retaining screw.

6. Remove the wheel sensor and cable from the brackets.

7. Unseat the grommet and pull the cable and connector through the wheel housing.

To install:

8. Insert the cable and connector through the wheel housing, then seat the grommet in position.

➡**New wheel sensors are equipped with a paper spacer that will properly gap the sensor when placed against the sensor ring.**

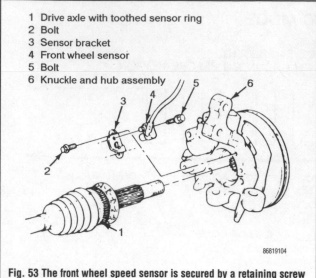

1 Drive axle with toothed sensor ring
2 Bolt
3 Sensor bracket
4 Front wheel sensor
5 Bolt
6 Knuckle and hub assembly

86819104

Fig. 53 The front wheel speed sensor is secured by a retaining screw

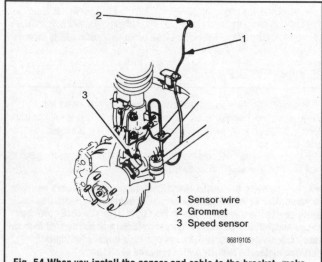

1 Sensor wire
2 Grommet
3 Speed sensor

86819105

Fig. 54 When you install the sensor and cable to the bracket, make certain the cable is clear of the steering and axle components

9. Install the sensor and cable to the bracket. Make certain the cable is clear of the steering and axle housing components.
10. Tighten the sensor retaining bolt to 53 inch lbs. (6 Nm).
11. If necessary, adjust the air gap to 0.028 in. (0.7mm) using a non-ferrous feeler gauge.
12. Tighten the sensor lockbolt to 18 inch lbs. (2 Nm).
13. Engage the wheel sensor connector.
14. Install the wheel and tire, hand-tighten the lug nuts.
15. Lower the vehicle, then tighten the lug nuts to 100 ft. lbs. (136 Nm).

PONTIAC 6000 STE

1. Unplug the sensor connector from the wiring harness.
2. To remove the wheel, loosen all the lug nuts at least one full turn, before raising the car.
3. Raise and safely support the vehicle.
4. Remove the wheel and tire.
5. Remove the sensor cables from the various clips and retainers.
6. Either remove the large cable grommets from there brackets or, if necessary, unbolt the bracket from the strut.
7. Remove the sensor retaining screw, then remove the sensor.
To install:
8. Coat the sensor body with anti–corrosion compound (GM 1052856 or an equivalent). Apply it where the sensor will contact the knuckle.

9. Install the sensor, then tighten the mounting bolt to 106 inch lbs. (12 Nm).
10. Position and install the cable into the grommets, clips and retainers. The cable must be secure in the retainers and clear of any moving parts. The cable must not be pulled too tight.
11. Connect the sensor to the wiring harness.
12. Install the wheel and tire, hand-tighten the lug nuts.
13. Lower the vehicle, then tighten the lug nuts to 100 ft. lbs. (136 Nm).

Rear Speed Sensor

PONTIAC 6000 AWD

◊ See Figure 55

1. Unplug the speed sensor connector in the front corner of the trunk compartment. If the right rear connector is to be disconnected, the spare wheel and tire must be removed.
2. Release the cable grommet. Carefully work the sensor cable and connector through the hole in the body panel.
3. To remove the wheel, loosen all the lug nuts at least one full turn, before raising the car.
4. Raise and safely support the vehicle.
5. Remove the wheel and tire.
6. Remove the sensor mounting bolt, then remove the sensor from the caliper. Slide the grommets out of the slots in the brackets and cable guide.
7. If the old sensor is to be reused, remove the paper spacer and any debris from the face of the sensor.
To install:
8. Install the sensor and tighten the retaining bolt to 80 inch lbs. (9 Nm). If reusing the old sensor, adjust the air gap.

➡**New wheel sensors are equipped with a paper spacer that will properly gap the sensor when placed against the sensor ring.**

9. Install the grommets into position on the brackets and cable guide.
10. Route the cable to avoid any contact with moving suspension components. Work the connector and cable up through the hole in the underbody, then fit the grommet into position in the hole.

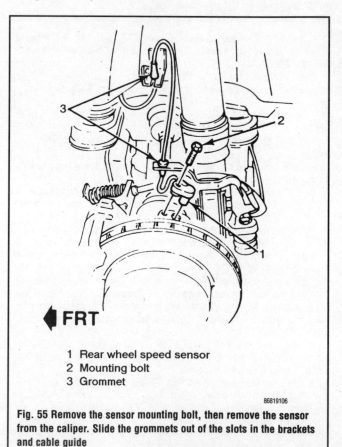

◄ **FRT**

1 Rear wheel speed sensor
2 Mounting bolt
3 Grommet

86819106

Fig. 55 Remove the sensor mounting bolt, then remove the sensor from the caliper. Slide the grommets out of the slots in the brackets and cable guide

11. Install the wheel and tire, hand-tighten the lug nuts. Lower the vehicle and tighten the lug nuts to 100 ft. lbs. (136 Nm).

12. Engage the wheel sensor connector to the wiring harness.

13. Install the spare wheel and tire if removed, then secure the trunk carpet.

Air Gap Adjustment

➡**Only the front and rear sensors on the Pontiac 6000 AWD are adjustable. On the Pontiac 6000 STE, the gap is not adjustable.**

1. To remove the wheel, loosen all the lug nuts at least one full turn, before raising the car.

2. Raise and safely support the vehicle.

3. Remove the wheel and tire.

4. Loosen the sensor adjustment bolt for the front or rear sensor.

5. Inspect the face of the sensor for abnormal wear or damage. If necessary, replace the sensor.

➡**New sensors come with a paper spacer which will properly gap the sensor when placed against the speed sensor ring.**

6. If the sensor is to be reused, clean the face of the sensor of all traces of the paper spacer, dirt, dust, etc.

To install:

7. Reposition the sensor, then adjust the air gap to 0.028 in. (0.7mm) using a non-ferrous feeler gauge.

8. Tighten the adjustment screw to 18 inch lbs. (2 Nm).

9. Install the wheel and tire, hand-tighten the lug nuts.

10. Lower the vehicle, then tighten the lug nuts to 100 ft. lbs. (136 Nm).

Hydraulic Unit

REMOVAL & INSTALLATION

Pontiac 6000 AWD

♦ **See Figure 56**

1. With the key **OFF**, disconnect the negative battery cable.

2. Depressurize the hydraulic accumulator.

3. Remove the wire clip from the return hose fitting and remove the return hose from the pump. Pull the return hose fitting out of the pump housing.

4. Remove the pressure hose bolt from the pump, then remove the hose and O-rings from the pump.

5. Remove the pump mounting bolt and separate the energy unit from the hydraulic unit.

6. Using 2 wrenches, disconnect the brake lines from the valve block and the hydraulic unit.

7. Disconnect the pushrod from the brake pedal.

8. Push the dust boot forward and off the rear half of the pushrod. Unscrew the 2 halves of the pushrod.

9. Remove the 2 hydraulic unit mounting bolts from the pushrod bracket.

10. Remove the hydraulic unit from the pushrod bracket. The front half of the pushrod will remain locked into the hydraulic unit.

To install:

11. Mount the hydraulic unit to the pushrod bracket and install the mounting bolts, then tighten the bolts to 37 ft. lbs. (50 Nm).

12. Thread the 2 parts of the pushrod together and reposition the dust boot.

13. Connect the pushrod to the brake pedal then tighten the nut to 27 ft. lbs. (37 Nm).

14. Using 2 wrenches, connect the brake lines to the hydraulic unit and the valve block. Tighten to 11 ft. lbs. (20 Nm).

15. Connect the energy unit to the pump unit, then install the pump mounting bolt.

16. Install the pressure hose and O-rings to the pump, then install the hose bolt and tighten it to 15 ft. lbs. (20 Nm).

17. Push the return hose fitting into the pump body and connect the return hose to the pump.

18. Install the wire clip to the return hose fitting.

19. Connect the wiring to the hydraulic unit.

20. Connect the negative battery cable.

21. Bleed the brake system.

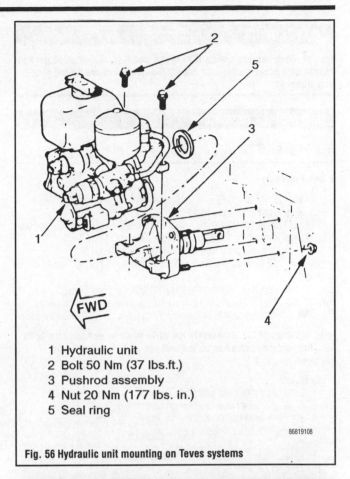

1 Hydraulic unit
2 Bolt 50 Nm (37 lbs.ft.)
3 Pushrod assembly
4 Nut 20 Nm (177 lbs. in.)
5 Seal ring

86819108

Fig. 56 Hydraulic unit mounting on Teves systems

✲✲ CAUTION

Do not move vehicle until a firm brake pedal is achieved. Failure to obtain firm brake pedal may result in personal injury and/or property damage.

Pontiac 6000 STE

1. With ignition switch **OFF**, disconnect the negative battery cable.

2. Depressurize the hydraulic accumulator.

3. Unplug all electrical connections at the hydraulic unit.

4. Remove the cross-car brace if equipped.

5. Remove the pump bolt and then move pump motor assembly to allow access to the brake lines.

6. Using 2 wrenches, disconnect the brake lines from the hydraulic unit and the valve body.

7. Push the dust boot forward, past the hex on the pushrod. Separate the pushrod into 2 sections by unscrewing it.

8. Remove the hydraulic unit mounting bolts at the pushrod bracket. Remove the hydraulic unit from the part of the pushrod may remain with the unit.

To install:

9. Position the hydraulic unit, then install new retaining bolts at the pushrod bracket. Tighten the bolts to 37 ft. lbs. (50 Nm).

10. From inside car, thread pushrod halves together and tighten. Reposition the dust boot and connect the pushrod to the brake pedal.

11. Install the brake lines to the valve block, then tighten to 106 inch lbs. (12 Nm).

12. Position the pump motor assembly on the hydraulic unit. Install the mounting bolt, then tighten to 10 ft. lbs. (13 Nm).

13. Install the cross-car brace if one was removed.

14. Engage the electrical harness to the hydraulic unit.

15. Connect the negative battery cable.

16. Bleed the brake system.

✳✳ CAUTION

Do not move vehicle until a firm brake pedal is achieved. Failure to obtain firm brake pedal may result in personal injury and/or property damage.

Valve Block Assembly

REMOVAL & INSTALLATION

▶ **See Figure 57**

1. With the ignition **OFF** disconnect the negative battery cable.
2. Depressurize the accumulator.
3. For Pontiac 6000 AWD, remove the hydraulic unit. For the Pontiac 6000 STE, drain or remove the brake fluid from the reservoir.
4. Unplug the electrical harness running to the valve block.
5. It may be necessary to disconnect the brake lines from the bottom of the valve block.
6. At the valve block, remove the nuts and the bolt with hex faces only. Remove the valve block assembly and O-rings by sliding the valve block off of the studs. Recover any O-rings or gaskets from the mounting points and/or the fluid line ports.

➡ **Do not attempt to disassemble the valve block by removing the bolts with the recessed drive heads, the unit cannot be overhauled or repaired.**

To install:
7. Lubricate the O-rings with brake fluid.
8. Install the valve block and O-rings onto the master cylinder body.
9. Install the nuts and the bolt, then tighten to 18 ft. lbs. (25 Nm).
10. Connect the brake lines to the bottom of the valve block if they were removed.
11. Reinstall the hydraulic unit if it was removed.
12. Connect the wiring harnesses.
13. Refill the system or reservoir to the correct level.
14. Connect the negative battery cable.
15. Bleed the brake system.

Pressure Warning Switch

REMOVAL & INSTALLATION

▶ **See Figure 58**

1. Disconnect the negative battery cable.
2. Depressurize the accumulator.
3. Unplug the electrical connector from the pressure warning switch.
4. Remove the pressure warning switch using tool J-35604 or an equivalent.
5. Remove the O-ring from the switch.

To install:
6. Lubricate a new O-ring with clean brake fluid.
7. Install the O-ring on the pressure warning switch.
8. Install the switch and tighten to 17 ft. lbs. (23 Nm). using the special tool.
9. Engage the electrical connector to the pressure warning switch.
10. Connect the negative battery cable.
11. Turn the ignition to the **ON** position. The BRAKE light should go out within 60 seconds.
12. Check for leakage around the switch.

Hydraulic Accumulator

REMOVAL & INSTALLATION

1. Disconnect the negative battery cable.
2. Depressurize the accumulator. Make certain the system is completely relieved of all hydraulic pressure.

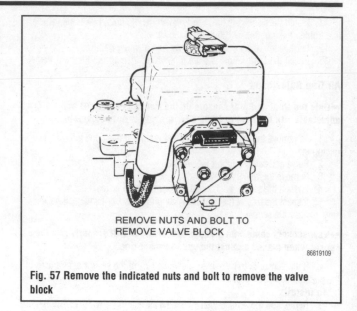

REMOVE NUTS AND BOLT TO
REMOVE VALVE BLOCK

86819109

Fig. 57 Remove the indicated nuts and bolt to remove the valve block

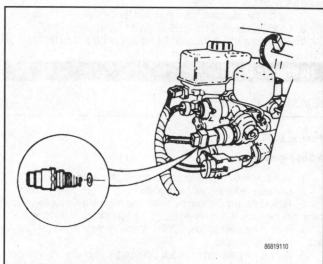

86819110

Fig. 58 Unplug the electrical connector from the pressure warning switch, then remove the switch

3. Unscrew the hydraulic accumulator from the hydraulic unit.
4. Remove the O-ring from the accumulator.

To install:
5. Lubricate a new O-ring with clean brake fluid and install it on the accumulator.
6. Install the accumulator, then tighten to 32 ft. lbs. (43 Nm), except on 6000 AWD tighten to 17 ft. lbs. (23 Nm).
7. Connect the negative battery cable.
8. Turn the ignition switch to the **ON** position. The BRAKE light should go out within 60 seconds.
9. Check for leakage around the accumulator.

Brake Fluid Reservoir and Seal

REMOVAL & INSTALLATION

1. Disconnect the negative battery cable.
2. Depressurize the accumulator.
3. Remove the return hose and drain the brake fluid into a container. Discard the fluid properly.
4. Unplug the 2 wire connectors from the fluid level sensor assembly.
5. Remove the reservoir–to–block mounting bolt.

6. Remove the reservoir from the hydraulic unit by carefully prying between the reservoir and the hydraulic unit.

7. Remove the seals and O-ring from the unit.

To install:

8. Lubricate the new seals and O-ring with clean brake fluid, then install them into the unit.

9. Push the reservoir into the master cylinder until it is fully seated.

10. Connect the reservoir to the valve block with the mounting bolt, then tighten to 45 inch lbs. (5 Nm).

11. Engage the 2 wire connectors to the reservoir cap.

12. Connect the return hose to the reservoir.

13. Refill the reservoir with clean brake fluid.

14. Connect the negative battery cable.

Pump Motor

REMOVAL & INSTALLATION

1. Disconnect the negative battery cable.
2. Depressurize the accumulator.
3. Remove the fluid from the reservoir.

✳✳ WARNING

Do not remove brake fluid from the reservoir using a syringe or other instrument which is contaminated with water, petroleum based fluids or any other foreign material. Contamination of the brake fluid may result.

4. Unplug the electrical connector from the pressure switch and the pump motor.

5. Remove the hydraulic accumulator and O-ring.

6. Disconnect the high pressure hose fitting connected to the pump.

7. Remove the pressure hose assembly and O-rings from the pump.

8. Disconnect the wire clip, then pull the return hose fitting out of the pump body.

9. Remove the pump mounting bolt and grommets attaching the pump motor assembly to the hydraulic unit.

10. Remove the pump motor assembly by sliding it off of the locating pin.

➡ **Replace the insulators if damaged or deteriorated.**

To install:

11. Position the pump motor assembly to the hydraulic unit.

12. Install the bolt attaching the pump motor assembly to the hydraulic unit, tighten to 71 inch lbs. (8 Nm).

13. Connect the return pressure hose to the pump. Push the return hose fitting into the pump body.

14. Install the wire clip to the return hose fitting.

15. Install the O-rings and the pressure hose to the pump, attach the hose bolt to the pump. Tighten the bolt to 15 ft. lbs. (20 Nm).

16. Install the O-ring and the hydraulic accumulator, tighten the accumulator to 17 ft. lbs. (23 Nm).

17. Engage the electrical connector to the pressure switch and the pump motor.

18. Connect the negative battery cable.

19. Refill the fluid reservoir with clean brake fluid.

Filling and Bleeding the System

SYSTEM FILLING

➡ **Do not allow the pump to run more than 60 seconds at a time. If the pump must run longer, allow the pump to cool several minutes between 60 second runs.**

With the ignition **OFF** and the negative battery cable disconnected, discharge the pressure within the accumulator. Remove the cap from the reservoir, then fill the reservoir to the correct level with DOT 3 fluid.

➡ **Use only DOT 3 brake fluid from a clean, sealed container. The use of DOT 5 silicone fluid is not recommended. Internal damage to the pump components may result.**

SYSTEM BLEEDING

Front brake circuits should be bled using pressure bleeding equipment. The pressure bleeder must be of the diaphragm type and must have a rubber diaphragm between the air supply and brake fluid.

✳✳ CAUTION

Do not move vehicle until a firm brake pedal is achieved. Failure to obtain firm brake pedal may result in personal injury and/or property damage

Front Brake Circuit

1. With the ignition switch **OFF**, disconnect the negative battery cable.
2. Depressurize the accumulator.
3. Remove the reservoir cap or disconnect the wiring sensor from the fluid level sensor and remove the sensor.
4. Install the special tool No. J-35798 in place of the cap or sensor.
5. Attach the brake bleeder to the adapter tool No. J-35798 and charge to 20 psi (138 kPa).
6. Attach a bleeder hose to one front bleeder valve and submerge the other end in a container of clean brake fluid.
7. Open the bleeder valve.
8. Allow the fluid to flow from the bleeder until no air bubbles are seen in the brake fluid.
9. Close the bleeder valve.
10. Repeat the previous steps on the other front bleeder valve.
11. Check the fluid level and fill as necessary.
12. Remove the brake bleeding equipment and adapters. Install the cap or sensor.

Rear Brake Circuit

1. Turn the ignition switch **OFF**.
2. Depressurize the accumulator.
3. Check the fluid level in the reservoir and fill as necessary.
4. Turn the ignition switch **ON** and allow the system to charge. (Listen for the pump motor, it will stop when the system is charged.)
5. Raise and safely support the vehicle.
6. Attach a clear bleeder hose to one of the rear bleeder valves and submerge the other end in a container of clean brake fluid.
7. Open the bleeder valve.

➡ **Do not allow the pump to run more than 60 seconds at a time. If it must run longer, allow it to cool down for several minuets between the 60 second runs.**

8. With the ignition **ON**, slightly depress the brake pedal for at least 10 seconds.

9. Allow the fluid to flow from the bleeder until no air bubbles are seen in the brake fluid. Repeat the step as necessary.

10. Close the bleeder valve.

11. Repeat the procedure for the other side.

12. Lower the vehicle.

13. Fill the reservoir with clean fluid and check the pedal for sponginess. Repeat the entire bleeding procedure to correct a sponginess condition. Check the warning lamps for any indication of a low fluid level.

ABS-VI ANTI-LOCK BRAKE SYSTEM (ABS)

Description and Operation

Anti-lock brakes provide the driver with 3 important benefits over standard braking systems: increased vehicle stability, improved vehicle steerability and potentially reduced stopping distances during braking.

The ABS-VI Anti-lock Braking System consists of a conventional braking system with a vacuum power booster, compact master cylinder, front disc brakes, rear drum brakes and interconnecting hydraulic brake lines augmented with the ABS components. The ABS-VI components consist of a hydraulic modulator assembly, Electronic Control Unit (ECU), a system relay, 4 wheel speed sensors, interconnecting wiring and an amber ABS warning light.

The ECU monitors inputs from the individual wheel speed sensors, then determines when a wheel or wheels are about to lock-up. The ECU controls the motors on the hydraulic modulator assembly to reduce brake pressure to the wheel about to lock-up. When the wheel regains traction, the brake pressure is increased until the wheel again approaches lock-up. The cycle repeats until either the vehicle comes to a stop, the brake pedal is released or no wheels are about to lock-up. The ECU also has the ability to monitor itself and can store diagnostic codes in a non-volatile (will not be erased if the battery is disconnected) memory. The ECU is serviced as an assembly.

The ABS-VI braking system employs 2 modes, the base (conventional) braking and the anti-lock braking. Under normal braking, the conventional part of the system stops the vehicle. When in the ABS mode, the system controls the 2 front wheels individually and the rear wheels together. If a rear wheel is about to lock-up, the hydraulic pressure to both wheels is reduced, controlling both wheels together. Since the vast majority of the braking is controlled by the front wheels, there is no adverse effect on vehicle control during hard braking.

PRECAUTIONS

Failure to observe the following precautions may result in system damage.
• Performing diagnostic work on the ABS-VI requires the use of a Tech I Scan diagnostic tool or equivalent. If unavailable, please refer diagnostic work to a qualified technician.
• Before performing electric arc welding on the vehicle, disconnect the Electronic Brake Control Module (EBCM) and the hydraulic modulator connectors.
• When performing painting work on the vehicle, do not expose the Electronic Brake Control Module (EBCM) to temperatures in excess of 185°F (85°C) for longer than 2 hrs. The system may be exposed to temperatures up to 200°F (95°C) for less than 15 min.
• Never disconnect or connect the Electronic Brake Control Module (EBCM) or hydraulic modulator connectors with the ignition switch ON.
• Never disassemble any component of the Anti-Lock Brake System (ABS) which is designated non-serviceable; the component must be replaced as an assembly.
• When filling the master cylinder, always use Delco Supreme 11 brake fluid or equivalent, which meets DOT 3 specifications; petroleum base fluid will destroy the rubber parts.

Onboard Diagnostics

The ABS-VI contains sophisticated onboard diagnostics that, when accessed with a bi-directional Scan tool, are designed to identify the source of any system fault as specifically as possible. There are many of diagnostic fault codes to assist the service technician with diagnosis. The last diagnostic fault code to occur is specifically identified, and specific ABS data is stored at the time of this fault. Additionally, using a bi-directional Scan tool, each input and output can be monitored, thus enabling fault confirmation and repair verification. Manual control of components and automated functional tests are also available when using a Scan tool. Details of many of these functions are contained in the following sections.

ENHANCED DIAGNOSTICS

Enhanced diagnostic information, found in the CODE HISTORY function of the bi-directional Scan tool, is designed to provide the service technician with specific fault occurrence information. For each of the first five (5) and the very last diagnostic fault codes stored, data is stored to identify the specific fault code number, the number of failure occurrences, and the number of drive cycles since the failure first and last occurred (a drive cycle occurs when the ignition is turned **ON** and the vehicle is driven faster than 10 mph). However, if a fault is present, the drive cycle counter will increment by turning the ignition **ON** and **OFF**. These first five (5) diagnostic fault codes are also stored in the order of occurrence. The order in which the first 5 faults occurred can be useful in determining if a previous fault is linked to the most recent faults, such as an intermittent wheel speed sensor which later becomes completely open.

During difficult diagnosis situations, this information can be used to identify fault occurrence trends. Does the fault occur more frequently now than it did during the last time when it only failed 1 out of 35 drive cycles? Did the fault only occur once over a large number of drive cycles, indication an unusual condition present when the fault occurred? Does the fault occur infrequently over a large number of drive cycles, indication special diagnosis techniques may be required to identify the source of the fault?

If a fault occurred 1 out of 20 drive cycles, the fault is intermittent and has not reoccurred for 19 drive cycles. This fault may be difficult or impossible to duplicate and may have been caused by a severe vehicle impact (large pot hole, speed bump at high speed, etc.) that momentarily opened an electrical connector or caused unusual vehicle suspension movement. Problem resolution is unlikely, and the problem may never reoccur. If the fault occurred 3 out of 15 drive cycles, the odds of finding the cause are still not good, but you know how often it occurs and you can determine whether or not the fault is becoming more frequent. If the fault occurred 10 out of 20 drive cycles, the odds of finding the cause are very good, as the fault may be easily reproduced.

By using the additional fault data, you can also determine if a failure is randomly intermittent or if it has not reoccurred for long periods of time due to weather changes or a prior repair. Say a diagnostic fault code occurred 10 of 20 drive cycles but has not reoccurred for 10 drive cycles. This means the failure occurred 10 of 10 drive cycles but has not reoccurred since. A significant environmental change or a repair occurred 10 drive cycles ago. A repair may not be necessary if a recent repair can be confirmed. If no repair was made, the service can focus on diagnosis techniques used to locate difficult to recreate problems.

DIAGNOSTIC PROCESS

When servicing the ABS-VI, the following steps should be followed in order. Failure to follow these steps may result in the loss of important diagnostic data and may lead to difficult and time consuming diagnosis procedures.

1. Using a bi-directional scan tool, read all current and history diagnostic codes. Be certain to note which codes are current diagnostic code failures. DO NOT CLEAR CODES unless directed to do so.

2. Using a bi-directional Scan tool, read the CODE HISTORY data. Note the diagnostic fault codes stored and their frequency of failure. Specifically note the last failure that occurred and the conditions present when this failure occurred. This "last failure" should be the starting point for diagnosis and repair.

3. Perform a vehicle preliminary diagnosis inspection. This should include:
   a. Inspection of the master cylinder for proper brake fluid level.
   b. Inspection of the ABS hydraulic modulator for any leaks or wiring damage.
   c. Inspection of brake components at all four (4) wheels. Verify no drag exists. Also verify proper brake apply operation.
   d. Inspection for worn or damaged wheel bearings that allow a wheel to wobble.
   e. Inspection of the wheel speed sensors and their wiring. Verify correct air gap range, solid sensor attachment, undamaged sensor toothed ring, and undamaged wiring. Especially at vehicle attachment points.
   f. Verify proper outer CV-joint alignment and operation.
   g. Verify tires meet legal tread depth requirements.

4. If no codes are present, or mechanical component failure codes are present, perform the automated modulator test using the Tech 1, T-100 or equivalent scan tool to isolate the cause of the problem. If the failure is intermittent and not reproducible, test drive the vehicle while using the automatic snapshot feature of the bi-directional Scan tool.

Perform normal acceleration, stopping, and turning maneuvers. If this does not reproduce the failure, perform an ABS stop, on a low coefficient surface such as gravel, from approximately 30–50 mph (48–80 kph) while triggering on any ABS code. If the failure is still not reproducible, use the enhanced diagnostic information found in CODE HISTORY to determine whether or not this failure should be further diagnosed.

5.   Once all system failures have been corrected, clear the ABS codes. The Tech 1 and T-100, when plugged into the ALDL connector, becomes part of the vehicle's electronic system. The Tech 1 and T-100 can also perform the following functions on components linked by the Serial Data Link (SDL):

- Display ABS data
- Display and clear ABS trouble codes
- Control ABS components
- Perform extensive ABS diagnosis
- Provide diagnostic testing for Intermittent ABS conditions.

Each test mode has specific diagnosis capabilities which depend upon various keystrokes. In general, five keys control sequencing: YES, NO, EXIT, UP arrow and DOWN arrow. The FO through F9 keys select operating modes, perform functions within an operating mode, or enter trouble code or model year designations.

In general, the Tech 1 has five test modes for diagnosing the anti-lock brake system. The five test modes are as follows:

MODE FO: DATA LIST- In this test mode, the Tech 1 continuously monitors wheel speed data, brake switch status and other inputs and outputs.

MODE F1: CODE HISTORY- In this mode, fault code history data is displayed. This data includes how many ignition cycles since the fault code occurred, along with other ABS information. The first five (5) and last fault codes set are included in the ABS history data.

MODE F2: TROUBLE CODES- In this test mode, trouble codes stored by the EBCM, both current ignition cycle and history, may be displayed or cleared.

MODE F3: ABS SNAPSHOT- In this test mode, the Tech 1 captures ABS data before and after a fault occurrence or a forced manual trigger.

MODE F4: ABS TESTS- In this test mode, the Tech 1 performs hydraulic modulator functional tests to assist in problem isolation during troubleshooting. Included here is manual control of the motors which is used prior to bleeding the brake system.

Press F7 to covert from English to metric.

DISPLAYING CODES

Diagnostic fault codes can only be read through the use of a bi-directional Scan tool. There are no provisions for Flash Code diagnostics.

CLEARING CODES

The trouble codes in EBCM memory are erased in one of two ways:
- Scan tool "Clear Codes" selection.
- Ignition cycle default.

These two methods are detailed below. Be sure to verify proper system operation and absence of codes when clearing procedure is completed. The EBCM will not permit code clearing until all of the codes have been displayed. Also, codes cannot be cleared by unplugging the EBCM, disconnecting the battery cables, or turning the ignition **OFF** (except on an ignition cycle default).

Scan Tool Clear Codes Method

1.   Select F2 for trouble codes.
2.   After codes have been viewed completely, the scan tool will display "CLEAR ABS CODES". Answer yes.
3.   The scan tool will then read "DISPLAY CODE HIST. DATA? LOST IF CODES CLEARED. NO TO CLEAR CODES". Answer no and codes will be cleared.

Ignition Cycle Default

If no diagnostic fault code occurs for 100 drive cycles (a drive cycle occurs when the ignition is turned **ON** and the vehicle is driven faster than 10 mph), any existing fault codes are cleared from the EBCM memory.

INTERMITTENT FAILURES

As with most electronic systems, intermittent failures may be difficult to accurately diagnose. The following is a method to try to isolate an intermittent failure especially wheel speed circuitry failures.

If an ABS fault occurs, the ABS warning light indicator will be ON during the ignition cycle in which the fault was detected. If it is an intermittent problem which seems to have corrected itself (ABS warning light OFF), a history trouble code will be stored. Also stored will be the history data of the code at the time the fault occurred. The Tech 1 must be used to read ABS history data.

Most intermittence are caused by faulty electrical connections or wiring, although occasionally a sticking relay or solenoid can be a problem. Some items to check are:

1.   Poor mating of connector halves, or terminals not fully seated in the connector body (backed out).
2.   Dirt or corrosion on the terminals. The terminals must be clean and free of any foreign material which could impede proper terminal contact.
3.   Damaged connector body, exposing the terminals to moisture and dirt, as well as not maintaining proper terminal orientation with the component or mating connector.
4.   Improperly formed or damaged terminals. All connector terminals in problem circuits should be checked carefully to ensure good contact tension. Use a corresponding mating terminal to check for proper tension.
5.   The J 35616-A Connector Test Adapter Kit must be used whenever a diagnostic procedure requests checking or probing a terminal. Using the adapter will ensure that no damage to the terminal will occur, as well as giving an idea of whether contact tension is sufficient.
6.   Poor terminal-to-wire connection. Checking this requires removing the terminal from the connector body. Some conditions which fall under this description are poor crimps, poor solder joints, crimping over wire insulation rather than the wire itself, corrosion in the wire-to-terminal contact area, etc.
7.   Wire insulation which is rubbed through, causing an intermittent short as the bare area touches other wiring or parts of the vehicle.
8.   Wiring broken inside the insulation. This condition could cause a continuity check to show a good circuit, but if only 1 or 2 strands of a multi-strand-type wire are intact, resistance could be far too high.

Checking Terminal Contact

When diagnosing an electrical system that uses Metri-Pack 150/280/480/630 series terminals (refer to Terminal Repair Kit J 38125-A and instruction manual J 38125-4 for terminal identification), it is important to check terminal contact between a connector and component, or between in-line connectors, before replacing a suspect component.

Frequently, a diagnostic chart leads to a step that reads Check for poor connection. Mating terminals must be inspected to ensure good terminal contact. A poor connection between the male and female terminal at a connector may be the result of contamination or deformation.

Contamination is caused by the connector halves being improperly connected, a missing or damaged connector seal, or damage to the connector itself, exposing the terminals to moisture and dirt. Contamination, usually in underhood or underbody connectors, leads to terminal corrosion, causing an open circuit or an intermittently open circuit.

Deformation is caused by probing the mating side of a connector terminal without the proper adapter, improperly joining the connector halves or repeatedly separating and joining the connector halves. Deformation, usually to the female terminal contact tang, can result in poor terminal contact causing an open or intermittently open circuit.

Follow the procedure below to check terminal contact.

1.   Separate the connector halves. Refer to Terminal Repair Kit J 38125-A instruction manual J 38125-4, if available.
2.   Inspect the connector halves for contamination. Contamination will result in a white or green buildup within the connector body or between terminals, causing high terminal resistance, intermittent contact or an open circuit. An underhood or underbody connector that shows signs of contamination should be replaced in its entirety, terminals, seals, and connector body.
3.   Using an equivalent male terminal from the Terminal Repair Kit J 38125-A, check the retention force of the female terminal in question by inserting and removing the male terminal to the female terminal in the connector body. Good terminal contact will require a certain amount of force to separate the terminals.
4.   Using an equivalent female terminal from the Terminal Repair Kit J 38125-A, compare the retention force of this terminal to the female terminal in question by joining and separating the male terminal to the female terminal in question. If the retention force is significantly different between the two female terminals, replace the female terminal in question, using a terminal from Terminal Repair Kit J 38125-A.

ABS Hydraulic Modulator Assembly

REMOVAL & INSTALLATION

To avoid personal injury, use the Tech I scan tool or equivalent to relieve the gear tension in the hydraulic modulator. This procedure must be performed prior to removal of the brake control and motor assembly.

1. Disconnect the negative battery cable.
2. Unplug the 2 solenoid electrical connectors and the fluid level sensor connectors.
3. Unplug the 6-pin and 3-pin motor pack electrical connectors.
4. Wrap a shop towel around the hydraulic brake lines and disconnect the 4 brake lines from the modulator.

➡**Cap the disconnected lines to prevent the loss of fluid and the entry of moisture and contaminants.**

5. Remove the 2 nuts attaching the ABS hydraulic modulator assembly to the vacuum booster.
6. Remove the ABS hydraulic modulator assembly from the vehicle.

To install:

7. Install the ABS hydraulic modulator assembly to the vehicle. Install the 2 attaching nuts and tighten to 20 ft. lbs. (27 Nm).
8. Connect the 4 brake pipes to the modulator assembly. Tighten to 13 ft. lbs. (17 Nm).
9. Engage the 6-pin and 3-pin electrical connectors and the fluid level sensor connector.
10. Properly bleed the system.
11. Connect the negative battery cable.

Control Unit

REMOVAL & INSTALLATION

1. Disconnect the negative battery cable.
2. Unplug the Electronic Control Unit (ECU) electrical connectors.
3. Remove the hex head screws attaching the ECU to the dash panel.
4. Remove the ECU from the dash panel.

To install:

5. Ensure all plastic grommets are properly located.
6. Install the ECU to the dash panel, aligning screw holes.
7. Install the hex head screws attaching the ECU.
8. Engage the ECU electrical connectors.
9. Connect the negative battery cable.

Speed Sensors

REMOVAL & INSTALLATION

Front Wheels

▶ **See Figure 59**

1. Disconnect the negative battery cable.
2. To remove the wheel, loosen all the lug nuts at least one full turn, before raising the car.
3. Raise and safely support the vehicle, then remove the wheel and tire.
4. Unplug the front speed sensor electrical connector.
5. Remove the hub and bearing assembly, then disconnect the speed sensor from the hub and bearing using a blunt flat bladed tool.

➡**When the speed sensor is removed it must be replaced, the sensor is damaged when being removed and cannot be reused. There are two parts to the speed sensor and they are only replaced as an assembly.**

To install:

6. Inspect the bearing for signs of water intrusion. If water has entered the bearing , the bearing must be replaced.
7. Apply Loctite® 620 to the mating surfaces of the wheel speed sensor where it contacts the hub and bearing assembly.

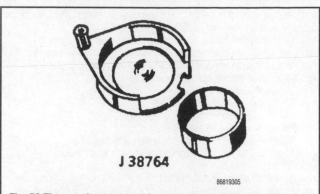

J 38764

86819305

Fig. 59 The speed sensor must be pressed onto the hub and bearing assembly. Tool J-38764 or its equivalent can be used to do this

8. Press the speed sensor onto the hub and bearing assembly with tool J-38764 or equivalent.
9. Install the hub and bearing assembly to the vehicle, then connect the speed sensor.
10. Install the wheel and tire. Hand-tighten the lug nuts.
11. Lower the vehicle, then tighten the lug nuts to 100 ft. lbs. (136 Nm).
12. Connect the negative battery cable.

Rear Wheels

➡**The rear integral wheel bearing and sensor assembly must be replaced as a unit.**

1. Disconnect the negative battery cable.
2. To remove the wheel, loosen all the lug nuts at least one full turn, before raising the car.
3. Raise and safely support the vehicle.
4. Remove the rear wheels, then remove the brake drums.
5. Remove the bolts and nuts attaching the rear wheel bearing and speed sensor. Rotate the axle flange to align the large hole with each of the bolt locations. Remove the bolt while holding the nut.

➡**With the rear wheel bearing and speed sensor attaching bolts and nuts removed, the drum brake assembly is supported only by the brake line connection. To avoid bending or damage to the brake line, Install two of the wheel bearing assembly bolts to secure the brake.**

6. Remove the rear wheel bearing and speed sensor assembly.
7. Unplug the rear sensor electrical connection.

To install:

8. Engage the rear speed sensor electrical connector.
9. Secure the bolts and nuts, attaching the rear wheel bearing, speed sensor and drum assembly to the suspension bracket. Rotate the axle flange to align the large hole with each bolt location. Install the bolt while holding the nut. Tighten the bolts to 46 ft. lbs. (63 Nm).
10. Install the brake drums.
11. Install the rear wheels. Hand-tighten the lug nuts.
12. Lower the vehicle, then tighten the lug nuts to 100 ft. lbs. (136 Nm).
13. Connect the negative battery cable.

Brake Control Solenoid Assembly

REMOVAL & INSTALLATION

1. Disconnect the negative battery cable.
2. Unplug the solenoid electrical connector.
3. Remove the Torx® head bolt.
4. Remove the solenoid assembly.

To install:

5. Lubricate the O-rings on the new solenoid with clean brake fluid.
6. Position the solenoid so the connectors face each other.
7. Press down firmly by hand until the solenoid assembly flange seats on the modulator assembly.

8. Install the Torx® head bolts. Tighten to 39 inch lbs. (5 Nm).
9. Engage the solenoid electrical connector.
10. Properly bleed the brake system.
11. Connect the negative battery cable.

Filling and Bleeding

BRAKE CONTROL ASSEMBLY

→Only use brake fluid from a sealed container which meets DOT 3 specifications.

1. Clean the area around the master cylinder cap.
2. Check fluid level in master cylinder reservoir and top-up, as necessary. Check fluid level frequently during bleeding procedure.
3. Attach a bleeder hose to the rear bleeder valve on the brake control assembly. Slowly open the bleeder valve.
4. Depress the brake pedal slowly until fluid begins to flow.
5. Close the valve and release the brake pedal.
6. Repeat for the front bleeder valve on the brake control assembly.

→When fluid flows from both bleeder valves, the brake control assembly is sufficiently full of fluid. However, it may not be completely purged of air. Bleed the individual wheel calipers/cylinders and return to the control assembly to purge the remaining air.

WHEEL CALIPERS/CYLINDERS

▶ See Figure 60

1. Prior to bleeding the rear brakes, the rear displacement cylinder must be returned to the top-most position. This can be accomplished using the Tech I scan tool or equivalent, by entering the manual control function and applying the rear motor. If a scan tool is unavailable, bleed the front brakes. Ensure the pedal is firm. Carefully drive the vehicle to a speed above 4 mph to cause the ABS system to initialize. This will return the rear displacement cylinder to the top-most position.
2. Clean the area around the master cylinder cap.
3. Check fluid level in master cylinder reservoir and top-up, as necessary. Check fluid level frequently during bleeding procedure.

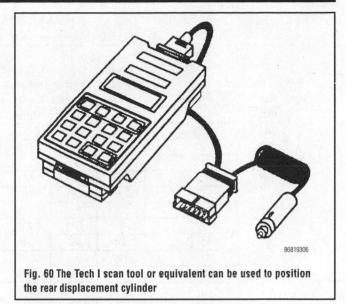

Fig. 60 The Tech I scan tool or equivalent can be used to position the rear displacement cylinder

4. Raise and safely support the vehicle.
5. Attach a bleeder hose to the bleeder valve of the right rear wheel and submerge the opposite hose in a clean container partially filled with brake fluid.
6. Open the bleeder valve.
7. Slowly depress the brake pedal.
8. Close the bleeder valve and release the brake pedal.
9. Wait 5 seconds.
10. Repeat until the pedal begins to feel firm and no air bubbles appear in the bleeder hose.
11. Bleed the remaining wheels in the following order:
- left rear
- right front
- left front
12. Lower the vehicle.

BRAKE SPECIFICATIONS
All measurements in inches unless noted

Year	Model		Master Cylinder Bore	Brake Disc Original Thickness	Brake Disc Minimum Thickness	Brake Disc Maximum Runout	Brake Drum Diameter Original Inside Diameter	Brake Drum Diameter Max. Wear Limit	Brake Drum Diameter Maximum Machine Diameter	Minimum Lining Thickness Front	Minimum Lining Thickness Rear
1982	All		0.874	NA	0.815	0.004	7.879	7.899	7.899	0.030	3
1983	All		0.874	NA	0.815	0.004	7.879	7.899	7.899	0.030	3
1984	All	1	0.874	NA	0.815	0.004	8.863	8.883	8.883	0.030	3
		2	0.944	NA	0.957	0.004	8.863	8.883	8.883	0.030	3
1985	Celebrity	1	0.875	0.885	0.815	0.004	7.879	7.929	7.899	0.030	3
		2	0.938	1.043	0.957	0.004	8.860	8.950	8.920	0.030	3
	Century	1	0.875	0.885	0.815	0.004	7.879	7.929	7.899	0.030	3
		2	0.938	1.043	0.957	0.004	8.860	8.950	8.920	0.030	3
	Cutlass Ciera	1	0.875	0.885	0.815	0.004	7.879	7.929	7.899	0.030	3
		2	0.938	1.043	0.957	0.004	8.860	8.950	8.920	0.030	3
1986	Celebrity	1	0.937	0.885	0.830	0.004	8.860	8.950	8.920	0.030	3
		2	0.937	1.043	0.972	0.004	8.860	8.950	8.920	0.030	3
	Century	1	0.875	0.885	0.815	0.004	8.860	8.909	8.880	0.030	3
		2	0.938	1.043	0.957	0.004	8.860	8.909	8.880	0.030	3
	Cutlass Ciera	1	0.875	0.885	0.815	0.004	8.860	8.909	8.880	0.030	3
		2	0.938	1.043	0.957	0.004	8.860	8.909	8.880	0.030	3
1987	Celebrity	1	0.937	0.885	0.830	0.004	8.860	8.950	8.920	0.030	3
		2	0.937	1.043	0.972	0.004	8.860	8.950	8.920	0.030	3
	Century	1	0.875	0.885	0.815	0.004	8.860	8.909	8.880	0.030	3
		2	0.937	1.043	0.957	0.004	8.860	8.909	8.880	0.030	3
	Cutlass Ciera	1	0.875	0.885	0.815	0.004	8.860	8.909	8.880	0.030	3
		2	0.938	1.043	0.957	0.004	8.860	8.909	8.880	0.030	3
1988	Celebrity	1	0.937	0.885	0.830	0.004	8.860	8.950	8.920	0.030	3
		2	0.937	1.043	0.972	0.004	8.860	8.950	8.920	0.030	3
	Century	1	0.874	0.885	0.815	0.004	8.866	8.946	8.920	0.030	3
		2	0.944	1.043	0.957	0.004	8.863	8.946	8.920	0.030	3
	Century wagon		0.944	1.043	0.957	0.004	8.863	8.909	8.877	0.030	3
	Cutlass Ciera	1	0.874	0.885	0.815	0.004	8.863	8.946	8.920	0.030	3
		2	0.944	1.043	0.957	0.004	8.863	8.946	8.920	0.030	3
	Cutlass Cruiser		0.944	1.043	0.957	0.004	8.863	8.909	8.877	0.030	3
1989	Celebrity	1	0.937	0.885	0.830	0.004	8.860	8.950	8.920	0.030	3
		2	0.937	1.043	0.972	0.004	8.860	8.950	8.920	0.030	3
	Century	1	0.874	0.885	0.815	0.004	8.866	8.946	8.920	0.030	3
		2	0.944	1.043	0.957	0.004	8.863	8.946	8.920	0.030	3
	Century wagon		0.944	1.043	0.957	0.004	8.863	8.909	8.877	0.030	3
	Cutlass Ciera	1	0.874	0.885	0.815	0.004	8.863	8.946	8.920	0.030	3
		2	0.944	1.043	0.957	0.004	8.863	8.946	8.920	0.030	3
	Cutlass Cruiser		0.944	1.043	0.957	0.004	8.863	8.909	8.877	0.030	3
	Cutlass Supreme	1	0.945	1.043	0.972	0.004	-	-	-	0.030	0.030
		2	0.945	0.492	0.429	0.004	-	-	-	0.030	0.030
1990	Celebrity	1	0.874	0.885	0.830	0.004	8.863	8.950	8.920	0.030	0.030
		2	0.944	1.043	0.972	0.004	8.863	8.950	8.920	0.030	0.030
	Century	1	0.874	0.885	0.815	0.004	8.866	8.946	8.920	0.030	3
		2	0.944	1.043	0.957	0.004	8.863	8.946	8.920	0.030	3
	Century wagon		0.944	1.043	0.957	0.004	8.863	8.909	8.877	0.030	3
	Cutlass Ciera	1	0.874	0.885	0.815	0.004	8.863	8.946	8.920	0.030	3
		2	0.944	1.043	0.957	0.004	8.863	8.946	8.920	0.030	3
	Cutlass Cruiser		0.944	1.043	0.957	0.004	8.863	8.909	8.877	0.030	3
	Cutlass Supreme		0.945	1.043	0.972	0.004	-	-	-	0.030	0.030
			0.945	0.492	0.429	0.004	-	-	-	0.030	0.030

91089C01

BRAKE SPECIFICATIONS
All measurements in inches unless noted

Year	Model	Master Cylinder Bore	Brake Disc			Brake Drum Diameter			Minimum Lining Thickness	
			Original Thickness	Minimum Thickness	Maximum Runout	Original Inside Diameter	Max. Wear Limit	Maximum Machine Diameter	Front	Rear
1991	Century [1]	0.874	0.885	0.815	0.004	8.866	8.946	8.920	0.030	[3]
	[2]	0.944	1.043	0.957	0.004	8.863	8.946	8.920	0.030	[3]
	Century wagon	0.944	1.043	0.957	0.004	8.863	8.909	8.877	0.030	[3]
	Cutlass Ciera [1]	0.874	0.885	0.815	0.004	8.863	8.946	8.920	0.030	[3]
	[2]	0.944	1.043	0.957	0.004	8.863	8.946	8.920	0.030	[3]
	Cutlass Cruiser	0.944	1.043	0.957	0.004	8.863	8.909	8.877	0.030	[3]
	Cutlass Supreme	0.945	1.043	0.972	0.004	-	-	-	0.030	0.030
		0.945	0.492	0.429	0.004	-	-	-	0.030	0.030
1992	Century [1]	0.874	0.885	0.815	0.004	8.866	8.946	8.920	0.030	[3]
	[2]	0.944	1.043	0.957	0.004	8.863	8.946	8.920	0.030	[3]
	Century wagon	0.944	1.043	0.957	0.004	8.863	8.909	8.877	0.030	[3]
	Cutlass Ciera [1]	0.874	0.885	0.815	0.004	8.863	8.909	8.880	0.030	[3]
	[2]	0.944	1.043	0.957	0.004	8.863	8.909	8.880	0.030	[3]
	Cutlass Cruiser	0.944	1.043	0.957	0.004	8.863	8.950	8.877	0.030	[3]
	Cutlass Supreme	0.945	1.040	0.972	0.004	-	-	-	0.030	0.030
		0.945	0.492	0.429	0.004	-	-	-	0.030	0.030
1993	Century [1]	0.874	0.885	0.815	0.004	8.866	8.946	8.920	0.030	[3]
	[2]	0.944	1.043	0.957	0.004	8.863	8.946	8.920	0.030	[3]
	Century wagon	0.944	1.043	0.957	0.004	8.863	8.909	8.877	0.030	[3]
	Cutlass Ciera [1]	0.874	0.885	0.815	0.004	8.863	8.909	8.880	0.030	[3]
	[2]	0.944	1.043	0.957	0.004	8.863	8.909	8.880	0.030	[3]
	Cutlass Cruiser	0.944	1.043	0.957	0.004	8.863	[3]	8.877	0.030	[3]
	Cutlass Supreme	0.945	1.040	0.972	0.004	-	-	-	0.030	0.030
		0.945	0.492	0.492	0.004	-	-	-	0.030	0.030
1994	Century	0.944	1.028	0.957	0.002	8.863	8.946	8.920	0.030	[3]
	Cutlass Ciera	0.944	1.028	0.957	0.002	8.860	8.909	8.880	0.030	[3]
	Cutlass Cruiser	0.944	1.028	0.957	0.002	8.860	8.909	8.880	0.030	[3]
	Cutlass Supreme	0.945	1.039	0.972	0.003	-	-	-	0.030	0.030
		0.945	0.492	0.429	0.003	-	-	-	0.030	0.030
1995	Century	0.944	1.028	0.957	0.002	8.863	8.946	8.920	0.030	[3]
	Cutlass Ciera	0.944	1.028	0.957	0.002	8.863	8.909	8.920	0.030	[3]
	Cutlass Cruiser	0.944	1.028	0.957	0.002	8.863	8.909	8.920	0.030	[3]
	Cutlass Supreme	1.000	1.039	0.972	0.003	-	-	-	0.030	0.030
		1.000	0.492	0.429	0.003	-	-	-	0.030	0.030
1996	Century	0.944	1.028	0.957	0.002	8.863	8.946	8.920	0.030	[3]
	Cutlass Ciera	0.944	1.028	0.957	0.002	8.863	8.909	8.920	0.030	[3]
	Cutlass Cruiser	0.944	1.028	0.957	0.002	8.863	8.909	8.920	0.030	[3]
	Cutlass Supreme	1.000	1.039	0.972	0.003	-	-	-	0.030	0.030
		1.000	0.492	0.429	0.003	-	-	-	0.030	0.030

1 Std.
2 Heavy duty
3 0.030 over rivet head: If bonded lining, use 0.062 from shoe
F - Front
R - Rear

91089C02

TORQUE SPECIFICATIONS

Component	US	Metric
Brake line brackets:	8 ft. lbs.	11 Nm
Caliper retaining bolts:	38 ft. lbs.	51 Nm
Front crossmember-to-body bolts:	103 ft. lbs.	140 Nm
Halfshaft end nuts:	184-192 ft. lbs.	250-260 Nm
Knuckle camber cam bolt:	140 ft. lbs.	190 Nm
Knuckle attaching bolts:	38 ft. lbs.	52 Nm
Lower ball joint pinch bolt:		
1982-84	40 ft. lbs.	50 Nm
1985-93	33 ft. lbs.	45 Nm
1994-96	38 ft. lbs.	52 Nm
Lower control arm bolts:	61 ft. lbs.	83 Nm
MacPherson strut shaft nut:	65 ft. lbs.	85 Nm
MacPherson strut-to-fender:	18 ft. lbs.	24 Nm
MacPherson strut-to-knuckle:	122-140 ft. lbs.	165-190 Nm
Rear shock-to-lower mount:		
1982-84	43 ft. lbs.	58 Nm
1985-86	35 ft. lbs.	47 Nm
1987-92	44 ft. lbs.	59 Nm
1993-96	53 ft. lbs.	72 Nm
Rear shock-to-upper mount:	16 ft. lbs.	22 Nm
Rear axle top bolt 6000 AWD:	148 ft. lbs.	200 Nm
Rear control arm-to-bracket:	84 ft. lbs.	115 Nm
Rear control bracket-to-underbody:	28 ft. lbs.	38 Nm
Rear hub and bearing assembly:	44 ft. lbs.	60 Nm
Rear jack pad mounting bolts:	18 ft. lbs.	25 Nm
Rear track bar at brace or underebody:	35 ft. lbs.	47 Nm
Rear coil spring track bolt:		
1982-92	44 ft. lbs.	60 Nm
1993-96	53 ft. lbs.	72 Nm
Rear leaf spring-to-cradle bolts:	61 ft. lbs.	83 Nm
Rear strut lower mount bolts:	148 ft. lbs.	200 Nm
Spring retention plate bolts:	15 ft. lbs.	20 Nm
Stabilizer insulator clamps-to-control arms:	32 ft. lbs.	43 Nm
Steering column mounting bolts:	18 ft. lbs.	25 Nm
Steering rack mounting bolts:	59 ft. lbs.	80 Nm
Steering wheel retaining nut:	30 ft. lbs.	41 Nm
Tie rod adjustment jam nut:	45 ft. lbs.	60 Nm
Tie rod nut:	43 ft. lbs.	58 Nm
Toe link sleeve tab bolt:	14 ft. lbs.	19 Nm
Toe link inner nut:	61 ft. lbs.	83 Nm
Wheel lug nuts:	100 ft. lbs.	140 Nm

91089C03

10

BODY AND TRIM

EXTERIOR

Doors

STRIKER ADJUSTMENT

▶ **See Figure 1**

1. Make sure the door is aligned properly. Apply modeling clay or body caulking compound to the lock bolt opening.
2. Close the door only enough so the striker bolt can form an impression into the clay/compound.
3. The impression should be centered fore and aft. The minimum allowance measurement for dimension is ³⁄₃₂ in. (2mm), the maximum allowance is ⁵⁄₃₂ in. (4mm). A spacer can be used to achieve the correct allowance, ³⁄₃₂ in. (2mm) or equivalent.
4. When adjustment is necessary, insert tool No. J-29843-9 or equivalent, into the star-shaped recess in the head of the striker retaining bolt and loosen. Repeat for the other striker bolts.
5. Shift the striker as required, then tighten the bolts to 34–46 ft. lbs. (46–62 Nm) for models through 1991, or 39 ft. lbs. (53 Nm) for 1992–96 models.

Hood

REMOVAL & INSTALLATION

▶ **See Figures 2 and 3**

1. Raise the hood. Install protective coverings over the fenders, to prevent damage to the paint and moldings.

2. Disconnect the underhood lamp wire.
3. Matchmark the position of the hinge on the hood to aid in alignment when hood is reinstalled.
4. With the hood supported, remove the hinge-to-hood screws on each side of the hood.
5. Remove the hood.
To install:
6. Align the hood with the marks made during removal.
7. Install the hood-to-hinge screws on each side of the hood, then tighten to 20 ft. lbs. (27 Nm).
8. Connect the underhood lamp wire.
9. Close the hood, then inspect for proper alignment. If not aligned properly, open the hood and repeat the previous tightening sequence.

ALIGNMENT

▶ **See Figure 4**

Fore-and-aft adjustment can be made at the hinge-to-hood attaching screws. Vertical adjustment at the front can be made by adjusting the rubber bumpers up or down.

Trunk Lid

REMOVAL & INSTALLATION

▶ **See Figure 5**

1. Prop the lid open, then place a protective covering along the edges of the rear compartment opening, this will prevent damage to the painted areas.

86810105

Fig. 1 In order to loosen the striker, insert a specialized driver into the star-shaped recesses of the three striker bolts

86810106

Fig. 2 Matchmark the position of the hinge on the hood to aid in alignment when the hood is reinstalled

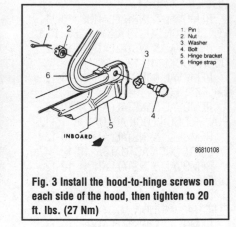

1. Pin
2. Nut
3. Washer
4. Bolt
5. Hinge bracket
6. Hinge strap

INBOARD

86810108

Fig. 3 Install the hood-to-hinge screws on each side of the hood, then tighten to 20 ft. lbs. (27 Nm)

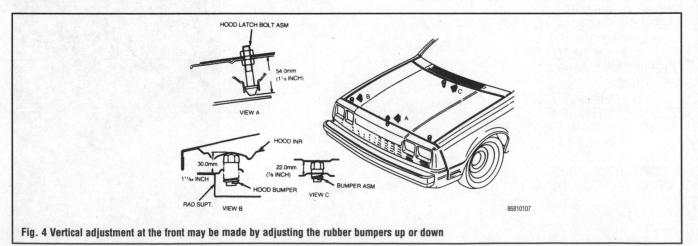

HOOD LATCH BOLT ASM

54.0mm (1¹⁄₈ INCH)

VIEW A

HOOD INR

30.0mm
1¹¹⁄₆₄ INCH

22.0mm (⁷⁄₈ INCH)

BUMPER ASM

HOOD BUMPER

RAD SUPT.   VIEW B

VIEW C

86810107

Fig. 4 Vertical adjustment at the front may be made by adjusting the rubber bumpers up or down

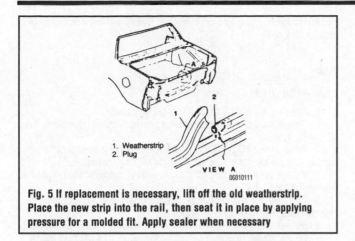

1. Weatherstrip
2. Plug

VIEW A

86810111

Fig. 5 If replacement is necessary, lift off the old weatherstrip. Place the new strip into the rail, then seat it in place by applying pressure for a molded fit. Apply sealer when necessary

2. Where necessary, disconnect the wiring harness from the lid.
3. Matchmark the location of the hinge strap attaching bolts to lid.
4. While a helper supports the lid, remove the hinge to lid bolts and remove the lid.

To install:

5. Before installing the trunk lid, inspect the weatherstrip for any deterioration, replace if necessary.
6. With an assistant, replace the lid into position. Install the bolts for mounting.
7. Tighten the hinge-to-lid attaching bolts 18–20 ft. lbs. (25–27 Nm).
8. Replace the wire harness, remove the prop, close the lid.
9. Inspect the lid for proper alignment. If not, open the lid, then loosen the bolts and tighten, repeat until the lid is aligned.

ADJUSTMENT

Fore and aft adjustment of the lid assembly is controlled by the hinge-to-lid attaching bolts. To adjust the lid, loosen the hinge-to-lid attaching bolts and shift the lid to the desired position; then tighten the bolts to 20 ft. lbs. (27 Nm).

Liftgate/Hatch

REMOVAL & INSTALLATION

♦ See Figures 6 and 7

❄❄ CAUTION

Do not attempt to remove or loosen the gas supports with the liftgate in any position other than fully open. This could cause personal injury.

1. Open and support the liftgate in the full open position.
2. Remove the lid and body side retaining clips from the ends of the gas support assemblies.
3. Disengage the attachment at each end of the gas supports, then remove them from the body.
4. On styles with heated glass or rear wiper-washer system, disconnect the wiring harness and hose from the washer assembly. Remove the washer nozzle if needed.
5. Remove the clip tabs and the drive pin which go through the hinge. Using a $5/32$ in. (4mm) diameter rod, place the end of the rod against the pointed end of the hinge pin, then strike rod firmly to shear retaining clip tabs and drive pin through hinge. Repeat this operation on the opposite side hinge, then with the aid of a helper, remove the liftgate from the body.

To install:

6. Before installing the liftgate/hatch, inspect the weatherstrip for any deterioration, replace if necessary.
7. Prior to installing hinge pins, install new retaining clips in notches provided in hinge pins. Position retaining clips so that tabs point toward head of pin.

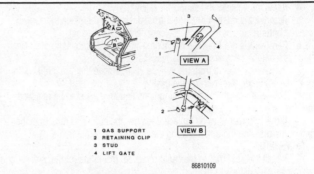

3
2
1
VIEW A

VIEW B

1 GAS SUPPORT
2 RETAINING CLIP
3 STUD
4 LIFT GATE

86810109

Fig. 6 Gas supports must be removed before removing the liftgate. Have a helper hold the liftgate in the up position while you remove the gas supports

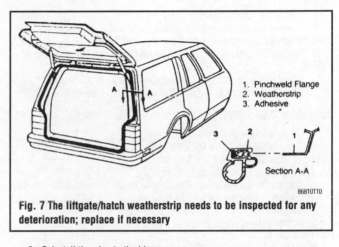

1. Pinchweld Flange
2. Weatherstrip
3. Adhesive

Section A-A

86810110

Fig. 7 The liftgate/hatch weatherstrip needs to be inspected for any deterioration; replace if necessary

8. Reinstall the pins to the hinge.
9. Install the wire harness, hose, and nozzle for models with heated glass and rear wiper assemblies.
10. Replace the gas shock assemblies, insert the retaining clips. Install the connectors to the gas support (pivot glass only).
11. Close the liftgate or pivot glass.

Bumpers

REMOVAL & INSTALLATION

Front

1982–91 MODELS

1. Remove the usually 4 retaining screws in each of the head light bezels and remove the bezels.
2. Raise the car and support it securely.
3. Remove the usually 6 push-on retainers from the bottom of the bumper and remove the 6 screws holding the retainer to each fender.
4. Remove the usually 4 push-on retainers from the outer molding and partially remove the outer molding from the fenders.
5. Remove the usually 2 sheet metal screws from the center bumper retainer, then remove the front bumper.
6. Remove the usually 8 retaining screws and bolts from the impact bar and remove the impact bar from its reinforcements.
7. To install, reverse the procedure above.

1992–93 MODELS

1. Disconnect the negative battery cable.
2. Remove the front headlights and side marker lamps.
3. Remove the grille. Partially disengage each end of the rubber strip on the bumper fascia.

4. Raise the vehicle and support it safely.

5. Remove the push-on retainers from the front fascia, then the screws from the bottom side of the fascia-to-fender and valance panel.

6. Remove the nut from the fascia stud-to-fender. Remove the push-on retainers from the retainers fascia-to-fender.

7. Remove the fascia from the vehicle, then remove the nuts holding the bar to the absorber, then remove the bar.

8. The reinforcements and parking lamp housings need to be removed from the bar.

9. If the absorber is to be replaced, remove the bolts and nuts from the front of the unit and the bolt attaching the rear bracket to the frame.

To install:

10. Install the absorber to the car, if removed. Install the reinforcements and parking lamp housings to the bar.

11. Connect the impact bar and the nuts holding the bar to the absorber.

12. Tighten the bar nuts to 20 ft. lbs. (27 Nm).

13. Install the front fascia to the car aligning the fascia studs-to-fender.

14. Secure the retainers for the fascia-to-fender. Push on the retainers to the retainer.

15. Secure the nuts to the fascia studs.

16. Connect the push-on retainers to the fascia. Install the rubber strip, then insert the screws to the bottom side of the fascia and fender.

17. Tighten the fascia nuts to 53 inch lbs. (6 Nm), and fascia screws to 18 inch lbs. (2 Nm).

18. Lower the car, then connect the negative battery cable.

19. Reset the clock, radio and any other accessories if required.

1994–96 SEDAN—BUICK

1. Raise and support the vehicle.

2. Remove the nuts to the fascia-to-fender.

3. Unfasten the absorber-to-impact bar nuts.

4. Remove the impact bar as an assembly.

5. Remove the bumper guards, then unfasten the fascia-to-impact bar screws.

6. Loosen and remove the air inlet seals.

7. Unfasten the license plate bracket, if equipped.

8. Unlock the push-on retainers on the top and bottom that secure the fascia-to-bumper.

9. Remove the fascia from the impact bar.

To install:

10. Install the rubber strip if removed, then position the fascia on the impact bar.

11. Install the push-on retainers attaching the fascia-to-impact bar.

12. Install the air inlet seals.

13. Reinstall the license plate bracket, if removed.

14. Install the fascia-to-impact bar screws.

15. Reinstall the bumper guards.

16. Lower the vehicle.

1994–96 SEDAN—OLDSMOBILE

1. Raise the vehicle and support it safely.

2. Remove the push-on retainers from the front fascia, then the screws from the bottom side of the fascia-to-fender and valance panel.

3. Remove the nut from the fascia stud-to-fender. Remove the push-on retainers from the retainers fascia-to-fender.

4. Remove the fascia from the vehicle, then remove the nuts holding the bar to the absorber, then remove the bar.

5. The reinforcements and parking lamp housings need to be removed from the bar.

6. If the absorber is to be replaced, remove the bolts and nuts from the front of the unit and the bolt attaching the rear bracket to the frame.

To install:

7. Install the absorber to the car, if removed. Install the reinforcements and parking lamp housings to the bar.

8. Connect the impact bar and the nuts holding the bar to the absorber.

9. Tighten the bar nuts to 20 ft. lbs. (27 Nm).

10. Install the front fascia to the car aligning the fascia studs-to-fender.

11. Secure the retainers for the fascia-to-fender. Push on the retainers to the retainer.

12. Secure the nuts to the fascia studs.

13. Connect the push-on retainers to the fascia. Install the rubber strip, then insert the screws to the bottom side of the fascia and fender.

14. Tighten the fascia nuts to 53 inch lbs. (6 Nm), and fascia screws to 18 inch lbs. (2 Nm).

15. Lower the vehicle.

Rear

1982–91 MODELS

1. Raise and support the car to a suitable work height.

2. Remove the 2 push-on retainer clips from each end of the molding, then remove the molding.

3. Remove the 4 wing nuts and electrical connectors from each of the tail lamp assemblies and remove the left and right tail lamp assemblies.

4. Remove the 5 wing nuts, detach the electrical connector and remove the back-up light assembly.

5. Open the trunk and remove the 2 retaining nuts from the left and right side reflectors, then remove the reflectors.

6. Remove the 7 retaining pins from the valance panel and remove the panel.

7. Disconnect the electrical connector and remove the 8 retaining nuts, 4 retaining bolts and 11 retaining pins from the rear bumper and remove the bumper.

8. Disconnect the electrical connector, and remove the 8 retaining nuts from the impact bar and energy absorber.

9. Remove the 8 retaining clips and remove the impact bar from the mounting support bracket.

10. To install, reverse to install.

11. Lower the vehicle.

1992–96 SEDAN—BUICK

1. Raise and support the vehicle.

2. Matchmark the nuts for assembly purposes.

3. Remove the nuts on each side that attach the fascia-to-rear quarter panel.

4. Support the rear bumper.

5. Unfasten the nuts which attach the impact bar to the absorber, then remove the fascia /impact bar assembly.

6. Remove the license plate bracket from the fascia.

7. Remove the push retainers securing the fascia-to-impact bar, remove the fascia.

8. Remove the fascia pad along with the attaching screws.

To install:

9. Install the fascia pad and the retaining screws, then tighten to 35 inch lbs. (4 Nm).

10. Reinstall the fascia-to-impact bar, insert the push-on retainers to the fascia.

11. Secure the license plate bracket to the fascia.

12. Install the impact bar/fascia to the absorber. Secure the attaching nuts to the scribed locations, then tighten the nuts to 20 ft. lbs. (27 Nm).

13. Insert the bumper fascia retaining nuts, then tighten to 89 inch lbs. (10 Nm).

14. Lower the vehicle.

1992–96 SEDAN—OLDSMOBILE

1. Raise and support the vehicle.

2. Unfasten the nuts from the end of the molding, then remove the molding.

3. Remove the tail lamp, back-up and side marker lamp assemblies.

4. Remove the retainers from the fascia-to-impact bar. Unfasten the screws, from the lower fascia-to-fender.

5. Loosen and remove the nuts from each side of the fascia studs to the fender.

6. Remove the screws from the fascia-to-fender. Unfasten the nuts from the reinforcement. Remove the impact bar and absorber from the vehicle.

7. Remove the rivets from the absorber, then the stud plates and retainers on the impact bar.

To install:

➡ **When installing the rear fascia, spread the outer "ears" by hand to prevent the ear mounting studs from scraping the paint surface.**

8. Reattach the stud plates and retainers to the impact bar.

9. Insert the absorber into the impact bar, then replace the rivets onto the absorber. Tighten the impact bar nuts to 21 ft. lbs. (29 Nm).

10. Install the fascia to the vehicle, then install the retainers to the fascia and impact bar.

11. Insert the screws to the fascia-to-fender. Install and tighten the nuts for the fender-to-fascia studs.

12. Secure the screws to the lower fascia and fender. Tighten the fascia screws and nuts to 89 inch lbs. (10 Nm).

13. Reinstall the back-up, side marker, and tail lamp assemblies.

14. Reattach the molding to the fascia, tighten with the nuts.

15. Lower the vehicle.

1992–96 WAGON—BUICK

1. Raise and support the vehicle. Scribe the locations of the nuts before disassembling for reassembly.

2. Remove the filler panel attaching nuts from each side of the vehicle, then remove the panel.

3. Disconnect the nuts that attach the impact bar and bumper guards to the absorber.

4. Remove the impact bar and bumper guards.

5. Remove the step pad, rubber strip and guards.

To install:

6. Install the step pad, rubber strip and guards onto the impact bar.

7. Reattach the impact bar-to-absorber, then insert and tighten the nuts on each side of the impact bar and bumper guards. Tighten the absorber nuts to 21 ft. lbs. (29 Nm), and the bumper guard nuts to 20 ft. lbs. (27 Nm).

8. Install the filler panels and nuts on each side, then tighten the nuts to 53 inch lbs. (6 Nm).

1992–96 WAGON—OLDSMOBILE

1. Disconnect the left side storage panel screw and remove the panel.

2. Remove the left side filler nuts.

3. Remove the spare tire panel and tire. Unfasten the filler panel to quarter panel nuts.

4. Raise the vehicle and support securely.

5. Remove the filler panel push-in retainers, along with the filler panel-to-quarter panel nuts.

6. Loosen and remove the nuts attaching the absorber to the impact bar, then remove the impact bar.

7. Remove the rubber strip and step pad.

To install:

8. Reinstall the rubber strip and step pad.

9. Install the nuts for the absorber-to-impact bar, then align the assembly and tighten the nuts to 20 ft. lbs. (27 Nm).

10. Attach the nuts on the filler panels-to-quarter panel, tighten them to 27 inch lbs. (3 Nm).

11. Insert the push-in retainers to the filler panel.

12. Lower the vehicle, then install the spare tire and tire panel.

13. Insert the nuts for the filler panel, tighten them to 54 inch lbs. (6 Nm).

14. Install the left side storage panel screw, then tighten to 21 ft. lbs. (29 Nm).

Grille

REMOVAL & INSTALLATION

◆ **See Figure 8**

1. Remove the retaining screws from the grille assembly.

2. Remove the grille from the front end panel.

To install:

3. Position the grille in the front end panel, then install the retaining screws.

Outside Mirrors

REMOVAL & INSTALLATION

Standard

◆ **See Figure 9**

1. Remove the door trim panel and detach the inner panel water deflector. With the glass in the down position, pull out the front portion of the glass run weatherstrip.

Fig. 8 After the retaining screws are removed, the grille can be pulled off. Be careful not to cut your hands, as the metal is sharp

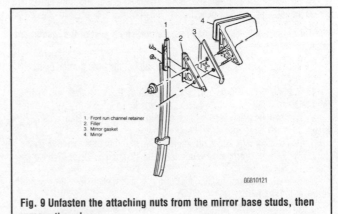

1. Front run channel retainer
2. Filler
3. Mirror gasket
4. Mirror

Fig. 9 Unfasten the attaching nuts from the mirror base studs, then remove the mirror

2. Remove the attaching bolts and screws from the front glass run channel lower retainer to filler, then rotate retainer rearward.

3. Remove the noise control patch to gain access to the screw at the belt, then remove the screw.

4. Remove the filler attaching screws at the top front of the window frame, then remove the mirror and filler from the door.

5. Remove the attaching nuts from the mirror base studs, then remove the mirror.

To install:

6. Be sure that the mirror gasket is aligned.

7. Replace the mirror and filler on the door. Install the filler attaching screws at the top front of the window frame. Attach the nuts to the mirror studs and tighten.

8. Install the screw at the belt, then insert the noise control patch.

9. Insert the retainer, then install the attaching bolts and screws to the front glass run channel lower retainer to filler.

10. Replace the front portion of the glass run weatherstrip, insert the inner panel water deflector, then reinstall the door trim panel.

Manual Remote

1. Remove the mirror remote control escutcheons and door trim panel. Detach the inner panel water deflector.

➡ **Right side remote mirror may require detaching part of the instrument panel.**

2. With the glass in the down position, pull out the front portion of the glass run weatherstrip.

3. Remove the attaching bolts and screws from the front glass run channel lower retainer to filler and rotate retainer rearward.

4. Remove the noise control patch to gain access to the 0.3 in. (7mm) screw at the belt and remove the screw.

5. Remove the filler attaching screws at the top front of the window frame.

6. Remove the mirror base with mirror and cable assembly from the door.

7. Remove the mirror to filler attaching nuts and remove the mirror and cable from filler.

To install:

8. Be sure cable is routed around front glass run channel retainer and installed to clip.

9. Install and connect the cable to the filler.

10. Attach the filler nuts to the mirror, then tighten to 72 inch lbs. (8 Nm).

11. Install the mirror base with the mirror and cable assembly to the door.

12. Insert the filler attaching screws to the top of the window frame, then install the screw to the belt.

13. Secure the noise control patch.

14. Attach the bolts and screws to the front of the glass run channel lower retainer and filler.

15. Install the glass run weatherstrip.

16. Attach the inner panel water deflector, door trim panel and mirror remote control escutcheon.

Electric Remote

1. Disconnect the negative battery cable.

2. Remove the mirror remote control escutcheons and door trim panel. Detach the inner panel water deflector and the electrical connector for the mirror.

➡**Right side remote mirror may require detaching part of the instrument panel.**

3. With the glass in the down position, pull out the front portion of the glass run weatherstrip.

4. Remove the attaching bolts and screws from the front glass run channel lower retainer to filler and rotate retainer rearward.

5. Remove the noise control patch to gain access to the 0.3 in. (7mm) screw at the belt and remove the screw.

6. Remove the filler attaching screws at the top front of the window frame.

7. Remove the mirror base with mirror and electric connector from the door.

8. Remove the mirror to filler attaching nuts and remove the mirror and electric wire from filler.

9. To install, reverse Steps 1 through 6. Be sure electric wire is routed around front glass run channel retainer and installed to the clip. Tighten the nuts to 72 inch lbs. (8 Nm).

10. Connect the negative battery cable, then reset the clock, radio and any other accessories if required.

Antenna

REMOVAL & INSTALLATION

Manual

1. Working from underneath the dash, disconnect the antenna cable from the radio.

2. Unscrew the antenna from the fender, then remove it from the car, with the cable attached.

To install:

3. Insert the new antenna cable lead into the fender wheel, then route the lead towards the radio. Attach the lead into the back of the radio.

4. Screw the antenna mast into the fender. Check operation.

Fixed

◆ **See Figure 10**

1. Remove the antenna mast from the base. Remove the trim piece from the antenna housing.

2. Disconnect the antenna housing mounting screws.

3. Loosen and remove the antenna lead-in cable, routing the cable out through the engine compartment.

4. Remove the antenna base assembly.

To install:

5. Install the base assembly. Route the lead-in cable through the engine compartment towards the radio.

6. Secure the antenna housing with the mounting screws and tighten to 18 inch lbs. (2 Nm).

7. Install the trim for the antenna housing. Install the antenna onto the base.

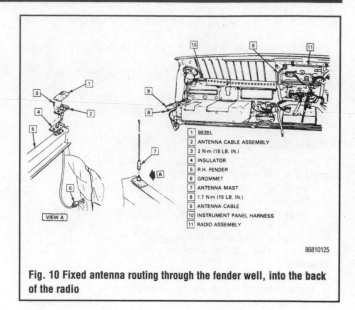

1	BEZEL
2	ANTENNA CABLE ASSEMBLY
3	2 N·m (18 LB. IN.)
4	INSULATOR
5	R.H. FENDER
6	GROMMET
7	ANTENNA MAST
8	1.7 N·m (15 LB. IN.)
9	ANTENNA CABLE
10	INSTRUMENT PANEL HARNESS
11	RADIO ASSEMBLY

86810125

Fig. 10 Fixed antenna routing through the fender well, into the back of the radio

Power

Because of the varied applications of power antennas, the following general power antenna removal and installation procedures are outlined. These removal steps can be altered as necessary.

FRONT MOUNTED TYPE

1. Disconnect the negative battery cable.

2. Remove the instrument panel sound absorber pad.

3. Disconnect the antenna lead-in and harness connector from the relay assembly.

4. Apply masking tape to the rear edge of the fender and door.

5. If required, remove the inner to outer fender retaining screws.

6. If required, raise the vehicle and support it safely; then remove the associated front wheel assembly.

7. Remove the lower rocker panel retaining screws, lower fender to body retaining bolt and remove the lower rocker panel, as required.

8. Remove the inner splash shield from the fender, as required.

9. Remove the upper antenna retaining nut, using an appropriately tool.

10. Remove the antenna to bracket retaining bolts, then remove the antenna.

To install:

11. Fit the antenna into position, then loosely install the antenna gasket and upper nut.

12. Loosely install the antenna to bracket retaining bolts.

13. Tighten the upper antenna retaining nut, using the appropriately tool, then tighten the antenna to bracket retaining bolts.

14. Complete installation in the reverse order of the removal procedure.

15. Apply silicone grease to the harness connector before reconnecting.

16. Connect the negative battery cable.

17. Check the operation of the antenna mast. Reset the clock, radio and any other accessories if required.

REAR MOUNTED TYPE

1. Disconnect the negative battery cable.

2. From inside the trunk, remove the trim panel from either the right or left rear wheel area.

3. Remove the antenna mounting bracket retaining screws.

4. Remove the upper antenna nut and bezel from the antenna, using an appropriately tool.

5. Remove the lead-in cable and wiring connector.

6. Remove the antenna assembly from the vehicle.

To install:

7. Fit the antenna to the vehicle, then connect the lead-in cable.

8. Install the nut and bezel to the antenna and mounting bracket retaining screws.

9. Apply silicone grease to the harness connector before reconnecting.

10. Install the trim panel and reconnect the negative battery cable.

11. Check the operation of the antenna mast. Reset the clock, if required.

Fenders

REMOVAL & INSTALLATION

1. Disconnect the negative battery cable.
2. It will be easier to service the fender with the hood removed.
3. Remove the wiper arms.
4. Remove the cowl vent panel to gain access to the upper fender-to-cowl bolts.

➡**An outer fender panel with plastic inner panel may be used. Care must be taken in handling the unsupported fender due to the lack of rigidity prior to installation.**

5. Disconnect the headlamp wire connector.
6. Disconnect the side marker lamp connector.

7. Remove the rocker panel molding, if used.
8. Remove the wheelhouse panel.
9. Remove the screws attaching the front end panel to the fender.
10. Unfasten the lower valance panel, if used on your vehicle.
11. With the fender removed carefully remove the molding and name plates.
To install:

➡**If the fender is not primed or undercoated as you desire it may be better to have this procedure done to the fender before installation.**

12. Transfer fender moldings and nameplates to new fender.
13. Install the fender assembly and tighten attaching bolts to 88 inch lbs. (10 Nm).
14. Install the lower valance if removed and tighten bolts to 18 inch lbs. (2 Nm).
15. Install the wheelhouse panel and the rocker panel if used.
16. Secure the headlamp and marker lamp wiring and connectors.
17. Reinstall the cowl vent panel and wiper arms.
18. Install the hood if removed and connect the battery cable.
19. Reset the clock and radio, along with any other accessories.

INTERIOR

Instrument Panel and Pad

REMOVAL & INSTALLATION

You may want to place a rag over the steering column to help prevent scratches. With vehicles equipped with tilt steering, it will help to lower the steering wheel all the way, then unscrew the tilt wheel lever. There is additional information on instrument panel and switches in Section 6 covering electrical components.

Century

♦ **See Figure 11**

1982–92 MODELS

1. Disconnect the negative battery cable.
2. Disconnect the speedometer cable and pull it through the firewall.
3. Remove the left side hush panel retaining screws and nut.
4. Remove the right side hush panel retaining screws and nut.
5. Remove the shift indicator cable clip.
6. Remove the steering column trim plate.
7. Put the gear selector in **L**. Remove the retaining screws and gently pull out the instrument panel trim plate.
8. Disconnect the parking brake cable at the lever by pushing it forward and sliding it from its slot.
9. Unbolt and lower the steering column.

10. Remove the gauge cluster retaining screws. Pull the cluster out far enough to disconnect any wires. Remove the instrument cluster.
To install:
11. Install the gauge cluster, connect the electrical connectors and install the retaining screws.
12. Position the steering column and install the retaining bolts.
13. Connect the parking brake cable at the lever.
14. Put the gear selector in **L**. Install the instrument panel trim plate.
15. Install the steering column trim plate.
16. Install the shift indicator cable clip.
17. Install the right side hush panel retaining screws and nut.
18. Install the left side hush panel retaining screws and nut.
19. Pull the speedometer cable through the firewall and connect to the speedometer.
20. Connect the negative battery cable.

1993–96 MODELS

1. Disconnect the negative battery cable.
2. Remove the left and right side sound insulators. Lower the steering column.
3. Disconnect the parking brake release cable.
4. Disconnect the harness connectors at the junction block.
5. Remove the speaker connections, then remove the A/C vacuum harness and temperature door cable.
6. Disconnect the engine harness connectors, then the antenna cable.
7. Remove the side window defogger hoses. Remove the bolts and screws holding the bulkhead connector.
8. Remove the bulkhead connector from the instrument panel.
9. Disconnect the windshield wiper motor and the brake master cylinder connectors, then unfasten the hoodlamp connection.
10. Disconnect the harness at the cowl by pulling the sides of the black clip out while pulling up on the clip.
11. To remove the harness, feed it throughout the cowl.
12. Unfasten the defroster/speaker grille by lifting up and out. Remove the two nuts on both inner sides of the steering column opening.
13. Unscrew the three screws at the bottom of the instrument panel, then remove the six screws at the defroster opening on top of the instrument panel.
14. Remove the instrument panel.
15. Reverse to install. Connect the negative battery cable, reset the clock and radio.

Celebrity

1. Disconnect the negative battery cable.
2. Remove instrument panel hush panel.
3. Remove vent control housing, as required.
4. On non-air conditioning vehicles, remove steering column trim cover screws and lower cover with vent cables attached. On air conditioning vehicles, remove trim cover attaching screws and remove cover.

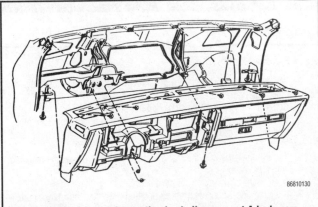

Fig. 11 Instrument panel mounting is similar on most A body cars— Century shown

86810130

5. Remove instrument cluster trim pad.

6. Remove ash tray, retainer and fuse block, disconnect wires as necessary.

7. Remove headlight switch knob and instrument panel trim plate. Disconnect electrical connectors of any accessory switches in trim plate.

8. Remove cluster assembly and disconnect speedometer cable, **PRNDL** and cluster electrical connectors.

To install:

9. Install cluster assembly and connect speedometer cable, **PRNDL** and cluster electrical connectors.

10. Install headlight switch knob and instrument panel trim plate. Connect electrical connectors of any accessory switches in trim plate.

11. Install ash tray, retainer and fuse block, connect electrical connectors.

12. Install instrument cluster trim pad.

13. On non-air conditioned vehicles, raise the cover with vent cables attached and install steering column trim cover screws. On air conditioned vehicles, install trim cover and attaching screws.

14. If removed, install vent control housing.

15. Install instrument panel hush panel.

16. Connect the negative battery cable.

Ciera and Cruiser

1982–92 MODELS

1. Disconnect the negative battery cable. Remove left instrument panel trim pad.

2. Remove instrument panel cluster trim cover.

3. Disconnect speedometer cable at transaxle or cruise control transducer, if equipped.

4. Remove steering column trim cover.

5. Disconnect shift indicator clip from steering column shift bowl.

6. Remove 4 screws attaching cluster assembly to instrument panel.

7. Pull assembly out far enough to reach behind cluster and disconnect speedometer cable.

8. Remove cluster assembly.

To install:

9. Install the cluster assembly.

10. Connect the speedometer cable.

11. Install the 4 screws attaching cluster assembly to instrument panel.

12. Connect shift indicator clip to steering column shift bowl.

13. Install the steering column trim cover.

14. Connect the speedometer cable at the transaxle or cruise control transducer, if equipped.

15. Install the instrument panel cluster trim cover.

16. Install the left instrument panel trim pad.

17. Connect the negative battery cable.

1993–96 MODELS

1. Disconnect the negative battery cable.

2. Remove the left and right sound insulators. Unfasten the accessory trim plate and remove the ash tray assembly.

3. Unfasten the connection to the lighter. Remove the instrument cluster trim plate and cluster assembly.

4. Remove the shift indicator clip from the steering column shift bowl, then remove the shift trim collar and trim plate, along with the lower steering column.

5. Remove the speaker grilles by unfastening the mounting screws.

6. Disconnect the ventilation system, pull the control assembly from the dash, then disconnect the wiring harness from the control assembly. Unfasten the temperature control cables.

7. Unfasten the steering column wiring harness from the steering column.

8. Remove the parking brake release handle.

9. Disconnect the side window defogger hoses from the heater outlet. Unfasten the bolts which attach the wiper motor to the cowl.

10. Disconnect the bulkhead connector at the cowl panel. Remove the lower instrument panel bolts.

11. Loosen, then remove the defroster grille by carefully prying the grille with a small prytool.

12. Remove the upper instrument panel screws.

13. Open the hood, then remove the clip in the engine compartment that holds the wiring harness to the cowl. Disconnect the wiring harness connectors in the engine compartment, then pull it through the cowl on the passengers side.

14. Tilt the instrument panel forwards, then remove the remaining electrical connections. Remove the instrument panel.

15. Reverse to install, then connect the negative battery cable. Reset the clock and radio along with any other accessories.

6000

1. Disconnect the negative battery cable, and remove the center and left side lower instrument panel trim plate.

2. Remove the screws holding the instrument cluster to the instrument panel carrier.

3. Remove the instrument cluster lens to gain access to the speedometer head and gauges.

4. Remove right side and left side hush panels, steering column trim cover and disconnect parking brake cable and vent cables, if equipped.

5. Remove steering column retaining bolts and drop steering column.

6. Disconnect temperature control cable, inner-to-outer air conditioning wire harness and inner-to-outer air conditioning vacuum harness, if equipped.

7. Disconnect chassis harness behind left lower instrument panel and ECM/PCM connectors behind glove box. Disconnect instrument panel harness at cowl.

8. Remove center instrument panel trim plate, radio, if equipped, and disconnect neutral switch and brake light switch.

9. Remove upper and lower instrument panel retaining screws, nuts and bolts.

10. Pull instrument panel assembly out far enough to disconnect ignition switch, headlight dimmer switch and turn signal switch. Disconnect all other accessory wiring and vacuum lines necessary to remove instrument panel assembly.

11. Remove instrument panel assembly with wiring harness.

To install:

12. Install instrument panel assembly with wiring harness.

13. Connect ignition switch, headlight dimmer switch and turn signal switch. Connect all other accessory wiring and vacuum lines.

14. Install upper and lower instrument panel retaining screws, nuts and bolts.

15. Connect neutral switch and brake light switch. Install the radio, if equipped, and install center instrument panel trim plate.

16. Connect chassis harness behind left lower instrument panel and ECM/PCM connectors behind glove box. Connect instrument panel harness at cowl.

17. Connect temperature control cable, inner-to-outer air conditioning wire harness and inner-to-outer air conditioning vacuum harness, if equipped.

18. Raise the steering column and install retaining bolts.

19. Install right side and left side hush panels, steering column trim cover and connect parking brake cable and vent cables, if equipped.

20. Install the instrument cluster lens.

21. Install the screws holding the instrument cluster to the instrument panel carrier.

22. Install the center and left side lower instrument panel trim plate.

23. Connect the negative battery cable, then reset the clock and radio.

Console

REMOVAL & INSTALLATION

♦ **See Figures 12 and 13**

1. Remove the shifter knob from the shifter by removing the retaining screw at the back of the knob.

2. Remove the screws at the sides and front of the console.

3. Open the console box and remove the retaining screw inside the box.

4. Remove the electrical connectors for the ashtray light (if supplied) and lighter.

5. Remove the ashtray at the rear of the console and remove the retaining screw behind the ashtray.

6. Remove the power seat control (if supplied).

7. Slide the upper console from it's position, then disconnect the courtesy light.

8. Remove the screws holding the lower console into place, then slide the console rearward slightly and remove.

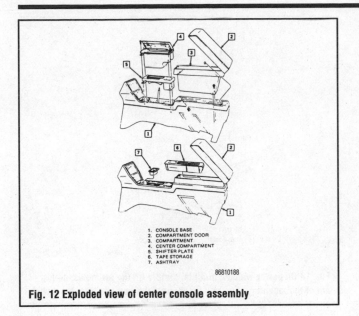

1. CONSOLE BASE
2. COMPARTMENT DOOR
3. COMPARTMENT
4. CENTER COMPARTMENT
5. SHIFTER PLATE
6. TAPE STORAGE
7. ASHTRAY

86810188

Fig. 12 Exploded view of center console assembly

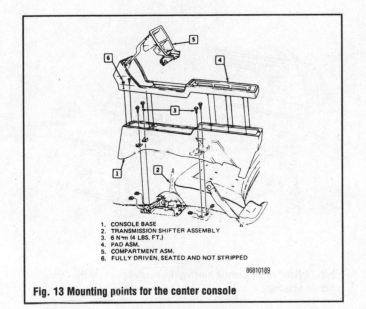

1. CONSOLE BASE
2. TRANSMISSION SHIFTER ASSEMBLY
3. 6 N·m (4 LBS. FT.)
4. PAD ASM.
5. COMPARTMENT ASM.
6. FULLY DRIVEN, SEATED AND NOT STRIPPED

86810189

Fig. 13 Mounting points for the center console

To install:

9. Install the lower console by attaching the mounting screws, tighten them to 54 inch lbs. (6 Nm).

10. Connect the electrical harness to the courtesy light.

11. Attach the upper console with the mounting screws in the front.

12. Connect the electrical harness to the ashtray light and lighter.

13. Insert the power seat control into the console, then attach the trim console plate.

14. On column shift, install the center compartment.

15. On console shift, attach the electrical harness to the shifter light, then attach the shifter trim plate.

16. Mount the two screws at the rear of the center compartment or the shifter trim plate.

17. Tighten the two screws belonging in the ashtray opening.

18. On vehicles with shift console, screw on the shifter knob, then install the snap ring holding the shift knob.

19. Install the ashtray, then install the armrest compartment.

Door Panels

REMOVAL & INSTALLATION

◆ **See Figures 14 thru 22**

1. Disconnect the negative battery cable.
2. Remove all door inside handles.
3. Remove door inside locking rod knob.
4. Remove screws inserted through door armrest and pull handle assembly into door inner panel or armrest hanger support bracket.
5. On styles with remote control mirror assemblies, remove the remote mirror escutcheons and disengage the end of the mirror control cable.
6. On styles with power window controls located in the door trim assembly, disconnect the wire harness at the switch assembly.
7. Remove the remote control handle escutcheons screws.
8. On styles with integral armrests, remove the screws inserted through the pull cup into the armrest hanger support.
9. Remove screws and plastic retainers from the perimeter of the door trim pad using tool BT-7323A or equivalent and a screwdriver. To remove the door trim panel, push trim upward and outboard to disengage it from the door inner panel at the belt line.
10. On styles with courtesy lamps located in the lower area of the trim panel, disconnect the wiring harness at the lamp assembly.

To install:

➡**Before installing the door trim panel, check that all trim retainers are securely installed to the panel and are not damaged. Replace damaged retainers as required.**

11. Connect electrical components where present.

12. To install the door trim panel, pull door inside handle inward; then position the trim panel to the inner panel, inserting door handle through hole in panel.

13. Position the trim panel to the door inner panel so trim retainers are aligned with the attaching holes in the panel and tap the retainers into the holes with a clean rubber mallet.

14. Install the armrest into the inner panel or armrest hanger support brackets. Assemble the locking rod knob, then all inner door handles.

15. Connect the negative battery cable, reset the clock and radio.

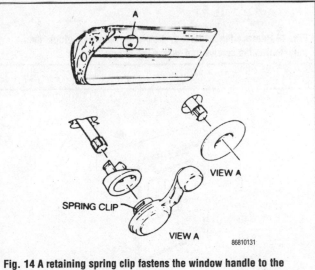

VIEW A

SPRING CLIP

VIEW A

86810131

Fig. 14 A retaining spring clip fastens the window handle to the spindle

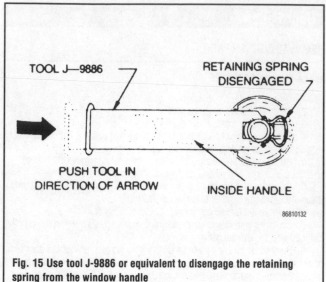

Fig. 15 Use tool J-9886 or equivalent to disengage the retaining spring from the window handle

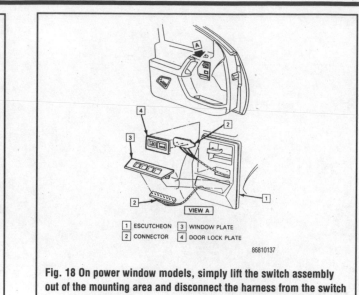

ESCUTCHEON — WINDOW PLATE — CONNECTOR — DOOR LOCK PLATE

Fig. 18 On power window models, simply lift the switch assembly out of the mounting area and disconnect the harness from the switch

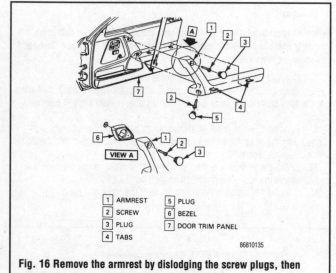

1	ARMREST	5	PLUG
2	SCREW	6	BEZEL
3	PLUG	7	DOOR TRIM PANEL
4	TABS		

Fig. 16 Remove the armrest by dislodging the screw plugs, then unfastening the screws that secure the armrest

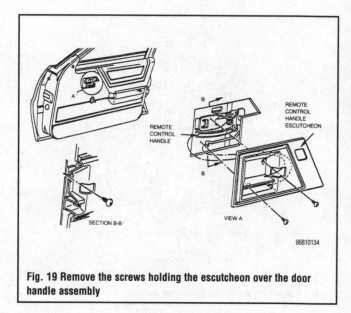

Fig. 19 Remove the screws holding the escutcheon over the door handle assembly

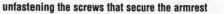

1. ESCUTCHEON ASSEMBLY - OUTSIDE REMOTE MIRROR
2. NUTS

Fig. 17 If your vehicle is equipped with a remote mirror, remove the mirror assembly, then the escutcheons. Disconnect the cable from the mirror head

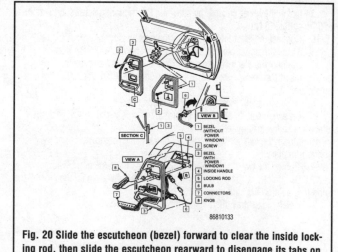

Fig. 20 Slide the escutcheon (bezel) forward to clear the inside locking rod, then slide the escutcheon rearward to disengage its tabs on the front from the trim panel. This will give you access to the wiring harness

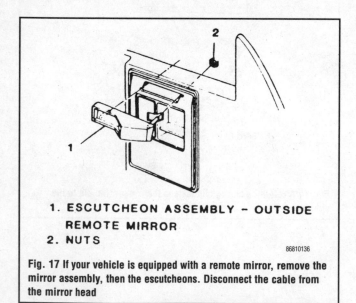

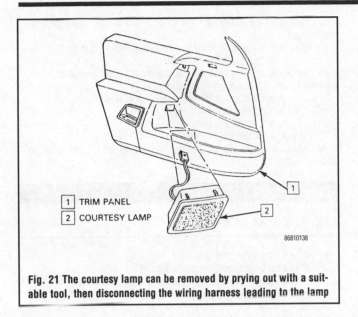

Fig. 21 The courtesy lamp can be removed by prying out with a suitable tool, then disconnecting the wiring harness leading to the lamp

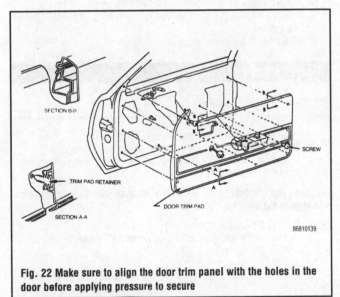

Fig. 22 Make sure to align the door trim panel with the holes in the door before applying pressure to secure

Headliner

REMOVAL & INSTALLATION

♦ See Figures 23, 24 and 25

1. Disconnect the negative battery cable.
2. Remove the dome lamp, courtesy lamp, coat hooks and sunvisors. On wagons remove the rear courtesy lamp.
3. Remove the quarter upper trim finishing panels using tool J-24595-C.
4. Remove the rear seat roof mounted shoulder belt retainers, as needed.
5. Remove the windshield pillar upper side roof rail and garnish moldings.
6. Remove the headlining hook and loop strips along the front and on the rear using tool J-2772-C.
7. Remove the push-in retainers. On wagons, remove the retainers from the rear of the headliner.
8. Remove the assembly through the right front door opening.

To install:

9. Care must be taken not to overflex the new liner when installing. Load the rear portion of the lining diagonally through the right front door opening.
10. Align the headlining with holes for the sunvisors and the interior lamps. Press into place, along the areas with hook and loop strips.

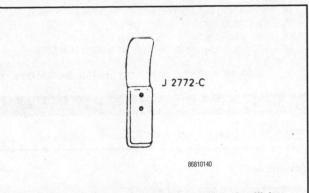

Fig. 23 Use tool J-2772-C or equivalent to remove the headlining hook and loop strips along the front and rear

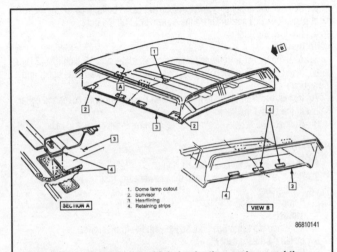

1. Dome lamp cutout
2. Sunvisor
3. Headlining
4. Retaining strips

Fig. 24 Align the headlining with holes for the sunvisors and the interior lamps. Press into place, along the areas with hook and loop strips

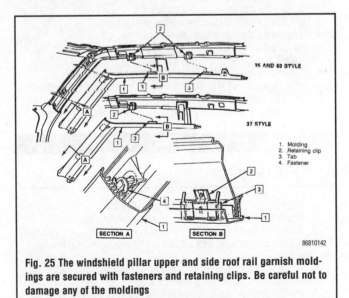

1. Molding
2. Retaining clip
3. Tab
4. Fastener

Fig. 25 The windshield pillar upper and side roof rail garnish moldings are secured with fasteners and retaining clips. Be careful not to damage any of the moldings

11. Install the retainers and the push-in retainers, to the rear of the headlining, on wagons.
12. Install the sunvisors and the interior lamps.
13. Install the windshield pillar upper and side roof rail garnish moldings.

14. Install the rear shoulder belt retainers, on the wagon, if needed.
15. Install the quarter trim finishing panels.
16. Install the coat hooks.
17. Make certain no wires for the lamps are pinched or installed incorrectly.
18. Connect the negative battery cable, then reset the clock and radio.

Ventilation Ducts and Hoses

REMOVAL & INSTALLATION

Oldsmobile

DEFROSTER/LEFT AND CENTER DUCT

1. Disconnect the negative battery cable.
2. Remove the left and right sound insulators. Unassemble the steering column collar and trim cover, along with the lower column collar.
3. Remove the upper and lower instrument panel bolts, then tilt the instrument panel forwards and unfasten the screws holding the duct.
4. Remove the duct.
To install:
5. Attach the duct with the mounting screws, tighten to 18 inch lbs. (2 Nm).
6. Insert the instrument panel into position and mount with the upper and lower bolts.
7. Install the steering column, then insert the column trim cover and collar. Reinstall the sound insulators.
8. Connect the negative battery cable, then reset the clock and radio.

RIGHT OUTLET DUCT

1. Disconnect the negative battery cable.
2. Remove the instrument panel, then remove the (usually) four screws mounting the duct.
3. Remove the duct.
To install:
4. Insert the duct into position, attach with the four screws.
5. Install the instrument panel.
6. Connect the negative battery cable, then reset the clock and radio.

Buick

1. Disconnect the negative battery cable.
2. Remove the instrument panel assembly.
3. Unfasten the hoses to the side window defoggers.
4. Unfasten the main duct bolts, then remove the duct.
5. Unfasten the side window defogger duct bolts, then remove the duct.
To install:
6. Install the side window defogger ducts and secure with bolts.
7. Insert the main duct with the bolts from removal. Install the hoses.
8. Install the instrument panel.
9. Connect the negative battery cable, then reset the clock and radio.

Door Locks

REMOVAL & INSTALLATION

1. Raise door window. Disconnect the negative battery cable.
2. Remove door trim panel and inner panel water deflector.
3. Disengage the inside lock rod, the inside handle-to-lock rod, lock cylinder-to-lock rod and the power lock actuator rod (power locks only) from the lock assembly.
4. On some models, remove the screw holding the door ajar switch-to-lock, then disconnect the connector from the lock.
5. Remove the lock screws, then lower the lock to disengage the outside handle-to-lock rod. Remove the lock from the door.
To install:
6. Align the lock cylinder gasket.

➡**Black lock cylinders should be lubricated with a light oil, all others should use a multi-purpose grease.**

7. First install the spring clips to the lock assembly, then install the lock into the door.
8. Install the lock screws, lower lock-to-outside handle, and the lock rod. Tighten the screws to 62 inch lbs. (7 Nm).
9. Install the following rods at the lock assembly, check the rod clips for any weak points or breakage, replace if needed:
   a. The power lock actuator rod, for power locks only.
   b. The lock cylinder to the lock rod.
   c. The handle to the lock rod.
   d. Install the inside locking rod.
10. Attach the water deflector. Connect the negative battery cable, reset the clock and radio.

Tailgate Lock

REMOVAL & INSTALLATION

1. Remove the liftgate inner trim panel.
2. Using a flat bladed tool, remove the lock cylinder retainer.
3. On power locks, remove the screws and clip from the actuator.
4. Pull the lock cylinder out, unfasten the lock rods from the cylinder.
To install:
5. Attach the actuator to the lock cylinder with the screws and clip.
6. Lubricate the lock cylinder, then insert into mounting hole. Attach the rods to the cylinder.
7. Install the liftgate inner trim panel.

Power Door Lock Actuator

REMOVAL & INSTALLATION

1. Raise the window. Disconnect the negative battery cable.
2. Remove the door trim panel and water deflector.
3. Locate the rivets holding the actuator. Drive out the rivets center pins, then drill out the rivets using a ¼ in. (6mm) drill bit.

➡**Some vehicle's door lock actuator are retained with ³⁄₁₆ in. rivets and will require the use of a ³⁄₁₆ in. drill bit.**

4. Remove the actuator from the lock rod.
5. Disconnect the actuator electrical connector and remove the actuator from the door.
To install:
6. Fit the actuator through the door access hole and install the actuator to the lock rod.
7. Fasten the actuator to the inner panel using ¼ x ½ in. aluminum peel type rivets. If rivets are not available, install U-clips on the regulator at the metal retainer locations. Be certain to install the clips with the clinch nuts on the outboard side of the retainers.
8. Reconnect the electrical connector to the actuator.
9. Install the door trim panel and water deflector, as required.
10. Reconnect the negative battery cable, then reset the clock and radio.

Tailgate Lock Actuator

REMOVAL & INSTALLATION

♦ **See Figure 26**

1. Disconnect the negative battery cable.
2. Open the tailgate, then position the glass fully upwards.
3. Remove the tailgate handle, inner trim panel and water deflector.
4. Remove the right side access hole cover, then disconnect the actuator electrical connector.
5. Locate the rivets holding the actuator. Drive out the rivets center pins, then drill out the rivets using a ¼ in. (6mm) drill bit.
6. Remove the actuator and rod from the upper lock lever.
To install:
7. Install the actuator assembly, then reconnect the upper lock lever.

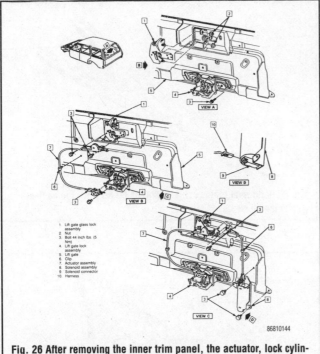

Fig. 26 After removing the inner trim panel, the actuator, lock cylinder and other nearby components are accessible

8. Secure the actuator using ¼—20 x 16 in. screws and nuts.
9. Reconnect the electrical connector, then install the access hole cover.
10. Install the water deflector, inner trim panel and tailgate handle.
11. Reconnect the negative battery cable, reset the radio and clock.

Door Glass and Regulator

REMOVAL & INSTALLATION

✳ CAUTION

When working on vehicle glass, always wear eye protection and gloves to reduce the risk of injury.

Door Glass (Coupe)

1. Remove the door trim panel and inner panel water deflector.
2. Raise the window to the full up position, then tape the glass to the door frame using cloth-backed tape.
3. Remove the bolts holding the lower sash channel to the regulator sash.
4. Remove the rubber down stop at the bottom of the door by pulling carefully.
5. Attach the regulator handle and run the regulator to the full down position. Remove the regulator sash by rotating 90° (one-quarter turn) and pulling outward.
6. While supporting the glass, remove the tape and lower the window to the full down position. Disengage the front edge of the glass from the glass run channel retainer. Slide the glass forward and tilt slightly to remove the guide from the retainer in the run channel.
7. Using care, raise the glass while tilting forward and remove glass inboard of the upper frame.
8. To install, reverse the steps. Use liquid soap solution on the rubber down stop before installing the trim parts, then check the window for proper operation and alignment.

Door Glass (Sedan and Wagon)

▶ See Figures 27 and 28

1. Remove the door trim panel and inner panel water deflector.
2. Raise the window to the full up position, then tape the glass to the door frame using cloth-backed tape.
3. Remove the bolts holding the lower sash channel to the regulator sash.
4. Attach the regulator handle and run the regulator to the full down position.
5. While supporting the glass, remove the tape, then lower the window to the half down position.
6. Wrap tape around the blade of tool J-245895B or equivalent. Insert a tool between the guide and the glass at the fastener and carefully pry apart.
7. Using care, raise the glass while tilting forward and remove glass inboard of the upper frame.
8. Remove the guide from the rear of the run channel weatherstrip metal retainer and discard of the guide.
To install:
9. Replace the guide on the glass by using heat on the guide with a hot air gun, or soak it in hot water for about one minute.
10. Install the guide to the glass by aligning to hole in glass, then carefully press the guide together at the fastener location.
11. Install the glass and lower it about halfway.
12. With one hand on bottom edge, rotate the glass rearward to snap the guide into the retainer.
13. Reinstall the regulator handle, then bolt the lower sash channel (on the window) to the regulator sash.
14. Install the water deflector.

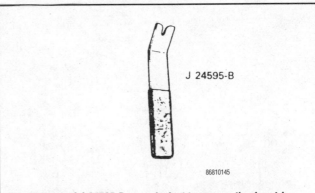

Fig. 27 Use tool J-24595-B or equivalent to remove the door trim pad and garnishes

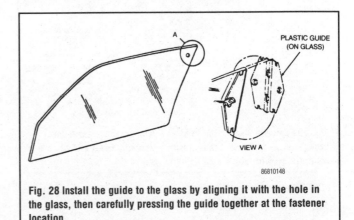

Fig. 28 Install the guide to the glass by aligning it with the hole in the glass, then carefully pressing the guide together at the fastener location

Regulator

MANUAL

▶ **See Figures 29, 30 and 31**

1. Remove the door trim panel and inner panel water deflector.
2. Raise the window to the full up position, then tape the glass to the door frame using cloth-backed tape.
3. Remove the lower sash bolts.
4. Punch out the center pins of the regulator rivet. Drill out the rivets using a ¼ in. (6mm) drill bit.
5. Remove the regulator through the rear access hole.

To install:

6. Use a hand rivet tool J-29022 or equivalent and install the regulator to the inner panel using ¼ in. x ½ in. aluminum peel type rivets, part No. 9436175 or equivalent.
7. If a hand rivet tool is not available, install U-clips on the regulator at the three attaching locations. Be sure to install the clips with cinch nuts on the outboard side of retainers.
8. Slide the regulator through the rear access hole, then align the regulator attaching clips with the holes in the inner panel. Attach regulator metal retainers with ¼ in.—20 x ½ in. (6mm—20 x 13mm) screws. Attach the housing part of the regulator with a ¼ in.—20 x ½ in. screws into ¼ in. (6mm—20 x 13mm) nuts with integral washers. Tighten the bolts to 90–125 inch lbs. (10–13 Nm).
9. Install the lower sash bolts.
10. Remove the tape from the door glass and frame.
11. Install the inner panel water deflector and door trim panel.

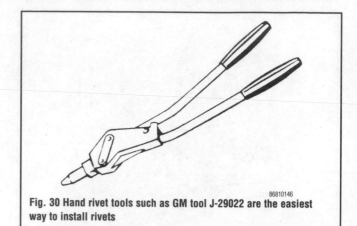

Fig. 30 Hand rivet tools such as GM tool J-29022 are the easiest way to install rivets

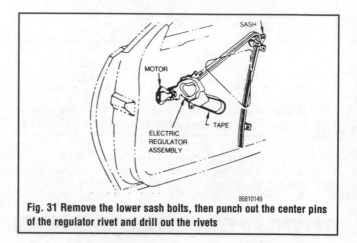

Fig. 31 Remove the lower sash bolts, then punch out the center pins of the regulator rivet and drill out the rivets

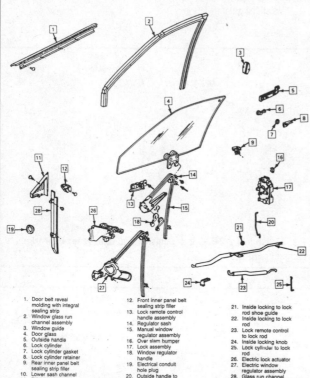

1. Door belt reveal molding with integral sealing strip
2. Window glass run channel assembly
3. Window guide
4. Door glass
5. Outside handle
6. Lock cylinder
7. Lock cylinder gasket
8. Lock cylinder retainer
9. Rear inner panel belt sealing strip filler
10. Lower sash channel
11. Filler assembly
12. Front inner panel belt sealing strip filler
13. Lock remote control handle assembly
14. Regulator sash
15. Manual window regulator assembly
16. Over slam bumper
17. Lock assembly
18. Window regulator handle
19. Electrical conduit hole plug
20. Outside handle to lock rod
21. Inside locking to lock rod shoe guide
22. Inside locking to lock rod
23. Lock remote control to lock rod
24. Inside locking knob
25. Lock cylinder to lock rod
26. Electric lock actuator
27. Electric window regulator assembly
28. Glass run channel lower front retainer

Fig. 29 Exploded view of the front door window glass assembly. Except for the motor and related components, manual and electric windows use virtually the same parts

ELECTRIC

▶ **See Figures 29, 30 and 31**

1. Remove the door trim panel and inner panel water deflector.
2. Raise the window to the full up position. Make sure to disconnect the negative battery cable before working with your electric window regulator.

3. Tape the glass to the door frame using cloth-backed tape.
4. Remove the lower sash bolts.
5. Punch out the center pins of the regulator rivet. Drill out the rivets using a ¼ in. (6mm) drill bit.
6. Remove the glass as stated previously, then move the regulator and motor assembly rearward, and remove the electric connector. Remove the regulator and motor assembly through the rear access hole.

To install:

7. Use a hand rivet tool J-29022 or equivalent and install the regulator to the inner panel using ¼ in. x ½ in. (6mm x 13mm) aluminum peel type rivets, part No. 9436175 or equivalent.
8. If hand rivet tool is not available, install U-clips on regulator at three attaching locations. Be sure to install clips with cinch nuts on outboard side of retainers.
9. Slide the regulator through the rear access hole and align the regulator attaching clips with the holes in the inner panel. Attach regulator metal retainers with ¼ in.—20 x ½ in. (6mm—20 x 13mm) screws. Attach housing part of regulator with ¼ in.—20 x ½ in. (6mm—20 x 13mm) screws into ¼ in. (6mm) nuts with integral washers. Tighten the bolts to 90–125 inch lbs. (10–13 Nm).
10. Install the lower sash bolts.
11. Remove the tape from the door glass and frame.
12. Install the inner panel water deflector and door trim panel.
13. Connect the negative battery cable.

Electric Window Motor

REMOVAL & INSTALLATION

1. Remove the door trim panel and inner panel water deflector.
2. Raise the window to the full up position and tape the glass to the door frame using cloth-backed tape.

3. Disconnect the negative battery cable.

4. Remove the lower sash bolts.

5. Punch out the center pins of the regulator rivet. Drill out rivets using ¼ in. (6mm) drill bit.

6. Move regulator and motor assembly rearward, then remove the electrical connector.

7. With the regulator in the door, drill out the regulator-to-motor rivets using a ⅛ in. (4mm) drill bit, then remove the motor.

To install:

8. Install and connect the window motor.

9. Use ³⁄₁₆ in. (5mm) rivets or ³⁄₁₆ in. (5mm) nuts and bolts to install the motor to the regulator.

10. Connect the electrical wiring, then install the regulator and door inner panel using a ¼ in. (6mm) rivets.

11. Install the lower sash bolts, tighten to 62 inch lbs. (7 Nm).

12. Install the water deflector and remove the tape from the window.

13. Connect the negative battery cable, reset the clock and radio.

Windshield and Fixed Glass

REMOVAL & INSTALLATION

If your windshield, or other fixed window, is cracked or chipped, you may decide to replace it with a new one yourself. However, there are two main reasons why replacement windshields and other window glass should be installed only by a professional automotive glass technician: safety and cost.

The most important reason a professional should install automotive glass is for safety. The glass in the vehicle, especially the windshield, is designed with safety in mind in case of a collision. The windshield is specially manufactured from two panes of specially-tempered glass with a thin layer of transparent plastic between them. This construction allows the glass to "give" in the event that a part of your body hits the windshield during the collision, and prevents the glass from shattering, which could cause lacerations, blinding and other harm to passengers of the vehicle. The other fixed windows are designed to be tempered so that if they break during a collision, they shatter in such a way that there are no large pointed glass pieces. The professional automotive glass technician knows how to install the glass in a vehicle so that it will function optimally during a collision. Without the proper experience, knowledge and tools, installing a piece of automotive glass yourself could lead to additional harm if an accident should ever occur.

Cost is also a factor when deciding to install automotive glass yourself. Performing this could cost you much more than a professional may charge for the same job. Since the windshield is designed to break under stress, an often life saving characteristic, windshields tend to break VERY easily when an inexperienced person attempts to install one. Do-it-yourselfers buying two, three or even four windshields from a salvage yard because they have broken them during installation are common stories. Also, since the automotive glass is designed to prevent the outside elements from entering your vehicle, improper installation can lead to water and air leaks. Annoying whining noises at highway speeds from air leaks or inside body panel rusting from water leaks can add to your stress level and subtract from your wallet. After buying two or three windshields, installing them and ending up with a leak that produces a noise while driving and water damage during rainstorms, the cost of having a professional do it correctly the first time may be much more alluring. We here at Chilton, therefore, advise that you have a professional automotive glass technician service any broken glass on your vehicle.

WINDSHIELD CHIP REPAIR

▶ See Figures 32 and 33

➡ **Check with your state and local authorities on the laws for state safety inspection. Some states or municipalities may not allow chip repair as a viable option for correcting stone damage to your windshield.**

Although severely cracked or damaged windshields must be replaced, there is something that you can do to prolong or even prevent the need for replacement of a chipped windshield. There are many companies which offer windshield chip repair products, such as Loctite's® Bullseye™ windshield repair kit. These kits usually consist of a syringe, pedestal and a sealing adhesive. The

syringe is mounted on the pedestal and is used to create a vacuum which pulls the plastic layer against the glass. This helps make the chip transparent. The adhesive is then injected which seals the chip and helps to prevent further stress cracks from developing

➡ **Always follow the specific manufacturer's instructions.**

TCCA0P00

Fig. 32 Small chips on your windshield can be fixed with an aftermarket repair kit, such as the one from Loctite®

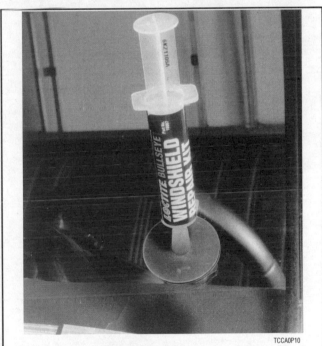

TCCA0P10

Fig. 33 Most kits use a self-stick applicator and syringe to inject the adhesive into the chip or crack

Inside Rear View Mirror

REPLACEMENT

The inside rear view mirror is permanently attached to the windshield. Should replacement become necessary, refer to your local dealer or a qualified technician for service. However, if the mirror simply falls off (due to faulty adhesive), reinstallation is possible using special rear view mirror adhesive, which is available at many automotive parts stores. Be sure to thoroughly clean the windshield and mirror mounting surfaces, and carefully follow the product's instructions.

Seats

REMOVAL & INSTALLATION

Front

♦ See Figure 34

1. Position the seat in the full forward position. If the car is equipped with six-way power seats, place the seat in the full forward and up position. When necessary to gain access to the adjuster-to-floor pan attaching nuts, remove the adjuster rear foot covers and or carpet retainers.
2. Remove the track covers where necessary, then remove the adjuster-to-floor pan rear attaching nuts. Position the seat in the full rearward position.
3. Remove the adjuster front foot covers, then remove the adjuster to floor pan front attaching nuts. Tilt the seat rearward and disconnect the feed wire connector.
4. Remove the seat assembly from the car.

To install:

5. Reinstall the seat into the car, then connect the wire connection.
6. Attach the seat with the adjuster-to-floor pan front nuts, then tighten the nuts to 18 ft. lbs. (24 Nm).
7. Position the seat in the full forward and up position, then attach the adjuster-to-floor pan rear nuts. Tighten the nuts to 18 ft. lbs. (24 Nm).
8. Reinstall the track covers, if removed.
9. Install the rear foot covers and the carpet retainers, if they were removed.

➡️ Inspect both seat adjusters making sure they are parallel and in phase with each other. This is where one adjuster reaches its maximum horizontal or vertical travel in a given direction, before the other adjuster. In the event they are out of phase.

10. Check the operation of the seat assembly for a full limit of travel.

Rear Stationary

♦ See Figure 35

1. Push the lower forward edge of the seat cushion rearward.
2. Lift upward and pull forward on the seat cushion frame to disengage the cushion frame wires from the retainers on the rear seat pan.
3. Remove the lower seat cushion from the vehicle.
4. At the bottom of the seatback, remove the anchor bolts securing the rear seat wire retainers.
5. Grasp the bottom of the seatback and swing toward to disengage the offsets on the upper frame bar from the hangers.
6. Lift the seatback upward and remove from vehicle.

To install:

7. Install the seat back into the car, make sure to have the seat belts on the outer sides of the seat, so they are exposed for use.

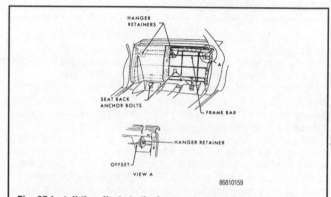

Fig. 35 Install the offsets to the hangers, secure the anchor bolts, then tighten to 89 inch lbs. (10 Nm)

8. Install the offsets to the hangers.
9. Secure all the anchor bolts, then tighten to 89 inch lbs. (10 Nm).
10. To install the rear seat cushion assembly, first pull the seat belts up so they will be exposed when the seat cushion is seated, then press down and rearward.

Folding Third Seat—Wagon

1. Remove the screws from the top side of the cushion.
2. Pull the top of the cushion outward and upward to remove.

To install:

3. Be sure to slot the lower rear of the cushion correctly into the back panel.
4. Install the cushion, then secure with the mounting screws.

Folding Split Second Seat—Wagon

1. Place the folding seatback into the down position, lift up the front flap of the carpet that covers the lower seatback.
2. Remove the cover(s) from the quarter inner trim panel(s).
3. Remove the bolt(s) from the seatback support.
4. Separate the split seatback by lifting forward and outwards.

To install:

5. It may be necessary to loosen and realign the second seatback striker(s). Tighten the striker(s) to 18 ft. lbs. (24 Nm).
6. Install the split seatback to the car, then install the bolts to the supports. Tighten the bolts to 18 ft. lbs. (24 Nm).

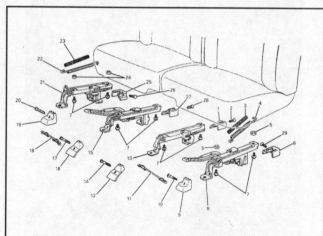

1	COVER, FRONT SEAT INNER ADJUSTER REAR TRACK	16	COVER, FRONT SEAT PASSENGER INNER ADJUSTER FRONT TRACK
2	BOLT/SCREW, FRONT SEAT INNER ADJUSTER REAR TRACK COVER	17	BOLT/SCREW, FRONT SEAT PASSENGER INNER ADJUSTER FRONT TRACK COVER
3	SILENCER, FRONT SEAT DRIVER ADJUSTER RETURN SPRING	18	WIRE, FRONT SEAT PASSENGER ADJUSTER
4	SPRING, FRONT SEAT DRIVER RETURN SPRING	19	COVER, FRONT SEAT PASSENGER OUTER ADJUSTER FRONT TRACK
5	SPACER, FRONT SEAT DRIVER OUTER ADJUSTER	20	BOLT/SCREW, FRONT SEAT PASSENGER OUTER ADJUSTER FRONT TRACK COVER
6	COVER, FRONT SEAT DRIVER OUTER ADJUSTER REAR TRACK	21	ADJUSTER ASSEMBLY, FRONT SEAT PASSENGER OUTER
7	BOLT/SCREW, FRONT SEAT	22	SPRING, FRONT SEAT PASSENGER RETURN SPRING
8	ADJUSTER ASSEMBLY, FRONT SEAT DRIVER OUTER	23	SILENCER, FRONT SEAT PASSENGER ADJUSTER RETURN SPRING
9	COVER, FRONT SEAT DRIVER OUTER ADJUSTER FRONT TRACK COVER	24	SPACER, FRONT SEAT PASSENGER OUTER ADJUSTER
10	BOLT/SCREW, FRONT SEAT DRIVER OUTER ADJUSTER FRONT TRACK COVER	25	COVER, FRONT SEAT PASSENGER OUTER ADJUSTER REAR TRACK
11	WIRE, FRONT SEAT DRIVER ADJUSTER	26	BOLT/SCREW, FRONT SEAT PASSENGER OUTER ADJUSTER REAR TRACK COVER
12	COVER, FRONT SEAT DRIVER INNER ADJUSTER FRONT TRACK	27	COVER, FRONT SEAT PASSENGER INNER ADJUSTER REAR TRACK
13	ADJUSTER ASSEMBLY, FRONT SEAT DRIVER INNER	28	BOLT/SCREW, FRONT SEAT PASSENGER INNER ADJUSTER REAR TRACK COVER
14	BOLT/SCREW, FRONT SEAT DRIVER INNER ADJUSTER FRONT TRACK COVER	29	BOLT/SCREW, FRONT SEAT DRIVER OUTER ADJUSTER REAR TRACK COVER
15	ADJUSTER ASSEMBLY, FRONT SEAT PASSENGER INNER		

86810158

Fig. 34 Exploded view of the mounting for a common manual seat assembly

7. Reinstall the covers to the quarter inner trim panels.
8. Install the carpet over the lower seatback.

Seat Belt Systems

REMOVAL & INSTALLATION

Floor Mount

1. Remove the cover from the anchor plate.
2. Remove the cover from the floor mounted retractor assembly.
3. Disconnect wiring from assembly, as needed.
4. Remove assembly.

To install:
5. Install the assembly. Tighten the retaining bolts to 31 ft. lbs. (42 Nm).
6. Connect the electrical wiring to the assembly.
7. Attach the cover to the floor mounted retractor assembly.
8. Attach the cover to the anchor plate.

Outboard Belts and Retractors

1. Remove door trim panel.
2. Remove screws securing intermediate guide to door.
3. Remove the intermediate guide.
4. Detach the electrical connectors.
5. Unfasten the nut securing the lap retractor.
6. Remove the lap retractor.
7. Unfasten the nut and screw securing the shoulder retractor.
8. Remove the shoulder retractor.
9. Remove or lower window as necessary.
10. Remove the cover, nut and spacer from D-ring and remove the D-ring.

To install:
11. Install the D-ring, and tighten the bolt to 21 ft. lbs. (28 Nm).
12. Reposition and install the D-ring covers.

13. Secure the shoulder retractor, then tighten to 31 ft. lbs. (42 Nm).
14. Install the lap retractor, then tighten to 31 ft. lbs. (42 Nm).
15. Connect the electrical connectors to the retractors.
16. Secure the intermediate guide and tighten to 44 inch lbs. (5 Nm).
17. Install the door trim panels.

Power Seat Motor

REMOVAL & INSTALLATION

1. Position the seat in the full forward position. If the car is equipped with six-way power seats, place the seat in the full forward and up position. When necessary to gain access to the adjuster-to-floor pan attaching nuts, remove the adjuster rear foot covers and or carpet retainers.
2. Remove the track covers where necessary, then remove the adjuster-to-floor pan rear attaching nuts. Position the seat in the full rearward position.
3. Remove the adjuster front foot covers, then remove the adjuster to floor pan front attaching nuts. Tilt the seat rearward and disconnect the feed wire connector.
4. Remove the seat assembly from the car.
5. Place the seat up side down on a clean surface.
6. Disconnect the vertical and horizontal drive cables from the motor.
7. Remove the retainer nut from the motor support bracket.
8. Remove the motor from the seat.

To install:
9. Position the motor in the motor support bracket.
10. Connect the vertical and horizontal drive cables.
11. Place the seat into the vehicle and connect the feed wire.
12. Position the seat in the position that makes installation of the retaining nuts easiest. Install the adjuster to floor pan attaching nuts, tighten to 15–21 ft. lbs. (20–28 Nm), then install the foot covers.

TORQUE SPECIFICATIONS

Component	US	Metric
Adjuster to seat frame bolt:	18 ft. lbs.	24 Nm
Air deflector:	80 inch lbs.	9 Nm
Bumper to absorber bolts:	18-25 ft. lbs.	24-34 Nm
Door hinge to body:	15-20 ft. lbs.	20-28 Nm
Door striker:		
1982-91	34-46 ft. lbs.	46-62 Nm
1992-96	39 ft. lbs.	53 Nm
Fender bolts upper:	89 inch lbs.	10 Nm
Fender bolts lower:	18 ft. lbs.	25 Nm
Folding second seatback lock stricker to back support:	34 ft. lbs.	46 Nm
Front seat center armrest:	9 ft. lbs.	12 Nm
Front seatbelt to anchor plate:	31 ft. lbs.	42 Nm
Front seatbelt to rocker:	31 ft. lbs.	42 Nm
High mounted stop light:	49 inch lbs.	5.5 Nm
Hood hinge to hood bolts:	20 ft. lbs.	27 Nm
Interia lock to seat back panel:	89 inch lbs.	10 Nm
Interia lock to seat bottom frame:	89 inch lbs.	10 Nm
Lockout plate to seat bottom:	9 ft. lbs.	12 Nm
Luggage carrier deck lid:	13 inch lbs.	1.5 Nm
Luggage carrier rail:	13 inch lbs.	1.5 Nm
Outer seatback hinge upper and lower bolts:	18 ft. lbs.	5.5 Nm
Outer slat retaining nuts:	49 inch lbs.	9 Nm
Outside mirror retaining nuts:	72-80 inch lbs.	8-9 Nm
Pivot glass bolts:	80 inch lbs.	6 Nm
Pivot glass lock, solenoid and acuator:	53 inch lbs.	6 Nm
Pivot glass screws to deflector:	80 inch lbs.	9 Nm
Pivot glass striker to glass assembly:	80 inch lbs.	9 Nm
Rear compartment lid lock and solenoid screws:	53 inch lbs.	6 Nm
Rear seat cushion retainer to floor pan:	89 inch lbs.	10 Nm
Rear seatback bolt:	89 inch lbs.	10 Nm
Reclining to seatback bolt:	31 ft.lbs.	42 Nm
Reclining seatback actuator assembly to cushion frame:	13 ft. lbs.	18 Nm
Reveal moulding to liftgate:	13 ft. lbs.	18 Nm
Seat adjuster-to-floor bolt:	13 ft. lbs.	18 Nm
Seat bottom-to-back frame:	80 inch lbs.	9 Nm
Seat motor and trans. support:	18 ft. lbs.	24 Nm
Seatback frame-to-cushion:	89 inch lbs.	10 Nm
Seatback lock assembly screw:	106 inch lbs.	12 Nm
Seatback lock striker and inner side bar stop:	34 ft. lbs.	46 Nm
Trunk lid retaining bolts:	18-20 ft. lbs.	25-27 Nm

91080C01

GLOSSARY

AIR/FUEL RATIO: The ratio of air-to-gasoline by weight in the fuel mixture drawn into the engine.

AIR INJECTION: One method of reducing harmful exhaust emissions by injecting air into each of the exhaust ports of an engine. The fresh air entering the hot exhaust manifold causes any remaining fuel to be burned before it can exit the tailpipe.

ALTERNATOR: A device used for converting mechanical energy into electrical energy.

AMMETER: An instrument, calibrated in amperes, used to measure the flow of an electrical current in a circuit. Ammeters are always connected in series with the circuit being tested.

AMPERE: The rate of flow of electrical current present when one volt of electrical pressure is applied against one ohm of electrical resistance.

ANALOG COMPUTER: Any microprocessor that uses similar (analogous) electrical signals to make its calculations.

ARMATURE: A laminated, soft iron core wrapped by a wire that converts electrical energy to mechanical energy as in a motor or relay. When rotated in a magnetic field, it changes mechanical energy into electrical energy as in a generator.

ATMOSPHERIC PRESSURE: The pressure on the Earth's surface caused by the weight of the air in the atmosphere. At sea level, this pressure is 14.7 psi at 32°F (101 kPa at 0°C).

ATOMIZATION: The breaking down of a liquid into a fine mist that can be suspended in air.

AXIAL PLAY: Movement parallel to a shaft or bearing bore.

BACKFIRE: The sudden combustion of gases in the intake or exhaust system that results in a loud explosion.

BACKLASH: The clearance or play between two parts, such as meshed gears.

BACKPRESSURE: Restrictions in the exhaust system that slow the exit of exhaust gases from the combustion chamber.

BAKELITE: A heat resistant, plastic insulator material commonly used in printed circuit boards and transistorized components.

BALL BEARING: A bearing made up of hardened inner and outer races between which hardened steel balls roll.

BALLAST RESISTOR: A resistor in the primary ignition circuit that lowers voltage after the engine is started to reduce wear on ignition components.

BEARING: A friction reducing, supportive device usually located between a stationary part and a moving part.

BIMETAL TEMPERATURE SENSOR: Any sensor or switch made of two dissimilar types of metal that bend when heated or cooled due to the different expansion rates of the alloys. These types of sensors usually function as an on/off switch.

BLOWBY: Combustion gases, composed of water vapor and unburned fuel, that leak past the piston rings into the crankcase during normal engine operation. These gases are removed by the PCV system to prevent the buildup of harmful acids in the crankcase.

BRAKE PAD: A brake shoe and lining assembly used with disc brakes.

BRAKE SHOE: The backing for the brake lining. The term is, however, usually applied to the assembly of the brake backing and lining.

BUSHING: A liner, usually removable, for a bearing; an anti-friction liner used in place of a bearing.

CALIPER: A hydraulically activated device in a disc brake system, which is mounted straddling the brake rotor (disc). The caliper contains at least one piston and two brake pads. Hydraulic pressure on the piston(s) forces the pads against the rotor.

CAMSHAFT: A shaft in the engine on which are the lobes (cams) which operate the valves. The camshaft is driven by the crankshaft, via a belt, chain or gears, at one half the crankshaft speed.

CAPACITOR: A device which stores an electrical charge.

CARBON MONOXIDE (CO): A colorless, odorless gas given off as a normal byproduct of combustion. It is poisonous and extremely dangerous in confined areas, building up slowly to toxic levels without warning if adequate ventilation is not available.

CARBURETOR: A device, usually mounted on the intake manifold of an engine, which mixes the air and fuel in the proper proportion to allow even combustion.

CATALYTIC CONVERTER: A device installed in the exhaust system, like a muffler, that converts harmful byproducts of combustion into carbon dioxide and water vapor by means of a heat-producing chemical reaction.

CENTRIFUGAL ADVANCE: A mechanical method of advancing the spark timing by using flyweights in the distributor that react to centrifugal force generated by the distributor shaft rotation.

CHECK VALVE: Any one-way valve installed to permit the flow of air, fuel or vacuum in one direction only.

CHOKE: A device, usually a moveable valve, placed in the intake path of a carburetor to restrict the flow of air.

CIRCUIT: Any unbroken path through which an electrical current can flow. Also used to describe fuel flow in some instances.

CIRCUIT BREAKER: A switch which protects an electrical circuit from overload by opening the circuit when the current flow exceeds a predetermined level. Some circuit breakers must be reset manually, while most reset automatically.

COIL (IGNITION): A transformer in the ignition circuit which steps up the voltage provided to the spark plugs.

COMBINATION MANIFOLD: An assembly which includes both the intake and exhaust manifolds in one casting.

COMBINATION VALVE: A device used in some fuel systems that routes fuel vapors to a charcoal storage canister instead of venting them into the atmosphere. The valve relieves fuel tank pressure and allows fresh air into the tank as the fuel level drops to prevent a vapor lock situation.

COMPRESSION RATIO: The comparison of the total volume of the cylinder and combustion chamber with the piston at BDC and the piston at TDC.

CONDENSER: 1. An electrical device which acts to store an electrical charge, preventing voltage surges. 2. A radiator-like device in the air conditioning system in which refrigerant gas condenses into a liquid, giving off heat.

CONDUCTOR: Any material through which an electrical current can be transmitted easily.

CONTINUITY: Continuous or complete circuit. Can be checked with an ohmmeter.

COUNTERSHAFT: An intermediate shaft which is rotated by a mainshaft and transmits, in turn, that rotation to a working part.

CRANKCASE: The lower part of an engine in which the crankshaft and related parts operate.

CRANKSHAFT: The main driving shaft of an engine which receives reciprocating motion from the pistons and converts it to rotary motion.

CYLINDER: In an engine, the round hole in the engine block in which the piston(s) ride.

CYLINDER BLOCK: The main structural member of an engine in which is found the cylinders, crankshaft and other principal parts.

CYLINDER HEAD: The detachable portion of the engine, usually fastened to the top of the cylinder block and containing all or most of the combustion chambers. On overhead valve engines, it contains the valves and their operating parts. On overhead cam engines, it contains the camshaft as well.

DEAD CENTER: The extreme top or bottom of the piston stroke.

DETONATION: An unwanted explosion of the air/fuel mixture in the combustion chamber caused by excess heat and compression, advanced timing, or an overly lean mixture. Also referred to as "ping".

DIAPHRAGM: A thin, flexible wall separating two cavities, such as in a vacuum advance unit.

DIESELING: A condition in which hot spots in the combustion chamber cause the engine to run on after the key is turned off.

DIFFERENTIAL: A geared assembly which allows the transmission of motion between drive axles, giving one axle the ability to turn faster than the other.

DIODE: An electrical device that will allow current to flow in one direction only.

DISC BRAKE: A hydraulic braking assembly consisting of a brake disc, or rotor, mounted on an axle, and a caliper assembly containing, usually two brake pads which are activated by hydraulic pressure. The pads are forced against the sides of the disc, creating friction which slows the vehicle.

DISTRIBUTOR: A mechanically driven device on an engine which is responsible for electrically firing the spark plug at a predetermined point of the piston stroke.

DOWEL PIN: A pin, inserted in mating holes in two different parts allowing those parts to maintain a fixed relationship.

DRUM BRAKE: A braking system which consists of two brake shoes and one or two wheel cylinders, mounted on a fixed backing plate, and a brake drum, mounted on an axle, which revolves around the assembly.

DWELL: The rate, measured in degrees of shaft rotation, at which an electrical circuit cycles on and off.

ELECTRONIC CONTROL UNIT (ECU): Ignition module, module, amplifier or igniter. See Module for definition.

ELECTRONIC IGNITION: A system in which the timing and firing of the spark plugs is controlled by an electronic control unit, usually called a module. These systems have no points or condenser.

END-PLAY: The measured amount of axial movement in a shaft.

ENGINE: A device that converts heat into mechanical energy.

EXHAUST MANIFOLD: A set of cast passages or pipes which conduct exhaust gases from the engine.

FEELER GAUGE: A blade, usually metal, or precisely predetermined thickness, used to measure the clearance between two parts.

FIRING ORDER: The order in which combustion occurs in the cylinders of an engine. Also the order in which spark is distributed to the plugs by the distributor.

FLOODING: The presence of too much fuel in the intake manifold and combustion chamber which prevents the air/fuel mixture from firing, thereby causing a no-start situation.

FLYWHEEL: A disc shaped part bolted to the rear end of the crankshaft. Around the outer perimeter is affixed the ring gear. The starter drive engages the ring gear, turning the flywheel, which rotates the crankshaft, imparting the initial starting motion to the engine.

FOOT POUND (ft. lbs. or sometimes, ft.lb.): The amount of energy or work needed to raise an item weighing one pound, a distance of one foot.

FUSE: A protective device in a circuit which prevents circuit overload by breaking the circuit when a specific amperage is present. The device is constructed around a strip or wire of a lower amperage rating than the circuit it is designed to protect. When an amperage higher than that stamped on the fuse is present in the circuit, the strip or wire melts, opening the circuit.

GEAR RATIO: The ratio between the number of teeth on meshing gears.

GENERATOR: A device which converts mechanical energy into electrical energy.

HEAT RANGE: The measure of a spark plug's ability to dissipate heat from its firing end. The higher the heat range, the hotter the plug fires.

HUB: The center part of a wheel or gear.

HYDROCARBON (HC): Any chemical compound made up of hydrogen and carbon. A major pollutant formed by the engine as a byproduct of combustion.

HYDROMETER: An instrument used to measure the specific gravity of a solution.

INCH POUND (inch lbs.; sometimes in.lb. or in. lbs.): One twelfth of a foot pound.

INDUCTION: A means of transferring electrical energy in the form of a magnetic field. Principle used in the ignition coil to increase voltage.

INJECTOR: A device which receives metered fuel under relatively low pressure and is activated to inject the fuel into the engine under relatively high pressure at a predetermined time.

INPUT SHAFT: The shaft to which torque is applied, usually carrying the driving gear or gears.

INTAKE MANIFOLD: A casting of passages or pipes used to conduct air or a fuel/air mixture to the cylinders.

JOURNAL: The bearing surface within which a shaft operates.

KEY: A small block usually fitted in a notch between a shaft and a hub to prevent slippage of the two parts.

MANIFOLD: A casting of passages or set of pipes which connect the cylinders to an inlet or outlet source.

MANIFOLD VACUUM: Low pressure in an engine intake manifold formed just below the throttle plates. Manifold vacuum is highest at idle and drops under acceleration.

MASTER CYLINDER: The primary fluid pressurizing device in a hydraulic system. In automotive use, it is found in brake and hydraulic clutch systems and is pedal activated, either directly or, in a power brake system, through the power booster.

MODULE: Electronic control unit, amplifier or igniter of solid state or integrated design which controls the current flow in the ignition primary circuit based on input from the pick-up coil. When the module opens the primary circuit, high secondary voltage is induced in the coil.

NEEDLE BEARING: A bearing which consists of a number (usually a large number) of long, thin rollers.

OHM: (Ω) The unit used to measure the resistance of conductor-to-electrical flow. One ohm is the amount of resistance that limits current flow to one ampere in a circuit with one volt of pressure.

OHMMETER: An instrument used for measuring the resistance, in ohms, in an electrical circuit.

OUTPUT SHAFT: The shaft which transmits torque from a device, such as a transmission.

OVERDRIVE: A gear assembly which produces more shaft revolutions than that transmitted to it.

OVERHEAD CAMSHAFT (OHC): An engine configuration in which the camshaft is mounted on top of the cylinder head and operates the valve either directly or by means of rocker arms.

OVERHEAD VALVE (OHV): An engine configuration in which all of the valves are located in the cylinder head and the camshaft is located in the cylinder block. The camshaft operates the valves via lifters and pushrods.

OXIDES OF NITROGEN (NOx): Chemical compounds of nitrogen produced as a byproduct of combustion. They combine with hydrocarbons to produce smog.

OXYGEN SENSOR: Use with the feedback system to sense the presence of oxygen in the exhaust gas and signal the computer which can reference the voltage signal to an air/fuel ratio.

PINION: The smaller of two meshing gears.

PISTON RING: An open-ended ring with fits into a groove on the outer diameter of the piston. Its chief function is to form a seal between the piston and cylinder wall. Most automotive pistons have three rings: two for compression sealing; one for oil sealing.

PRELOAD: A predetermined load placed on a bearing during assembly or by adjustment.

PRIMARY CIRCUIT: the low voltage side of the ignition system which consists of the ignition switch, ballast resistor or resistance wire, bypass, coil, electronic control unit and pick-up coil as well as the connecting wires and harnesses.

PRESS FIT: The mating of two parts under pressure, due to the inner diameter of one being smaller than the outer diameter of the other, or vice versa; an interference fit.

RACE: The surface on the inner or outer ring of a bearing on which the balls, needles or rollers move.

REGULATOR: A device which maintains the amperage and/or voltage levels of a circuit at predetermined values.

RELAY: A switch which automatically opens and/or closes a circuit.

RESISTANCE: The opposition to the flow of current through a circuit or electrical device, and is measured in ohms. Resistance is equal to the voltage divided by the amperage.

RESISTOR: A device, usually made of wire, which offers a preset amount of resistance in an electrical circuit.

RING GEAR: The name given to a ring-shaped gear attached to a differential case, or affixed to a flywheel or as part of a planetary gear set.

ROLLER BEARING: A bearing made up of hardened inner and outer races between which hardened steel rollers move.

ROTOR: 1. The disc-shaped part of a disc brake assembly, upon which the brake pads bear; also called, brake disc. 2. The device mounted atop the distributor shaft, which passes current to the distributor cap tower contacts.

SECONDARY CIRCUIT: The high voltage side of the ignition system, usually above 20,000 volts. The secondary includes the ignition coil, coil wire, distributor cap and rotor, spark plug wires and spark plugs.

SENDING UNIT: A mechanical, electrical, hydraulic or electro-magnetic device which transmits information to a gauge.

SENSOR: Any device designed to measure engine operating conditions or ambient pressures and temperatures. Usually electronic in nature and designed to send a voltage signal to an on-board computer, some sensors may operate as a simple on/off switch or they may provide a variable voltage signal (like a potentiometer) as conditions or measured parameters change.

SHIM: Spacers of precise, predetermined thickness used between parts to establish a proper working relationship.

SLAVE CYLINDER: In automotive use, a device in the hydraulic clutch system which is activated by hydraulic force, disengaging the clutch.

SOLENOID: A coil used to produce a magnetic field, the effect of which is to produce work.

SPARK PLUG: A device screwed into the combustion chamber of a spark ignition engine. The basic construction is a conductive core inside of a ceramic insulator, mounted in an outer conductive base. An electrical charge from the spark plug wire travels along the conductive core and jumps a preset air gap to a grounding point or points at the end of the conductive base. The resultant spark ignites the fuel/air mixture in the combustion chamber.

SPLINES: Ridges machined or cast onto the outer diameter of a shaft or inner diameter of a bore to enable parts to mate without rotation.

TACHOMETER: A device used to measure the rotary speed of an engine, shaft, gear, etc., usually in rotations per minute.

THERMOSTAT: A valve, located in the cooling system of an engine, which is closed when cold and opens gradually in response to engine heating, controlling the temperature of the coolant and rate of coolant flow.

TOP DEAD CENTER (TDC): The point at which the piston reaches the top of its travel on the compression stroke.

TORQUE: The twisting force applied to an object.

TORQUE CONVERTER: A turbine used to transmit power from a driving member to a driven member via hydraulic action, providing changes in drive ratio and torque. In automotive use, it links the driveplate at the rear of the engine to the automatic transmission.

TRANSDUCER: A device used to change a force into an electrical signal.

TRANSISTOR: A semi-conductor component which can be actuated by a small voltage to perform an electrical switching function.

TUNE-UP: A regular maintenance function, usually associated with the replacement and adjustment of parts and components in the electrical and fuel systems of a vehicle for the purpose of attaining optimum performance.

TURBOCHARGER: An exhaust driven pump which compresses intake air and forces it into the combustion chambers at higher than atmospheric pressures. The increased air pressure allows more fuel to be burned and results in increased horsepower being produced.

VACUUM ADVANCE: A device which advances the ignition timing in response to increased engine vacuum.

VACUUM GAUGE: An instrument used to measure the presence of vacuum in a chamber.

VALVE: A device which control the pressure, direction of flow or rate of flow of a liquid or gas.

VALVE CLEARANCE: The measured gap between the end of the valve stem and the rocker arm, cam lobe or follower that activates the valve.

VISCOSITY: The rating of a liquid's internal resistance to flow.

VOLTMETER: An instrument used for measuring electrical force in units called volts. Voltmeters are always connected parallel with the circuit being tested.

WHEEL CYLINDER: Found in the automotive drum brake assembly, it is a device, actuated by hydraulic pressure, which, through internal pistons, pushes the brake shoes outward against the drums.

MASTER INDEX